T0189256

Communications
in Computer and Information Science   **644**

Commenced Publication in 2007
Founding and Former Series Editors:
Alfredo Cuzzocrea, Dominik Ślęzak, and Xiaokang Yang

More information about this series at http://www.springer.com/series/7899

Lin Zhang · Xiao Song
Yunjie Wu (Eds.)

Theory, Methodology, Tools and Applications for Modeling and Simulation of Complex Systems

16th Asia Simulation Conference
and SCS Autumn Simulation Multi-Conference
AsiaSim/SCS AutumnSim 2016
Beijing, China, October 8–11, 2016
Proceedings, Part II

 Springer

Editors
Lin Zhang
Beihang University
Beijing
China

Yunjie Wu
Beihang University
Beijing
China

Xiao Song
Beihang University
Beijing
China

ISSN 1865-0929   ISSN 1865-0937   (electronic)
Communications in Computer and Information Science
ISBN 978-981-10-2665-2   ISBN 978-981-10-2666-9   (eBook)
DOI 10.1007/978-981-10-2666-9

Library of Congress Control Number: 2016946015

Printed on acid-free paper

This Springer imprint is published by Springer Nature
The registered company is Springer Science+Business Media Singapore Pte Ltd.

Preface

AsiaSim/SCS AutumnSim 2016 (the 2016 International Simulation Multi-Conference) was a joint conference of the 16th Asia Simulation Conference and the 2016 Autumn Simulation Multi-Conference. The Asia Simulation Conference (AsiaSim) is an annual international conference started in 1999. In 2011, the Federation of Asian Simulation Societies (ASIASIM) was set up and the AsiaSim became an annual conference of ASIASIM. The SCS Autumn Simulation Multi-Conference (SCS AutumnSim) is one of the premier conferences of the Society for Modeling and Simulation International (SCS), which provides a unique opportunity to learn about emerging M&S applications in many thriving fields. AsiaSim/SCS AutumnSim 2016 was the first conference jointly sponsored by ASIASIM and SCS and organized by the China Simulation Federation (CSF), Science and Technology on Special System Simulation Laboratory (STSSSL), and Beihang University (BUAA). It was also co-sponsored by the China Simulation Federation (CSF), the Japanese Society for Simulation Technology (JSST), the Korea Society for Simulation (KSS), the Society for Simulation and Gaming of Singapore (SSAGSG), the International Association for Mathematics and Computers in Simulation (IMACS), the Chinese Association for Artificial Intelligence (CAAI), China Computer Federation (CCF), the China Electrotechnical Society (CES), the China Graphics Society (CGS), and the China Ordnance Society (COS).

This conference is a big event that provides a unique opportunity to learn about emerging M&S research achievements and applications in many thriving fields, focusing on the theory, methodology, tools and applications for M&S of complex systems; it provides a forum for the latest R&D results in academia and industry.

The papers contained in these proceedings address challenging issues in M&S theory and methodology, model engineering for system of systems, high-performance computing and simulation, M&S for smart city, robot simulations, M&S for intelligent manufacturing, military simulation, as well as cloud technologies in simulation applications.

This year, AsiaSim/SCS AutumnSim received 639 submissions. Submissions came from around 15 countries and regions. After a thorough reviewing process, 267 papers were selected for presentation as full papers, with an acceptance rate of 41.8 %. These papers are published in the proceedings in the four volumes, 643–646. Volume 643 mainly addresses the issues of basics of M&S theory and methodology. Volume 644 discusses M&S for intelligent manufacturing and military simulation methods. In Vol. 645, cloud technologies in simulation applications, simulation and big data techniques are covered. And Vol. 646 presents M&S applications and simulation software.

The high-quality program would not have been possible without the authors who chose AsiaSim/SCS AutumnSim 2016 as a venue for their publications. Also, we would like to take this opportunity to thank the ASIASIM Federation for allowing us to host AsiaSim 2016 in Beijing.

We also thank the members of the Program Committee for their valuable effort in the review of the submitted papers. Finally, we would also like to thank our technical co-sponsors and sponsors. Your contributions and support have helped to make AsiaSim/SCS AutumnSim 2016 a memorable and successful event.

We hope that you enjoy reading and benefit from the proceedings of AsiaSim/SCS AutumnSim 2016.

October 2016   Lin Zhang
                                                         Xiao Song
                                                         Yunjie Wu

Organization

Sponsors

Federation of Asian Simulation Societies (ASIASIM)
The Society for Modeling & Simulation International (SCS)

Co-Sponsors

China Simulation Federation (CSF)
Japanese Society for Simulation Technology (JSST)
Korea Society for Simulation (KSS)
Society for Simulation and Gaming of Singapore (SSAGSG)
International Association for Mathematics and Computers in Simulation (IMACS)
Chinese Association for Artificial Intelligence (CAAI)
China Computer Federation (CCF)
China Electrotechnical Society (CES)
China Graphics Society (CGS)
China Ordnance Society (COS)

Organizers

China Simulation Federation (CSF)
Science and Technology on Special System Simulation Laboratory (STSSSL)
Beihang University (BUAA)

Honorary Chairs

Chuanyuan Wen, China
Robert M. Howe, USA
Yukio Kagawa, Japan
Sadao Takaba, Japan
Sung-Joo Park, Korea
Tianyuan Xiao(†), China

General Chairs

Bo Hu Li, China
Qinping Zhao, China

Deputy General Chair

Agostino Bruzzone, Italy

General Co-chairs

Satoshi Tanaka, Japan
Jonghyun Kim, Korea
Axel Lehmann, Germany
Zicai Wang, China
Xianxiang Huang, China

Program Committee Chair

Lin Zhang, China

Program Committee Co-chairs

Bernard Zeigler, USA
Tuncer Ören, Canada
Ralph C. Huntsinger, USA
Xiaofeng Hu, China
Soo-Hyun Park, Korea
H.J. Halin, Switzerland
Kaj Juslin, Finland
Roy E. Crosbie, USA

Ming Yang, China
Xiaogang Qiu, China
Satoshi Tanaka, Japan
Jin Liu, China
Min Zhao, China
Shiwei Ma, China
Francesco Longo, Italy
Agostino Bruzzone, Italy

Program Committee

Anxiang Huang, China
Yoonbae Kim, Korea
Yu Yao, China
Fei Xie, USA
Toshiharu Kagawa, Japan
Giuseppe Iazeolla, Italy
Mhamed Itmi, France
Haixiang Lin, Netherlands
Henri Pierreval, France
Hugh HT Liu, Canada
Wolfgang Borutzky, Germany
Jong Sik Lee, Korea
Xiaolin Hu, USA
Yifa Tang, China

Wenhui Fan, China
Bernard Zeigler, USA
Mingduan Tang, China
Long Wang, China
ChaoWang, China
Doo-Kwon Baik, Korea
Shinsuke Tamura, Japan
Pierre Borne, France
Ratan Guha, USA
Reinhold Meisinger, Germany
Richard Fujimoto, USA
Ge Li, China
Jinhai Sun, China
Xinping Xiong, China

Changjian Bi, China
Jianguo Cao, China
Yue Dai, China
Minrui Fei, China
Chen Guo, China
Fengju Kang, China
Guoxiong Li, China
Jin Liu, China
Shiwei Ma, China
Jipeng Wang, China
Zhongjie Wang, China
Hongjun Zhang, China
Qinping Zhao, China
Guomin Zhou, China
Gary S.H. Tan, Singapore
Francesco Longo, Italy
Hong Zhou, China
Shin'ichi Oishi, Japan
Zhenhao Zhou, China
Beike Zhang, China
Alain Cardon, France
Xukun Shen, China
Yangsheng Wang, China
Marzuki Khalid, Malaysia
Sergio Junco, Argentina
Tieqiao Wen, China
Xingsheng Gu, China
Zhijian Song, China
Yue Yang, China

Yongsheng Ding, China
Huimin Fan, China
Ming Chen, China
Javor, Andras, Hungary
Nabendu Chaki, India
Koji Koyamada, Japan
Osamu Ono, Japan
Yunjie Wu, China
Beiwei Guo, China
Ni Li, China
Shixuan Liu, China
Linxuan Zhang, China
Fei Tao, China
Lei Ren, China
Xiao Song, China
Xudong Chai, China
Zonghai Chen, China
Yuhao Cong, China
Guanghong Gong, China
Zhicheng Ji, China
Weidong Jin, China
Bo Hu Li, China
Ma Ping, China
Shaojie Mao, China
Zhong Su, China
Jianping Wu, China
Min Zhao, China
Huizhou Zheng, China

Organization Committee Chair

Yunjie Wu, China

Organization Committee Co-chairs

Shixuan Liu, China
Zaijun Shi, China
Linxuan Zhang, China
Ni Li, China
Fei Tao, China

Beiwei Guo, China
Xiao Song, China
Weijing Wang, China
Lei Ren, China

General Secretaries

Shixuan Liu, China
Xiao Song, China

Special Session Chairs

Ni Li, China
Linxuan Zhang, China

Publication Chairs

Shiwei Ma, China
Xiao Song, China

Publicity Chairs

Fei Tao, China
Baiwei Guo, China

Awards Committee Chairs

Lin Zhang, China
Axel Lehmann, Germany

Awards Committee Co-chair

Yifa Tang, China

Awards Committee Members

Sung-Yong Jang, Korea
Wenhui Fan, China
Xiao Song, China

Contents – Part II

Military Simulation

HMI & Robot Simulations

Model-Free Adaptive Iterative Learning Control Based on Data-Driven for Noncircular Turning Tool Feed System

Zhao Yunjie[1], Cao Rongmin[1(✉)], and Zhou Huixing[2]

[1] School of Automation, Beijing Information Science
and Technology University, Beijing 100192, China
rongmin_cao@163.com
[2] College of Engineering China Agricultural University, Beijing 100083, China

Abstract. In practical applications, noncircular turning tool feed system repeat the same control tasks over a finite time interval. But it does not have the ability to improve the tool position error from past repeated operations. This paper will use Partial Form Dynamic Linearization based Model-Free Adaptive Iterative Learning Control (PFDL-MFAILC) algorithm in noncircular turning tool feed. PFDL-MFAILC is a data-driven iterative learning control algorithms. The design of noncircular turning tool feed controller is just rely on input and output data. Simulation of PFDL-MFAILC algorithm show that the noncircular turning tool feed position error is improved as the number of repetitions increases. By contrast with PID control algorithm, position tracking accuracy of PFDL-MFAILC algorithm is significantly better than traditional PID control algorithm. After 60 iterations, the steady-state error of PFDL-MFAILC algorithm is much lower than the steady-state error of the PID algorithm. PFDL-MFAILC algorithm achieve the goal that improving position precision of noncircular turning tool feed and making noncircular turning tool feed have self-learning ability from past repeated operations.

Keywords: Model-free adaptive control · Iterative learning control · Noncircular turning tool feed system · Linear motor servo system

1 Introduction

Shipbuilding is an important industry in development of marine resources and national defense construction. With increasing demand for maritime transport, technology of shipbuilding has been rapid developed [1]. Diesel is the power part of ship. Cooperation of piston and cylinder can determine the performance of diesel. Improve accuracy of piston will increase diesel's power and reduce its fuel consumption.

Piston is typical noncircular component and it have complex surface. Currently, noncircular turning is an effective way to machine the piston in high precision. Linear motor is an important part of noncircular turning tool feed system. However, the traditional algorithm such as PID control can not learn from the past repeated operations. As a result, although the noncircular turning tool feed system runs many times, the position error would be same without any improvement.

© Springer Science+Business Media Singapore 2016
L. Zhang et al. (Eds.): AsiaSim 2016/SCS AutumnSim 2016, Part II, CCIS 644, pp. 3–10, 2016.
DOI: 10.1007/978-981-10-2666-9_1

MFAILC is a data-driven algorithm. The basic idea of the approach is shown as follows [2–4]: First, the data model with a simple incremental form is given by introducing the concept of PG along the iteration axis. Then, the data model based MFAILC scheme is designed. Theoretical analysis show that the tracking error converges monotonically to zero along the iteration axis although the initial errors are randomly varying with iterations [5].

Therefore, this article will apply partial form dynamic linearization based model-free adaptive iterative learning control(PFDL-MFAILC) to noncircular turning tool feed system.

2   Partial Form Dynamic Linearization (PFDL) Data Model in the Iteration Domain

SISO nonlinear discrete-time system that operates repeatedly can be written as follows:

$$y(k+1, i) = f(y(k,i), y(k-1, i)\ldots, y(k-n_y, i), u(k,i), u(k-1, i)\ldots, u(k - n_u, i)) \tag{1}$$

Where $u(k,i)$ is control system input and $y(k,i)$ is control system output at sampling time k of the ith iteration, n_y, n_u are two unknown positive number, and $f(\cdots)$ is an nonlinear function.

Denote $\mathbf{U}_L(k,i)$ as a vector consisting of all control input signal within a moving time window $[K - L + 1, K]$ of the ith iteration. The integer L is called control input linearization length constant [5].

$$\mathbf{U}_L(k,i) = [u(k,i), u(k-1, i) \cdots, u(k-L+1, i)]^T$$

PFDL data model in the iteration domain is done in the following two assumptions.

Assumption 1. Nonlinear system (1) partial derivative respect to the variables from the $(n_y + 2)th$ to the $(n_y + L + 1)th$, namely, $u(k,i), u(k-1, i), \cdots, u(k-L+1, i)$, are continuous.

Assumption 2. When $|\Delta u(k,i)| \neq 0$, system (1) conforms the generalized *Lipschitz* condition along the iteration axis, that is,

$$|\Delta y(k+1, i)| \leq b\|\Delta \mathbf{U}_L(k,i)\| \tag{2}$$

where $\Delta y(k+1, i) = y(k+1, i) - y(k+1, i-1), \Delta \mathbf{U}_L(k,i) = \mathbf{U}_L(k,i) - \mathbf{U}_L(k,i-1)$; $b > 0$ is a finite positive constant.

Consider nonlinear system (1) satisfying Assumptions 1 and 2. If $\|\Delta \mathbf{U}_L(k,i)\| \neq 0$, then there exists Pseudo Gradient (PG): $\mathbf{\Phi}_L(k,i)$. PG is a vector, which contains a number of time-varying parameters. Therefore the system (1) can be transformed into the following PFDL-MFAILC data model:

$$\Delta y(k+1,i) = \mathbf{\Phi}_L^T(k,i)\Delta \mathbf{U}_L(k,i) \tag{3}$$

where

$$\mathbf{\Phi}_L(k,i) = [\Phi_1(k,i),\Phi_2(k,i),\cdots,\Phi_L(k,i),]^T$$
$$\Delta \mathbf{U}_L(k,i) = [\Delta u(k,i),\Delta u(k-1,i),\cdots\Delta u(k-L+1,i)]^T$$

3 Controller Algorithm

Given a desired trajectory $y_d(k)$, The goal is to find a series of appropriate control input signal $u(k,i)$, so that with the number of iteration i increase, the tracking error $e(k+1,i) = y_d(k+1) - y(k+1,i)$ continues to decrease.

Consider the cost function of the control input as follows:

$$J(u(k,i)) = |e(k+1,i)|^2 + \lambda|u(k,i) - u(k,i-1)|^2 \tag{4}$$

where $\lambda > 0$ is introduced to restrain the changing rate of the control input.

Using the optimal condition $(\partial J/(\partial u(k,i))) = 0$, we have

$$u(k,i) = u(k,i-1) + \frac{\Phi_1(k,i)}{\lambda + |\Phi_1(k,i)|^2}[\rho_1 e(k+1,i-1) - \sum_{j=2}^{L}\rho_j\Phi_j(k,i)\Delta u(k$$
$$-j+1,i)] \tag{5}$$

where $\rho \in (0,1]$ is added to make the CFDL-MFAILC algorithm (5) more general.

4 PG Iterative Updating Algorithm

Since $\mathbf{\Phi}_L(k,i)$ is not available, controller algorithm (5) cannot be applied directly. Thus, we present a cost function of PG estimation as

$$J(\mathbf{\Phi}_L(k,i)) = \left|\Delta y(k+1,i-1) - \mathbf{\Phi}_L^T(k,i)\Delta \mathbf{U}_L(k,i-1)\right|^2 + \left\|\hat{\mathbf{\Phi}}_L(k,i)(k,i-1)\right\|^2 \tag{6}$$

where $\mu > 0$ is a weighting factor.

Minimizing (6) with respect to $\mathbf{\Phi}_L(k,i)$ according to the optimality condition and using the above matrix inversion lemma give

$$\hat{\mathbf{\Phi}}_L(k,i) = \hat{\mathbf{\Phi}}_L(k,i-1) + \frac{\eta\Delta \mathbf{U}_L(k,i-1)}{\mu + \|\Delta \mathbf{U}_L(k,i-1)\|^2}(\Delta y(k+1,i-1) - \hat{\mathbf{\Phi}}_L^T(k,i$$
$$-1)\Delta \mathbf{U}_L(k,i-1)) \tag{7}$$

Where the parameter $\eta \in (0, 2]$ is added to make the Pseudo Gradient (PG) estimation algorithm more generic. The $\hat{\Phi}_L(k, i)$ is the estimation of unknown PG $\Phi_L(k, i)$.

5 PFDL-MFAILC Algorithm Simulation of Noncircular Turning Tool Feed System

In noncircular turning tool feed system, the structure conclude current loop control, speed loop control and position loop control. The current loop and speed loop are achieved by linear motor driver, position loop is achieved by controller [1]. Therefore, the controlled plant in this paper are linear motor driver and linear motor.

From reference [1], control input is voltage signal, control output is linear motor position signal. After system identification, linear motor and its drive transfer function is written as follows:

$$G(s) = \frac{7437.7769(s - 928.2)}{(s+474)(s+474)(s+6.404)}$$

Z-transformation:

$$G(z) = \frac{0.001811z^2 - 0.00363z - 0.002546}{z^3 - 2.239z + 1.625z - 0.385}$$

Set sampling time interval is 1 ms, the differential equation is written as follows:

$$\begin{aligned} y(k) &= 2.2386y(k-1) - 1.6246y(k-2) + 0.385y(k-3) \\ &+ 0.0018u(k-1) - 0.0036u(k-2) - 0.0025u(k-3) \end{aligned} \tag{8}$$

To facilitate the operation, formula (8) is written as follows:

$$\begin{aligned} y(k+3) &= 2.2386y(k+2) - 1.6246y(k+1) + 0.385y(k) \\ &+ 0.0018u(k+2) - 0.0036u(k+1) - 0.0025u(k) \end{aligned}$$

5.1 PID Algorithm Simulation of Noncircular Turning Tool Feed System

PID algorithm is a traditional control algorithm and it is widely used in industrial control. Setting sinusoidal signal as linear motor's desired output position curve [6–9]. The sinusoidal signal's amplitude is 2 mm, frequency is 0.5 Hz. System step: $k \in [1, 4000]$. Step interval is 1 ms. Figure 1 shows tracking performance of PID algorithm after tuning PID parameters to the best and position error of PID algorithm. Where $y_d(k)$ represents the desired output position curve, $y(k)$ represents the actual output position curve. As can be seen from Fig. 1, the maximum position error is about 60μm. With the increase of sampling time, the Steady-State Error is about 27μm.

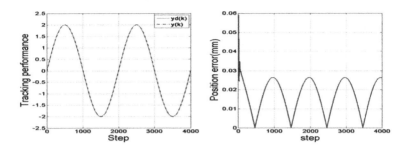

Fig. 1. Tracking performance of PID algorithm

5.2 PFDL-MFAILC Algorithm Simulation of Noncircular Turning Tool Feed System

Setting sinusoidal signal as noncircular turning tool feed desired output position curve [10–12]. The sinusoidal signal's amplitude is 2 mm, frequency is 0.5 Hz. System step: $k \in [1, 4000]$ step interval is 1 ms. The parameters in PFDL-MFAILC are set to $L = 2, \lambda = 1, \eta = 1, \rho_1 = \rho_2 = 1, \mu = 1$. In order to compare with PID algorithm, set the voltage signal value in PID as PFDL-MFAILC algorithm input in the first iteration. Set the initial output position value as $y(1, i) = y_d(1), y(2, i) = y_d(2), y(3, i) = y_d(3)$

Where $y_d(1), y_d(2), y_d(3)$ represents desired output position value in sampling time 1, 2, 3, where $y(1, i), y(2, i), y(3, i)$ represent set initial output position value at time instant 1, 2, 3 of the *ith* iteration.

Figure 2 shows tracking performance in PFDL-MFAILC algorithm after iterating 60 times. Where $y_d(k)$ is desired output position curve, $y(k)$ is actual output position curve. Figure 3 shows maximum position error and partial view of maximum position error as iteration number increase. From Fig. 3, the maximum position error of the linear motor is gradually decreased and converge to 20µm as iteration number increase.

Figure 4 shows noncircular turning tool feed position error after iterating 20,30,40,50 times. From Fig. 4, the maximum position error occurs in initial sampling time, and as iteration number increases, the Steady-State Error decreases rapidly. Figure 5 shows position error curve and partial view of position error after iterating 60 times. From partial view of Fig. 5, the Steady-State Error can be converged to 13 nm after 60 iterations.

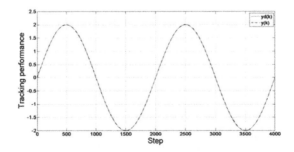

Fig. 2. Tracking performance in PFDL-MFAILC algorithm

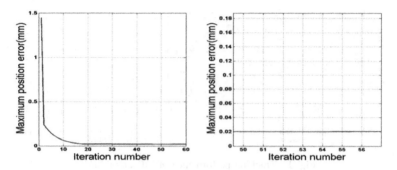

Fig. 3. Maximum position error in PFDL-MFAILC algorithm

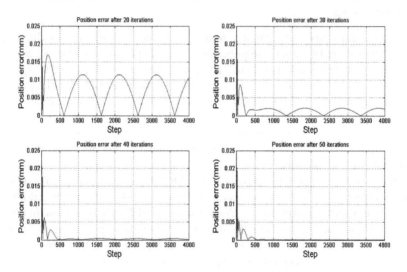

Fig. 4. Position error after 20,30,40,50 iterations

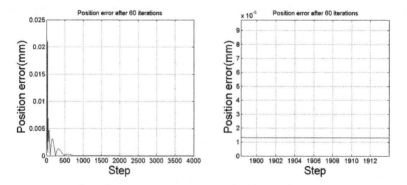

Fig. 5. Position error after 60 iterations

6 Conclusion

Due to noncircular turning tool feed does not have self-learning ability to improve its position error, this paper use PFDL-MFAILC algorithm in noncircular turning tool feed system. After simulating linear motor position error in PID algorithm and PFDL-MFAILC algorithm, the results show that maximum error is about 60μm in PID algorithm and Steady-State Error is about 27μm in PID algorithm. Linear motor maximum position error is about 20μm in PFDL-MFAILC algorithm. The steady-state error is just about 13 nm in PFDL-MFAILC algorithm after 60 iterations. From result of simulation, PFDL-MFAILC algorithm position error is much lower than PID algorithm as iteration increase. It achieve the goal that improving positional accuracy of noncircular turning tool feed system and making noncircular turning tool feed have self-learning ability.

In the future, PFDL-MFAILC algorithm will be used in practical applications. Robustness of noncircular turning tool feed system will be enhanced in order to deal with practical interference.

Acknowledgment. This work is supported by Beijing Natural Science Foundation of China (4142017), International Cooperation Project of National Natural Science Foundation of China (61120106009) and The National Natural Science Foundation of China (61261160497).

References

1. Zheng, D.: Research on derived CNC lathe system for large-sized non-circular middle-convex and varying oval piston. China Agricultural University, Beijing (2014)
2. Jin, S.-t.: On model free learning adaptive control and applications. Beijing Jiaotong University, Beijing (2008)
3. Zheng, J.: Model-free adaptive control with noise attenuation based on modified wavelet threshold denoising methods. Beijing Jiaotong University, Beijing (2016)
4. Guo, W.-p.: Application research of model free adaptive predictive control in grinding process. Hebei University of Technology, Hebei (2015)
5. Hou, Z.S., Jin, S.T.: Model Free Adaptive Control Theory and Applications. Science Press, Beijing (2013)
6. Cao, R.M.: Motion Control System Design and Implement Based on Data-Driven. National Defense Industry Press, Beijing (2012)
7. Yanhui, W.: Study on Model Free Adaptive Control for Nonlinear Systems. Yanshan University, Hebei (2015)
8. Cao, R.M., Zhou, H.X., Hou, Z.S.: Synthesis iterative learning control for noncircular turning tool feed. Electric Drive **09**, 42–46 (2012)
9. Lei, W.: Design and Experimental Study of Poly Magnet Linear Voice Coil Motor. China Agricultural University, Beijing (2014)

10. Hou, M.: Research on high-precision high-speed high-frequency linear motor control method. China Agricultural University, Beijing (2016)
11. Zhang, Y.: The research of the error compensation and the technology of feedforward control for the permanent magnet synchronous linear motor. North University of China (2016)
12. Liu, Y.: Data-driven terminal iterative learning control with variant uncertainties. Qingdao University of Science and Technology (2016)

Vibration Characteristic Analysis and Optimization of Heavy Load High Voltage Circuit Breaker Contact

Aibin Zhu[1(✉)], Wencheng Luo[1], Jianwei Zhao[2], and Dayong He[1]

[1] Key Laboratory of Education Ministry for Modern Design & Rotor-Bearing System, Xi'an Jiaotong University, Xi'an 710049, China
abzhu@mail.xjtu.edu.cn,
{luo0409,hedayong}@stu.xjtu.edu.cn
[2] School of Mechanical Electronic and Information Engineering,
China University of Mining and Technology (Beijing), Beijing 100083, China
zhaojianwei@cumtb.edu.cn

Abstract. The steady and rapid action of contact directly determines the overall performance of high voltage circuit breaker robot in closing and opening process. The current high-voltage circuit breaker robot reveals obvious contact vibration during use. In order to alleviate the ablation of contact due to the electric arc which is caused by the contact vibration, this essay establishes a forced vibration model of damped three degrees of freedom system through citing a new high-voltage circuit breaker, and analyzes the impacts of the mass and equivalent stiffness proportion among static contact, moving contact and support frame on the contact vibration frequency and amplitude by adopting Dunkerly and matrix iteration methods. Through adding vibration measuring instrument in the contact for experimental verification, the results show that appropriate and reasonable optimization of the mass proportion and equivalent stiffness proportion among static contact, moving contact and support frame can effectively reduce the amplitude of the first order of the main vibration mode, thus significantly alleviating the ablation of contact under the premise of effectively ensuring the opening speed to meet the conditions. The study results can remarkably reduce the vibration of high voltage circuit breaker contact, and then improve the overall performance of high voltage circuit breaker robot.

Keywords: High voltage circuit breaker · Three degrees of freedom system · Equivalent stiffness · The first order vibration mode · Opening speed

1 Introduction

High voltage circuit breaker (hereafter referred to as HVCB) is an important control and protection robot in the power system, its main role is to effectively control and protect power transmission lines and electrical apparatus [1–3]. In order to meet the

---

A. Zhu, W. Luo, J. Zhao and D. He — Co-first authors: they contribute equally to this research.

© Springer Science+Business Media Singapore 2016
L. Zhang et al. (Eds.): AsiaSim 2016/SCS AutumnSim 2016, Part II, CCIS 644, pp. 11–19, 2016.
DOI: 10.1007/978-981-10-2666-9_2

kinetic characteristic of contact, the closing speed must be quick enough to decrease the arcing time of pre-breakdown, so as to alleviate the ablation of contact surface [4, 5]. But on the other hand, excessive closing speed will cause contact vibration which also can leads to the ablation of contact surface. Therefore, the vibration characteristics simulation of HVCB contact can help to ease the closing elastic vibration, opening bounce [6], and improve the working life of HVCB robot.

In terms of reducing the contact vibration of HVCB robot, the domestic scholars have done some preliminary studies. Yang-Wu carried on the theoretical analysis and simulation of hydraulic operating mechanism opening buffer [7]. Xu-Jian Yuan established the relationship among the speed characteristic, contact overshoot and rebound amplitude, and achieved effective inhibition of contact overshoot and bounce through calibrating the default value [8]. Qian-Jia Li analyzed the impact phenomena and calculation methods of moving component of HVCB operating mechanism during processing, and analyzed the best mass ratio of the two colliding part under the different requirements [9]. Lin concluded that increasing contact spring stiffness coefficient can limit the closing vibration [10]. Zhang et al. [11], Fu and Hao [12] researched the fault diagnosis methods based on vibration signal.

The above research results are effective for simple operation system, especially for low-voltage circuit breaker mechanism motion characteristics where opening speed is not seen as important. However, it is dramatically difficult to obtain good vibration damping effect for HVCB robot with intricate mechanical structure and numerous mechanical components. Besides that, this method will prolong design cycle and augment the product cost. Especially for heavy load HVCB robot researched in this paper, the structure is shown in Fig. 1, and the comparison parameter with the traditional CT20 HVCB is shown in Table 1. It can be seen from the Table 1 that the new type circuit breaker can endure 550 kV voltage level or higher voltage level, and the closing spring operating power is nearly 6KN, which is almost twice what the

Table 1. The parameter comparison between CT20 HVCB and new type HVCB

Parameter comparison	Opening power/KN	Closing power/KN	Opening speed/m/s	Closing speed/m/s	Applied voltage grade/KV
CT20	1.8	3.2	4.5~5.5	2.5~3.5	40~252
New type	3.8	5.9	7.8~9.2	3~4	550~800

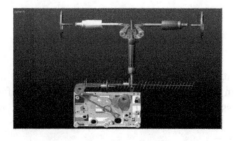

Fig. 1. The structure of high voltage circuit breaker

traditional CT20 HVCB can provide. Additionally, the new type HVCB has more than 300 components and fast closing speed, it needs to endure bigger closing impact with, so the method of adding buffer almost has no effect on the new circuit breaker.

Given that the contact vibration condition, this essay establishes a forced vibration model of damped three degrees of freedom system based on vibration mechanics theory, and analyzes the impacts of the mass and equivalent stiffness ratio among static contact, moving contact and support frame on the contact vibration frequency and amplitude by adopting Dunkerly and matrix iteration methods. Through adding vibration measuring instrument in the contact for experimental verification, the results show that reasonable optimization of the mass and equivalent stiffness ratio among static contact, moving contact and support frame can effectively reduce the amplitude of the first order vibration mode, thus significantly alleviating the ablation of contact.

1.1   The Establishment of Vibration Mechanical Model

Motion differential equation of damped multiple-degree-of-freedom system is Eq. (1):

$$M\ddot{x} + C\dot{x} + Kx = P(t) \tag{1}$$

Where mass matrix M, stiffness matrix K, damping matrix C are all $n \times n$ square matrices, x, $\dot{x}$, $\ddot{x}$ and $P(t)$ are all n-dimensional vector. The specific form of reaction equation as the following:

$$\begin{bmatrix} m_{11} & m_{12} & \cdots & m_{1n} \\ m_{21} & m_{22} & \cdots & m_{2n} \\ \vdots & \vdots & \ddots & \vdots \\ m_{n1} & m_{2n} & \cdots & m_{nn} \end{bmatrix} \begin{bmatrix} \ddot{x}_1 \\ \ddot{x}_2 \\ \vdots \\ \ddot{x}_n \end{bmatrix} + \begin{bmatrix} c_{11} & c_{12} & \cdots & c_{1n} \\ c_{21} & c_{22} & \cdots & c_{2n} \\ \vdots & \vdots & \ddots & \vdots \\ c_{n1} & c_{2n} & \cdots & c_{nn} \end{bmatrix} \begin{bmatrix} \dot{x}_1 \\ \dot{x}_2 \\ \vdots \\ \dot{x}_n \end{bmatrix} + \begin{bmatrix} k_{11} & k_{12} & \cdots & k_{1n} \\ k_{21} & k_{22} & \cdots & k_{2n} \\ \vdots & \vdots & \ddots & \vdots \\ k_{n1} & k_{2n} & \cdots & k_{nn} \end{bmatrix} \begin{bmatrix} x_1 \\ x_2 \\ \vdots \\ x_n \end{bmatrix} = \begin{bmatrix} P_1(t) \\ P_2(t) \\ \vdots \\ P_n(t) \end{bmatrix} \tag{2}$$

Where c_{ij} in the matrix C is called the damping influence coefficient, its meaning is the corresponding force applied on the i-coordinate to make the system generate unit speed only on the j-coordinate.

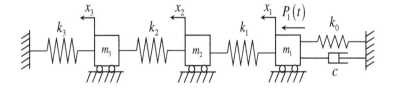

Fig. 2. Forced vibration model of damped three degrees of freedom system

In Fig. 2, the paper establishes a forced vibration model of damped three degrees of freedom system. In the process of collision, the moving contact m_1 under the force

$P_1(t)$ collides with the static contact m_2, the support frame of the static contact is m_3. Respectively, the equivalent spring stiffness between moving contact and static contact is k_1, between the stationary contacts and the support frame is k_2 and between the support frame and the ground is k_3.

Combined with the Eqs. (1) and (2) to obtain the specific form of the forced vibration model's motion equation, the matrix form of the differential equation as the following:

$$
\begin{bmatrix} m_1 & 0 & 0 \\ 0 & m_2 & 0 \\ 0 & 0 & m_3 \end{bmatrix} \begin{bmatrix} \ddot{x}_1 \\ \ddot{x}_2 \\ \ddot{x}_3 \end{bmatrix} + \begin{bmatrix} c & 0 & 0 \\ 0 & 0 & 0 \\ 0 & 0 & 0 \end{bmatrix} \begin{bmatrix} \dot{x}_1 \\ \dot{x}_2 \\ \dot{x}_3 \end{bmatrix} + \begin{bmatrix} k_1 + k_2 & -k_2 & 0 \\ -k_2 & k_2 + k_3 & -k_3 \\ 0 & -k_3 & k_3 \end{bmatrix} \begin{bmatrix} x_1 \\ x_2 \\ x_3 \end{bmatrix} = \begin{bmatrix} P_1(t) \\ P_2(t) \\ P_3(t) \end{bmatrix}
$$
(3)

To solve the first-order vibration mode's natural frequency by adopting Dunkerly and matrix iteration methods [13], the completed method is demonstrated as the following. First, record $n \times n$ square matrix A as the dynamic matrix of the system, which is defined as $A = FM = K^{-1}M$. In order to prevent elements of the iteration vector become too big or too small during the iterative process, the vector needs to be normalized after each iteration step, i.e., replaces the last element with 1. The concrete calculating steps of matrix iterative method as the following:

(1) Select the initial iteration vector X_1, replace the last element with 1;
(2) Iterate matrix X_1, and make new vector Y_1 normalization;
(3) Repeat Eq. (4) iteration equation

$$
Y_r = AX_r, X_{r+1} = \frac{1}{(Y_r)_n} Y_r
$$
(4)

If there is $X_{r+1} = X_r$ within the permissible error range, take X_{r+1} or X_r as the first-order vibration mode. Therefore, the first order natural frequency is shown as the following:

$$
\lambda_1 = \frac{(Y_r)_n}{(X_r)_n} = \frac{(Y_r)_n}{1}, \omega_1 = \frac{1}{\sqrt{(Y_r)_n}} = \frac{1}{\sqrt{\lambda_1}}
$$
(5)

2 The Analysis of Contact Vibration Mechanical Model

Based on the previous analysis, the vibration mechanics characteristics of the contact is determined primarily by the mass of static contact m_1, moving contact m_2 and support frame m_3 and equivalent stiffness ratio k_1, k_2, k_3 between them. However, how will this six parameters affect the vibration characteristics of the contact and the influence extent need to be further explored and analyzed.

Barkan has made some discussion on dynamical processing of contact closing bounce [14]. He proposed a three degrees of freedom energy transmission model for the analysis of contact collision. The main result obtained from the model is that when $k_2/k_1 = 1 = m_3/m_1$, the kinetic energy associated with the collision can be transmitted and retained to the support frame to the full extent during the collision. On the basis of Barkan's work, the author further analyzes the impacts of the mass ratio m_3/m_2 and equivalent stiffness ratio k_3/k_1 on the contact vibration frequency and amplitude.

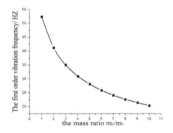

Fig. 3. The mass ratio influence

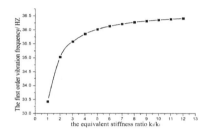

Fig. 4. The equivalent stiffness ratio influence

In order to quantitatively analyze the impact of the collision parts mass ratio on the first order of the vibration mode's natural frequency, this essay gradually increase the mass ratio m_3/m_2 from 1 to 10, and then calculate the natural frequency for each mass ratio. In Fig. 3, in the course of the mass ratio m_3/m_2 increasing step by step, the first order natural vibration frequency decreases first quickly, then slowly and finally levels off. The vibration frequency varies in a larger range from 52 Hz to 18 Hz. From the above analysis, it can come to the conclusion that through appropriately increasing the mass ratio between support frame and static contact, the vibration impact can be quickly transmitted to the support frame so as to weaken the contact vibration.

Similarly, in order to quantitatively analyze the impact of the equivalent stiffness ratio k_3/k_1 on the first order of the vibration mode's natural frequency, this essay gradually increase the equivalent stiffness ratio k_3/k_1 from 1 to 12, and then calculate the natural frequency for each equivalent stiffness ratio. In Fig. 4, in the course of the equivalent stiffness ratio k_3/k_1 increasing step by step, the first order vibration frequency increases first quickly, then slowly and finally levels off. The vibration frequency varies in a small range from 32 Hz to 37 Hz. From the above analysis, it can come to the conclusion that through appropriately decreasing the equivalent stiffness ratio, the vibration can be reduced. And the impact of the equivalent spring stiffness ratio on the main vibration frequency of the first order is less than the mass ratio on the vibration frequency.

Considering the double contact structure of the new type HVCB, it is measured by the physical prototype of HVCB: $m_2 = 22.174$ kg , $m_1 = 37.392$ kg , $m_3 = 67.764$ kg. Through increasing or decreasing the mass of non-critical structural components, the author readjusts the mass ratio among static contact, moving contact, flange plate and support frame. After optimization, $m_1 = 64.428$ kg, $m_2 = 21.276$ kg, $m_3 = 66.391$ kg. Taking the optimization of the flange plate mass as an example, the author reduces the

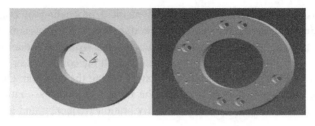

(a) Before optimizatio   (b) After optimization

Fig. 5. The comparison of flange plate mass before and after optimization

flange plate overall mass through cutting holes in non-critical structural position as shown in Fig. 5. However, taking the real situation of mass ratio and material stiffness into account, the author finally determines $m_3/m_2 = 3$ and $k_3/k_1 = 10$ as the best approach.

3   The Results and Analysis of Contact Vibration Model Test

3.1   The Settings of Test Apparatus

In order to verify the accuracy of three degrees of freedom vibration model, the author conducts experiment research on the physical prototype of HVCB robot by using vibration analyzer. Through installing vibration sensors on the HVCB contact, the author respectively measures the contact vibration situation before and after the mass and equivalent stiffness optimization of static contact, moving contact, flange plate and support frame. And the author simultaneously records X direction transverse vibration of the contact in the process of opening and closing. Physical prototype and measurement method is shown in Fig. 6. Measuring principle is shown in Fig. 7.

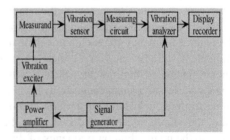

Fig. 6. Measurement methods   **Fig. 7.** Measuring principle

The author first sets 10 as the gradient for the range of 0 Hz to 100 Hz and 100 for the range of 100 Hz to 1000 Hz. Then under the different excitation vibration frequency, the author records the first order vibration frequency of contact and compares the experiment result with the model simulation result.

3.2   The Analysis of Experimental Results Before and After Optimization

The vibration response which is motivated by the external vibration in X direction is shown in Fig. 8. Before optimization, in the process of the excitation frequency gradually increasing from 0.1 Hz to 10 Hz, the amplitude increases slowly, then from 10 Hz to 30 Hz process, the amplitude increases rapidly, and there is a very remarkable peak at 31 Hz, from 31 Hz to 100 Hz, the amplitude decreases rapidly, and from 100 Hz to 1000 Hz, the amplitude slowly decreases to its original level. After the optimization, in the process of the excitation frequency gradually increasing from 0.1 Hz to 10 Hz, the amplitude increases slowly, then from 10 Hz to 20 Hz, the amplitude increases rapidly, and there is a very remarkable peak at 23 Hz, from 23 Hz to 100 Hz, the amplitude decreases rapidly, and from 100 Hz to 1000 Hz, the amplitude slowly decreases to its original level. Through the above analysis, it comes to the conclusion that the contact first order resonance frequency decreases from 31 Hz to 23 Hz after the optimization. The analysis shows the experimental results is consistent with the theoretic simulation results, and the maximum relative error is less than 5 %.

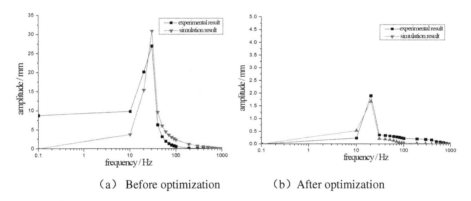

(a) Before optimization   (b) After optimization

Fig. 8. The comparison of simulation and experiment results before and after optimization

Table 2. The comparison of simulation and experiment results before optimization

Performance parameter	Simulation	Experiment	Absolute error	Relative error/%
Frequency/Hz	22.74	23.61	0.87	3.67
Amplitude/mm	1.67	1.81	0.14	8.38

Table 3. The comparison of simulation and experiment results after optimization

Performance parameter	Simulation	Experiment	Absolute error	Relative error/%
Frequency/Hz	31.65	33.18	1.53	4.83
Amplitude/mm	30.89	28.46	2.43	7.87

As shown in Table 2, before optimization, the resonance amplitude measured by experiment is 28.46 mm and by simulation is 30.89 mm. Therefore, the simulation results agree with the experimental results essentially, and the maximum relative error of the average amplitude is less than 10 %. In Table 3, after optimization, the resonance amplitude measured by experiment is 1.81 mm and by simulation is 1.67 mm, and the maximum relative error of the average amplitude is less than 10 %. In conclusion, given that the experimental result curves agree with the simulation result curves better before and after optimization, the experiment results can prove the effectiveness of the forced vibration model simulation of damped three degrees of freedom system. In addition, after optimization, the ablation of the contact surface is greatly reduced and finally the service life of HVCB robot is improved.

Compared with the conclusion in Qian-Jia Li's essay [9], the kinetic energy associated with the collision can be transmitted and retained to the support frame to the full extent during the collision. Additionally, the mechanical transmission efficiency has been improved by 5 %.

4 Conclusion and Future Works

A forced vibration model of damped three degrees of freedom is proposed to achieve the contact vibration frequency and amplitude. Dunkerly and matrix iteration methods is adopted to calculate the first order vibration frequency. Both the simulation results and calculation results are verified by experiment. Experiment results show that the resonance amplitude of the physical prototype can be reduced from 28.46 mm to 1.67 mm after the optimization of the mass and equivalent stiffness proportion among static contact, moving contact and support frame, and the maximum relative error of average amplitude is less than 10 %. In conclusion, the study results can effectively reduce the amplitude of the first order of the main vibration mode, thus significantly alleviating the ablation of contact, and finally improve the overall performance of HVCB robot.

The future works of this study will continue the theoretical research on contact vibration model to further promote the performance of the heavy load HVCB. Meanwhile, the future works will concentrate on the ablation time to strengthen the approach of alleviating the ablation of contact.

References

1. Dai, Y., Zhang, M., Fan, K., et al.: Investigation of series-connected IGBTs in fast high-voltage circuit breaker. J. Fus. Energy **34**(6), 1406–1410 (2015)
2. Garzon, R.D.: High voltage circuit breakers: design and applications. Vacuum 214–218 (2002)
3. Zheng, X.-G.: Principle and application of high voltage circuit breaker, pp. 15–34. Tsinghua University Press, Beijing (2000)
4. Arabi, S., Trepanier, J.Y., Camarero, R.: Transient simulation of nozzle geometry change during ablation in high-voltage circuit breakers. J. Phys. D Appl. Phys. **48**(4), 22–114 (2015)

5. Godin, D., Trepanier, J.Y., Reggio, M., et al.: Modeling and simulation of nozzle ablation in high-voltage circuit-breakers. J. Phys. D Appl. Phys. **33**(20), 2583–2590 (2000)
6. Xu, K.X.: Optimization and simulation for spring actuator of high-voltage circuit breaker. Dalian Univ. Technol. 21–25 (2012)
7. Wu, Y., Zhe, R.-M., Chen, D.-G., et al.: Optimum design of high-voltage circuit breakers based on mechanism dynamic features simulation. J. Xi'an Jiaotong Univ. **36**(12), 1211–1214 (2002)
8. Yuan, X.-J., Lei-Wei, T.-G., et al.: Research on opening contact overshoot and rebound suppression methods of vacuum circuit breakers with permanent magnet actuator. High Volt. Appar. **51**(3), 22–27 (2015)
9. Li, Q.-J., Gang, G.-Y.: Analysis of mechanical impact in operating device for HV circuit breaker. High Volt. Appar. **39**(6), 20 (2001)
10. Lin, X., Cao, C., Bin, L.I., et al.: Dynamic simulation and opening bouncing analysis of vacuum circuit breaker with permanent magnetic actuator. High Volt. Appar. **39**(7), 1–5 (2013)
11. Zhang, P., Zhao, S.T., Shen, L., et al.: Research on vibration and acoustic joint mechanical fault diagnosis method of high voltage circuit breaker based on improved EEMD. Power Syst. Prot. Control **42**(8), 77–81 (2014)
12. Fu, C., Hao, J.: On-line monitoring system based on vibration signal of high voltage circuit breaker. J. Multimedia **9**(4), 598–603 (2014)
13. Ni, Z.-H.: Vibration Mechanics, pp. 277–286. Xi'an Jiaotong University Press, Xi'an (1989)
14. Barkan, P., Mcgarrity, R.V.: A spring-actuated, cam-follower system: design theory and experimental results. J. Manuf. Sci. Eng. **87**(3), 279–286 (1965)

Gait Planning and Simulation of Four Rocker-Arms Inspection Robot for Fully-Mechanized Workface in Thin Coal Seam

Jianwei Zhao, Deyong Shang[✉], and Qu Yuanyuan

School of Mechanical Electronic and Information Engineering,
China University of Mining and Technology, Beijing, China
shangdy1983@126.com

Abstract. A inspection robot with four rocker-arms was designed adapting to the environment of fully-mechanized workface in thin coal seam. The walking mechanism and relevant parameters were determined according to the function requirements of the robot. Two sets of walking gaits were planned specifically for the four rocker-arms and were simulated virtually using ADAMS. By observing the behaviors of rocker-arms and analyzing the centroid displacement of the robot during the movements, both of the two sets of walking gaits were verified to be reasonable, one of them is recommended based on its better stability.

Keywords: Thin seam · Inspection robot · Simulation · Gait planning

1 Introduction

The thin coal resource, with great economic exploitation value, is abundant and distributes widely in china. However, due to the narrow space of thin coal seam workface, installation, operation and maintenance of equipment manually become more difficult. The typical environment of thin coal seam workface was shown in Fig. 1. The maintenance workers squat and examine the working condition of shearer group, hydraulic supports and other equipment [1]. While some workface is so narrow that workers have to crawl through, which harms the health of maintenance workers obviously, especially when they have to work for a long time under this harsh environment.

In order to alleviate the labor intensity of maintenance workers, it is urgent to design a kind of inspection robot, which can adapt the environment of fully mechanized workface in thin coal seam, and replace or accomplish the inspection work auxiliary. The desired inspection robot, whose structure is shown in Fig. 2, can adapt all kinds of terrain environment of the working face with better obstacle crossing ability. It is composed of walking mechanism and operating arm. The walking mechanism is driven by crawler and consists of four rocker-arms assembled in front and rear respectively which mainly assist crossing obstacles.

© Springer Science+Business Media Singapore 2016
L. Zhang et al. (Eds.): AsiaSim 2016/SCS AutumnSim 2016, Part II, CCIS 644, pp. 20–28, 2016.
DOI: 10.1007/978-981-10-2666-9_3

Fig. 1. Workers overhaul equipment in thin coal seam workface

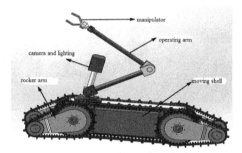

Fig. 2. The structure of the inspection robot

2 Performance Indicators

In view of particularity of the environment of thin coal seam workface, the aforementioned inspection robot must satisfy the performance indicators shown in Table 1.

Table 1. Main performance indicators of inspection robot

Item	Performance indicators
Boundary dimension $l \times b \times h$(mm)	rocker-arm fully extended $750 \times 340 \times 160$
	rocker-arm shrinkage $540 \times 340 \times 160$
Total mass	31 kg
Working speed	0.5 m/s
Maximum permissible gradient	30°
Maximum height of surmountable obstacle	180 mm
Rotation angle of front and rear rocker-arm	±360°
Endurance	2 h

3   Structure of Walking Mechanism

The inspection robot consists of three parts, including robot body, left and right master drive tracks,as well as front and rear rocker-arms tracks. As shown in Fig. 3, The inspection robot has six DC motors in total, which two of them drive the two rear-wheels respectively to realize the function of going forward and differential turning. The other four DC motors drive the four rocker-arms respectively to assist the inspection robot get through a variety of complicated terrains [2–4]. The employ of four rocker-arms modular design in this case is based on its conveniences for maintenance and replacement. Symmetrical structure layout [5, 6] is applied to make the centroid of the robot coincide with its geometric center, so that to improve the robot's stability when crossing obstacles.

Fig. 3.   The structure design diagram for inspection robot

4   Four Rocker-Arms Gait Planning

Generally, there are at least three driven joints in each leg for the omni-directional quadruped robot. Unlikely, the four rocker-arms of the designed inspection robot in this paper are driven by four DC motors separately, which means they can only revolve around the main body of the robot. The expected walking manner as any quadruped robot does is realized through reasonably planning the rotation angle and swinging sequence of the four rocker-arms.

4.1   The Assumption of Gait Planning

When planning the static gait for the four rocker-arms robot, the following assuming conditions are proposed [7, 8].

- The structure of inspection robot is symmetrical, the centroid of robot is located on the body geometric center; the influence to the robot's centroid position by the rotation of the rocker-arms is neglected.
- The step length of four swinging legs are equal and the time that one step takes is the same, that is to say, two-side swing is symmetrical.
- There is no relative sliding for the contact point between swinging leg and the ground.
- Assume an initial state of the inspection robot when walking.

4.2 The Gait Figure

In order to keep robot's walking stability in one gait period, not only the revolving sequence and rotation angle of each rocker-arm need to be planned reasonably, but also their positions against to the robot's main body are necessarily adjusted at the same time. Thus, the sufficient stability margin could be guaranteed during the proceeding.

The gait figure is used to describe the walking manner of the inspection robot in one motion period, it reflects the revolve sequencing of each rocker-arms and their position against to robot's main body. Assumed that the inspection robot left front rocker-arm as rocker-arm 1, then the rocker-arm2, rocker-arm3 and rocker-arm4 respectively according to clockwise direction, In order to keep the robot moving stably, the four rocker-arms rotate and move forward in turn according to the gait planning. We must ensure that at least three rocker-arms support the robot simultaneously, Define that the gait 3-1-4-2 refers to the rotation sequence of the rocker-arm that the rocker-arm 3 rotate at first, then the rocker-arm 1, rocker-arm4, and rocker-arm2 rotate respectively. The gait 3-1-4-2 diagram is shown in Fig. 4. This set of gait adjusts the centroid location only once in one period when the robot proceeds, which is simple to control, easy to realize and of high walking efficiency.

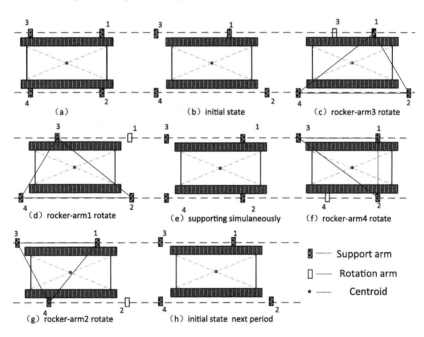

Fig. 4. The motion diagram of the gait 3-1-4-2. The gait marked as 1-4-2-3 was planned and is shown in Fig. 5. In one gait period, the robot adjusts the location of centroid position twice a period when the four rocker-arms supporting robot body simultaneously.

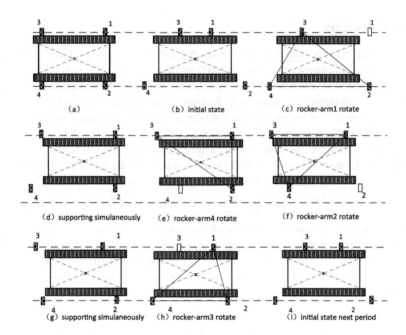

Fig. 5. The motion diagram of the gait 1-4-2-3

4.3   The Virtual Simulation

In order to verify the rationality and validity of the gait planning, the two sets of gaits were virtual simulated using ADAMS. To display clearly, the rocker link was hidden during the simulation. The front view of simulation of the two sets of gaits are shown in Figs. 6 and 7, respectively. And the simulation results show that both the two sets of gaits were reasonable.

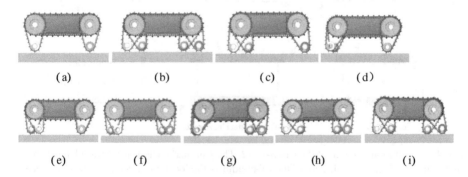

Fig. 6. The simulation diagram of gait 1-4-2-3

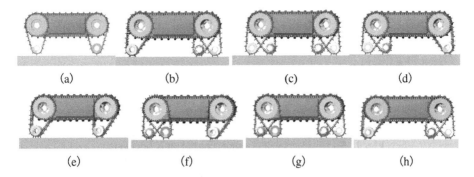

Fig. 7. The simulation diagram of gait 3-1-4-2

4.4 Sequence Diagram for Control Rocker-Arm

The duty ratio of the both planned gaits is $85/100 = 0.85$, the move distance of each step and the motor rotary angle are related to the initial position of the robot. In order to ensure the movement stability, set the initial position of the robot arm randomly to rotate $20°$.

The gait 1-4-2-3 sequence diagram of the robot is shown in Fig. 8(a), and the 3-1-4-2 gait is shown in Fig. 8(b), horizontal solid line represents the rocker arm in the supporting state.

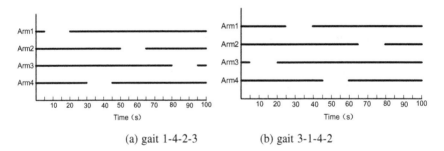

(a) gait 1-4-2-3   (b) gait 3-1-4-2

Fig. 8. The gait sequence diagram for one cycle

4.5 Analysis on Simulation

The two sets of gaits planning were virtual simulated in three cycles using the ADAMS, the centroid displacement curve diagram of the robot in the walking direction (X orientation) is shown in Fig. 9. Simulated result shows that the robot displacement in the horizontal direction is 225.6 mm under the gait 3-1-4-2 by one cycle, and the horizontal displacement is 225.6 mm for the gait 1-4-3-2. Meanwhile, the gait 3-1-4-2 shows more smoothly than gait 1-4-3-2.

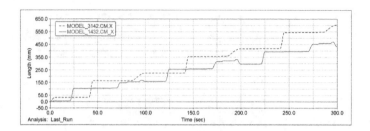

Fig. 9. The displacement of robot centroid on X orientation

The centroid displacement curve in the vertical direction (Y orientation) of the robot is shown in Fig. 10. The amplitude value of both two sets of gait are the same and the maximum value is 12.1 mm, while the fluctuation number of the 3-1-4-2 gait is obviously less than the gait 1-4-3-2.

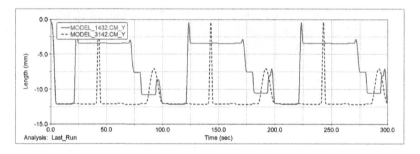

Fig. 10. The displacement of robot centroid on Y orientation

The centroid displacement curve in Z direction is shown in Fig. 11. Gait 3-1-4-2 offsets from the initial position further than the gait 1-4-3-2 does, and it turns to deviate gradually from the planned route after moving several cycles.

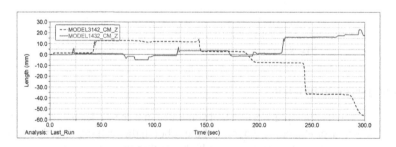

Fig. 11. The displacement of robot centroid on Z orientation

4.6 Stability Margin Calculation

Generally, the stability margin of the robot depends on the distance between the centroid location and the supporting side boundary in forward direction [9, 10], as the distance denoted by 'S' illustrated in Fig. 12. The size of the margin is an important indicator to judge the stability performance of the robot.

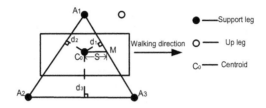

Fig. 12. Stability margin of the robot move direction

By exporting the tangency points data of four rocker-arms from ADAMS, The robot stability margin curve in three gait cycle is plotted and shown in Fig. 13. The results indicate that within the 65–80 s, the minimum stability margin of the gait 1-4-3-2 was 11.40 mm, and the minimum stability margin of the gait 3-1-4-2 was 35.91 mm.

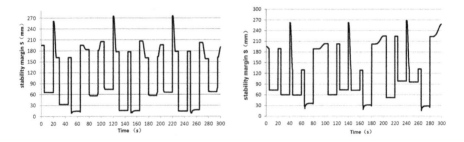

Fig. 13. Stability margin of the robot with the (a) gait 1-4-2-3 and (b) gait 3-1-4-2

5 Conclusions

The structure of this inspection robot cannot achieve omnidirectional walking, and its stability and flexibility were not as good as the quadruped robot. For the robot-arm structure, we planned the gait 3-1-4-2 and gait 1-4-2-3, and two kinds of three walking gait cycle had been virtual simulation. The centroid of the robot's displacement in the X, Y, Z direction and the stability margin had been analysed, the results showed that the gait 3-1-4-2 was more stable and easy to control. The planning gait can realize the robot body posture adjustment and obstacle crossing function in fully mechanized workface, which put forward higher requirements to the control system of inspection robot.

References

1. Shang, D.: Research on kinematics joint type mobile robot platform for thin coal seam inspection. In: Applied Mechanics and Materials, vol. (651–653), pp. 818–821 (2014)
2. Li, Y., Ge, S., Zhu, H., et al.: Obstacle-surmounting mechanism and capability of four-track robot with two swing arms. ROBOT **32**(3), 157–164 (2010)
3. Lee, W., Kang, S., Kim, M., Shin, K.: Rough terrain negotiable mobile platform with passively adaptive double-tracks and its application to rescue missions. In: Proceedings of the 2005 IEEE International Conference on Robotics and Automation, Barcelona, Spain, pp. 1591–1596 (2005)
4. Kim, J., Lee, C., Kim, G.: Study of machine design for a transformable shape single-tracked vehicle system. Mech. Mach. Theory **45**, 1082–1095 (2010)
5. Duan, X.-G., Huang, Q., Li, J.: Small sized ground mobile robot with surmounting obstacle function. J. Mach. Des. **23**(4), 38–41 (2006)
6. Moosavian, S.A.A., Kalantari, A.: Experimental slip estimation for exact kinematics modeling and control of a tracked mobile robot. In: 2008 IEEE/RSJ International Conference on Intelligent Robotics and Systems, Nice, France, pp. 95–100 (2008)
7. Elshamli, A.: Mobile Robots Path Planning Optimization in Static and Dynamic Environments. University of Guelph (2004)
8. Buehler, M., Battaglia, R., Cocosco, A., et al.: Scout: a simple quadruped that walks, climbs, and runs. In: IEEE International Conference on Robotics and Automation, pp. 1707–1712. IEEE, Piscataway, NJ, USA (1998)
9. Wang, X., Li, P.: Research on joint positions and robot stability of an omnidirectional crawling quadruped robot. China Mech. Eng. **16**(17), 1561–1565 (2005)
10. Tsai, L.W.: Kinematics of a three DOF platform with three extensible limbs. In: Lenarcic, J., Parenti-Castell, V. (eds.) Recent Advances in Robot Kinematics, pp. 401–410. Kluwer Academic Publishers, Amsterdam (1996)

Self-balancing Robot Design
and Implementation Based on Machine Vision

Yingnian Wu[✉] and Xinli Shi

School of Automation, Beijing Key Laboratory of High Dynamic Navigation
Technology, Beijing Information Science & Technology University,
Beijing, China
wuyingnian@bistu.edu.cn

Abstract. Self-balancing robot based on machine vision with two wheels
sometimes can be more flexible and saving space than four wheels. We present
design scheme and experiment implement of self-balancing robot based on
machine vision in the paper. The robot can get road information by CCD
camera, then process the image by algorithm to get the road path information
and the robot can safely and reliably auto-drive along the road. Based on
machine vision the self-balancing robot does not need person to control it, and it
can reduce the human disturbance which can greatly improve the efficiency and
safety of the system. The system needs to deal with lots of tasks under CPU
resource limitation. We have considered the task scheduling under CPU
resource limitation through experiment and theory prove. It is proved that the
system has good intelligence and anti-interference ability by experiments and
competition.

Keywords: Self-balancing robot · Machine vision · Task scheduling

1 Introduction

With the development of new information technology, more and more robots have been
used in factory. Self-balancing robot based on machine vision with two wheels sometimes can be more flexible and saving space than four wheels. It has the function of
automatic driving, and automatic identification of road information. It can get the environment around itself based on the camera. There are black lines in both edges of the road.
The robot can safely and reliably auto-drive along the road. Based on machine vision the
self-balancing robot does not need person to control it, and it can reduce the human
disturbance which can greatly improve the efficiency and safety of the system [1–4].

2 System Model and Stability Discussion

Figure 1 is the real system of the self-balancing robot. We can take the robot as a
physical pendulum model which centroid weight is m and pendulum length is *L*, and
take the motor and its driver system as coil spring model. We can discuss the pendulum
stability from the perspective of the potential energy curve.

L. Zhang et al. (Eds.): AsiaSim 2016/SCS AutumnSim 2016, Part II, CCIS 644, pp. 29–37, 2016.
DOI: 10.1007/978-981-10-2666-9_4

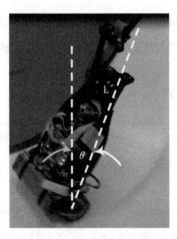

Fig. 1. Real system of the self-balancing robot.

Suppose the system satisfying Hooke's law, which assumes that the restoring force of the motor and the tilt angle is proportional to the actual situation. In the real system, when there is a deviation between the setting angle and the real angle of the robot, the motor will timely correct the angle. So we assume the angel between setting angel and real angel of the robot is less than 5 degree. The restoring force of the motor is proportional linear relationship to the inclination angle.

Set the motor torque of the robot inverted pendulum model:

$$L_b = -k\theta \qquad (1)$$

The elastic potential energy is

$$E_{pb} = \int_0^\theta k\theta d\theta = \frac{1}{2}k\theta^2 \qquad (2)$$

The gravitational potential energy is

$$E_{pg} = mgL(\cos\theta - 1) \qquad (3)$$

The total potential energy is

$$E_p = \frac{1}{2}k\theta^2 + mgL(\cos\theta - 1) \qquad (4)$$

Balance position is corresponding to the extreme value of the potential energy curve, so set $E_p = U(\theta)$, we can get the possible existing equilibrium position by derivative of θ.

$$\frac{dU}{d\theta} = k\theta - mgL\sin\theta = mgL\left(\frac{k}{mgL}\theta - \sin\theta\right) \tag{5}$$

Set $\frac{dU}{d\theta} = 0$, there exist 3 cases, case 1: $\frac{k}{mgL} > 1$, only if $\theta=0$, there exists a stationary point; case2: $\frac{k}{mgL} < 1$, there exist 3 stationary points, $\theta=0$ and $\theta = \pm\theta_0$. case3: The critical state between the case 1 and case 2.

The stability of the equilibrium position is decided by $\frac{d^2U}{d\theta^2}$.

$$\frac{d^2U}{d\theta^2} = k - mgL\cos\theta \tag{6}$$

(1) When $\frac{k}{mgL} > 1$ and $\theta=0$, $\frac{d^2U}{d\theta^2} > 0$, $E_p = U(\theta)$ exists minimum value, equilibrium is stable.

(2) When $\frac{k}{mgL} < 1$ and $\theta=0$, $\frac{d^2U}{d\theta^2} < 0$, $E_p = U(\theta)$ is corresponding to the potential energy maximum value, equilibrium is unstable.

(3) When $\frac{k}{mgL} < 1$ and $\theta = \pm\theta_0$, $\frac{d^2U}{d\theta^2} < 0$, which can prove, equilibrium is stable [5].

3   Hardware System Design

There are 6 modules in the self-balancing robot based on machine vision systems: micro-controller module, wireless communication module, machine vision module, inertial sensing module, power module, and motor drive & control module (Fig. 2).

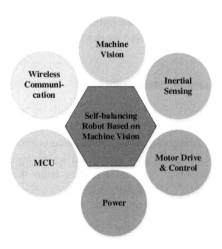

Fig. 2. Robot system scheme

3.1 Power and Motor Drive & Control Module

The main functionality of the power module is to supply power for the micro controller, all sensors and motor driver modules. The robot uses Ni-Cr battery for power supply, which has good specialty for big electricity discharging. The specified voltage for the battery is 7.2 V, which can be up to 8.4 V with fully charging. The deceasing voltage under load is small, which makes benefit for the robot to move stably.

The CCD camera, micro controller, encoder, blue tooth, accelerometer and gyroscope module are all powered at 5 V, hence the regulator module is only made up of LM2940 regulator chip, which is relatively simple and has small effect on the gravity center of the robot.

The motor drive & control module is made up of BTS7970B double circuit using light coupling, so that it can be isolated from the power supply on CPU and effectively protect the CPU. The drive circuit has a small size and leads to good driving ability and effective braking.

3.2 Micro-Controller Module

The micro-controller is the brain of the intelligent robot. It controls the robot to perform various actions as pre-settings, receives the information gathered by all sensors, processes all received information, and transfers the processed information to corresponding actuators.

The robot uses the 16 bit MC9S12XS128 MCU as its control core. The main frequency is 16 MHz, which can be frequency doubling increased to 96 MHz by the phase locked loop inside the MCU. The interrupt of MCU has seven priorities and its kernel supports priority dispatching, which can access the whole memory space up to 8 MB.

MC9S12XS128 is a 16 bits MCU, which has a limitation on processing speed and resource comparing to 32 bits MCU. We optimized the program and system during research and applied simple and effective methods to implement expected functions.

3.3 Wireless Communication Module

The main function of wireless communication module is to transmit the data from MCU to the superior workstation. The blue tooth is the protocol for short distance communication. Generally, the communication distance is about 10 meters at the open area and the communicating speed gets lower and lower upon longer distance. The system applies the blue tooth to transmit the data from the robot to the superior workstation so that debugging and status monitoring can be performed.

3.4 Machine Vision Module

The robot applies CCD camera to get the road information during moving. There are black border lines on both sides of the road. According to the road border lines information gathered by the camera, the robot can move automatically between the border lines. The CCD camera OV7620MVA applies self-adoption power supply at 5 V/3.3 V, no need to increase the voltage to 12 V, which makes the regulator circuit simple, the regulator module lighter, and the gravity center lower. Also, the camera uses 2.8 mm/95 wide lucid lens to ensure a high quality for the images.

3.5 Inertial Sensing Module

The robot controls the motor speed by gathering and processing the data from inertia sensing module, hence controls its balance and moving speed. The inertia sensing module consists of accelerometer, gyroscope and encoder.

The accelerometer and gyroscope module uses MMA7361 and ENC03 chips, a triple axis accelerometer and a single axis gyroscope module. This module applies a hardware Kalman filter. The Kalman filter can merge the signals from accelerometer and gyroscope.

The encoder is 512 lines triple axis MINI incremental rotating encoder with small size. When the disk with optics graphic pattern and rotating axle rotate at the same time, the corresponding light getting through the two aperture will appear as passing through and intercepting status, hence the angle displacement can be transformed to corresponding pulse signal [6], and then figure out the moving speed of the robot.

4   Software System Design

The software system of the robot consists of main function module, one-millisecond interrupt system module and video field interrupt system module.

The main function module is the frame of the whole program and the base for both one-millisecond interrupt system and field interrupt system module. The one-millisecond interrupt module is a program based on MC9S12XS128 one-millisecond interrupt hardware, and millisecond interrupt will occur every mil-lisecond. The field interrupt system is used to process image information from the CCD camera. During the idle time for CPU to process the main program, it will process the one-millisecond interrupt program or field interrupt program at regular intervals. If there is any conflict for the two programs, process the field interrupt program as higher priority.

4.1   Main Function Module

Figure 3 illustrates how the main program works. It starts to wait for interrupt right after initialization. MC9S12XS128 totally has 55 interrupt with different priorities, and the one with highest priority is reset interrupt. The robot only uses two different priority interrupt, i.e., field interrupt and one-millisecond interrupt. That is, the core board will run the field interrupt, or one-millisecond interrupt, or stay idle right after the initialization.

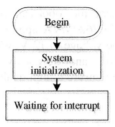

Fig. 3. Main function module diagram

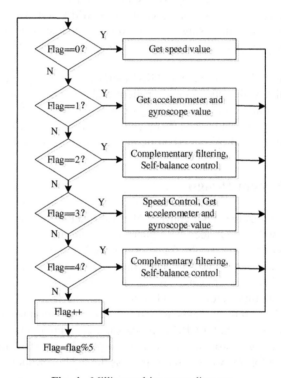

Fig. 4. Millisecond interrupt diagram

4.2   One-Millisecond Interrupt Module

Figure 4 illustrates the one-millisecond interrupt module. One-millisecond interrupt means one interrupt at every millisecond, that is, it will process interrupt regardless of whether the interrupted task is completed or not. It requires that the tasks assigned during each interrupt could not last longer than one millisecond, otherwise, the CPU could not dispatch the tasks well. Flag is the flag specified for millisecond interrupt. Getting the robot speed, the value of accelerometer and gyroscope, complementary filter, self-balance control and speed control are all corresponding sub functions.

4.3   Field Interrupt Module

The field interrupt has higher priority than the millisecond interrupt. The module consists of function to capture video and process the image and function for direction control.

4.3.1   Video Capture and Image Process Function

Firstly, the camera will capture one frame image of the road track. Then the CPU will process the 128 pixel point on the first line of the frame image and make it binaryzation. The reason to get the value of the first line is because we found it can make the robot perspective with less disturbance point from many tests on the image controlling. After obtaining the 128 binaryzation data, it will retrieve the data of this line from both left and right sides to find the junction of the black line on left and right sides and the white track, and return a value. After that, it will figure out if the track is straight or curve even sharp curve according to the range of returned value, then get a middle value corresponding to different processing algorithm. Moreover, to remedy the deviation caused by getting a single line, the algorithm applies *fake multiple lines processing* method, that is, to store the middle value, superpose multiple middle values with different proportions according to straight or curve track, and get the final middle value. All these proportion values are the optimized values after many tests.

4.3.2   Direction Control Function

The direction control function gets the middle value from the Video capture and image process function. Then it figures out whether current track is straight or curve even sharp curve by checking if the difference is big between current middle value with the next one. By combining the middle value with PID parameters and adjusting the PID parameters, it can adjust the stability of the direction control function.

4.4   The Task Scheduling Under CPU Resource Limitation

To save the cost, the system applies a lower main frequency CPU. As the system is composed of multiple sub systems, we must arrange the task scheduling reasonably to ensure the system running reliably. So we measured the actual tasks execution time by experiments after system designing. We measured the execution time of each function and figured out whether a CPU static task scheduling can be performed by setting a pin to high level at the beginning and setting it to low level at the end of the function, and using dual-trace oscilloscope to measure the high level time of each function. The actual execution time of each task was obtained by averaging the ten times measurement results.

According to the setting, the polling interval for above five tasks is 5 ms. Above tasks will be executed within the millisecond interrupt function periodically by sequence. The field interrupt has higher priority than millisecond interrupt, so the CPU will pause the millisecond interrupt immediately and start the field interrupt if the field interrupt comes. It costs less than 7 ms to read one image data, and the interval between reading each frame image is 16.67 ms (Table 1).

Table 1. Task execution time

Task no.	Measure value(μs)											Average (μs)
0	Speed_Read	20	19	20	18	22	20	23	17	21	19	19.9
1	Get_ADResult	165	152	148	162	150	156	158	142	150	164	154.7
2	Datehandle	18	23	15	19	20	22	16	21	17	20	19.1
	Stand_Control	162	149	154	157	142	160	162	145	152	155	153.8
3	Speed_Control	13	17	22	25	18	15	21	24	16	18	18.9
	Get_ADResult	157	162	150	162	158	165	148	152	160	156	157.0
	SpeeedControlOutput	20	15	22	26	18	25	16	22	15	19	19.8
4	Datehandle	16	14	18	22	25	20	15	24	25	17	19.6
	Stand_Control	160	155	162	164	158	148	142	145	152	152	153.8

There are 6 tasks including 5 polling tasks and one field interrupt task. According to optimal RM task scheduling theorem [7, 8], the occupancy of the tasks is,

$$
\begin{aligned}
U &= \sum_{i=1}^{n} \frac{c_i}{h_i} \\
&= (\frac{19.9}{5} + \frac{154.7}{5} + \frac{19.1 + 153.8 + 18.9}{5} + \frac{157 + 19.8}{5} + \frac{19.6 + 153.8}{5}) \times 10^{-3} + \frac{7}{16.67} \\
&= 0.5632 < n(2^{\frac{1}{n}} - 1) = 6 \times (2^{\frac{1}{6}} - 1) = 0.7348
\end{aligned}
$$

The system tasks can be scheduled.

To realize the goal as much as possible and avoid the impact among internal interrupts in MC9S12XS128, we only transformed 182 columns per line during image data transformation. Although to obtain the road path information by gathering only one line data will lead to more errors, we have to keep doing like that as we found the robot cannot self-balance when reading more than one lines of image data. Fortunately, we can remedy it by increasing fault tolerance and adjusting PID parameters during direction control.

5 Conclusion

The auto-balanced robot based on machine vision has been designed and experimented in the paper. Based on machine vision the self-balancing robot does not need person to control it, and can reduce the human disturbance which greatly improves the efficiency and safety of the system. The system needs to deal with lots of tasks such as getting the robot speed, getting the value of accelerometer and gyroscope, complementary filter, self-balance control and speed control, capture video and process the image and direction control etc. We have considered the task scheduling under CPU resource limitation through experiment and theory prove. The works in the paper has attended the national robot competition based on machine vision won the second prize. It is proved that the system has good intelligence and anti-interference ability by experiments and competition.

Acknowledgments. This work is supported by the BISTU Graduate Education Quality Project (5111623305),BISTU Course Construction and Teaching Reform Project (2014KG22, 2015KGZD06, 2016JGYB15, 2014JG08).

References

1. Umar, F., Usman, M.A., Athar, H., et al.: Design and implementation of a fuzzy logic controller for two wheeled self-balancing robot. Adv. Mater. Res.: MEMS, NANO and Smart Syst. **403-408**, 4918–4925 (2012)
2. Osama, J., Mohsin, J., et al.: Modelling control of a two-wheeled self-balancing robot. In: International Conference Proceedings on Robotics and Emerging Allied Technologies in Engineering, pp. 191–199 (2014)
3. Yuli, C., Yikai, S., et al.: Research on two wheeled self-balanced robot based on variable universe fuzzy PID control. Comput. Simul. **30**(2), 347–350 (2013)
4. Wenjian, L., Hang, Z., et al.: Design and implementation of control system for two-wheeled self-balancing robot. J. Electron. Meas. Instrum. **27**(8), 750–759 (2013)
5. Shouxian, S.: Stability and bistability in physical systems (I). Phys. Eng. **12**(03), 1–5,10 (2002)
6. Wen, M., Hong, Y., et al.: Application of incremental encoder in impulse measurement with compound pendulum. Chin. J. Sci. Instrum. **28**(1), 140–144 (2007)
7. Shouping, G., Wei, Z., et al.: Networked Control Systems and Application. Publishing House of Electronics Industry, Beijing (2008)
8. Wu, Y., Song, X., Gong, G.: Real-time load balancing scheduling algorithm for periodic simulation models. Simul. Model. Pract. Theor. **52**(1), 123–134 (2015)

M&S for Intelligent Manufacturing

Energy Optimization Characteristic Analysis of Electromechanical Actuator on More Electric Aircraft

Liang Liu[1], Zheng Cao[2(✉)], Lirong Sun[1], and Yuanjun Zhou[2]

[1] 601 Aircraft Design Institute, Shenyang, China
{liuliang10.16,sunlirong}@163.com
[2] School of Automation Science and Electrical Engineering, Beihang University, Beijing, China
caozheng1203158@163.com, zhouyuanjun@buaa.edu.cn

Abstract. As the concept of more electric aircraft is mentioned, electrical power on aircraft can gradually replace hydraulic energy, pneumatic energy and other secondary energy, in order to achieve the purpose of saving energy. This paper is illustrated by the example of electromechanical actuator, analyzes the energy consumption of equipment and power loss of energy transmission. Appling in multi-domain modeling, it compares power loss with the traditional hydraulic actuator. As well as, it analyzes power loss of the secondary energy transformation device system including generator and hydraulic pump. The results of simulation show that aircraft actuator with electrical energy optimize energy utilization, especially for large passenger aircraft.

Keywords: Energy optimization · Electromechanical actuator · More electric aircraft

1 Introduction

The power of modern aircraft has two forms: the main power and the secondary power [1]. The main power is produced by aviation engine, and the secondary power is mainly electrical energy, hydraulic energy and pneumatic energy provided by aircraft equipments and control systems. Compared with other forms of energy, electricity is easy to transport, distribute, and transform. Therefore, the concept of more electric aircraft is put forward [2, 3], which uses electricity to replace hydraulic, pneumatic and other secondary power. The typical system of more electric aircraft is the flight control system, and the power equipment is electromechanical actuator belonged to transient high-power consumption equipment [4]. Multi-domain modeling is widely adopted, it solves problem between different physical domains [5–7]. The energy management is mentioned [8], however it don not compare with other different energy. The transient behavior is shown in aircraft dynamic systems and its influence [9]. This paper is taken electromechanical actuator energy consumption system and energy transformation device system as examples. Compared with traditional hydraulic actuator and hydraulic pump, the power change and loss of energy consumption of equipment and transmission are analyzed by multi-domain modeling.

© Springer Science+Business Media Singapore 2016
L. Zhang et al. (Eds.): AsiaSim 2016/SCS AutumnSim 2016, Part II, CCIS 644, pp. 41–52, 2016.
DOI: 10.1007/978-981-10-2666-9_5

2   The Energy Consumption of Actuator in Flight Control System

The typical system of more electric aircraft is flight control system. The flight control system which is composed of energy transmission device and energy consumption device applies electrical energy or hydraulic energy to drive actuator.

2.1   The Structure of Electromechanical Actuator Energy Consumption System

The electromechanical actuator is mainly made up of power electronic device, motor and mechanical device. The energy is produced by airborne power, transmitted by cable, through inverter, motor and reducer, eventually sent to aircraft rudder surface. The power flow of electromechanical actuator energy consumption system is shown in Fig. 1.

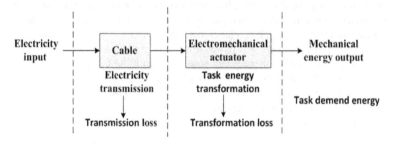

Fig. 1.   The power flow of electromechanical actuator energy consumption system

2.2   The Structure of Hydraulic Actuator Energy Consumption System

The structure of hydraulic actuator energy consumption system is relatively simple, and the hydraulic actuator is mainly composed of hydraulic actuator cylinder. The energy is produced by hydraulic source, transmitted by oil pipeline, and sent to aircraft rudder surface. The power flow of hydraulic actuator energy consumption system is shown in Fig. 2.

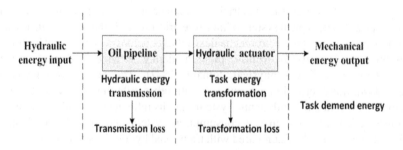

Fig. 2.   The power flow of hydraulic actuator energy consumption system

3   The Power Loss Analysis of Electromechanical Actuator

According to the power flow of electromechanical actuator energy consumption system, power loss mainly has two parts: one is power transmission part, the other is electromechanical actuator part. On the basis of electromechanical actuator structure, the loss of the second part mainly includes power loss of power electronic device (inverter), motor and mechanical transmission device.

3.1   The Power Loss of Electricity Transmission

The power loss of electricity transmission refers to power loss of transmission cable, and formula is:

$$\Delta p_{cs} = I^2 R \tag{1}$$

where heat loss of transmission cable is related to current through cable and resistance of cable.

3.2   The Power Loss of Electromechanical Actuator

1. The power loss of electronic device (inverter)
   The power loss of electronic device (inverter) includes conduction loss Δp_{on} and switching loss Δp_{sw} of power switching devices, namely

$$\Delta p_{iv} = \Delta p_{on} + \Delta p_{sw} = K_{iv} I_C \tag{2}$$

   The loss factor K_{tv} is related to power voltage, switching frequency, conduction voltage drop, and rise time and fall time of switching device which depends on type of IGBT.
2. The power loss of motor
   The motor is usually permanent magnet brushless dc motor, loss of which mainly includes copper loss, iron loss, and mechanical loss. The power loss is:

$$\Delta p_{mot} = \Delta p_{cu} + \Delta p_{fe} + \Delta p_{m0} = 2r_a I_a^2 + \left(k_{fe} + T_{m0} \right) \Omega_r \tag{3}$$

   where r_a is phase winding resistance, I_a is phase winding current, Ω_r is rotor angular velocity, T_{m0} is no-load torque, and k_{fe} is for iron loss coefficient of motor.
3. The power loss of mechanical transmission device
   The mechanical transmission device is made up of speed reducer and screw. The loss is produced by friction. Assuming that friction of reducer and screw is constant under different speed, the power loss is

$$\Delta p_{dr} = T_f \Omega_a = T_f \frac{\Omega_r}{k_\Omega}$$

(4)

In Eq. (4), T_f is friction torque, Ω_a is rudder angular velocity, Ω_r is rotor angular velocity of motor, and k_Ω is reduction ratio of gear.

3.3   The Simulation of Electromechanical Actuator Energy Consumption System

For the power consumption characteristics of electromechanical actuator, it applies multi-physics region modeling. The electromechanical actuator is position servo control system, and the output power with 25° deflection control of rudder surface is shown in Fig. 3. The actuator needs large torque when it starts and forms larger pulse power. As the hinge torque of rudder load changes, the output power gradually increases.

1. The power loss of electromechanical actuator
   The power loss of electromechanical actuator is shown in Fig. 4. Due to large pulse current when actuator starts, it forms pulse copper loss and when actuator brakes, it forms small amplitude pulse copper loss.
2. The power loss of transmission cable
   The transmission cable is selected with density of 5 A/mm², and length of 10 m. The power loss is shown in Fig. 5.

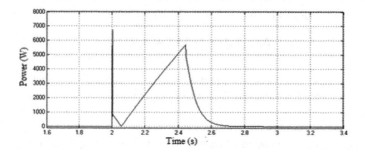

Fig. 3.   The output power of electromechanical actuator energy consumption system

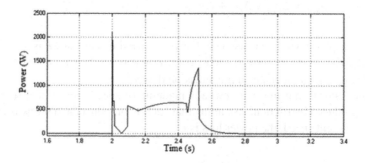

Fig. 4.   The loss of electromechanical actuator

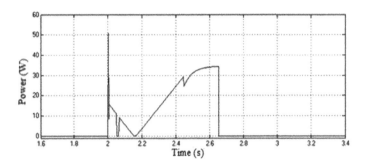

Fig. 5. The loss of transmission cable

4   The Hydraulic Actuator Energy Consumption System

For the characteristic analysis of power loss, electromechanical actuator energy consumption system could compare with hydraulic actuator energy consumption system. Similar to the power flow of electromechanical actuator system, the power loss of hydraulic actuator system is divided into two parts: the first is transmission loss of oil pipeline, the second is power loss of hydraulic actuator.

4.1   The Power Loss of Hydraulic Transmission

The hydraulic transmission uses oil pipeline. The oil is sticky and has resistance in process of flow. In order to overcome the resistance, transmission should produce energy loss and the main performance is pressure loss. The pressure loss in hydraulic system could be divided into two types: one is frictional pressure loss, the other is local pressure loss.

1. The frictional pressure loss
   When oil flows in the straight tube, due to friction force between liquid and pipe wall or turbulent flow, the collision between particles leads to pressure loss. The pressure loss is:

$$\Delta p_\lambda = \lambda \frac{l}{d} \frac{\rho v^2}{2} \tag{5}$$

   Where Δp_λ is frictional pressure loss, l is pipe length, d is pipe diameter, v is fluid flow velocity, ρ is liquid density, and λ is frictional resistance coefficient.
2. The local pressure loss
   When oil flows through local obstacle (bend or joint), due to suddenly changes in direction and speed of fluid flow, in local part it forms vortex which is produced by collision and friction between hydraulic oil point or particle and solid wall, and generates pressure loss, the formula is:

$$\Delta p_\zeta = \zeta \frac{\rho v^2}{2} \tag{6}$$

In Eq. (6), Δp_ζ is local pressure loss, ξ is local resistance coefficient, v is fluid flow velocity, and ρ is liquid density.

Therefore loss of oil pipeline transmission is:

$$\Delta P_{cs} = \Delta p_s q = \left(\sum \Delta p_\lambda + \sum \Delta p_\zeta \right) q \tag{7}$$

Where q is for liquid flow through pipeline.

4.2   The Power Loss of Hydraulic Actuator

The traditional hydraulic actuator directly uses hydraulic source. The servo valve controls the size of liquid flow rate to drive piston movement and aircraft rudder surface movement. The cylinder of hydraulic actuator mostly makes input hydraulic energy become output mechanical energy, however, there is small part loss with the form of oil leakage and mechanical friction loss.

1. The oil leakage loss
   The differential pressure of hydraulic actuator cylinder causes internal leakage and leakage flow is proportional to working pressure difference, thus the oil leakage flow Δq_a is:

$$\Delta q_a = \lambda_c (p_1 - p_2) = \lambda_c \Delta p \tag{8}$$

Where λ_c is leakage coefficient which is related with equivalent diameter and length of leak oil, as well as dynamic viscosity of oil, and Δp is pressure difference on both piston sides.

Therefore, the oil leakage loss ΔP_{a1} is:

$$\Delta P_{a1} = \Delta q_a (p_1 - p_2) = \lambda_c \Delta p^2 \tag{9}$$

2. The mechanical loss
   The mechanical loss is friction torque loss produced by relative motion between artifacts of hydraulic actuator. Generally friction F_f is constant, and the mechanical loss is:

$$\Delta P_{a2} = F_f v_a \tag{10}$$

Where v_a is movement speed of piston.

4.3   The Simulation of Hydraulic Actuator Energy Consumption System

Based on the above theoretical analysis, the multi-physics region modeling should be established, simulated and analyzed. In order to compare with electromechanical actuator, movement requirement of aircraft rudder surface should be in accordance with electromechanical actuator, namely control surface deflection is 25°. The output power of hydraulic actuator system is shown in Fig. 6.

1. The power loss of hydraulic actuator
   As is shown in Fig. 7, the hydraulic source pressure of hydraulic actuator basically remains unchanged, due to the constant loss caused by leakage. The mechanical loss which is proportional to speed mainly changes.
2. The power loss of transmission oil pipeline
   The transmission oil pipeline is selected with diameter of 5 mm and length of 10 m. The number of bend is 2: one is 90° and the other is 45°. The power loss is shown in Fig. 8.

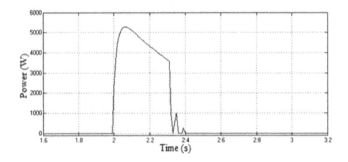

Fig. 6.   The output power of hydraulic actuator energy consumption system

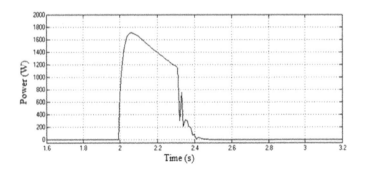

Fig. 7.   The loss of hydraulic actuator

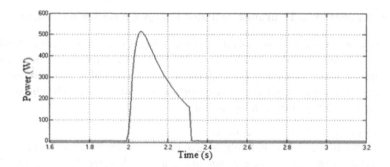

Fig. 8. The loss of transmission pipeline

5　The Power Loss Analysis of Energy Transformation Device

The transformation devices of electrical energy and hydraulic energy on the aircraft are generator and hydraulic pump driven by the engine. The devices transform mechanical energy to secondary energy.

5.1　The Power Loss of Generator

The 270 V DC generator is composed of the synchronous generator and rectifier. The power loss of generator includes copper loss, iron loss and mechanical loss.

1. The copper loss
   The copper loss contains generator resistance loss and conduction loss of rectifier diode. The loss formula is:

$$\Delta p_{Cu} = \Delta p_a + \Delta p_d = m\left(R_a + 2R_d\right)I_a^2 \tag{11}$$

Where m is winding phase number, R_a is phase winding resistance, R_d is the equivalent resistance of rectifier diode and I_a is current RMS of phase winding.

2. The iron loss
   The iron loss of generator is related to magnetic flux density and magnetic field frequency which is proportional to motor speed. The aviation generator could adjust voltage by excitation, further regulate the output voltage to keep stability. The iron loss is:

$$\Delta p_{Fe} = kn \tag{12}$$

In Eq. (12), n is motor speed and k is related proportional coefficient.

3. The copper loss of generator excitation
   In 3-levels aviation generator, the flux of main generator is provided by exciter and the loss should be defined as the excitation loss. The loss of exciter also has copper loss and iron loss, but far less than copper loss and iron loss of main generator.

The iron loss is similar to the main generator, which is proportional to speed, and usually ascribes to iron loss of main generator. The copper loss is decided by the excitation current of main generator. The exciter copper loss of exciter is:

$$\Delta p_{Cuf} = R_f I_f^2 \tag{13}$$

Where R_f is resistance of excitation circuit including winding resistance of main generator excitation, winding resistance of excitation armature and equivalent winding resistance of rotated rectifier diode.

4. The mechanical loss of generator

   The mechanical loss of generator is friction torque loss, which is proportional to speed of generator, as follows:

$$\Delta p_m = \Delta T \Omega = \frac{2\pi}{60} \Delta T n \tag{14}$$

Where ΔT is friction torque loss which has constant torque characteristic and n is speed of generator.

5.2   The Power Loss of Hydraulic Pump

This section discusses modeling method for hydraulic pump. The hydraulic pump should be able to produce large enough power and form stable hydraulic pressure source. The hydraulic source applies controllable variable pump with closed-loop control to ensure pressure stability. The power loss of hydraulic pump could be divided into two parts: volume loss and the mechanical loss.

1. The volume loss of hydraulic pump

   The volume loss refers to internal leakage caused by pressure difference of hydraulic pump, which is proportional to the working pressure difference and inverse proportional to liquid viscosity. The formula is:

$$\Delta p_{vp} = \Delta q p_p = \frac{p_p^2}{R} \tag{15}$$

In Eq. (15), R is liquid volume which is decided by oil viscosity, equivalent diameter and length of leak oil, and generally it is constant in actual system. The p_p is pressure difference of hydraulic pump.

2. The mechanical loss of hydraulic pump

   The mechanical loss is friction torque loss caucused by relative motion between the inside components. The loss expression is:

$$\Delta p_{mp} = 2\pi n \Delta T \tag{16}$$

Where n is rotated speed of hydraulic pump, and ΔT is equivalent torque of mechanical loss which is constant.

6 The Performance Comparison of Energy

6.1 The Comparison of Actuator Power Loss

According to analysis of results in Sects. 3 and 4, the power loss data of actuators with different energy is summarized in Table 1. The average power of energy consumption is average of actuator movement time. The data from the table reflects that power loss energy of hydraulic actuator is 54 % more than electromechanical actuator, however power loss of transmission with pipeline is 8 times. The total loss of hydraulic actuator is almost 80 % more than electromechanical actuator.

Table 1. The comparison of equipment energy consumption

Equipment	Loss	Peak power (kW)	Energy loss (kJ)	Average power (kW)
Electromechanical actuator	Actuator	2.12	0.31	0.07
	Cable	0.05	0.012	0.003
	Total	2.17	0.322	0.073
Hydraulic actuator	Actuator	1.7	0.48	0.12
	Pipeline	0.51	0.1	0.025
	Total	2.21	0.58	0.145

Therefore, the power loss characteristics of energy consumption system with electromechanical and hydraulic actuator are:

(1) In the same flight mission, energy utilization of electromechanical actuator does not have obvious advantage. According to results of flight control system, it is almost the same in terms of power consumption.

(2) The transmission loss of electricity which is copper loss depends on resistance of cable. However, the transmission loss of hydraulic energy which is pressure loss depends on resistance of pipeline, and structure of transmission system is more complex, leading to a lot of loss. Therefore, in the long distance transmission, energy loss of electricity transmission is much lower than hydraulic transmission, namely the efficiency is much higher.

6.2 The Comparison of Transformation Device

According to analysis of Sect. 5, the power loss characteristics of generator and hydraulic pump system are:

(1) The power loss of generator includes copper loss, iron loss and mechanical loss. The copper loss is main loss which is proportional to the square of output current, meaning that the loss is small when generator works with the light load, therefore the efficiency of generator is higher.

(2) The power loss of hydraulic pump includes volume loss and mechanical loss, which has little relationship to output power, meaning that the efficiency is highest when hydraulic pump works in the rated power. Due to constant loss in light load, the efficiency is very low. Obviously, the actuator is short-time working equipment. With hydraulic energy, the output power is low in most of time, and the loss basically remains unchanged, which is not beneficial to energy utilization.

7 Conclusions

This paper analyzes the energy consumption characteristics of electromechanical actuator on more electric aircraft and compares with the hydraulic actuator. For the actuator which is transient power consumption equipment of flight control system, in the same flight mission, electromechanical actuator compared with hydraulic actuator does not have obvious advantage on energy utilization. However, actuator with electrical energy has large advantage on transmission. The transmission distance of cable is longer, the loss is smaller compared with oil pipeline. Therefore, the advantage of energy transmission makes EMA realize optimization of energy utilization for large aircraft.

Acknowledgement. This research was financially supported by Aeronautical Science Foundation (2014ZC01002).

References

1. Feiner, L.J.: Power-by-wire aircraft secondary power systems. In: Proceedings of 12th AIAA/ IEEE Digital Avionics Systems Conference, pp. 439–444. Institute of Electrical and Electronics Engineers, New York (1993)
2. Mario, R., Atephen, J.: Aircraft electrical system architectures to support more-electric aircraft. In: Avionic & Systems Conference, pp. 17–19 (2004)
3. Weimer, J.A.: The role of electric machines and drives in the more electric aircraft. In: 2003 IEEE International Electric Machines and Drives Conference, IEMDC 2003, vol. 1, pp. 11–15, 1-4 June 2003
4. Botten, S.L., Whitly, C.R., King, A.D.: Flight control actuation technology for next-generation all-electric aircraft. Technol. Rev. J. Millennium Issue, Fall/Winter 55–67 (2000)
5. Beater, P., Clauss, C.: Multi-domain systems: pneumatic, electronic and mechanical subsystems of pneumatic drive modeled with Modelica. In: Proceedings of the 3rd International Modelica Conference, Linkoping, Sweden, pp. 369–376 (2003)
6. Georigou, I.T., Romeo, F.: Multi-physics dynamics of a mechanical oscillator coupled to an electro-magnetic circuit. Nonlinear Dyn. Eng.: Model. Anal. Appl., Int. J. Non-Linear Mech. **70**, 153–164 (2015)
7. Bechmann, B., Wiesman, H.: Advanced modeling of electromagnetic transients in power systems. In: Proceedings of the Modelica Workshop 2000, Lund, Sweden, pp. 93–97 (2000)

8. O'Connell, T., Russell, G., McCarthy, K., Lucus, E.: Energy management of an aircraft electrical system. In: The 46th AIAA/ASME/SAE/ASEE Joint Propulsion Conference & Exhibit, Nashville, TN, 25–2 July 2010
9. Phan, L.L.: A methodology for the efficient integration of transient constraints in the design of aircraft dynamic systems. Ph.D. thesis, School of Aerospace Engineering, Georgia Institute of Technology, Atlanta, GA (2010)

Reliability Analysis of Multi-state System from Time Response

Weihua Zhang[1(✉)], Yongfeng Fang[1], and Kong Fah Tee[2]

[1] School of Mechanical Engineering,
Guizhou University of Engineering Science, Bijie 551700, China
{zhangwh_2016, fangyf_9707}@126.com
[2] Department of Engineering Science,
University of Greenwich, Kent ME4 4TB, UK
K.F.Tee@gre.ac.uk

Abstract. In this paper, firstly, it is discrete the engine output and constructed the Markov random process with the discrete state and continuous time. Secondly, we constructed a model of the multi-state Markov model and determined the transition intensity. Thirdly, we computed the expected of the engine capacity deficiency and the forced outage by the method.

Keywords: Reliability · Multi-state · System · Time response · Markov

1 Introduction

In the engineering practice, most systems are acted on their works under the kinds of their units, which units is limited, additional, the state of these units are diverse, so a system is shown a multi-state by these reasons, that such the system is called a multi-state system (MSS) (Levitin and Lisnianski 2001). The MSS is widely used in the reliability evaluation of the power systems, engine systems and electronic products systems (Mosleh 1991). The reliability of the MSS have been studied, the basic research methods were provided, but these studies have some limit and is start. In addition, because of the complexity of the MSS, the studying has some difficulties, therefore, the articles about the reliability of the MSS is little for now. Recently, the multi-state reliability of the engine is assessed by using the two-state system (Fang et al. 2014), but the assessment result of the engine is error if the reliability of the engine unit has special, or at least limited. The contents of Markov chain and semi-Markov chain become rich in research, theory is quite perfect, gradually. The reliability of the system was studied by using the Markov chains (MC) and semi-Markov Chain (SMC) (Trivedi 2001, Zhang and Wu 2012), reliability of system, availability of system, average operating time of system may be obtained. People studied the reliability of the of the coal-fired generating to be used a single Markov model (Hamoud and Yiu 2015, Jmamal et al. 2015). The reliability problems of the system with the discrete state (DS) and the time continuous (TC) was studied by using the Markov model (MM) with DS and TC (Shnurkov and Ivanov 2015, Atchade 2014). The DS and TC Markov models have been used to assess the reliability of other systems (Fang et al. 2013). The reliability of the multi-state

© Springer Science+Business Media Singapore 2016
L. Zhang et al. (Eds.): AsiaSim 2016/SCS AutumnSim 2016, Part II, CCIS 644, pp. 53–62, 2016.
DOI: 10.1007/978-981-10-2666-9_6

(MS) elements generator system were studied by using the DS and TC Markov model, The result that was predicted has a good effect for the short-term forecasting.

In this paper, we studied the MS random process of the engine unit according to the DS and TC MM and the SMM from the actual reliability of the engine system, we established the multi-state Markov model (MSMM) and accessed the MS the reliability of the engine from time response using the method. Finally, the method is shown by using an engineering practical case.

2 The Multi-state Markov Model

T is the Service deadline of an engine unit, we used the interval $[0, e]$ to indicate the output energy of the engine, e is the engine's maximum output energy in the time t. It is shown that the random process is continuous time and the continuous state, we used the discrete state to substituted it whom is noted as $E(t)$.

(1) We noted two special state of the engine as 1, N they are corresponding to $e_1 = 0$ the engine is failed complete and $e_N = e$ that the engine is outputted normally, respectively.

(2) We divided the interval $[0, e]$ to $N - 2$ sub-interval, the every sub-interval's length is $\Delta e = \frac{e}{N-2}$.

(3) If $E(t) \in ((i - 1)\Delta e, (i - 1)\Delta e], i = 2, \cdots, N - 1$, we noted the state of $E(t)$ is $i(i = 2, 3, \cdots N - 1)$ in t, g_i is its output energy.

(4) The work energy g_i in state i is the average of the interval $((i - 1)\Delta e, (i - 1)\Delta e]$.

Through about quantitative processing, the continuous state and the continuous of the original random process $E(t)$ is translated to the DS and TC of the random process $E_D(t)$, the random process $E_D(t)$ has $N(N = 1, 2, \cdots, N)$ different outputting level g_i, while the random process $E_D(t)$ is expressed by using the Markov stochastic process (MSP), its transition stats is shown as Fig. 1.

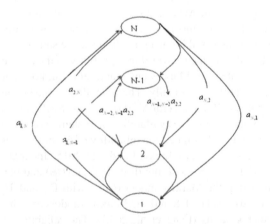

Fig. 1. The generation unit is established to MSMM

It is shown as Fig. 1, $a_{i,j}$ is the state i translating to the state j, $a_{N-1,N-2}$ is the state $N-1$ translating to the state $N-2$, the other and so on. Each state i are corresponding to the output energy g_i of the engine. T_i^m is the mth sojourn time at the state i of the unit. $\{T_i^{(1)}, T_i^{(2)}, \cdots, T_i^{(k_i)}\}$ is the sample of the unit service period. k_{ij} is the unit number from state i translating to the state j, k_i is the sojourn number in the state i of the unit. We can obtained the transfer intensity $a_{i,j}$ using the real number that will be observed from the discrete state and time continuous stochastic process.

3 The Transfer Intensity of the Engine Unit Will be Determined

$E_D(t)$ is a DS and TC Markov process, we neglected the translation time of the unit state from $i\,j(i \neq j)$, the transfer moment only is interested, so $E_D(t)$ is considered as a DS and time discrete (TD) random process, it is noted as $E_{Di}(n), n = 0, 1, 2, \cdots$, its transition probability of one step is noted as $\pi_{ij}, i,j = 1, 2, \cdots N$.

The unit from state i translating to the state $j(i \neq j)$ whose The cumulative probability distribution function is as follow.

$$Q_{ij}(t) = 1 - e^{-a_{ij}t} \tag{1}$$

The probability of the first transfer of the unit state from i to j before the moment t is noted as $H_{ij}(t), i,j = 1, \cdots, N$, the random process $E_D(t)$ whose the nuclear matrix $H(t)$ of will be consisted by all $H_{ij}(t)$.

$$H_{ik}(t) = \int_0^t [1 - Q_{i1}(u)] \cdots [1 - Q_{ik-1}(u)][1 - Q_{ik+1}(u)] \cdots [1 - Q_{ik-1}(u)] dQ_{ik}(u) \tag{2}$$

From Eqs. (1) and (2), it is obtained as follow.

$$H_{ik}(t) = \frac{a_{ik}}{\sum\limits_{j=1}^n a_{ij}} [1 - e^{-\sum\limits_{j=1}^N a_{ij}t}] \tag{3}$$

The unit sojourn time T_i whose cumulative probability distribution function in the state i is as follow.

$$Q_i(t) = \sum\limits_{k=1}^N H_{ik}(t) = 1 - e^{-\sum\limits_{j=1}^N a_{ij}t} \tag{4}$$

From Eq. (4), the T_i is obeyed to the exponential distribution, $Q_i(t)$ mean is follow.

$$T_{imean} = \frac{1}{\sum\limits_{j=1}^{n} c_{ij}} = \frac{1}{A} \tag{5}$$

Where $A = \sum\limits_{j=1}^{n} a_{ij}$.

The mean that is obtained by using the observation samples is noted as follow.

$$\hat{T}_{imean} = \frac{\sum\limits_{j=1}^{k_i} T_i^{(j)}}{k_i} \tag{6}$$

It is obtained by using Eqs. (5) and (6) as follow.

$$\hat{A} = \frac{1}{\hat{T}_{imean}} = \frac{k_i}{\sum\limits_{j=1}^{k_i} T_i^{(j)}} \tag{7}$$

We can obtain the transition probability of one step to use the embedded Markov random processing.

$$\pi_{ij} = \lim_{t \to \infty} H_{ij}(t) \tag{8}$$

On the formula was simplified as follow.

$$\pi_{ij} = \frac{c_{ik}}{\sum\limits_{j=1}^{N} c_{ij}} \tag{9}$$

It is obtained by using the above equation.

$$a_{ik} = \pi_{ij} \sum\limits_{j=1}^{N} a_{ij} \tag{10}$$

The single transition intensity in the state i can be obtained by using Eq. (10).

We can obtain the transition probability of single step of the embedded Markov chain (EMC) using the unit work energy which can be observed in the random process.

$$\hat{\pi}_{ik} = \frac{k_{ik}}{k_i} \tag{11}$$

We can compute the transition intensity by using Eqs. (7), (10) and (11).

$$\hat{a}_{ik} = \pi_{ik}\hat{C} = \frac{k_{ik}}{k_i}\frac{1}{\hat{T}_{imean}} = \frac{k_{ik}}{\sum\limits_{j=1}^{k_i} T_i^{(j)}}, i,k = 1,\cdots,N \tag{12}$$

For the MSM system that has N states, it has as follow.

$$\sum_{j=1}^{N} a_{ij} = 0 \tag{13}$$

So:

$$\hat{a}_{ii} = -\sum_{\substack{j=1 \\ i \neq j}}^{N} a_{ij} \tag{14}$$

Above all, there is an algorithm for model of the MSM system that has N states.

Step 1. The system will be quantitative processed by using the method in the 2nd part content.

Step 2. The unit in the every state i total sojourn time is computed.

$$T_{\sum_i} = \sum_{m=1}^{k_i} T_i^{(m)} \tag{15}$$

Step 3. The transition intensity of the state from i to state j can be computed by using Eqs. (16) and (17).

$$\hat{a}_{ij} = \frac{k_{ij}}{T_{\sum_i}}, i \neq j. \tag{16}$$

$$\hat{a}_{ii} = -\sum_{\substack{j=1 \\ i \neq j}}^{N} a_{ij} \tag{17}$$

4   The MSMM and the Engine Short Time Reliability

4.1   The Transition Intensity Will be Computed

Commonly, a fuel engine output power of is 288 kW, its service deadline is $T = 5$ years, the Markov will be established by using the above algorithm.

$e_1 = 0$ kW, $e_4 = 288$ kW can be computed by using the method.

$$\Delta e = \frac{288}{4-2} = 144 \text{ kW} \qquad (18)$$

Then the output energy of the engine can be divided to two intervals as $[0, 144]$ kW, $[144, 288]$ kW.

The remainder two output level is $e_2 = 123$ kW, $e_3 = 241$ kW, respectively. The state transition intensity $\hat{a}_{ij}$ from state i to the state j as follow.

$$\begin{bmatrix} -0.0933 & 0.0800 & 0.0133 & 0 \\ 0.0294 & -0.3823 & 0.3235 & 0.0294 \\ 0 & 0.0288 & -0.3846 & 0.3558 \\ 0.0002 & 0.0001 & 0.0007 & 0.0010 \end{bmatrix} \qquad (19)$$

The number of the transition and the sojourn time is shown in Table 1.

Table 1. The transition number, residence time

States	1	2	3	4	Work energy (kW)	Accumulation time $T_{\sum_i}$ (h)
1	0	6	1	0	0	75
2	1	0	11	1	123	34
3	0	3	0	37	241	104
4	6	4	28	0	288	40711

4.2   MSS Model of Four-State

The state transition for four state of the MM is as the follow figure. The state 1, 2, 3 and 4 steady state probability is respectively shown as follows (Fig. 2).

$$P_1 = 0.0018, P_2 = 0.0008, P_3 = 0.0025, P_4 = 0.9949 \qquad (20)$$

The probability $P_i(t), (i = 1, 2, 3, 4)i$ is computed after the differential equations (21a)–(21d) is solved.

$$\frac{dP_1(t)}{dt} = -(a_{12} + a_{13} + a_{14})P_1(t) + a_{21}P_2(t) + a_{31}P_3(t) + a_{41}P_4(t) \qquad (21a)$$

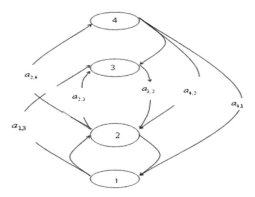

Fig. 2. Engine unite is divided to four-state MSS

$$\frac{dP_2(t)}{dt} = a_{12}P_1(t) - (a_{21} + a_{23} + a_{24})P_2(t) + a_{32}P_3(t) + a_{42}P_4(t) \tag{21b}$$

$$\frac{dP_3(t)}{dt} = a_{13}P_1(t) + a_{23}P_2(t) - (a_{31} + a_{32} + a_{34})P_3(t) + a_{43}P_4(t) \tag{21c}$$

$$\frac{dP_4(t)}{dt} = a_{14}P_1(t) + a_{12}P_2(t) + a_{13}P_3(t) - (a_{41} + a_{42} + a_{43})P_4(t) \tag{21d}$$

The probability of the state i can be obtained by solving the differential equation (21) under the special initial conditions in any time, the reliability of the engine can be computed too.

According to the probability of the state, the engine stability probability when its state is the state i can be obtained by using the follow equation.

$$p_i = \lim_{t \to \infty} P_i(t), (i = 1, 2, 3, 4) \tag{22}$$

4.3   The Engine Reliability from Time Response

For the engine system, the evaluation for the rate of the work outage (ROW) of the engine is an important. ROW is a whole failure probability for the engine, that is to say the engine work energy is zero, its function about time that is stopped at the state one as follow.

$$ROW(t) = P_1(t) \tag{23}$$

Of course, the result of *ROW(t)* depend on the initial conditions.
It is clearly, the initial conditions can be preset as follows.

$$P_1(0) = 0, P_2(0) = 0, P_3(0) = 0, P_4(4) = 1 \tag{24}$$

The result computed is shown in the Fig. 3. It is shown that the engine will be gone to stability after 81 h, the stability probability at the state 1 is as follow in this time.

$$p_1 = \lim_{t \to \infty} P_1(t) = 0.0018 \tag{25}$$

If the initial conditions can be preset as follows.

$$P_1(0) = 0, P_2(0) = 0, P_3(0) = 1, P_4(4) = 0 \tag{26}$$

ROW(t) is shown as Fig. 4.

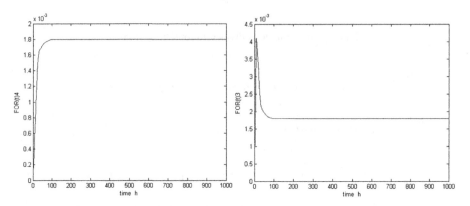

Fig. 3. ROW(t) under the initial condition (24) in the 1000 time

Fig. 4. ROW(t) under the initial condition (26) in the 1000 time

If the initial conditions can be preset as follows.

$$P_1(0) = 0, P_2(0) = 1, P_3(0) = 0, P_4(4) = 0 \tag{27}$$

ROW(t) is shown as Fig. 5.
If the initial conditions can be preset as follows.

$$P_1(0) = 1, P_2(0) = 0, P_3(0) = 0, P_4(4) = 0 \tag{28}$$

ROW(t) is shown as Fig. 6.

It is shown in Figs. 3, 4, 5 and 6, the *ROW* of the engine is stabilized 0.0018 under the initial conditions (24), (26), (27) and (28). It is also shown in the four figures, the maximum for *ROW* under the initial conditions (26)–(28) is larger more than the maximum for *ROW* under the initial conditions (24), it is because the engine will be more happened malfunction. Obviously, the engine has been turn to the fault state while it is begun to run under the Eq. (27), it is confirmed to the actual situation.

When $W = 200$ kW at the 1000th h, the state would transits to the state 2, the work energy could not reach to 123 kW, it is to say, that the deficiency capacity (DC) will produce.

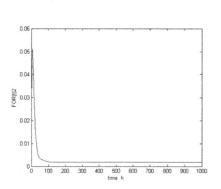

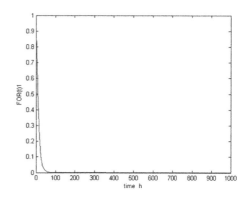

Fig. 5. ROW(t) under the initial condition (27) in the 1000 time

Fig. 6. ROW(t) under the initial condition (28) in the 1000 time

$$DC2 = (W - 123) = 76 \text{ kW} \tag{29}$$

If the state become to the state 1, the work energy can not reach the required, it is to say, that the DC) will produce as follow.

$$DC1 = (W - 0) = 200 \text{ kW} \tag{30}$$

The expected deficiency capacity (EDC) is too a function from time response, it is shown as follow.

$$EDC(t) = P_2(t)DC2 + P_1(t)DC1 \tag{31}$$

The EDC is shown in Figs. 7, 8, 9 and 10 under the initial condition (24), (26), (27) and (28).

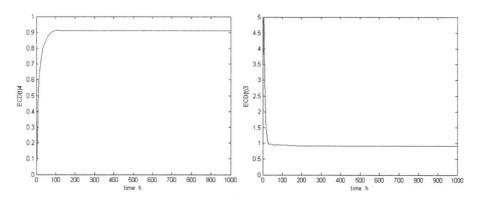

Fig. 7. EDC(t)4 under the initial condition (24) in the 1000 time

Fig. 8. EDC(t)3 under the initial condition (26) in the 1000 time

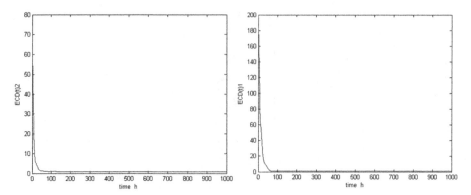

Fig. 9. EDC(t)2 under the initial condition (26) in the 1000 time

Fig. 10. EDC(t)1 under the initial condition (28) in the 1000 time

5   Conclusion

For the MS engine system, we discrete the engine system and quantization processed, we constructed the multi-state Markov model. We given the algorithm of transition intensities according to the observed data. The ROW and the EDC of the engine changing over time can be calculate by the method. This method can be applied to calculate the generator system failure rate changes from time response and the output of the energy deficit expectations. Finally, it is shown that the method is feasibility, effectiveness and practicability by using an engineering practical example.

Acknowledgments. The work was supported by the Foundation from the Excellent Talent of Bijie University (G2015003), the Science Technology Foundation of Guizhou Province, China ([2014] 2001), projects Department of Education of Guizhou Province, China (Qian Jiao Ke he KY zi [2014] 238) and the Fundamental Research Funds for Southwest University (XDJK2014C108).

References

Mosleh, A.: Common cause failures: an analysis methodology and examples. Reliab. Eng. Syst. Saf. **34**(3), 249–292 (1991)

Fang, Y., Tao, W., Tee, K.F.: A reliability based work model of repairable k/n (G) system. Comput. Concr. **12**(6), 775–783 (2013)

Hamoud, G.A., Yiu, C.: One Markov model for spare analysis of distribution power transformers. IEEE Trans. Power Syst. **3**(1), 1–6 (2015)

Shnurkov, P.V., Ivanov, A.V.: Analysis of a discrete semi-Markov model of continuous inventory control with periodic interruptions of consumption. Discrete Math. Appl. **25**(1), 414–420 (2015)

Atchade, Y.F.: Estimation of high-dimensional partially-observed discrete Markov random fields. Electron. J. Stat. **8**(2), 2242–2263 (2014)

Zhang, X., Wu, X.: Mission reliability allocation of spaceflight TT&C system based on adaptive particle swarm optimization. J. Aerosp. Power **27**(9), 2147–2154 (2012)

Simulation Optimization of Manufacturing System Including Assemble Lines and Material Handling Systems

Li Xiang[1,2], Chen Qing-xin[1], Yu Ai-lin[1(✉)], and Zhang Hui-yu[1]

[1] Guangdong Provincial Key Laboratory of Computer Integrated Manufacturing System
Guangdong, University of Technology, Guangzhou 510006, China
138231i@sina.com, gdutcims_16@126.com
[2] College of Electronic Information and Electrical Engineering, Xiangnan University,
Chenzhou 423000, Hunan, China

Abstract. Customized equipment manufacturing enterprises use cellular manufacturing system, material handling system transfer material between the units. It is difficult to obtain this type of manufacturing system accurate solution of optimization problem by traditional mathematics methods. This paper establish simulation model about process-assemble and material handling system based on computer simulation. Because the model has much variable and coupling influence, this paper uses sensitivity analysis method based on orthogonal experiments, determines the parameters optimization direction and the influence discipline between parameters, proposes a heuristic optimization method based on the optimization goal and practical constraints. Analysis shows that the proposed optimization method, which can be effective and reasonable configuration enterprise resources.

Keywords: Assemble unit · Material handling system · Computer simulation · Sensitivity · Simulating optimization

1 Introduction

Most custom equipment manufacturing enterprise in accordance with the request of a customer order, production process with the method of process oriented manufacturing unit, unit through the material handling system between materials handling system (MHS). This kind of production structure, it will encounter all sorts of problems in practice, from the perspective characteristics of unit itself, by more than one processing unit of former level assembly unit jointly determine their own work; in terms of the structure of production system, the traditional way of manufacturing cell based on group technology without considering load balance, a single level before and after the production situation of manufacturing unit has greatly affected the production situation of manufacturing unit, and high intensity of logistics makes the scale manufacturing unit performance before and after the volatility increases, logistics transportation strength too low can cause resource waste logistics system, for mechanical parts piled up in front of the manufacturing unit. So, analysis manufacturing unit and try to eliminate the bottleneck constraint function, the rational allocation of logistics resources, considering

© Springer Science+Business Media Singapore 2016
L. Zhang et al. (Eds.): AsiaSim 2016/SCS AutumnSim 2016, Part II, CCIS 644, pp. 63–70, 2016.
DOI: 10.1007/978-981-10-2666-9_7

the complex production system and logistics system, the regularity of internal cooperation can with smaller cost significantly increase the productivity of the whole.

Previous studies single focus on the production process or logistics performance characteristics of the process, ignore the tight coupling effect on each other. The literature [1] of logistics system simulation were discussed and related research areas, logistics system simulation was divided into production logistics system simulation, Logistics distribution system simulation and supply chain simulation. Traditional simulation methods of applied mathematics model, using the analytical method to calculate system steady state performance. For example Srinivasan and Bozer [2] have used mathematical model to analyzed the influence of the production process and logistics system to the WIP; Li et al. [3] have used Markov stochastic process theory to establish a multi-level queuing network node status model of flow shop and buffer capacity optimization heuristic optimization algorithm is put forward. Another kind of simulation method using computer simulation technology, for example Wang et al. [4] compared the mathematical analytical method and computer simulation to study the characteristics of logistics system and its advantages and disadvantages; Huang et al. [5] have used Plant Simulation software realized the Simulation of the assembly line optimization; Zhou [6] have used Plant Simulation software to establish a general MTO enterprises mixed flow assembly line material distribution system simulation model, optimization of distribution system of transport cars and cache area.

Summarizes related literature study, mathematical model set scenes often differ with the actual situation is larger, and the present stage can only be used for small problem can solve, as the problem size increases NP - Hard problem. In this paper, application of computer simulation technology, the establishment of containing between unit and unit assembly material transportation system simulation model, the sensitivity of parameters calculated by using the orthogonal experiment method, to determine the parameters optimization sequence, analysis the influence law of MHS system on the production of the whole system, and then based on the optimization goal and practical constraints, a heuristic optimization method is proposed.

2   Assembly Production Logistics System Simulation and Analysis

2.1   Scenario Description

Consider a processing scene: contains processing unit, a manufacturing enterprise logistics transportation system between unit and unit assembly, the cache in a unit of area is limited. Materials processing unit respectively according to certain material buffer before rate achieve unit, processing is completed in the workpiece buffer waiting for transportation to the special workpiece cache area before the assembly unit, leaving the system assembly in the finished product after the completion of the cache area. In this kind of manufacturing system, both the production - cooperation relationship: assembly unit assembly unit must satisfy variety for assembly artifacts exist at the same time, the different types of artifacts in independent processing unit manufacturing; and material transportation system between the units and production units to cooperate relationship: transport the car will be completed machining unit of artifacts to the workpiece buffer before the assembly unit, the car may be in place waiting for processing after the completion of the loading processing units, may also be in the assembly cache area waiting to unload all the goods, it shows that the car work status is affected by the working state of the two levels before and after the production unit, and the car transport needs certain time which affects the level before and after work. Processing unit of the workpiece cache area, for example, the car did not timely dislodged artifacts, machining center is blocked; the car without the piece to assemble unit in time, lack of certain kinds of workpiece assembly unit will not work, causing hunger assembly unit. So for this kind of complex production system, we need to production, the assembly unit and transportation system simulation at the same time reflects the strong coupling among, get more in line with the actual situation of data.

A simple production system model is set up as follows in Fig. 1. It contains the parts of A and B are independent of each other processing unit; to assemble part A and part B of the assembly unit; the processing unit to complete parts transportation to the transportation system of assembly unit.

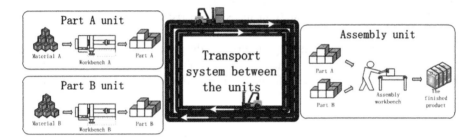

Fig. 1. Contains processing and assembling production logistics system diagram

2.2 The Simulation Model

According to the diagram shown in Fig. 1 of the manufacturing system, set up based on Tecnomatix Plant Simulation 8.2 Simulation software of the Simulation model, as shown in Fig. 2, the basic hardware configuration is as follows: 2.0 GHz dual-core CPU, 4 GB of memory hardware environment.

Simulation model of the assumptions are as follows:

Hypothesis 1. The processing unit of workpiece A and B all ave a workbench. Processing stage belongs to the first come first service type can be processed at a time and a workpiece. Processing time obey exponential distribution.

Hypothesis 2. The Poisson distribution is subject to the same material to material limited buffer before the processing unit.

Hypothesis 3. The assembly unit has A workbench, work stage, there are two artifacts limited buffer, hold A part respectively, B parts. Assembly bench only when at the same time have A & B parts to assembly, assembly time obey exponential distribution. After completion of assembly in infinite buffer after assembling unit, sign the whole machining process is complete.

Hypothesis 4. Unit between transportation systems consists of two car, the car according to the principle of load balancing transport artifacts, each transport number of artifacts between 1 to maximum loading capacity C. Loading and unloading time, run a circle time obey negative exponential distribution.

Hypothesis 5. In order to ensure the production line balance, the processing rate of assembly unit > machining rate of unit; logistics transportation system does not become the bottleneck of the whole system, set up the car transport equivalent (speed x maximum capacity) is greater than the unit before and after the treatment rate; two parallel lines, cache before assembly area, two car parameter Settings are the same.

3   Simulation Optimization Method

3.1   The Simulation Optimization

As the research model contains a lot of uncertain factors, relationships between factors, so the simulation method and optimization method to optimize the combination of the principle is shown in Fig. 3. Mainly includes two parts: the optimization evaluation algorithm and simulation model, simulation model is first get the system performance index, the optimization evaluation algorithm to get the performance index of validation constraints, modify the system parameters, the simulation model using the modified system parameters to get a new performance index, so repeatedly, until the expiration

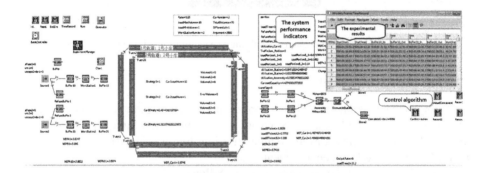

Fig. 2. Simulation model

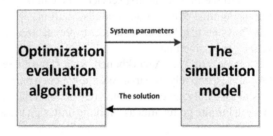

Fig. 3. The principle diagram of the simulation optimization

of the optimization evaluation algorithm to satisfy certain conditions, the system parameters is the optimal solution.

3.2   Heuristic Optimization Methods

Productivity is finished in manufacturing system per unit time the number of artifacts, task rejection rate is the ratio of manufacturing system refused to new orders, reflecting the comprehensive utilization rate of the system and line balance. Results found from Table 2, output, WIP and production cycle were increased with increase buffer, on the other hand, reduce the cache area will make productivity, WIP, production cycle is reduced. Enterprises in order to improve competitiveness, on the premise of guarantee the productivity should try to shorten the production cycle.

Above calculation shows that the sensitivity of variables will influence the performance of the system, the greater the sensitivity value shows that the impact on the performance of the system, the more obvious, at the same time also shows that the influence of other variables is bigger also, so these variables should be optimized first, the rest of the variables can quickly get optimal value.

To sum up, the cycle for production optimization goal of heuristic optimization method as shown in Fig. 4. Simulation initial value is set to a larger value (right now), the maximum capacity of 1 C car, according to the above calculation, the sensitivity of value from big to small in turn choose need to modify the buffer zone, and then according to set the parameters of the simulation, to evaluate the performance index, productivity, rejection rate is greater than the preset constraints, I, the sensitivity higher number of buffer zone of the constraint is loose, because the need for a buffer zone which smaller sensitivity numerical optimization allowance. If meet the constraint conditions will reduce the choice to optimize the cache area, a new simulation; otherwise restore to the last parameter Settings and to choose to optimize the cache area. In order to get the optimization results quickly, after the system level cache area initial size set for the first level cache area optimization results of 1.5 times. All of the cache area after the optimization, record the results of simulation

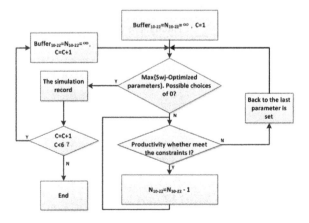

Fig. 4. Heuristic optimization method

with a set of car capacity and buffer size optimization results. Increase the car volume 1, according to the same steps to obtain a set of optimization results, until five car capacity optimization results, the experiment ended.

3.3 Instance Analysis and the Experimental Results

Through the optimization method, the final performance of the system output is not less than 90 % and rejection rate is not more than 10 % as constraint conditions, optimize product average production cycle and the system average captain. System set order input rate of $\lambda = 0.9/h$. Processing rate $\mu_1 = 1/h$, assembly processing rates $\mu_3 = 1.1/h$, MHS transportation system as a whole processing rates $\mu_2 = 1.2/h$, if enter the orders cannot be rejected.

The part of results of simulation was shown in Table 1, ordinal optimization cache area according to the sensitivity value. From the results can be found that after the optimization of the first buffer, the average 15 % to 15 % drop in production cycle; after optimization of the second buffer, fell to 85 % average production cycle, on average the captain and the improvement of the production cycle a lot; optimize the third cache area, average captain and production cycle basic has not changed. This is because the first cache optimization, constraint condition is relatively loose, not optimized buffer still in a state of excessive input, to the work pieces piled up in wireless buffer, causing average captain and production cycle is too large, the optimization of the second buffer zone, because the latter is MHS transportation system, batch processing way can make the level before and after the coupling relationship in the buffer zone, the optimization, the coupling relationship between enhancement obviously improved the optimization, on average, captain, the third end of a buffer in the system, after the class without blocking phenomenon, so the optimization of the cache area to improve the system performance is not obvious. Summary data found that from infinite buffer to the final optimized buffer, the system average captain fell 86.5 %, production cycle is reduced by 89 % on average, a 8 % drop in productivity at the same time, rejection rate rose 9 %, significantly improve product production cycle and other performance degradation in the acceptable range, the optimization effect is better.

Table 1. The simulation results

The car max capacity	Buffers	Throughput	Leading time	Average length
1	∞,∞,∞	99 %	161.38	312.74
1	8,∞,∞	93 %	138.94	244.76
1	8,10,∞	91 %	18.04	40.32
1	8,10,15	91 %	18.01	40.31
3	∞,∞,∞	98 %	182.79	353.98
3	8,∞,∞	93 %	167.62	295.78
3	8,10,∞	90 %	20.39	48.25
3	8,10,15	90 %	20.1	47.75
5	∞,∞,∞	99 %	181.05	359.21
5	8,∞,∞	93 %	147.49	268.10
5	8,10,∞	89 %	22.89	55.25
5	8,10,15	89 %	23	55.14

Figure 5 is the tendency of the system performance index for the experimental process. Each curve represents the use of a specification of the car, the optimization of buffer effect the average production cycle and rejection rate of the system. Can be found from the figure, each curve trend is basically the same, every time optimization of index system of influence range is similar, but the curve between don't coincide.

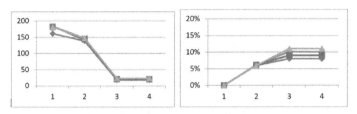

(a) The average production cycle optimization trend chart (b) Rejection rate change trend chart

Fig. 5. Performance of the system change trend chart

Table 2 is the set for different car capacity conditions, in turn, according to the optimal buffer and the sensitivity value of the final optimization results. Can learn from the results, the performance of the system such as the sensitivity calculation the conclusion is the same, with the decrease of the maximum load car, system performance improvement. But consider from the actual situation, the car capacity of 3 when overall system performance in the acceptable range, and MHS set reasonable, overall is in a better balance.

Table 2. The optimization results of different capacity of the car

The car max capacity	Buffers	Throughput	Leading time	Average length
1	8,10,15	91 %	18.01	40.31
2	8,10,15	91 %	19.12	44.23
3	8,10,15	90 %	20.1	47.75
4	8,10,15	90 %	21.56	52.08
5	8,10,15	89 %	23.00	55.14

4   Conclusions

In this paper, through the establishment of both assembly unit and simulation model of MHS, the sensitivity analysis of the orthogonal experiment method, calculating the sensitivity of parameters on the performance of the system to determine the optimization direction, and then use the heuristic optimization method to optimize system parameters. This optimization method using the sensitivity optimization direction, from the choice of empirical formula optimization parameter, improve the efficiency of optimization, on the other hand reveals the influence law of manufacturing system between the internal parameters, especially the MHS transport system parameter is set to total system can influence law. From the experimental results in this paper, the rational allocation method of resources for the enterprise has been provided effectively.

This project was supported by the National Natural Science Foundation (No. 51375098; 61573109; 71572049) and Aid program for Science and Technology Innovative Research Team in Higher Educational Institutions of Hunan Province china.

References

1. Li, Y.-X., Hu, X.-P., Xiong, Y.: Overview on logistics system simulation. J. Syst. Simul. **07**, 1411–1416 (2007)
2. Srinivasan, M.M., Bozer, Y.A.: Which one is responsible for WIP: the workstations or the material handling system. Int. J. Prod. Res. **30**(6), 1369–1399 (1992)
3. Li, X., Chen, Q.-X., Mao, N.: Buffer allocation optimization for multistage flow shop based on queuing network model. Comput. Integr. Manuf. Syst. **20**(4), 890–897 (2014)
4. Wang, Y., Cai, L.-N., Yue, X.-J.: The development of the logistics system design using simulation. Manuf. Autom. **09**, 5–8 (2004)
5. Huang, F., Zhu, W., Bai, B., Li, B.: Research on assembly line modeling and simulation optimization. In: Xiao, T., Zhang, L., Fei, M. (eds.) AsiaSim 2012, Part I. CCIS, vol. 323, pp. 20–27. Springer, Heidelberg (2012)
6. Zhou, J.-P.: Mixed flow simulation and optimization of the assembly line material distribution. Mech. Electr. Eng. Technol. **40**(8), 25–28 (2011)

A Hybrid Particle Swarm Optimization Algorithm for Solving Job Shop Scheduling Problems

Qiaofeng Meng$^{(\boxtimes)}$, Linxuan Zhang, and Yushun Fan

State CIMS Engineering Research Center at Tsinghua University, Beijing 100084, China
wwmmyymmqqff@163.com

Abstract. This paper proposes a new hybrid PSO optimization algorithm, which fuses GA and simulated annealing (SA) into the PSO algorithm. The crossover and mutation mechanism of GA algorithm make the new hybrid algorithm keep the diversity of population and retain the good factors in the population to jump out of local optimum. The sudden jump probability of SA also guarantees the diversity of the population, thus preventing local minimum of the hybrid PSO algorithm. This new hybrid algorithm is used to minimize the maximum completion time of the scheduling problems. The simulation results show that the performance of hybrid optimization algorithm outperforms another hybrid PSO algorithm. The hybrid PSO algorithm is not only in the structure of the algorithm, but also the search mechanism provides a powerful way to solve JSSP.

Keywords: Job shop scheduling problem · Particle swarm optimization · Simulated annealing · Maximum completion time

1 Introduction

Job Shop scheduling problem (JSSP) is demonstrated to be a classic NP-hard combinatorial optimization problem [1] which plays an important role in computer integrated manufacturing system and has vital effect on production management and control system. As one class of typical production scheduling problems, JSSP has attracted many scholars to study this field for last decades. It consists of a finite jobs set, J_i (i = 1, 2, …, n) to be processed on a finite machine set M_k (k = 1, 2, …, m) [2]. According to its production routine, each job is processed on machines with a given processing time, and each machine can process only one operation for each job [3]. JSSP can be thought of as the allocation of resources over a specified time to perform a predetermined collection of tasks [4].

Many different heuristics algorithms are developed for this problem in last decades. With the development of intelligent technology, more and more evolutionary algorithms have been applied to JSSP and have got many good results.

Phanden et al. [5] present a simulation-based genetic algorithm approach for JSSP, with and without restart scheme. Meng and Zhou [6] put forward immune genetic algorithm adopting timely dynamic vaccination and the shutdown criteria. Sun and Xiong [7] introduced the Metropolis sampling criteria in simulation annealing algorithm into algorithm, and proposed three kinds of hybrid PSO algorithms integrating simulation

© Springer Science+Business Media Singapore 2016
L. Zhang et al. (Eds.): AsiaSim 2016/SCS AutumnSim 2016, Part II, CCIS 644, pp. 71–78, 2016.
DOI: 10.1007/978-981-10-2666-9_8

annealing to solve part of FT problems and LA problems. Bank et al. [8] studies a permutation flow shop scheduling problem with deteriorating jobs. Gao et al. [9] designs a hybrid intelligence algorithm based on Particle Swarm algorithm and the Taboo Search algorithm (TS-PSO). Through particle swarm and Taboo search algorithm combined, the results show that this algorithm has very good accuracy of convergence, and embodies the obvious superiority compared with the traditional scheduling algorithm.

The simulated annealing (SA) is a generic probabilistic meta heuristic to solve global optimization problems. This algorithm can be applied in discrete spaces and combinatorial optimization problems. The simulated annealing method successfully solves the problem of classical Shop Job [10, 11], which guarantees the optimality, but the computational efficiency is poor.

Through the latest literature review, we found that hybrid approaches have effective performance than single one. We combine PSO with GA and SA not only making use of the fast research ability of PSO, but also increasing the individual diversity of population by utilizing the global search ability of GA and SA, which guarantees that the PSO algorithm could effectively jump out of the local optimal solution. The PSO convergence rate is fast but its accuracy is inferior. SA is of powerful generality and easy to be realized. Nevertheless, its computational time is long and efficiency is lower. Taking complementarities between PSO algorithm, GA and SA algorithm may have an advantage than each single algorithm. In this paper a new hybrid PSO algorithm (NHPSO) combined with GA and simulated annealing algorithm is developed to solve JSSP with minimization of the maximum completion time.

The paper is organized as follows. Next section is problem definition in which the formulation and notations used in the paper are described. In Sect. 3 a hybrid PSO algorithm is proposed including the main idea, the key steps and the whole procedure. In Sect. 4, a comparison between the results of our NHPSO with another HPSO is examined. Finally, Sect. 5 is devoted to conclusions and recommendation for future studies.

2 Problem Formulation

The job-shop scheduling problem considers how to determine the time of beginning processing, the time of finishing processing or the processing order of all the work pieces in order to optimize the processing performance index on the prerequisite of meeting the process constraint [12]. In general, the job shop problems can be described as follows. There are a set of jobs $J = \{1, 2, \ldots, n\}$ and a set of machines $M = \{1, 2, \ldots, m\}$ to be scheduled. Each job consists of a predetermined sequence of task operations, each of which needs to be processed without preemption for a given period of time on a given machine. The required machine and the fixed processing time characterize each operation. There are several constraints on jobs and machines: Each job must visit each machine exactly once; There are no precedence constraints among the operations of different jobs; Each operation cannot be commenced until the processing is completed, if the precedent operation is still being processed; Tasks of the same job cannot be processed concurrently and each job must visit each machine exactly once.

The mathematical model of the JSSP can be described as follows.

$$\min \max_{1 \leq k \leq m} \left\{ \max_{1 \leq i \leq n} C_{ik} \right\} \tag{1}$$

s.t. $\quad C_{ik} - T_{ik} + M\left(1 - a_{ihk}\right) \geq C_{ih} \qquad i = 1, 2, \cdots, n, \qquad h, k = 1, 2, \cdots, m \tag{2}$

$$C_{jk} - C_{ik} + M\left(1 - x_{ijk}\right) \geq T_{jk} \qquad i, j = 1, 2, \cdots, n, \qquad k = 1, 2, \cdots, m \tag{3}$$

$$C_{ik} \geq 0, i = 1, 2, \cdots, n, \qquad k = 1, 2, \cdots, m \tag{4}$$

$$a_{ihk} = 0 \, or \, 1 \qquad i = 1, 2, \cdots, n, \qquad h, k = 1, 2, \cdots, m \tag{5}$$

$$x_{ijk} = 0 \, or \, 1 \qquad i, j = 1, 2, \cdots, n, \qquad k = 1, 2, \cdots, m \tag{6}$$

$$a_{ihk} = \begin{cases} 1, if \, machine \, h \, processes \, workpiece \, i \, earlier \, than \, machine \, k \\ 0, others \end{cases} \tag{7}$$

$$x_{ijk} = \begin{cases} 1, if \, workpiece \, i \, processed \, by \, machine \, k \, earlier \, than \, workpiece \, j \\ 0, others \end{cases} \tag{8}$$

Where, (1) defines the objective function is to minimize make span. (2) defines the machining sequences of all the processes of every work piece, that is each operation can't be commenced until the processing is completed, if the precedent operation is still being processed. (3) represents the sequences of the machines processing every work piece determined by the process constraint conditions, which is a machine can only handle one job at a time. Among them, C_{ik} and T_{ik} respectively represent the time of finishing processing and the processing time of the work piece i on machine k, and M is a enough big positive number in order to ensure the inequalities of (2) and (3) can be established. In this model, using M we can get different constrain conditions. The constraint of a_{ihk} and x_{ijk} is defined in (5), (6), (7) and (8).

3   The Hybrid PSO Algorithm to Solve JSSP

Particle swarm optimization algorithm is one of the latest evolutionary optimization techniques which are developed by Kennedy and Eberhart [13]. PSO algorithm is based on communication and interaction between the members which is named as particle determines its position by combining the history of its own best location with those of other members of the swarm. The efficiency of PSO is so much higher than other algorithm that it has a large number of applications in recent years. However, PSO also has some disadvantages such as easy to fall into local extreme point, late in evolution slow convergence and so on. Therefore, this paper produces a new hybrid PSO (NHPSO) algorithm which importing the idea of genetic algorithm and SA to overcome the shortcomings of the particle swarm algorithm. The crossover and mutation operators explore new regions of search space to keeping some of the current information at the same time.

We use SA to enhance the local search capability [14] of the NHPSO. The hybrid algorithm will not only retain the advantages of GA, PSO and SA but also desert the defects of the three approaches.

The idea of PSO algorithm is adopted in the main frame of hybrid algorithm. Each particle in the swarm represents a solution to the problem and it is defined with its position and velocity.

The new hybrid algorithm started from a set of randomly generated initial solution to search for the global optimal solution, followed by mutation and crossover operation to generate a new set of particles, and then used the SA algorithm to search in local solution space. The evolutionary process repeated over and over again until the termination condition is satisfied, and the performance of the algorithm is greatly improved.

The process of the hybrid algorithm is as follows.

Step1 Initialization. Randomly generated initial particle swarm, initial mutation rate, simulated annealing initial temperature and other parameters.
Step2 Calculate the population fitness value.
Step3 Adjust the individual optimal fitness value.
Step4 Perform mutation, crossover operations and local search operations.
Step5 If the algorithm reaches the maximum algebra, then the algorithm is over, otherwise go to Step2.

The main components of the hybrid algorithm are introduced as followed.

3.1 Randomly Generated Initial Population of Particles

The hybrid algorithm begins with randomly generating particles of population according to the matrix of work piece and procedure, which represents all possible solution of a problem that are considered as candidate solutions. In order to increase the randomness of the initial group of particles, the strategy of exchanging position inside the particle is used.

3.2 Individual Optimal Particle Variation

The algorithm carries on mutation operator according to the mutation rate. Each particle randomly generated two mutation positions, and exchanged the individual of the two random position of the particle. The particle variation diagram is shown in Fig. 1. For example, the algorithm sets three times variants and randomly generates 3 pairs of the locations for the best individual particle p_{best}, such as 3 and 5, 7 and 10, 11 and 15. Then it exchanges the position of the corresponding process, namely the exchange 4 and 3, 1 and 6, 6 and 1, resulting in variation of the optimal particle.

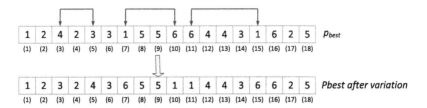

Fig. 1. The particle variation diagram

3.3 Cross

Using the idea of preserving the good gene in the genetic algorithm, a fragment of the individual optimal particle is retained in the next generation of particles, i.e., the particle crossing, as shown in Fig. 2. Specified a stochastic fragment (4)–(8) in an optimal particle p_{best}, that is, the procedure sequence (2, 4, 3, 6, 5). Firstly we delete the procedures successively in the individual particles which equal to the procedure of the fragments, i.e., remove (2, 4, 3, 6, 5) on position (1, 2, 5, 3, 4). Then we insert the sequence (2, 4, 3, 6, 5) into the individual particles in the rest of the sequence corresponding to the position, the retention position of (2, 4, 3, 6, 5) in the optimal particle, so as to produce a new generation of particle.

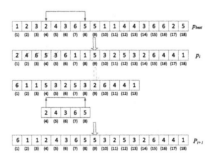

Fig. 2. The particle cross diagram

3.4 Local Search by SA Operator

The hybrid algorithm (NHPSO) runs SA operator after it finds an optimal solution. With the initial temperature declining continually, the algorithm search in the neighborhood of the optimal solution. If the solution searching by SA operator in the neighborhood of the current optimal solution is better than the current solution, it will replace the optimal solution according to a certain probability. The algorithm repeats this process until the temperature drops to a specific temperature.

4 Simulation

We simulate the effect of the important parameters on the performance of the hybrid algorithm, which is helpful to set up the appropriate parameters in the application of the algorithm to obtain better results. Mutation rate is an important parameter in the hybrid particle swarm algorithm because it plays an important role in maintaining the diversity of the population. Mutation rate is too big, the search direction easy to deviate from the previous search results. While mutation rate is too small, the algorithm will fall into local optimum easily. In order to test the effects of different mutation rate to the target value, we run a simulation which set up 10 mutation rate, that is MutPSO = [0.35 0.4 0.45 0.5 0.55 0.6 0.65 0.7 0.75 0.8]. The simulation results show that the maximum complete time reached the minimum value when the mutation rate is 0.5. The cross frequency is another important parameter in the hybrid particle swarm algorithm. More crossing, the next generation of particles group changing more than current particle swarm, then the algorithm will jump out of local optimum more easily. However, if cross frequency is too big, the particle swarm of the algorithm will lose some excellent characteristics. In order to find the appropriate crossover frequency, we set 10 crossover frequencies, that is CrossPSO = [1 2 3 4 5 6 7 8 9 10]. From the simulation results, we knew that the algorithm reaches the minimum target value when crossover frequency is 3 or 4. Therefore, the parameters in the NHPSO are set as follows. The particle swarm size swarmNum = 120, the initial temperature initT = 1000, and the temperature cooling coefficient a = 0.97, CrossPSO = 3, the Mutationrate MutPSO = 0.5.

We also perform experiments to compare our proposed new hybrid PSO (NHPSO) algorithm with another hybrid particle swarm optimization (HPSO) proposed by Sha et al. [15]. Table 1 summarizes these results for different sizes of benchmark problems obtained from the OR-Library [16]. As can be seen from the table, the new PSO(NHPSO) is significantly better than HPSO to solve JSSP problems of different scales.

Table 1. The computational results

Benchmark	n	m	Makespan (HPSO)	Makespan (NHPSO)
ft06	6	6	58	56
ft10	10	10	1045	998
ft20	20	5	1196	1175
abz5	10	10	1341	1275
abz6	10	10	1026	988
abz7	20	15	689	664
la01	10	5	712	703
la16	10	10	1045	981
la17	10	10	890	823
la35	30	10	1906	1893
la36	15	15	1297	1275
la20	10	10	951	920
orb01	10	10	1095	1062
orb05	10	10	996	973

The solution to ft10 is shown by Gantt chart in Fig. 3. The magenta blocks in the figure indicate the operation arrangement, the numbers below which represent the specific operation, such as 20 represents the first operation of the second job, and the 109 represents the tenth operation of the tenth job.

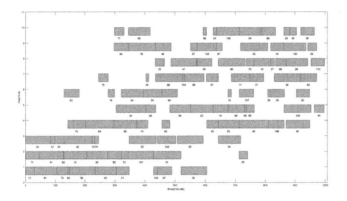

Fig. 3. The optimal solution of the FT10 10 × 10 problem

5   Conclusion

To improve the disadvantages for particle swarm optimization (PSO) algorithm such as easy to fall into local optimal solution, slow convergence speed in the late evolutionary and poor accuracy optimization and so on, this paper puts forward a novel PSO algorithm (NHPSO) which fuses GA and SA into PSO to solve the problem of JSSP. The new hybrid PSO incorporates the crossover and mutation mechanism of GA to increase the diversity of particles and retains the excellent factor of each generation of particle swarm to help the algorithm to escape from local optimal value, using property of probabilistic jumping of SA algorithm to avoid falling into the local optimum value, which facilitates the new algorithm extend the search scope to unexplored region, and enhances global search ability. In order to verify the performance of the new algorithm, we compare the maximum completion time of the new hybrid PSO algorithm (NHPSO) with another HPSO. The simulation results show that the maximum completion time of the hybrid PSO algorithm proposed in this paper has obvious advantages. The algorithm proposed in this paper can be applied to all sizes of job shop scheduling problem and effectively avoid trapping in local optimal solution. With some modification, the NHPSO can be applied to solve the flexible job shop scheduling problem. We will attempt to apply NHPSO to deal with multiple objectives JSSP in future research.

Acknowledgements. The work was supported by the Aviation Science Fund of China No. 20141625003).

References

1. Garey, M.R., Sethi, R.: The complexity of flowshop and jobshop scheduling. Math. Oper. Res. **1**(1), 117–129 (1976)
2. Geyik, F., Cedimoglu, I.H.: The Strategies and parameters of tabu search for job-shop scheduling. J. Intell. Manuf. **15**, 439–448 (2004)
3. Chen, J.C., Wu, C.-C., Chen, C.-W., Chen, K.-H.: Flexible job shop scheduling with parallel machines using genetic algorithm and grouping genetic algorithm. Expert Syst. Appl. **39**, 10016–10021 (2012)
4. Surekha, P., Sumathi, S.: Solution to the job shop scheduling problem using hybrid genetic swarm optimization based on (λ, 1)-interval fuzzy processing time. Eur. J. Sci. Res. **64**(2), 168–188 (2011)
5. Phanden, R.K., Jain, A., Verma, R.: A genetic algorithm-based approach for flexible job shop scheduling. Appl. Mech. Mater. **110**, 3930–3937 (2012)
6. Meng, L., Zhou, C.: Application of job shop based on immune genetic algorithm. In: Pan, J.-S., Snasel, V., Corchado, E.S., Abraham, A., Wang, S.-L. (eds.) Intelligent Data Analysis and Its Applications, Volume I. AISC, vol. 297, pp. 317–322. Springer, Heidelberg (2014)
7. Sun, Y., Xiong, H.: Job-shop scheduling problem based on particle swarm optimization algorithm. Sens. Transducers **16**, 116 (2012)
8. Bank, M., Ghomi, S.M.T.F., Jolai, F., et al.: Application of particle swarm optimization and simulated annealing algorithms in flow shop scheduling problem under linear deterioration. Adv. Eng. Softw. **47**(1), 1–6 (2012)
9. Gao, H., Kwong, S., Fan, B., et al.: A hybrid particle-swarm tabu search algorithm for solving job shop scheduling problems. IEEE Trans. Industr. Inf. **10**(4), 2044–2054 (2014)
10. Laarhoven, P.J.M.V., Aarts, E.H.L., Lenstra, J.K.: Job shop scheduling by simulated annealing. Oper. Res. **40**(1), 113–125 (1992)
11. Satake, T., Morikawa, K., Takahashi, K., Nakamura, N.: Simulated annealing approach for minimizing the makespan of the general job-shop. Int. J. Prod. Econ. **60–61**, 515–522 (1999)
12. Wang, L.: Shop Scheduling with Genetic Algorithm. Tsinghua University Press, Beijing (2003)
13. Kennedy, J., Eberhart, R.: Particle swarm optimization. In: IEEE International Conference on Neural Networks, Proceedings, vol. 4, pp. 1942–1948 (1995)
14. Kirkpatrick, S., Gelatt, C.D., Vecchi, M.P.: Optimization by simulated annealing. Science **220**(4598), 671–680 (1983)
15. Sha, D.Y., Hsu, C.Y.: A hybrid particle swarm optimization for job shop scheduling problem. Comput. Ind. Eng. **51**(4), 791–808 (2006)
16. Beasley, J.E.: OR-Library: distributing test problems by electronic mail. J. Oper. Res. Soc. **41**(11), 1069–1072 (1990)

A Chaotic Differential Evolution Algorithm for Flexible Job Shop Scheduling

Haijun Zhang[1(✉)], Qiong Yan[2], Guohui Zhang[2], and Zhiqiang Jiang[1]

[1] School of Mechatronics Engineering,
Zhengzhou University of Aeronautics, Zhengzhou, China
{tengda83,joan2055}@163.com
[2] School of Management Engineering,
Zhengzhou University of Aeronautics, Zhengzhou, China
120811921@qq.com, nodone@163.com

Abstract. To solve the flexible job shop scheduling problem (FJSP), a chaotic differential evolution algorithm (CDEA) is proposed with makespan minimization criterion. In the CDEA, logistic mapping is used to generate chaotic numbers for the initialization, because it is helpful to diversify the CDEA population and improve its performance in preventing premature convergence to local minima. A compositive operation-machine-based (COMB) encoding method is employed to reduce computational burden. Meanwhile, a self-adaptive double mutation scheme and an elitist strategy in the selection operator are introduced to balance the population diversity and the convergence rate. The performance of schedules is evaluated in terms of makespan and relative error. The results are compared with different well-known algorithm from open literatures. The results indicate that the proposed CDEA is effective in reducing makespan because the small value of relative error and the faster convergence rate are observed.

Keywords: Flexible job shop scheduling · Chaotic · Differential evolution

1 Introduction

With the market diversification and global competitiveness, modern manufacturing enterprises face increasing challenge with opportunity of complex products and the changeable market. Flexible production is an effective mode of production to meet the challenge, which has the ability to switch rapidly from the manufacture of one product to another. This mode can increase the economic efficiency of enterprises through the rational allocation and the efficient use of resources. There are often conflicts between the artificial scheduling and the actual production. Although the flexible production can enhance the flexibility and responsiveness of enterprises, shorten the production cycle, improve equipment utilization and product quality, the production planning and control of the enterprise has made a very high demand. FJSP is a key issue of resource optimization allocation, which plays an important role in the entire production process.

FJSP is an extension of the classical job shop scheduling problem (JSP), which is one of the most difficult problems proved to be a NP-hard problem [1]. At present, the solution strategy of FJSP includes the hierarchical approach and the integrated approach.

© Springer Science+Business Media Singapore 2016
L. Zhang et al. (Eds.): AsiaSim 2016/SCS AutumnSim 2016, Part II, CCIS 644, pp. 79–88, 2016.
DOI: 10.1007/978-981-10-2666-9_9

In the integrated approach, the assignment on the machines and the sequencing of the jobs are treated simultaneously. For example, Yazdani et al. proposed a parallel variable neighborhood search (PVNS) algorithm for FJSP [2]. Xing et al. proposed a knowledge-based ant colony optimization for FJSP [3]. Wang et al. proposed a bi-population based estimation of distribution algorithm for FJSP [4]. Zhao proposed a hybrid algorithm mixed with bilevel neighborhood search and GA for solving FJSP [5]. Zhong et al. proposed a method based on niching and particle swarm optimization algorithms for multi-objective FJSP [6].

Many researchers have been active in the study of FJSP, which made great achievements. With the development of swarm intelligence algorithms, differential evolutionary algorithm (DEA) is an evolutionary algorithm introduced by Storn and Price [7] for optimization over continuous spaces. Since its invention, DEA has been applied with high success on many numerical optimization problems outperforming other more popular population heuristics including GAs [8]. In this paper, the use of a new method based on DEA called the chaotic DEA (CDEA) is investigated for solving FJSP.

The rest of this paper is organized as follows: The FJSP formulation is introduced in Sect. 2. Section 3 illustrates the method encoding and decoding of CDEA individuals. In Sect. 4, the proposed CDEA is described in detail. Computational results over known test instances and discussion are presented in Sect. 5. Finally, the conclusion and future research of this paper are given in Sect. 6.

2   Formulation of FJSP

A general FPSP may be formulated as follows: there is a set of NJ jobs to be processed on NM machines. Each job consists of a predefined sequence of operations. The execution of each operation requires one machine out of a set of given machines with the different processing times. Thus, FJSP consists of assigning an operation to a machine, aiming to obtain a feasible sequence of jobs on the machine to optimize a certain objective. A typical objective of this process is to minimize the total completion time (makespan) required for all jobs. The following notations are used for the formulation of FJSP:

Objective:

$$Min \ CT_{max} \tag{1}$$

Subject to:

$$CT_{max} \geq \sum_{m \in M_{ij}} CT_{ijm} \ \forall i, j = NO_i; \tag{2}$$

$$ST_{ijm} \geq 0, CT_{ijm} \geq 0 \ \forall i, j, m; \tag{3}$$

$$CT_{ijm} = ST_{ijm} + P_{ijm} \cdot V_{ijm}^1; \tag{4}$$

$$\sum_{m \in M_{ij}} V_{ijm}^1 = 1 \quad \forall i, j; \tag{5}$$

$$\sum_{m \in M_{ij}} ST_{ijm} \geq \sum_{m \in M_{i(j-1)}} CT_{i(j-1)m} \quad \forall i, \forall j = 2, \cdots, NO_i; \tag{6}$$

$$ST_{hgm} \geq CT_{ijm} \quad if \ V_{ijhgm}^2 = 1. \tag{7}$$

NJ	Number of jobs
NM	Number of machines
O_{ij}	The jth operation of job i
M_{ij}	Set of available machine is assigned to operation O_{ij}
NO_i	Number of all operations of job i
PT_{ijm}	Processing time of operation O_{ij} on machine m
ST_{ijm}	Start time of operation O_{ij} on machine m
CT_{ijm}	Completion time of operation O_{ij} on machine m
i, h	Indexes of jobs $i, h = 1, 2, \cdots, NJ$
m	Indexes of machines $m = 1, 2, \cdots, NM$
j, g	Indexes of operations $j, g = 1, 2, \cdots, NO_i$
V_{ijm}^1	Decision variable 1, if operation O_{ij} was performed on machine m, it is set to 1, otherwise 0
V_{ijhgm}^2	Decision variable 2, if operation O_{ij} precedes operation O_{hg} on machine m, it is set to 1, otherwise 0

In the mathematical model, the expression (1) is the objective of the model to minimize the makespan. The constraint (2) determines the completion times of the jobs. The constraint (3) states the starting and completion times of operation on machine m equal to 0 if operation O_{ij} is not assigned to machine m. The constraint (4) calculates the completion time of operation O_{ij}. The constraint (5) ensures that an operation is performed on one and only one machine. The constraint (6) ensures that no precedence relationship is violated, i.e. the operation O_{ij} on machine m is not started before the operation O_{ij-1} has been completed. The constraint (7) ensures that operations O_{ij} and O_{hg} cannot be done at the same time on any machine.

3   Representation of FJSP

The individual in the CDEA population is corresponding to the solution of the FJSP. Decoding and encoding of the individual are very important to the CDEA. This paper employs a novel compositive operation-machine-based (COMB) method.

In this paper, a real number encoding system is proposed. For the example, consider an instance of the problem with 2 jobs and 4 machines given in Table 1. The position of individual is represented by a real number. The integer part is used to assign the operations of each job to the machine and fractional part is used to sequence of the operations on each machine. In the following we show the above instance with a permutation of $\Pi = \{0.25, 3.64, 2.12, 2.44, 3.14\}$, which is generated using logistic map function:

Step 1: Calculate the number of machine $|M_{ij}|$ which is available to operation O_{ij}, as shown in the last column of Table 1.

Step 2: Sequencing of available machines for an operation according to the increasing order of processing time. That is the machine priority matrix. If a machine cannot process the operation, the corresponding processing time is set to infinity.

Step 3: Each real number in the permutation Π are separated by the fractional part and the integer part, as shown in the 2nd and 3rd row of Table 3.

Step 4: Calculate the remainders when the above integer values are divided by the corresponding $|M_{ij}|$. The remainders are as the priority levels, as shown in the 4th row of Table 3. Then according to Table 2, the available machine is selected corresponding to the priority level, as shown in the 5th row of Table 3.

Step 5: The process order of operations to be scheduled on the same machine depends on the value of the fractional values.

Table 1. An example of jobs and processing times

Jobs	Operat-ions	Available machines & processing times				Number of available machines
		M1	M2	M3	M4	
Job1	O_{11}	2	3	5	6	4
	O_{12}	—	4	—	8	2
Job2	O_{21}	3	—	6	—	2
	O_{22}	4	5	6	—	3
	O_{23}	—	5	7	11	3

Note:" — " indicates that the operation cannot be processed the corresponding machine

Table 2. A machine priority matrix

Jobs	Operations	Priority Level			
		0	1	2	3
Job1	O_{11}	M1	M2	M3	M4
	O_{12}	M2	M4	M1	M3
Job2	O_{21}	M1	M3	M2	M4
	O_{22}	M1	M2	M3	M4
	O_{23}	M2	M3	M4	M1

Using the COMB method, each individual in the population is guaranteed to be eligible.

Table 3. An example of individual encoding and decoding

Operations	$O_{1,1}$	$O_{1,2}$	$O_{2,1}$	$O_{2,2}$	$O_{2,3}$
Individual	0.25	3.64	2.12	2.44	3.14
Fractional	0.25	0.64	0.12	0.44	0.14
Integer	0	3	2	2	3
Mod	0	1	0	2	0
Machines	M1	M4	M1	M3	M2

4 Chaotic Different Evolution Algorithm (CDEA)

4.1 Chaotic Initialization

The initialization of population has a great impact on the quality and efficient of evolutionary algorithms. Chaos is a kind of characteristic of nonlinear systems, which is a bounded unstable dynamic behavior that exhibits sensitive dependent on initial conditions and includes infinite unstable periodic motions [9]. The purpose of chaotic numbers as a substitute of random numbers in CDEA is a powerful strategy to diversify the CDEA population and improve its performance in preventing premature convergence to local minima.

The logistic map illustrated in Eq. (8) is used instead of random number generator in the CDEA, as it is one of the simplest dynamic systems which demonstrate chaotic behavior where Z_n is the value of chaotic variable in nth iteration:

$$Z_n = \mu \cdot Z_{n-1} \cdot (1 - Z_{n-1}) \tag{8}$$

where μ is the bifurcation parameter of chaotic system.

From Fig. 1, it can be observed that chaotic numbers have higher degree of disorder which facilitates high diversity in the individuals and thus helps the algorithm to converge rapidly towards the solution.

4.2 Self-adaptive Double Mutation Operator

An effect of mutant individual is to perturb the target individual in order to avoid being stuck in the local convergence. Therefore, this paper defines the diversity of individual position (*DIP*) of population:

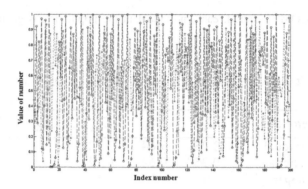

Fig. 1. Comparison between random numbers and chaotic numbers

$$DIP = \frac{1}{N}\sum_{n=1}^{N}\sqrt{\frac{1}{I}\sum_{k=1}^{I}(x_{n,k}^{(g)} - x_{best,k})^2} \qquad (9)$$

where $I = \sum_{i=1}^{NJ} NO_i$, g is the generation index, N is the size of population, $n = 1, 2, \ldots, N$ is the index of individual, $j = 1, 2, \ldots, I$ is the index of individual dimension, $best$ denotes the current best individual $X_{best} = \left(x_{best,1}, x_{best,2}, \ldots, x_{best,j}, \ldots x_{best,I}\right)$.

As shown in Eq. (10), if $DIP \le \varepsilon(\varepsilon$: a user-defined threshold), CDEA employs either DE/rand/1/bin scheme (Eq. (10.a)) as the mutation operator, otherwise DE/best/2/bin scheme (Eq. (10.b)).

$$\bar{x}_{n,k}^{(g)} = \begin{cases} x_{\alpha,k}^{(g)} + F \times (x_{\beta,k}^{(g)} - x_{\gamma,k}^{(g)}) & DIP \le \varepsilon \quad (a); \\ x_{best,k}^{(g)} + F \times [(x_{\alpha,k}^{(g)} - x_{\beta,k}^{(g)}) + (x_{\gamma,k}^{(g)} - x_{\delta,k}^{(g)})] & DIP > \varepsilon \quad (b). \end{cases} \qquad (10)$$

4.3   Crossover Operator

The crossover operator is applied to form a trial individual $U_n^{(g)}$ against a target individual $X_n^{(g)}$. In the case, either a dimension of the target individual or that of the mutant individual $\overline{X}_n^{(g)}$ is adopted, with a user-defined probability CR, as the corresponding dimension of the trial individual.

$$u_{n,k}^{(g)} = \begin{cases} \bar{x}_{n,k}^{(g)} & rand(0, 1) \le CR \ or \ k = rand[1, I], \\ x_{n,k}^{(g)} & otherwise. \end{cases} \qquad (11)$$

4.4   Elite-Selection Operator

The traditional selection operator is replaced here by the "elite-preserving mechanism" proposed by Deb et al. [10] in this paper. This mechanism is applied to CDEA as follows: without taking any decision based on a pair of a target individual and its trial individual only, all the target and trial individuals are first combined, and then the combined individuals are sorted according to their qualities (makespans). Finally, the first 15 % of the best individuals of the combined individuals are extracted as the population in the next generation.

5   Numerical Experiments and Discussion

5.1   Experimental Setup

The proposed CDEA procedure was coded using C# programming language and run on an AMD CPU 2.29 GHz PC. To illustrate the effectiveness and performance of the CDEA, the benchmark instances [11] from other papers are adopted in the experiment. These instances include 10 open problems for FJSP. After much experimental effort with the combination of settings, and taking into account both the convergence speed, as well as, the diversity of population, the threshold of $DIP{:}\varepsilon = 0.30$, the scale of population $N = 100$, the scaling parameter $F = 0.90$ and the crossover rate $CR = 0.50$. To be fair with the stochastic behavior of the heuristics, it was decided to run each of them 10 times over each instances of the benchmarks problems and report the best result. The proposed CDEA terminates when the number of iterations reaches to the maximum value 200 or the algorithm finds the known optimum results. The relative error (RE) is employed to evaluate the quality of results from the algorithms. The formula of RE is as follows (13):

$$RE = \left(\frac{CT_{best} - LB}{LB}\right) \times 100\% \tag{13}$$

where CT_{best} denotes the best result by the algorithm, LB denotes the present known lower bound value of optimum results.

5.2   Results and Discussions

In Table 4, comparison of makespan obtained by CDEA to the results of the GA [12], PVNS [2] and BBO [13] on the instances is made. Table 4 indicates that CDEA produces better results for 9 out of 10 problems, where CDEA produces better than other heuristics for problems MK06 and MK10. Most heuristics give better solution than CDEA for problem MK07. Table 4 also illustrates the comparisons the RE results of heuristics. The 11th row shows that the RE of CDEA is smaller than those of other heuristics. It illustrates that the results by CDEA are closest to the optimal values in average.

Table 4. The experimental results of heuristics

Problem name	n×m	(LB,UB)	PVNS(Yazdani et al., 2010)		GA(Pezella et al., 2008)		BBO(Rahmati et al., 2012)		CDEA	
			CT	RE	CT	RE	CT	RE	CT	RE
MK01	10×6	(36,42)	40	11.11%	40	11.11%	40	11.11%	40	11.11%
MK02	10×6	(24,32)	26	8.33%	26	8.33%	28	16.67%	26	8.33%
MK03	15×8	(204,211)	204	0.00%	204	0.00%	204	0.00%	204	0.00%
MK04	15×8	(48,81)	60	25.00%	60	25.00%	64	33.33%	60	25.00%
MK05	15×4	(168,186)	173	2.98%	173	2.98%	173	2.98%	173	2.98%
MK06	10×15	(33,86)	60	81.82%	60	81.82%	66	100.00%	58	75.76%
MK07	20×5	(133,157)	141	6.02%	141	6.02%	144	8.27%	144	8.27%
MK08	20×10	(523,558)	523	0.00%	523	0.00%	523	0.00%	523	0.00%
MK09	20×10	(299,369)	307	2.68%	307	2.68%	310	3.68%	307	2.68%
MK10	20×15	(165,296)	208	26.06%	208	26.06%	230	39.39%	201	21.82%
Average				16.40%		16.40%		21.54%		15.59%

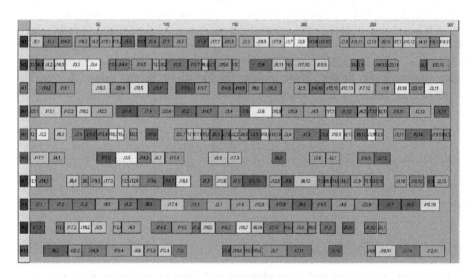

Fig. 2. Gannt chart of problem MK09 (makespan = 307)

Gantt chart of the obtained solution for MK09 by CDEA is illustrated in Fig. 2 (makespan = 307). The convergence curve is drawn for problem MK09 set in Fig. 3. Figure 3 illustrates the comparison of the performance of initialization method. It is conceivable to note that CDEA algorithm improves the makespan, and the best makespan, equal to 307, is reached after 104 iterations. It can also be observed from Fig. 3 that the objective value converges towards the optimal value faster when the

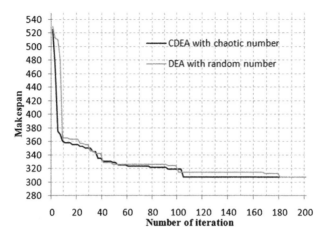

Fig. 3. The convergence curves of DEA and CDEA for problem MK09

chaotic numbers are used for initialization of the individual. This is because of higher degree of disorderness of the chaotic number s which facilitates high diversity in the individual and helps the heuristics to converge rapidly towards the optimal value. The computational results validate the proposed CDEA's effectiveness.

6   Conclusions

In this paper, we solve the flexible job-shop scheduling problem with a novel differential evolution algorithm that is based on chaotic numbers of initialization and a compositive operation-machine-based (COMB) method of encoding. Numerical experiments with the proposed heuristic were performed for ten instance of FJSP to find the optimal solutions. The results show that the proposed CDEA obtains better solutions for instances, while comparing with the existing algorithms that solve the same instances. One can also verify that, the chaotic number of initialization can improve the proposed CDEA converge towards the optimal value faster.

Acknowledgements. This paper is partially supported by Aviation Foundation of China (2015ZG55018); Soft Science Research Project of Henan Province (132400410782); Key Science Research Project of Higher Education of Henan Province (15A630050); Technological Development Project of Zhengzhou City (20140583).

References

1. Kacem, I., Hammadi, S., Borne, P.: Approach by localization and multi-objective evolutionary optimization for flexible job-shop scheduling problems. IEEE Trans. Syst. Man Cybern. **32**(1), 1–13 (2002)
2. Yazdani, M., Amiri, M., Zanfieh, M.: Flexible job-shop scheduling with parallel variable neighborhood search algorithm. Expert Syst. Appl. **37**(1), 678–687 (2010)

3. Xing, L.N., Chen, Y.W., Wang, P., et al.: A knowledge based ant colony optimization for flexible job shop scheduling problems. Appl. Soft Comput. **10**(3), 888–896 (2010)
4. Wang, L., Wang, S., Xu, Y., et al.: A bi-population based estimation of distribution algorithm for the flexible job-shop scheduling problem. Comput. Ind. Eng. **62**(4), 917–926 (2012)
5. Zhao, S.K.: Bilevel neighborhood search hybrid algorithm for the flexible job shop scheduling problem. J. Mech. Eng. **51**(14), 175–184 (2015)
6. Zhong, Y.J., Yang, H.C., Mo, R., et al.: Optimization method of flexible job-shop scheduling problem based on niching and particle swarm optimization algorithms. Comput. Integr. Manuf. Syst. **21**(12), 3231–3238 (2015)
7. Storn, R., Price, K.: Differential evolution – a simple and efficient heuristic for global optimization over continuous spaces. J. Global Optim. **11**, 341–354 (1997)
8. Kaelo, P., Ali, M.M.: A numerical study of some modified differential evolution algorithms. Eur. J. Oper. Res. **171**, 674–692 (2006)
9. Wong, K., Man, K.P., Li, S., Liao, X.: More secure chaotic cryptographic scheme based on dynamic look-up table. Circ. Syst. Sig. Process. **24**(5), 571–584
10. Deb, K., Agarwal, S., Pratap, A., et al.: A fast and elitist multi-objective genetic algorithm: NSGA-II. IEEE Trans. Evol. Comput. **6**(2), 182–197 (2002)
11. Brandimarte, P.: Routing and scheduling in a flexible job shop by tabu search. Ann. Oper. Res. **41**(3), 157–183 (1993)
12. Pezella, F., Morganti, G., Ciaschetti, G.: A genetic algorithm for the flexible job-shop scheduling problem. Comput. Oper. Res. **35**(10), 3202–3212 (2008)
13. Rahmati, S.H.A., Zandieh, M.: A new biogeography-based optimization (BBO) algorithm for the flexible job shop scheduling problem. Int. J. Adv. Manuf. Technol. **58**(9–12), 1115–1129 (2012)

Modeling and Simulation for Super Large Twin-Propeller Twin-Rudder Ship and Its Course ADRC

Chen Guo, Demin Wang[✉], and Yongzheng Li

Information Science and Technology College,
Dalian Maritime University, Dalian, China
wangdemin1990@126.com,
dmuzheng@163.com

Abstract. Taking a super large twin-propeller twin-rudder container ship as research object, according to mechanism of MMG modeling, a mathematical model of ship motion for a super large ship with twin-propeller and twin-rudder is established. The validity of the ship model is verified by completing turning test. The maneuverability of the ship is discussed under several working conditions when left propeller and right propeller have the same speed and different speed. The active disturbance rejection control algorithm is adopted in the design of ship course controller and simulation calculation is accomplished. Fuzzy control algorithm is used to improve conventional active disturbance rejection controller (ADRC), which is applied to above ship course control. The simulation results show that the improved ADRC has better control performance, fast response and better control accuracy obtained.

Keywords: Twin-propeller twin-rudder ship · Ship motion mathematical model · Ship maneuverability · Active disturbance rejection control · Fuzzy control

1 Introduction

At present the trend of container ship maximization and intelligence is becoming more and more obvious. With the advent of Maersk's Triple E container ship with twin-propeller and twin-rudder, some new issues of steering and control for super large container ship are proposed. The super large twin-propeller twin-rudder ship could take advantages of flexible operation to overcome problems of manipulation and control. The super large twin-propeller twin-rudder ship can turn in the smaller water area. However, there is not too much research works for this super shape and equipage container ship. Many new issues are worthy of being studied. Simulation researches on modeling and control for this type super large ship with twin-propeller and twin-rudder have important theory value and practical significance.

© Springer Science+Business Media Singapore 2016
L. Zhang et al. (Eds.): AsiaSim 2016/SCS AutumnSim 2016, Part II, CCIS 644, pp. 89–99, 2016.
DOI: 10.1007/978-981-10-2666-9_10

2 Maneuvering Mathematical Model of Twin-Propeller Twin-Rudder Ship

In this paper, the study is focused on the problem of ship motion in the horizontal plane. The plane motion coordinate system for the twin-propeller twin-rudder ship is shown in Fig. 1.

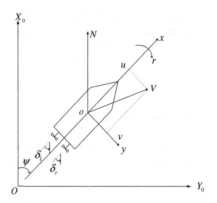

Fig. 1. Ship plane motion coordinate system

The mathematical equation of the ship motion with three degrees of freedom is written in the following equations [1]:

$$\left.\begin{aligned}
m(\dot{u} - rv) &= X_{H_0} + X_P + X_R + X_{wind} + X_{current} \\
m(\dot{v} + ru) &= Y_{H_0} + Y_P + Y_R + Y_{wind} + Y_{current} \\
I_{zz}\dot{r} &= N_{H_0} + N_P + N_R + N_{wind} + N_{current} - Y \cdot x_C
\end{aligned}\right\} \quad (1)$$

Where, subscripts H_0, P, R, $wind$ and $current$ refer to bare hull, propeller, rudder, wind and current respectively. $-Y \cdot x_C$ is N's revision of the ship's center of gravity.

2.1 Hull Hydrodynamic Forces and Moments

The hydrodynamic forces and moments acting on the bare hull include inertia force and viscous force. Inertia forces and moments are expressed as follows:

$$\left.\begin{aligned}
X_I &= -(m_x\dot{u} - m_yvr) \\
Y_I &= -(m_y\dot{v} + m_xur) \\
N_I &= -(J_{zz}\dot{r} + (m_y - m_x)uv)
\end{aligned}\right\} \quad (2)$$

Where, m_x and m_y represent the added mass of x axis and y axis respectively, J_{zz} is the added moment of inertia of ship around Z axis. Above parameters are calculated by Zhou Zhaoming regression formula [2].

In this paper, the main study is ship course control in ocean going, which belongs to the ordinary-speed field motion state. Kijima model is used to calculate viscous forces and moments as follows [1],

$$
\left.
\begin{aligned}
X_H &= X(u) + X_{vv}v^2 + X_{vr}vr + X_{rr}r^2 \\
Y_H &= Y_v v + Y_r r + Y_{|v|v}|v|v + Y_{|r|r}|r|r + \\
&\quad Y_{vvr}v^2 r + Y_{vrr}vr^2 \\
N_H &= N_v v + N_r r + N_{|v|v}|v|v + N_{|r|r}|r|r + \\
&\quad N_{vvr}v^2 r + N_{vrr}vr^2
\end{aligned}
\right\}
\tag{3}
$$

2.2 Mathematical Model of Twin Propellers

In MMG model, hydrodynamic term of propeller includes longitudinal force X_P, transverse force Y_P and transverse moment N_P.

Longitudinal forces X_P is calculated using the following equation,

$$
X_P = (1 - t_p)(T_l + T_r)
\tag{4}
$$

Where, t_p is thrust deduction factor, T_l is left propeller thrust, T_r is right propeller thrust.

The research object of this paper is an inner-rotating twin- propeller twin-rudder container ship, the transverse force generated by left and right propellers is almost offset, which can be neglected. The transverse moment is expressed as follows,

$$
N_P = (1 - t_p)\frac{b}{2}(T_l - T_r)
\tag{5}
$$

Where, b is the distance between two propellers.

In this study, the mathematical model of twin propellers is shown as follows [3],

$$
\left.
\begin{aligned}
X_P &= (1 - t_p)(T_l + T_r) \\
N_P &= (1 - t_p)\frac{b}{2}(T_l - T_r)
\end{aligned}
\right\}
\tag{6}
$$

2.3 Mathematical Model of Twin Rudders

The mathematical model of twin rudders is shown as follows [4, 5],

$$
\left.\begin{aligned}
X_R &= -\{(1-t_R)(F_{N(l)}\sin\delta_l + F_{N(r)}\sin\delta_r)\} \\
Y_R &= -\{(1+a_H)(F_{N(l)}\cos\delta_l + F_{N(r)}\cos\delta_r)\} \\
N_R &= -\{(x_R + a_H x_H)(F_{N(l)}\cos\delta_l + F_{N(r)}\cos\delta_r)\} \\
&\quad -\frac{b}{2}(1-t_R)(F_{N(l)}\sin\delta_l - F_{N(r)}\sin\delta_r)
\end{aligned}\right\}
\tag{7}
$$

Where, t_R is rudder resistance coefficient, $F_{N(l)}$ is left rudder pressure, $F_{N(r)}$ is right rudder pressure, δ_l is left rudder angle, δ_r is right rudder angle. This twin-propeller twin-rudder ship is equipped two steering engines driving two rudders, so the mathematical model of left steering engine and right steering engine is established as below:

$$
\left.\begin{aligned}
T_E\dot{\delta}_l &= \delta_{El} - \delta_l \\
T_E\dot{\delta}_r &= \delta_{Er} - \delta_r
\end{aligned}\right\}
\tag{8}
$$

Where, δ_{El} is left command rudder angle, δ_{Er} is right rudder angle, T_E is steering engine time constant. The range of the rudder angle is $\left|\delta_{\{l,r\}}\right| \le 35°$, dual steering engines: $T_E = 2$, $\left|\dot{\delta}\right| \le 3°/s$ [6]. Because the course control is studied for the ocean voyage, two rudders operated jointly and two propellers are at same speed.

2.4　Turning Test

Simulation result of full load right turning is shown in Fig. 2. Each parameter is set as follows, Initial ship speed $V = 23\text{kn}$, left propeller revolution $n = 76.5r/\text{min}$, right propeller revolution $n = 76.5r/\text{min}$.

The comparison between simulation result and real data is shown in Table 1.

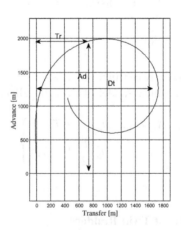

Fig. 2. Simulation result of right turning test

Table 1. Comparison of right turning test result

Turning parameters	Real data	Simulation result	Error
Advance A_d(m)	1979	1987	8 (0.02L$_{pp}$)
Transfer T_r(m)	774	868	94 (0.24L$_{pp}$)
Tactical diameter D_T(m)	1746	1727	19 (0.05L$_{pp}$)

According to the comparison between simulation result and real ship data in Table 1, the error of advance A_d is 0.02 L$_{pp}$, the error of transfer T_r is 0.24 L$_{pp}$, the error of tactical diameter D_T is 0.05 L$_{pp}$, each error is in a reasonable range. Maneuvering mathematical model of twin-propeller twin-rudder ship can meet simulation test requirements.

2.5 Maneuverability Study Under Multi-operating Conditions

The super large twin-propeller twin-rudder ship is designed with twin engines, twin propellers and twin rudders. Two propellers not only can be operated jointly, but also can be operated independently, so the ship with twin-propeller and twin-rudder is able to have more operation modes.

In the conditions of two rudders operated jointly, two propellers at different speeds, the analysis and research on the maneuverability of the ship during right turning motion are shown in Tables 2 and 3.

Table 2. Turning parameters when the rudder angle is 35°

Left propeller revolution (r/min)	Right propeller revolution (r/min)	Rudder angle (°)	Steady diameter (m)	Turning period (s)
76.5	76.5	35	1254	298
76.5	65	35	1095	281
76.5	51	35	910	256

Table 3. Turning parameters when the rudder angle is 25°

Left propeller revolution (r/min)	Right propeller revolution (r/min)	Rudder angle (°)	Steady diameter (m)	Turning period (s)
76.5	76.5	25	1799	367
76.5	65	25	1521	336
76.5	51	25	1228	300

According to the above simulation data, the right turning experiments are carried out at two different rudder angles (the left propeller is inside propeller and the right propeller is outside propeller). Compared with the situation which two propellers have the same speed, the situation which outside propeller speed is greater than that of inside one can achieve smaller steady diameter and shorter turning period.

When the speed difference between the left and right propellers increases, the steady diameter reduces and the turning period decreases. But the difference is not as bigger as better, and this study find that the turning quality can keep good performance only the speed difference in a certain range.

During the process of turning and the speed difference between the inside and outside propellers changing in a reasonable range, when the outside propeller speed is greater than the inner propeller speed, the turning quality is improved. Speed difference of inside and outside propellers can increase the effect of turning moment, which is equivalent to add the effect of rudder and it is conducive to reducing the load of rudder. So, the independent operation of twin propellers can have more flexible maneuverability.

3   Ship Course Active Disturbance Rejection Controller

The active disturbance rejection controller (ADRC) is composed of tracking differential (TD), extended state observer (ESO), nonlinear state error feedback control law (NLSEF) and disturbance compensation. Its structure is shown in Fig. 3, the dashed part is ADRC [7–9].

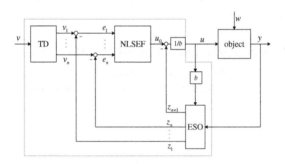

Fig. 3.   Structure diagram of ADRC

3.1   Design of Nonlinear Active Disturbance Rejection Controller

The nonlinear active disturbance rejection controller (NLADRC) algorithm is designed as follows,

$$\text{TD}\begin{cases} \dot{x}_1 = x_2 \\ \dot{x}_2 = fhan(x_1 - v, x_2, r, h_0) \end{cases} \tag{9}$$

$$\text{ESO} \begin{cases} e = z_1 - y \\ \dot{z}_1 = z_2 - \beta_{01}e \\ \dot{z}_2 = z_3 - \beta_{02}fal(e, a_1, \delta) + bu \\ \dot{z}_3 = -\beta_{03}fal(e, a_2, \delta) \end{cases} \tag{10}$$

$$\text{NLSEF} \begin{cases} e_1 = x_1 - z_1, e_2 = x_2 - z_2 \\ u_0 = \beta_1 fal(e_1, a_3, \delta) + \beta_2 fal(e_2, a_4, \delta) \end{cases} \tag{11}$$

$$u = \frac{u_0 - z_3}{b} \tag{12}$$

3.2 Design of Linear Active Disturbance Rejection Controller

There are many parameters need to be adjusted in the NLADRC and it also uses a large number of nonlinear functions, which makes the changes of parameters have great influence on the control effect. In addition, the parameter tuning can only be achieved by experience. In this paper, a linear active disturbance rejection controller (LADRC) is designed.

The LADRC algorithm is designed as follows.

$$\text{LESO} \begin{cases} e = z_1 - y \\ \dot{z}_1 = z_2 - \beta_{01}e \\ \dot{z}_2 = z_3 - \beta_{02}e + bu \\ \dot{z}_3 = -\beta_{03}e \end{cases} \tag{13}$$

$$u_0 = \beta_1(v - z_1) - \beta_2 z_2 \tag{14}$$

$$u = u_0 - \frac{z_3}{b} \tag{15}$$

3.3 Simulation of Ship Course Active Disturbance Rejection Controller

In order to verify control effect of two controllers designed in front, simulation experiments of course control are carried out under interference condition.

Ship parameters are set as follows, initial ship speed is $V = 23$kn, left propeller revolution and right propeller revolution are $n = 76.5r/\text{min}$, draft is 16 m, initial course angle is $0°$, target course angle is $20°$.

Wind and flow parameters are set as follows, wind speed is 15m/s, wind direction is $30°$, flow velocity is 2m/s, flow direction is $10°$.

Simulation results of LADRC and NLADRC are shown in Fig. 4.

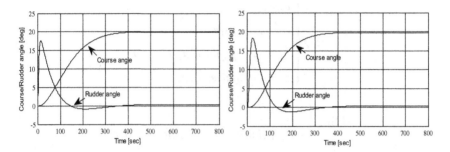

Fig. 4. Simulation results of LADRC and NLADRC under interference condition

Conclusions can be drawn from Fig. 4, under interference condition, LADRC and NLADRC can reach the specified course, and achieve the control of ship course. But these two kinds of conventional active disturbance rejection controllers reach the target course for a little long time. The rudder angle of LADRC at the initial moment changes quickly and there is a small steady-state error in NLADRC.

4 Design of Improved Fuzzified Active Disturbance Rejection Controller

In order to improve the quality of controller and enhance the adaptability of controller, fuzzy control algorithm is introduced to improve the conventional ADRC. The parameters β_1 and β_2 of NLSEF in ADRC could achieve automatic adjustment [10]. The structure of fuzzified ADRC is shown in Fig. 5.

As shown in Fig. 5, the inputs of fuzzy controller are error e_1 and the change of the error e_2, and the outputs are correction coefficient $\Delta\beta_1$ and $\Delta\beta_2$ of NLSEF.

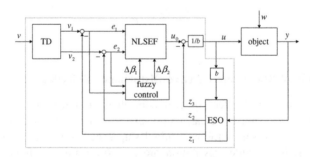

Fig. 5. Structure diagram of fuzzified ADRC

4.1 Simulation of Fuzzified Linear Active Disturbance Rejection Controller

Under interference condition, the simulation results comparisons of fuzzified linear active disturbance rejection controller (FLADRC) and conventional LADRC are shown in Fig. 6.

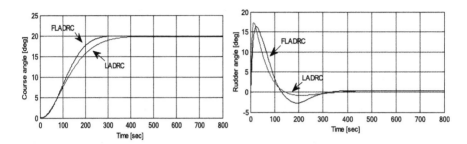

Fig. 6. Simulation results of FLADRC and LADRC under interference condition

From Fig. 6(a), the FLADRC has shorter time than the conventional LADRC to reach the target course and does not produce overshoot. From Fig. 6(b), the maximum rudder angle of the FLADRC is obviously reduced than that of conventional LADRC. So FLADRC could avoid the drastic change of the rudder angle at the initial time, and the rudder angle curve is more stable and smooth. The improved LADRC can realize the ship course control more quickly and almost without overshoot.

4.2 Simulation of Fuzzified Nonlinear Active Disturbance Rejection Controller

Under interference condition, the simulation result comparisons of fuzzified nonlinear active disturbance rejection controller (FNLADRC) and conventional NLADRC are shown in Fig. 7.

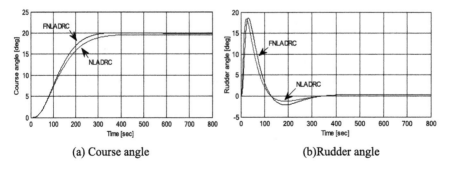

(a) Course angle   (b)Rudder angle

Fig. 7. Simulation results of FNLADRC and NLADRC under interference condition

From Fig. 7, the maximum steering angle is almost the same. When the FNLADRC achieve stability, there is no static error, and the response speed is accelerated. The improved NLADRC achieves good control effect under interference condition.

From all the above simulation results, we can come to conclusions that the introduction of fuzzy control algorithm could overcome shortcomings appeared in the process of ship course conventional ADRC. The response speed is further accelerated, the output of rudder angle is smoothed and the static error is eliminated. The ADRC improved by fuzzy control algorithm has excellent features of fast response, no overshoot and strong anti-interference ability. The fuzzified ADRC has a more significant effect on ship course control.

5   Conclusions

In this paper, the simulation research is focused on modeling and course active disturbance rejection for super large twin-propeller twin-rudder container ship. The mathematical model of ship with three degrees of freedom for super large twin-propeller twin-rudder ship is established and verified. In the representative ship turning test process, the ship maneuverability is calculated and analyzed in the condition of two propellers have different rotating speeds. The results of simulation prove that the large ship with twin-propeller twin-rudder has more flexible maneuverability. Conventional LADRC and NLADRC for above ship course steering are designed and the simulation calculations for demonstrating the validity are performed under interference conditions. The authors put fuzzy set algorithm into use to improve ADRC and get fuzzified ADRC. The simulation results show that the fuzzified ADRC has faster response speed, higher control precision and stronger robustness. It is effective and feasible for such super large size ship course control.

Acknowledgements. This work was supported by the National Nature Science Foundation of China (Nos. 51579024,61374114) and the Fundamental Research Funds for the Central Universities (DMU no. 3132016311).

References

1. Jia, X.-L., Yang, Y.-S.: Mathematical Model of Ship Motion: Modeling and Identification. Dalian Maritime University Publishing House, Dalian (1999)
2. Zhou, Z.-M., Sheng, Z.-Y., Feng, W.-S.: On maneuverability prediction for multipurpose cargo ship. Ship Eng. **06**, 21–29 (1983)
3. Khanfir, S., Hasegawa, K., Lee, S.K.: Mathematical model for maneuverability and estimation of hydrodynamic coefficients of twin-propeller twin-rudder ship. Jpn. Soc. Nav. Archit. Ocean Eng. **07**, 57–60 (2008)
4. Khanfir, S., Nagarajan, V., Hasegawa, K., et al.: Estimation of mathematical model and its coefficients of ship maneuverability for a twin-propeller twin-rudder ship. In: Proceedings of MARSIM 2009, pp. 159–166 (2009)

5. Lee, S.K., Fuiino, M.: Assessment of a mathematical model for the manoeuvring motion of a twin-propeller twin-rudder ship. Int. Shipbuild. Prog. **50**(01), 109–123 (2003)
6. Du, L.-H.: A study on the maneuverability of twin screws and twin rudders vessel. Dalian Maritime University (2005)
7. Han, J.-Q.: Active Disturbance Rejection Control Technique—The Technique for Estimating and Compensating the Uncertainties. National Defense Industry Press, Beijing (2013)
8. Han, J.-Q.: Active disturbance rejection control technology. Front. Sci. **1**, 24–31 (2007)
9. Ruan, J.-H., Li, Y.-B.: ADRC based ship course controller design and simulations. In: 2007 IEEE International Conference on Automation and Logistics, pp. 2731–2735. IEEE (2007)
10. Gai, J.-T., Huang, S.-D., Huang, Q.: A new fuzzy active-disturbance rejection controller applied in PMSM position servo system. In: 2014 17th International Conference on Electrical Machines and Systems (ICEMS), pp. 2055–2059. IEEE (2014)

Aircraft Takeoff Taxiing Model
Based on Lagrange Interpolation Algorithm

Meng Zhang[✉], Yiping Yao[✉], and Hong Wang

College of Computer, National University of Defense Technology,
Changsha, Hunan, China
zhangmeng_sim@163.com, ypyao@nudt.edu.cn

Abstract. Research on aircraft takeoff taxiing model has a great significance upon evaluation of aircraft performance, design of airport runway and warfare simulation. Because the aircraft takeoff taxiing is a complex nonlinear process, existing numerical calculation models are ordinarily based on the energy method or assumption of moment equilibrium, which leads to complex modeling process and low precision. In this paper, we establish a takeoff taxiing model by numerical integration method which is easy to implement, and obtain the parameters of running distance calculation formula based on Lagrange interpolation algorithm [1]. At the end of this paper, we use the characteristic parameters of a specific aircraft as model inputs to validate the correctness and accuracy of this model by comparing the model output and actual flight data.

Keywords: Takeoff taxiing model · Warfare simulation · Lagrange interpolation algorithm · Numerical integration

1 Introduction

Takeoff taxiing is the first step of flight and a process of aircraft continuous acceleration on the runway until leave ground [2]. Aircraft takeoff taxiing model can imitate the taxiing course in different environmental conditions, according to the given engine thrust parameters and aerodynamic parameters [3]. Developing aircraft takeoff taxiing model is very meaningful: (1) it can calculate aircraft takeoff performance [4], including takeoff distance, taxiing time and takeoff speed, these are very helpful to the development of aircraft and the design of airport runway; (2) it can also be used to estimate the survival probability of aircraft during takeoff period, through combat simulation.

Takeoff taxiing is a complex acceleration process. Aircraft will be affected by gravity, runway support force, friction, air resistance, lift and engine thrust at each moment, and these forces will even change with the velocity. And the aerodynamic parameters of aircraft, such as instantaneous thrust, lift coefficient and drag coefficient, will also be affected by different of state of the aircraft. According to the characteristics above, we first use Lagrange interpolation algorithm to calculate the instantaneous thrust, lift and drag coefficient of taxiing distance calculation formula. Then we determine the takeoff speed through iterative method with high-precision termination

© Springer Science+Business Media Singapore 2016
L. Zhang et al. (Eds.): AsiaSim 2016/SCS AutumnSim 2016, Part II, CCIS 644, pp. 100–108, 2016.
DOI: 10.1007/978-981-10-2666-9_11

conditions. Finally, we use numerical integration method to establish the aircraft takeoff taxiing model based on the running distance calculation formula.

The remainder of this paper is organized as follows. In Sect. 2, the related work is shown. In Sect. 3, the key algorithm used in the model is introduced. In Sect. 4, the process of modeling aircraft takeoff taxiing is described. In Sect. 5, the correctness of this model is proved by an experiment. In the last section, a summary is made for this paper.

2   Related Work

As the takeoff taxiing is an important part of aircraft flight and the modeling of takeoff taxiing is important for aircraft development, runway design and warfare simulation, many researchers have proposed lots of schemes and technologies.

At present, there are many methods to establish the numerical model of the aircraft takeoff taxiing, such as look-up table method, analytic method, numerical integration method, energy method [5] and so on. Using table checking method to establish the takeoff taxiing model can accurately simulate aircraft takeoff taxiing process, but creating tables of different parameters for looking up needs a lot of flight tests, resulting in high modeling costs. Analytical method builds takeoff taxiing model based on the assumption of moment equilibrium [6] and needs to consider the force of the aircraft at every moment, and they will lead to complex modeling process and large calculation. In addition, the output data of aircraft takeoff taxiing model established by energy method [7] is rough and users cannot get the exact location of the aircraft during takeoff taxiing process. Numerical integral method combined with the advantages of energy method and analytical method, can be very convenient to build takeoff taxiing model.

Using numerical integral method to build takeoff taxiing model can have a good practical effect. But the selections of dynamic parameters, aerodynamic parameters and movement parameters of existing models are based on the fixed engine performance and aerodynamic characteristic curves or some fixed values, so the precision of models are not high. In literature [8], Johnson gets instantaneous thrust of aircraft by modeling aircraft engine using the similarity method, but the method is not universal and the modeling process is complex. In literature [7], the author uses empirical data to calculate the lift and drag coefficient of taxiing model, which results in low precision.

The establishment of takeoff taxiing model using numerical method needs to determine the takeoff speed of aircraft. The literature [9] points out that iterative method can be used to determine the takeoff speed, but the iterative process and the termination conditions are not specified. The literature [7] generates the formula of takeoff speed based on the assumption that the lift force is equal to the gravity at the moment of leaving ground, but the assumption does not take into account the rising acceleration of the aircraft.

In this paper, we first use Lagrange interpolation algorithm to calculate the instantaneous thrust and lift and drag coefficient. Then determine the takeoff speed of aircraft using iterative method. Finally, we use numerical integration method to establish the aircraft takeoff taxiing model based on the running distance calculation formula.

3 Key Algorithm

Establishing aircraft takeoff taxiing model according to running distance calculation formula needs to know the instantaneous thrust of engine under actual air pressure and temperature of airport. However, the general aircraft performance specification only gives a few thrust curves of engine in the international standard atmosphere, as shown in Fig. 1. Therefore, we use Lagrange 2D interpolation algorithm to determine the actual instantaneous thrust of engine. Its basic principles and procedures are as follows:

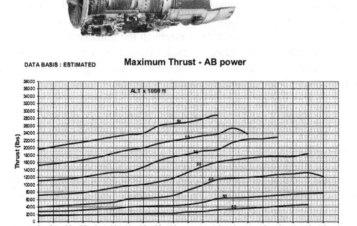

Fig. 1. Thrust curve of engine F100-PW-200

Let $n+1$ distinct interpolation points (nodes) $x_0, x_1, \cdots, x_n$, be given $y_0, y_1, \cdots, y_n$, together with corresponding numbers, which may or may not be samples of a function $y = f(x)$. Let Π_n denote the vector space of all polynomials of degree at most n. The classical problem addressed here is that of finding the polynomial $y = p_n(x) \in \Pi_n$ that interpolates $y = f(x)$ at the points $x_0, x_1, \cdots, x_n$, i.e.,

$$p_n(x_k) = y_k, \quad k = 0, 1, \cdots, n$$

The problem is well-posed; i.e., it has a unique solution that depends continuously on the data. Moreover, as explained in virtually every introductory numerical analysis text, the solution can be written in Lagrange form:

$$p_n(x) = \sum_{i=0}^{n} f(x_i) l_i(x) = f(x_0) l_0(x) + f(x_1) l_1(x) + \cdots + f(x_n) l_n(x) \tag{1}$$

And $l_i(x)$ is Lagrange basic polynomial:

$$l_i(x) = \prod_{j=0, j\neq i}^{n} \frac{(x - x_j)}{(x_i - x_j)}, i = 0, 1, \cdots, n \qquad (2)$$

Let $n = 3$, the Lagrange interpolation polynomial is:

$$p_3(x) = \frac{(x - x_1)(x - x_2)}{(x_0 - x_1)(x_0 - x_2)} y_0 + \frac{(x - x_0)(x - x_2)}{(x_1 - x_0)(x_1 - x_2)} y_1 + \frac{(x - x_0)(x - x_1)}{(x_2 - x_0)(x_2 - x_1)} y_2 \qquad (3)$$

2D Lagrange interpolation is actually a surface interpolation of a two-variable function; it can be realized by the ideal of dimension reduction [10]. Let two-variable function $z = f(x, y)$, calculate estimated value z at point (x, y), the specific method can be carried out according to the following steps:

1. Find three nearest interpolation points x_i, x_{i+1}, x_{i+2} to x;
2. Let $x = x_i$, find three nearest interpolation points y_i, y_{i+1}, y_{i+2} to y, calculate estimated value $z_1 = p_3(y)$ at points (y_i, z_i), (y_{i+1}, z_{i+1}) and (y_{i+2}, z_{i+2}) with formula (3);
3. Let $x = x_{i+1}$ and x_{i+2}, get z_2 and z_3 by the same way;
4. Calculate estimated value $z = p_3(x)$ at points (x_i, z_1), (x_{i+1}, z_2) and (x_{i+2}, z_3) with formula (3).

4 Modeling Process

By consulting the open literature [9] we can know that in a small period of time, the distance increment Δs and the velocity increment ΔV have the following relationship:

$$\Delta s = \frac{(V - V_w)\Delta V}{\left[\frac{nP_s(H_p, M)\cos(\alpha + \varphi)}{mg}\right] - f - \theta - \frac{(C_x - fC_y)\rho_s SV^2}{2mg}} \times \frac{1}{g} \qquad (4)$$

In formula (4): m is aircraft mass; g is gravitational acceleration; V_w is the wind-speed along running direction; n is the number of engine; $P_s(H_p, M)$ is instantaneous thrust of one engine, which is related with airport pressure altitude H_p and instantaneous Mach M; α is angle of attack; φ is installation angle of engine; f is friction coefficient of airport runway; θ is average slope of airport runway; C_x is lift coefficient; C_y is drag coefficient; ρ_s is air density; S means wing area.

To establish aircraft takeoff taxiing model using numerical integral method, we must determine all parameters in the formula (4). Parameters: m, n, α, φ, S can be found in aircraft specification; V_W, f, θ can be assigned according to the actual situation of airport. According to the laws of thermodynamics, ρ_s can be determined by the following formula:

$$\rho_s = \rho_0 \times \frac{P_s}{P_0} \times \frac{T_0}{T_s} \qquad (5)$$

In formula (5): ρ_0 means standard atmospheric density; P_0 is standard sea level atmospheric pressure; T_0 is Kelvin temperature 273.15 K; P_s actual atmospheric pressure at the airport; T_s airport actual Kelvin temperature.

4.1 Instantaneous Thrust

The instantaneous thrust of the engine P_s is related to the pressure altitude of the aircraft H_p and the instantaneous Mach M. Referring to the thrust characteristic curve in the international standard atmosphere given by aircraft specification, we can know the instantaneous thrust $P(H_i, M_j)(i = 1, 2, \cdots, s; j = 1, 2, \cdots, t)$ at some typical height and Mach points (H_i, M_j). As long as we know the pressure altitude of airport H_p and instantaneous Mach M, we can calculate the instantaneous thrust using 2D Lagrange interpolation introduced in Sect. 3 of this paper. The airport pressure altitude H_p is related to the actual atmosphere of the airport P_s, and the relationship is:

$$H_p = \frac{1 - (P_s/P_0)^{1/5.25588}}{225577} \times 10^5 \qquad (6)$$

Instantaneous Mach M is the ratio of aircraft instantaneous velocity V and actual sound velocity v_s, and the calculation formula of v_s is as follows:

$$v_s = \sqrt{1.4 \times 287 \times T_s} \qquad (7)$$

4.2 Lift and Drag Coefficient

The lift coefficient and drag coefficient are related to the angle of attack of aircraft, and the relationships are generally expressed by lift curve and polar curve. According to the characteristics of lift curve and polar curve, the lift coefficient and drag coefficient can be calculated by Lagrange three-point interpolation method. The approach is, finding the lift coefficient $C_{y(i)}(i = 0, 1, \cdots, p)$ corresponding to angle of attack α_i from the lift curve given by the aircraft specification, then calculating lift coefficient C_y about α using the following formula:

$$C_y = \sum_{i=r}^{r+2} \left\{ \left[\prod_{\substack{j=r \\ j \neq i}}^{r+2} \frac{\alpha - \alpha_j}{\alpha_i - \alpha_j} \right] \times C_{y(i)} \right\} \qquad (8)$$

α_r, α_{r+1}, α_{r+2} are the nearest points of α. Similarly, we can find the drag coefficient $C_{x(i)}(i = 0, 1, \cdots, q)$ correspond to lift coefficient $C_{y(i)}$ from the polar curve, then calculate drag coefficient C_x about C_y using the following formula:

$$C_x = \sum_{i=l}^{l+2} \left\{ \left[\prod_{\substack{j=l \\ j \neq i}}^{l+2} \frac{C_y - C_{y(j)}}{C_{y(i)} - C_{y(j)}} \right] \times C_{x(i)} \right\} \tag{9}$$

$C_{y(l)}$, $C_{y(l+1)}$, $C_{y(l+2)}$ are the nearest points of C_y.

4.3 Takeoff Speed

As the lift equals to gravity when the aircraft leaves ground, we can know that:

$$\frac{1}{2} C_{y2} \rho_s S V_t^2 + n P_s\left(H_p, M_t\right) \sin(\alpha_2 + \varphi) = mg \tag{10}$$

In this formula, C_{y2} is the lift coefficient at that moment; α_2 is the angle of attack; M_t is the instantaneous mach. From formula (10), we can get takeoff speed V_t:

$$V_t = \sqrt{\frac{2\left[mg - nP_s\left(H_p, M_t\right)\sin(\alpha_2 + \varphi)\right]}{\rho_s S C_{y2}}} \tag{11}$$

As $P_s\left(H_p, M_t\right)$ is the actual instantaneous thrust corresponding to the takeoff speed V_t when the aircraft leaves ground and V_t is unknown, we can use iterative method to solve it. The iterative equation is as follows:

$$V_{t(k+1)} = \sqrt{\frac{2[mg - nP_s\left(H_p, M_{t(k)}\right)\sin(\alpha_2 + \varphi)]}{\rho_s S C_{y2}}} \tag{12}$$

And initial condition is $V_{t(0)} = \sqrt{\frac{2mg}{\rho_s S C_{y2}}}$; termination condition is $\left|V_{t(k+1)} - V_{t(k)}\right| < 10^{-6}$. The speed $V_{t(k+1)}$ at the end of iteration is what we want.

4.4 Takeoff Taxiing Model

Aircraft takeoff taxiing can be divided into two phases [11], in phase I aircraft will run with three wheels. With the increase of speed, aircraft will lift the front wheel, running with two wheels, this is the phase II. The speed of the aircraft to lift its front wheel is V_r, which is 0.8 times the takeoff speed V_t. Now we take phase I as an example to establish its numerical integration model; we assume that in this phase, the aircraft angle of attack is α_1, and the corresponding lift and drag coefficient are C_{y1} and C_{x1}. Divide velocity interval $[V_w, V_r]$ into l identical cells with size ΔV_1, and in each cell we assume that velocity V and engine thrust $P_s(H_p, M)$ remain unchanged, and is the estimated value corresponding to the velocity at the left endpoint of the cells. Using numerical integration method we can get:

$$\Delta V_1 = \frac{V_r - V_w}{l} \tag{13}$$

$$\Delta S_i = \frac{(V_i - V_W)\Delta V_1}{\left[\dfrac{nP_s(H_p, M_i)cos(\alpha_1 + \varphi)}{mg}\right] - f - \theta - \dfrac{(C_{x1} - fC_{y1})\rho_s S V_i^2}{2mg}} \times \frac{1}{g} \tag{14}$$

$$V_{i+1} = V_i + \Delta V_1, V_0 = V_w \tag{15}$$

$$S_{i+1} = S_i + \Delta S_i, S_0 = 0 \tag{16}$$

$$t_{i+1} = t_i + \frac{\Delta S_i}{V_i}, t_0 = 0 \tag{17}$$

According to the above formula, we can get the speed V_i and the distance S_i at time t_i in phase I. The modeling method of phase II is the same as phase I, but the angles of attack are different and the initial state of phase II is the termination state of phase I. Aircraft takeoff taxiing model is the combination of the this two phase models.

5   Validation

Based on the modeling process above, we developed aircraft takeoff taxiing model using C++ programming language. This program can simulate the takeoff taxiing processes of various aircrafts under different environmental conditions. In order to prove the correctness of this model, we take the characteristic parameters of a certain aircraft as the model input, and compare the output data of the model and the actual test data. Figure 2

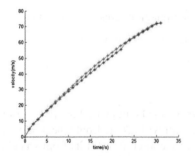

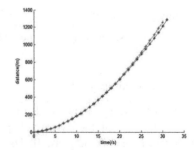

Fig. 2. The velocity curves of the model output and flight test

Fig. 3. The aircraft taxiing distance curves of model output and flight test

shows the velocity curves of the model and aircraft. Through analysis, we find that the maximum absolute error of the output data and the actual flight data is approximately 2.5 m/s, and the maximum relative error is about 4.7 %. Figure 3 shows the aircraft taxiing distance curves. Through the comparison of the two curves we can find that the calculation results and actual measurement are very close. The calculation running distance is 1263 m, and the actual measurement is approximately 1257 m. Thus, we can say that the aircraft takeoff taxiing model is correct and high-precision.

The physical characteristics of this aircraft as shown in Table 1. Airport environmental data as shown in Table 2. Aerodynamic characteristics and thrust characteristic as shown in Tables 3 and 4.

Table 1. Physical characteristics of aircraft

Mass	60×10^3 kg
Number of Engine	2
Wing Area	$164.5m^2$
Installation Angle	$0°$
Stop AOA	$4°$
Takeoff AOA	$8°$

Table 2. Airport environmental data

Air Pressure	96525 Pa
Temperature	22.3°C
Wind Speed	2.0m/s
Gravity	9.8m/s^2
Average Slope	−0.0011
Friction	0.025

Table 3. Aerodynamic characteristics of aircraft

AOA/°	Lift coefficient	Drag coefficient
0	0.459	0.052
2	0.623	0.058
4	0.908	0.069
6	0.967	0.080
8	1.171	0.097
10	1.316	0.122
12	1.422	0.151

Table 4. Thrust characteristic of aircraft

Height/m	Mach	Thrust/N	Height/m	Mach	Thrust/N	Height/m	Mach	Thrust/N
0	0.0	93133	1000	0.0	85762	2000	0.0	77196
0	0.1	88303	1000	0.1	80556	2000	0.1	72793
0	0.2	84870	1000	0.2	77959	2000	0.2	71102
0	0.3	82980	1000	0.3	76244	2000	0.3	69514
0	0.4	82005	1000	0.4	75705	2000	0.4	69423

6 Conclusion

This paper shows the detail process of establishing aircraft takeoff taxiing model by numerical method. First of all, we summarize the limitations and the low-precision problems of the existing modeling methods. Then we introduce the principle of

Lagrange interpolation algorithm, as well as the steps of solving the 2D interpolation problems with Lagrange three-point interpolation algorithm. After that, we expound the method of determining the parameters in distance calculation formula and the process of establishing aircraft takeoff model. Finally, we prove the correctness and accuracy of the takeoff taxiing model, by comparing the model output data with the actual flight data of a specific aircraft.

References

1. Berrut, J.-P., Trefethen, L.N.: Barycentric Lagrange interpolation. SIAM Rev. **46**(3), 501–517 (2004)
2. Gu, H.-B.: Dynamic model of aircraft ground handling. Acta Aeronautica Astronautica Sinica **22**(2), 163–167 (2001)
3. Rolfe, J.M., Staples, K.J.: Flight Simulation, pp. 56–89. Cambridge University Press, Cambridge (1986)
4. Li, X.-y., Xing, X.: Design & implementation of civil transport takeoff performance program. J. Civil Aviation Univ. China **26**(1), 8–13 (2008)
5. Hua, Z.: Research on aircraft engine modeling for flight simulation. Nanjing University of Aeronautics and Astronautics (2010)
6. Shui, Q.-c., Wang, Q.-h.: A mathematical model used to calculate the takeoff performance for an aircraft. Flight Dyn. **19**(4), 70–74 (2001)
7. Fang, Z.-p.: Aircraft Flight Dynamics, p. 6. Beijing University of Aeronautics and Astronautics Press, Beijing (2005)
8. Johnson, S.A.: A simple dynamic engine model for use in a real-time aircraft simulation with thrust vectoring. NASA Technical Memorandum 4240 (1990)
9. Song, H.-y., Cai, L.-c., Zheng, R.-h.: Numerical value integral improvement algorithm of aircraft take-off running distance. J. Traffic Transp. Eng. **7**(2), 24–28 (2007)
10. Xiao, B., Zhang, H., Zhang, C.-z., Heng, J.: Multi-dimension interpolation algorithm and its simulation application. J. Syst. Simul. (2008)
11. Waters, M., Anthony, M.G.: Propulsion System Modeling and Takeoff Distance Calculations for a Powered-Lift Aircraft with Circulation-Control Wing Aerodynamics. AIAA-2009-1258 (2009)

Precise Geometrical Alignment of Assembly Design from Tolerance Simulation Perspective

Muhammad Kashif Nawaz[1,2], Lihong Qiao[1,2(✉)], and Jianshun Wu[1,2]

[1] School of Mechanical Engineering and Automation, Beihang University, Beijing, China
kashif.n@hotmail.com, lhqiao@buaa.edu.cn
[2] Engineering Research Centre of Complex Product Advance Manufacturing System,
Ministry of Education, Beijing, China
923137300@qq.com

Abstract. Precision geometry alignment with rigorous deviation is one of the key assembly issues to be designed in product development. Propagation of tolerances causes large misalignment in assemblies leading to a cast-off and undesirable product functionality. There is always an imperativeness to calculate the assembly characteristic with tighter tolerances for functionally critical dimensions so that geometry imperfections can be compensated. Tolerance analysis and simulation techniques have been utilized by designer supporting such problem solving process. In this paper, a precise geometrical alignment of assembly design has been performed with the help of tolerance simulation. Both worst case and statistical tolerance analysis approaches are applied to provide design alternatives. In this research, a two-component thin walled alignment assembly structure has been chosen to present the design by tolerance simulation procedures. Tolerance ranges have been calculated and recommendations have been provided comparing the worst case and statistical analysis results.

Keywords: Tolerance simulation · Product design · Assembly

1 Introduction

As the technological developments effloresce, performance requirements are becoming tighter and tighter and the need for precision assemblies also increases. This ongoing evolution of precision assemblies demands the need to have a quantitative design tool for tolerance specification. Tolerance analysis merges engineering design with manufacturing capabilities by providing a quantitative evaluation of tolerance specifications vis-à-vis design and manufacturing [1].

Development of mathematical models and methods of tolerance analysis has been an engrossing problem for the researchers during recent times [2–5]. In this regard, there has been much focus, too, on precision assembly tolerance analysis for coupling slots of thin walled assemblies [6]. It has been pointed out in the literature that with respect to the performance of precision assemblies, sometimes there is a degradation on account of systematic and random errors where the later includes machining errors and assembly/adjustment errors. Hence, some mechanical errors compensation is

© Springer Science+Business Media Singapore 2016
L. Zhang et al. (Eds.): AsiaSim 2016/SCS AutumnSim 2016, Part II, CCIS 644, pp. 109–117, 2016.
DOI: 10.1007/978-981-10-2666-9_12

inherently included in the design. However, it is not known at design stage that what will be the magnitude of these errors for critical dimensions and what is going to be the exact variation so the quantifiability of this problem demands a definite level of cogitation. This generates the need of tolerance simulation for such products.

In this paper, tolerance analysis for a two-component assembly with functionally important alignment slots has been performed using 3DCS tolerance analyst. It is hoped that this study is going to provide a quantifiable effect of individual tolerances upon critical dimensions and hence, it will be a useful information to design reasonable tolerance ranges for functionally important dimensions of such assemblies.

2   Tolerance Simulation Assisted Product Assembly Design

2.1   The General Framework of Tolerance Simulation Assisted Product Assembly

Tolerance analysis has been at the heart of precision assembly design process during recent times. Figure 1 elaborates the process where part geometries are created in CAD packages with tolerance ranges and assemblies are developed using mate relationships. To quantify the accumulated effects of individual tolerances as well as prediction of significant contributors, tolerance analysis plays an indispensable role. It uses worst case scheme considering extremes of dimensions as well as statistical distributions. For a thin walled assembly design which has demanding requirements of alignment, a customized tolerance analysis process flow has been elucidated with the help of a flow chart beneath.

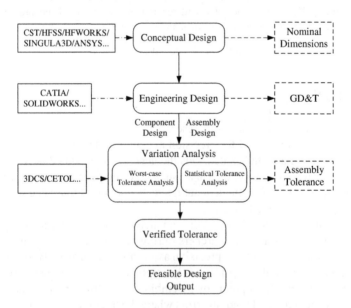

Fig. 1. Flow chart of precise assembly tolerance simulation

The structure can be modeled and simulated using various simulation tools such as HFSS, CST studio, Ansys etc. Depending upon the design requirements; shape, size and geometrical features are calculated and simulated. Each geometrical feature has to perform a specific role in the overall structure and its inaccuracy, dislocation or misalignment can degrade the product's performance a great deal, especially, at higher frequencies. Since at this stage, quantifiable information is not available for cumulative effect of variation in the final assembly, the tolerances are assigned based on experience and structure is simulated to obtain simulation results. After this as shown in Fig. 1, solid modeling of individual components and assembly is performed using a CAD package and tolerances are allocated considering the machining capabilities. After the development of CAD solid model, it is imperative to obtain a quantifiable information about individual tolerances impact on critical dimensions of final assembly hence 3DCS variation analyst comes into play.

Using 3DCS, both worst case and statistical tolerance analyses have been performed and results are compared. The reason for utilizing 3DCS variation analyst is its robustness and unique capability to provide a quantifiable comparison for an under consideration case study using both worst case and statistical approach. This approach has not only validated the idea behind this research but also provided a logical background for the given recommendations. Results of feasible design output for target assembly dimensions have been interpreted and data is sent to designer to add design compensations. Hence, a feasible tolerance range has been achieved which is not arbitrary but is based upon facts and figures.

2.2   Assembly Design of Precise Geometrical Alignment Components

Suitable tolerances are considered to be one of the key parameter during the product development of precision assemblies. It further helps preventing remanufacturing and achieving slot position and dimensions with desired accuracy. In this regard, a slotted structure assembly has been selected for tolerance analysis and simulation. For such kind of structures, a slight variation in alignment can lead to rejection of the assembly resulting a catastrophic failure to the project. A detailed view of components and critical dimensions has been shown in Fig. 2 below.

For such assemblies, slots are cut in the metallic walls using CNC milling and wire EDM respectively for functional requirements. It is imperative to develop the assembly in such a way that slot positions, angles, offsets and dimensions are extremely close to design limits with minimum possible variations in terms of tolerances. One of the components is fitted at front face of assembly having radiating slots and the other is assembled behind having feeding slots as shown in Fig. 2(b).

In this assembly, there are two critical dimensions to be achieved with ultimate accuracy. Firstly it is the structure height and then it is the angular symmetry or parallelism of both plates as shown above as Target-1 and Target-2 respectively in Fig. 2(c) and (d). It is desired to calculate the feasible tolerance ranges for Target-1 and Target-2 dimensions so that necessary adjustments can be done in structural design process.

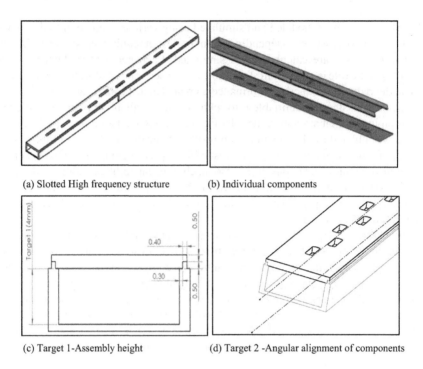

(a) Slotted High frequency structure   (b) Individual components

(c) Target 1-Assembly height   (d) Target 2 -Angular alignment of components

Fig. 2. Assembly model of high frequency structure

3   Procedure of Tolerance Simulation

3.1   3DCS Variation Analysis Process

3DCS has been widely utilized for precision assemblies in aerospace industry for tolerance analysis and simulation [8], that's why it has been used in this paper to streamline assembly tolerances. Process flow of 3DCS variation analyst is elaborated in Fig. 3. This kind of simulation model has five input elements namely Component geometry, Assembly sequence, Tolerances, Measurements and simulation explained beneath:

Step 1: First of all, part Geometry defines the various features being analyzed. There may be a feature not affecting assembly tolerances, however, to have a comprehensive analysis, all geometries under consideration are selected.

Step 2: Another step during tolerance simulation is the selection of sequence of assembly. It defines how parts locate to one another and in which order parts are assembled called "Moves". Moves are added to the model to represent all steps during build process. Similar assembly with different components assembly sequence provides different tolerance analysis results. Hence, it is considered as an important step in the process.

Step 3: Tolerances define the variation from nominal geometry within specified limits. It may be unilateral, bilateral or geometric tolerances. Tolerances of individual components are linked through assigned moves. Through moves, tolerances of individual parts combine and lead to variation in overall assembly.

Step 4: Measurements are taken which track the assembly variation. In fact, measurements will quantify the tolerance range.

Step 5: Simulation is run to obtain and analyze the results, which concludes the process.

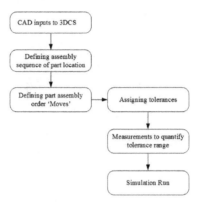

Fig. 3. 3DCS simulation process diagram

3.2   The Simulation Model for Tolerance Simulation of Precision Assembly

During the simulation, it is imperative to break down the specifications and translate into a form that can be used in tolerance analysis so following are the dimensions with tolerances that were taken into account as inputs for moves for both parts as shown below in Fig. 4 and Table 1.

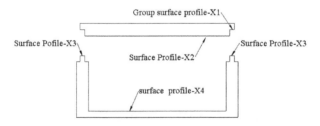

Fig. 4. Input surfaces for moves

Table 1. Input surfaces tolerances

Part	Feature	Tolerance
Front plate	Group surface profile-X1	±0.04
Front plate	Surface profile-X2	±0.04
Back plate	Surface profile-X3	±0.04
Back plate	Surface profile-X4	±0.04

After setting the inputs for moves to assemble both the components, the measurements were taken to quantify a range of tolerance for both target measurements. Details of measurements are as follows in Fig. 5.

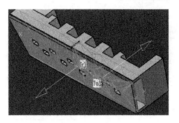

Fig. 5. Measurement for Target 1- assembly height

Likewise measurement was done for Target-2 to quantify a range of tolerance for angular alignment of both plates as shown in Fig. 6(a) and (b):

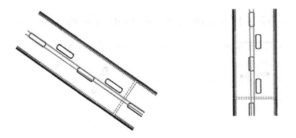

(a) Angular measurement for Target-2   (b) Parallelism of both plates

Fig. 6. Measurements for Target-2 dimensions

4   Analysis Results

Sensitivity report for worst case scenario suggests that for Target-1 i.e. the height of assembly, surface profile X2 and surface profile X4 have equal and significant effect i.e. 44.44 % while surface profile X3 has relatively low influence of 11.11 % as shown in Table 2 below:

Table 2. Sensitivity report for worst case analysis

Index	Tolerance	Part	Range	Percentage
1	Surface profile X2	Front plate	0.08	44.44 %
2	Surface profile X4	Back plate	0.08	44.44 %
3	Surface profile X3	Back plate	0.08	11.11 %

This means that these two surface profiles are the significant variation contributors towards achieving the accurate assembly height.

Similarly, for Target-2 i.e. angular alignment of both plates, the GD&T of back plate has contribution of 100 % and no other measurement has a contribution towards this target angular alignment.

Figure 7(a) gives a clear understanding of worst case simulation for Target-1 showing a probability distribution and range of tolerance for assembly height in the assembly. Similarly, Fig. 7(b) shows worst case simulation for Target-2 highlighting a probability distribution and a tolerance range for angular alignment of plates.

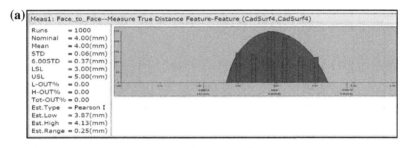

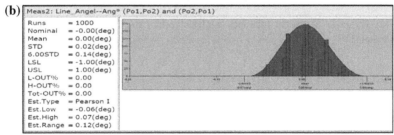

Fig. 7 (a) Target-1- Worst case simulation results. (b) Target-2- Worst case simulation results

Considering Fig. 7(a), nominal size was 4.00 mm and mean value is also 4.00. The distribution spread is from 3.87 minimum to 4.13 maximum showing an estimated tolerance range of 0.25. Similarly, Fig. 7(b) shows the simulation results for Target-2. It shows that for this angular measurement, variation is from −0.06° to 0.07° hence an estimated range of tolerance for angular variation is 0.12° for worst case.

Figure 8(a) and (b) highlight the statistical tolerance analysis results respectively for Target-1 and Target-2. In Fig. 8(a) above, normal distribution shows that estimated lower range is 3.94 mm and higher range is 4.06 mm, highlighting a total range of 0.13 mm for nominal size of 4.00 mm. For worst case, this range was 0.25 mm. This highlights that in case of statistical tolerance analysis, the range of tolerance is almost half of the worst case tolerance range. Figure 8(b) shows that for this angular measurement, variation is from −0.02° to 0.03° hence an estimated range of tolerance for angular variation is 0.05°. For worst case, it was 0.12° so this shows that for angular measurement, a much closer tolerance range has been obtained using statistical tolerance analysis approach.

(a)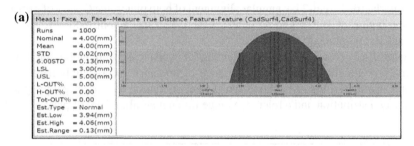

(b)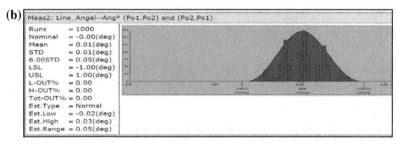

Fig. 8 (a) Target-1- Statistical tolerance analysis results (b) Target-2- Statistical tolerance analysis results

5   Conclusion

A logical approach towards a precision assembly tolerance was presented based upon tolerance analysis. For this, both worse case tolerance analysis and statistical tolerance analysis were performed using 3DCS variation analyst. The results show that for height and angular alignment of the under consideration assembly; statistical tolerance analysis provides feasible tolerance range providing much accuracy which is required for such dimensionally sensitive assemblies. Since both analyses have been performed using 3DCS, it is quite obvious to compare and conclude about the optimal tolerance analysis scheme. Similarly, for multiple arrays, there is a scope of research to perform three dimensional tolerance analysis as well.

Acknowledgments. This work is supported by the National Science Foundation of China (Grant 51575031), National High-Tech. R&D Program of China (No. 2015AA042101) and Beijing Municipal Education Commission. The authors would like to express their appreciation to the agencies.

References

1. Jerome, B., Jean, Y.D., Regis, B., Patrick, M.: Statistical tolerance analysis of bevel gear by tooth contact analysis and Monte Carlo simulation. Mech. Mach. Theory **42**, 1326–1351 (2007)
2. Marziale, M., Polini, W.: A review of two models for tolerance analysis of an assembly: Jacobian and torsor. Int. J. CIM **24**(1), 74–86 (2011)
3. Laperrière, L., Desrochers, A.: Modeling assembly quality requirements using Jacobian or screw transforms: a comparison. In: Proceedings of the IEEE International Symposium on Assembly and Task Planning, pp. 330–336. IEEE (2001)
4. Ameta, G., Serge, S., Giordano, M.: Comparison of spatial math models for tolerance analysis: tolerance-maps, deviation domain, and TTRS. J. Comput. Inf. Sci. Eng. **11**(2), 021004 (2011)
5. Chen, H., Jin, S., Li, Z., et al.: A comprehensive study of three dimensional tolerance analysis methods. J. CAD **53**, 1–13 (2014)
6. Liu, J., Jiang, Y.J., Yang, C.S., Sun, W.F.: Tolerance analysis of coupling slot of WG slot array. In: 3rd IEEE International Symposium on Microwave, Antenna, Propagation and EMC Technologies for Wireless Communications, pp. 647–650. IEEE (2009)
7. Na, L., Baoyan, D., Zheng, F.: Effect of random error on the radiation characteristic of reflector antenna based on two dimensional fractal. Int. J. Antennas Propag. **2012**, Article ID 543462 (2012)
8. Wang, W., Yu, H., Shafeeu, A., Gu, T.: Research on aircraft components assembly tolerance design and simulation technology. In: 3rd International Conference on Material, Mechanical and Manufacturing Engineering (IC3ME), pp. 2140–2145 (2015)

RUL Prediction of Bearings Based on Mixture of Gaussians Bayesian Belief Network and Support Vector Data Description

Qianhui Wu, Yu Feng, and Biqing Huang[✉]

Department of Automation, Tsinghua University, Beijing 100084, China
hbq@tsinghua.edu.cn

Abstract. This paper presents a method to predict the remaining useful life of bearings based on theories of Mixture of Gaussians Bayesian Belief Network (MoG-BBN) and Support Vector Data Description (SVDD). Our method extracts feature vectors from raw sensor data using wavelet packet decomposition (WPD). The features are then used to train the corresponding MoG-BBN and SVDD model. Genetic algorithm is employed to determine the initial value of training algorithm and enhance the stability of our model. The two models are combined to acquire a good generalization ability. The effectiveness of the proposed method is verified by actual bearing datasets from the NASA prognostic data repository.

Keywords: Wavelet packet decomposition · Mixture of Gaussians Bayesian Belief Network · Genetic algorithm · Support Vector Data Description · Remaining useful life

1 Introduction

Bearings are one of the most commonly used components in mechanical equipment. Due to their high failure rate, the working condition of bearings directly affects the safety of the whole equipment. RUL prediction of bearings plays a key role in condition based maintenance (CBM) [1], as it can effectively anticipate bearing failure, reduce the maintenance cost as well as increase the productivity.

Since the condition monitoring data is available, this paper focuses on the data-driven methods [2]. Under this framework, a variety of previous researches about bearings prognostic and RUL prediction has been conducted, including artificial networks [3–5], hidden Markov models (HMM) [6, 7], support vector machines [8–10], etc. Huang *et al.* [5] trained the back propagation neural networks which focus on ball bearings' degradation periods by the MQE indicator obtained from SOM, then applied WAFT technology to make RUL prediction. Tobon-Mejia *et al.* [6] proposed a method based on the Mixture of Gaussian Hidden Markov Models, in which hidden states are used to represent the failure modes of bearings. The RUL can be estimated straightly by the stay durations in each state. Shen *et al.* [8] took the fuzziness of degradation into account and proposed a damage severity index (DSI) based on fuzzy support vector data description (FSVDD), which can indicate the growth of degradation with running time.

© Springer Science+Business Media Singapore 2016
L. Zhang et al. (Eds.): AsiaSim 2016/SCS AutumnSim 2016, Part II, CCIS 644, pp. 118–130, 2016.
DOI: 10.1007/978-981-10-2666-9_13

In addition, Zhang *et al.* [11] constructed a Mixture of Gaussians Bayesian Belief Network (MoG-BBN) to characterize the degradation state by the condition monitoring data from sensors. However, the initial values of the parameters used in model training have a great impact on the accuracy of the RUL prediction. Hence, the stability and generalization of the model are reduced. To overcome this deficiency, this paper proposed a RUL prediction method based on the MoG-BBN and SVDD. The novelty of this paper lies in two respects. First, genetic algorithm is used to find the optimal initial value when training the MoG-BBN model so that the stability of the model enhances significantly. Second, a method based on SVDD are presented to estimate the RUL when the MoG-BBN model does not work well, which improve the generalization capability and the prediction accuracy.

The remainder of the paper is organized as follows: Sect. 2 introduces the methodology proposed for remaining useful life prediction of bearings. Section 3 carries out experiments on actual bearing data from NASA to examine the effectiveness of the proposed method. Section 4 concludes the work.

2 Methodology

The framework of the methodology is shown in Fig. 1. It can be divided into two phases: the off-line phase and the on-line phase. During the off-line phase, the raw data is processed to extract features, and then these features are used to train the MoG-BBN model and the SVDD model. During the on-line phase, the processing of the real-time vibration signal from sensors to extract features remains the same. Then, the features

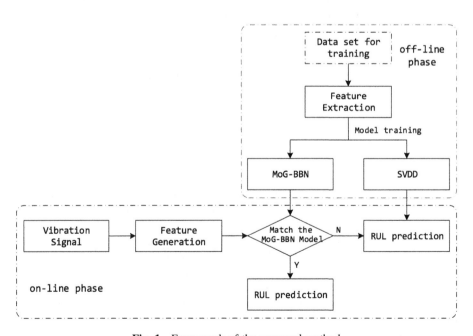

Fig. 1. Framework of the proposed method

are fed into the MoG-BBN model to characterize the degradation state. Some measures will be taken to determine whether the trained MoG-BBN model matches well with current component. If matching well, it comes to the RUL prediction step directly. Otherwise, the features will be fed into the SVDD model to get a better model performance and robustness. Finally, the RUL estimation will be implemented.

2.1 Feature Extraction

Wavelet packet decomposition (WPD) is an effective technique in signal analysis. It has sufficient high-frequency resolution, which contains the most useful fault information of bearings [12]. WPD can be considered as a tree, and its root is the original signal. By recursively applying the wavelet transform, WPD can automatically choose the appropriate frequency scale according to the characteristics of the analyzed signal, further decompose the high and low frequency data, and divide the spectrum band into several levels [7].

Based on excellent properties described above, WPD method is used to extract features from the raw vibration data of bearings in this paper. Assume that the decomposition level is l, then there will be $L = 2^l$ nodes on the last level. Let f_{it} represent the ith node of the last level, the feature vector at time t can be described as following.

$$\mathbf{f} = (f_{1t}, f_{2t}, \ldots, f_{Lt})^T \tag{1}$$

Note that a normalization process based on the mean and standard deviation of the raw data should be applied to the result of WPD before training the model in order to improve the generalization capability.

2.2 The Mixture of Gaussians Bayesian Belief Network

Structure. Figure 2 illustrates the MoG-BBN structure where D and M are discrete variables, and O is a continuous variable. In this structure, D represents the degradation states which cannot be directly observed, $D \in \{1, 2, \ldots a\}$. a is the maximum degradation state number. In this paper, a is set to 3, representing healthy, sub-healthy, and faulty states. M represents the distinctive Gaussian distributions for each state D, $M \in \{1, 2, \ldots b\}$, where b is the number of components in mixed Gaussian distribution. O represents the observation vector corresponding to a degradation state.

Note that M is the connection of the degradation state D and the observation O, which makes MoG-BBN a suitable tool, because it transforms continuous observations from monitoring sensors to discrete degradation states of physical components. From the above definition, once the probability $P(D|O)$ is known, the degradation state can be recognized, and then RUL of bearings can be estimated.

Let $\mathbf{o}$ be a realization of O. According to Fig. 2, the definition of conditional probability and the total probability formula, the value of $P(D|O)$ can be calculated as following.

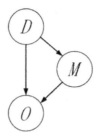

Fig. 2. Mixture of Gaussian Bayesian belief network.

$$P(D|O = \mathbf{o}) = \frac{P(D)\sum\limits_{M} P(M|D)P(O = \mathbf{o}|D, M)}{\sum\limits_{X} P(D)\sum\limits_{M} P(M|D)P(O = \mathbf{o}|D, M)} \tag{2}$$

Note that, the values of $P(D)$, $P(M|D)$ and $P(O|D, M)$ must be inferred by EM algorithm shown below.

EM Algorithm. A declaration of the variables used in the estimation procedure is given first.

- π_d: the initial distribution of degradation state D, and $\pi_d = P(D = d)$ for $d \in \{1, 2, \ldots, a\}$.
- C_{dm}: mixture coefficient of the mth Gaussian distribution for degradation state d, where $C_{dm} = P(M = m|D = d)$, for $d \in \{1, 2, \ldots, a\}$, $m \in \{1, 2, \ldots, b\}$.
- μ_{dm}: mean vector of the mth Gaussian distribution for degradation state d.
- Σ_{dm}: covariance matrix of the mth Gaussian distribution for degradation state d.

To compute $P(O|D, M)$, suppose O_d is the distribution of an observation O generated by degradation state d, then

$$O_d = \sum_{m=1}^{b} C_{dm} N(\mu_{dm}, \Sigma_{dm}), 1 \leq d \leq a \tag{3}$$

The statistical values of the above parameters can be inferred via training data sets and the EM algorithm. Given an observation sequence $\mathbf{o} = \{\mathbf{o}^{(1)}, \mathbf{o}^{(2)}, \ldots, \mathbf{o}^{(N)}\}$, where N denotes the length of the sequence, the EM algorithm is divided into the Expectation-Step and the Maximization-Step.

- Expectation-Step: for each pair of (d, m, n), with $n \in \{1, 2, \ldots, N\}$,

$$
\begin{aligned}
\omega_{dm}^{(n)} &= P(D^{(n)} = d, M^{(n)} = m|\mathbf{o}^{(n)}, \pi_d, C_{dm}, \mu_{dm}, \Sigma_{dm}) \\
&= \frac{P(\mathbf{o}^{(n)}|D^{(n)} = d, M^{(n)} = m, \mu_{dm}, \Sigma_{dm})P(D^{(n)} = d, M^{(n)} = m, \pi_d, C_{dm})}{\sum\limits_{d=1}^{a}\sum\limits_{m=1}^{b} P(\mathbf{o}^{(n)}|D^{(n)} = d, M^{(n)} = m, \mu_{dm}, \Sigma_{dm})P(D^{(n)} = d, M^{(n)} = m, \pi_d, C_{dm})}
\end{aligned} \tag{4}
$$

- Maximization-Step: update the above parameters as follows,

$$\pi_d = \frac{1}{N}\sum_{n=1}^{N}\sum_{m=1}^{b}\omega_{dm}^{(n)}$$

$$C_{dm} = \frac{1}{N\pi_d}\sum_{n=1}^{N}\omega_{dm}^{(n)}$$

$$\mu_{dm} = \frac{\sum\limits_{n=1}^{N}\omega_{dm}^{(n)}\mathbf{o}^{(n)}}{\sum\limits_{n=1}^{N}\omega_{dm}^{(n)}} \tag{5}$$

$$\Sigma_{dm} = \frac{\sum\limits_{n=1}^{N}\omega_{dm}^{(n)}\left(\mathbf{o}^{(n)} - \mu_{dm}\right)\left(\mathbf{o}^{(n)} - \mu_{dm}\right)^{T}}{\sum\limits_{n=1}^{N}\omega_{dm}^{(n)}}$$

Let $\lambda = (\pi, \mathbf{C}, \mu, \Sigma)$. The process is repeated until $\left|P(\mathbf{o}|\lambda^{t}) - P(\mathbf{o}|\lambda^{t-1})\right| < \xi$ or iteration number exceeds the maximum value set in advance. The threshold $\xi = 10^{-4}$ is used in the experiment section of this paper.

Initial Value Optimization Based on Genetic Algorithm. The initial value of π and $\mathbf{C}$ can be generated randomly from a uniform distribution, while μ and Σ can be acquired through clustering methods for training samples. Due to the fact that the initial values of π and $\mathbf{C}$ have a great impact on the model obtained by training, in this paper, an initial value optimization method based on genetic algorithm is proposed.

Encoding. According to what is proposed in [13], encoding methods of GA can be classified into two main approaches: binary encoding and float encoding. Taking into account the convenience and accuracy, floating encoding is adopted in this paper. Suppose that the maximum degradation state number in the MoG-BBN model is a, and mixed Gaussian distribution number for each state is b. The numbers of total parameters to optimize related to π and $\mathbf{C}$ are a and $a \cdot b$, respectively. Then there are $a \cdot (b+1)$ decimal floating numbers constituting an individual.

Fitness function. Corresponding to the fitness of the individuals to the environment, the value of this function reflects the fitness of the individuals in terms of measurement indicators. In this paper, the fitness function depicts the accuracy of the models generated by different individuals when identifying the degradation states.

Selection. According to each individual's fitness, the strategy of RWS is to calculate the probability that the gene is inherited from the individual by the offspring, and based on that probability, the offspring population is randomly selected in the parent generation. The higher the fitness of the parent is, the greater the probability that its genes will be selected to be inherited to the offspring will be. Let the fitness of the ith individual be f_i, and the population quantity be *pop*. The probability that this individual will be selected is

$$P_i = \frac{f_i}{\sum\limits_{i=1}^{pop} f_i} \tag{6}$$

A method based on Roulette Wheel Selection (RWS) is used in this paper: let the first to the kth individuals be a part of the next generation directly on the basis of the fitness sorting (from large to small). And the rest $pop - k$ individuals can be generated by genic recombination and mutation of $pop - k$ pairs that are selected from the current population by RWS method.

Crossover. This paper use Arithmetic crossover to produce a new individual. Assume that two individuals of the parent are X_A and X_B, then the new individual generated by arithmetic crossover operator is as following, where γ is the parameter, which is commonly set to 0.5.

$$\begin{cases} X'_A = \gamma X_B + (1 - \gamma) X_A \\ X'_B = \gamma X_A + (1 - \gamma) X_B \end{cases} \tag{7}$$

Mutation. Mutation is a genetic operator which is used to maintain genetic diversity. To ensure the convergence, the mutation operator used in this paper adds or subtracts a small random number to the original floating number. This random number is called step width. Bigger step width leads to faster evolution speed at the beginning. However, it will be more difficult to converge at the end. In order to speed up the evolution and ensure that the genetic algorithm can be more accurate when converging to the optimal solution at the same time, a method that the step width changes dynamically is taken.

The steps of float coding genetic algorithm for the optimization of the initial values of π and $\mathbf{C}$ can be summarized as following.

(a) Randomly generate the initial population consisting of *pop* individuals.
(b) Calculate and sort the fitness of each individual in the current population, from large to small.
(c) Let the first to the kth individuals be a part of the next generation directly on the basis of the fitness sorting. Generate the rest $pop - k$ individuals by genic crossover and mutation of $pop - k$ pairs that are selected from the current population by RWS method. Note that the step width in the mutation process decreases gradually with the iteration. Besides, if necessary, additional measures should be taken to ensure that the values of float genes related to π and $\mathbf{C}$ are significant after crossover and mutation, respectively.
(d) If the resulting solution tends to be stable in a certain range or the number of iterations reach the maximum value, exit and the optimal solution is gotten. Otherwise, turn to step (b).

2.3   Support Vector Data Description

Assume a training set containing n vectors of objects $\{\mathbf{x}_i, i = 1, 2, \ldots, N\}$. The optimization objective of the SVDD method is to find the minimum-volume hypersphere containing all or most possible target data points in feature space, and it can be described as following:

$$\min_{R,c,\xi} R^2 + C\sum_{i=1}^{N} \xi_i \tag{8}$$
$$s.t. (x_i - c)^T (x_i - c) \leq R^2 + \xi_i, \ \xi_i \geq 0, i = 1, 2, \ldots, N$$

where c is the center of the hypersphere, and ξ_i is slack variable, cooperating with the penalty constant C to make the trade-off between the radius R and the number of data points that lie out of the hypersphere [14]. Construct the Lagrangian:

$$L(R, c, \alpha_i, \xi_i) = R^2 + C\sum_{i=1}^{N} \xi_i - \sum_{i=1}^{N} \alpha_i\{R^2 + \xi_i - (x_i^2 - 2cx + c^2)\} - \sum_{i=1}^{N} \gamma_i \xi_i \tag{9}$$

Where $\alpha_i \geq 0$ and $\gamma_i \geq 0$. Set the partial derivatives of Eq. (9) to 0.

$$\frac{\partial L}{\partial R} = 0, \quad \therefore \sum_{i=1}^{N} \alpha_i = 1$$
$$\frac{\partial L}{\partial c} = 0, \quad \therefore c = \sum_{i=1}^{N} \alpha_i x_i \tag{10}$$
$$\frac{\partial L}{\partial \xi_i} = 0, \quad \therefore C - \alpha_i - \gamma_i = 0$$

With Eqs. (9) and (10), the objective function can be reconstructed:

$$\max L(\alpha) = \sum_{i=1}^{N} \alpha_i(x_i \cdot x_i) - \sum_{i=1,j=1}^{N} \alpha_i \alpha_j(x_i \cdot x_j)$$
$$s.t. \sum_{i=1}^{N} \alpha_i = 1, 0 \leq \alpha_i \leq C \tag{11}$$

In practice, the inner product $(x_i \cdot x_j)$ is replaced by a kernel function $K(x_i \cdot x_j)$ that satisfies Mercer's theorem. In this paper, the RBF kernel function is used, and then Eq. (11) is transformed to the following form:

$$\max L(\alpha) = \sum_{i=1}^{N} \alpha_i K(x_i \cdot x_i) - \sum_{i=1,j=1}^{N} \alpha_i \alpha_j K(x_i \cdot x_j)$$

$$s.t. \sum_{i=1}^{N} \alpha_i = 1, 0 < \alpha_i < C \tag{12}$$

The value of α_i can be obtained by solving Eq. (12). Target data points corresponding with $0 < \alpha_i < C$ are support vectors. Then the radius R of the hypersphere can be acquired by any support vector x_{sv}.

$$R^2 = K(x_{sv} \cdot x_{sv}) - 2 \sum_{i=1}^{N} \alpha_i K(x_i \cdot x_{sv}) + \sum_{i=1,j=1}^{N} \alpha_i \alpha_j K(x_i \cdot x_j) \tag{13}$$

2.4 RUL Prediction

To predict the RUL in the on-line phase, two curves (the degradation state curve and the radius curve) must be obtained first in the off-line phase.

Degradation State Curve. By EM algorithm, the parameters π, **C**, μ and Σ of the MoG-BBN are estimated, which allows us to obtain the state sequence of the training data through Eq. (2), and the degradation state curve (Fig. 3). The time duration for which the component in the off-line phase has been in each state can be computed based on the curve, as Eq. (14),

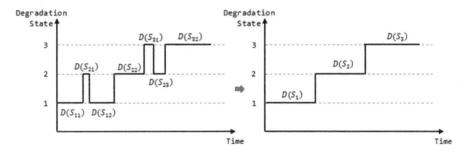

Fig. 3. The degradation state curve of the MoG-BBN.

$$T(S_d) = \sum_{\omega=1}^{\Omega} T(S_{d\omega}) \tag{14}$$

where $T(S_d)$ stands for the total time duration of the state d, Ω represents the number of consecutive visits.

Radius Curve. Suppose that the training set contains N vectors of objects $\{x_1, x_2, \ldots, x_N\}$, and the objects $\{x_1, x_2, \ldots, x_{n_0}\}$ correspond to the healthy state at the beginning. The SVDD models are trained sequentially with each sub data set $\{x_1, x_2, \ldots, x_n\}$, $n \in \{n_0, n_1, \ldots, N\}$, to get the corresponding SVDD hypersphere's radius R_n. Then we obtain the radius change $\mathbf{R} = \{R_{n_0}, R_{n_1}, \ldots, R_N\}$ with the time evolution, as shown in Fig. 4.

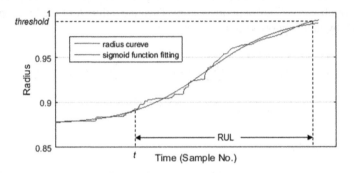

Fig. 4. Radius curve and the Sigmoid function fitting.

RUL Prediction. To predict the remaining useful life of the component in the real-time signal in the on-line phase, first we characterize the degradation state of the component by Eq. (2), then we determine whether current state of the component match the trained MoG-BBN model. Concretely, supposed that the characterized degradation state is s at time t while the degradation state is $\bar{s}$ according to the right part of Fig. 3 (obtained by training data). If s is equal to $\bar{s}$, it matches the model, otherwise it doesn't.

Denote $L(t)$ as the prediction of remaining useful life at time t. If s is equal to $\bar{s}$, $L(t)$ can be computed as following.

$$
\begin{aligned}
L(t) &= \sum_{d=1}^{a} P(D = d)L_d(t) \\
&= \sum_{d=1}^{a} P(D = d)\left(\sum_{i=d}^{a} T(S_i) - \bar{T}_d(t)\right)
\end{aligned}
\tag{15}
$$

In Eq. (15), $L_d(t)$ denotes the RUL when the component is in the degradation state d, and $\bar{T}_d(t)$ denotes the past time for which the component has been in the degradation state d.

When s is not equal to $\bar{s}$, the Sigmoid function curve fitting will be implemented by the radius curve obtained by SVDD. Figure 4 illustrates how the RUL at time t is estimated.

3 Experiments and Discussions

The RUL prediction method of bearings proposed previously is tested by the condition monitoring data from NASA's prognostics data repository [2]. During the experiments, raw data of bearing 1 and bearing 4 in the test #2 are used, and both of them can be considered failed at the end.

First, wavelet packet decomposition was applied to the data, where the number of decomposition levels is set to 3 and the wavelet base is db4 (Fig. 5). Then two experiments were implemented: in experiment #1, the raw data collected from bearing 1 was divided into training data and test data, in experiment #2 the dataset of bearing 1 was used to as training data and the dataset of bearing 4 was used as test data. A detailed discussion of the experiment #1, and the results of both experiments are given as following.

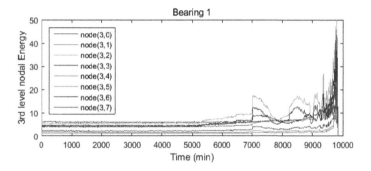

Fig. 5. WPD is applied to raw signal of bearing 1.

In the off-line phase, the sojourn time of each state of the trained MoG-BBN model is shown in Table 1, the radius curve is shown in Fig. 6. The reason why the radius curve starts at 4500 min is that the former data was collected when the bearing was in the healthy state. And the SVDD model was first trained at 4500 min with all the former data. Sigmoid function was used in the curve fitting of the radius curve, for the bearing has in the healthy state for a long time according to Table 1, and in this period, the radius growth of the hypersphere is slow, while at the end of bearings' life cycle, the slack variable ξ_i in the objective function of SVDD makes the radius grow slow, too. From Fig. 6, we can observe that the radius curve fits well with the Sigmoid function.

Table 1. Sojourn time of each degradation state in Expt. #1

Degradation state	1	2	3
Sojourn time (min)	5090	1890	2870

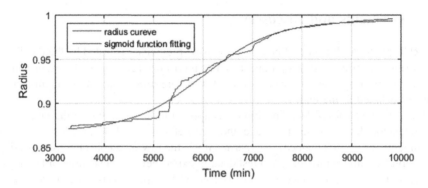

Fig. 6. Radius curve generated by the training data.

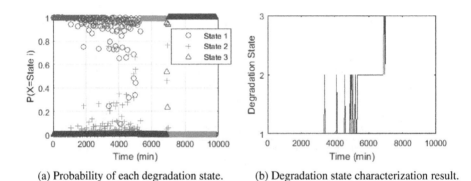

(a) Probability of each degradation state.   (b) Degradation state characterization result.

Fig. 7. Degradation state characterization in Expt. #1.

In the on-line phase, Fig. 7 depicts how the degradation states are characterized after the validate data are fed into the MoG-BBN model. We could observe that the bearing had been in the healthy state for almost 50 % of its whole lifetime, which matches the result in Table 1. It can be explained that the training data and validate data is collected from the same bearing.

The RUL prediction results of the method based on MoG-BBN without GA and the method proposed by this paper are compared in Figs. 8 and 9.

From Figs. 8 and 9, we can observe that the predicted remaining useful life converges at the end of predictions. With the optimization of the initial value by genetic algorithms and the combination of the SVDD model, our method has an excellent performance in the RUL predictions of bearings. It has higher prediction accuracy, and better generalization ability and robustness as well.

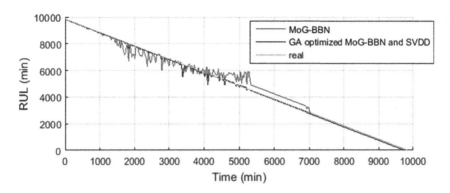

Fig. 8. RUL prediction result of experiment #1.

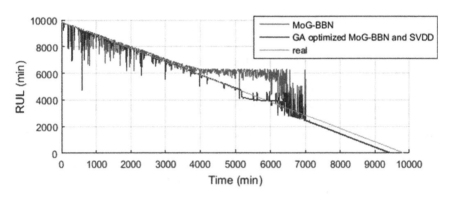

Fig. 9. RUL prediction result of experiment #2.

4   Conclusions

A method based on the MoG-BBN and SVDD for RUL prediction of bearings is proposed in this paper. WPD is chosen to extract features because it has sufficient high-frequency resolution, which contains the most useful fault information of bearings. The MoG-BBN model is a useful tool to predict the RUL with high accuracy when the work condition of bearings in on-line phase is very similar to the training data. However, different initial value may lead to different performance, the genetic algorithm is used to overcome this deficiency and acquire good stability with randomly generated initial parameters. And, an appropriate combination of the MoG-BBN and the SVDD model could improve the generalization capability and ensure the accuracy of the prediction at the same time.

Acknowledgement. This work was supported by the National Hig-Tech. R&D (863) Program (No. 2015AA042102) in China.

References

1. Jammu, N.S., Kankar, P.K.: A review on prognosis of rolling element bearings. Int. J. Eng. Sci. Technol. **3**(10), 7497–7503 (2011)
2. Lee, J., Qiu, H., Yu, G., Lin, J.: Rexnord Technical Services. IMS, University of Cincinnati. "Bearing Data Set", NASA Ames Prognostics Data Repository, NASA Ames Research Center, Moffett Field, CA (2007). http://ti.arc.nasa.gov/project/prognostic-data-repository
3. Gebraeel, N.Z., Lawley, M.A.: A neural network degradation model for computing and updating residual life distributions. IEEE Trans. Autom. Sci. Eng. **5**(1), 154–163 (2008)
4. Tian, Z., Wong, L., Safaei, N.: A neural network approach for remaining useful life prediction utilizing both failure and suspension histories. Mech. Syst. Signal Process. **24**(5), 1542–1555 (2010)
5. Huang, R., Xi, L., Li, X., et al.: Residual life predictions for ball bearings based on self-organizing map and back propagation neural network methods. Mech. Syst. Signal Process. **21**(1), 193–207 (2007)
6. Tobon-Mejia, D.A., Medjaher, K., Zerhouni, N., et al.: Hidden Markov models for failure diagnostic and prognostic. In: Prognostics and System Health Management Conference (PHM-Shenzhen), pp. 1–8. IEEE (2011)
7. Tobon-Mejia, D.A., Medjaher, K., Zerhouni, N., et al.: A data-driven failure prognostics method based on mixture of Gaussians hidden Markov models. IEEE Trans. Reliab. **61**(2), 491–503 (2012)
8. Shen, Z., He, Z., Chen, X., et al.: A monotonic degradation assessment index of rolling bearings using fuzzy support vector data description and running time. Sensors **12**(8), 10109–10135 (2012)
9. Wang, H., Chen, J.: Performance degradation assessment of rolling bearing based on bispectrum and support vector data description. J. Vibr. Control **20**(13), 2032–2041 (2014)
10. Sloukia, F., El Aroussi, M., Medromi, H., et al.: Bearings prognostic using mixture of gaussians hidden Markov model and support vector machine. In: 2013 ACS International Conference on Computer Systems and Applications (AICCSA), pp. 1–4. IEEE (2013)
11. Zhang, X., Kang, J., Jin, T.: Degradation modeling and maintenance decisions based on Bayesian belief networks. IEEE Trans. Reliab. **63**(2), 620–633 (2014)
12. Wald, R., Khoshgoftaar, T.M., Sloan, J.C.: Using feature selection to determine optimal depth for wavelet packet decomposition of vibration signals for ocean system reliability. In: 2011 IEEE 13th International Symposium on High-Assurance Systems Engineering (HASE), pp. 236–243. IEEE (2011)
13. Zhang, T., Zhang, H., Wang, Z.: Float encoding genetic algorithm and its application. J. Harbin Inst. Technol. **32**(4), 59–61 (2000)
14. Tax, D.M.J., Duin, R.P.W.: Support vector data description. Mach. Learn. **54**(1), 45–66 (2004)

Military Simulation

Decision-Making Modeling of Close-In Air-Combat Based on Type-2 Fuzzy Logic System

Hua-xing Wu[1,2(✉)], Wei Huang[2], Peng Zhang[2], and Fengju Kang[1]

[1] Marine College, North Western Polytechnical University,
Xi'an 710072, China
[2] Aeronautics and Astronautics Engineering Institute of AFEU,
Xi'an 710038, China

Abstract. To increase the credibility of decision-making model for close-in air-combat, a type-2 fuzzy logic system (FLS) based approach is introduced into its production rule base, which traditionally neglects the uncertainty of human cognition. By defining its interval type-2 Gaussian membership function for its inputs and outputs, and renovating the traditional production rules into type-2 fuzzy rules, the type-2 FLS model is quickly built. The model employs interval type-2 fuzzy sets to simplify the fuzzy operation and type-reduction while keeping the uncertainty of experiential knowledge. Simulation results show the feasibility and credibility of this approach.

Keywords: Type-2 fuzzy logic system · Uncertainty · Close-in air combat · Decision-making model

1 Introduction

To simulate the decision-making behavior of computer generated force (CGF) in the domain of close-in air-combat, one common method is building a production rule base by knowledge and experience from experts of matter [1]. However, a pilot's situation awareness (SA) is usually uncertain due to the violent dynamics and antagonism of close-in air combat. A pilot often makes decisions intuitively and indefinitely, and his decisions are not always optimal. Thus, CGFs using fixed production rules defined with clear bounds will decrease its credibility [2].

So, fuzzy logic (FL) that can reason under uncertainty is widely introduced by the decision-making area of air-combat. In [3, 4], FL is combined with Petri nets to represent tactical decisions of air-combat. In [5, 6], FL is integrated into Bayesian network to model situation awareness and decision-making of air-combat. In [7, 8], FL is also introduced into Neural networks for decision-making of air-combat. But all these methods aim at optimal decisions and rely on traditional rule base. They require rigorous rules and parameters insides their network architecture, leaving out of consideration for variety and flexibility of human's cognitive behavior, and making little use of knowledge of different air-combat experts. That leads to incredibility and extensibility of CGFs and limits the range of application of FL.

© Springer Science+Business Media Singapore 2016
L. Zhang et al. (Eds.): AsiaSim 2016/SCS AutumnSim 2016, Part II, CCIS 644, pp. 133–143, 2016.
DOI: 10.1007/978-981-10-2666-9_14

In [9, 10], a tri-level decision-making model is proposed to represent the dog-fighting behavior of pilots in consideration of ambiguity of expert's experience. But its FL rules are based on type-1 membership functions, and are mainly applied to flight control and section of tactics maneuver.

As shown in [11–13], type-1 FL based on type-1 membership functions is insufficient for representation of rule's uncertainty which evidently exists in pilot's cognitive behavior and experiential knowledge, J. M. Mendel extend type-1 FL into type-2 FL which is based on more ambiguous rules. Type-2 FL can describe uncertainty of human's cognition by adding another dimension to fuzzy rules. However, type-2 FL is more computably complex than type-1 FL, and it is less used in real-time simulation domain so far.

In this paper, we proposed a simplified type-2 FL method to represent the uncertain of decision-making model of air-combat while improving the computing efficiency.

2 Decision-Making Model of Air-Combat Based on Traditional Rules

In the process of one vs. one close-in air-combat, a pilot decides what kind of tactics by his judgment on attacking situation for own-ship against the target, which mainly depends on two angles between own-ship heading, target's heading and line of sight (LOS) [14], as shown in Fig. 1.

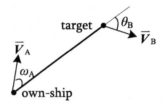

Fig. 1. Angles between LOS and headings of both aircraft

Where ω_A is angle between LOS and own-ship heading, θ_B is angle between LOS and target's heading. For traditional CGF simulation, these two angles are used along with maneuverability of both ships, to select the proper tactical maneuvers, which can be defined by the following pseudo-codes:

```
If   ωₐ≤ω₁ and θ_B≤θ₁, Then tactics 1;
Elseif  ωₐ>ω₂ and θ_B>θ₂, Then tactics 5;
Elseif  ωₐ+θ_B≤π/2, Then tactics 2;
Elseif  ωₐ+θ_B≤π, Then tactics 3;
Else  tactics 4.
```

Here, $0 \leq \theta_1 < \pi/2 < \theta_2 \leq \pi, 0 \leq \omega_1 < \pi/2 < \omega_2 \leq \pi$.

These simplified rules originate from practice and are easily implemented and widely applied. But they have no consideration about the uncertainty of experiential knowledge, and neglect the indeterminacy of awareness of space position and attitude angles. So it leads to lack of tactical variety, and makes people easily perceive that the adversary is a CGF and not a human pilot. This shortcoming heavily degrades the credibility of trailing simulation [2].

So, to fully use original rules and extend its ability to handle uncertainty, type-2 FL is applied to enhance air-combat decision-making.

3 Modeling Air-Combat Decision-Making Based on Type-2 FLS

3.1 Type-2 FLS

A type-2 fuzzy set $\widetilde{A}$ is expressed by type-2 membership function $\mu_{\widetilde{A}}(x, u)$ [15], that is:

$$\widetilde{A} = \left\{ \left((x, u), \mu_{\widetilde{A}}(x, u) \right) | \forall x \in X, \forall u \in J_x \subseteq [0, 1] \right\} \tag{1}$$

Where, x is the membership value of element x that belong to input universe X. Its range J_x is called primary membership of x, which is a limitary set. $\mu_{\widetilde{A}}(x, u)$ is the membership corresponding to value of primary membership u, also called secondary membership, subject to $0 \leq \mu_{\widetilde{A}}(x, u) \leq 1$. Secondary membership represents the further uncertainty of input x belong to fuzzy set $\widetilde{A}$.

As shown by Fig. 2, type-2 FLS is similar to type-1 FLS. It is consist of input fuzzifier, rule base, inference engine, type reducer and defuzzifier [11].

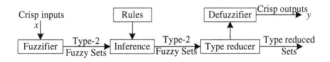

Fig. 2. Components of type-2 FLS

Unlike type-1 FLS, the inputs of type-2 FLS can be crisp number, type-1 fuzzy number, or type-2 fuzzy number. The antecedent and consequent of rule is represented by type-2 fuzzy sets, so it can handle the input noise and the uncertainty of rules. Type FLS also reason by "if then" sentences, that enables it not only can inherits experiential knowledge from traditional rule base but also can add ambiguity of language from experiential experience.

The inference of type-2 FLS is as follows: first translates the inputs into type-2 fuzzy sets, synthesizes the inputs and antecedents of rule to form firing sets, then takes fuzzy operation between firing sets and consequent of rule, outputs type-2 fuzzy sets which will be type-reduced into type-1 fuzzy sets, and finally produces crisp outputs via defuzzifier [16].

Given that $X = [x_1, x_2, \ldots, x_p]$, the output of the first rule is a type-2 membership function:

$$\mu_{\tilde{B}^l}(y) = \mu_{\tilde{G}^l}(y) \prod \left\{ \left[\coprod_{x_1 \in X_1} \left(\mu_{\tilde{X}_1}(x_1) \prod \mu_{\tilde{F}_1^l}(x_1) \right) \right] \right.$$
$$\left. \prod \cdots \prod \left[\coprod_{x_p \in X_p} \left(\mu_{\tilde{X}_p}(x_p) \prod \mu_{\tilde{F}_p^l}(x_p) \right) \right] \right\}, \quad y \in Y \tag{2}$$

where, $\mu_{\tilde{G}^l}(y)$, $\mu_{\tilde{X}_p}(x_p)$, $\mu_{\tilde{F}_p^l}(x_p)$ is type-2 membership functions of consequent, input, and antecedent respectively. The sign $\prod$ indicates intersection between fuzzy sets, which usually employs minimal or multiple operation. The sign $\coprod$ indicates union between fuzzy sets, which usually employs maximal operation [17]. The firing intension by input x_i against rule l is a type-1 fuzzy set, described by:

$$\mu_{F_i^l}(x_i) = \coprod_{x_i \in X_i} \left(\mu_{\tilde{X}_i}(x_i) \prod \mu_{\tilde{F}_i^l}(x_i) \right) \tag{3}$$

If there are M rules, the membership function of type-2 fuzzy set $\widetilde{B}$ will be:

$$\mu_{\tilde{B}}(y) = \coprod_{l=1}^{M} \mu_{\tilde{B}^l}(y) \tag{4}$$

As shown by the above formulas, the computation of common type-2 FLS is very complex and inefficient. That drives us to simplify the membership function of both antecedent and consequent. An available approach is to employ interval type-2 membership functions and construct interval type-2 fuzzy sets.

If $\forall x \in X, \forall u \in J_x \subseteq [0, 1]$, while $\mu_{\tilde{A}}(x, u) = 1$, a type-2 membership function is called interval type-2 membership function, thus fuzzy set $\widetilde{A}$ becomes an interval type-2 fuzzy set [16].

$$\widetilde{A} = \int_{x \in X} \int_{u \in J_x} 1/(x, u), \quad J_x \subseteq [0, 1] \tag{5}$$

The secondary membership of interval type-2 fuzzy set is equal to 1, which makes primary membership become one interval set and indicates the same uncertainty of primary membership. Interval type-2 fuzzy set simplifies the complex type-2 fuzzy set while keeping the uncertainty of knowledge and language at the time [18].

3.2   Inputs and Outputs of Decision-Making Model for Close-In Air-Combat

In a certain time of air-combat, a pilot is usually unsure of real inputs about ω_A and θ_B, which make it hard to depict by crisp numbers. Here, we use type-1 fuzzy number to

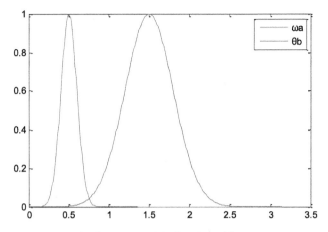

Fig. 3. Membership function of inputs

represent them, assuming that their membership function are both Gaussian, as shown by Fig. 3.

The mean and standard deviation for input Gaussian membership function can be adjusted if needed. Usually evaluated deviation of θ_B will be bigger than that for ω_A, and will increase as θ_B increases. It provide an approach describing random noises of sensors and uncertainty of spacial awareness by pilots.

Consider that both ω_A and θ_B is divided into 4 intervals in traditional rules, we define both input antecedents by 4 interval type-2 fuzzy sets, each of them is described by type-2 Gaussian membership function with uncertain standard deviation. As shown by shaded areas in Fig. 4, the type-2 fuzzy set corresponding to ω_A includes 4 interval type-2 fuzzy sets: $\tilde{A}_1$, $\tilde{A}_2$, $\tilde{A}_3$ and $\tilde{A}_4$.

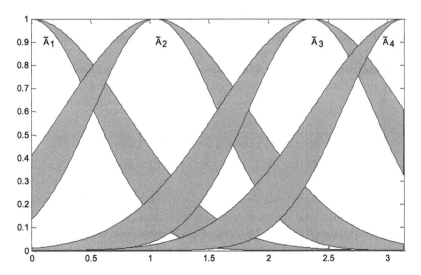

Fig. 4. Interval type-2 fuzzy sets for the antecedents of ω_A

The same approach can be used to obtain interval type-2 fuzzy sets for the antecedents of θ_B, $\widetilde{B}$.

For close-in air-combat question, the consequent sets for deciding rules are tactical decisions that only can be described with discrete values(such as 0,1,2,3,4). These discrete outputs can be converted into type-2 fuzzy sets. As shown by Fig. 5, the consequent is divided into 5 type-2 fuzzy sets: $\widetilde{C}_1$, $\widetilde{C}_2$, $\widetilde{C}_3$, $\widetilde{C}_4$ and $\widetilde{C}_5$.

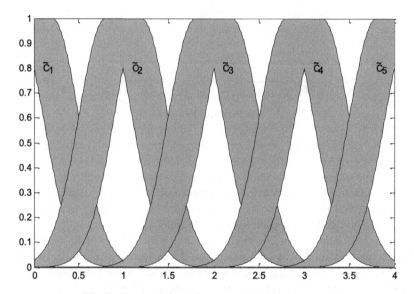

Fig. 5. Interval type-2 fuzzy sets for the consequent

3.3   Rules for Decision-Making Model of Close-In Air-Combat

As proposed by above, the fuzzy rule used for air-combat decision making includes two antecedents and one consequent. Every antecedent includes 4 type-2 fuzzy set. The consequent includes 5 type-2 fuzzy set. So the rule base can maximally embrace 16 rules. Thus, type-2 fuzzy rule base for the question can be built quickly in the following form:

```
Rule1: If (ωₐ is A₁) and (θ_B is B₁) then (y is C₁)
Rule2: If (ωₐ is A₄) and (θ_B is B₄) then (y is C₅)
......
```

It is comprehensible and similar to traditional rules that carry forward the traditional experienced knowledge. The type-2 fuzzy outputs of these rules must be type-reduced. Commonly used methods include centroid type-reducer, height type-reducer and center-of-sets type-reducer. Here, we used center-of-sets type-reducer to compute the output, as shown by the following formulas:

$$C^l = \int_{\theta_1 \in J_{y_1}} \cdots \int_{\theta_N \in J_{y_N}} \left[\prod_{i=1}^{N} (f_{y_i}(\theta_i)) \right] / \frac{\sum_{i=i}^{N} y_i \theta_i}{\sum_{i=i}^{N} \theta_i} \tag{6}$$

where, C^l is the centroid of the consequent set for the lth rule, and it is a type-1 fuzzy set. Since C^l is irrelevant to actual inputs, it can be computed ahead.

For type-2 interval fuzzy set of the consequent as shown in Fig. 5, their secondary membership $f_{y_i}(\theta_i)$ is equal to 1. So we can calculate their type-reduced sets, as shown by the following Table 1.

Table 1. Type-reduced result for the consequent sets of the type-2 fuzzy rules

Consequent set	Type-reduced C^l	Centroid of the set
$\widetilde{C}_1$	[0.1562,0.3700]	0.2631
$\widetilde{C}_2$	[0.7970,1.2066]	1.0018
$\widetilde{C}_3$	[1.7935,2.2065]	2.0000
$\widetilde{C}_4$	[2.7934,3.2030]	2.9982
$\widetilde{C}_5$	[3.6300,3.8438]	3.7369

3.4 Computing Approach of Output for Decision Making Model

On the basis of inputs, outputs and consequent sets defined above, type-2 FLS can be built quickly to model the decision-making for close-in air-combat. The type-reduced outputs of type-2 FLS is an interval fuzzy set that can't be provided by traditional type-1 FLS. It is an important tool that can be used to model uncertainty of rules. We used center-of-sets defuzzifier to compute the type-reduced output, as shown by the following formulas:

$$Y_{\cos} = \frac{\sum_{l=1}^{M} \left[C^l \prod_{i=1}^{p} \left(\mu_{F_i^l}(x_i) \right) \right]}{\sum_{l=1}^{M} \left[\prod_{i=1}^{p} \left(\mu_{F_i^l}(x_i) \right) \right]} \tag{7}$$

Where $\mu_{F_i^l}(x_i)$ is the firing set in formula (3).

Because we use type-1 Gaussian membership function to process the inputs of interval type-2 FLS and simply the firing operation between inputs and antecedents, so the firing sets can be simplified into interval sets, whose bounds can be expressed as the following formula [19]:

$$\begin{cases} \underline{f}_k^l = \exp\left(-\dfrac{\left(m_k^l - x_k'\right)}{2\left(\sigma_{X_k}^2 + \sigma_{k1}^{l2}\right)}\right) \\ \bar{f}_k^l = \exp\left(-\dfrac{\left(m_k^l - x_k'\right)}{2\left(\sigma_{X_k}^2 + \sigma_{k2}^{l2}\right)}\right) \end{cases} \tag{8}$$

Where x_k' and σ_{X_k} is the mean and standard deviation of input Gaussian membership function respectively. m_k^l, σ_{k1}^l and σ_{k2}^l is mean and standard deviation of antecedent type-2 Gaussian membership function respectively, subjected to $\sigma_{k1}^l < \sigma_{k2}^l$.

The interval $[\underline{f}_k^l, \bar{f}_k^l]$ is also the firing set for input set X_k against the lth rule. By minimal operation among all firing set, we get the firing set as follows:

$$[\underline{f}^l, \bar{f}^l] = [\min(\underline{f}_1^l, \ldots, \underline{f}_p^l), \min(\bar{f}_1^l, \ldots, \bar{f}_p^l)] \tag{9}$$

Where p is the counts of antecedents. Then, formula (7) can be simplified into the following formula (10).

$$Y_{\cos} = [y_l, y_r] = \int_{y_1 \in [C_l^1, C_r^1]} \cdots \int_{y_1 \in [C_l^M, C_r^M]} \int_{f^1 \in [\underline{f}^1, \bar{f}^1]} \cdots \int_{f^M \in [\underline{f}^M, \bar{f}^M]} 1 \left/ \dfrac{\sum\limits_{i=i}^{M} y^i f^i}{\sum\limits_{i=i}^{M} f^i} \right. \tag{10}$$

Where M is the number of rules, $[C_l^i, C_r^i]$ is type-reduced set of the lth rule pre-computed by via formula (6). Formula (10) can be calculated by classical KM algorithm that is detailedly described in Ref [19]. Not only the interval set $Y_{\cos}$ can be used as output of type-2 FLS, but also the centroid of $Y_{\cos}$, which is replaced by $(y_l + y_r)/2$.

4   Simulation and Analysis

We built a type-2 FLS by computing approach described above, to make decisions for close-in air-combat at variable conditions. For example, when ω_A and θ_B is represented by different crisp number, we have computed the output values of type-2 FLS, as shown by Fig. 6.

As Fig. 6 shows, the upper curved surface represents the upper bounds of the output of type-2 FLS, the bottom curved surface represents the lower bounds, and the middle represents the centroid. Different from traditional rule base whose decision output is fixed at certain condition, but the decision output of type-2 FLS may be variable at a range even at the same condition. It can output decisions like type-1 FLS using the middle centroid. It can also output decisions randomly between the upper and lower bounds.

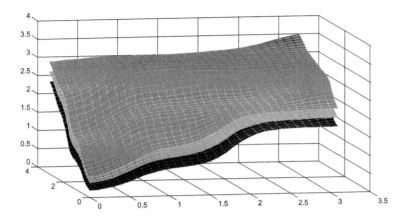

Fig. 6. Decision outputs when inputs are crisp numbers

For another example, when ω_A and θ_B is fuzzy sets as show in Fig. 4, the output interval of Type-2 FLS is [1.2380, 1.9638], the crisp output of its center-of-sets defuzzifier is 1.6009. That means the decision-making output has uncertainty between consequent fuzzy set $\widetilde{C}_2$ and $\widetilde{C}_3$. If we select maneuver tactics only by crisp output, we may get results similar to those in Refs. [3, 4]. But we can make decisions with some preference that reflects the subjectiveness of pilot, such as courage and skill, etc. Because the output of type-2 FLS includes a interval, it provides the availability to various selection, which make it more flexible and human-like than traditional type-1 FLS.

On the basis of variable selection of Type-2 FLS, a aircraft CGF can employ corresponding flexible maneuvers to control the flight model [10], that produce suitable trajectory against the target. Here, we omit the production from decisions to maneuver (that is not the topic in this paper) and just present the example trajectories of two aircraft in 1vs1 close-in air-combat, as shown in Fig. 7. Among them, one is the

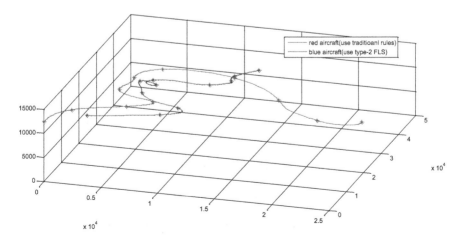

Fig. 7. Demonstration of 1vs1 close-in air-combat simulation

trajectory of blue aircraft that make decision by type-2 FLS; another is of red aircraft only using traditional fixed rules.

Figure 7 show that blue aircraft selects maneuvers more flexibly and suitably than the red one. Moreover, many results from our 1vs1 close-in air-combat simulation show that blue aircraft prefer to select aggressive maneuvers than red aircraft at various initial conditions when it uses the upper value of interval output of type-2 FLS. That shows that the rules based on type-2 FLS is more flexible and credible than traditional fixed rules, and type-2 FLS can extend the variety of decision-making model of CGFs. Furthermore, simplified interval type-2 fuzzy rules greatly improve the computing efficiency, which enables the model to run in about 15 ms in MATLAB.

5   Conclusion

Because of the computing complexity of type-2 FLS, its application in real-time CGF simulation is extremely scanty. In this paper, we use interval type-2 FLS as the decision-making model of close-in air combat, taking full consideration for the uncertainty of sensor inputs, experiential knowledge and human's preference. The results demonstrate that type-2 FLS is an efficient and credible approach to model decision-making in air-combat simulation.

Acknowledgment. In this paper, the research was sponsored by the National Nature Science Foundation (Project No. 61472441, 61573373).

References

1. Mulgund, S.S., Harper, K.A., Zacharias, G.L.: SAMPLE: situation awareness model for pilot-in-the-loop evaluation. In: Proceedings of the 9th Computer Generated Forces and Behavior Representation, Orlando, FL, pp. 377–388 (2000)
2. Patchett, C.: The performance of an intelligent agent in a simulated air combat environment. In: Proceedings of the 12th Conference on Computer Generated Force and Behavior Representation (2003)
3. Zhang, Y., Yang, R., Wu, M., et al.: Air combat tactics decision-making based on intuitionistic fuzzy Petri net. Comput. Eng. Appl. **48**(30), 224–228 (2012)
4. Shi, Z.-F., Zhang, A., Liu, H.-Y., He, S.-Q., He, Y.-P.: Study on air combat tactics decision-making based on fuzzy Petri nets. J. Syst. Simul. **19**(1), 63–66 (2007)
5. Yu, Z.-X., Hu, X.-X., Xia, W.: Foe intention inference in air combat based on fuzzy dynamic Bayesian network. J. Hefei Univ. Technol. (Nat. Sci. Ed.) **36**(10), 1210–1216 (2010)
6. Shi, J.-G., Gao, X.-G., Li, X.-M.: Modeling air combat situation assessment by using fuzzy dynamic Bayesian network. J. Syst. Simul. **18**(5), 1093–1096 (2006)
7. Li, M., Jiang, C.-S., Yang, C.: A fuzzy-neural network method of occupying attack seat in air combat of attacker. Fire Control Command Control **27**(3), 18–20 (2002)
8. Chang, Y., Jiang, C., Chen, Z.: Decision-making based on fuzzy neural network for air combat of multi-aircraft against multi-target. Electron. Opt. Control **18**(4), 13–17 (2011)
9. Bo, T., Peng, Z.-Q., Liu, X.-L., Wang, Z.-Z., Huang, K.-D.: Study on fuzzy rule based human behavior modeling for air combat simulation. J. Syst. Simul. **14**(4), 440–443 (2002)

10. Bo, T.: Research on Human Behavior Representation of Fighter Dogfight Combat. National University of Defense Technology, Changsha (2002)
11. Mendel, J.M.: Type-2 fuzzy sets and systems: an overview. IEEE Comput. Intell. Mag. **2**(2), 20–29 (2007)
12. Garibaldi, J.M., Ozen, T.: Uncertain fuzzy reasoning: a case study in modelling expert decision making. IEEE Trans. Fuzzy Syst. **15**(1), 16–30 (2007)
13. Ozen, T., Garibaldi, J.M.: Effect of type-2 fuzzy membership function shape on modelling variation in human decision making. In: IEEE International Conference on Fuzzy Systems, July 2004
14. Burgin, G.H., Sidor, L.B.: Rule-based air combat simulation. NASA CR-4160 (1988)
15. Weibin, Z., Huaizhong, H., Wenjiang, L.: Traffic flow forecast based on type-2 fuzzy logic approach. J. Xi'an Jiaotong Univ. **41**(10), 1160–1164 (2007)
16. Zheng, G., Xiao, J., Jiang, Q., Wang, S.: Research on theory and application of type-2 fuzzy logic systems. J. Hefei Univ. Technol. (Nat. Sci. Ed.) **32**(7), 966–971 (2009)
17. Karnik, N.N., Mendel, J.M.: Operation on type-2 fuzzy sets. Fuzzy Syst. **122**(7), 327–348 (2001)
18. Mendel, J.M.: Uncertain Rule-Based Fuzzy Logic Systems: Introduction and New Directions. Prentice-Hall, Upper Saddle River (2001)

Research on Multi-dimension and Multi-view Integrated Modeling of Operational System of Systems

Li Kou[✉], Lili Yin, and Wenhui Fan

Department of Automation, Tsinghua University, Beijing, China
{Kou113,yll15}@mails.tsinghua.edu.cn, fanwenhui@tsinghua.edu.cn

Abstract. The construction of joint operational system had become the important content of military modernization and preparations for military struggle. Comprehensive and accurate model of Operational System of Systems (OSoS) had become the key fundamental work. The most OSoS models which were constructed in single view had a weak integrated degree and could not accurately describe the system capacity. According to this problem, the framework and method of Multi-dimension and Multi-View Integrated OSoS Modeling was put forward. The OSoS was described in terms of lifecycle, generality, multi-view and multi-dimension. These models were integrated effectively. The emergence, dynamics and openness of OSoS were well reflected.

Keywords: Multi-dimension and multi-view · Integrated modeling · Operational System of Systems

1 Introduction

Under the current conditions of informatization, the widespread use of information technology has subverted the traditional concept of Operational System of Systems. The battlefield is also extended to the sea, land, air, sky, electromagnetic and other multi-dimensional space. Confrontation is also showing more and more obvious systematic feature. Ron Johnson, the deputy director of Boeing Advanced Systems Engineering and Technology Department, defined the system as: the system of systems (SOS) [1], namely "super-system". The elements constituting this "super system" is a complex, independent system, they interact with each other to complete a mission together. Therefore, OSoS can be defined as a dynamic complex system, which can adapt to the dangerous environment. It is composed of sensors with independent characteristics, command control, communications, fire, security and other systems (entities, nodes, elements, sub-network) [2]. And these component systems have relatively independent functions, they can self-administer, self-operate for their own purposes. Because of the emergence property, OSoS is able to show some features that other component systems don't have. OSoS is also loose coupling, each component system, function and behavior can be dynamically added or removed during the operation of the system.

OSoS modeling and simulation is aimed to reveal the law of true OSoS's construction, evolution, against in the informative conditions, and improve the effectiveness evaluation of OSoS. It has been one of the extremely urgent research topics in the

© Springer Science+Business Media Singapore 2016
L. Zhang et al. (Eds.): AsiaSim 2016/SCS AutumnSim 2016, Part II, CCIS 644, pp. 144–157, 2016.
DOI: 10.1007/978-981-10-2666-9_15

military sphere. Based on this background, the establishment of a comprehensive and accurate description model of the OSoS has become one of the most critical basic works. At present, there are many researches about modeling theory and methods of OSoS in the overseas and in the domestic.

The theories and methods for OSoS modeling all describe the OSoS in a few aspects. And they are in the conceptual modeling stage of demand analysis and system design, can't fully reflect the characteristics of OSoS in terms of OSoS's dynamic modeling and the mapping with simulation models. For example, Zachman, CIM-OSA, DoDAF and C4ISR framework lack the modeling for the OSoS's emergence, dynamics and openness; The description for the OSoS's property, procedures and resource models based on the complex network approach is not detailed enough. Therefore, we put forward an integrated method for OSoS modeling based on the integrated enterprise modeling theory [7] proposed by professor Fan Yushun in Qinghua University, which combines with the advantages of all theoretical approaches. This method uses the multi-view and multi-level description form, giving a description of the OSoS structure and component function based on the complex network's multi-Agent modeling theory, and correlating each view through a process view. This paper finally analyses the key indicators in system-of-systems efficiency based on the knowledge associated graph mining method.

2   Integrated Modeling Framework of OSoS

The integration of OSoS is the coordination of OSoS's each component system and each function. Only the organic integration could share information, could make the right decisions in a short time. Therefore, integration is the main method to constitute the whole, to constitute the system. Similarly, achieving the integration of OSoS's description in different aspects, in different dimensions and in different views, to form the

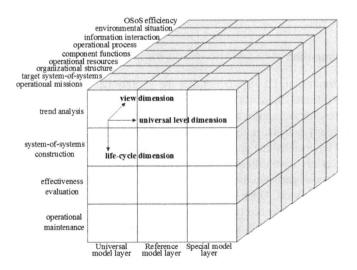

Fig. 1. The integrated modeling architecture of OSoS

integrated OSoS model is also a key method to improve the model description's comprehensiveness and accuracy. The system architecture of OSoS integrated modeling is shown in Fig. 1. It is a three dimensional cube structure consist of view dimension, universal level dimension and life-cycle dimension.

2.1 Life-Cycle Dimension

The introduce of the life-cycle dimension into the OSoS modeling framework, can be divided into four stages according to the implementation process of the combat missions: trend analysis, system-of-systems construction, effectiveness evaluation, and operational maintenance. According to the different demands of each stage, use different modeling methods to build models with different purposes, views and granularity.

In the life cycle of modeling, the relationship between the views in different stages uses the modeling method of deriving from the upper to the lower step by step. But in practice, because the understanding of the system is gradually mature and the various models are constantly changing during the system confrontation process, there are still relatively frequent iterative process in the system modeling during the different stages of the life cycle. The OSoS model is evolving constantly.

2.2 Universal Level Dimension

OSoS is a large system composed of a lot of operational units. Each operational entity is organized and managed according to the categories in practice. So the object-oriented method can be used in modeling through the classified description of the models according to their degree of universality, which is better for the analysis and management of the operational entity model. Thus constitute one dimension in the modeling framework, namely universal level dimension. In the universal level dimension, the operational entity models can be divided into three layers: universal model layer, reference model layer and special model layer.

2.3 View Dimension

In the view dimension, OSoS model takes the operational process view as the core, including operational missions, target system-of-systems, organizational structure, operational resources, component functions, information interaction, sys-tem-of-systems efficiency and the multi-view model of environmental situation view. Each view, created by establishing and improving gradually, describes the OSoS characteristics and behaviors from different angles. They are interrelated, mutually referenced, mutually influenced and take the process view as the core to control and maintain the consistency with models. Operational mission view: OSoS is composed of the operational systems to complete a certain operational mission. Operational missions, the basis of the construction of the OSoS, determines the composition and operation of the OSoS.

3   Integrated Modeling Method of OSoS

3.1   Modeling Method of Life Cycle Dimension

The life cycle of the OSoS can be divided into four stages, including situation analysis stage, system-of-systems construction stage, efficiency evaluation stage, operation and maintenance stage, as shown in Fig. 2. In the situation analysis stage, it is mainly carried out to assign operational missions, analyze environment situation and analyze the target system-of-systems to select the hit target according to the missions and environment. In the system-of-systems construction stage, it is mainly carried out to build the organizational structure, component function, information interaction and operational resources used according to the operational missions and selected targets, and on the above basis to describe the operational procedures. In the efficiency evaluation stage, it is mainly carried out to analyze the system-of-systems efficiency to help making decision, such as the topology structure of each component unit of OSoS, system-of-systems complexity, component system's critical level and so on. In the operation and maintenance stage, it is mainly carried out to record the resulting data provided for the follow-up stage's analysis by running the OSoS model.

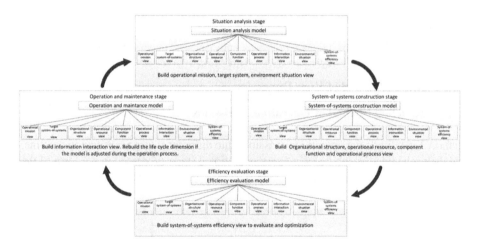

Fig. 2. The life cycle dimension of OSoS modeling

3.2   Modeling Method of Universal Level Dimension

Universal level dimension is the space dimension of the integrated modeling framework of OSoS. Its modeling method is similar to the object-oriented approach, taking the entity existing in operational system as an object to manage; The objects can be abstracted as classes according to their properties, and the objects are the examples of these classes. So they can be divided into universal model, reference model and special model according to the universal degree of each component model of OSoS. By constructing the basic building blocks of the OSoS modeling at different stages, different modeling view can establish the basic model component library. On this basis abstract the reference model of OSoS according to the model's category, and then inherit and modify the reference model to form a specific model, as shown in Fig. 3.

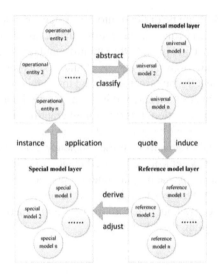

Fig. 3. The evolutionary process of universal level dimension's model

3.3   Modeling Method of View Dimension

3.3.1   Modeling Method of Operational Missions

The description of operational missions uses the Analytic Hierarchy Process (AHP) method. First divide the operational missions into different stages according to the time, and then schedule the sub tasks in every operational stage expressed in the form of the "task tree", as shown in Fig. 4.

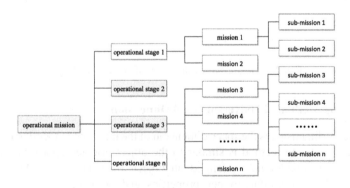

Fig. 4. The AHP method of operational missions modeling

The formal description of operational missions can be abstracted as the following form:

$$\text{Task} = < T_{ID}, T_{Name}, T_{Des}, T_{STime}, T_{ETime} >$$

$$\text{Stage} = < S_{ID}, S_{Name}, S_{Des}, S_{STime}, S_{ETime}, T_{ID} >$$

$$\text{STask} = < ST_{ID}, ST_{Name}, ST_{Des}, ST_{STime}, ST_{ETime}, S_{ID} \backslash ST_{ID} >$$

"Task" representing operational missions, is described by the task code, task name, task description, start time and end time; "Stage" representing operational stage, is described by stage code, stage name, stage description, start time, end time and task code it belongs to; "STask" representing subtasks, is described by subtask code, name, description, start time, end time and the stage/task code it belongs to.

3.3.2   Modeling Method of Operational Resource

Operational resource view mainly describes the classification and structure of operational resources, resource quantity and quality. It also has extensive relations with the organization structure, component function and information interaction view, which will be described in detail in the following chapters. As a part of military system, operational resources have a complete classification method and encoding rules, so it can be modeled in the form of "resource tree" according to the category that the operational resource belongs to, as shown in Fig. 5.

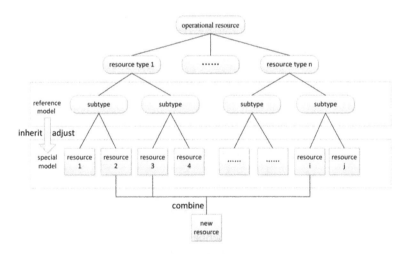

Fig. 5. Modeling method of operational resource

The formal description of operational resources can be abstracted as the following form:

$$\text{Resource} = < R_{ID}, R_{Name}, R_{Type}, R_{Att}, R_{Number} >$$

$$ZResource = < ZR_{ID}, ZR_{Name}, ZR_{Type}, ZR_{Att}, ZR_{Number}, R_{ID} >$$

"Resource" representing resource entity, is described by number, name, type, attribute, quantity, etc. "ZResource" representing combined resources, is described by number, name, type, attribute, quantity and number of sub resource.

3.3.3 Modeling Method of Component Function

The main purpose of component function modeling is to describe the function of OSoS, that is to explain the specific activities which is must carried out to complete a task. These activities consist of operational entity or the basic functional unit of operational resource. These basic function units can be abstracted as an action of the entity. This action completes the processing of the input information in a certain constraint (control), mainly through the occupation and consumption of certain operational resources (mechanism), and finally get the output information. These basic functional units are combined together to construct the function of the OSoS. The modeling of component function can use IDEF0 modeling method, which is a graphical model established by structured analysis method, and can be decomposed and combined to describe the logical structure of the system-of-systems function according to the hierarchy, as shown in Fig. 6.

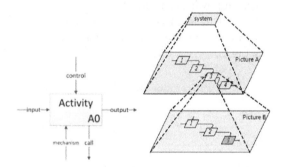

Fig. 6. The function activity diagram of IDEF0

The formal description of component functions can be abstracted as follows:

$$UnitFun = < F_{ID}, F_{Name}, F_{Par}, R_{ID}, T_{ID}, Condition >$$

$$SysFun = < UnitFun_1, UnitFun_2, \cdots, UnitFun_n >$$

"UnitFun" representing the basic function unit, is described by function number, function name, function parameter, implementation object of function activities, resources used and implementing condition. "SysFun" representing the system function, is composed of the ordered two tuple of the basic function unit. This kind of representation method can describe the autonomy and interactivity characteristics of each component system of OSoS, which provides a framework for the modeling based on multi-Agent.

3.3.4   Modeling Method of Organization Structure

From the perspective of topology, this article abstracts operational unit as sensing, fire, commands and communication system node, and abstracts the information (or material, energy) interaction between these systems as edge. Thus the OSoS is abstracted as a OSoS network. The connection diagram of the OSoS network is shown in Fig. 7.

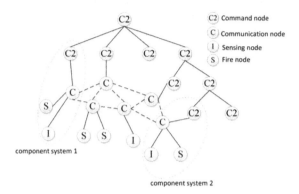

Fig. 7. The connection diagram of the OSoS network

This network can be expressed by a n × n matrix M, where n is the number of nodes of OSoS network. The matrix element M_{ij} = 1 represents there is a connection between node i and j. M_{ij} = 0 means there is no connection between node i and j. This matrix is a symmetric matrix. It can be expressed in two-dimensional array in data structure. It also can be expressed as a linked list when it is a sparse matrix.

The formal description of the organization structure contains two types of view: component view and structure view, separately representing the operational unit nodes and the node network between them, which is described as:

$$\text{Organization} =< U, UR >$$

$$U =< C2_1, C2_2, \cdots, C2_n, I_1, I_2, \cdots I_n, S_1, S_2, \cdots S_n, C_1, C_2, \cdots C_n >$$

$$UR_{ij} = \begin{cases} 1 & i\, to\, j\, connected \\ 0 & i\, to\, j\, unconnected \end{cases}$$

$$UR = \begin{bmatrix} 1 & \cdots & 0 \\ \vdots & \ddots & \vdots \\ 0 & \cdots & 1 \end{bmatrix}$$

U represents the collection of entity nodes in the OSoS, which is respectively composed of charge nodes, sensor nodes, fire nodes and communication nodes. UR is the matrix of the directed graph of the hierarchical network. The entity unit nodes can be associated with the operational resources and component function nodes, which will be described in the following chapters.

3.3.5   Modeling Method of Information Interaction

Information interaction model mainly describes the underlying data structure and the information flow condition. The information flows between each network node of OSoS are generally classified as information sharing, information reporting and order making. These three kinds of information flow can be respectively realized by the method of broadcast, multicast and P2P, which forms the directed graph of information exchange in the network structure of the OSoS.

The underlying data structure of the information interaction model describes the logical relationship of the related data in the database, generated in the running process of each view model of OSoS. It provides a standard and framework for effective recording and management of data model. It is an important foundation for the establishment of the information systems and the implementation of information integration of OSoS. It can be described by the IDEF1X or ER diagram method, as shown in Fig. 8.

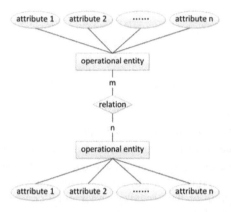

Fig. 8.   The example of information model

On the basis of the underlying data structure, the operational entity will share or sent its own or other's property value to update other's or its own property value when the information exchange occurs between the operational entities, in order to complete the information exchange process. The formal description of information exchange view can be also divided into two parts: the underlying data structures and information exchange model, which can be abstracted as follows:

$$Entity = < E_{ID}, E_{Name}, E_{Atts} >$$

$$Relation = < Relation_{ID}, Relation_{Name}, E_{ID_i}, E_{ID_j} >$$

$$Info = < Info_{ID}, Info_{Name}, Info_{Type}, M >$$

"Entity" representing operational entity, is respectively represented by entity number, entity name and attribute set. "Relation" representing the relationship between entities, is respectively represented by the relationship number, name and related entity's number. "Info" representing the interactive information, is composed of the information number, name, type and interaction matrix M. Interaction matrix M is established based on organization structure model. The information interaction between the nodes also can be represented by matrix. When $M_{ij} = 1$, it represents that the information of entity i interacts with entity j, and entity j updates its own attributes according to the value of interaction matrix at the same time.

Information interaction matrix:

$$M = \begin{bmatrix} 0 & \cdots & 1 \\ \vdots & \ddots & \vdots \\ 1 & \cdots & 0 \end{bmatrix}$$

3.3.6   Modeling Method of Environmental Situation

Operational entity is running in a certain battlefield environment. It can be affected by environmental factors, and it also has an impact on the battlefield environment at same time. In different battlefield environment, the operational effect achieved is completely different. The new operational styles that gradually develop in the modern war reinforce the importance of the environmental situation, such as the electronic countermeasure and electromagnetic interference. It can play a key role sometimes. Therefore, the modeling of environmental situation should also be included in the OSoS model, and should be described as a separate view. The environmental situation view only describes the natural and artificial environment that don't have the subjective initiative. The description of operational target is detailed in the target system-of-systems view. In this article, the environmental situation is divided into the natural environment and the battlefield situation, as shown in Fig. 9. The natural environment can be divided into geographical factors, meteorological factors, etc. The battlefield situation can be divided into land situation, sea situation, air situation and space situation.

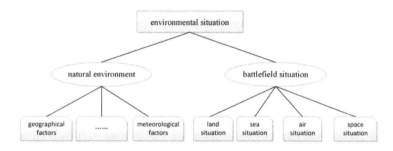

Fig. 9.   The categories of environmental situation model

The formal description of the environmental situation view can be abstracted as:

$$Env = < Env_{ID}, Env_{Name}, Env_{Atts}, Area, Time, Entities >$$

$$Env_{Atts} = < Att_{ID}, Att_{Name}, Att_{Value} >$$

$$\text{Area} =< \text{Point}_1, \text{Point}_2, \cdots, \text{Point}_n >$$

"Env" representing environmental situation model, is respectively described by number, name, attribute set, function area, reaction time and perceptive object. Attribute set is described by attribute number, name and attribute value. Function area is described by the closed spaces composed of a series location points.

3.3.7   Modeling Method of Operational Process

Operational process is the core view of the multi-view modeling, and is also the link to build the model of OSoS. Through the operational process view model, the other scattered, independent view models can be associated and integrated. The complete description of the OSoS is formed finally, as shown in Fig. 10.

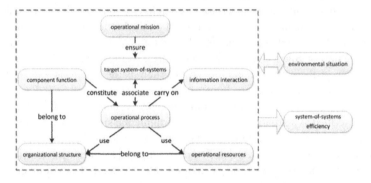

Fig. 10. The integrated relationship between views

In the operational process of the OSoS, select the target from the target system-of-systems view according to operational mission view, and plan the operational process according to the target; Organizational structure view provides the executor of the activities to operational process view; Resource view provides resources used in activities to operational process view; Each activity in the operational process is a realization of a component function of the system. Therefor an operational process can be described through a combination of functions. And it reflects the logical relationship between the operational entities' function domain at the same time; Operational process should also reflect the execution relations and conditions between the functions of each component. During this process the information is generated and interact with each other; In the operational process, it is important to fully consider the influence of the environment situation and system, and calculate the system-of-systems efficiency of the OSoS according to the data of OSoS such as the organization structure, information exchange and operational resource.

The main method of operational process modeling is the scientific deployment of operational resources based on operational missions, operational targets and system constraints, in order to make operational units organize together tightly and play their respective functions at an ordered time and in a reasonable place. And the data and information generated is recorded in the process. Its basic unit is action, and action is also a bridge associating and integrating other view models. This paper uses "5W1H" method to describe the operational actions, respectively including the six aspects of operational missions and targets (what), operational units (who), operational time (when), operational area (where), operational constraints (why), operational mode (how), thus setting up a one-to-one relationship with other view models. And the operational process can be described by the action network diagram. The action network diagram is a directed diagram composed of nodes and connecting arcs. The nodes represent actions, and the connecting arcs represent the order relationship between the actions, thus forming a sequence diagram composed of the operational actions, as shown in Fig. 11.

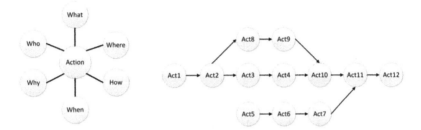

Fig. 11. The schematic diagram of operational process model

The formal description of the operational process view can be abstracted as:

$$\text{Process} =< \text{Act}_1, \text{Act}_2, \cdots, \text{Act}_n >$$

$$\text{Sequence}_{ij} =< \text{Act}_i, \text{Act}_j >$$

$$\text{Act}_i =< \text{Condition}_i, \text{Function}_i, \text{actT}_i, \text{actPostion}_i >$$

$$\text{actT} =< \text{actT}_1, \text{actT}_2, \cdots, \text{actT}_n >$$

$$\text{actPostion} =< \text{actPostion}_1, \text{actPostion}_2, \cdots, \text{actPostion}_n >$$

$$\text{Condition} =< \text{Condition}_1, \text{Condition}_2, \cdots, \text{Condition}_n >$$

"Process" means that operational process is composed of a series of activities. These activities are connected by the connecting arcs ("Sequence"); Activities should perform the corresponding function under certain condition ("Condition") and in the corresponding position ("actPostion") and the corresponding time ("actT"). Trigger conditions "Condition" can be divided into automatic trigger, manual trigger, message trigger and time trigger. Activities execute time only when the time is triggered. The other activities can calculate their executed time according to the activity triggered by the time.

3.3.8   Modeling Method of System-of-Systems Efficiency

With the increasing maturity of data mining technology, the related knowledge of efficiency evaluation of OSoS can be got from the perspective of data, by mining the data generated during the process of OSoS operation or simulation. The main method is to construct knowledge association diagrams ("Knowledge Map") using the sample data. Data mining method based on knowledge association diagram is mainly to calculate the joint entropy and the number of connections of each parameter by finding the correlated parameters of the OSoS. It can describe the whole system's uncertainty and complexity and recognize the key variables and the uncontrollable variables of the system, and thus find the key elements of the OSoS. Due to limited space, the specific method will be introduced in another article.

3.3.9   Modeling Method of Target System-of-Systems

Because the system structure and system function of the target system-of-systems are consistent with the OSoS, the target system-of-systems can be modeled with the same method. The modeling of the target system-of-systems can also be described from life cycle dimension, universal level dimension and view dimension. After completing the description, the confrontation exercise of the OSoS and the target system-of-systems model can be achieved by the simulation method, to test the effectiveness of OSoS model.

4   Conclusion

OSoS model is the media via which people understand and know the OSoS, is the bridge between operational research experts and military personnel. The integrated modeling method fully describes the evolution of the OSoS in its life cycle from the perspective of multi-dimension and multi-view. These can help study the operational rules of the OSoS. This paper also puts forward a method to analyze the efficiency of the OSoS from the perspective of data mining.

The next work mainly includes the following aspects: The first one is studying the mapping method between integrated OSoS model and executable model; The second one is studying the component modeling method based on Agent based on the correlation between organizational structure, operational resources and component function view; The third one is designing the system-of-systems confrontation simulation based on the integrated OSoS model to verify the model's correctness and efficiency index from the perspective of simulation data.

References

1. Johnson, R.: Dynamic Complexity in System of Systems. Engineering and Technology, Advanced Systems. The Boeing Company, Chicago (2007)
2. Wei-xin, J.I.N.: Complex Network Modeling and Simulating of the OSoS of Systems. Electronic Industry Press, Beijing (2010)

3. Zachman, J.A.: A framework for information systems architecture. IBM Syst. J. **26**(3), 276–292 (1987)
4. ESPRIT Consortium AMICE: CIMOSA: Open System Architecture for CIM. Springer, Berlin (1993)
5. C4ISR Architecture Working Group. C4ISR Architecture Framework Version 2.0. Department of Defense, USA (1997)
6. DoD Architecture Framework Working Group. DoD Architecture Framework Version 1.5 Volume I: Definitions and Guidelines. Department of Defense, USA (2007)
7. Fan, Y.-S.: Integrated Enterprise Modeling Method and System. China Electric Power Press, Beijing (2007)

An External Rendering Algorithm for IR Imaging Simulation of Complex Infrared Scene

Peng Wang[1](✉), Ge Li[1], Xibao Wang[1], and Dongling Liu[2]

[1] National University of Defense Technology, Changsha, Hunan, China
wangpeng_nudt@nudt.edu.cn
[2] Liaoning University, Shenyang, Liaoning, China

Abstract. The performance of Infrared System is mainly determined by targets' infrared radiation characteristic, ambient complex environment's infrared radiation characteristic and the infrared radiation contrast between them. Meanwhile these factors are also influenced by geography location, weather condition, season and the time of a day. The IR imaging simulation system has the advantage of convenience, safety, lower cost etc. Using computer to simulate complex infrared scene has been more and more popular. In this paper, a new external rendering algorithm is proposed. This paper focuses on the designment and implementation of the external rendering of the complex scene for the IR imaging simulation. Finally, the effectiveness of the proposed algorithm is validated through an example.

Keywords: Infrared scene synthesis · External rendering · Complex infrared scene · IR imaging simulation

1 Introduction

In the IR imaging simulation of the complex scene, the conditions of the targets, background and atmosphere are complex. The infrared imaging sensor creates the infrared radiation image by receiving the infrared radiation signals from the scene. The radiation of the atmosphere and the atmospheric attenuation of radiation transmission both have impacts on the infrared radiation image [1]. To create the imaging model of the complex scene, we should not only consider the characteristics of the physics, radiation of the targets and background, but also need to consider the complex characteristics of the environment, atmosphere and some other objects [2, 3]. This paper presents a new external rendering algorithm for IR imaging modeling of the complex infrared scene. We give a detailed description of the implementation of the external rendering and the various ways of establishing an infrared scene using the proposed algorithm.

This work is supported by the National Nature Science Foundation of China (Grant No. 61374185).

L. Zhang et al. (Eds.): AsiaSim 2016/SCS AutumnSim 2016, Part II, CCIS 644, pp. 158–166, 2016.
DOI: 10.1007/978-981-10-2666-9_16

2   The Proposed External Rendering Algorithm

The external rendering algorithm proposed by this paper is implemented by using the infrared environment model. This algorithm also needs the sensor objects and the emitter/reflector objects. The sensor object is mainly used to convert the received infrared signal into a displayable image signal. It needs the information of the targets and background provided by the infrared environment model. The target object represents the concrete instances of the targets existing in the simulation system, such as fighters, ground vehicles, missiles, clutters and so on. The infrared environment model is mainly used to respond to the requests sent by the sensor objects. It also manages and calculates the signal sent by the target objects. Ultimately it provides the accurate information to the sensor objects. The infrared environment model is in charge of the generation, transmission and collection of the infrared signals emitted by the targets and background.

When the infrared environment model receives the request messages from the sensors, it would firstly determine which objects are in the sensor's field of view by calling the spatial service interface. Then it sends the request messages to all the objects in the sensor's field of view to request their infrared signals. After receiving the infrared signals from all the objects, the infrared environment model synthesizes the signals in a suitable way, and applies the atmospheric effects by calling the atmosphere service interface. After all the processing, the infrared environment model returns the information of the images to the sensor. The communication flow and data flow of the whole infrared simulation system is shown in Fig. 1.

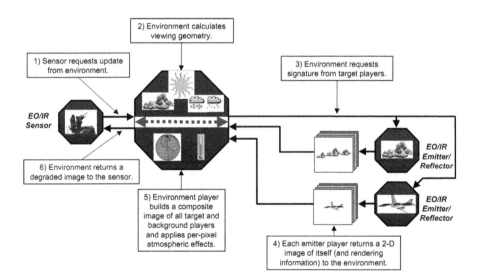

Fig. 1. Data communication flow chart of the proposed infrared simulation algorithm

2.1 The Segmentation and Aggregation of Targets

For the imaging of the complex infrared scene, the main deficiency of the external rendering is the modeling and processing of the optical interactions between the targets [4, 5]. So only with the reasonable segmentation and aggregation of the targets in the scene, we can create the synthetic infrared scene with sufficient fidelity to meet practical requirements [6]. There are many different ways to do the segmentation and aggregation of the targets for external rendering. We enumerate and analyses four main kinds of these methods.

1. Every Object a Separate Model

In this method, we regard each emitter or reflector in the scene as an independent model and treat each target as an independent emitter/reflector. This method has the lowest inherent fidelity, but it can satisfy the requirements of most IR imaging simulation applications. This method can't model the shadow of the ground or targets caused by the other targets.

2. Targets as Separate Models and Other Objects as a Single Model

In this method, we divide the objects into two classes: target objects and non-target objects. The non-target objects are defined as the any objects except the targets, such as interference, clouds and background. We regard each target objects as a separate model, and all the other objects as a single model.

3. EO Critically Coupled Objects as a Single Model

In this method, we regard the critical coupling scene objects as a single model. It is necessary to build the correct model of the optical interactions of the separating objects in the space. If we aggregate these objects to be a single model, we should build the model of the optical interactions, because these optical interactions will affect the total radiation energy.

4. Entire Environment as a Single Model

In this method, we regard all the targets in the scene as a single model. The requirement of the fidelity for this method is very strict. This enables us to take any necessary heat and optical interaction into account when modeling the entire scene.

The Fig. 2 summarizes the generation mechanism of the infrared images. This figure shows us the kinds of infrared signals that can be aggregated by the four methods mentioned above. We can see that even in the worst case, most of the light sources can be modeled.

2.2 The Synthesis of IR Images

The targets are always in the midst of a certain background. It is necessary to do the synthesis of the infrared radiation images of the targets and background [7]. Only in this way can we analyze the infrared radiation contrast of targets and background [8]. The main characteristic of the proposed external rendering is that it can synthesize the

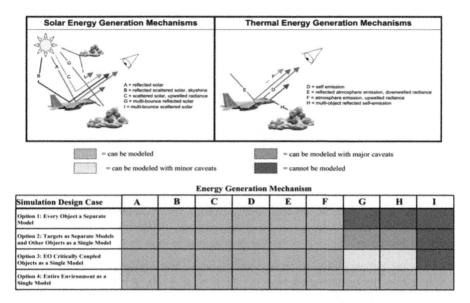

Fig. 2. The energy generation mechanism of the external rendering algorithm

feature images of many objects in the right way when the atmospheric transmission effect of infrared radiation is taken into consideration. The information related to performing this function is as shown in Fig. 3.

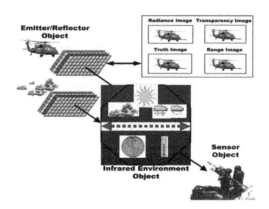

Fig. 3. The schematic diagram of the rendering algorithm

After rendering the emitters and reflectors in the sensor's field of view, the infrared environment model requests the feature images of these emitters and reflectors. Every emitter/reflector will transmit its own four rendering images or two-dimensional matrixes to the infrared environment model, including radiance image, transparency image, truth image and range image.

The radiance image is a pixel array which has a unit with photo flux rate of radiation. The transparency image is an image of the sensor's field of view which is closed by the given emitters or reflectors. It is mainly used to consider the occlusion between the targets. The truth image is a coded image similar to the transparency image. It describes the types of the target objects which are founded in the sensor's field of view. It is a kind of coding for the emitters/reflectors, and we can use it to distinguish all the objects in the imaging simulation system. The range image is an array of distance values. It describes the distance between the sensor objects and the emitters/reflectors. The infrared environment model uses these distance values to operate the atmospheric effect on each pixel [9]. All the images are all stored in the form of two-dimensional arrays, and the sizes are determined by the sample sizes of the sensor in the azimuth direction and the pitching direction.

The IR image synthesis process finally exports one radiance image, one transparency image, one truth image and one range image. These images contain all the objects in the sensor's field of view. The specific calculation process is shown below.

1. Define the radiance images, transparency images, truth images and range images returned by the emitters/reflectors as $\{S_i\} \supset \{R_i, F_i, D_i, T_i\}, 1 \leq i \leq n$. Then we should determine the minimum distance values of every range image $R_{M(1)}, R_{M(2)},$ $\ldots, R_{M(i)}, \ldots, R_{M(n)}$:

$$R_{M(i)} = \min_{1 \leq k \leq x, 1 \leq 1 \leq y}[R_i(k,l)](1 \leq i \leq n) \tag{1}$$

Here k and l mean that the pixel is located at row k, column l; $R_i(k,l)$ is the distance value of the pixel at the position (k,l) of ith range image. Then sort the minimum distance values in descending order. The sorted minimum distance values are as follows: $R_{M(L1)} \geq R_{M(L2)} \geq \cdots \geq R_{M(Li)} \geq \cdots \geq R_{M(Ln)}$, here $1 \leq Li \leq n(1 \leq i \leq n)$. The order of the range images, radiance images, transparency images and truth images corresponding to the minimum distance values also need to be adjusted as follows: $\{S_{Li}\} \supset \{R_{Li}, F_{Li}, D_{Li}, T_{Li}\}, 1 \leq Li \leq n(1 \leq i \leq n)$.

2. Then take a pixel point $P(k,l)$ of the rendering image as an example, here k and l denote the position of the pixel in the image. So the distance value, radiance value, transparency value and truth value at this position of each rendering image are $\{R_{P(i)}, F_{P(i)}, D_{P(i)}, T_{P(i)}\}, 1 \leq i \leq n$. Here the definitions of $R_{P(i)}, F_{P(i)}, D_{P(i)}, T_{P(i)}$ are as follows:

$$R_{P(i)} = R_{Li}(k,l) \ (1 \leq i \leq n) \tag{2}$$

$$F_{P(i)} = F_{Li}(k,l) \ (1 \leq i \leq n) \tag{3}$$

$$D_{P(i)} = D_{Li}(k,l) \ (1 \leq i \leq n) \tag{4}$$

$$T_{P(i)} = T_{Li}(k,l) \ (1 \leq i \leq n) \tag{5}$$

Then we sort the distance values of the pixels at the given position with the bubble sort algorithm and make them sorted in the descending order. The sorted distance values are $R_{P(L1)} \geq R_{P(L2)} \geq \cdots \geq R_{P(Li)} \geq \cdots \geq R_{P(Ln)}$, here $1 \leq Li \leq n (1 \leq i \leq n)$. Correspondingly we adjust the order of the radiance values, transparency values and truth values $\{S_{P(Li)}\} \supset \{R_{P(Li)}, F_{P(Li)}, D_{P(Li)}, T_{P(Li)}\}, 1 \leq i \leq n$. Finally, all the pixels are traversed by this method in order to adjust the radiance value, distance value, transparency value and truth value of each pixel.

3. Once the final order of the pixels is determined, the radiance value of each pixel of the final synthetic image can be calculated. The calculation of the radiance value at any position of the synthetic image should begin from the top-level pixel, then propagate the radiance value of the second top-level pixel in turn forward, and end at the bottom-level pixel. Now the details are as follows: firstly we should calculate the synthetic radiance value of the far pixel and the near pixel at the given position. The synthetic value can be determined by follows:

$$\text{Rad}_{\text{syn}} = \left(\text{Rad}_{\text{far}} \times \text{Tran} + \text{Rad}_{\text{path}}\right) \times \text{D}_{\text{near}} + \text{Rad}_{\text{near}} \tag{6}$$

Here Rad_{far} represents the radiance value of the far pixel, and Rad_{near} is the radiance value of the near pixel. $Tran$ and Rad_{path} are the ratio of atmosphere transmission and the path radiation between these two pixels. D_{near} is the transparency value of the near pixel and Rad_{syn} is the synthetic radiance value of these two pixels. Then the result Rad_{syn} is assigned to Rad_{near} which can be used in the next step of the synthesis of the radiance value, namely the synthesis of the radiance value of the pixel next to the near pixel. Repeat this process until the pixel is the bottom pixel. Finally the distance value, transparency value and truth value are respectively equal to the distance value, transparency value and truth value of the bottom-level pixel.

4. When the final synthetic image of the emitters/reflectors is got, the atmospheric effects should be added to each pixel of the synthetic image. The specific calculation method is as follows:

$$\text{Rad}_{\text{after}} = \text{Rad}_{\text{syn}} \times \text{Tran}' + \text{Rad}'_{\text{path}} + \text{D}_{\text{syn}} \times \left(\text{Rad}'_{\text{sky}} - \text{Rad}'_{\text{path}}\right). \tag{7}$$

Here Rad_{syn} and D_{syn} respectively represent the radiance value and transparency value of the pixel in the synthetic image. $Tran'$, Rad'_{path} and Rad'_{sky} respectively represent the values of the ratio of atmospheric transmission, path radiation and sky radiation from the pixel point to the sensor object. Rad_{after} is the radiance value that has been added the atmospheric effects.

3 Simulation Example

We take the infrared imaging simulation of the helicopter as an example to verify the effectiveness of the proposed external rendering algorithm. As it is shown in Fig. 4, a reconnaissance plane equipped with an infrared sensor is monitoring the helicopter. In this infrared imaging simulation, we should take the terrain object, tree objects and atmospheric effects into account.

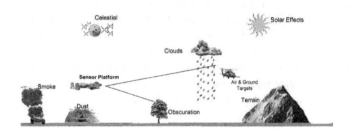

Fig. 4. Schematic diagram of the simulation scenario

3.1 Simulation Implementation

We take advantage of the CAD technology to create the 3D geometric models of the targets, trees and terrain. The geometric profile uses the mixed surface structure with the element of triangles and quadrangles. In the process of generating the target, we generate these unit structures with the mixed surface structures and generate the complete target's geometry shape by the combination of these unit structures. Then we process the hidden line block of each surface structure by the coordinate transformation according to the viewing angle, height and the distance between the surface structure and the sensor. In this way we can get the geometric view of the target. We use the Z-buffer algorithm to generate the geometric view of the target.

After generating the 3D geometric models of the target, we assign the radiation brightness values to the model to represent the infrared radiation characteristics of the target. But the radiance images haven't considered the atmospheric transmission effects. We store these infrared radiance images in the infrared image database. The whole process is as shown in Fig. 5.

3.2 Simulation Result

We store the simulation results in a database and we use the tool called SigView provided by JMASE to display the results [9]. The results are as shown in Fig. 6.

From Fig. 6 we can see that there are four kinds of objects (target object, terrain object, tree objects and environment object) to be simulated. The radiance images, range images, truth images and transparency images are regarded as the inputs for the infrared sensor object. The infrared environment object's outputs are synthetic radiance images, range images and truth images.

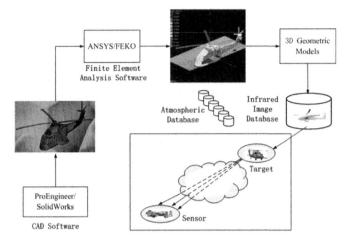

Fig. 5. The process of creating the target model

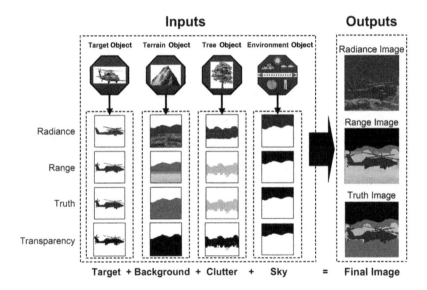

Fig. 6. The result of the infrared imaging simulation

From this example, it can be seen that the design and implementation of the infrared environment model can correctly simulate the infrared imaging of the target and background. The relationship of the radiation intensity and interaction between the targets and the background can be clearly seen in the infrared images.

4 Conclusions

In this paper, we propose an external rendering algorithm for IR imaging modeling of the complex infrared scene. We study the segmentation and aggregation of the targets in the complex scene, and enumerate four applicable methods. We also propose a practical method of the synthesis of the IR Images. We also analyze and implement the external rendering algorithm with a case. Finally, we validate the effectiveness of the proposed method through case study. The future research work includes the distributed algorithm of the external rendering to improve the fidelity and the scalability.

References

1. Accetta, J.S., et al.: The Infrared and Electro-Optical Handbook. SPIE Optical Engineer Press, Bellingham (1993)
2. Balfour, L.S., Bushlin, Y.: Semi-empirical model based approach for IR scene simulation. In: Isral (1997)
3. Zhang, J.-Q., Fang, X.-P.: Infrared Physics. Xidian University Publishing House, Xi'an (2004)
4. Fan, J., Yang, J.: Development of infrared imaging detecting technology. Infrared Laser Eng. **41**(12), 3145–3153 (2012)
5. Dobbs, B.M.: The Incorporation of Atmospheric Variability into DIRSIG. Center for Imaging Science Rochester Institute of Technology, USA, 16 January 2005
6. Crow, D.R.: High fidelity phenomenology modeling of infrared emissions from missile and aircraft exhaust plumes. SPIE **2741**, 242–250 (1996)
7. Tofanl, A.: Absolute and contrast infrared signature from missile nose. SPIE **1362**, 231–242 (1991)
8. Bushlin, Y., et al.: Variance properties in IR background images. In: SPIE, vol. 1967 (1993)
9. Liang, S.: Research on EO/IR Environment Simulation System. National University of Defense Technology (2005)

An Improved Genetic Algorithm in Shipboard Power Network Planning

Zhi-peng Hui[⊠] and Xin Ji

Naval Armament Academy, Beijing, China
hzpeng117@163.com, jixin441@126.com

Abstract. In order to optimize the survivability of shipboard power system, a bi-level programming model was proposed. The master programming model had the topological structure of shipboard power network and electric nodes layouts as decision variables and optimal power system survivability as the objective function. The slave programming model was to minimize the total length of power cables in order to optimize the layouts of them. The standard genetic algorithm was improved to be the solving method of shipboard power network planning. Two genetic operators, which are repairing operator and equivalence operator respectively, are proposed and added to genetic algorithm. The repairing operator was proposed to deal with the infeasible solutions such as isolated nodes, isolated islands and loops, and the equivalence operator was proposed to optimize the scale of electric nodes. A computational example verified the validity and practicality of the improved genetic algorithm and the programming model.

Keywords: Shipboard power system · Power network planning · Power system survivability · Bi-level programming · Genetic algorithm

1 Introduction

Shipboard power network planning can improve the survivability and power supplying continuity of shipboard power system (SPS). As for the SPS with small capacity and scale, quantity of alternative design plans meeting the requirements of total design and stability is relatively small. Therefore, with traditional design methods which utilize basic experience and check of industrial experience, the designers can work out the proper design plan for it. However, modern SPS is becoming more and more complex, from the prospect of capacity, load type and network structure. It would be a time consuming and laborious task, and the optimality of plan worked out in terms of survivability, stability, reliability and economic cannot be ensured, if designing power network of large SPS with traditional methods.

In terrestrial power system (TPS), power grid planning is usually separated into power transmission network planning [1, 2] and power distribution network planning respectively [3, 4], because of the separation of electric market. In power grid planning, economic indicators are treated as the main evaluating indicators, such as costs on network investment and operation, equipments depreciation, and line loss. Meanwhile, some planning models have the minimum economic loss as objective function, which is usually caused by power shortage and interruption.

© Springer Science+Business Media Singapore 2016
L. Zhang et al. (Eds.): AsiaSim 2016/SCS AutumnSim 2016, Part II, CCIS 644, pp. 167–179, 2016.
DOI: 10.1007/978-981-10-2666-9_17

Because of the differences existing between SPS and TPS in terms of operating ambient and mode, the power transmission network and distribution network of SPS should be in combination to ensure the global optimality of planning solution achieved, and decision variables should contain both of topological structure and elements layouts of power network. Additionally, for SPS of warships fulfilling battle efforts, the performance of its survivability is in direct relation to its maneuverability and the ability of combating and self-defense. Therefore, in power network planning of SPS, requirement on SPS survivability should be taken into great account [5–7], whereas the economic requirements of it should be treated as secondary ones.

The genetic algorithm (GA), as an adaptive algorithm for global optimization and probabilistic searching, can simulate the behaviors of inheritance and mutation of natural species. With prominent features of implicit parallelism, global optimality, adaptivity and high robustness, GA is extensively used for terrestrial power grid planning at the present [8, 9].

In this dissertation, the standard GA is improved to be the solving method of shipboard power network planning, which make sure the algorithm converge into feasible solutions and scale of power nodes be optimized. A computational test of a typical SPS verifies the validity and practicality of the solving method proposed.

2 Programming Model for Shipboard Power Network Planning

Shipboard power network programming is to plan the topological structure and layouts of electric nodes and power cables to ensure the optimal survivability of SPS, with the known conditions as follows:

- Layouts and usage of cabins;
- Layouts, quantity, capacity and load distribution of power plants;
- Layouts and electric parameters of loads known.

The decision variables are not mutually independent of each other. The layouts of power cables cannot be worked out before the network topological structure and layouts of electric nodes are planned. Therefore, a bi-level programming model is established to plan the shipboard power network. The master programming model has the power network topological structure and electric nodes layouts as the decision variables, and the optimal power system survivability as objective function. The slave one has the layouts of power cables as decision variables, and the minimum total length of power cables as objective function.

2.1 The Master Programming Model

The requirements on SPS survivability are to ensure the power supply of loads in combating ambient, the maximum running loads with power system regionally damaged while under attack and power supply continuity of vital loads with power system heavily damaged. Consequently, under the consideration of the importance of loads, the minimum mathematical expectation of loads out of service with power system damaged is set as the objective function of master programming model.

In order to calculate the value of objective function, the shipboard electrical loads are classified into vital ones and normal ones. Accordingly, the objective function of master programming model can be demonstrated as

$$\min V = \sum_{l_i \in L_{g1}} \frac{P_{g2}^{\max}}{P_{g1}^{\min}} \cdot p_{L,i} \cdot P_{L,i} + \sum_{l_j \in L_{g2}} p_{L,j} \cdot P_{L,j} \tag{1}$$

where, L_{g1} and L_{g2} are set of vital loads and normal loads respectively; $P_{L,i}$ is the rated power of load l_i; $p_{L,i}$ is the non-operating probability of load l_i; $P_{g2}^{\max}$ is the maximum value of rated power of normal loads; $P_{g1}^{\min}$ is the minimum value of rated power of vital loads.

As is shown in Eq. (1), with the same non-operating probabilities of loads, contribution of the outage of a vital load to V is not less that of an arbitrary normal load, even if its rated power is minimal. Obviously, the lower the value of V is, the better the survivability of SPS is.

The constraints of master programming model can be classified into types as follows:

- Constraints to the topological structure of power transmission network;
- Constraints to the topological structure of power distribution network;
- Constraints to the capacities of power cables;
- Constraints to the quantities of outlets of distribution boards;
- Constraints to the hierarchies of power distribution.

2.2   The Slave Programming Model

As the decision variables of slave programming model, layouts of power cables mean the laying routes of power cables. In this programming model, the minimum total length of power cables is set as objective function. To simplify the procedure of calculation, basic assumptions are proposed as below:

- Laying route of each power cable passes the geometric center of each related cabin;
- The laying direction of horizontally laid cables should parallel to or be across the keel-line;
- The laying direction of cables penetrating decks should be across the decks.

Let the cabins that cable *No. i* passes through in turn be $\{c_{i,1}, \ldots, c_{i,k}, \ldots, c_{i,S}\}$ and coordinates of geometric center of cabin $c_{i,k}$ be $(x_{c_{i,k}}, y_{c_{i,k}}, z_{c_{i,k}})$, according to the basic assumptions, the length of the cable section $(c_{i,k-1} \leftrightarrow c_{i,k})$ can be demonstrated as

$$l_{i,k-1} = \left| x_{c_{i,k-1}} - x_{c_{i,k}} \right| + \left| y_{c_{i,k-1}} - y_{c_{i,k}} \right| + \left| z_{c_{i,k-1}} - z_{c_{i,k}} \right| \tag{2}$$

Now that the length of cable c_i is

$$l_i = \sum_{j=1}^{S-1} l_{i,j} \tag{3}$$

Then the total length of cables is

$$L_T = \sum_{i=1}^{N} l_i = \sum_{i=1}^{N} \sum_{j=1}^{S-1} l_{i,j} \tag{4}$$

where N represents the quantity of power cables on the ship. Therefore, the objective function of slave programming model can be presented as

$$\min L_T = \sum_{i=1}^{N} \sum_{j=1}^{S-1} l_{i,j} \tag{5}$$

3 Improved GA in Shipboard Power Network Planning

3.1 Framework of Shipboard Power Network Planning

The standard GA serves as the solving method of slave programming of shipboard power network and the improved one is applied to solving the master programming. Flow chart of GA used for shipboard power network planning is shown in Fig. 1. Methods of coding [10] and coping with constraints [11] of programming models are pivotal techniques in the application of GA, which are expounded in detail vide infra.

3.2 Coding Mode for Master Programming

Shipboard power transmission network is composed of main distribution boards, jumper power cables, and intermediate electric nodes as well. As for the intermediate electric nodes, they not only transmit electric energy but also increase the number of connecting paths between arbitrary two distribution boards. Obviously, the quantity of intermediate electric nodes should be confirmed before running master programming. Assuming that connection between arbitrary two distribution boards can only be carried out through intermediate electric nodes and letting the number of distribution nodes be N, the number of intermediate electric nodes can be confirmed under circumstances as follows:

- $N = 1$: the number of intermediate electric nodes is 0;
- $N = 2$: the number of intermediate electric nodes is 2;
- $N \geq 3$: if the distribution boards can be connected with each other directly, according to the assumption proposed, the number of intermediate electric nodes is C_N^2.

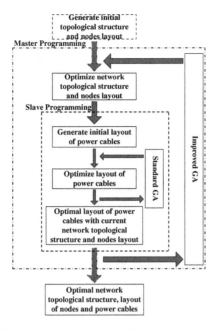

Fig. 1. Flow chart of power network planning process with GA

The coding of topological structure of power transmission network and intermediate electric nodes layouts are conducted with three types of matrices defined:

- Matrix A: This matrix is defined to describe the adjacent relationship between main distribution boards and intermediate electric nodes. Matrix element $a_{i,j} = 1$ if main distribution board *No. i* is connected to intermediate electric node *No. j*, and $a_{i,j} = 0$ if not. Apparently, dimension of A is $N \times C_N^2$.
- Matrix B: This matrix is defined to describe the adjacent relationship between intermediate electric nodes. Matrix element $b_{i,j} = 1$ if intermediate electric nodes *No. i* and *No. j* are connected by power cable, and $b_{i,j} = 0$ if not. Obviously, dimension of B is $C_N^2 \times C_N^2$ and B is symmetric. Thus, just the upper triangular zone of B can describe the adjacent relationship between intermediate electric nodes completely.
- Vector C: This vector is to describe layouts of intermediate electric nodes. Vector element c_i represents the number of cabin where intermediate electric node *No. i* is laid. Therefore, the dimension of C is C_N^2.

Figure 2 shows the zonal shipboard power transmission network and parts of its coding scheme. There are 6 intermediate electric nodes in this network, where intermediate electric node *No. 5* and *No. 6* are not drawn in this figure because they are not connected to any nodes.

Shipboard power distribution network is a typical radial network, where each sub-distribution board has only one other distribution board above it electrically. It is assumed that the quantity of sub-distribution boards equals to that of cabins, and

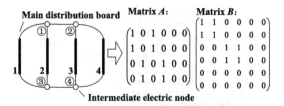

Fig. 2. Sketch map and partial coding of zonal shipboard power transmission network

sub-distribution boards and cabins are of one to one correspondence. Thus, when topological structure of power distribution network is planned, the planning of layouts of sub-distribution boards is also completed at the same time.

Let the quantities of sub-distribution boards, loads and vital loads be N_d, N_l and N_v respectively, the topological structure and sub-distribution boards layout of power distribution network can be described by three types of defined vectors:

- Vector D: This vector is defined to describe the connective relationship between sub-distribution boards. Vector element d_i represents the number of sub-distribution board that is electrically above sub-distribution board *No. i*, and is of the dimension of N_d. Thus, matrix D related to power distribution network shown in Fig. 3 is $(8,8,4,0,8,7,0,0,4)^T$.

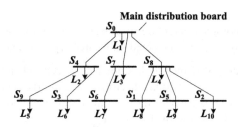

Fig. 3. Sketch map of radial shipboard power distribution network

- Vector E: This vector describes the power supply of normal loads and regular power supply of vital loads. Vector element e_i represents the number of sub-distribution board that load *No. i* is connected to. The dimension of E is N_l. Thus, the corresponding E of power distribution network shown in Fig. 3 is $(0,4,7,8,9,3,6,1,5,2)^T$.
- Vector F: This vector indicates the setting of backup power supply of vital loads, and has the dimension of N_v. Vector element f_i represents the number of the sub-distribution board as the backup power supply of vital load *No. i*.

3.3   Repairing Operator

The mutation operator and crossover operator in GA may generate plenty of infeasible solutions that disobey constraints to topological structure of shipboard power network.

Penalty function method is the traditional method to solve this problem. However, if the penalty term is set too weak, there still will be some infeasible solutions generated. If the penalty term is set too strong, the competiveness of superior individuals will be weakened, thus operational efficiency of GA will decline. As a result, this method does not fit for shipboard power network planning. Therefore, the repairing operator is proposed and added to standard GA in order to deal with infeasible solutions. This operator has no additional requirements on coding mode and operation of crossover operator and mutation operator.

In shipboard power transmission network, main distribution boards are connected to each other via intermediate electric nodes and jumper power cables. Two kinds of following infeasible solutions will be generated due to the operation of crossover operator and mutation operator:

- Isolated node: This kind of nodes represents the non-reference main distribution boards which are not connected to any other intermediate electric nodes.
- Isolated island: The connected domain that does not contain reference main distribution board.

The reference main distribution board mentioned above represents the main distribution board that is labeled beforehand. Operational procedures of the repairing operator are as follows:

- Repairing the isolated nodes: Connect the isolated node searched out to an arbitrary intermediate electric node to turn it into isolated island or make it interconnected with reference main distribution board. Run this step repeatedly until there is no isolated node in the power transmission network;
- Repairing the isolated island: Select one intermediate electric node randomly in the isolated island found and connect it to any node in the connected domain containing reference main distribution board. Run this step repeatedly until there is no isolated island in the power transmission network.

Procedures of repairing the infeasible solutions in power transmission network are shown in Fig. 4, where main distribution board S_0 is the reference one.

In Shipboard power distribution network, each sub-distribution board has a corresponding distribution board related to it. That is to say, each sub-distribution board has a corresponding feeder line related to it. Assuming that there be N_S distribution boards, there will be $N_S - 1$ feeder lines in power distribution network. As for the

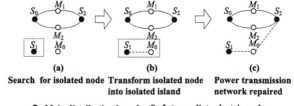

(a)
Search for isolated node

(b)
Transform isolated node into isolated island

(c)
Power transmission network repaired

● –Main distribution board   ○ –Intermediate electric node

Fig. 4. Operational procedure of repairing operator acted on intermediate electric nodes

domain that does not contain main distribution board, it will contain N_d feeder lines, assuming that there be N_d distribution boards. It means this domain must contain a "loop". Procedures of repairing loops are as follows:

- Search for the domain containing main distribution board in the power distribution network, and let this domain be represented as T;
- Search for the loops in the network. Randomly select one distribution board in the loop searched out, and connect it to an arbitrary distribution board in T and return to the step 1). If there is no loop found in the network, it means repairing of power distribution network is finished.

This repairing procedure is shown in Fig. 5, where distribution board *No. 0* is the main distribution board.

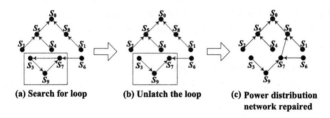

(a) Search for loop   (b) Unlatch the loop   (c) Power distribution network repaired

Fig. 5.   Operational procedure of repairing operator acted on sub-distribution boards

3.4   Equivalence Operator

According to the assumption proposed above, quantity of intermediate electric nodes and sub-distribution boards are set beforehand. It means they will not vary throughout the whole planning process if there is no additional operation is conducted, which goes back on the aims of shipboard power network planning. Therefore, the equivalence operator is proposed and added to GA to solve this problem.

As for the power transmission network, equivalence operator acts on three kinds of intermediate electric nodes as follows:

- Intermediate electric node that is not connected with main distribution board. This kind of nodes takes no efforts, so the equivalence operator removes them directly.
- Intermediate electric node that is connected to only one jumper power cable. This kind of nodes does not play a part in transmitting and redistributing electrical energy, so the equivalence operator removes them directly.
- Intermediate electric node that is connected to only two jumper power cables. This node equals to one jumper power cable, so the equivalence operator remove this node and connect the two nodes connected to it with one jumper power cable.

The operational procedures of equivalence operator acted on intermediate electric nodes are shown in Fig. 6.

As for power distribution network, equivalence operator acts on two kinds of sub-distribution boards as follows:

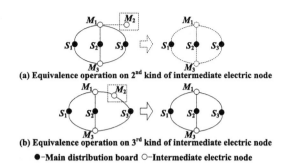

(a) Equivalence operation on 2nd kind of intermediate electric node

(b) Equivalence operation on 3rd kind of intermediate electric node

●-Main distribution board   ○-Intermediate electric node

Fig. 6. Operational procedure of equivalence operator acted on intermediate electric nodes

- The sub-distribution board which has no normal loads and sub-distribution boards connected to it and is not set as the regular power supply of vital loads. If there exists vital load having it as backup power supply, the equivalence operator will set the distribution board that is electrically above the sub-distribution board mentioned as the backup power supply of this load and remove this distribution board.
- The sub-distribution board which has only one sub-distribution board below it electrically and no normal loads connected to it, and is not set as the regular power supply of vital loads. If there exists vital load having it as backup power supply, set the distribution board that is electrically above the sub-distribution board mentioned as the backup power supply of this load, interconnect the distribution boards above it and below it respectively, and remove this board.

The operational procedures of equivalence operator acted on sub-distribution boards are shown in Fig. 7.

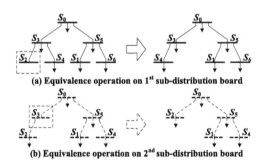

(a) Equivalence operation on 1st sub-distribution board

(b) Equivalence operation on 2nd sub-distribution board

Fig. 7. Operational procedure of equivalence operator acted on sub-distribution boards

3.5   Coding Mode for Slave Programming

According to the network topological structure and nodes layouts worked out in master programming, layouts of terminals of power cables can be known. Rest on the constraints of slave programming model, search for backup layout plans of each power cable and coding them with binary code. Combine the related binary code of backup layouts of each power cable together in sequence and the coding of power cables can be obtained.

4   Computational Test

A computational test is conducted on a simplified existed warship. This ship has the length of 195 m, width of 30 m, 3 decks with 5 m deck height and contains 39 cabins among which cabin No. 12, No. 21 and No. 36 are not allowed to be laid with power cables. Each cabin is cuboid and tridimensional measurements of cabins- length(L), width(W) and height(H), are shown in Table 1. This power system contains 2 power plants, and the generators in the two plants are laid in cabin No. 13 and No. 34 respectively. The two plants all have the capacity of 1.6 MW. There are 52 loads in this power system, where load No. 20, No. 26, No. 32 and No. 44 are vital ones, and the rest loads are normal ones. Rated power(P) and layouts of loads are shown in Table 2.

As is shown in Fig. 8, in the optimal design scheme of this shipboard power network, the two main distribution boards are connected together with two jumper power cables, which are laid along cabins of starboard and larboard respectively. Vital loads have the nearby distribution boards as regular power supplies and the distribution boards under the other plant as backup power supplies, as is shown in Table 3.

Table 1. Tridimensional measurements of cabins

Cabin	3-D size/m			Cabin	3-D size/m		
	L	W	H		L	W	H
1	15.00	20.00	5.00	21	20.00	15.00	5.00
2	20.00	22.00	5.00	22	10.00	30.00	5.00
3	20.00	22.00	5.00	23	25.00	25.00	5.00
4	27.00	22.00	5.00	24	45.00	15.00	5.00
5	24.00	11.00	5.00	25	30.00	15.00	5.00
6	24.00	11.00	5.00	26	15.00	15.00	5.00
7	25.00	25.00	5.00	27	20.00	30.00	5.00
8	30.00	15.00	5.00	28	11.00	15.00	5.00
9	30.00	15.00	5.00	29	9.00	15.00	5.00
10	15.00	30.00	5.00	30	20.00	15.00	5.00
11	20.00	15.00	5.00	31	20.00	30.00	5.00
12	20.00	15.00	5.00	32	10.00	15.00	5.00
13	10.00	30.00	5.00	33	10.00	15.00	5.00
14	10.00	30.00	5.00	34	10.00	30.00	5.00
15	20.00	30.00	5.00	35	15.00	30.00	5.00
16	10.00	30.00	5.00	36	9.00	15.00	5.00
17	10.00	15.00	5.00	37	11.00	15.00	5.00
18	10.00	15.00	5.00	38	20.00	15.00	5.00
19	15.00	30.00	5.00	39	10.00	30.00	5.00
20	20.00	15.00	5.00				

Table 2. Rated powers and layouts of loads

Load	Cab	P/kW	Load	Cab	P/kW	Load	Cab	P/kW
1	1	27	19	14	43	37	28	49
2	2	31	20	14	65	38	29	50
3	2	40	21	15	51	39	30	50
4	3	20	22	15	35	40	30	61
5	4	32	23	16	48	41	31	45
6	4	35	24	17	51	42	31	23
7	5	32	25	18	26	43	32	46
8	6	38	26	19	65	44	33	43
9	7	36	27	20	50	45	34	53
10	8	42	28	21	53	46	35	49
11	8	50	29	22	43	47	35	37
12	9	44	30	22	41	48	36	43
13	10	59	31	23	35	49	37	53
14	10	21	32	24	46	50	38	30
15	11	25	33	24	51	51	39	55
16	12	51	34	24	39	52	39	44
17	13	47	35	25	47			
18	13	35	36	27	37			

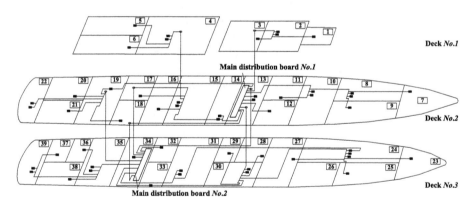

Fig. 8. Sketch map of optimal shipboard power network

Table 3. Normal and backup sources of vital loads

Load	Regular source		Backup source	
	Distribution board	Cabin	Distribution board	Cabin
20	1	13	10	15
26	11	19	1	13
32	7	24	13	31
44	2	34	8	28

As is shown in Table 4, compared with the best scheme in initial species group, performance of power system survivability of the planned scheme is optimized prominently. The mathematical expectation value of loads out of service is reduced by 32.0 %; total length of power cables is reduced by 40.8 %, and the scale of distribution boards is optimized to a certain extent. Additionally, in the iterative process of GA, 72.3 % of the individuals disobey the constraints in average and the repairing operator transforms them into feasible solutions totally.

Table 4. Indicators comparison of planning schemes

Schemes	Indicators		
	V/kW	L_T/m	Quantity of distribution boards below Plant *No. 1* & *No. 2*
Before planning	204.37	2132.0	19 & 20
After planning	138.97	1261.5	6 & 7

5 Conclusion

A bi-level model for shipboard power network planning is proposed, which has the optimal performance of power system survivability as the objective function. The master programming model has the topological structure and electric nodes layout as decision variables, and the minimum mathematical expectation of loads out of service with power system damaged as the objective function. The slave programming model has layout of power cables as decision variables and minimum total length of power cables as objective function.

Solve the problem of shipboard power network planning with GA and have it improved. Repairing operator is proposed to deal with infeasible solutions generated by traditional genetic operators, and equivalence operator is proposed to optimize the scale of electric nodes in the network. The computational test on an existing shipboard power network verifies the practicality and effectiveness of this planning method.

References

1. Merrill, H.M., Wood, A.J.: Risk and uncertainty in power system planning. Electr. Power Energy Syst. **13**, 81–90 (1991)
2. Romero, R., Monticelli, A., Garcia, A.: Test system and mathematical models for transmission network expansion planning. IEEE Proc. Gener. Transm. Distrib. **1**, 27–36 (2002)
3. Tang, Y.: Power distribution system planning with reliability modeling and optimization. IEEE Trans. Power Syst. **11**, 181–189 (1996)
4. Ramirez, J., Bernal, J.L.: Reliability and costs optimization for distribution networks expansion using an evolutionary algorithm. IEEE Trans. Power Syst. **16**, 111–118 (2001)

5. Zivi, E.: Distributed intelligence for automated survivability. In: ASNE Reconfiguration and Survivability Panel Session, pp. 283–287 (2005)
6. Bagley, D., Youngs, R.: Energy metric for platform systems resource management and survivability analysis. In: ASNE Reconfiguration and Survivability Panel Session, pp. 322–328 (2005)
7. Glaeser, J.: Specifying and assessing survivability in early stage ship design. In: ASNE Reconfiguration and Survivability Panel Session, pp. 126–134 (2005)
8. Edson, L.S., Hugo, A.G., Jorge, M.A.: Transmission network expansion planning under an improved genetic algorithm. IEEE Trans. Power Syst. **15**, 1168–1175 (2000)
9. Miranda, V., Ranito, J.V., Proenca, L.M.: Genetic algorithm in optimal multistage distribution network planning. IEEE Trans. Power Syst. **9**, 1927–1933 (1994)
10. De Jong, K.A.: An Analysis of the Behavior of a Class of Genetic Adaptive Systems. University of Michigan, Michigan (1975)
11. Bracken, J., Gill, J.M.M.: Mathematical programs with optimization problems in the constraints. Oper. Res. **21**(1), 37–44 (2004)

Modeling and Simulation of Four-Point Source Decoying System

Bai Fu-zhong[⊠], Cao Fei, and Tang Jun-yao

Rocket Force University of Engineering,
No.2, Tongxin Road, Baqiao District,
Xi'an 710025, China
942549997@qq.com

Abstract. This paper first analyzes the principle of four-point source decoying system to confront passive radar seeker (PRS) of anti-radiation missile (ARM). Then by establishing the decoying system model, the amplitude and phase of the compound electric field of various radiation sources in the PRS dynamic process are calculated and simulated, the simulation conclusion is analyzed. Finally the coordinates of the intersection point between the normal line of the synthetic wavefront with the ground are derived, and a quantitative simulation based on the system model is given. The simulation results show that the four-point source decoying system can not only protect the radar target, but also effectively avoid the bait attack.

Keywords: Four-point source decoy · Anti-Radiation Missile (ARM) · Bait · Compound electric field

1 Introduction

With the rapid development of modern science and technology, high-tech war has been an indisputable fact. ARM as a set of discovery, tracking and destroying radar in one of the hard-kill weapons is particularly important to win electromagnetic airpower in modern warfare, which plays an active role in the Vietnam War, the Gulf War and the Kosovo War, and it has been ground air defense radar "nemesis" and "killer". To survive and to play its effectiveness, radar must take measures to defend the ARM.

Active decoying system is a widely used and widely recognized as the effective method. Two-point source decoying system is generally used for theoretical analysis, which is not reliable and safe in practical application. Three-point source decoying system is a more practical active decoying system, that the safety performance of it than two-point source decoying system has increased, and easy to control, low cost. Four-point source decoying system is a good system to protect radar. With the distance of radiation field to ARM decreasing, the radar is easy to break away from the field of view of ARM, and ARM will track the three decoy synthetic field. So radar is in a safe area. Therefore, this paper mainly analyzes the four-point source decoying system.

© Springer Science+Business Media Singapore 2016
L. Zhang et al. (Eds.): AsiaSim 2016/SCS AutumnSim 2016, Part II, CCIS 644, pp. 180–187, 2016.
DOI: 10.1007/978-981-10-2666-9_18

2 Introduction to the Four Point Source

Four-point source decoying system is built on the basis of two inherent defects. One is low resolution that is aroused by the diameter limit of PRS. The other one is difficult to correct the flight attitude that is aroused by high speed in short distance. So, first of all, the principle of ARM passive radar seeker is analyzed.

2.1 Passive Radar Seeker (PRS) Principle

The main function of PRS is through carrier frequency, pulse width and pulse repetition frequency, signal modulation characteristics, pulse arrival time, pulse arrival characteristics of the radiation source signal determine signal sorting and target position. Once the ARM is launched, the effect of tracking and destroying the target is largely dependent on the direction finding capability of the seeker. PRS direction finding system is generally used in a monopulse system. PRS in order to meet the real-time performance, it is generally used in a monopulse direction finding system which does not require long integration time or demodulation processing 2. The methods of direction finding mainly include amplitude comparison monopulse direction finding, phase comparison monopulse direction finding, phase-amplitude comparison monopulse direction finding and holographic direction finding.

Amplitude comparison direction finding system precision is low, generally only do coarse system. Phase comparison direction finding system has the advantages of simple structure, high precision, good real-time performance, strong ability to adapt to the signal form. However, there is a contradiction between direction finding accuracy and direction finding angle ambiguity, namely the baseline is long, precision is high, but more prone to fuzzy point. Due to the limitation of the arm of the projectile diameter size, long baseline antenna can not be installed in the seeker. So generally the phase-amplitude comparison direction finding system is used to solve the problem of multi-valued ambiguity of phase comparison direction finding and the low accuracy of amplitude comparison direction finding. It is also widely used in ARM radar seeker. Spatial spectrum estimation is in vigorous development and research phase. Each finding methods have different advantages and disadvantages, and also depend on the specific circumstances in practical applications.

2.2 Four-Point Source Decoying System Analysis

The four-point source decoying system is the target radar signals and the three bait signal to interfere with the incoming ARM, so that the tracking and pointing point of ARM is located at a certern point of the target radar in the range of four-point source. So as to protect the function of radar target. Before PRS distinguishes each radiation source, the aiming direction of ARM toward the power centroid of four-point source decoying system. When the opening angle of ARM that reach each radiation source relative to itself is more than PRS minimum resolvable angle $\Delta\theta(\Delta\theta = 0.9\Delta\theta_R, \Delta\theta_R$ is the angle of resolution of PRS antenna, $\Delta\theta_R = 0.9\Delta\theta_{0.5}$, is the width of the antenna beam of PRS), ARM enters a stable state and PRS begins to deflect a radiation source. Because the missile at a high speed maneuvering flight conditions is not only difficult to timely adjust the attitude, but also can not aim the radiation source before touching the ground, which leads to be decoyed.

3   Four-Point Source Decoying System Model

The four-point source decoying system model is establishing shown in Fig. 1, X-axis points north, Z-axis perpendicular to the ground up, Y-axis is determined as the right guidelines. Target radar is located at the origin of coordinate $O(0,0,0)$, the coordinate of the bait 1 is $O_1(x_1, y_1, z_1)$, the coordinate of the bait 2 is $O_2(x_2, y_2, z_2)$, the coordinate of the bait 3 is $O_3(x_3, y_3, z_3)$, and ARM is located at $A(x_A, y_A, z_A)$. The radar signal received by the PRS is:

$$E_0 = E_{00} \cos(\omega_0 t - \frac{2\pi}{\lambda_0} R_0) \tag{1}$$

The bait signal received by the PRS is:

$$E_i = E_{0i} \cos(\omega_i t - \frac{2\pi}{\lambda_i} R_i + \varphi_{i0}) \tag{2}$$

In the formulas (1) and (2), E_{00} is the intensity peak of electric field of radar, and E_{0i} is the intensity peak of electric field of the i-th bait. ω_0 is the angle frequency of electric field of radar. ω_i is the angle frequency of electric field of the i-th bait. λ_0 is the wavelength of electric field of radar. λ_i is the wavelength of electric field of the i-th bait. R_0 is the distance from the radar to the PRS. R_i is the distance from the i-th bait to the PRS. φ_{i0} is the initial phase difference of the electric field between the i-th bait and the radar. R_0 and R_i can be calculated as:

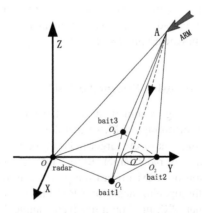

Fig. 1.   Four-point source decoying system mode

$$R_0 = (x_A^2 + y_A^2 + z_A^2)^{1/2} \tag{3}$$

$$R_i = [(x_A - x_i)^2 + (y_A - y_i)^2 + (z_A - z_i)^2]^{1/2} \tag{4}$$

The phase of each radiation source at the PRS for the synthetic field is:

$$\varphi = \arctan \frac{\sum\limits_{i=0}^{3} E_{0i} \sin \varphi_i}{\sum\limits_{i=0}^{3} E_{0i} \cos \varphi_i} \tag{5}$$

The amplitude of each radiation source at the PRS for the synthetic field is:

$$E = [(\sum\limits_{i=0}^{3} E_{0i} \sin \varphi_i)^2 + (\sum\limits_{i=0}^{3} E_{0i} \cos \varphi_i)^2]^{1/2} \tag{6}$$

In Eqs. (5) and (6), $\varphi_i = \omega_i t - \frac{2\pi}{\lambda_i} R_i + \varphi_{i0}$ $(i = 0, 1, 2, 3)$, $\varphi_{00} = 0$. The normal equation of synthetic wavefront is:

$$\frac{x - x_A}{\varphi'_{x_A}} = \frac{y - y_A}{\varphi'_{y_A}} = \frac{z - z_A}{\varphi'_{z_A}} \tag{7}$$

$\varphi'_{x_A}, \varphi'_{y_A}, \varphi'_{z_A}$ in the Eq. (7) is the partial derivative at point A (x_A, y_A, z_A). According to Eqs. (1) to (7) can be obtained:

$$x = \frac{\sum\limits_{i=0}^{3} \sum\limits_{k=0}^{3} E_{0i} E_{0k} \frac{x_k z_A - x_A z_k}{R_k \lambda_k} \cos(\varphi_i - \varphi_k)}{\sum\limits_{i=0}^{3} \sum\limits_{k=0}^{3} E_{0i} E_{0k} \frac{z_A - x_A}{R_k \lambda_k} \cos(\varphi_i - \varphi_k)} \tag{8}$$

$$y = \frac{\sum\limits_{i=0}^{3} \sum\limits_{k=0}^{3} E_{0i} E_{0k} \frac{y_k z_A - y_A z_k}{R_k \lambda_k} \cos(\varphi_i - \varphi_k)}{\sum\limits_{i=0}^{3} \sum\limits_{k=0}^{3} E_{0i} E_{0k} \frac{z_A - y_A}{R_k \lambda_k} \cos(\varphi_i - \varphi_k)} \tag{9}$$

Because the monopulse seeker of ARM tracks the normal direction of the electromagnetic wavefront, so Eqs. (8) and (9) can determine the tracking direction of the ARM flight at every time.

Assuming that the effective receiving area of PRS for each radiation signal is 1m2, the impedance of the receiving antenna is 1 Ω. A(x_A, y_A, z_A) is 3:

$$E_i = \sqrt{60 P_i G_i F(\theta_i)} \Big/ R_i \quad (i = 0, 1, 2, 3) \tag{10}$$

In Eq. (10), $F(\theta_i)$ is the normalized antenna function of the radiation source, θ_i is the angle between the line of ARM and the radiation source and the Z axis. P_i is the power of each radiation source. G_i is the antenna gain of each radiation source.

When the three baits radiation antenna is an ideal omnidirectional antenna, namely, the direction function $F(\theta_i)$ $(i = 1, 2, 3)$ is 1. The sinc function model is used to target radar antenna pattern:

$$F(\theta) = \begin{cases} \dfrac{\sin(\alpha\theta/\Delta\theta_0)}{\alpha\theta/\Delta\theta_0} & |\theta| \leq \theta_0 \\ g_1 \times \dfrac{\sin(\alpha(\theta+\theta_1)/\Delta\theta_0)}{(\alpha(\theta+\theta_1)/\Delta\theta_0)} & \theta_0 < |\theta| \leq \theta_2 \\ g_2 & |\theta| > \theta_2 \end{cases} \tag{11}$$

In Eq. (11), $\theta_0 = \Delta\theta_0$ is the right zero point of the mainlobe of unbiased beam, $\theta_1 = \Delta\theta_0 + \Delta\theta_1$ is the center of first sidelobe on the right side of unbiased beam. $\theta_2 = \Delta\theta_0 + 2\Delta\theta_1$ is the zero point of first sidelobe on the right side of unbiased beam. When the parameters is set to $\alpha = 2.783$, $\Delta\theta_0 = 2°$, $\Delta\theta_1 = 1°$, $g_1 = -20 \, \text{dB}$, $g_2 = -40 \, \text{dB}$. The antenna pattern is shown in Fig. 2.

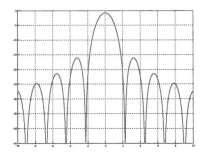

Fig. 2. Target radar antenna pattern

Suppose the distribution of the four-point source decoying system is as follows: target radar is located at the origin of the coordinate $O(0,0,0)$, the coordinate of the bait 1 is $O_1(100,300,0)$ (the unit is m, the same below), the coordinate of the bait 2 is $O_2(0,500,0)$, the coordinate of the bait 3 is $O_3(-100,300,0)$, ARM is located at A $(400,20000,300)$, the wavelength of each radiation source is 3 cm, the initial phase of the radiation signal is 0 °, 30 °, 45 °, 60 °, respectively. The radiation power of target radar is 50 kW, and the gain is 30 dB. The radiation power of each bait is 45 kW, and the gain is 32 dB. So the synthetic amplitude and phase of PRS in the flight process of ARM can be gotten in a four-point source decoying system. As shown in Figs. 3 and 4.

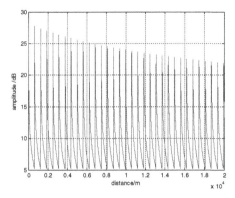

Fig. 3. Amplitude of the synthetic field at PRS

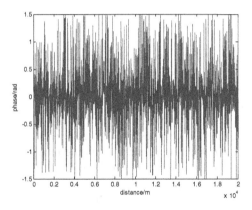

Fig. 4. Phase of the synthetic field at PRS

The amplitude of the composite field increases slowly with the decrease of the distance, and jumps once every 600 m. The phase of the composite field changes roughly between −1.5–1.5 rad. The effect of this change on the decoying system needs to be further studied.

4 Simulation Analysis of Effect for Four-Point Source Decoying System

In the case of the above model, the formulas (8) and (9) are simplified. So the coordinates O' of the intersection point between the normal of synthetic wavefront and the ground are getted.

$$x' = \frac{\frac{x_1\beta_1}{K_1}B + \frac{x_2\beta_2}{K_2}C + \frac{x_3\beta_3}{K_3}D}{A + \frac{\beta_1}{K_1}B + \frac{\beta_2}{K_2}C + \frac{\beta_3}{K_3}D} \tag{12}$$

$$y' = \frac{\frac{y_1\beta_1}{K_1}B + \frac{y_2\beta_2}{K_2}C + \frac{y_3\beta_3}{K_3}D}{A + \frac{\beta_1}{K_1}B + \frac{\beta_2}{K_2}C + \frac{\beta_3}{K_3}D} \tag{13}$$

And

$$A = 1 + \beta_1 \cos \Delta\varphi_{01} + \beta_2 \cos \Delta\varphi_{02} + \beta_3 \cos \Delta\varphi_{03}$$

$$B = \cos \Delta\varphi_{01} + \beta_1 + \beta_2 \cos \Delta\varphi_{12} + \beta_3 \cos \Delta\varphi_{13}$$

$$C = \cos \Delta\varphi_{02} + \beta_1 \cos \Delta\varphi_{12} + \beta_2 + \beta_3 \cos \Delta\varphi_{23}$$

$$D = \cos \Delta\varphi_{03} + \beta_1 \cos \Delta\varphi_{13} + \beta_2 \cos \Delta\varphi_{23} + \beta_3$$

$\beta_i = \frac{E_{0i}}{E_{00}}$ $(i = 1,2,3)$, $K_i = \frac{R_i\lambda_i}{R_0\lambda_0}$ $(i = 1,2,3)$, $\cos \Delta\varphi_{ik} = \cos(\varphi_i - \varphi_k)$ $(i,k = 0,1,2,3)$.

When ARM is far away from the target radar and the bait, it can be considered $E_{01} = E_{02} = E_{03}$, $\lambda_0 = \lambda_1 = \lambda_2 = \lambda_3$, $R_0 \approx R_1 \approx R_2 \approx R_3$.   So $\beta = E_{01}/E_{00} = E_{02}/E_{00} = E_{03}/E_{00}$, $K = K_1 = K_2 = K_3 = 1$. Assuming that $\cos \Delta\varphi_{ik}$ $(i,k = 0,1,2,3)$ obeys the uniform distribution in the range of 0 to 2π, so the value of x' and y' can be gotten. The calculation results are shown in Figs. 5 and 6.

From Figs. 5 and 6, the x/x_1 changes basically near zero, namely bait 1 and bait 3 in a safe area. When $\beta > 0.43$, x/x_1 increases with the increase of the β, namely the target radar farther away from the aiming point. Then it can be explained that the effect of the four-point source decoying system is obvious, so that the target radar and baits are safe. The model and layout of the active decoying system designed by the above mentioned are reasonable.

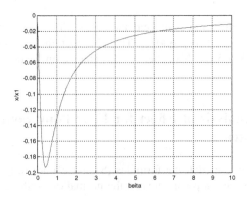

Fig. 5. Change of x/x_1

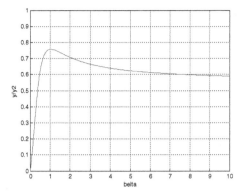

Fig. 6. Change of y/y_2

5   Concluding Remarks

Through the above analysis, the establishment of four source decoying system model need to consider the radiated power, antenna gain, antenna pattern, wavelength, phase difference and distance etc. from the radiation source to the PRS. In order to effectively reduce the hit probability of ARM to the target radar, the design and layout of bait can be optimized by modeling and simulation, and a more effective four-point source decoying system can be constructed. The research of this paper provides reference for the development of decoying system and the improvement of equipment.

References

1. Xiao, B.-L., Yang, L.-D., Zhang, C.: Method of decoy setting in two-source decoy radiation simulation test. Mod. Electron. Tech. **35**(1), 4–7 (2012)
2. Zou, J., Gao, K., Zhang, E.: Research on Angle Measurement Model of anti-radiation missiles PRS under coherent decoys. Przeglad Elektrotechniczy (2012)
3. Liu, K., Xu, S., Liu, M., Zou, N.: Study on compound electric field of four-point source decoy anti-radiation missile. J. Projectiles Rockers Missiles Guidance **30**(4), 244–246 (2010)
4. Li, X., Yuan, Z.-W., Yang, B.: Design of antiradar missile decoy system arrange project and decoying effect analysis. Syst. Eng. Electron. **27**(3), 439–445 (2005)
5. Zheng, M.-s., Ying, Z.-a.: Embattling mode simulation and evaluation of enticing system of multi-points sources for disturbing anti-radiation missile. Comput. Simul. **23**(6), 16–19 (2006)

The Optimized Design on the Tails of a Miniature Guided Rocket Projectile

XiaoQian An and JunFang Fan[✉]

Beijing Key Laboratory of High Dynamic Navigation Technology,
Beijing Information Science and Technology University, Beijing 100101, China
1308043309@qq.com, wyhffjf@bistu.edu.cn

Abstract. From local war fares in recent times, miniature guided munition is playing an increasingly important role in modern wars. This paper proposed a miniature guided rocket projectile which is portable by a soldier. In order to study the influence on the aerodynamic characteristics of the projectile effected by its tails, this article carried on a numerical simulation on the projectile under different kinds of tails, knife edge rear tails and large area flat rear tails, and the lift coefficients, drag coefficients and pitching moment coefficients of the projectile aerodynamic shape are obtained as well as flow field characteristics and the surface pressure distribution when the angle of attack changes. The results showed that, compared with the knife edge rear tails, the flat rear tails have effective enough windward area and wing surface shape which has a good resistance effect. The projectile has a good static stability and good aerodynamic characteristics with enough high lift within a small scope of angle of attack. This research will perform as the theoretical basis for the choice of miniature guided rocket tails and the analysis of its flying stability.

Keywords: Miniature guided rocket projectile · Knife edge rear tails · Large area flat rear tails · Aerodynamic characteristics

1 Introduction

In the recent massive high-tech local wars, such as the Gulf War, the Afghanistan war and the Iraq war, in order to destroy some fixed or moving armored targets, earthworks and some valuable point-targets, as a highly efficient precision-guided weapon, miniature guided rocket projectile can more meet the need of modern battles [1]. In addition, with the development of new materials, new technology and electronic information and precision guidance technology, some small load platforms have emerged, such as unmanned aerial vehicle and stealth aircraft, etc. Due to the limit of load capacity and

This work is supported by National Natural Science Foundation (NNSF) of China under Grant (61201417), the Beijing Nova Program (Z151100000315073, xxjh2015B041), the Importation and Development of High-Caliber Talents Project of Beijing Municipal Institutions (CIT&TCD201504055), and Outstanding Young Talents of Beijing (2015000026833ZK03).

© Springer Science+Business Media Singapore 2016
L. Zhang et al. (Eds.): AsiaSim 2016/SCS AutumnSim 2016, Part II, CCIS 644, pp. 188–195, 2016.
DOI: 10.1007/978-981-10-2666-9_19

mobility, miniature guided munitions with strict size and weight requirements are developed [2]. The structural design of miniature guided rocket projectile is simple, which have some advantages, such as small volume, light weight, low cost, high precision as well as small collateral damage and man-portable. When conflict occurs in the low intensity asymmetric warfare mountains, cities and other complex environments, miniature guided rocket projectiles can destroy armor protection system with a low cost and suppress enemy fire rapidly, which has become a decisive assault weapon in short-range combat.

With the same space size constraints, this paper proposed a miniature guided missile and completed its aerodynamic shape with knife edge rear tails and large area flat tails. Through fluid mechanics simulation, this article analyzed the aerodynamic characteristics within the scope of small angle of attack. The experimental results showed that, the axial folded flat rear tails can provide enough effective tail surface area and the wing surface can well increase the resistance, which can provide high overload for projectile and the projectile has good static stability. The results provide an important reference for the tail structure design of miniature guided missile.

2   Aerodynamic Layout Design

The shape layout design of missile is very important in the process of overall designing. According to the configuration and control characteristics of tails and rudders along the missile body, there are some typical layouts, such as tail type layout, koala type layout, normal type layout and duck type layout, etc. [3]. Considering the demand of launch system, this paper used the duck type which has a high control efficiency, and proposed a miniature guided rocket projectile with two kinds of tail structure, the radial folded knife edge rear tails and axial folded large area flat rear tails, as shown in Figs. 1 and 2.

Fig. 1. The projectile model with knife edge tails

Fig. 2. The projectile model with large area flat rear tails

From the figure above, the overall structural design of missile is simple, compact and slender. Along the longitudinal axis, the body is followed by Seeker, Electric steering engine (including four slices duck rudder), Inertial Measurement Unit (IMU), Bomb onboard computer system and On-board recorder cabin, Batteries, Warhead, Two levels of engine and Tail section. The projectile is launched by a launching canister, which can not only increase the reliability of the system and firing accuracy, but also can make it easy to transport, extend the storage period and reduce the space requirements. Especially, based on the emission requirements the slender projectile shape can effectively reduce the flight resistance, get a higher speed and have a wide firing range. From the development point of view, the design of the semicircle warhead has more advantages in subsonic flight conditions. Four slices duck tails can be embedded into the body at ordinary times and a certain sweepback design can not only improve the lift-to-drag ratio of missile moderately, but also increase firing range. After the engine working, the four canards can cooperate the four rear wings to provide balance and high lift for the projectile [4].

3   Aerodynamic Simulation

3.1   Pneumatic Geometric Modeling

The rear tails proposed in this paper are fixed by base, connecting shaft and the torsional spring and stay in folding state at ordinary times. In order to optimize the tail structure design, it needs analyzing the flight characteristics of the projectile with two kinds of tail structure. Within a small scope of angle of attack, the air flow field around the missile is very complicated and the accurate aerodynamic parameters are very difficult to obtain though theoretical analysis method. At the same time, the traditional wind tunnel test has a long cycle and a high cost in many flight conditions. In recent years, with the rapid development of computer technology, it is possible to study such problems using computational fluid dynamics numerical simulation method [5].

First of all, according to the geometry size of basic structure components of the missile, import the corresponding geometric point, connect the each section point into line, and then rotate the line into surface and expand surface to body, Finally, though the Boolean operations a miniature guided missile model is realized. The three-dimensional model of missile body with the knife edge rear tails is shown below. (The missile body model with large area flat rear tails is in the same way) (Fig. 3).

3.2   The Meshing

We assume that the flow field around the projectile is steady and invariable under different flight conditions. In order to describe the flow field around truly, it is very reasonable using the unstructured grid method. Based on the aerodynamic shape and flow field characteristics the grid density is set. As the key parts to provide the aerodynamic force of missile, the tails shape is more complex, thus we can moderately increase grid density to improve the calculation accuracy [6]. The boundary of the entire outer layer flow field is 10 times long the body model and the meshing is shown in Fig. 4.

Fig. 3. 3-D modeling   **Fig. 4.** The flow field grid

3.3   The Numerical Simulation

3.3.1   Flying Conditions

- The Mach number $Ma = 0.5, 0.7$;
- The canard deflection angle $\delta = 0°, 4°, 6°, 8°$;
- The angle of attack $\alpha = 2°, 4°, 6°, 8°$.

3.3.2   The Simulation Method

The simulation uses density solver, explicit format finite volume method and relatively simple Spalart-Allmaras single equation turbulent model. When we carry on the calculation, the default Roe-FDS flux difference method and Second Order Upwind to discrete space method are introduced. At same time, the Aerodynamic Monitor is used to calculate residual error and discriminate the convergence of the solution [7].

4   The Simulation Results

4.1   The Static Stability Analysis

The miniature guided rocket projectile proposed by this paper is fired by two levels of engine. The first level engine is used to send the missile out safely, and then the missile opens its canard fins and flies into a safe distance with no control. A moment later, the secondary engine is started which it is used to push the projectile reaching top speed and then the canard fins are expanded. In this phase, the projectile stays in low stability. Thus choosing the state ($\delta = 0°$, $\alpha = 2°$) and the simulation results are as follows,

Table 1. The aerodynamic characteristics of missile under two wing structure when $\delta = 0°, \alpha = 2°$

Wing type	Lift coefficient	Drag coefficient	Pressure center coefficient	Pitching moment coefficient	Static stability
Knife edge rear tails (case 1)	0.2636	0.4792	0.4526	−0.0079	The static stable missile (1.3 %)
Large edge flat rear tails (case 2)	0.3614	0.5063	0.4726	−0.0146	The static stable missile (3.5 %)

According to the simulation results, we can see that pitching moment coefficients of the missile under two kinds of rail structure are negative, thus the missile is static stable and the static stability of the missile under two rear tail structure were 1.3 % and 3.5 % respectively. It is easy to conclude that, compared to the knife edge rear tails, the flat tails are helpful to make pressure center back and improve the static stability. According to the theoretical research and engineering practice experience, the static stability of the missile directly affects the stability and mobility of the missile. Generally, the missile with bigger static stability will have better movement stability and poor mobility. On the contrary, the missile with smaller static stability will have poor movement stability and better mobility [8]. Therefore, from Table 1, within the same spatial structure launch tube, the large area flat wing structure can provide projectile with high lift and high static stability that could satisfy the requirement of mobility and maneuverability.

4.2   Lift and Resistance Characteristics

The lift and drag coefficient change curve of the projectile under two kinds of tail structures are shown in Figs. 5 and 6. It can be seen that, within same Mach number and different canard deflection angles, the lift and drag coefficients of the rocket projectile are sensitive to angle of attack increasing with the increase of angle of attack.

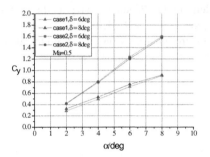

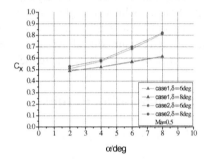

Fig. 5. The lift coefficient change curve   **Fig. 6.** The drag coefficient change curve

At the same time, within the same flight condition, the lift-to-drag effect of flat tails is higher than that of the knife edge tails. Combing with the principles of missile flight, it can be concluded that the windward area and the surface shape of tails have great influence on the lift and drag produced by the missile. The bigger the exposed effective area, and the stronger the lift and drag coefficients [9].

In addition, the surface flow field and pressure diagram of the projectile under two kinds of tail structure are shown below.

From Figs. 7 and 8, as the structure of knife edge tail is complex, when the missile flies in the subsonic speed, the mutual influence between tail blade and body will make the flow field around projectile more complex, and the shock wave generated by the air flow congestion will make the lift coefficient small; while the missile under the flat tail structure almost has no choked air flow, so this tail structure can provide high enough lift for the projectile.

Fig. 7. The longitudinal flow field under two kinds of tail structure

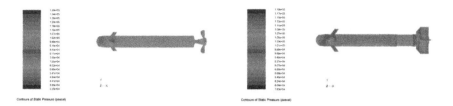

Fig. 8. The longitudinal constant pressure diagram under two kinds of tail structure

4.3 Pitching Moment Characteristics

From what has been discussed above, the flat tails is superior to the knife edge tail structure. Therefore, we selected the flat tail structure for further analyzing the aerodynamic characteristics, and the results are as follows:

From Fig. 9, we can see that the pitching moment coefficients of the missile under the flat tails reduce with the increase of angle of attack, and the values are sensitive to angle of attack varying from positive to negative, which clearly shows the changing process of projectile from unstable into stable state.

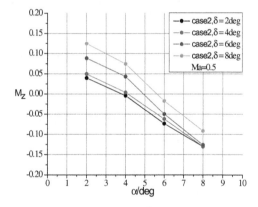

Fig. 9. The change curve of pitching moment coefficient under the large area flat rear tails

From the Fig. 10, within the same Mach number, the balance angles of attack increase linearly with the increase of the rudder deflection, while they tend to be same under the same canard deflection angle and different Mach number. It can be seen that when $\delta = 8°$, then the maximum of balance angle of attack is about $5.6°$, and the missile still has a good control effect. According to the flight mechanics and the lift coefficients resulted from the simulation, when the missile flying at zero meter altitude and $Ma = 0.5$, the maximum available overload is not less than 2.5 g, while the missile flying at 5000 meters altitude, the maximum available overload is about 1.2 g. So within a small scope of angle of attack, this miniature guided rocket projectile has high mobility, which can meet the needs of guide control in the entire shooting.

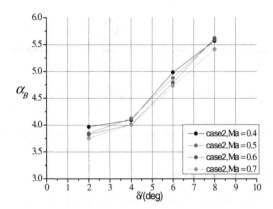

Fig. 10. The change curve of balance angle of attack under the large area flat rear tails

5   Conclusion

This paper completed aerodynamic shape design of a miniature guided rocket projectile under two kinds of tail structure. Though analyzing its aerodynamic characteristics by means of the aerodynamic simulation calculation, we can draw the following conclusions:

(1) The axial folded flat tail wings can provide enough effective tail surface area, which can not only increase the resistance but also can provide a high overload for projectile. At the same time, with the rear rail structure, the projectile has good static stability

(2) Due to the folding way limitation, the radial folded knife edge rear tails is relatively close to the missile body, which leads that it is difficult to design the wing surface shape. At the same time, the missile has low stability for the strong interference among the wing surface, and the missile has low resistance effect.

This research will have a certain guiding significance on the optimized design of the miniature guided rocket projectile rear tails.

References

1. Song, Y.-R., Jiang, Q., Guan, S.-Y.: Foreign small multi-purpose missile development. J. Tactical Missile Technol. **6**, 6–11 (2012)
2. Sun, B.-C., Fan, J.-F.: The guidance system design of strapdown small munitions. J. Infrared Laser Eng. **43**(6), 1960–1965 (2014)
3. Gu, L.-X., Wen, B.-H.: Missile General Design Principle. Northwestern Polytechnical University Press, Xi'an (2004)
4. Silton, S.I., Fresconi, F.: Effect of canard interactions on aerodynamic performance of a fin-stabilized projectile. J. Spacecraft Rockets **52**(5), 1430–1442 (2015)
5. Chen, W.-D., Tang, X.-P., Zeng, K., Wu, X.-D.: The missile aerodynamic characteristics based on engineering and numerical method. J. Aerosp. Comput. Technol. **42**(3), 1–5 (2012)

6. Hu, Z.-P., Liu, R.-Z., Guo, R.: The influence from two typical tail shape on the aerodynamic characteristics of without umbrella end sensitive. J. Nanjing Univ. Sci. Technol. **36**(5), 739–744 (2012)
7. Yu, Y.: The Introductory and Advanced Tutorial of FLUENT. Beijing Institute of Technology Press, Beijing (2008)
8. Guo, F.-T., Wang, C.-Q., Guo, J.-Z.: The theoretical study about the impact of RSS on maneuverable missile overall performance. J. Tactical Missile Technol. (6), 4–7 (2008)
9. Zhou, Z.-C., Zhao, R.-X.: The aerodynamic characteristics of smart bullet experimental with different tail. Exp. Fluid Mech. **24**(4) (2010)

The Customized Human Body Modeling and Its Application in Damage Model Simulation

Yidi Gao and Xiajun Jiang[(✉)]

College of Computer Science and Technology,
Nanjing University of Aeronautics and Astronautics, Nanjing, China
{gaoyidi,xiajunja}@nuaa.edu.cn

Abstract. Human body customization is an important task in computer graphics and computer simulation recently. The existing human body modeling methods may generate distorted model or generate a human body model that does not match the target measurements. These shortcomings are improved in this paper. This human body modeling module includes two parts: analyzing the linear relationship between human body shapes and measurements, and human shape modeling according to the target measurements. Instead of analyzing the linear relationship between measurements and the whole human body shapes, we segment each model into 16 rigid parts, and learn the mapping between 3D body shapes of each part and their measurements. By using the above method, we can obtain a new human body model with the control of target measurements. The reconstructed human models are used as infantry battle formation in the damage simulations.

Keywords: Human body modeling · Anthropometry · Damage model

1 Introduction

In recent years, with the continuous development of the theory and technology in virtual reality field, the 3D human body modeling has become an important task in animation and computer graphics. Virtual human is the representation of the geometric characteristics and behavior characteristics of human in the virtual environment (space generated by computer), 3D human body has become more and more deeply and widely used in many fields, such as sports, fashion design, animation and game production. Therefore, the need for customized 3D human body model has been increased.

Since human body modeling is used more and more in different applications, many methods have been proposed consequently to customize human body models. However, it is still nontrivial to quickly and easily generate high-quality body models with simple specifications. The main content of this paper is to propose a method that can easily generate personalized human body model with 7 human measurements, and these generated models are used as infantry battle formation in the damage model simulations. According to the human body measurements, our method generates a human body model based on a scanned human body example dataset, which improves

© Springer Science+Business Media Singapore 2016
L. Zhang et al. (Eds.): AsiaSim 2016/SCS AutumnSim 2016, Part II, CCIS 644, pp. 196–206, 2016.
DOI: 10.1007/978-981-10-2666-9_20

the accuracy of the generated human body model. We segment each example model into 16 parts to increase the diversity of the training dataset of human body model greatly, because these body parts from different examples can be combined into one body model. The method in this paper can also be used to generate the human body model in a more precise way.

The rest of the paper is organized as follows. We firstly review the related work in Sect. 2. And secondly we introduce our method and its application in Sects. 3 and 4. We demonstrate the experimental results in Sect. 5. Finally the conclusion of this paper and discussion of the future work is given in Sect. 6.

2   Related Work

In this section, we describe the details and limitations of the existing methods for generating customized human models in different applications.

In the garment computer aided design (GCAD) field, it is necessary to have a model that represents the individual customer's body shape and dimensions [1]. In the late 1980s, whole body scanner system was introduced to the clothing industry [2]. After that, the human body measurement technology has developed from manual method to automatic method, contact type to non-contact type. Anthropometric sizing surveys have been carried out world-widely using body scanners. There exist a lot of human body example datasets, such as SizeUSA dataset and CAESAR dataset. The accuracy of the scanned customer's human body is high, but it needs expensive professional equipment and customers must go to a specific spot to have their bodies scanned. So researchers proposed example-based human body modeling method, which is wildly used in recent years. This kind of method usually constructs human body by analyzing the distribution of real human body shapes scanned by scanner systems. Zhu et al. [1] proposed a human body customization method based on orthogonal-view monocular photos. They used two customer's orthogonal-view images to extract the measurements of user. And then they built RBF networks to learn the mapping from 2D size features to 3D shape features. Finally a developed deformation algorithm was used to build a high-resolution model. Zhang et al. [3] also used example-based human body modeling method. Based on the scanned example meshes, they created an initial 3D model using the example-oriented radial basis function model that maps the set of 30 measurements estimated from several input measurements to the body shape space. And this initial 3D model was refined by constrained optimization to create the target model.

3D human body model also has been wildly used in the applications of motion simulation and animation. A human body model in these kinds of applications needs to model the human body's shape and posture variation at the same time. The SCAPE model is a popular framework for modeling human body in different shapes and poses. It aligned a template model with each mesh in the training dataset and then modeled the rigid and non-rigid deformation component. Shape deformation component using principal component analysis (PCA) modeled shape differences across different individuals [4]. But SCAPE model still has drawbacks, it only considers a single subject in different poses, which means the non-rigid deformations are only considered as a function of pose without taking the physique differences from person to person into account. Therefore, visual artifacts may occur when transferring deformations from a masculine to a non-masculine person. To solve this problem, Hasler et al. [5] proposed a statistical model that encode both shape and pose in the rotation and translation invariant surface encoding. As a result, people in different shape may cause different deformation when their poses are the same. These two popular methods can estimate the poses and shapes of naked meshes, which are not wildly used in virtual reality applications. Based on Hasler's work, Neophytou and Hilton [6] proposed a three layered model of human body and garment deformation. This kind of modeling method is able to model human shape, pose and garment. Firstly, they used 3D human body models obtained by scanning human subjects in tight clothes in a variety of poses to train the shape and pose deformation. And then they used animated mesh sequences of dressed actors to train the garment deformation. It considered garment deformations as the residual transformations between a naked mesh and the dressed mesh of the same subject. Finally they synthesized new dressed meshes with the information of pose, shape and garment of new subjects.

Human body modeling also plays an important role in anthropometry and ergonomics. As mentioned above, anthropometric sizing surveys can be done using body scanners. Koo et al. [7] selected 63 anthropometric landmarks and manually extract the 3D position of these landmarks from each example model. They were able to extract 13 anthropometric measurements with the help of landmarks and reshape human body model through these measurements. Lai et al. [8] proposed a method that extracts body size based on point cloud data. This method segmented the de-noised human body in standard coordinate into 6 parts and automatically recognized three kinds of human landmarks: the global extreme points, the local extreme points and the points that do not have obvious characteristics. The human body measurements can be calculated based on the identified relative landmarks. Tsoli et al. [9] proposed model-based anthropometry method to estimate the measurements of 3D body models in both standing and sitting poses. They extracted features including limb lengths, circumferences, and statistical features of global shape from the registered models rather than from the scanned models. They also learned a mapping from these features to measurements using regularized linear regression. They proved that the global shape features of human body model are good for predicting linear measurements with experiments.

3   Human Body Modeling Method

In this section, we introduce the human body modeling method in our application. In order to improve the existing human body modeling methods, we propose a new method that is able to accurately and fully reflect the human body shape characteristic to build customized human body model. And the steps of this method are summarized as follows (Fig. 1):

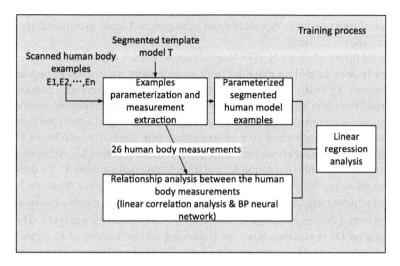

Fig. 1. Outline of our modeling methodology

1. We extract 26 measurements from each registered 3D human body example and then segment each example mesh into 16 parts. According to the definition of the "China adult human body size" (GB10000-88), we manually extract 35 anthropometric landmarks on the scanned surface. So that the set of 26 human body measurements can be extracted from each mesh model automatically based on these landmarks. By calculating convex hull length and breadth of cross sections which contain the landmark points and are perpendicular to the skeleton, we are able to obtain the full measurement set. According to the landmarks and key measurements, the models are divided into 16 rigid regions: head, breast, waist, hip and two thighs, calves, feet, forearms, upper arms and hands. The landmarks and measurements are shown in Fig. 2. After obtaining the full measurement set, statistical analysis on these measurements is done to model the linear correlation between different kinds of human measurements via Pearson correlation coefficient:

$$r_{i,j} = \frac{1}{n-1} \sum_{k=1}^{n} \left(\frac{m_k^i - \bar{m}^i}{s_{mi}} \right) \left(\frac{m_k^j - \bar{m}^j}{s_{mj}} \right), \tag{1}$$

where $r_{i,j}$ is the linear correlation between measurement m_i and m_j, s is the standard deviation of each measurement and n is the number of examples in training dataset. We choose the pairs of measurements with strong linear relationship as the input and output pairs, and use linear regression to model their correlation. While selecting the input measurements, we need to guarantee that the linear relationship between the input measurements is weak and the input measurement should be easy to measure from people. After obtaining the measurements that have strong linear relationship with the input measurements, we use BP neural networks to build the non-linear relationship mapping between the input measurements and other measurements.

The set of measurements extracted from examples and input measurements in bold type are shown in Table 1.

2. Statistical information analysis of shape features on each rigid body part of example meshes is done to build a mapping from measurement parameters to human shape parameters. We firstly determine the type of control measurement parameter for each rigid region in a way similar to [10] and obtain the deformation parameters of all regions. A template model is used as a reference model to obtain the parametric representation of each rigid part of examples. Our method is similar to Hasler's encoding pattern: we encode each triangle as a transformation U_i and then split up the transformation into a rotation R_i and a stretching deformation S_i. To construct a relative encoding for the rotation matrix R_i, we use the relative rotations between pairs of adjacent triangles: $R_{i,j} = R_i \cdot R_j^{-1}$. Then we convert relative rotation matrix and stretching deformation matrix to one 15×1 vector d_i for triangle i. The shape deformation D_k is parameterized by combining all the vectors of triangles in part k. Then we use principal component analysis (PCA) to analyze the shape features of each part. Linear regression is used to learn the linear mapping between the measurements of each part and local shape features.

3. Customized model generation. Users can input 7 measurements to generate a customized human body model. Firstly, we use trained BP neural network and linear function to estimate the full set of 26 measurements from 7 input measurements. Secondly, through the linear mapping learned from step 2, the deformation parameters of the human body are calculated, and the initial model is obtained according to the measurement set. Finally, we modify the generated new model with a non-linear optimal method. The generated model is projected on 3D space, and adjustment is done to reduce the measurement error by changing the position of landmarks and the corresponding points on key measurements.

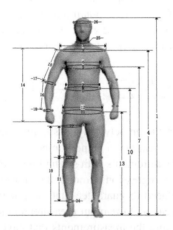

Fig. 2. Landmarks and anthropometric measurements extracted from each model. Red dots represent landmarks at the back of model. (Color figure online)

4   Application in Damage Model Simulation

We adapt the customized human bodies generated by the proposed method into the damage modeling for a kind of grenade. In the simulation, hundreds of fragments of the grenade scatter from the explosive point, and some fragments can hit the bodies in the generated battle formation.

The simulation process of the damage model using customized human bodies is shown in Fig. 3. Firstly, we input 7 anthropometric measurements for each human body, and they are: height, shoulder girth, breast girth, waist girth, hip girth, arm length, neck girth. Then, we use our human body modeling algorithm to generate customized human bodies. The process of this step is shown in Fig. 4. These generated bodies consist of triangular meshes and surfaces. Next, we generate the infantry battle formation needed by the damage simulation. Each triangular battle formation includes three customized human bodies. Finally, the triangular meshes of each human body are used to calculate whether a grenade fragment hit the corresponding body or not.

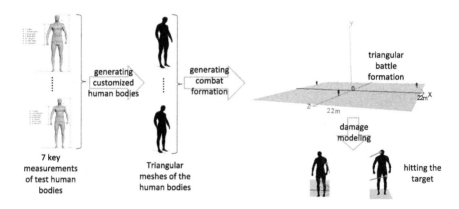

Fig. 3. Simulation process of the damage model using customized human bodies.

In the damage simulation, the fragment trajectories are defined as rays, and the origin of the rays is the explosive point. When a fragment hits the human model, a collision between the trajectory ray and a triangular mesh of the human model can be tested. Figure 4 shows such collision detection. A triangular mesh is composed of three vertices: P0, P1 and P2. P is any point in the interior or edge of the triangle. Parameters u and v satisfy the following conditions: (1) u >= 0, (2) v >= 0, (3) u + v <= 1. The equation of point P is defined as follows.

$$P = (1 - u - v)P_0 + uP_1 + vP_2 \qquad (2)$$

The equation of the point P on the ray is also defined as follows.

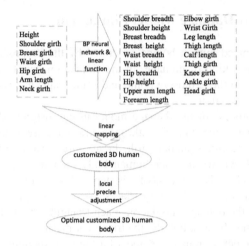

Fig. 4. Customized human body modeling based-on 7 selected anthropometric measurements

$$P = O + Dt \tag{3}$$

When the two equations are equal, the ray intersects with the triangle. Figure 4 and Eq. 4 show such condition. Moore and Wilhelms [11] provided the details of the above algorithm (Fig. 5).

$$O + Dt = (1 - u - v)P_0 + uP_1 + vP_2 \tag{4}$$

Figure 6 shows the 9 reconstructed human models of the infantry battle formation in a damage model simulation. The simulation space is a 110 m *110 m rectangle.

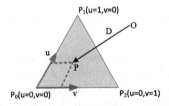

Fig. 5. Collision detection between a triangular mesh and a ray

5 Experiments and Results

In this section, the results of the human body modeling method proposed in this paper are presented. We use the data set proposed by Hasler et al. [5], and use the scanned male body models as the training data set. We select 9 scanned male models as the test dataset, of which the height ranges from 165 cm to 190 cm and the body mass index (BMI) is in normal range.

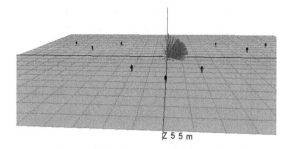

Z 5 5 m

Fig. 6. Three triangular battle formations and one explosive point.

Table 1. Measurements for 9 selected humans.

	No1 (mm)	No2 (mm)	No3 (mm)	No4 (mm)	No5 (mm)	No6 (mm)	No7 (mm)	No8 (mm)	No9 (mm)
Height	**1904.51**	**1869.96**	**1834.76**	**1805.79**	**1776.92**	**1735.26**	**1797.38**	**1755.51**	**1654.04**
Shoulder girth	**1134.11**	**1091.87**	**1102.08**	**1097.3**	**1082.51**	**932.886**	**1078.34**	**1081.42**	**1064.56**
Shoulder height	1582.32870	1533.87378	1504.88352	1481.02422	1457.24727	1432.93664	1474.09785	1439.61427	1356.04492
Shoulder breadth	466.29171	459.15661	445.92630	452.92458	443.45280	429.40440	441.75303	437.05897	425.64242
Breast girth	**962.942**	**958.81**	**974.812**	**958.571**	**958.222**	**876.562**	**977.607**	**1000.97**	**959.665**
Breast height	1431.37151	1404.29076	1376.70053	1353.99346	1331.36476	1308.71110	1347.40159	1314.58332	1235.04977
Breast breadth	330.50205	327.32279	325.72604	322.18856	313.47444	311.39047	321.89570	335.22897	323.64797
Waist girth	**769.388**	**736.562**	**799.406**	**741.654**	**783.835**	**673.584**	**827.464**	**782.172**	**778.975**
Waist height	1276.61046	1231.59106	1206.10096	1185.12232	1164.21609	1154.04798	1179.03221	1148.71203	1075.23246
Waist breadth	274.43162	276.82518	290.44958	265.88938	289.98506	272.89103	294.20184	280.86097	289.57779
Hip girth	**1038.67**	**984.403**	**1055.17**	**937.895**	**997.137**	**964.834**	**938.939**	**987.979**	**982.75**
Hip height	1040.44620	998.41155	1007.60757	938.52252	941.59264	954.21309	993.75871	911.86835	861.76822
Hip breadth	372.22356	352.26192	378.29295	335.15435	356.94601	345.06363	335.53838	353.57732	351.65388
Arm length	**525.583**	**603.044**	**514.781**	**539.2**	**503.022**	**568.525**	**571.901**	**507.36**	**486.748**
Upper arm length	166.81468	209.06052	160.92346	174.24115	154.51032	190.23448	192.07569	156.87618	145.63477
Forearm length	224.61470	231.03777	212.56596	208.83882	207.84972	230.07382	223.87937	207.89608	207.42927
Elbow girth	294.96242	277.17756	279.68419	282.81227	284.53809	254.95813	277.85929	284.58559	240.99314
Wrist girth	173.40220	160.79773	170.36896	169.33249	169.23567	146.45120	161.93521	169.24983	159.06299
Leg length	908.84967	877.33973	855.42512	837.38914	819.41543	813.47899	832.15329	806.08611	742.91351
Thigh length	433.44130	421.99051	410.32429	400.72286	391.15457	397.34733	397.93556	384.05872	350.42886
Calf length	365.09482	357.36251	349.48474	343.00123	336.54011	327.21658	341.11907	331.74854	309.03950
Thigh girth	609.31982	575.73586	619.53110	546.95368	593.61649	563.62529	547.59977	577.94892	574.71288
Knee girth	370.53497	351.71399	364.62219	348.09762	359.53762	328.17741	352.72164	359.58088	347.14100
Ankle girth	224.56414	214.94443	219.06553	216.11802	216.15413	201.89986	212.99711	216.17274	215.56027
Neck girth	**373.424**	**361.925**	**385.785**	**364.167**	**386.147**	**308.011**	**346.783**	**389.713**	**358.777**
Head girth	540.53802	527.95929	537.71059	533.84011	532.87318	477.07299	509.38161	532.91311	532.71002

Table 1 includes 26 anthropometric measurements for 9 test human models. The 7 key measurements are in bold type, and we use them as input data shown in Fig. 4. Table 2 shows the relative errors between the measurements of reconstructed model and the measurements of the test models. The relative errors are calculated by the following equation:

$$\text{relative error} = \frac{m_r - m_t}{m_t} \times 100\% , \tag{5}$$

where m_r is the measurement of reconstructed model, and m_t is the corresponding measurements of the test model.

The maximum absolute value of the relative errors is 9.82 in Table 2, which is shown in bold type. The experimental results indicate that our method can achieve good accuracy.

Table 2. The relative errors between the measurements of reconstructed model and the measurements of the test model.

	No1 (%)	No2 (%)	No3 (%)	No4 (%)	No5 (%)	No6 (%)	No7 (%)	No8 (%)	No9 (%)
Shoulder height	0.65	1.32	0.74	−1.02	−1.18	0.76	0.58	−0.16	0.87
Shoulder breadth	−0.89	−1.63	0.54	−0.20	−0.23	0.88	−1.57	1.14	1.34
Breast height	1.63	1.75	1.31	−0.77	−0.59	1.67	0.93	−0.30	0.83
Breast breadth	0.44	0.12	−1.33	2.12	−0.72	−1.82	−0.57	−0.23	0.75
Waist height	0.87	0.57	0.68	−0.57	−0.91	1.05	1.62	−0.24	0.21
Waist breadth	0.267	0.14	0.38	1.38	−0.49	−1.38	0.27	−0.18	−0.26
Hip height	1.69	1.69	1.96	0.59	−1.55	1.35	0.65	−1.24	−2.27
Hip breadth	0.40	2.26	3.01	−0.15	2.00	2.06	1.37	−2.88	−0.48
Upper arm length	−9.46	0.051	1.96	2.36	5.86	5.65	2.27	−3.45	−0.09
Forearm length	−0.34	4.59	−5.81	6.25	−0.31	−0.05	2.60	3.73	−0.79
Elbow girth	5.18	−0.77	−3.54	−7.07	−6.13	−7.45	−1.02	−2.97	4.14
Wrist girth	6.04	6.36	1.17	−5.66	−6.84	−4.92	−2.62	2.73	**−9.82**
Leg length	1.50	0.30	0.48	−1.45	−0.19	2.64	1.17	−2.91	−0.91
Thigh length	2.23	1.23	1.04	−2.91	2.71	3.07	0.24	−2.65	−5.07
Calf length	1.81	−0.95	−1.60	4.99	0.01	2.89	1.75	−3.17	−1.38
Thigh girth	−1.05	−2.87	1.07	1.93	1.45	−1.12	0.80	0.97	0.97
Knee girth	2.52	−3.18	3.12	−4.71	3.89	−5.01	1.86	−4.87	−3.62
Ankle girth	6.76	2.70	6.06	−5.84	1.36	−4.56	−0.54	−1.89	−8.68
Head girth	−1.96	0.35	1.78	−0.73	−1.34	1.21	−2.40	1.45	−0.76

6   Conclusion and Future Work

In this section, we introduce the advantages and disadvantages of our method and give applications of our method. The main contributions of our paper are listed as follows: (1) we cut down the number of input measurements when generating new customized human body model, (2) we proposed the segmented human body modeling method, and (3) we give a damage modeling application using the realistic human body model. Our application can be used in battlefield environment simulation and animation games. But our generated human body models are all in a standard standing pose, which makes the simulating environment unconnected to real-world situations in some way. Our future work will tackle this problem, to model human body in multiple poses and postures. Combined with the model of soldier's behavior pattern on the battle field [12] and complex and realistic crowd behaviors [13], we can carry out the overall visual simulation of battlefield environment and riot controlling in city environment.

Acknowledgments. This paper was supported by Natural Science Foundation of Jiangsu Province (No. BK20140826) and Collaborative Innovation Center of Novel Software Technology and Industrialization.

References

1. Zhu, S., Mok, P.Y., Kwok, Y.L.: An efficient human model customization method based on orthogonal-view monocular photos. Comput.-Aided Des. **45**(11), 1314–1332 (2013)
2. Istook, C.L.: 5–three-dimensional body scanning to improve fit. In: Advances in Apparel Production, pp. 94–116 (2008)
3. Zhang, Y., Zheng, J., Magnenat-Thalmann, N.: Example-guided anthropometric human body modeling. Vis. Comput. Int. J. Comput. Graph. **31**(12), 1615–1631 (2015)
4. Anguelov, D., Srinivasan, P., Koller, D., et al.: SCAPE: shape completion and animation of people. ACM Trans. Graph. **24**(3), 408–416 (2005)
5. Hasler, N., Stoll, C., Sunkel, M., et al.: A statistical model of human pose and body shape. In: Computer Graphics Forum, pp. 337–346 (2009)
6. Neophytou, A., Hilton, A.: A layered model of human body and garment deformation. In: International Conference on 3D Vision, pp. 171–178. IEEE (2015)
7. Koo, B.Y., Park, E.J., Choi, D.K., et al.: Example-based statistical framework for parametric modeling of human body shapes. Comput. Ind. **73**, 23–38 (2015)
8. Lai, J., Bo, W., Quan, F.U., et al.: Automatic extraction method of human body sizes based on 3D point clouds. J. Cent. S. Univ. **45**(8), 2676–2683 (2014)
9. Tsoli, A., Loper, M., Black, M.J.: Model-based anthropometry: predicting measurements from 3D human scans in multiple poses. In: 2014 IEEE Winter Conference on Applications of Computer Vision (WACV), pp. 83–90. IEEE Computer Society (2014)
10. Yang, Y., Yu, Y., Zhou, Y., et al.: Semantic parametric reshaping of human body models. In: International Conference on 3D Vision, pp. 41–48. IEEE (2014)
11. Moore, M., Wilhelms, J.: Collision detection and response for computer animation. In: Computer Graphics (SIGGRAPH 1988 Proceedings), pp. 289–298 (1988)

12. Xue, Q., Deng, Q., Sun, J., Gao, H.: Research on behavior model of virtual soldier. In: Xiao, T., Zhang, L., Fei, M. (eds.) AsiaSim 2012, Part I. CCIS, vol. 323, pp. 1–6. Springer, Heidelberg (2012)

13. Liang, J.H., Meng, L., Fu, Y.W., et al.: A behavior based crowd simulation framework for riot controlling in city environment. Commun. Comput. Inf. Sci. **402**, 61–70 (2013)

Research on Image Stitching Algorithm for UAV Ground Station Terminal

Hou Jinmeng[1,2(✉)] and Su Zhong[1,2]

[1] Beijing Key Laboratory of High Dynamic Navigation Technology, Beijing, China
Skylly_monkey@163.com, sz@bistu.edu.cn
[2] Beijing Information Science and Technology University, Beijing, China

Abstract. With the development of small UAV, the ground station system is gradually improving. In order to realize the large field of view and wide angle detection of multi targets in the reconnaissance area, the image stitching module is integrated into the terminal of the ground station. Therefore, studying a real-time and efficient image matching algorithm is particularly important. This paper puts forward an improved algorithm based on SIFT (Scale Invariant Feature Transform) feature matching, which joins the UAV aerial parameters to estimate the overlapped region of the aerial images to reduce the sampling time, and adopts gauss quadratic D^2OG feature detection operator instead of DOG operator to simplify the structure of the pyramid. Finally, we use the RANSAC algorithm to complete the precise image matching. Through the simulation results we can see that the proposed algorithm can reduce the complexity of data processing, simplify the area of feature matching, and meet the needs of the system on time.

Keywords: Ground stations · Image stitching · Overlapping domain calculation · Feature extraction

1 Introduction

UAV (Unmanned Aerial Vehicle, UAV) mounted photoelectric pod can get sequence of reconnaissance video sequence of image frames, in order to achieve ground station terminal easy observation aerial images and obtain information about the target area, we need to further expand the field of view range. While ground image captured by the imaging device UAV due to its shooting distance is much greater than the ups and downs of the ground itself, so that the imaging device can be approximated on the drone captured the scene on the same plane, which makes image stitching as possible.

Image stitching mainly using existing equipment such as computers will have over-lapping areas of two or more images for a large seamless image stitching technology [1].

This work is supported by The National Natural Science Foundation of China (Grant NO. 61261 160497); Beijing Science and Technology Project (Grant NO. Z131100005313009); Beijing Municipal Commission of Education (Grant NO. TJSHG201510772017).

© Springer Science+Business Media Singapore 2016
L. Zhang et al. (Eds.): AsiaSim 2016/SCS AutumnSim 2016, Part II, CCIS 644, pp. 207–215, 2016.
DOI: 10.1007/978-981-10-2666-9_21

It breaks through the traditional limitations of image capture device, and is widely used in aerospace, medical image analysis, computer vision, video surveillance and other fields, which is a very important field of image processing of the current branch. So the development of UAV image stitching has received more and more attention at home and abroad, and has become a hot spot of image processing [2].

Image matching criterion is the most important part of the whole UAV image stitching system, which is the basis of pattern recognition, motion monitoring, computer vision and other image processing techniques. The core of image registration is to determine an optimal transformation, so that we can get spatially aligned at different times, different perspectives of the same scene taken. There are some common registration methods such as based on gray information, based on transform domain and based on feature [3]. According to UAV Ground Station problems such as low efficiency in the process of image stitching and workload complex, study on a geometric calibration method on the basis of image stitching algorithm SIFT, which can directly use the UAV flight state parameters to correct the original image, and then using the improved feature matching algorithm based on D^2OG feature points. The algorithm used D^2OG zero crossing detection to replace the DOG extreme point detection, simplifies the structure of DOG Pyramid, optimizes the process of stitching, and meets the requirement of real-time performance in the premise of ensuring the quality of stitching [4–6].

2   Image Stitching Review

The UAV image stitching includes image preprocessing, image registration and image fusion of three parts. Image preprocessing is deal with deformity, distortion, low contrast, in the process of image acquisition and transmission, and make the image united to a coordinate system, so that to measure the coordinate information of the target [7]. The pretreatment methods commonly used histogram processing, image smoothing, image enhancement, and Fourier transform and so on. Image registration refers to the match between the images to extract information, to find the best match in the extracted information, and to complete alignment, image stitching success mainly to see the image registration. Fused image refers to the registration after the image stitching and smooth boundary, so that the image natural transition. Image stitching process is shown in Fig. 1.

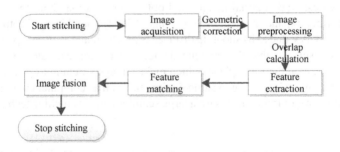

Fig. 1. Image stitching process

3   Overlapping Area Calculation

Due to the relatively small size UAV, and the poor stability and the ability to resist the wind, in the process of taking pictures will inevitably tilt, shake, and the camera itself are geometric distortion of the lens, so first of all is to make image geometric correction for UAV [8]. The UAV flight attitude angle including pitch angle α, roll angle β and yaw angle γ, which uses UAV body coordinate system $P\text{-}X_PY_PZ_P$ relative to the ground coordinate system $E\text{-}X_EY_EZ_E$ to measure the rotation of the relationship, the attitude Angle coordinate system are shown in Fig. 2.

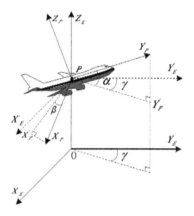

Fig. 2. Position coordinate system

Through analysis, we can know that UAV aerial image angle variation is mainly due to UAV flight advance distance and flight steering, whereas the sequence of frames for stitching images in rotation angle of the aircraft is not a short time too. Considering height, pitch, yaw, roll, and other aspects of parameter information, you can create geometric correction model is as follows:

$$
\begin{bmatrix} x \\ y \\ -f \end{bmatrix}_S = R(H)R(\gamma)R(\beta)R(\alpha) \begin{bmatrix} \dot{x} \\ \dot{y} \\ -f \end{bmatrix}_S
\tag{1}
$$

Where, f denotes a focal length of the imaging, $R(\alpha)$, $R(\beta)$, $R(\gamma)$ and $R(H)$ are rotation matrix parameters for each flight, $(\dot{x}, \dot{y})$ is an original image pixel $\dot{p}$ coordinates in the image coordinate system, (x, y) is the point p coordinate after the point $\dot{p}$ geometric correction in the coordinate system.

Through geometric correction, two images can be converted to the same plane coordinates using the image information center. Among them, the positive direction of the y is the direction of flight, and then we use the coordinates of the center of the image and the image size information, determine the coordinates of the four corners of the image, and through the center of the direction of displacement r judge the trend of the image, at last used img2 two vertex coordinates of point and parallel to the x line to determine the starting position of the overlapping area of the img1. Then just finding a match within the overlapping area characteristics can realize the whole image registration. The overlap region Calculation algorithm flowchart is as follows (Fig. 3):

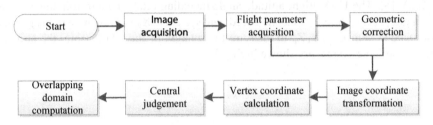

Fig. 3. Overlapping region calculation flowchart

4 Feature Matching Based on D²OG Algorithm

4.1 Scale Space Construction and Feature Point Determination

In 1984, Koendetink proved that the only transform nuclear scale conversion is Gaussian convolution kernels, then Lindeberg et al. further demonstrated the Gaussian kernel is the only nuclear [9]. Two-dimensional Gaussian function is defined as follows:

$$G(x, y, \sigma) = \frac{1}{2\pi\sigma^2} e^{-(x^2+y^2)/2\sigma^2} \tag{2}$$

The original image is defined as $I(x, y)$, make it convolution with a Gaussian convolution kernel, we can get the Gaussian scale space.

$$L(x, y, \sigma) = G(x, y, \sigma)I(x, y) \tag{3}$$

Wherein, (x, y) representative image corresponding to the coordinates of the pixel space, σ is the scale factor space.

Based on Gaussian scale space sampling, the establishment of Gaussian pyramid, and then Gaussian pyramid of the adjacent layer is presupposed get DOG pyramid, as follows:

$$D(x, y, \sigma) = L(x, y, k\sigma) - L(x, y, \sigma) \tag{4}$$

The DOG function making difference operation once again, you can get the second order differential of Gaussian pyramid function is as follows D²OG.

$$D^2(x, y, \sigma) = D(x, y, k\sigma) - D(x, y, \sigma) \tag{5}$$

The details of the construction process D²OG operator is shown on Fig. 4.

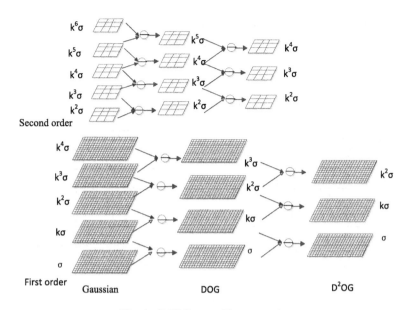

Fig. 4. D2OG pyramid construction

By Eq. (5) we can know D^2OG is a second order differential of Gaussian functions, we find the corresponding zero point guide function is to solving a function of demand DOG algorithm extreme points as:

$$\frac{\partial D}{\partial \sigma} \approx \frac{D(x, y, k\sigma) - D(x, y, \sigma)}{k\sigma - \sigma} = \frac{D^2(x, y, \sigma)}{k\sigma - \sigma} \tag{6}$$

Because $k\sigma - \sigma$ not zero, so $\frac{\partial D}{\partial \sigma} = 0 \Leftrightarrow D^2(x, y, \sigma) = 0$. Zero is the image to be matched feature points of D^2OG.

The feature points is to determine the characteristics of the detection D^2OG second order Gaussian pyramid pixel difference absolute value close to zero. First, you need to set a suitable threshold T, and compared the second order Gaussian pixel absolute difference with the threshold value, if within the threshold range it is recorded as a feature point, and also we should store the cover point scale. Select the threshold value T is a key, if T too big, may lead to an increase in the number of feature points result in a false match, in contrast, it is not enough to express the feature point distribution information. So it is need to make several trials comparing select the optimal value. In this paper, through a number of large number of experiments we found that the value of T in 200–500 when you can get better results.

4.2 Feature Point Matching

Via the above methods we can calculate the feature point,then use SIFT algorithm to realize feature points matching. First, in order to ensure the consistency of the key points in its neighborhood, we have introduced a feature descriptor, Axis direction of the image will be adjusted to be consistent with the main direction of the feature point. Then make the feature point as the center, and choose a nearby region of 8 × 8, as shown in Fig. 5 on the left side.

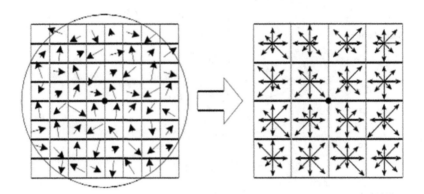

Fig. 5. The generation of feature vector

Statistical respectively modulus and gradient direction of each pixel by eight directions (0° to 45° to 360° per direction), and then calculated the accumulated value to form a seed point, shown on the right in Fig. 5.

After generating the SIFT feature vectors, we use the Euclidean distance of a key feature vector as the similarity measure. Take frame image of a critical point, and find the nearest top two key points in the image to be matched with the nearest, In these two key points, if the most recent close distance divided by time distance is less than a certain percentage threshold, the acceptance of this pair of matching points.

5   Simulation and Analysis

In order to verify the improved feature matching algorithm stitching effect, we conducted a series of simulation experiments using MATLAB on PCS. In experiments I select a set of resolution of 582 * 337 of the original image, and then use geometric correction for matching overlap area of images, where we use D^2OG feature detection operator for feature point extraction, description, and matching. The following Fig. 6 gives the original images, coarse matching rendering, precise matching effect, and the final image stitching effect.

According to the results, after the original image preprocessing and feature points extraction, we can get the coarse matching image as a1, then get the precise matching image as b1 after using RANSAC algorithm, finally obtain the stitching image as shown in figure c1.

In addition choosing an another scenario picture of resolution of 600 * 450, I do the same with the pictures, where we get the feature points throw pretreatment, then

Original image (First)

a1 (Coarse matching)   b1 (Precise matching)

c1 (Stitching effect chart)

Fig. 6. Stitching image (1)

we obtained transformation matrix, and finally achieved the image stitching. The same as above, all kinds of rendering images are shown in Fig. 7.

We analyzed the experimental results from the aspects of the feature point detecting time, the matched number and the correct rate, where the feature point detecting time is the sum of the time to be matched two radiation image feature detection, the matched number means for matching the number of the fine after the match, and the correct rate refers to the proportion of fine match after match correctly. The above stitching effect shows, while maintaining the original sift algorithm precision, scale and rotation invariance, etc., this algorithm can meet the practical requirements of the time. On the one hand, due to the overlap region is calculated during preprocessing, matching feature

Original image (Second)

a2 (Coarse matching)   b2 (Precise matching)

c2 (Stitching effect chart)

Fig. 7. Stitching image (2)

points on the scope make relevant points less than the original algorithm involved in matching, so the overall time will reduce. On the other hand, the improved D^2OG algorithm needs to calculate the zero on the feature point layer, which simplifies the complexity of the process data, reducing the joining together of the time.

6 Conclusion

Based on the sift algorithm, considering the extraction of feature points and the registration time and so on various aspects factor, we improved the extraction region and the determination of the extreme points. By introducing motion parameters and the zero point of first order differential instead of extreme value point method, we achieved good effect for image stitching, and is suitable for the real-time system. In the following system design, we can consider using the method of long scale image, and reduce the amount of data processing, so as to improve the time of feature points extraction.

References

1. Di, Y., Chen, Y., Chen, Y., et al.: A summary of the image stitching algorithm for UAV. Comput. Appl. **31**(1), 170–174 (2011)
2. Di, Y., Chen, Y., Chen, Y., et al.: UAV image stitching algorithm review. J. Comput. Appl. **31**(1), 170–174 (2011)
3. Yang, G., Zhang, H., Yang, Y.L.: Study of image stitching based on the method of finite difference. In: Congress on Image and Signal Processing, CISP 2008, vol. 4, pp. 436–440. IEEE (2008)
4. Ke, Y., Sukthankar, R.: PCA-SIFT: a more distinctive representation for local image descriptors. In: Proceedings of the 2004 IEEE Computer Society Conference on Computer Vision and Pattern Recognition, CVPR 2004, vol. 2, pp. II-506–II-513. IEEE (2004)
5. Lowe, D.G.: Object recognition from local scale-invariant features. In: The Proceedings of the Seventh IEEE International Conference on Computer Vision, vol. 2, pp. 1150–1157. IEEE (1999)
6. Lowe, D.G.: Distinctive image features from scale-invariant keypoints. Int. J. Comput. Vis. **60**(2), 91–110 (2004)
7. Li, Q., Zhang, B.: A fast matching algorithm based on image gray scale. J. Softw. **17**(2), 216–222 (2006)
8. Xie, L.Y.: The geometric correction of aerial photographs of the digital map. J. Northwest. Poly Tech. Univ. **19**(4), 617–620 (2001). Prime Minister
9. Lindeberg, T.: Feature detection with automatic scale selection. Int. J. Comput. Vis. **30**(2), 79–116 (1998)

Improved Clonal Selection Algorithm Optimizing Neural Network for Solving Terminal Anti-missile Collaborative Intercepting Assistant Decision-Making Model

Jin-ke Xiao[1(✉)], Wei-min Li[1], Xin-rong Xiao[2], and Cheng-zhong Lv[1]

[1] Air Force Engineering University, Xi'an 710051, China
xjk_6688@163.com
[2] South China University of Technology, Guangzhou 510640, China

Abstract. Programming terminal high-low collaborative intercepting strategy scientifically and constructing assistant decision-making model with self-determination and intellectualization is one key problem to enhance operational efficiency. Assistant decision-making model has been constructed after analysis on collaborative intercepting principle; then Improved Clonal Selection Algorithm Optimizing Neural Network (ICLONALG-NN) is designed to solve the terminal anti-missile collaborative intercepting assistant decision-making model through introducing crossover operator to increase population diversity, introducing modified combination operator to make use of information before crossover and mutation, introducing population update operator into traditional CLONALG to optimize Neural Network parameters. Experimental simulation confirms the superiority and practicability of assistant decision-making model solved by ICLONALG-NN.

Keywords: Terminal anti-missile system · Collaborative intercepting · Assistant decision-making · Clonal Selection Algorithm · Neural network

1 Introduction

Ballistic Missile (BM) fight course consists of boost course, middle course and terminal course according to its fight phase, therefore constructing multi-layer Ballistic Missile Defense System (BMDS) has already been inevitable and intercepting in terminal course is the last chance [1, 2]. In order to improve terminal interception probability, on one hand, we should carry research on how to exploit the operational capability of terminal anti-missile intercepting systems; on the other hand, we should design terminal collaborative intercepting strategy of high-low intercepting system including recombining intercepting resource to maximize intercepting efficiency [3, 4].

Collaborative intercepting in terminal anti-missile system is combination intercepting mode against BM according to some collaborative regulation implemented by terminal high and low (high-low) intercepting system [5, 6]. In addition, terminal high-low intercepting system intercept Middle-Range Ballistic Missile (MRBM) at firstly and Short-Range Ballistic Missile (SRBM) secondly mostly and respectively,

© Springer Science+Business Media Singapore 2016
L. Zhang et al. (Eds.): AsiaSim 2016/SCS AutumnSim 2016, Part II, CCIS 644, pp. 216–231, 2016.
DOI: 10.1007/978-981-10-2666-9_22

therefore the collaborative intercepting could increase intercepting chance and enhance operational efficiency greatly. Then, how to program terminal high-low collaborative intercepting strategy in limited time interval scientifically is the real military decision-making problem which is urgent to be solved.

There are military collaborative applications at present including air combat [7–9] and multi-sensor cooperative planning [10–13]. These applications give us some inspirations for collaborative intercepting in terminal anti-missile system. However, there are few literatures on collaborative intercepting in terminal anti-missile system except midcourse guidance design for collaborative intercepting [14]. Therefore, collaborative intercepting assistant decision-making model with self-determination and intellectualization is constructed in this paper from the view of advancing integrative terminal high-low collaborative intercepting operational efficiency.

2 Related Principle

Firstly, command control, battle management and communication (C2BMC) system programs firepower plan [15–19] based on operational information including accurate missile early-warning information, object defense grade information and intercepting system status information, then distributes customizing intercepting assignment into high-low intercepting system. Secondly, high-low intercepting system launch interception missiles and put combination interception in practice considering intercepting capability and intercepting chance. Thirdly, the killing evaluation report is fully assessed based on ground-based radar information, which mainly includes killing BM operational process of interception missile launched by intercepting system. High-low collaborative intercepting process is demonstrated in Fig. 1.

Five operational validity principles of Terminal High-Altitude Area Defense (THAAD) and PAC-3 collaborative intercepting are proposed by American army, which represents typical terminal high and low intercepting system. Five operational validity principles clarify the probability of every operational scene at length, standardize basic theory of launching pattern and ascertain the launching quantity during THAAD and PAC-3 collaborative intercepting. Detailed theories are described as follows:

Grade 0 is no defense grade, that is to say no interception mission is launched against BM.

Grade 1 is low defense grade, that is to say single interception chance pattern including THAAD or PAC-3 launches one interception missile.

Grade 2 is middle defense grade, that is to say two interception chances pattern includes (A) high interception pattern: high intercepting system launches two interception missiles; (B) low interception pattern: low intercepting system launches two interception missiles; (C) high-low collaborative intercepting pattern: high-low intercepting system launches one interception missile respectively and collaboratively.

Grade 3 is higher defense grade, that is to say three interception chances pattern includes (A) high priority collaborative intercepting pattern: high-low intercepting system launch two and one interception missiles respectively; (B) low priority

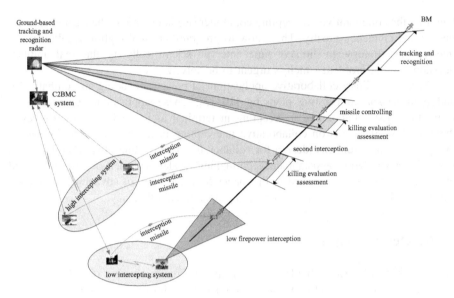

Fig..1. Process of terminal high-low collaborative intercepting

collaborative intercepting pattern: high-low intercepting system launch one and two interception missiles respectively.

Grade 4 is highest defense grade, that is to say high-low intercepting system launch two interception missiles collaboratively.

Terminal high-low intercepting system will intercept with highest efficiency usually for that BM has high destruction and anti-missile system has the last intercepting chance in terminal course.

Whereas terminal high-low intercepting systems locate in different geography, then how to program high-low collaborative intercepting grade for assigned BM to maximize collaborative intercepting operational efficiency is almost the most important decision-making problems with the limited interception missile resource.

Some decision-making approaches including Analytic Hierarchy Process (AHP), fuzzy multiple attribute decision-making are applied in similar problems. However, these approaches should calculate attribute weight, which results in two problems: one problem is how to calculate attribute weight and the other problem is how to make use of experience from a great deal of historical data. Artificial Neural Network is proposed from simulation on information processing approach of brain information process and information memory. Here Improved Clonal Selection Algorithm Optimizing Neural Network (ICLONALG-NN) is proposed to solve terminal high-low collaborative intercepting assistant decision-making problem based on collaborative intercepting experience database provided by domain expert, which will provide collaborative intercepting online with decision-making support.

3   Formulation Design

3.1   Model Formulation

While terminal anti-missile collaborative intercepting assistant decision-making should choose collaborative intercepting grade with self-determination and intellectualization based on the BM threat assessment degree, perfect collaborative intercepting assistant decision-making need support from other database. Then some decision-making indexes are selected according to comprehensive, pertinent and comparable principles.

At first, three indexes including range, penetration capability and arriving time, are selected, which describe BM threat from different sides. Then, the index distance from BM falling point is used to decide different collaborative intercepting strategy when the distance from BM falling point is different.

Terminal anti-missile collaborative intercepting grade is divided into Grade 2, Grade 3 and Grade 4 by many domain experts considering that C2BMC system distributes interception missiles comprehensively and intelligently.

Collaborative intercepting decision-making logic flow is demonstrated in Fig. 2.

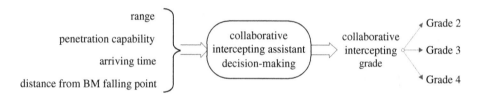

Fig..2. Collaborative intercepting assistant decision-making logic flow

Terminal anti-missile collaborative intercepting assistant decision-making model takes range, penetration capability, arriving time, distance from BM falling point as inputs and takes collaborative intercepting grade as outputs. Furthermore, the measures to solve assistant decision-making model can been seen in the following Sections.

3.2   Model Quantitative Inputs and Outputs

3.2.1   Quantitative Inputs

Range: early-warming information includes BM range information and the range is restricted below 3000 km [1, 20] for that terminal high-low intercepting system mainly intercept MRBM and SRBM.

Penetration capability: penetration capability is an index measuring the warhead capability of penetrating anti-missile intercepting system anti-block area without scathe and penetration capability is lead by warhead maneuverability [21], electromagnetism interference [22], some fake warhead [23] and otherwise ways and means. The more the penetration capability is, the larger threat degree of warhead to defense object is and vice versa. Penetration capability $p \in (0, 1)$ can been acquired from integrating intelligence and early-warming information. $p = 0.6$ means the probability that warhead penetrates anti-missile intercepting system anti-block area without scathe is 0.6.

Arriving time: arriving time is the time interval between time of C2BMC system receiving BM early-warming and time of BM falling point. The more the arriving time t is, the larger threat degree of warhead to defense object is and vice versa.

Distance from BM falling point: the distance h from defense object to BM falling point reflects shoot precision. The smaller h is, the higher threat degree is, the higher collaborative intercepting grade is and vice versa.

3.2.2   Quantitative Outputs

Model output results will select particular collaborative intercepting grade and one vector $L = (l_1, l_2, l_3)$ is taken to describe collaborative intercepting grade, which is defined as follows in Eq. (1):

$$l_i = \begin{cases} 1, \text{collaborative intercepting is Grade } (i+1) \\ 0, \text{collaborative intercepting is not Grade } (i+1) \end{cases} \quad i = 1, 2, 3 \qquad (1)$$

Where l_1, l_2 and l_3 subject to $\sum_{i=1}^{3} l_i = 1$, For example, $L = (0, 1, 0,)$ is collaborative intercepting Grade 3.

4   Model Solution

4.1   Neural Network

Back Propagation (BP) Neural Network [24–26] with input layer, hidden layer and output layer is demonstrated in Fig. 3 as follows:

Where $X = [x_{i1}, x_{i2}, \ldots, x_{in}]^T \in R^n$ $i = 1, 2, \ldots, n$ is n network input data, $Y = [y_1, y_2, \ldots, y_m]$ is network output, h is the number of hidden layer, $W_1 = [w_{i1}, w_{i2}, \ldots, w_{ih}]$ and $W_2 = [w_{j1}, w_{2j}, \ldots, w_{hj}]$, $j = 1, 2, \ldots, m$ is weight from input nodes to hidden nodes and weight from hidden nodes to output nodes respectively, B is

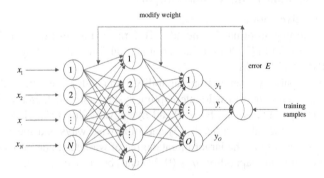

Fig..3. Principle of BP neural network

neuron threshold vector, $f(\cdot)$ is activation function of hidden layer, then output matrix from input layer to hidden layer is $X' = f(W_1 \cdot X)$ and output matrix from hidden layer to output layer is $Y' = W_2 \cdot X'$; $E = \left\| Y - Y' \right\| = \frac{1}{2} \sum_{k=1}^{m} (y_k - \hat{y}_k)^2$ is network output error function and the training of neural network is the searching W_1, W_2 and B to minimize E.

4.2 ICLONALG-NN Illustration

Slow convergence phenomenon often appears during training neural network with traditional gradient descent algorithm. Clonal Selection Algorithm (CLONALG) [27, 28] is a optimization algorithm with distinguishing, self-adjust and immune memory capability inspired from immune phenomenon that antibody in biological immune system eliminates invading antigen. Improved Clonal Selection Algorithm (ICLO-NALG) introduces crossover operator to increase population diversity and introduces modified combination operator to make use of information before crossover and mutation, therefore ICLONALG is proposed to optimize neural network leading to the birth of ICLONALG-NN model.

Here objective function E is considered as antigen in ICLONALG and full neural network parameters are considered as antibody in ICLONALG, the optimization process is searching the best objective function $f(\cdot)$ through eliminating invading antigen and producing antibody with high affinity through selecting operator and other immune operator.

The complex nonlinear optimization relation between every evaluate index and collaborative intercepting grade could be described by ICLONALG-NN, which enjoys super nonlinear management capability with precision and speediness and will enjoys applausive applications in multi-input and multi-output terminal anti-missile collaborative intercepting assistant decision-making model.

Furthermore, the basic solving process is demonstrated as follows:

(1) construct terminal anti-missile collaborative intercepting assistant decision-making model, this model takes evaluation indexes as inputs and takes collaborative intercepting grade as outputs;
(2) design executing steps of ICLONALG-NN;
(3) train and test ICLONALG-NN with samples.

The network parameters to be optimized are $W = [W_1, W_2, B]$, where $W_1 = [w_{i1}, w_{i2}, \ldots, w_{ih}]$, $W_2 = [w_{j1}, w_{2j}, \ldots, w_{hj}]$, $i = 1, 2, \ldots, n$, $j = 1, 2, \ldots, m$ and B is neural neuron threshold vector. Then the ICLONALG-NN flowchart is demonstrated in Fig. 4.

Executing steps of ICLONALG-NN are undertook priority analysis as follows:

Step 1: initializing population

Full neural network parameters $W = [W_1, W_2, B]$ are coded in floating-point format, which is the

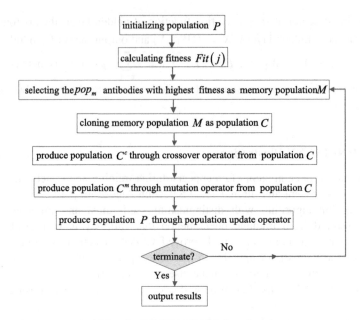

Fig. 4. ICLONALG-NN flowchart

corresponding problem space, therefore antibody population P is initialized with population scale *pop*.

Step 2: calculating fitness $Fit(j)$

Fitness $Fit(j)$ is set to reciprocal of objective function E_j according to Eqs. (2) and (3).

objective function

$$minE_j = \sum_{k=1}^{T}\sum_{i=1}^{m}\frac{\left(y_i^k - \hat{y}_i^k\right)^2}{2} \tag{2}$$

$$Fit(j) = \frac{1}{E_j} \tag{3}$$

Where j is the jth individual in population, y_i^k and $\hat{y}_i^k$ is the expected outputs and practical outputs in kth training mode respectively; m is the number of neuron in output layer; T is the number of training samples.

Step 3: producing memory population

Memory population M is produced through selecting the best pop_m antibodies from antibody population P according to their fitness.

Step 4: clone operator

Population C is produced through cloning memory population M.

The higher the antibody fitness, the more cloning antibody population, the proportional cloning operator is in Eq. (4).

$$clone_j = \text{Int}\left[clone * \frac{f(j)}{\sum f(j)}\right] \qquad (4)$$

Where $clone$ is the antibody population cloning scale, $clone = \sum clone_i$ and $\text{Int}(\cdot)$ is the elements to

the nearest integers which can be seen in Matlab 7.11.0.

Step 5: crossover operator: population C^c is produced from population C through crossover operator.

Select crossover point randomly in every antibody and set variable x and $x^{'}$ as before and after crossover operator, which are produced through linear crossover in Eq. (5).

$$\begin{cases} x_1^{'} = rx_1 + (1-r)x_2 \\ x_2^{'} = rx_2 + (1-r)x_1 \end{cases} \qquad (5)$$

Where $r \in [0, 1]$ is a random number.

Step 6: mutation operator: population C^m is produced from population C through mutation operator.

Select mutation point randomly in every antibody and set variable x and $x^{'}$ as before and after mutation operator, which are produced through nonuniformity mutation in Eqs. (6) and (7).

$$x^{'} = \begin{cases} x + \Delta[g_c, r(k) - x], sign = 0 \\ x - \Delta[g_c, x - l(k)], sign = 1 \end{cases} \qquad (6)$$

$$\Delta(g_c, y) = yr\left(1 - \frac{g_c}{T}\right)^b \qquad (7)$$

Where Δ is calculating variable function, y is the distance from x to lower or upper bounds, g_c is evolution iteration at present, T is the maximum iteration, r is the coefficient with an nonuniformity adjusting function. The larger evolution iteration is, the larger probability $\Delta(g_c, y)$ converges at 0. Therefore, algorithm could search the problem space at the evolvement early stage abroadly and algorithm remains local high search precision at the evolvement later stage.

Step 7: population update operator

Combine population C, population C^c and population C^m into C^{new} in Eq. (8) to make full use of antibody information before crossover operator, mutation operator and inject new antibody information into population.

$$C^{new} = [C, C^c, C^m, D] \qquad (8)$$

Firstly produce antibody population P' by selecting *pop* antibodies from population C^{new} according to their fitness, then produce antibody population P by replacing the lowest fitness antibodies in population P' with population D, which is produced randomly with population scale d.

Step 8: repetition

Repeat Step 3 ∼ Step 7 until the maximum iteration T.

4.3   Applying ICLONALG-NN to Solve Decision-Making Model

Here BP Neural Network is adopt in ICLONALG-NN and takes four indexes including range, penetration capability, arriving time and distance from BM falling point as inputs, collaborative intercepting grade including Grade 2, Grade 3 and Grade 4 as outputs. Furthermore, BP Neural Network has single hidden network, the neuron number is set to be 9 according to "$2N + 1$" method proposed by Hecht-Nielsen [29, 30] and transferring function is Sigmoid function in every neuron. Therefore topology structure 4-9-3 BP Neural Network with 4 inputs, 9 hidden layers and 3 outputs is demonstrated in Fig. 5, which is also applied in experimentation 1.

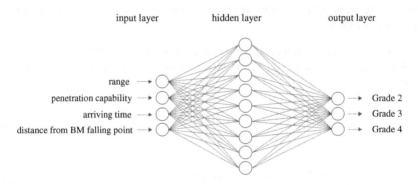

Fig. 5. BP neural network in experimentation 1

And the BP Neural Network parameters include w_1, w_2 and b_1, b_2, which are weight from input layer to hidden layers, weight from hidden layers to output layer and every neuron threshold of hidden layer, output layer respectively. These parameters could be optimized by ICLONALG.

5   Analysis on Simulation Results

5.1   Experimentation 1

Collaborative intercepting data information provided by terminal anti-missile collaborative intercepting domain expert is considered as training samples and testing samples. Three group row data are testing samples including data from row No. 30 to row No. 32, the other row group data are training samples in Table 1. ICLONALG-NN, CLONALG-NN are adopt to solve the problem and the network parameters are set as follows: $T = 300$, $pop = 50$, $pop_m = 20$, $clone = 100$, $d = 5$.Firstly, the network input data is in normalization processing according to Eq. (9).

$$I_{ij} = \frac{I_{ij} - \min I_{\cdot j}}{\max I_{\cdot j} - \min I_{\cdot j}} \tag{9}$$

Where I_{ij} is the input data in Table 1, i is row serial number, j is column serial number, $\max I_{\cdot j}$, $\min I_{\cdot j}$ are the maximum and minimum of the jth column data respectively.

Then, train the Neural Network with the data in Table 1 and draw the global error curve figure demonstrated in Fig. 6.

Global network error comparison of ICLONALG-NN and CLONALG-NN could be found in upper subfigure in Fig. 6, the network error comparison in first half training process and latter half training process are demonstrated in lower left subfigure and lower right subfigure respectively. The convergence speed of ICLONALG-NN is faster than that of CLONALG-NN, for that ICLONALG-NN already appears convergence before 50 iterations while CLONALG-NN almost appears convergence after 200 iterations. In addition, the global network error precision of ICLONALG-NN almost reaches 10^{-6} while that of CLONALG-NN could reach just 10^{-2}, therefore, the optimization capability of ICLONALG is higher than that of CLONALG obviously.

The experimental results confirms the higher optimization capability of ICLONALG than that of CLONALG, for that ICLONALG amends the defect of lower local optimization capability and prematurity convergence through the modified crossover operator, modified mutation operator and modified population update operator which leads to improve optimization capability. Furthermore, testing results of ICLONALG-NN with training samples and testing samples confirm the consistency between expectation outputs and practical outputs with minimum network error.

In conclusion, the response speed and the evaluation precision of ICLONALG-NN are better than that of CLONALG-NN, the trained ICLONALG-NN could better reflect the correlativity between input samples and output samples, which could enjoy applausive application in terminal anti-missile collaborative intercepting assistant decision-making model.

Table 1. Collaborative intercepting data provided by domain expert

Serial number	s	p	t	h	Expectation outputs	Practical outputs	Remarks
1	2700	0.95	61	50	(0,0,1)	(0.0000,0.0000,1.0000)	Training
2	800	0.55	152	79	(0,1,0)	(0.0004,0.9996,0.0000)	
3	1100	0.58	69	55	(0,1,0)	(0.0000,1.0000,0.0000)	
4	2400	0.55	111	65	(0,1,0)	(0.0000,1.0000,0.0000)	
5	800	0.55	99	352	(1,0,0)	(1.0000,0.0000,0.0000)	
6	800	0.55	199	123	(1,0,0)	(1.0000,0.0000,0.0000)	
7	900	0.60	73	66	(0,1,0)	(0.0001,0.9999,0.0000)	
8	800	0.60	75	118	(1,0,0)	(1.0000,0.0000,0.0000)	
9	800	0.56	179	93	(1,0,0)	(0.9996,0.0004,0.0000)	
10	800	0.58	108	115	(1,0,0)	(1.0000,0.0000,0.0000)	
11	800	0.55	380	400	(1,0,0)	(1.0000,0.0000,0.0000)	
12	1000	0.60	70	57	(0,1,0)	(0.0000,1.0000,0.0000)	
13	800	0.59	71	63	(0,1,0)	(0.0000,1.0000,0.0000)	
14	800	0.64	280	400	(1,0,0)	(1.0000,0.0000,0.0000)	
15	1000	0.60	64	54	(0,1,0)	(0.0000,1.0000,0.0000)	
16	800	0.55	143	101	(1,0,0)	(0.9997,0.0002,0.0000)	
17	800	0.55	179	101	(1,0,0)	(0.9999,0.0001,0.0000)	
18	1000	0.68	71	51	(0,0,1)	(0.0000,0.0000,1.0000)	
19	1500	0.90	75	51	(0,0,1)	(0.0000,0.0000,1.0000)	
20	900	0.55	280	79	(0,1,0)	(0.0001,0.9999,0.0000)	
21	800	0.55	280	163	(1,0,0)	(1.0000,0.0000,0.0000)	
22	1100	0.63	66	54	(0,1,0)	(0.0000,1.0000,0.0000)	
23	800	0.58	135	98	(1,0,0)	(1.0000,0.0000,0.0000)	
24	800	0.55	139	172	(1,0,0)	(1.0000, 0.0000, 0.0000)	
25	800	0.55	199	170	(1,0,0)	(1.0000, 0.0000, 0.0000)	
26	2500	0.61	135	303	(1,0,0)	(0.0000,0.0001,1.0000)	
27	1700	0.66	115	55	(0,1,0)	(0.0000,1.0000,0.0000)	
28	1500	0.60	60	54	(0,1,0)	(0.0000,1.0000,0.0000)	
29	1300	0.55	63	314	(1,0,0)	(1.0000,0.0000,0.0000)	
30	900	0.65	60	53	(0,1,0)	(0.0000,1.0000,0.0000)	Testing
31	1200	0.80	62	51	(0,0,1)	(0.0000,0.0001,1.0000)	
32	1000	0.55	63	314	(1,0,0)	(1.0000,0.0000,0.0000)	

5.2 Experimentation 2

Comparing with traditional air defense command automation system, high-speed characteristic BM sets a still higher demand on the rapid reaction capability and autonomous operation speed of C2BMC system; these requirements also sets a still higher demand on collaborative intercepting design in C2BMC system.

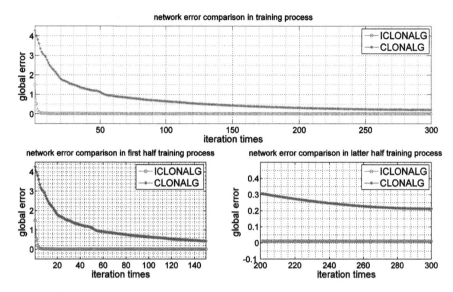

Fig. 6. Network error comparison of ICLONALG-NN and CLONALG-NN

Table 2. Terminal anti-missile collaborative intercepting grade

Evaluation index	Grade 1	Grade 2	Grade 3	Grade 4
Range/kilometer	<600	600 ~ 1000	1000 ~ 2000	2000 ~ 3000
Arriving time/second	>150	128 ~ 150	72.0 ~ 120	<72.0

Here the experiment 2 is designed to validate the universality of ICLONALG-NN. Operational system designers usually simplify assistant decision-making model considering the BM high-speed, which will put high real-time characteristic requirement forward for terminal anti-missile collaborative intercepting assistant decision-making. Here range and arriving time are the model inputs and collaborative intercepting grade 1, grade 2, grade 3 and grade 4 are the model outputs, which are demonstrated as $(1,0,0,0)$, $(0,1,0,0)$, $(0,0,1,0)$ and $(0,0,0,1)$ respectively.

Terminal anti-missile collaborative intercepting grade determinant criterion is in Table 2 according to domain expert and the training samples are randomly produced in Table 3. Critical value of all the collaborative intercepting grade in Table 3 are used once while the collaborative intercepting grades relative to critical values are 0.5 and the other collaborative intercepting grades are 0.

Terminal anti-missile collaborative intercepting assistant decision-making model is constructed according to ICLONALG-NN designing criterion. Topology structure 2-5-4 BP Neural Network with 2 inputs, 5 hidden layers and 4 outputs is demonstrated in Fig. 7, whose neuron number of single hidden network is set to be 9 according to "$2N + 1$" method proposed by Hecht-Nielsen and transferring function is Sigmoid function in every neuron.

Table 3. Neural Network training samples produced randomly

Serial number	s	t	Expectation outputs	Practical outputs
1	300	181.0	(1,0,0,0)	(0.9999,0.0001,0.0000,0.0000)
2	350	172.7	(1,0,0,0)	(0.9985,0.0013,0.0000,0.0000)
3	380	168.1	(1,0,0,0)	(0.9833,0.0155,0.0000,0.0000)
4	400	160.7	(1,0,0,0)	(0.9817,0.0146,0.0000,0.0000)
5	500	155.5	(1,0,0,0)	(0.9746,0.0283,0.0000,0.0000)
6	600	150.0	(0.5,0.5,0,0)	(0.5217,0.4912,0.0000,0.0000)
7	650	147.2	(0,1,0,0)	(0.0147,0.9947,0.0000,0.0000)
8	700	143.9	(0,1,0,0)	(0.0011,0.9999,0.0000,0.0000)
9	780	139.8	(0,1,0,0)	(0.0002,1.0000,0.0000,0.0000)
10	860	135.5	(0,1,0,0)	(0.0000,1.0000,0.0003,0.0000)
11	900	130.3	(0,1,0,0)	(0.0000,0.9983,0.0114,0.0000)
12	1000	128.0	(0,0.5,0.5,0)	(0.0000,0.5003,0.4941,0.0000)
13	1100	120.6	(0,0,1,0)	(0.0000,0.0000,0.9994,0.0000)
14	1300	107.4	(0,0,1,0)	(0.0000,0.0000,0.9999,0.0000)
15	1500	95.9	(0,0,1,0)	(0.0000,0.0000,1.0000,0.0000)
16	1700	86.5	(0,0,1,0)	(0.0000,0.0000,0.9999,0.0000)
17	1900	75.9	(0,0,1,0)	(0.0000,0.0000,0.9958,0.0000)
18	2000	72.0	(0,0,0.5,0.5)	(0.0000,0.0000,0.5126,0.5117)
19	2200	67.0	(0,0,0,1)	(0.0000,0.0000,0.0000,1.0000)
20	2300	53.8	(0,0,0,1)	(0.0000,0.0000,0.0000,1.0000)
21	2500	35.0	(0,0,0,1)	(0.0000,0.0000,0.0000,1.0000)
22	2700	29.5	(0,0,0,1)	(0.0000,0.0000,0.0000,1.0000)
23	2900	21.0	(0,0,0,1)	(0.0000,0.0000,0.0000,1.0000)

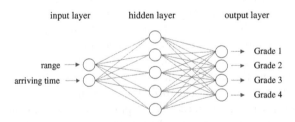

Fig. 7. BP neural network in experimentation 2

Training ends when the global network error precision of ICLONALG-NN almost reaches 10^{-3} after 300 iterations. The training results are in the right practical outputs column in Table 3 and the trained Neural Network could reflect the relationship between the sample inputs and the sample outputs. Therefore, terminal anti-missile collaborative intercepting grades are determined by ICLONALG-NN model, which are demonstrated in Table 4.

The test samples evaluation results that are consistent with terminal anti-missile collaborative intercepting grades criterion include serial number 1, serial number 2,

Table 4. evaluation on test samples

Serial number	s	t	Practical outputs	Grade
1	500	161.3	(0.0002,0.9998,0.0000,0.0000)	Grade 2
2	980	138.7	(0.0000,0.9558,0.0769,0.0000)	Grade 2
3	1400	125.6	(0.0000,0.0000,0.9999,0.0000)	Grade 3
4	1200	114.4	(0.0000,0.0000,0.9999,0.0000)	Grade 3
5	2800	61.9	(0.0000,0.0000,0.0000,1.0000)	Grade 4
6	1900	110.6	(0.0000,0.0000,0.9955,0.0022)	Grade 3
7	950	69.7	(0.0000,0.0000,1.0000,0.0000)	Grade 3
8	2200	34.8	(0.0000,0.0000,0.0000,1.0000)	Grade 4
9	1100	106.7	(0.0000,0.0000,1.0000,0.0000)	Grade 3

serial number 4, serial number 5, serial number 6, serial number 8 and serial number 9. Then the evaluation results of serial number 3 and serial number 7 should be analysed as follows at length for the reasons that their range and arriving time belong to different collaborative intercepting grade.

(1) range 1400 km belongs to Grade 3 and is almost in middle interval $[1000, 2000]$, which are the lower and upper bounds of range in Grade 3 considering serial number 3. However, arriving time $t = 125.6$ belongs to Grade 2 and is nearer to 128, which is both the upper bound of range in Grade 3 and lower bound of range in Grade 2, therefore, the evaluation result that collaborative intercepting grade belongs to Grade 3 is reasonable.

(2) range 950 km belongs to Grade 2 and is nearer to 1000, which is both the upper bound of range in Grade 2 and lower bound of range in Grade 3. However, arriving time $t = 69.7$ belongs to Grade 4 and is nearer to 72, which is both the upper bound of range in Grade 4 and lower bound of range in Grade 3, therefore, the evaluation result that collaborative intercepting grade belongs to Grade 3 is more reasonable.

ICLONALG-NN could evaluate terminal anti-missile collaborative intercepting grades, whose results are reasonable completely. The method could reflect the relationship between the multi-indexes and collaborative intercepting grades for that this method could solve different indexes evaluation result incompatible problems appearing in multi-indexes evaluation system.

Furthermore, ICLONALG-NN model are constructed to evaluate terminal anti-missile collaborative intercepting grades practically based on the training samples provided by domain experts and the model could be easily updated through increasing new training samples or increasing some evaluation indexes. Therefore, the model is practical and applicable in common currency. The more complex model, the more training time, therefore the operational time limit requirement should be considered before designing practical ICLONALG-NN. In conclusion, ICLONALG-NN will enjoy high applause in the future application.

6 Conclusions

Terminal anti-missile collaborative intercepting assistant decision-making model is constructed and ICLONALG-NN is proposed to solve the model. Crossover operator and population update operator are introduced into ICLONALG to produce antibodies with high affinity in large probability. Then experiment results demonstrate algorithm remarkable effectiveness in the application. In practical missile defense operational process, the proposed model parameters in paper are fixed to collaborative intercepting software module. C2BMC system could program collaborative intercepting after target assignment automatically based on collaborative intercepting programming, which will satisfy real-time collaborative intercepting requirement.

To promote the development on the theory and application of ICLONALG-NN, our future research will focus on the two points below.

(1) The basic theory of the ICLONALG-NN. Biology immune theory and Neural Network theory should be explored at length to enhance the optimization capability, in addition, control parameters play an significant role in algorithm performance, therefore, relative research should be carried on through theoretical analysis and experiments.
(2) ICLONALG-NN application in classification. Apply ICLONALG-NN to some engineering problems including pattern recognition, threat assessment, cluster analysis.

References

1. Xu, S.K., Liu, J.H., Wei, X.Z., Li, X., Guo, G.: Wideband electromagnetic characteristics modeling and analysis of missile targets in ballistic midcourse. Sci. China Technol. Sci. **55**(6), 1655–1666 (2012)
2. Prabhakar, N., Kumar, I.D., Tata, S.K., Vaithiyanathan, V.: A simplified guidance for target missiles used in ballistic missile defence evaluation. J. Inst. Eng. (India): Ser. C **94**(1), 31–36 (2013)
3. Xiao, J.-K., Li, W.-M., Liu, B., Lv, C.-Z.: Analysis on operational planning key technology in aerospace defense system. Aerodyn. Missile J. **11**(2), 51–55 (2015)
4. Wang, S., Li, W.-M., Xiao, J.-K.: Dynamic analysis on American ballistic missile defense system. Aerodyn. Missile J. **12**(12), 27–31 (2014)
5. Wang, G., Wang, M.-Y., Yang, S.-C., Wu, L.-F.: Research of anti-missile battle management technique. Mod. Defence Technol. **40**(1), 26–30 (2012)
6. Xiao, J.-K., Wang, G., Fu, Q., Li, Y.-L.: Research on technology requirement of C2BM in anti-missile system. Aerodyn. Missile J. **9**(9), 57–61 (2012)
7. Chen, X., Wei, X.-M., Xu, G.-Y.: Cooperative air combat decision making for multiple UCAV based on decentralized invite auction algorithm. J. Syst. Simul. **24**(6), 1257–1266 (2014)
8. Pan, H., Wang, W., Qiu, X., Zhang, X.: Target assignment in multi·aircraft cooperative air combat based on distributed calculation. Electron. Opt. Control **20**(1), 32–35 (2013)

9. Chen, Z., Wang, L., Jia, Z.-Y.: The network effect of beyond-visual-range coordinated air combat. Command Control Simul. **35**(1), 11–17 (2013)
10. Rz, W., Tx, S., Wp, J.: Collaborative sensing mechanism for intelligent sensors based on tuple space. Ruan Jian Xue Bao/J. Softw. **26**(4), 790–801 (2015)
11. Fu, Q., Wand, G., Xiao, J.-K., Guo, X.-K., Wei, G.: Research on multrsensor cooperative tracking of high-speed aerospace vehicle. Syst. Eng. Electron. **36**(10), 2007–2012 (2014)
12. Jie, T., Jiang, T., Jinke, X.: Research on collaborative planning of theater anti-missile sensors. Tactical Missile Technol. **8**(5), 49–53 (2013)
13. Jia, C., Changqiang, H., Xiang, G., Jie, H.: Target tracking by multi-sensor cooperation method based on distributed Nash Q-learning. J. SE Univ. (Nat. Sci. Ed.) **42**(Suppl 2), S60–S65 (2012)
14. Lu, C., Shen, L.-C., Xie, H.-B.: Midcourse guidance design of collaborative intercepting of two interceptors for exo-atmospheric interception. Navig. Control **13**(2), 17–22 (2014)
15. Zhang, C., Zhu, Q., Kuang, X.: Development overview of the US ballistic missile defense C2BMC system. J. Acad. Equipment **23**(3), 60–63 (2012)
16. Yao, Y., Li, Z.: Research on C2BMC system operational view based on DoDAF. J. Acad. Equipment Command Technol. **22**(3), 76–81 (2011)
17. Li, J., Zhang, Z., Xu, L.: The capability of US C2BMC system. J. Acad. Equipment **24**(5), 78–82 (2013)
18. Yao, Y., Li, Z., Wang, L.: Design of C2BMC simulation system based on HLA. J. Acad. Equipment **22**(2), 84–88 (2011)
19. Xiao, J.K., Wang, G., Liu, C.Y., Yang, S.C.: Research on requirement analysis of C2BM in terminal anti-missile system based on DoDAF. Fire Control Command Control **38**(8), 13–17 (2013)
20. Prabhakar, N., Kumar, I.D., Tata, S.K., Vaithiyanathan, V.: A simplified guidance for target missiles used in ballistic missile defence evaluation. J. Inst. Eng. India Ser. C **94**(1), 31–36 (2013)
21. Guo, K.Y., Sheng, X.Q.: Precise recognition of warhead and decoy based on components of micro-Doppler frequency curves. Sci. China Inf. Sci. **55**(4), 850–856 (2012)
22. Chanyal, B.C.: Octonionic matrix representation and electromagnetism. J. Korean Phys. Soc. **65**(11), 1715–1728 (2014)
23. Golubev, V.K., Medvedkin, V.A.: Dynamic cutting of AMg6 aluminum alloy casings of warhead cones. Strength Mater. **34**(1), 99–101 (2002)
24. Lu, J., Huang, G.-L., Li, S.-Z.: A study of maneuvering control for an air cushion vehicle based on back propagation neural network. J. Shanghai Jiaotong Univ. (Sci.) **14**(4), 482–485 (2009)
25. Jin, H., Sujun, W., Peng, Y.: Prediction of contact fatigue life of alloy cast steel rolls using back-propagation neural network. JMEPEG **22**(12), 3631–3638 (2013)
26. Ruan, G., Tan, Y.: A three-layer back-propagation neural network for spam detection using artificial immune concentration. Soft. Comput. **14**(2), 139–150 (2010)
27. Chang, T.-Y., Shiu, Y.-F.: Simultaneously construct IRT-based parallel tests based on an adapted CLONALG algorithm. Appl. Intell. **36**(4), 979–994 (2012)
28. Zheng, J., Chen, Y., Zhang, W.: A Survey of artificial immune applications. Artif. Intell. Rev. **34**(1), 19–34 (2010)
29. Izeboudjen, N., Bouridane, A., Farah, A., Bessalah, H.: Application of design reuse to artificial neural networks: case study of the back propagation algorithm. Neural Comput. Appl. **21**(7), 1531–1544 (2012)
30. James Ting-Ho, L.: Functional model of biological neural networks. Cogn. Neurodyn. **4**(4), 295–313 (2010)

Optimal Controller Design and Simulation Analysis of Inertially Stabilized Platform for Airborne Remote Sensing

Delin Zeng$^{(\boxtimes)}$ and Kai Xiao

College of Aerospace Science and Engineering,
National University of Defense Technology, Changsha, China
18670387476@163.com

Abstract. In order to isolate interference and, keep the line of sight of imaging load in inertial coordinate system, applying an inertially stabilized platform as a joint between aircraft and load is best choice. But it is difficult to design the controller of inertially stabilized platform for airborne remote sensing, because of its large mass and volume, which results low structural resonance interference. Based on the complex frequency domain analysis of various disturbances, a novel optimal controller design method is put forward. Firstly, the dual loop control structure is obtained by modeling main interference and ignoring the inessential disturbance. Secondly, the configuration of controller is determined considering the complexity and tracking performance. Moreover, constraints conditions are designed after analyzing the nyquist stability criterion and the influence of structural resonance. Finally, objective function about the evaluation index of anti-interference ability is proposed and, the controller optimal design is completed by using genetic algorithm. Simulation experiment is implemented based on a realistic prototype system and, the optimal controller design method is proved simple, effective and practical for engineering using.

Keywords: Complex frequency domain · Dual-loop control system · Optimal controller design · Genetic algorithm · Disturbance-rejection

1 Introduction and Background

In order to isolate interference and, keep the line of sight of imaging load in inertial coordinate system, applying an inertially stabilized platform as a joint between aircraft and load is best choice. The structure of the tri-axial inertially stabilized platform for airborne remote sensing is shown in Fig. 1. Imaging load is installed in the internal gimbal, namely, the azimuth gimbal in Fig. 1, as well as POS, gyro and other sensors. Sensors measure the attitude and angular velocity information and, feed back to the control system, after calculating, control signal is input to the motor by power amplifier circuit and then, control torque is generated to achieve high precision control [1–5].

The Inertially stabilized platform for airborne remote sensing always has a large volume and quality, because of the high resolution imaging load installed in it, and needs large control torque, which complicates the structure of system and introduces the exceeding interference. Therefore, we must apply the gear transmission mechanism,

© Springer Science+Business Media Singapore 2016
L. Zhang et al. (Eds.): AsiaSim 2016/SCS AutumnSim 2016, Part II, CCIS 644, pp. 232–247, 2016.
DOI: 10.1007/978-981-10-2666-9_23

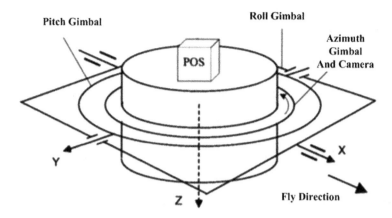

Pitch Gimbal

Roll Gimbal

Azimuth
Gimbal
And Camera

POS

Y

X

Z

Fly Direction

Fig. 1. Typical structure of tri-axial inertially stabilized platform for airborne remote sensing

to achieve high precision control, leading to a significant reduction in the structural resonance frequency of the system. However, the toque disturbance-rejection capability is approximately proportion to the bandwidth of the stabilization loop, which is limited by the structural resonance. The increased pressure, caused by the large quality, deteriorates the lubrication condition between bearing contact surfaces, resulting in a great increase of friction interference. The application of the large reduction ratio gear increases the counter electromotive force disturbance. In addition, the elastic force, which is come from non-rigid structure of the system, such as cable, the circuit noise interference, and so on, making disturbance-rejection property of control system particularly important [6–10].

The structure of control system of Inertially stabilized platform for airborne remote sensing is usually the dual-loop control structure, namely, the speed stable loop and the position stable loop. The control bandwidth of the velocity stabilization loop is, as a rule, far greater than the one of position stabilized loop, furthermore, except for tracking the input signal, generated by position loop controller, speed stable loop must acting to suppress interference. Therefore, velocity stabilization loop controller design is most important. Due to inertially stabilized platform parameters cannot be obtained accurately in actual engineering application, the controller design mainly uses the frequency domain analysis and PID method. This method has very strong practicability and reliability. However, these two methods are relatively rough design and, usually, cannot obtain optimal controller parameters, furthermore, cannot explain the anti-interference performance exactly. Adaptive control, fuzzy control, robust control methods are researched, in order to deal with the unknown parameters condition, and are gotten some achievement. However, the control system, come from advanced design methods above, are always complex and, in actual engineering, will bring new problems [11–16].

Based on the analysis of the complex frequency domain and considering the influence of the structure resonance, this paper proposes a novel optimal controller design method, which transforms the controller design problem to multi-objective issue and, considers the disturbance-rejection ability as an optimal target, using genetic algorithm to complete the design. The paper is organized as follows. The analysis of disturbance, system modeling and simplification are illustrated in Sect. 2; the main idea of the optimal design method of controller is described deeply in Sects. 3 and 4; in Sect. 5 simulation studies of the characteristic of a more realistic system is performed; finally, the effectiveness of the optimal design method is investigated through simulation studies.

2   Analysis of Disturbance and Modeling and Simplification of System

2.1   Negligible Disturbance

In practical engineering applications, there is a lot of interference, whose influence is very small to control accuracy, to highlight the main interference, this interference should be ignored. In aerial remote sensing work, due to the effect of control system, tri-axial gimbals are moving small around the inertial equilibrium position and, because of the small angular motion of aircraft, the angle and angular velocity between gimbals are keeping very small. Accordingly, the coupling effect can ignore, for that they are come from the high order terms of small quantities above, and the controller design of each axis can be separately carried on. Processing and installation error is unavoidable, but after careful design, processing, assembling and, the latter debugging and dynamic balance experiment, can limiting the disturbance to a very small rang, thus, we can ignore these disturbances in controller design. Noise of control circuit and sensor is also a factor affecting the control accuracy, while, in aerial remote sensing task, better performance of devices are usually selected and, the using of filter, so that the impact of noise can be not considered. By the analysis above, we can greatly simplify the factors, which need to be considered carefully in controller design.

2.2   LuGre Friction Model

Friction torque of inertially stabilized platform with large load is considerable, usually in few Nm and, and due to the low frequency interference caused by the angular motion of aircraft makes the low-speed friction effect particularly distinctness. At present, the research on the friction model has a lot of work, in which the LuGre model represents the highest level of the current, which fully reflects the low-speed friction effect, strict-back effect and zero-speed dynamic performance. The LuGre friction model has been applied to the inertial stabilization platform [17].

$$\begin{cases} z = \omega_r - \frac{\sigma_0 |\omega_r|}{g(\omega_r)} \bullet z \\ M_f = \sigma_0 z + \sigma_1 \dot{z} + \sigma_2 \omega_r \end{cases} \tag{1}$$

Where ω_r is relative angular velocity between gimbal and the base, z is internal friction state, which indicates the mean displacement of contact bristle, and usually has the follow formulation.

$$g(\omega_r) = M_c + (M_s - M_c)e^{-\left(\frac{\omega_r}{\omega_s}\right)^2} \tag{2}$$

The formula uses the exponential form to reflect the zero-speed friction dynamic, M_c is coulomb friction torque, M_s is the greatest static friction torque and, ω_s is strict-back constant, which can represent the negative slope of strict-back property combined with exponential form. M_f is friction torque, composed of three parts, first part is proportional to the internal friction state and σ_0 is scaling factor, stand for stiffness of bristle; the second part is caused by the change of internal state and σ_1 is micro-damp factor; the last part is viscous friction torque, and the coefficient is σ_2.

2.3 Motor Drive Model

The disturbance, caused by the counter electromotive of motor, amplified by large reduction ratio, causes greater impact to the control system accuracy, which needs analysis deeply. We can establish the model:

$$\begin{cases} U_c - U_e = L\dot{I} + RI \\ T_c = IK_iN \\ J\dot{\omega} = T_c - M_d \end{cases} \tag{3}$$

Where U_c is control input voltage, $U_e = K_eN\omega_r$ is counter electromotive of motor and, K_e is the coefficient, N is gear reduction ratio. I is motor current, L is motor inductance and R is motor resistance. Where T_c is motor output torque, which is proportional to current and, the scaling factor is K_i. $\dot{\omega}$ is absolute angular acceleration, M_d is interference torque, mainly caused by friction [18].

2.4 Structural Resonance Model

The introduction of gear transmission system greatly limits the bandwidth of the control system, which is a great threat to the stability of the control system. In order to consider the influence of the structural resonance, usually, a second order transform function is used to replace the structural resonance.

$$G_r = \frac{\omega_n^2}{s^2 + 2\zeta\omega_n + \omega_n^2} \tag{4}$$

Where ω_n is free frequency, which can be used to represent the structural resonance frequency, ζ is damp ratio, which can represent the influence of structural resonance. Based on the modeling and analysis above, we can complete the design of control system with the block diagram as shown in Fig. 2 [19].

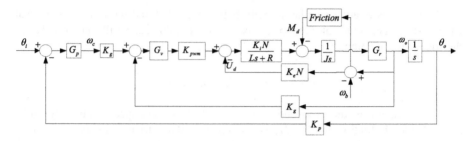

Fig. 2. Structure block diagram of control system

3 Optimal Design Method and Controller Design of Velocity Stable Loop

In the dual- loop control structure of Fig. 2, in addition to tracking the input signal, the speed stabilization loop must restrain the interference, so it must be carefully designed. G_r is represent the structural resonance as shown in Fig. 2, However, the second order transmission function increased two order of the system, greatly complicating the system. In order to simplify the control system and make the controller much easier, we can replace G_r by a constraint condition about closed-loop bandwidth, which is discussed in detail in follow sections. So, we can complete the optimization design of the speed stability loop controller with block diagram 3.

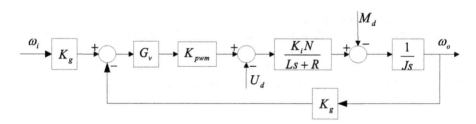

Fig. 3. The sketch map of optimal controller design of speed stability loop

3.1 The Structure of Controller G_v

From Fig. 3, we can get transfer function of output angular velocity versus input control signal:

$$G_{\omega_0/\omega_c} = \frac{K_i N K_{pwm} K_g G_v}{Js(Ls+R) + K_i N K_{pwm} K_g G_v} \tag{5}$$

Transfer function of tracking error to input angular velocity:

$$G_{e_\omega/\omega_c} = \frac{JK_g s(Ls+R)}{Js(Ls+R)+K_iNK_{pwm}K_gG_v} \tag{6}$$

The change of output angular velocity caused by counter electromotive disturbance is:

$$G_{\omega_0/U_d} = \frac{-K_iN}{Js(Ls+R)+K_iNK_{pwm}K_gG_v} \tag{7}$$

And the change of output angular velocity caused by equivalent interferential torque is:

$$G_{\omega_0/M_d} = \frac{-(Ls+R)}{Js(Ls+R)+K_iNK_{pwm}K_gG_v} \tag{8}$$

From (6), we can get steady state error of signal tracking is:

$$e_{\omega ss} = \lim_{s \to 0} \frac{JK_g s^2(Ls+R)\omega_i(s)}{Js(Ls+R)+K_iNK_{pwm}K_gG_v} \tag{9}$$

In order to achieve the effective tracking, tracking error should be keeping zero or as small as possible. Formula (9) indicates that the speed loop can't achieve effective tracking if the input signal is accelerated or even higher order signal. It is not allowed for system. To solve the confliction, the controller G_v must contain integral term, and the higher order the integral term is, the better tracking performance the system has. However, the higher order integral term can complex and reduce the stability of the system. From (7), we can get steady state output caused by counter electromotive interference:

$$\omega_{U_d ss} = \lim_{s \to 0} \frac{-K_iNsU_d(s)}{Js(Ls+R)+K_iNK_{pwm}K_gG_v} \tag{10}$$

Formula (9) indicates that control system can absolutely suppress the impulse and step interference but not the ramp or higher order disturbance if G_v without integral term. When G_v has first order integral term, the system can suppress the ramp interference, and when G_v has second order integral term, the system can deal with the higher interference. (Analysis about equivalent disturbance torque is the same as the counter electromotive interference.)

Based on the analysis above, fully considering the simpleness of the speed stabilization loop, tracking and disturbance-rejection performance, we let G_v be:

$$G_v = \frac{K_v(s+a)(s+b)}{s^2} \tag{11}$$

Where $K_v, a, b \in R^+$.

3.2   Optimal Design and Determination of Controller Parameters

3.2.1   Analysis of Stability and Stability Constraint Condition

Taking the formula (11) to Fig. 3, we can get open-loop transfer function:

$$G_{vopen} = \frac{K_{pwm}K_gK_iNK_v(s+a)(s+b)}{Js^3(Ls+R)} \tag{12}$$

The nyquist curve is shown in Fig. 4, when taking the general numerical values of the parameters in the model.

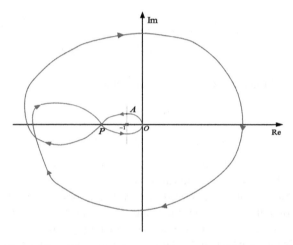

Fig. 4. Open-loop Nyquist curve of speed stabilization loop

According to the nyquist stability criterion, the control system is stable when point P is on the left side of point $(-1, 0)$. In order to ensure the control system stable and with enough stable margin, the point P should be on the left side of point $(-2, 0)$. Put $s = j\omega$ into formula (12), we can get the stability constraint condition.

$$\frac{C_1K_v\left[Lab - (a+b)R - L\omega_p^2\right]}{J\omega_p^2\left(L^2\omega_p^2 + R^2\right)} \ll -2 \tag{13}$$

3.2.2   Constraint Condition of Structural Resonance

To ensure the normal operation of the system not excite the structure resonance and, having enough margin of control system, ordinarily, have the inequation $\omega_{vb} \leq \omega_n$, where ω_{vb} is the control closed-loop bandwidth of velocity stabilization loop, ω_n is the structural resonance frequency. (The detail illustration of the advantage of the inequation is in the Sect. 5.) Taking the inequation into (5), and using the 3 dB bandwidth definition, we can get the constraint condition.

$$-JL^2\omega_{vb}^4 - 2LC_1K_v\left(ab - \omega_{vb}^2\right) - JR^2\omega_{vb}^2 + 2RC_1K_v(a+b) \leq 0 \qquad (14)$$

3.2.3 Analysis of Disturbance-Rejection Ability and Optimal Object Function

In order to analyze the influence between the value of K_v, a, b and the anti-interference ability of system, put $s = j\omega$ into formulas (7) and (8), and we can get exceeding output response signal's amplitude caused by disturbance.

$$\begin{cases} \left|G_{\omega_o/u_d}\right| = \sqrt{\dfrac{C_2^2\omega^4}{[JL\omega^4 + C_1K_v(ab-\omega^2)]^2 + [C_1K_v(a+b)-JR\omega^3]^2}} \\ \left|G_{\omega_o/M_d}\right| = \sqrt{\dfrac{L^2\omega^6 + R\omega^4}{[JL\omega^4 + C_1K_v(ab-\omega^2)]^2 + [C_1K_v(a+b)-JR\omega^3]^2}} \end{cases} \qquad (15)$$

For a certain frequency interference signal, the smaller the $\left|G_{\omega_o/u_d}\right|$ and $\left|G_{\omega_o/M_d}\right|$ is, the better the ability to suppress the interference is, thus, we can put forward an evaluation index S, which is composed of the $\left|G_{\omega_o/u_d}\right|$ and $\left|G_{\omega_o/M_d}\right|$, to represent the ability to suppress the disturbance of system.

$$S = \sqrt{\sum_{\omega=0}^{\omega=\omega_d} \left|G_{\omega_o/u_d}\right|_\omega^2} + \sqrt{\sum_{\omega=0}^{\omega=\omega_d} \left|G_{\omega_o/M_d}\right|_\omega^2} \qquad (16)$$

Where ω, ω_d are disturbance frequency and max disturbance frequency, respectively. They are determined by the actual conditions. If in an actual system, interference of some frequency or frequency domain is more than ones of residual frequency domain, we can add more weight to the amplitude response of S in these frequencies. The smaller S is, the better ability to suppress disturbance is.

3.2.4 Design of Controller Based on Genetic Algorithm

Based on the analysis above, we can transform the issue of controller design into multi-objectives optimal problem. Genetic algorithm, because of its high efficiency and global optimality which is widely applied to multi-objective optimization problems. So, we can use genetic algorithm to get optimal design of controller. Let S be the objective function, formula (13) and (14) be the nonlinear constraint condition, and $K_v, a, b > 0$ be the linear constraint condition. After programming and calculating, we can obtain optimal controller.

At the end of this chapter, we get the optimal controller design flow chart 5 (Fig. 5).

4 Controller Design of Position Stable Loop

Control system of position stabilization loop is shown in Fig. 6.

Unlike the speed stability loop controller design, the main function of the position stability loop is to track the input signal without the need to consider the interference

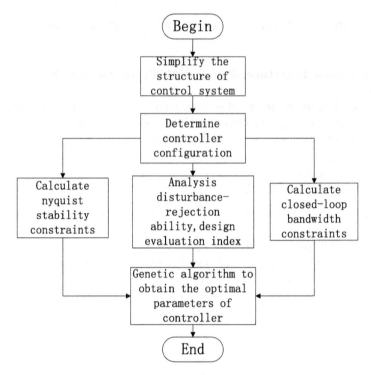

Fig. 5. Optimal design flow chart of controller of speed stability loop

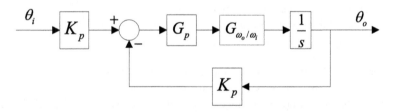

Fig. 6. Control system block diagram of position stabilization loop

suppression. Furthermore, design of G_p is based on the design of G_v, thus, the design of G_p is much easier.

Like the design of G_v, first is to determine the controller configuration. Considering the simpleness and tracking performance of position stabilization loop, let the configuration of controller G_p is (the detail discuss is similar to the determination of configuration of G_v):

$$G_p = \frac{K_G(s+c)}{s} \qquad (17)$$

Where $K_G, c \in R^+$. The selection of controller parameters must ensure the stability requirements and control bandwidth constraints. From Fig. 6, formula (5), (11) and (17), open-loop transfer function of position stability loop can be obtained.

$$G_{popen} = \frac{C_1 K_v K_G K_p (s+a)(s+b)(s+c)}{Js^5 (Ls+R) + C_1 K_v s^2 (s+a)(s+b)} \qquad (18)$$

Bringing G_v, whose parameters are known, and numerical values of related parameters, the nyquist curve of G_{popen} is shown in the Fig. 7.

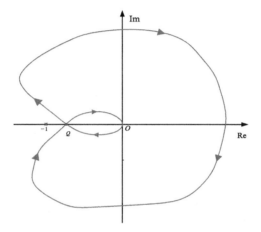

Fig. 7. Nyquist curve of open-loop transfer function of position stable loop.

According to the nyquist stability criterion and enough stability margin requirements, point Q, in Fig. 7, should be on the right side of point $(-0.5, 0)$, namely

$$Q_{Re} \geq -0.5 \qquad (19)$$

To ensure the tracking and disturbance-rejection performance of the controller G_v, the control closed-loop bandwidth should satisfy the inequation:

$$\omega_p \leq \frac{1}{10} \omega_{vb} \qquad (20)$$

Where ω_p is the closed-loop bandwidth of position stability loop.

The values of the G_p have little influence on the system anti-interference ability, furthermore, there are only two parameters in G_p, thus, we can use simple search method to complete design.

5 Simulation and Analysis

5.1 Simulation Parameters and Controller Design Results

Based on the technical parameters of a practical principle prototype, the simulation parameters, that are need in control block diagram 2, are shown in Table 1.

Table 1 Simulation parameters of a practical principle prototype

Parameter symbol	Value	Parameter symbol	Value
Motor inductance L	8.6 * 2.2e-4 (H)	Second order Damping ζ	0.1
Motor resistance R	8.6 (Ω)	Counter electromotive K_e	0.01
Current torque Coefficient K_i	0.181	Coulomb friction torque M_c	1.71 (Nm)
Reduction ratio N	120	Maximal static friction M_s	3.42 (Nm)
Moment of inertia J	1.65 (Kg•m^2)	Strict-back coefficient ω_s	0.03
Gyro scale factor K_g	2 * 0.694 * 2^{19}/20	Bristle stiffness coefficient σ_0	1500 (N/m)
PWM coefficient K_{pwm}	28/937	Micro-damping σ_1	11 (Ns/m)
Structural response frequency ω_n	30 (Hz)	Viscous coefficient σ_2	27 (Ns/rad)
POS scale factor K_g	180/π	Interference frequencies ω	0 $\sim$ 20 rad/s

In genetic algorithm, let population size 300, crossover probability 0.8 and the Mutation probability 0.2. The fitness function is based formula (16). Putting all simulation parameters into the optimal controller design method, we get that $G_v = 0.02(s+2)(s+2.735)/s^2$. The closed-loop control bandwidth of the speed stabilization loop is $\omega_{vb} = 5.98$ (Hz), which is very close to $\omega_n/5$, ensures the structural resonance constraints, responsive velocity and disturbance-rejection performance. Bring G_v in the nyquist curve, we can get that the point P is $(-28.45, 0)$, indicates that control system has large stability margin. Put G_v into the position stabilized loop, using the design method in Sect. 4, we can get $G_p = 0.05497(s+0.1)/s$. And closed-loop control bandwidth of position stabilization loop is 0.5714 Hz, which satisfies the bandwidth constraint condition and is close to the ultimate value, namely, $\omega_{pb} \approx \omega_{vb}/10$. Point Q, as shown in Fig. 7, is $(-8 \times 10^{-4}, 0)$, indicates that system has large stability margin.

5.2 Simulation and Analysis

In order to illuminate the effectiveness of the optimal design method, the contrast controller is designed by the traditional method such as PID and Frequency Response method. The speed stability loop controller G_v has a great influence on the performance of the system, thus, the simulations as follows are mainly in the speed stability loop.

5.2.1 Stability and Closed-Loop

Introduce the second order structure resonance term to the speed stability loop, as shown in Fig. 2, and put into different controllers, that satisfy the nyquist constraints but make system with different closed- loop bandwidth, we can get the step response as shown in Fig. 8.

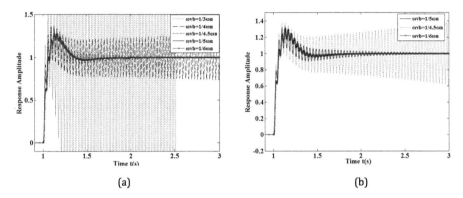

(a)   (b)

Fig. 8. Step response with different closed loop control bandwidth. In plot (a), $\omega_n = 60\pi(rad/s)\zeta = 0.1$, as in Table 1, While $\omega_n = \omega_n - \Delta\omega$ and $\zeta = \zeta - \Delta\zeta$ in plot (b).

From Fig. 8(a), we can know that system is stable when $\omega_{vb} \leq \omega_n/5$, and the system is unstable when $\omega_{vb} \geq \omega_n/4$. Figure 8 also shows the condition, when ω_{vb} is slightly greater than $\omega_n/5$, although system is stable at the beginning, system will lost the stable because of slightly changes of the structural resonance parameters such as ω_n and ζ, as shown in figure (b). As a result, controller G_v must satisfy the inequation of $\omega_{vb} \leq \omega_n/5$.

5.2.2 Tracking Error and Configuration of Controller G_v

Based on the simulation model, using traditional controller design methods, remaining all conditions unchanged, we can get various types of contrast controllers: type-0 contrast controller $G_{v0} = 0.01$, type-1 contrast controller $G_{v1} = 0.01(s+5)/s$ and type-2 contrast controller $G_{v2} = 0.01(s+5)^2/s^2$. Let velocity stabilization loop tracking step, ramp and acceleration signal, respectively, with different types of controllers, we can get the response curves as shown in Fig. 9.

Figure 9 indicates that: Tracking performance of type-2 controller is much better than the type-0 and type-1 controllers. Compare the tracking performances of the optimal controller G_v and contrast type-2 controller G_{v2}, the former is better.

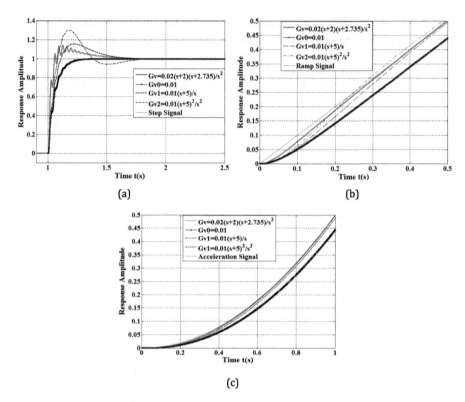

Fig. 9. Responses of different input signal of controllers with different configuration. Plot (a) shows response of step input and, in (b) illuminates the response about ramp input, while in (c) is talking about the case of accelerated input signal.

5.2.3 Disturbance-Rejection Performance

Put optimal controller G_v and contrast controller G_{v2} into formula (15), respectively, we can get the response plot of disturbance as shown in Fig. 10.

Figure 10 indicates that the ability, to suppress disturbance, of optimal controller is much stronger than the one of contrast controller. Introduce second order structural resonance term, models of counter electromotive interference and LuGre friction model, whose parameter is in the Table 1. And using chirp signal, whose frequencies is $0 \sim 20$ rad/s, as angular motion of aircraft, we can get the step response curves as shown in Fig. 11.

The optimal controller design method improves the anti-interference performance of system about 20 %.

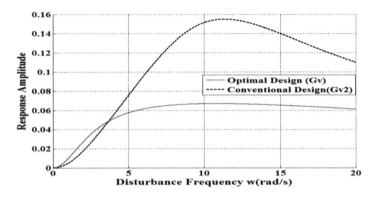

Fig. 10. Responses of disturbances with different frequencies of two controllers

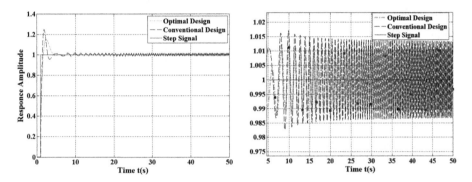

Fig. 11. Simulation plot of responses of disturbance about two controllers

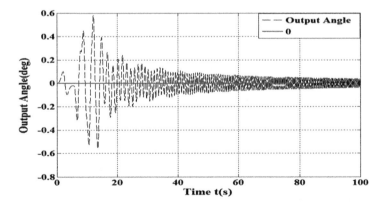

Fig. 12. Simulation of disturbance suppression of actual sensing working

5.3 Simulation of Position Stabilized Loop

Bring designed controller G_v and G_G in control system as shown as Fig. 2, keep all simulation condition is the same as above, let the input signal 0, and the angular motion disturbance of aircraft is a sine signal with 1degree and 1 Hz, then we can get Fig. 12.

Figure 12 shows that, in aerial photography, control system can keep the line of sight of the optical load in a small rang, less than 0.05 degree. In summary, the proposed optimal controller design method is simple and effective, which is suitable for engineering application.

6 Summary and Conclusions

Based on the complex frequency domain analysis of disturbance about inertially stabilized platform, modeling the interference of motor counter electromotive, friction and structural resonance, respectively, a novel optimal controller design method is developed, which is designed with the target of the strongest ability to suppress disturbance and proved effective. Combined with a practical prototype system, some conclusions are got by simulation. The proposed type-2 configuration of controller has more advantages, considering the complexity of the system and the tracking performance of the signal; the constraint conditions of bandwidth and stability, that are put forward after analyzing the open-loop nyquist stability criterion and the influence of structural resonance, ensure the stability and robust performance of system; the optimal controller with best disturbance-rejection performance is obtained, by applying the genetic algorithm, which is implemented by proposed objective function about the evaluation index of anti-interference ability. Finally, Contrast simulation, which is implemented between optimal controller and conventional controller, indicates that the anti-interference performance of system is improved about 20 % by using the optimal controller design method.

References

1. Lin, Z.-C., Liu, K., Zhang, W.: Inertially stabilized platform for airborne remote sensing using magnetic bearings. IEEE/ASME Trans. Mechatron. **c**, 1083–4435 (2015)
2. Hilkert, J.M.: Inertially stabilized platform technology concepts and principles. IEEE Control Syst. Mag. 21–46 (2008)
3. Liao, H.B., Fan, S.-X., Hei, M.: Modeling and parameter identification for electro-optical stabilized platform servo systems. Opt. Precis. Eng. **2**, 477–483 (2015). (in Chinese)
4. Pang, X.-L., Fan, D.-P., Teng, X.-D.: Realization of digital airborne opto-electronic servo-system. Opto-Electron. Eng. **3**, 10–15 (2007)
5. Liu, Q., Er, L.-J., Liu, J.-K.: Overview of characteristics, modeling and compensation of nonlinear friction in servo systems. Syst. Eng. Electron. **24**, 45–50 (2002)
6. Masten, M.K.: Inertially stabilized platforms for optical imaging systems. IEEE Control Syst. Mag. **2**, 47–63 (2008)
7. Lin, Z., Liu, K.: Inertially stabilized line-of-sight control system using a magnetic bearing with vernier gimbaling capacity. In: Optical Design and Testing VI. SPIE, Beijing (2014)

8. Li, S.-S., Zong, M.-Y.: Design of control system based on PID of three-axis inertially stabilized platform for airborne remote sensing. J. Jilin Univ. **7**, 275–279 (2011)
9. Yin, R., Fang, J.-C., Zhong, M.-Y.: Dynamic modeling and simulation of inertial stabilized platform for aerial remote sensing system. J. Chin. Inertial Technol. **12**, 676–685 (2011)
10. Mu, Q., Liu, G., Lei, X.: A RBFNN-Based Adaptive Disturbance Compensation Approach Applied to Magnetic Suspension Inertially Stabilized Platform. http://dx.doi.org/10.1155/2014/657985
11. Zhu, M.-C., Liu, H., Zhang, X., et al.: Adaptive feed-forward control for inertially stabilized platform. Opt. Precis. Eng. **1**, 141–147 (2015)
12. Hilkert, J.M.: Adaptive control system techniques applied to inertial stabilization systems. In: Acquisition, Tracking, and Pointing V, pp. 190–206 (1990)
13. Gibson, S., Tsao, T.-C.: Adaptive Jitter control for tracker line of sight stabilization. In: Advanced Wave-Front Control: Methods, Devices, and Applications VII (2010)
14. Lee, H.-P., Yoo, I.-E.: Robust control design for a two-axis gimbaled stabilization system. IEEE **2008**, 1–7 (2008)
15. Jark, M.: Fuzzy controller for line-of-sight stabilization systems. OpticalEngineering **43**(6), 1340–1394 (2004)
16. Morales, R., Sira-Ramírez, H., Feliuc, V.: Adaptive control based on fast online algebraic identification and GPI control for magnetic levitation systems with time-varying input gain. Int. J. Control **87**(8), 1604–1621 (2014)
17. Zhou, X.-Y., Liu, W.: Parameter identification of friction model on inertially stabilized platform for aerial remote sensing application. J. Chin. Inertial Technol. **12**, 710–714 (2013)
18. Dongliang, Liu, Yanfei, Cui, Meibin, Chen: Research of back-EMF estimation for brushless DC motor. Trans. China Electrotech. Soc. **6**, 52–58 (2013)
19. Hilkert, J.M.: A reduced-order disturbance observer applied to inertially stabilized line-of-sight control. In: William, E.T., Paul, F M. (eds.) Acquisition, Tracking, Pointing, and Laser Systems Technologies XXV (2011)

Cooperative Task Assignation for R/S UAVs Based on Binary Wolf Pack Algorithm

Yonglan Liu[1($\boxtimes$)], Weimin Li[1], Husheng Wu[2], and Chengzhong Lv[1]

[1] Air and Missile Defense College,
Air Force Engineering University, Xi'an, Shaanxi, China
liuyonglancol.hi@163.com,
{2576000402,1101596177}@qq.com
[2] Armed Police Force Engineering University, Xi'an, Shannxi, China
852693678@qq.com

Abstract. Reconnaissance and Strike Integrated Unmanned Aerial Vehicles (briefed as R/S UAVs) have operational capabilities of performing many kinds of missions. Aiming at its cooperative task assignation problem, Binary Wolf Pack Algorithm (briefed as BWPA) is proposed to solve the problem. Firstly, model of task assignation is built on the degree of threaten and the degree of hard to attack that time-sensitive targets have. Secondly, basing on Wolf Pack Algorithm (briefed as WPA) and taking binary coding as entry point, BWPA is introduced, which abstracts a productive rule for leading wolf, a renewable mechanism for whole wolf pack, and three intelligent behaviors of scouting, summoning and beleaguering. Lastly, through flexible dealing with task list of time-sensitive targets and coding of R/S UAVs, BWPA is adopted to solve the problem of task assignation. Simulation results show that proposed model is verified, and BWPA has astringency and global optimization capability, is effective to solve the problem of cooperative task assignation of UAVs.

Keywords: Task assignation · Reconnaissance and strike integrated unmanned aerial vehicles · Binary wolf pack algorithm

1 Introduction

With rapid development of information technology, unmanned aerial vehicles' capabilities are improved and extended, whose application in military field is paid high attention. As the main developing direction of unmanned aerial vehicles' technology, R/S UAV integrates reconnaissance platform and strike platform, has many capabilities such as reconnaissance, surveillance, target acquisition, and real-time striking, greatly shortening the time from detecting target to destroying [1]. It is expected to carry out surprise striking effect to high value and time-sensitive targets. Problem of cooperative task assignation is still a hot topic in the study field of UAVs at present [2, 3]. Methods of cooperative task assignation that more often used are dynamic programming, branch and bound, intelligent optimization algorithm, task assignation based on contract net, and so on [2, 4]. Dynamic programming, and branch and bound, are applied to the problem of small scale and simple task assignation. The method of task assignation

© Springer Science+Business Media Singapore 2016
L. Zhang et al. (Eds.): AsiaSim 2016/SCS AutumnSim 2016, Part II, CCIS 644, pp. 248–261, 2016.
DOI: 10.1007/978-981-10-2666-9_24

based on contract net has a simple principle, but is limited to that each bargaining must be dependent and linear [5], and always conflicts with personal benefit in pursuing the optimal whole operational effectiveness. Intelligent optimization algorithm does not rely on specific model, and is easy to be implemented, has a low computing complexity and a superior performance, and so on. WPA, belongs to intelligent optimization algorithm, realizes the global optimization through simulating hunting behaviors of cooperative searching based on job distribution of the wolf pack and distribution mode for prey, and has better computational robustness and global searching ability [6, 7].

This paper will adopt the discrete form of WPA, that is BWPA, to solve the problem of cooperative task assignation for multi-R/S UAVs.

2 Simulation Models

2.1 Problem of Cooperative Task Assignation for R/S UAVs

Problem of cooperative task assignation for UAVs, belongs to complex combinational optimization problem, aimed at achieve task efficiency as high as possible at the cost as low as possible. Problem includes task set that each UAV performs, sequence and time of performing task.

Background of the research is that multi-R/S UAVs cooperatively perform air to air (land) tasks. Assuming that there might appear many time-sensitive targets in an operational airfield (land field), which is transpired through intelligence means. According to the degree of threaten, time-sensitive targets can be divided into three types of light degree of threaten, medium degree of threaten, and serious degree of threaten. According to the state of time-sensitive targets, that is the degree of hard to attack, those targets can be divided into three types of easy to attack, medium, and hard to attack. Some of time-sensitive targets can be attacked directly; some of them may need to be confirmed before being attacked, some important targets may need to be damage evaluated after being attacked. Aiming at important time-sensitive target, three tasks of confirming, attacking and damage evaluating need to be done in an order. Accordingly, operational task can be resolved into tasks that one R/S UAV can perform, gaining a series of task set.

Typical characteristic of time-sensitive target is that motion state of target will change over time, thus leads to the change of degree of threaten and degree of hard to attack. This determines that for time-sensitive target, cooperative task assignation is not suited for long time planning, should be partitioned into many short time segments for planning, to ensure the validity of cooperative task assignation. Model of assignation that built is applied to each time segment, but only thing to note here is that the degree of threaten and the degree of hard to attack of target change, which means that the priority degree of task assignation changes.

Evaluation index of cooperative task assignation scheme is that in any time segment of planning, the income that R/S UAVs gain is largest.

Related parameters in the problem of cooperative task assignation for multi-R/S UAVs can be represented as:

$V = \{V_1, V_2, \ldots V_{N_V}\}$ is the set of R/S UAVs, N_V is the quantity of R/S UAVs.

$G = \{G_1, G_2, \ldots G_{N_G}\}$ is the set of time-sensitive targets, N_G is the quantity of time-sensitive targets.

$T = \{\Delta t_1, \Delta t_2, \cdots \Delta t_{N_T}\}$ is the set of time segments for task assignation. In different time segment, state of time-sensitive targets will change. N_T is the quantity of time segments for task assignation. In any time segment, a time-sensitive target will be assigned to a R/S UAV.

$M_{g_i} = \{M_{g_{i1}}, M_{g_{i2}}, \ldots M_{g_{iN_m}}\}$ is the task set of time-sensitive target G_i that R/S UAVs will perform, N_m is the quantity of tasks.

$x_{g_i, V_j, \Delta t_k} \in \{0, 1\}$ is that if in Δt_k segment, time-sensitive target G_i is assigned to R/S UAV V_j, then $x_{g_i, V_j, \Delta t_k} = 1$; else $x_{g_i, V_j, \Delta t_k} = 0$.

$f_{\Delta t_k}(g_i, V_j, M_{g_{i,m}})$ is the income that R/S UAV V_j gains through performing $M_{g_{i,m}}$ to time-sensitive target G_i in Δt_k segment. Revenue function is:

$$f_{\Delta t_k}(g_i, V_j, M_{g_{i,m}}) = \lambda f_{T,\Delta t_k}(g_i, V_j, M_{g_{i,m}}) + (1 - \lambda) f_{A,\Delta t_k}(g_i, V_j, M_{g_{i,m}}) \quad (1)$$

Thereinto, λ is the weight, $f_{T,\Delta t_k}(g_i, V_j, M_{g_{i,m}})$ is the income that R/S UAV V_j gains according to the degree of time-sensitive target's threaten, through performing $M_{g_{i,m}}$ for time-sensitive target G_i in Δt_k segment. $f_{A,\Delta t_k}(g_i, V_j, M_{g_{i,m}})$ is the income that R/S UAV V_j gains according to the degree of hard to attack, through performing $M_{g_{i,m}}$ for time-sensitive target G_i in Δt_k segment. Value of λ is among the interval of $(0, 1)$, if the value is close to 1, then income that is gained through performing task for time-sensitive target with serious degree of threaten, takes up a great portion, meaning that time-sensitive target with serious degree of threaten tends to be attacked; if the value is close to 0, then income that is gained through performing task for time-sensitive target with easy to attack, takes up a great portion, meaning that time-sensitive target with easy to attack tends to be attacked. According to dividing types of the degree of threaten and the degree of hard to attack, the income that is gained through attacking the type of target, can be represented in form of segmented function, as follows:

$$D_T = \begin{cases} 3 & \text{light degree of threaten} \\ 6 & \text{medium degree of threaten} \\ 9 & \text{serious degree of threaten} \end{cases} \quad (2)$$

$$D_A = \begin{cases} 8 & \text{easy to attack} \\ 5 & \text{medium} \\ 2 & \text{hard to attack} \end{cases} \quad (3)$$

Thereinto, D_T represents that divided by the degree of threaten; D_A represents that divided by the degree of hard to attack. Both of them represent the income of performing reconnaissance for time-sensitive target.

For time-sensitive target, task is performed in the order of reconnaissance confirming, fire attacking and damage evaluating. Only if time-sensitive target is detected and confirmed, the following fire attacking and damage evaluating can be performed. Therefore, income that gained through performing the task of reconnaissance confirming is largest, then following by performing the task of fire attacking, last by performing the task of damage evaluating. So revenue function is:

$$f_{T,\Delta t_k}(g_i, V_j, M_{g_{i,m}}) = D_{T,\Delta t_k} \times \frac{N_m - m + 1}{N_m} \tag{4}$$

$$f_{A,\Delta t_k}(g_i, V_j, M_{g_{i,m}}) = D_{A,\Delta t_k} \times \frac{N_m - m + 1}{N_m} \tag{5}$$

Thereinto, values of $D_{T,\Delta t_k}$ and $D_{A,\Delta t_k}$ depend on the state of time-sensitive target G_i; value of m depends on the type of task that R/S UAV V_j performs for time-sensitive target G_i.

In conclusion, problem of cooperative task assignment of many R/S UAVs can be depicted as:

$$\max F = \sum_{i=1}^{N_G} \sum_{j=1}^{N_V} \sum_{m=1}^{N_m} f_{\Delta t_k}(g_i, V_j, M_{g_{i,m}}) \qquad i \in N_G, k \in N_T, m \in N_m \tag{6}$$

$$s.t. \quad x_{g_i, V_j, \Delta t_k} \in \{0, 1\} \quad j \in N_V \tag{7}$$

$$\left(\sum_{i=1}^{N_G} x_{g_i, V_j, \Delta t_k} \right) \cap \left(\sum_{j=1}^{N_V} x_{g_i, V_j, \Delta t_k} \right) = 1 \tag{8}$$

$$\sum_{k=1}^{N_T} \sum_{j=1}^{N_V} x_{g_i, V_j, \Delta t_k} = g_{i, N_m} \tag{9}$$

Thereinto, formula (6) represents that in Δt_k segment, the income that R/S UAVs gain is largest. Formulas (7), (8) and (9) are constraint conditions. Among, formula (7) represents the constraint of integer decision variable; formula (8) represents in any Δt_k segment, only a time-sensitive target G_i will be assigned to a R/S UAV V_j, and a R/S UAV V_j only can perform one task; formula (9) represents that for each time-sensitive target G_i, there are g_{i,N_m} tasks that are performed, ensuring that task set of each time-sensitive target can be completed.

2.2 Binary Wolf Pack Algorithm

Here only briefly introduces the principles of WPA, places great emphasis on the study of applying BWPA to the problem of cooperative task assignation.

Fundamental Principles of WPA. Wolves, as a social animal, have specific job distributions, and maintain the survive and development of whole wolf pack through unity and cooperation. As described in Fig. 1, wolf pack has three types of leading

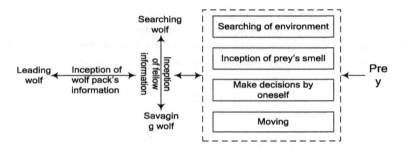

Fig. 1. Hunting model of wolf pack

wolf, searching wolf and savaging wolf, taking on separate different job distribution. WPA adopts design method of bottom to top based on the artificial wolf and path structure of cooperative searching based on job distribution of the wolf pack [6, 8]. It carries out whole hunting process of the wolf pack, through individual perception of prey's smell, searching of environmental information, sharing and interacting among different individuals, and making decisions by oneself based on job distribution of individual.

From whole hunting process of the wolf pack, WPA abstracts three intelligent behaviors of scouting, summoning and beleaguering, a productive rule for leading wolf that the winner can dominate its all, and a renewable mechanism for whole wolf pack that named survival of the stronger. Detail description of three intelligent behaviors, a productive rule for leading wolf and a renewable mechanism for whole wolf pack in continuous space, refers to doctrine [6]. These won't be explained here.

Principles of BWPA. Transform from continuous space to discrete space can be carried out by special coding. On the basis of WPA in continues space, WPA in discrete space, that is BWPA, can be obtained by introducing the concept of binary coding and doing some modification of related definitions. Three intelligent behaviors and survival mechanism in discrete space will be described at length in the following.

Parameter Meanings and Basic Definitions. For convenient to describe, some parameter meanings and basic definitions in discrete space are given in the first place [7].

Discrete space, also named European space, denoted as $D_{N \times m}$; N is the quantity of artificial wolves; location $\mathbf{X}_i$ of artificial wolf i in discrete space is expressed by $(x_{i1}, x_{i2}, \cdots, x_{ij}, \cdots, x_{im})$ in the form of binary coding, where $i = 1, 2, \ldots,$ $N; j = 1, 2, \ldots, m$; m is the length of binary coding of artificial wolf's location; value of element x_{ij} among $\mathbf{X}_i$ only can be 0 or 1. Density of prey's smell that artificial wolf perceives is the objective function value, expressed by $Y = f(\mathbf{X})$.

Definition 1: Distance. Distance between artificial wolf p and artificial wolf q is Manhattan distance, that is:

$$L(p,q) = \sum_{j=1}^{m} |x_{pj} - x_{qj}| \, p, q \in \{1, 2, \cdots, N\} \tag{10}$$

Definition 2: Reverse. Reverse of element x_{ij} among $\mathbf{X}_i$, is that turn original value of x_{ij} into its reverse value 0 or 1, that is:

$$x_{ij}^T = \begin{cases} 1, & x_{ij} = 0 \\ 0, & x_{ij} = 1 \end{cases} \tag{11}$$

Definition 3: Motion operator [7]. M is the location set of coding that reversed, and can not be none, which represents motion range of artificial wolf in discrete space; r is the quantity of coding location that reversed, which represents motion step; motion operator $\Gamma(\mathbf{X}_i, M, r)$ represents that randomly choose r coding location from M and reverse the value of r coding location.

$$\mathbf{X}_i = \{1, 0, 0, 1, 1, 0\} \qquad M = \{3, 5\} \quad r = 1$$

Then $\Gamma(\mathbf{X}_i, M, r) = \{1, 0, 1, 1, 1, 0\}$ or $\{1, 0, 0, 1, 0, 0\}$

Related Description of Intelligent Behaviors and Rules. BWPA is developed on the basis of WPA, including a productive rule for leading wolf, a renewable mechanism for whole wolf pack, and three intelligent behaviors of scouting, summoning and beleaguering.

(1) A productive rule for leading wolf. In initial solution space, artificial wolf with the optimal objective function value will be seen as leading wolf. Taking notes objective function value of the optimal wolf after each iteration, if it is superior to the objective function value of leading wolf in previous iteration, then the location of leading wolf is replaced with location of the optimal wolf. If there are many wolves with optimal objective function value, then leading wolf is produced by a random choice of these wolves. What needs to note here is that leading wolf directly enters into the next iteration, without joining in the three intelligent behaviors.

(2) A renewable mechanism for whole wolf pack. According to the natural law of survival that survival of the fittest, R artificial wolves with worst objective function value in the algorithm will be deleted, meantime, new R artificial wolves will be added randomly. Value of R affects the diversity of whole wolf pack, if it is large, the diversity can be maintained well; but if it is too large, BWPA tends to random searching. Therefore, value of R should be random integer among the interval $[\frac{N}{2\beta}, \frac{N}{\beta}]$, β represents the renewed ratio factor of whole wolf pack. New artificial wolves may go beyond the limit of task constraint, so artificial wolf's location $\mathbf{X}_i = (x_{i1}, x_{i2}, \cdots, x_{ij}, \cdots, x_{im})$ without meet the conditions, should repeat to carry out motion operator $\mathbf{X}_i^* = \Gamma(\mathbf{X}_i, M, 1)$, until meet the conditions. Value of M is:

$$M(k) = \begin{cases} j, \ k = k+1, \ j = j+1, \ x_{ij} = 1 \\ null, \ k = k, \ j = j+1, \ x_{ij} = 0 \end{cases} \tag{12}$$

Thereinto, $j = 1, 2, \cdots, m$, initial value of k is 1; null represents the none; final value of k is the quantity of elements that the set M includes.

(3) Scouting behavior. Objective function value of searching wolf i is Y_i. If $Y_i > Y_{lead}$ (objective function value of leading wolf), then let $Y_{lead} = Y_i$, which means the searching wolf i becomes leading wolf. If $Y_i < Y_{lead}$, then searching wolf i tries to move one step toward h directions for scout, and its location $\mathbf{X}_i$ carries out motion operator $\Gamma(\mathbf{X}_i, M, step_a)$ for h times. In the meantime, taking notes objective function value Y_{ip} of searching wolf i in each trial move, and comparing the objective function value before move with that after move, the decision of whether to move can be made. If searching wolf i moves, then it moves one step toward the p^* direction with largest value of Y_{ip} and its location $\mathbf{X}_i$ is updated. Until $Y_i > Y_{lead}$, or scouting times T go beyond the limit T_{max}, the process will not be repeated. Among, taking diversity of searching wolves into consideration, value of h may be the random integer among the interval $[h_{min}, h_{max}]$; $M = \{1, 2, \cdots, m\}$; $step_a$ is scouting step of searching wolf; $p \in H$, $H = \{1, 2, \cdots, h\}$.

(4) Summoning behavior. When heard of the summoning of leading wolf, savaging wolf will spontaneously move quickly toward leading wolf's location $\mathbf{X}_d$ at a bigger raiding step $step_b$. Updating formula of location $\mathbf{X}_i$ of savaging wolf i is

$$\mathbf{X}'_i = \Gamma(\mathbf{X}_i, M, step_b) \tag{13}$$

Value of M in formula (13) is:

$$M(k) = \begin{cases} j, k = k+1, \ j = j+1, \ x_{dj} \neq x_{ij} \\ null, k = k, \ j = j+1, \ x_{dj} = x_{ij} \end{cases} \tag{14}$$

Thereinto, $j = 1, 2, \cdots, m$, initial value of k is 1; null represents the none; M is the set of coding locations where savaging wolf's location $\mathbf{X}_i$ is not different from leading wolf's location $\mathbf{X}_d$. If M is none, then motion operator $\Gamma(\mathbf{X}_i, M^*, 1)$ is carried out randomly for one times, here $M^* = \{1, 2, \cdots, m\}$.

Assumed that objective function value of savaging wolf i is Y_i. Similar to the behavior of searching wolf, if $Y_i > Y_{lead}$, then let $Y_{lead} = Y_i$, which means savaging wolf i becomes leading wolf. If $Y_i < Y_{lead}$, then savaging wolf i won't continue to raid, until the distance between savaging wolf i and leading wolf d_{is} is less than the judging distance d_{near}, and turn into beleaguering behavior. Among, $d_{near} = \lceil m/\omega \rceil$, ω is the distance judging factor, $\lceil * \rceil$ represents round up to an integer.

(5) Beleaguering behavior. Savaging wolf and searching wolf obey the command of leading wolf and beleaguer the prey. View leading wolf's location $\mathbf{X}_d$ as location of the prey, updating formula of location $\mathbf{X}_i$ of artificial wolf i that carries out the beleaguering behavior is:

$$\mathbf{X}'_i = \Gamma(\mathbf{X}^*_i, M^*, step_c) \tag{15}$$

Thereinto, $\{1, 2, \cdots, m\}$; $\mathbf{X}^*_i = \Gamma(\mathbf{X}_i, M, step_c)$, the method of set the value of M refers to formula (14); $step_c$ is the beleaguering step of artificial wolf i. Specific meanings of motion operator $\Gamma(\mathbf{X}_i, M, step_c)$ and $\Gamma(\mathbf{X}^*_i, M^*, step_c)$, along with M are referred to doctrine [7].

Comparing objective function value of artificial wolf before carrying out beleaguering behavior with that after carrying out beleaguering behavior, then greedy decision can be made.

Scouting step $step_a$, raiding step $step_b$ and beleaguering step $step_c$ are integers, which mean elaborate degrees of searching the optimal solution, when artificial wolves have different job distributions. These steps' relationship in the coding space where length is m, is:

$$\lceil m/10 \rceil \geq step_b \geq step_a \geq step_c = 1 \tag{16}$$

2.3 Process Design of Cooperative Task Assignation for Multi-R/S UAVs Based on BWPA

Aiming at any Δt_k segment, problem of cooperative task assignation for multi-R/S UAVs can be expressed as:

$$\max F = \sum_{i=1}^{N_G} \sum_{j=1}^{N_V} \sum_{m=1}^{N_m} f_{\Delta t_k}(g_i, V_j, M_{g_{i,m}})$$

$$= \lambda \sum_{i=1}^{N_G} \sum_{j=1}^{N_V} \sum_{m=1}^{N_m} f_{T, \Delta t_k}(g_i, V_j, M_{g_{i,m}}) + (1 - \lambda) \sum_{i=1}^{N_G} \sum_{j=1}^{N_V} \sum_{m=1}^{N_m} f_{A, \Delta t_k}(g_i, V_j, M_{g_{i,m}})$$

$$\tag{17}$$

As formula (9) is the constraint of completing task in the whole time, so it can be resolved into any time segment, and considered through updating the initial task set in iteration. Here focuses on task assignment of the current time segment, and mainly considers the constraints (7) and (8).

Due to special performance, R/S UAVs can be thought to carry out any of three tasks of reconnaissance confirming, fire attacking and damage evaluating. Inspired by doctrine [9] and [10], a kind of one dimensional binary coding $\mathbf{X}_i$ is designed to express the scheme of task assignation.

$$Y = (Y_1, Y_2, \cdots Y_{GD}, Y_{GD+1}, Y_{GD+2}, \cdots Y_{GD+GA}, Y_{GD+GA+1}, Y_{GD+GA+2}, \cdots Y_{GD+GA+GV})$$

$$X = (X_1, X_2, \cdots X_{GD}, X_{GD+1}, X_{GD+2}, \cdots X_{GD+GA}, X_{GD+GA+1}, X_{GD+GA+2}, \cdots X_{GD+GA+GV})$$

$$\mathbf{X}_i = (x_{i1}, x_{i2}, \cdots, x_{ij}, \cdots, x_{im})$$

Thereinto, GD, GA 和 GV among the subscript of X separately express the sorties of UVAs that demand to carry out tasks of reconnaissance confirming, fire attacking and damage evaluating to all targets. X represents the total set of all tasks after being resolved, that is total sorties of R/S UAVs that demand. According to relations of one to one corresponding, location of X can be coded in binary, noting that length of coding takes the largest as a standard. When the length of coding is short, invalid 0 can be added before the coding, For example $X_1 = 2$, $X_2 = 4$, then those binary coding are (010) and (110). Coding scheme of $\mathbf{X}_i$ may be obtained by corresponding binary coding to location coordinate of artificial wolf. Meantime, there is a group of target numbering vector Y that corresponding with X, which is determined by task table of battle targets.

In order to understand the meaning of the coding, an example is inducted to explain. Assumed that 4 R/S UAVs will carry out battle tasks to 3 time-sensitive targets, task table of target G that waited to attack is shown in Table 1. In model of task assignation, numbering of target G_i is $i = 1, 2, 3$; numbering of V_j is $j = 1, 2, 3, 4$; $k = 1, 2, 3$ separately is reconnaissance confirming, fire attacking and damage evaluating. Coding of UAV V is shown in Table 2.

Table 1. Task table of target G that waited to attack

Numbering of target G	Type of task		
	Sorties of reconnaissance	Sorties of attacking	Sorties of evaluating
1	1	1	1
2	1	1	1
3	1	1	1
Sorties of single type of task	3	3	3

Then the target numbering vector Y of battle task can be obtained, as shown in Fig. 2. Values of GD, GA and GV separately are $GD = 3$; $GA = 3$; $GV = 3$.

If binary coding of location $\mathbf{X}_i = (0, 0, 0, 1, 0, 0, 0, 1, 1, 0, 0, 1,\ 0, 0, 0, 0, 1, 0,$ $0, 0, 0,\ 0, 0, 0,\ 0, 0, 0)$ is numbering of UAVs that will perform tasks, scheme of task assignation can be achieved from the Fig. 2. According to transforming process of binary to decimal, $X = (0, 4, 3, 1, 0, 2, 0, 0, 0)$ be obtained by transforming with three of $\mathbf{X}_i$ as a group, expressing that UAVs with numbering 4 and 3 will carry out the task of reconnaissance confirming to time-sensitive target 2 and 3; UAVs with numbering 1 and 2 will carry out the task of fire attacking to time-sensitive target 1 and 3.

Table 2. Coding of UAV V

Numbering of UAV V	Binary coding		
1	0	0	1
2	0	1	0
3	0	1	1
4	1	0	0

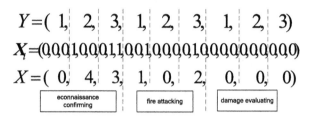

$$Y=(\ 1,\ 2,\ 3,\ 1,\ 2,\ 3,\ 1,\ 2,\ 3)$$
$$X_i=(000100001100100000100000000000)$$
$$X=(\ 0,\ 4,\ 3,\ 1,\ 0,\ 2,\ 0,\ 0,\ 0)$$

Fig. 2. Sketch of coding

Process of cooperative task assignation of many R/S UAVs based on BWPA is designed as following:

Step 1: Preparing for data. Attributes of time-sensitive G_i $(i = 1, 2, \cdots, N_G)$ in the planning time segment Δt_k are confirmed, including degree of threaten and degree of hard to attack, along with task set that waited to carry out. Referred to Table 1, target numbering of task table is done and vector Y is obtained, whose length is L_Y. Referred to Table 2, binary coding of UAV $V_j(j = 1, 2, \cdots, N_V)$ is done, and the length of coding is L_V. Therefore, the length of coding of artificial wolf's location $\mathbf{X}_i$ is $m = L_Y \times L_V$.

Step 2: Initializing related parameters. Setting the size of wolf pack N, artificial wolf's initial location $\{\mathbf{X}_i\}$, largest iteration times $k_{\max}$, scouting step $step_a$, raiding step $step_b$ and beleaguering step $step_c$, largest scouting times $T_{\max}$, distance judging factor ω, renewed ratio factor of whole wolf pack β.

Step 3: Scouting behavior. Objective function value of artificial wolf can be obtained through formula (17). Artificial wolf with the optimal objective function value becomes leading wolf, others become searching wolf, and carry out scouting behavior. Until $Y_i > Y_{lead}$ or $T > T_{\max}$, scouting process won't be repeated.

Step 4: Summoning behavior. All artificial wolves except leading wolf are seen as savaging wolf, raiding toward location of the prey according to formula (13). If $Y_i > Y_{lead}$ in the raiding process, then savaging wolf i becomes leading wolf, and carries out the summoning behavior; else, savaging wolf i continues to raiding, till $d_{is} < d_{near}$, and turns into beleaguering behavior.

Step 5: Beleaguering behavior. According to formula (15), location of artificial wolf i that joins into beleaguering behavior is updated. Comparing objective function value of artificial wolf before carrying out beleaguering behavior with that after carrying out beleaguering behavior, then greedy decision can be made.

Step 6: Renewal of wolf pack. According the productive rule of leading wolf, location of leading wolf is undated. Meantime, according to the renewable mechanism for whole wolf pack, the whole wolf pack is renewed. And new added artificial wolf's location that does not meet the conditions of constraints is renovated.

Step 7: Judging whether task assignation in current time segment is over or not. Making a judgment of whether objective function value meets the demand of optimum precision or reaches the largest iteration times k_{max}. If meets, optimal solution of cooperative task assignation, which is location of leading wolf, can be output; else turns to step 3.

Step 8: Judging that whether to start task assignation of next time segment or not. Combined with the real situation of completing task in current planning time segment, task set of next time segment can be judged. If task set is not none, then turns to step1, the whole process of task assignation in the above is repeated; if task set is none, the whole tasks are completed, and task assignation is over.

3 Simulation and Discussion

An operational scene is produced randomly, consisting of 5 time-sensitive targets. For each time-sensitive target, tasks of reconnaissance confirming, fire attacking and damage evaluating are carried out. Distribution of time-sensitive targets is shown in Fig. 3, attributes of targets in current planning time segment is described in Table 3. Assuming that there are 3 R/S UAVs responsible for carrying out tasks in current planning time segment, binary coding of which are (01), (10) and (11). So the length of coding is 2, value of weight λ is 0.6.

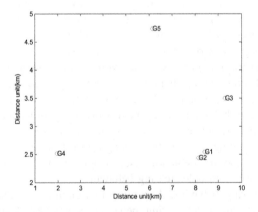

Fig. 3. Distribution of time-sensitive targets

BWPA is adopted to solve the problem of cooperative task assignation in operational scene. Setting the size of wolf pack $N = 100$, largest iteration times $k_{max} = 100$, largest scouting times $T_{max} = 10$, judging distance $d_{near} = 6$, $step_a = 2$, $step_b = 3$, $step_c = 1$, renewed ratio factor of whole wolf pack $\beta = 3$. Target numbering vector $Y = (1, 2, 3, 4, 5, 1, 2, 3, 4, 5, 1, 2, 3, 4, 5)$ that corresponding with each $\mathbf{X}_i$ can be obtained directly from the Table 3, expressing that the total sorties of tasks needed to carry out are 15, the former 5 sorties are targets that corresponding to task of reconnaissance; in-between 5 sorties are targets that corresponding to task of attacking; the last 5 sorties are targets that corresponding to task of damage evaluating. Artificial wolf's location $\mathbf{X}_i$ is expressed by binary coding $(x_{i1}, x_{i2}, \ldots, x_{ij}, \ldots, x_{im})$, $i = 1, 2, \ldots, N$, $j = 1, 2, \ldots, m$, $N = 100$, $m = 15 \times 2 = 30$, besides $x_{ij} \in \{0, 1\}$. By using BWPA to solve the above problem in current planning time segment, the evolution curve of income be achieve, as shown in Fig. 4.

Known from Fig. 4, after iterated for 16 times, the algorithm converges on the optimal solution. The optimal solution obtained is $\mathbf{X}_{best} = (0, 1, 0, 0, 0, 0, 1, 1, 1, 0, 0, 0, 0, 0, 0, 0, 0, 0, 0, 0, 0, 0, 0, 0, 0, 0, 0, 0, 0, 0)$, optimal value of function F is 22.6. Result of cooperative task assignation in current planning time segment is achieved, as described in Table 4.

Table 3. Attributes of time-sensitive targets in current planning time segment

Numbering of target G	Degree of threaten	Degree of hard to attack	Task list that waited to carry out		
			Reconnaissance confirming	Fire attacking	Damage evaluating
1	Serious	Hard	1	1	1
2	Medium	Medium	1	1	1
3	Light	Easy	1	1	1
4	Serious	Medium	1	1	1
5	Serious	Easy	1	1	1

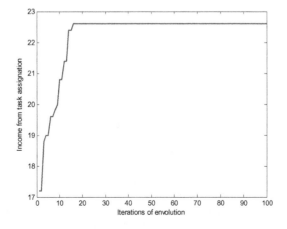

Fig. 4. Evolution curve of income from task assignation

Table 4. Task assignation in current planning time segment

Numbering of target G	Type of task	Numbering of UAV V (binary coding)
	Reconnaissance confirming	
1	1	1(01)
2		
3		
4	1	3(11)
5	1	2(10)

Known from Table 4, 3 R/S UAVs prefer to carry out the task of reconnaissance confirming to those time-sensitive targets with serious degree of threaten, in order to carry out the task of fire attacking in next time segment, according with the actual conditions basically. Therefore, model that built and solution method can provide helpful reference for task assignation and to solve other related problem.

4 Conclusions and Future Work

In studying the problem of cooperative task assignation for multi-R/S UAVs, model of cooperative task assignation is built, and BWPA is adopted to solve the problem. Simulation proves the validity of the model, and that BWPA has good astringency and global optimization capability, suitable for combinational optimization problem. Study of this paper is expected to provide a extensive thought and method for solving problems that are similar to resource allocation problem. Shortage of the study is that load problem and continuation of the flight that R/S UAV faced with are not taken into consideration, which will be the important contents of next study.

References

1. Li, G., Ren, S., Ma, Y.: Development review of R/S UAVs. J. Aviat. Space Reconnaissance **33**(1), 17–19 (2011)
2. Ye, W., Fan, H., Zhu, A.: Mission Planning for Unmanned Aerial Vehicles. National Defense Industry Press, Beijing (2011)
3. Chen, C., Xing, L., Tan, Y.: Improved genetic algorithm for cooperative multi air vehicle mission planning. Ordance Ind. Autom. **29**(9), 28–31 (2010)
4. Long, T., Shen, L., Zhu, H., Niu, Y.: Distributed task allocation and coordination technique of multiple UCAVs for cooperative tasks. Ordance Ind. Autom. **33**(7), 731–737 (2007)
5. Ye, Y.: Cooperative task planning method for multi-UAVs. National University of Defense Technology, Changsha, October 2005
6. Wu, H., Zhang, F., Wu, L.: New swarm intelligence algorithm-wolf pack algorithm. Syst. Eng. Electron. **35**(11), 2430–2438 (2013)
7. Wu, H., Zhang, F., Zhan, R., et al.: A binary wolf pack algorithm for solving 0-1 knapsack problem. Syst. Eng. Electron. **36**(8), 1160–1167 (2014)

8. Ye, Y., Yin, J., Feng, Z., Cao, B.: Wolf-pack algorithm for business process model syntactic and semantic structure verification in the workflow management environment. In: 2010 IEEE Asia-Pacific Services Computing Conference. TongJi University, Shanghai (2010)

9. Yao, M., Wang, X., Zhao, M.: Cooperative combat task assignment optimization design for unmanned aerial vehicles cluster. J. Univ. Electron. Sci. Technol. China **42**(5), 723–727 (2013)

10. Wu, H.: Wolf pack algorithm and its application. Airforce Engineering University, Xi'an, December 2014

A Filtering Method of Laser Radar Imaging Based on Classification of Curvature

Xin Yuan[(✉)] and Qing Li

Beijing Key Laboratory of High Dynamic Navigation Technology,
Beijing Information Science and Technology University, Beijing, China
820291253@qq.com, liqing@bistu.edu.cn

Abstract. A point cloud data filtering method of laser radar imaging based on classification of curvature is investigated to resolve the deficiencies of the massive 3D point cloud data model filtering using single method. This method divides the region of point cloud data model by the average Gaussian curvature value in neighbor of the sampling point, and then the adaptive median filtering and adaptive bilateral filtering method are used for different region types. Static and dynamic targets are adopted respectively in simulation experiments, experiments show the method can effectively remove the noise of targets under the different motion states, it can also keep details of point cloud data models, and this method has better filtering performance compared with the single filtering method.

Keywords: Radar imaging · Classification of curvature · Adaptive median filtering · Dynamic targets

1 Introduction

With the development of 3D imaging techniques, 3D laser radar with quick acquisition to massive 3D coordinate data [1] of the scanned area is widely used in the environment, communications, aerospace and other fields. Laser radar can get the point cloud data of probe target fast, with high precision and high distribution [2] with no contacts with target. But compared to the laser radar hardware updates [3], processing method of point cloud data is not mature, systematic.

The key step of point cloud data processing is the data preprocessing, which can provide reliable point cloud data to the model reconstruction, and provide a good foundation to build a high precision model [4].

2 Point Cloud Data Filtering

Filtering of point cloud data model is the significant part of 3D point cloud data preprocessing and modeling, it's used to eliminate scattered point cloud noise points effectively, smooth the point cloud model surface and keep the original details of the

Supported by The National Nature Science Foundation of China (Grant No. 61261160497).

L. Zhang et al. (Eds.): AsiaSim 2016/SCS AutumnSim 2016, Part II, CCIS 644, pp. 262–270, 2016.
DOI: 10.1007/978-981-10-2666-9_25

geometric feature of the sampling surface at the same time, it can also avoid any bad influence of noise on the subsequent processing [5]. Therefore, it is particularly important to maintain the characteristic information of the model while filtering.

The point cloud data is a spatial discrete geometric point set obtained by 3D scanning equipment, and it is represented by a series of spatial point data on the object surface. The point cloud is represented by a set $P = \{p_i\}_{i \in \text{index}(P)}$, where $p_i \in R^3$, $i \in \text{index}(P)$ means the index of the spatial sampling point in the 3D point cloud model (usually expressed in $[1, n]$, n is the number of sampling points in the set P). Points and its related surface characteristics is the basic unit of point cloud, there are a various forms of point cloud due to the different principles of different scanning equipment (as shown in Fig. 1): scattered point cloud, scanning line point cloud, array point cloud and grid point cloud. The scattered point cloud is mainly studied in this paper.

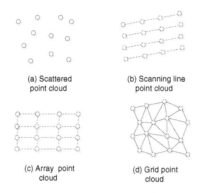

(a) Scattered point cloud

(b) Scanning line point cloud

(c) Array point cloud

(d) Grid point cloud

Fig. 1. The arrangement form of point cloud

At present, the filtering algorithm of point cloud data has been widely studied at home and abroad. Desbrun [6] proposed a method based on the mean curvature flow, it solved the problem of vertex drift, but this isotropic method makes target feature inevitable bending; Alexa [7] established a mobile minimum quadratic surface (MLS) for point cloud surface model, but this method needs large amount of calculation, and it's difficult to maintain the detailed features of the point cloud model. In this paper, a filtering method based on the classification of curvature is adopted, it divides the region of point cloud data model by the average Gaussian curvature value in neighbor of the sampling point, and then the adaptive median filtering and adaptive bilateral filtering method are used for different region types.

3 A Filtering Method Based on Classification of Curvature

Studies about scattered point cloud data filtering is mainly divided into two categories at present, one is to turn scattered point cloud data into grid model, and then use the filtering method of grid model to filter the point cloud data; another is to filter the point cloud data directly. The main filtering methods include: Laplace filtering, mean curvature flow and bilateral filtering.

3.1 K-Nearest Neighbor (KNN)

K neighbor is a kind of adaptive neighbor estimation method, which can deal with the irregular sampling surface with high reliability.

Definitions: assuming a given point cloud $P = \{p_i\}_{i \in index(P)}$, $p_i \in R^3$, for any one of these sampling points $p_i \in P$, then the k - points which are nearest in space with this point are called the KNN of point p_i. Recorded as $N(p_i)$. As shown in Fig. 2.

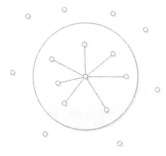

Fig. 2. Point cloud neighbor

If $\wedge$ is an arrangement and satisfies the condition

$$\|p_\wedge - p\| > 0, \|p_{\wedge(k)} - p\| \leq \|p_{\wedge(k+1)} - p\|, \quad k \in [1, n-1] \tag{1}$$

Then, the KNN of $N(p_i)$ is

$$Np_i = \{\wedge(1), \wedge(2), \cdots \wedge(k)\} \tag{2}$$

Where the neighbor radius is

$$r_p^k = \max_k \{\|p_{\wedge(k)} - p\|\}, k \in [1, n] \tag{3}$$

The KNN of each sampling point in the point cloud model is only related to the sampling point, and independent of the neighbor of the other sampling points in the k-point cloud model.

Kd-tree and spatial grid method are widely used in KNN search algorithm at present, and the kd-tree is adopted to search k nearest neighbor points of points cloud in this paper.

3.2   Overall Plan

By comparing the Gauss curvature value of the sampling point and average size of the Gaussian curvature values in the sampling point KNN, the whole laser radar point cloud is divided into smooth neighbor region and sharp characteristic neighbor region. Average Gauss curvature k- nearest neighbor is:

$$\bar{K} = \frac{1}{k}\sum_1^k |K_i| \tag{4}$$

Where the K_i means the Gauss curvature value at each point in the KNN.

If the Gauss curvature at point p, K is less than $\bar{K}$, then we can make the decision that the point p is a point in smooth neighbor regionals, otherwise, If the Gauss curvature at point p, K is greater than $\bar{K}$, then this point is determined as a point in sharp characteristic neighbor region.

A general method for laser radar filtering based on curvature classification is: using the average Gauss curvature value in the neighbor of the sampling point as the dividing criterion of the smooth neighbor region and the sharp characteristic neighbor region, the adaptive median filtering method is used to model the laser radar point cloud data in the smooth neighbor region and the adaptive bilateral filtering method is used to model the laser radar point cloud data in the sharp characteristic neighbor region (Fig. 3).

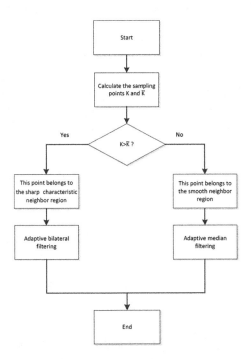

Fig. 3. The overall process

3.3   Adaptive Median Filtering

Median filter is a kind of nonlinear signal processing technology can restrain the noise effectively, which is based on the theory of order statistics. For the median filter, as long as the spatial density of impulse noise is small, the performance would be very good (p_a, p_b should be less than 0.2 based on experience). Adaptive median filtering can be used to process the impulsive noise with greater probability. It depends on certain conditions to change the value of S_{xy} in the filter processing. The output of the filter is a single value, which is used to replace the pixel value of the point (x, y). The point (x, y) is a special point after the given time window S_{xy} is centered. Adaptive median filtering algorithm works in two layers, defined as the layer A and the layer B.

$$\text{Layer A}: A_1 = z_{mid} - z_{min}, \quad A_2 = z_{mid} - z_{max}$$

If $A_1 > 0$ and $A_2 < 0$, then turn to layer B, otherwise increase the size of window $\leq S_{max}$, if the size of window $< S_{max}$, then repeat layer A, otherwise export z_{mid}.

$$\text{Layer B}: B_1 = z_{xy} - z_{min}, \quad B_2 = z_{xy} - z_{max}$$

If $B_1 > 0$ and $B_2 < 0$, then export z_{xy}, otherwise export z_{mid}.

As the z_{min} means the minimum value of gray level in S_{xy}, z_{max} means the maximum value of gray level in S_{xy}; z_{mid} means the mean value of gray level in S_{xy}; z_{xy} means the value of gray level at point (x, y); S_{max} means the maximum allowed size of S_{xy}.

3.4   Adaptive Bilateral Filtering

The bilateral filtering algorithm was propose by Tomasi and Manduchi in 1998, this algorithm process the image noise by combining the spatial neighbor information and gray similarity value, it controls the motion of current point in the normal vector to prevent the excessive contraction of the point cloud.

Firstly, calculate the local neighbor of each point, secondly, estimate the normal vector according to the local neighbor, and then represent the geometric feature information of the point cloud surface according to the changes of normal vector between neighbor point, determine the degree of impacts of the points in the neighbor to current point by the degree of similarity of the normal vectors. The more similar the normal vectors are, the greater the impacts are. Filtering values can be calculated according to the normal value and the value of distance factors weight. Bilateral filtering operator can be expressed as below:

$$d = \frac{\sum_{p_i \in N_{(p)}} W_a\left(\|p_i - p'\|\right) W_b\left(\left|<\vec{n_i}, \vec{n}> - 1\right|\right) <\vec{n}, p - p_i>}{\sum_{p_i \in N_{(p)}} W_a(\|p_i - p'\|) W_b\left(\left|<\vec{n_i}, \vec{n}> - 1\right|\right)} \tag{5}$$

Where $N_{(p)}$ means the point set of the neighbor of p and $p_i \in N_{(p)}$. p' means the projection of p on s. W_a and W_b mean the Gauss filtering functions in space domain and in frequency domain in bilateral filtering function as the Gaussian filtering of the local neighbor tangent surface where the sampling points are located and the Gaussian filtering on the normal height field respectively, they can be expressed as below:

$$W_a(x) = e^{-\frac{x^2}{2\sigma_1^2}} \tag{6}$$

$$W_b(x) = e^{-\frac{x^2}{2\sigma_2^2}} \tag{7}$$

σ_1, σ_2 mean the Gauss filtering coefficient in space domain and in frequency domain separately, they reflect the area of influence of Gauss filtering function on tangential and normal directions when calculating bilateral filtering function values of the sampling points.

The maximum value of the distance between points in KNN and the sampling point is taken as the value of σ_1:

$$\sigma_1 = \max\|p_i - p'\|, \quad i \in [1, k] \tag{8}$$

The standard deviation of the height between points in KNN and the tangent plane is taken as the value of σ_2:

$$\sigma_2 = \sqrt{\frac{1}{k-1}\sum_{i=1}^{k}(\varepsilon_i - \bar{\varepsilon})^2}, \quad \varepsilon = <\vec{n}, p - p_i> \tag{9}$$

The adjustment function of the sampling point location is shown below:

$$P = p + dn \tag{10}$$

Where P means the location after adjustment, d means the distance that pending points adjusted in the direction of the normal vector, n means the normal vector of sampling points at p.

4   Simulation Experiments and Results Analysis

In the simulation experiment, the filtering method, proposed in this paper, based on median filtering and curvature classification is used to deal with the static target reality scene and the dynamic target reality scene, the results of experiments are compared in this paper (Table 1).

4.1   Static Target Simulation

An office laboratory is used as a static scene in static target simulation experiment, and the results are shown in Fig. 4.

Table 1. Configuration of experimental environment

Name	Parameter
Radar	Velodyne VLP-16
CPU	Core(TM)i7-3517UE@2.20GHz
RAM	8.0G
Hard disk	240G
Debugger	Microsoft Visual Studio 2008 MATLAB R2015b

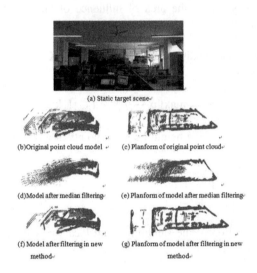

(a) Static target scene

(b)Original point cloud model   (c) Planform of original point cloud

(d)Model after median filtering   (e) Planform of model after median filtering

(f) Model after filtering in new method   (g) Planform of model after filtering in new method

Fig. 4. Simulation experiment 1 (147783 data points)

4.2   Dynamic Target Simulation

The experimental scene of the dynamic target is shown in Fig. 5: the Traveler IV is moving from the radar to the far side in the direction of the arrow.

The laser radar point cloud models during the whole movement process of Traveler IV are shown in Fig. 5, there are 11 frames point cloud data in the whole movement process, each single frame data is filtered respectively, 4 frame processing results selected randomly are shown in Fig. 6.

4.3   Results Analysis

The simulation experiments above are carried out under static and dynamic scenes separately, the environmental characteristics of experiment 1 are more complex, and the number of points cloud is huge, when it comes to experiment 2, the amount of data point cloud is greatly increased because of the presence of moving objects. There are many redundant points and noise points in original point cloud which is derived from the original image in simulation experiment, some of them do not belong to the object

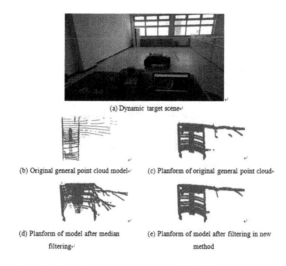

(a) Dynamic target scene

(b) Original general point cloud model

(c) Planform of original general point cloud

(d) Planform of model after median filtering

(e) Planform of model after filtering in new method

Fig. 5. Simulation experiment 2 (349458 data points)

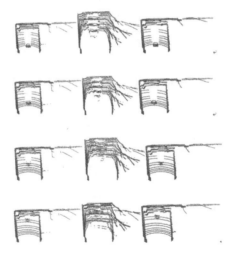

Fig. 6. Each single frame data and filtering (The first column represent the original point cloud of No. 1, 4, 7, 11 frames, the second column represents the results of the medium filtering, the third column represents the results of filtering proposed in this paper)

and there are also some noise caused by the external environment, the discreteness of laser beam or some other factors.

Compare and analysis of the results of the median filter and the filtering method based on the curvature classification of original point cloud data model:

For median filter: It's obviously that the edge is blurred, sharp features fade and filtering effect is not ideal in the complex environment characteristics of experiment 1 (Fig. 4 d, e). In experiment 2 (Fig. 5 d), although part of the redundant points do not belong to the object are removed, but this leads to a clutter of point cloud model, the filtering effect is poor.

The simulation results of point cloud model filtering method based on the classification of curvature compared have been greatly improved compared with the median filtering method in edge and sharp features remain, details can be shown well and filtering effect is quite ideal.

The filtering process of the single frame point cloud data model in Fig. 6 is in fact equivalent to the processing of the static target in different position of the Traveler IV in the movement process. The simulation results show that the method is also suitable for filtering the dynamic object.

5 Conclusions

The filtering method of laser radar imaging based on classification of curvature proposed in this paper realize the processing of massive 3D point cloud data filtering well, edge characteristics are kept while the details are shown well, this filtering method is applicable to both the static object and the dynamic object process. It plays an important role in the preprocessing of 3D point cloud data, besides, it can be extended to the carrier detection, SLAM and other fields.

References

1. Yan, J.-F., Deng, K.-Z., Xing, Z.-Q.: 3D laser scanning point cloud filtering based on least squares fitting. Bull. Surveying Mapp. **05**, 43–46 (2013)
2. Chai, G.-B., Zhang, J.-Q., Zhang, X., Guo, B.-T.: Study of dynamic scenes model for laser imaging radar simulation. J. XiDian Univ. **41**(2), 107–113 (2014)
3. Bo, Y., Guo, L., Qian, X.-L., Zhao, T.-Y.: A new adaptive bilateral filtering. J. Appl. Sci. **30**(5), 517–523 (2012)
4. Wang, X.-K., Li, F.: Improved adaptive median filtering. Comput. Eng. Appl. **46**(3), 175–176 (2010)
5. Zhang, X.-M., Xu, B.-S., Dong, S.-Y.: Adaptive median filtering for image processing. J. Comput. Aided Des. Comput. Graph. **17**(2), 295–299 (2005)
6. Desbrun, M., Meyer, M, Schröder, P., Barr, A.H.: Implicit fairing of irregular meshes using diffusion and curvature flow. In: Proceeding of SIGGRAPH, pp. 317–324. ACM Press, New York (1999)
7. Alexa, M., Berh, J., Cohen-Or, D., et al.: Computing and rendering point set surfaces. IEEE Trans. Vis. Comput. Graph. **9**(1), 3–15 (2003)

The Database Architecture Design of the Satellite Simulation Platform

Guannan Sun, Qipeng Hu[✉], and Xin Lin

School of Automation Science and Electrical Engineering,
Beihang University, Beijing, China
w18679104034@126.com, 1539257426@qq.com, lx@buaa.edu.cn

Abstract. The database architecture is classified as database, database management system and users. The database management system is composed of several core modules named as internal mode, external mode, and mapping relations. Database design is discussed as conceptual model design and physical model design respectively. Important technologies such as database connection pool and ORM mapping framework database in database access layer are discussed specially. At last, design validations are presented.

Keywords: Distributed simulation system · Satellite simulation · Database management system

1 Introduction

The development of simulation has been deeply influenced by computer and network technology, and led to the application of distributed simulation system which consists of lots of network nodes and subsystems to realize complex simulation tasks. Distributed simulation standards, such as SIMNET, DIS, HLA [1] has been developed and used widely in simulation field. With the development and application of network database architecture in cooperation level distributed systems [2, 3], the program architecture base on network database has been also applied in distributed simulation system in recent years which is ideal for mass data system design [4, 5].

As we developing satellite simulation platform [6], network database architecture is adopted to store mass data produced in simulation process and coordinate all application terminals in simulation system.

2 Database Architecture

Database architecture is designed as a pure object-oriented paradigm. The database server is concerned as a core node in the architecture, provides data storage and data distribution services for other simulation nodes. Simulation nodes act as database terminals, and exchange data with database directly. Communication among simulation nodes is disabled. All data exchange among terminals should be transferred through database server. Because

© Springer Science+Business Media Singapore 2016
L. Zhang et al. (Eds.): AsiaSim 2016/SCS AutumnSim 2016, Part II, CCIS 644, pp. 271–278, 2016.
DOI: 10.1007/978-981-10-2666-9_26

coordination works among terminals are reduced significantly, system scalability and cross-platform capability are improved greatly.

The database architecture design rules of distributed simulation system are as shown below:

(1) Entity data models are divided into two levels, respectively static data model and dynamic data model. These two levels interact by certain data structures, such as trees, hash tables, and so on;
(2) Entity initialization and its algorithm calculation are allocated to different terminals to reduce system coupling;
(3) Entity static data and dynamic data are processed in different ways to reduce the data redundancy and improve the hit rate.

As shown in Fig. 1, database is the foundation of architecture and provides the abstraction and storage of various types of simulation data. To meet simulation task and system requirements, we chose relational database MySQL as the underlying database. The database management system is composed of several core modules which responsible for important functions such as data sharing platform management, data storage and data interaction. These core modules include: internal mode, external mode, and mapping relations.

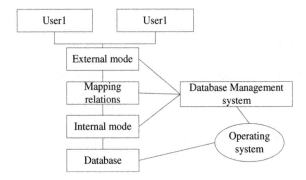

Fig. 1. Database architecture

Internal mode module is the interface to operate and access the underlying database. For example, SQL language is a typical internal mode interface. The internal model allows application program manipulate the database directly, meanwhile developers should master the internal mode interface language. Internal mode limits system scalability, portability, and the secondary development of the system.

External mode module is the interface provided to user to access the database and has characteristics of clear and easy to understand, and allows users to access the database without mastering professional database knowledge.

Mapping relations module is a bridge between external and internal mode module. It converts external commands to internal commands through mapping rules, and converts internal mode search results to acceptable data type of external mode.

3   Database Design

3.1   Conceptual Model Design

The conceptual model design of database concentrates on consolidating users' requirements and analyzing the mutual relationship among real world entities. First, entity
initialization data were sent to satellite simulation platform, then the model should be
resolved, computed and stored by simulation platform. At last the results would be
presented to users in 2D/3D map windows. In addition, simulation platform would store
real-time entity state information to data sharing platform. Figure 2 shows the ER
diagram which describes the logical relationship between simulation system and scenes.

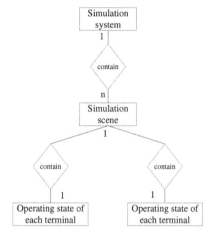

Fig. 2.   Simulation system ER diagram

3.2   Physical Model Design

One of the main features of relational database is the ability to set primary key and
foreign key constraints, to make a table field dependent on primary key or foreign key,
which can reduce data redundancy, avoid erroneous data to some extent. Database
architecture described in this paper uses a normalized database relation form (Normal
Forms: NF) called 3NF to design database, and each table in the database has a unique
indivisible primary key, each non-primary attribute in the table is strictly depend on the
primary key.

4   Database Access Layer

4.1   Database Connection Pool

When access database, creating a database connection requires a lot of resources, and
the time consuming is even more than the time required for database query. While the

system is running, creating and shutting down of database connection frequently will lead to inefficiency and waste of resource. To solve this problem, we design a database connection pool to reuse database connection which can greatly improve the efficiency.

Database connection pool model is shown in Fig. 3. When a user requests access to database, connection pool will assign a connection to the use. When the user no longer access the database, the connection will be released to connection pool, then the connection pool decides to keep idle connection or destroy it. Connection pool does not limit the number of users. However it controls the total number of connections. When connection application exceeds the total number of connections, the application thread would enter blocking state until some connections are released. Thus the efficiency of existing connections can be guaranteed.

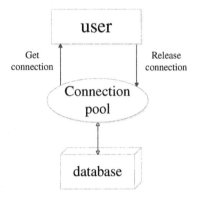

Fig. 3. Database connection pool model

The main tasks of database connection pool include:

(1) Pre-distribution management. The database connection pool initialize several idle connections when initialization and set the default number.

(2) Idle connections management. Connection pool always maintains a certain amount of idle connections. When the user issues a connection request, connection pool will assigns an idle connection to the user directly. Time consumption wasted in creating a new connection is avoided. If user release a connection to connection pool, the connection pool would keep it as idle if the maximum number of idle connection is not exceeded, otherwise directly destroy it.

(3) Create new connection. At runtime of database connection pool, sometimes new connection should be created. After creation completed, the child thread which creates new connection would enter blocked state, and would wake up again when next new connection should be created.

(4) Close connection. The connection pool has the ability to close connections to avoid memory exhaustion caused by excessive idle connections.

(5) Connectivity test. Database connection pool can judge whether the connection is turned on.

4.2   ORM Mapping Framework

Because MySQL database adopts relational data model while application program uses the object-oriented design methods, ORM (Object Relation Method) [7] was introduced to map between object-oriented model and relational model. In ORM framework, we can manipulate relational databases through object-oriented interface.

ORM mapping acts as a bridge to deal with the data type conversion issue between object and relation model. The ORM framework design references Hibernate framework which is a commonly used framework in lightweight Java EE application development, takes some adjustment and simplification as need.

The object-oriented models are developed by using program language C#, and the relational database using MySQL. Except for basic data types, mapping methods are designed for custom data types. Each custom data type represents an entity in the scenario. Besides database mapping functionality, custom data types also assumed complex simulation tasks.

In the system design process, template methods are adopted to implement simulation entities and program codes for the reason that most of them are very similar.

Program developer need not to master database knowledge if database administrator (DBA) provides suitable mapping mechanism under ORM framework. ORM framework is advantageous to decouple the system mission and suitable for team works. However ORM framework also constrains developers on accessing database. So MySQL statement interface is provided to access database directly, improves system scalability and flexibility. Developers can access the database in internal mode command. In this case the data retrieved from database are also the internal mode data type which needs to convert to corresponding external mode.

5   Operating Validations

5.1   Database Operating Validation

The underlying database uses relational database MySQL and operate in windows system. The basic configuration of MySQL is saved in the My.ini file. When configuration completes, we could set all data tables in satellite simulation platform. Setting results are shown in Fig. 4.

5.2   ORM Mapping Mechanism Validation

Figures 5, 6 and 7 shows the ORM mapping between custom data type and relational database. First, Fig. 5 shows all tables in the database, and queries the records in the ScenarioInit table.

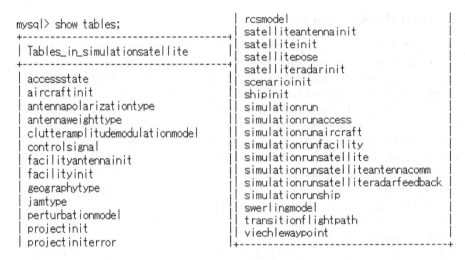

Fig. 4. Database entity table design

Fig. 5. Database display

Next, open the parameter input terminal.

Click the "open" button and pop out "Select Scene" window, select the scenario which named "ScenarioInit" and open it, as shown in Fig. 6. The sub-window at the left side of main window "Scene Structure" displays all scenario entities. Move the mouse to the scenario entity in "scenarioStructure" window, and the "Properties" window at the right side of the main window will appear all the configuration parameters of the entity. As a example we change the author property from ScenarioInit into mrsun and click the "Save Changes" button, complete the mapping from memory to database. Then view the ScenarioInit contents, we can see the authorproperties are modified which means data mapped successfully.

Fig. 6. Parameter window display

6 Conclusion and Prospect

The design and implementation of database architecture supports well the development of satellite simulation platform, reduces the coupling of each simulation terminal, improves system stability, facilitates the expansion of system, and accomplished corresponding simulation functions. In the foreseeable future, the storage and analysis of mass data produced in simulation process will be a trend in distributed simulation. Our further works include: transfer current relational database to non-relational database, migrate existing servers located on the PC to server with mass data processing capabilities, explore data mining algorithm with simulation characteristics and so on.

References

1. Pedrielli, G., Sacco, M., Terkaj, W., Tolio, T.: An HLA-based distributed simulation for networked manufacturing systems analysis. J. Simul. **6**, 237–252 (2012)
2. Grad, B., Bergin, T.J.: History of database management. IEEE Ann. Hist. Comput. **31**(4), 3–5 (2009)
3. Stonebraker, M., Brown, P., Zhang, D., Becla, J.: SciDB: a database management system for applications with complex analytics. Comput. Sci. Eng. **15**(3), 54–62 (2013)
4. Huang, Y., Gannon, D.: A comparative study of web service-based event notification specifications. In: Proceedings of the International Conference on Parallel Processing Workshops (ICPP) (2006)

5. Chandy, K.M.: Towards a theory of events. In: Processing of the DEBT, Toronto, Ontario, Canada (2007)
6. Sun, G., Su, Q., Lin, X.: Distributed simulation system framework designed based on STK. In: China Simulation Conference 2015 (2015)
7. Li, D., Yi, Z., Wang, H.: The ORM framework of Java EE based on hibernate. Electron. Technol. **2**(25) (2010)

Cooperative Searching Strategy
for Multiple Unmanned Aerial Vehicles Based
on Modified Probability Map

Qiwang Huang, Jian Yao, Qun Li, and Yifan Zhu$^{(\boxtimes)}$

College of Information System and Management,
National University of Defense Technology, Changsha, Hunan, China
nudthqw@163.com

Abstract. Cooperative target-searching of multiple Unmanned Aerial Vehicles
(UAVs) in uncertainty environment is an important research area in multi-UAVs
cooperative control. The objective of multi-UAVs searching is to obtain the
information of the searched area, decrease the uncertainty of this area and find
the hidden targets as fast as possible. This paper introduces a new framework for
UAV search operations and proposes a new approach to solve multi-UAVs
cooperative searching problem. Aimed at the characteristics of the multi-UAVs
cooperative searching problem, the modified probability map based cooperative
searching strategy was discussed in detail. Based on the existing algorithms, the
cooperative strategy was divided into three key parts, which are probability map
initialization, probability map updating and the rules of UAV transfer. The
search effectiveness of the Multi-UAVs system in the condition of Multi-target
was analyzed based on the method of ABMS (Agent Based Modeling and
Simulation). Simulation results demonstrated the effectiveness of the algorithm.

Keywords: Unmanned aerial vehicle · Searching · Cooperative control ·
Probability map

1 Introduction

With the development of technology and information age war, UAV (unmanned aerial
vehicle) become the best choice to accomplish boring and dangerous tasks [1]. In recent
years, UAV is widely used in battlefield reconnaissance, maritime search and rescue.
Researchers are devoting significant attention to the study of autonomous unmanned
aerial vehicles (UAVs) working cooperatively to accomplish an objective [2–6].

Cooperative control of multiple UAVs applies to settings where teams of UAVs
cooperate to accomplish a common objective. It has been shown that a collaborative
team of autonomous aerial and ground vehicles can provide more effective operational
capabilities to accomplish hard and complex tasks than are available through independent control of each individual vehicle [7–9]. A critical problem in realizing such
multivehicle systems is to develop coherent and efficient coordination and control
algorithms to maneuver each vehicle so that the team as a whole can produce complex,
adaptable, and flexible group behaviors.

© Springer Science+Business Media Singapore 2016
L. Zhang et al. (Eds.): AsiaSim 2016/SCS AutumnSim 2016, Part II, CCIS 644, pp. 279–287, 2016.
DOI: 10.1007/978-981-10-2666-9_27

Multi-UAV cooperative search problems are typically formulated by gridding the environment into a set of cells [10–14]. Each of the cells contains some information that a target exists in or not that cell. The search problems are then solved with the information about each of the cells. However, there will be uncertainty in the information, due to poor intelligence or noisy sensors. Traditional probability map cannot accurate represent the probability of a target in or not in one cell. To solve that problem, this paper extends the traditional probability map into three dimensional data structure.

This paper focuses on the multi-UAV cooperative search problem where a team of UAVs moves in an environment of known extent seeking targets of interest and gathering information about the environment. The UAVs only have limited or nonexistent a priori information about the target distribution in the environment.

The structure of this paper is as follows. Section 2 introduces how to representation the dynamic environmental. Section 3 discusses how to initial and Update the modified probability map. Section 4 then describes the case study, demonstrates the benefits of the approach with several numerical simulations. Section 5 summarizes the conclusions and future work.

2   Environmental Representation

We represent the environment using $M \times N$ probabilistic maps divided into rectangle cells, C_j, $j \in (1,2...M \times N)$. The value of a cell records the probability that a particular event is true at that cell location. Our model uses two types of maps, depicted in Fig. 1. UAV occupancy maps record the probability (called UAV occupancy probability (UOP), that a teammate UAV occupies a particular cell. Target occupancy maps record the probability (called target occupancy probability (TOP)), that a target occupies a particular cell. Since these probabilities occur in two-dimensional Cartesian space, they represent probability mass functions (PMFs). The PMF values for a given map, summed over all map cells, equal unity.

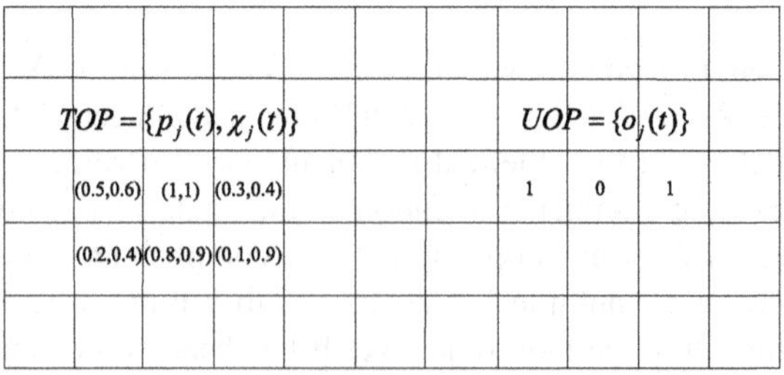

$TOP = \{p_j(t), \chi_j(t)\}$					$UOP = \{o_j(t)\}$		
(0.5,0.6)	(1,1)	(0.3,0.4)			1	0	1
(0.2,0.4)	(0.8,0.9)	(0.1,0.9)					

Fig. 1. Probabilistic maps

3 Modified Probability Map Method

3.1 Probability Map Initialization and Updating

Before Multi-UAVs system searches the targets, probability map must be initialized. If the search area is totally unknown to us the target exist probability, environment certainty probability and UAV occupancy probability were initial as $p_j(0) = \chi_j(0) = o_j(0) = 0$.

- Target exist probability updating:

Let us first describe how a UAV updates its TOP map based on sensor readings. As a UAV flies, its sensor scans the cells within the sensor's FOV. The sensor's FOV covers M cells. The sensor registers either detection or no detection at each time step. Since the sensor's FOV covers multiple cells, a detection event may be triggered due to a detection event in one, some, or all cells within the FOV. We use the following definitions in our TOP map update equations:

(1) event that a target is in cell C_j: A_j;
(2) event that a target is not in cell C_j: $\bar{A}_j$;
(3) event that detection occurs in FOV_i: B_{FOV_i};
(4) event that no detection occurs in FOV_i: $\bar{B}_{FOV_i}$;
(5) event that detection occurs in cell C_j: D_j ;
(6) event that no detection occurs in cell C_j : $\bar{D}_j$;
(7) detection probability: P_d, $P_d = P(D_j|A_j)$, $\bar{P}_d = 1 - P_d = P(\bar{D}_j|A_j)$;
(8) false alarm probability: P_f, $P_f = P(D_j|\bar{A}_j)$, $\bar{P}_f = 1 - P_f = P(\bar{D}_j|\bar{A}_j)$;
(9) The prior probability: TOP_j, $TOP_j = P(A_j)$;
(10) The posterior probability: TOP'_j, $TOP'_j = P(A_j|event)$, $event \in \{B_{FOV_i}, \bar{B}_{FOV_i}\}$.

TOP update when detection is declared: For this event, we want the probability that a target is in a certain cell given detection is declared. We write Bayes rule as follows:

$$TOP'_j = P(A_j|B_{FOV_i}) = \frac{P(B_{FOV_i}|A_j)P(A_j)}{P(B_{FOV_i})}, j \in \{1, 2, \ldots, M \times N\}$$

$$= \begin{cases} \dfrac{(1 - \bar{P}_d \cdot \bar{P}_f^{N-1})P(A_j)}{\sum\limits_{n \in FOV_i} (1 - \bar{P}_d \cdot \bar{P}_f^{N-1})P(A_n) + \sum\limits_{n \notin FOV_i} (1 - \bar{P}_f^N)P(A_n)} & for\, j \in FOV_i \\[3em] \dfrac{(1 - \bar{P}_f^N)P(A_j)}{\sum\limits_{n \in FOV_i} (1 - \bar{P}_d \cdot \bar{P}_f^{N-1})P(A_n) + \sum\limits_{n \notin FOV_i} (1 - \bar{P}_f^N)P(A_n)} & for\, j \notin FOV_i \end{cases} \quad (1)$$

TOP update when no detection is declared: For a no detection event, we write Bayes rule as follows:

$$TOP'_j = P(A_j|\bar{B}_{FOV_i}) = \frac{P(\bar{B}_{FOV_i}|A_j)P(A_j)}{P(\bar{B}_{FOV_i})}, j \in \{1, 2, \ldots, M \times N\}$$

$$= \begin{cases} \dfrac{\bar{P}_d \cdot \bar{P}_f^{N-1} \cdot P(A_j)}{\sum\limits_{n \in FOV_i} \bar{P}_d \cdot \bar{P}_f^{N-1} \cdot P(A_n) + \sum\limits_{n \notin FOV_i} \bar{P}_f^N \cdot P(A_n)} & for\, j \in FOV'_i \\[6mm] \dfrac{\bar{P}_f^N \cdot P(A_j)}{\sum\limits_{n \in FOV_i} \bar{P}_d \cdot \bar{P}_f^{N-1} \cdot P(A_n) + \sum\limits_{n \notin FOV_i} \bar{P}_f^N \cdot P(A_n)} & for\, j \notin FOV_i \end{cases} \quad (2)$$

Therefore, Target exist probability Updating equation as follows:

$$p_j(t+1)$$

$$= \begin{cases} \dfrac{(1 - \bar{P}_d \cdot \bar{P}_f^{N-1})p_j(t)}{\sum\limits_{n \in FOV_i} (1 - \bar{P}_d \cdot \bar{P}_f^{N-1})p_j(t) + \sum\limits_{n \notin FOV_i} (1 - \bar{P}_f^N)p_j(t)} & for\, j \in FOV_i \, and \, B_{FOV_i} \\[6mm] \dfrac{(1 - \bar{P}_f^N)p_j(t)}{\sum\limits_{n \in FOV_i} (1 - \bar{P}_d \cdot \bar{P}_f^{N-1})p_j(t) + \sum\limits_{n \notin FOV_i} (1 - \bar{P}_f^N)p_j(t)} & for\, j \notin FOV_i \, and \, B_{FOV_i} \\[6mm] \dfrac{\bar{P}_d \cdot \bar{P}_f^{N-1} \cdot p_j(t)}{\sum\limits_{n \in FOV_i} \bar{P}_d \cdot \bar{P}_f^{N-1} \cdot p_j(t) + \sum\limits_{n \notin FOV_i} \bar{P}_f^N \cdot p_j(t)} & for\, j \in FOV_i \, and \, \bar{B}_{FOV_i} \\[6mm] \dfrac{\bar{P}_f^N \cdot p_j(t)}{\sum\limits_{n \in FOV_i} \bar{P}_d \cdot \bar{P}_f^{N-1} \cdot p_j(t) + \sum\limits_{n \notin FOV_i} \bar{P}_f^N \cdot p_j(t)} & for\, j \notin FOV_i \, and \, \bar{B}_{FOV_i} \end{cases} \quad (3)$$

Environment certainty probability and occupancy probability updating

In order to direct the search for targets, it is important to quantify the degree to which each cell's TOP is based on knowledge rather than ignorance. We do this by defining a *certainty* variable $\chi_j(t)$, for each C_j. Each observation by a UAV in C_j updates the certainty as:

$$\chi_j(t+1) = \begin{cases} \eta \cdot \chi_j(t) & for\, j \notin FOV_i \\ \chi_j(t) + 0.5 \cdot (1 - \chi_j(t)) & for\, j \in FOV_i \end{cases} \quad (4)$$

Each cell C_j UAV updates occupancy probability as:

$$o_j(t+1) = \begin{cases} 1 & for\, j \in FOV_i \\ 0 & for\, j \notin FOV_i \end{cases} \quad (5)$$

3.2   UAV Transfer

UAVs move autonomously in the environment, searching, cooperating with other UAVs via the Probability Map, making decisions, and performing tasks. At time, t, every cell in the environment has the information of target exist probability, environment certainty probability and UAV occupancy probability. UAV_i choose path according the following object function:

$$G_i(t) = \omega_1 \sum_{C_j \in S_i} p_j^i(t) + \omega_2 \sum_{C_j \in S_i} (1 - \chi_j^i) p_j^i(t) + \omega_3 \sum_{C_j \in S_i} (1 - o_j^i(t)) \qquad (6)$$

Where ω_1, ω_2, ω_3 is weight coefficient, $p_j^i(t)$, χ_j^i and $o_j^i(t)$ is target exist probability, environment certainty probability and occupancy probability. S_i is the path that UAV_i transfer at a time step, depicted in Fig. 2.

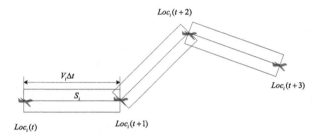

Fig. 2. UAV transfer rule

4   Case Study

The search area is 280 km × 160 km divide into 280 × 160 cells。 There are 20 targets in the search area. There is a team of 4 identical UAVs moving synchronously in discrete time and continually sensing the environment using their sensors. The initialization scenario depicts in Fig. 3. The vehicles are assumed to be equipped with reliable communication capabilities so that they can exchange sensing information among the group without any error or delay. The team of UAVs use modified probability map (MPM) strategy, greed strategy and random strategy to search the task area in different simulation runs.

The simulation model is developed by MASS (Multi-agent Simulation System) based on the method of ABMS (Agent Based Modeling and Simulation). MASS is an agent-based, time-stepped, stochastic, multimission-level model specifically designed to help evaluate the military utility of C4ISR systems. Figure 4 shows the simulation interface. The weight coefficient in every scenario was $W = [\omega_1, \omega_2, \omega_3] = [0.4, 0.4, 0.3]$ for each UAV. To avoid the random number influencing the simulation results, each scenario will be run 100 times, and we use the average of the 100 times as the result of each scenario.

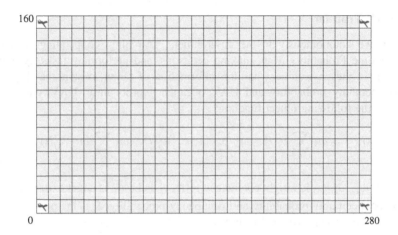

Fig. 3. UAV initial location and search area

Fig. 4. Simulation of multi-UAVs

On the basis of the simulation, we get the results. The performance of different strategy in each scenario was measured with the found targets along simulation time. Figure 5 shows the comparison of found targets in the condition of static targets between probability map (PM) strategy and modified probability map (MPM) strategy, and Fig. 6 shows the comparison of found targets in the condition of dynamic targets between probability map (PM) strategy and modified probability map (MPM) strategy. Figure 7 shows the comparison of found targets in the condition of static targets between three different strategies, and Fig. 8 shows the comparison of found targets in the condition of dynamic targets between three different strategies.

By Figs. 5 and 6 we can note that, modified probability map (MPM) strategy can find more targets than probability map (PM) strategy. MPM extend the traditional PM by add occupancy probability avoid UAVs searching the same cell, so that UAVs can find more targets in the same searching time.

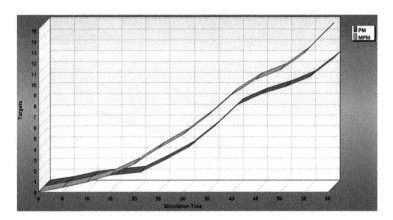

Fig. 5. Comparison of PM and MPM in the condition of static targets

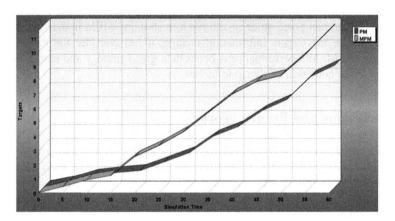

Fig. 6. Comparison of PM and MPM in the condition of dynamic targets

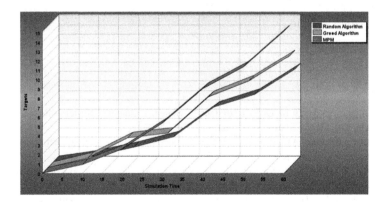

Fig. 7. Comparison of MPM and other algorithms in the condition of static targets

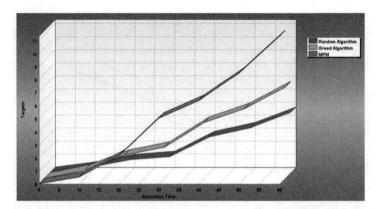

Fig. 8. Comparison of MPM and other algorithms in the condition of dynamic targets

By Figs. 7 and 8 we can note that, modified probability map (MPM) strategy can find more targets than greed strategy and random strategy. MPM update the TOP and MOP map while the targets information change, it has consider the targets state's dynamic so that MPM's performance is better than greed strategy and random strategy especially in the condition of dynamic targets.

5   Conclusions and Future Work

This paper introduces a new framework for UAV search operations and proposes a new approach to solve multi-UAVs cooperative searching problem. We testify our model and algorithm based on ABMS (Agent Based Modeling and Simulation), the result proves that the TOP and MOP map is effective for the Cooperative target-searching of multiple Unmanned Aerial Vehicles problem. This method was then compared in numerical simulations to Random and Greed Algorithm, and was shown to be more successful in the condition of dynamic targets than static targets. Future work will extend this approach to the case of limiting communication and the influence of the communication capability.

References

1. Office of the Secretary of Defense of United States. Unmanned Systems Roadmap 2007–2032. DoD of United States, Washington, USA (2007)
2. Blackmore, L., Ono, M., Williams, B.C.: Chance-constrained optimal path planning with obstacles. IEEE Trans. Robot. **27**(6), 1080–1094 (2011)
3. Richards, A., How, J.P.: Decentralized model predictive control of cooperating UAVs. In: IEEE Conference on Decision and Control, Bahamas, pp. 4286–4291 (2004)
4. Bertuccelli, L.F., How, J.P.: Robust UAV search for environments with imprecise probability maps. In: IEEE Conference on Decision and Control (2005, to appear)

5. Yang, Y., Minai, A., Polycarpou, M.: Evidential map-building approaches for multi-UAV cooperative search. In: American Control Conference (2005)
6. Ma, Y., Ma, X., Song, X.: A case study on air combat decision using approximated dynamic programming. Math. Probl. Eng. (2014)
7. Scheidt, D., Stipes, J., Neighoff, T.: Cooperating unmanned vehicles. Presented at IEEE International Conference on Networking, Sensing and Control, Tuscon, AZ (2005)
8. Chandler, P., Rasmussen, S., Pachter, M.: UAV cooperative path planning. In: Proceedings of AIAA Guidance, Navigation, and Control Conference and Exhibit, Denver, CO, pp. 1255–1265 (2000)
9. Chandler, P., Pachter, M.: Hierarchical control for autonomous teams. In: Proceedings of AIAA Guidance, Navigation, and Control Conference and Exhibit, Monterey, CA, pp. 632–642 (2001)
10. Pachter, M., Chandler, P.: Challenges of autonomous control. IEEE Control Syst. Mag. **18** (4), 92–97 (1998)
11. Jin, Y., Minai, A., Polycarpou, M.: Cooperative real-time search and task allocation in UAV teams. In: IEEE Conference on Decision and Control (2003)
12. Jun, M., D'Andrea, R.: Probability map building of uncertain dynamic environments with indistinguishable obstacles. In: IEEE American Control Conference (2003)
13. Krokhmal, P., Murphey, R., Pardalos, P., Uryasev, S.: Robust decision making: addressing uncertainties in distributions. In: Butenko, S., et al. (eds.) Cooperative Control: Models Applications and Algorithms, pp. 165–185. Kluwer Academic Publishers, Berlin (2003)
14. Polycarpou, M., Yang, Y., Passino, K.: A cooperative search framework for distributed agents. In: IEEE International Symposium on Intelligent Control (2001)

Design of Target Aircraft Auto Air-Combat Tactics Decision System

Kungang Yuan, Dengdi Liu, Daogang Jiang, Zhiwei Zhang, and Xiang Lei[✉]

Air Force Command College, Beijing, China
240669315@qq.com

Abstract. Aiming at the air-combat simulation training, refer to tactics that pilot use in actual air-combat, integrated air-combat knowledge and rules from BVR(Beyond-Visual-Range) to WVR(Within-Visual-Range) were established according to air situation, threat environment and airborne weapon performance. An expert system for target aircraft air-combat tactics decision was designed and developed by using Maneuver Sequence Automation (MSA) method based on basic flight maneuvers, an autonomous air-combat tactical simulation system was also established by using Visual C++ and Open Scene Graph (OSG). This study provided a high fidelity virtual opponent for simulation combat training, early-warning and detection, target recognition, information fusion etc.

Keywords: Target aircraft · Auto Air-combat · Tactical decision

1 Introduction

High fidelity virtual opponent aircraft is becoming more and more important in simulation combat training, early-warning and detection, target recognition, information fusion etc. moreover, as virtual opponent of air combat simulation, the target aircraft need to execute many behaviors automatically in acute variety air conditions, such as offensive/defensive maneuver flight, weapon eject, electronic jamming and so on [1].

In this paper, according to the characteristic of air combat that it usually begin from beyond-visual-range(medium range) to in-visual-range(short range dogfight), consider the air condition, threat environment and airborne weapon performance of target aircraft, integrated air-combat knowledge and rules were established and an expert system was adopted to develop typical tactical maneuvers select an decision. Meanwhile, these tactical maneuvers of target aircraft were decomposed into basic flight maneuvers using Maneuver Sequence Automation (MSA) method.

2 Auto Air Combat Tactics Decision of Target Aircraft

2.1 Main Framework

In modern times, air combat involved with many elements, knowledge and rules such as information disposal maneuver flight, weapon use and so on. Thus the expert system

This research is sponsored by Aeronautical Science Fund (NO. 20115189003)

L. Zhang et al. (Eds.): AsiaSim 2016/SCS AutumnSim 2016, Part II, CCIS 644, pp. 288–296, 2016.
DOI: 10.1007/978-981-10-2666-9_28

was selected to develop the auto air combat tactics decision; the main framework of this system is shown as Fig. 1.

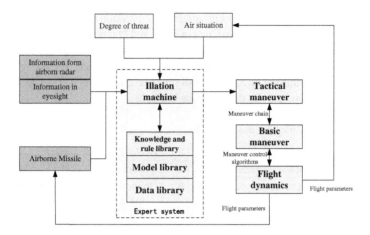

Fig. 1. The auto air combat tactics decision system framework based on expert system

Typical expert system [2] includes leastwise knowledge library, database, model library and reasoning-machine. In this paper, the knowledge library deposits air combat situation information and corresponding tactical maneuvers in those air situations. In tactical maneuvers, the fire control behaviors like weapon ejecting were included. The database saves performance data for both sides of countermeasures, such as aircrafts, airborne radars, medium range interception missiles, dogfight missiles and so on. The model library includes all kinds of models for calculating air situations, radar detect range, eye range, medium missile, dogfight missile, threat judgment, target distribute and so on. These information from database and current calculated state parameters were input into reasoning machine, and the reasoning machine matches these information and the preconditions of integrated air-combat knowledge and rules, then reason and output tactical maneuvers of target aircraft. The purpose of tactical maneuvers is to create advantage offensive situations and break away from disadvantage situations for target aircraft. Tactical maneuvers are integrated use of basic flight manuevers airborne equipments and weapons.

2.2 Establishment of Integrated Air Combat Tactical Rules

In many papers, the beyond-visual-range(BVR) air combat and within-visual-range(WVR) air combat were researched separately when built air combat rules. However, it is not very accord with fact, because air combat usually begins with BVR, through many complex conversions and decisions it goes to WVR air combat. Meanwhile, in some situations, the BVR and WVR air combat exist at the same time, in these situations, the aircraft can use medium range interception missiles to attack its opponents as well as use dogfight missiles, it also maybe in face of threat from medium missiles and dogfight missiles. So it is important to consider BVR and WVR air combat together and establish proper knowledge and rules that integrated from BVR(Beyond-Visual-Range) to WVR.

According to air combat process, a parameter method [3] was adopted to describe knowledge and rules from BVR through medium conversion to WVR, these rules were described by "integrated situations of air combat" and "tactical maneuvers". The integrated situations of air combat include many elements such as relative position of any aircrafts, information from radar/eye, and weapon performance. By doing these, the tactical decisions are running through the full process of air combat. Typical "integrated situations of air combat" can be described as Table 1.

Table 1. Parameter describe of integrated situations of air combat (I)

ID	Radar/medium missile information	ID	Eye/dogfight missile information
1	Opponent is out of the radar detect range	A	Opponent is out of the eye sight
2	Radar find opponent, but not yet track and acquisition	B	Opponent is in the eye sight, but out of the dogfight missile's attack range
3	Radar acquisition, but opponent out of medium missile's attack range		
4	Radar acquisition, and opponent in medium missile's attack range	C	Opponent is in the eye sight and in the dogfight missile's attack range

In Table 1, the radar, eye sight and the medium, dogfight missile range are integrated to form the "integrated situations of air combat", and using parameter I to describe these situations, the value of I includes A1–A4, B1–B4, C1–C4 (totally 12 situations), the value of I contains almost all situations that a target aircraft faced and is considered as one input parameter of reasoning machine in tactical decision expert system. The inputs of reasoning machine also include the threat degree and the weapon loaded. The threat degree can also be considered in the "integrated situations of air combat" of opponent aircraft that the target aircraft faced, using parameter D, it can be described as Table 2.

Table 2. Parameter describe of threat degree (d)

ID	Threat situations faced	Threat degree
1	In A1–A3, B1–B3 of opponent aircraft	light
2	In A4 or B4 and enter the medium missile's attack range of opponent	medium
3	In C1–C4 and enter the dogfight attack range of opponent	severe
4	Opponent's medium missile is ejected	Very severe
5	Opponent's dogfight missile is ejected	Fearfully severe

As for the factor of weapon loaded by target aircraft, considering that aircraft loads two kind typical weapons in general condition, namely medium interception missile and dogfight missile, the remained number of missiles can be used as a parameter to describe the influence of weapon loaded as an input of reasoning machine. See Table 3.

Table 3. Parameter describe of the number of remained missiles (M)

ID	Remained number of airborne missiles
1	Remained number of medium missiles/dogfight missiles are n/x
2	Remained number of medium missiles/dogfight missiles are n/0 (no dogfight missile remained)
3	Remained number of medium missiles/dogfight missiles are 0/n (no dogfight missile remained)
4	Remained number of medium missiles/dogfight missiles are 0/0 (no missile remained)

Corresponding to parameters I, D and M, there are 240 conditions for each target aircraft, for each condition, a confirm tactical maneuver can be executed. Typical tactical maneuvers and their conversions can be formed from basic tactics in real air combat. For offensive tactics, the basic process such as search, find, attack, etc. these typical tactics and corresponding I and M are shown in Fig. 2.

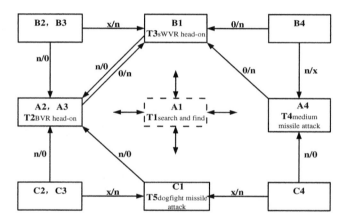

Fig. 2. Offensive tactical maneuvers and conversions based on air combat process

It can be shown in Fig. 2 that air combat usually begin from situation A1 (that is, opponent is out of the eye sight and radar detect range, in Table 1), in that situation, the tactical maneuver T1 (search and find maneuver) should be executed, during the reasoning process, the air situation are changed and corresponding tactical maneuvers are executed according to conversions shown in Fig. 2.

In these tactical maneuvers, five typical offensive tactical maneuvers are:
T1: search and find tactical maneuver, executed in situation A1
T2: BVR head-on and encounter tactical maneuver, executed in situation A2, A3
T3: WVR head-on and encounter tactical maneuver, executed in situation B1
T4: medium missile attack tactical maneuver, executed in situation A4
T5: dogfight missile attack tactical maneuver, executed in situation C1

In other air situations, combined with the parameter M, these five tactical maneuvers can be confirmed using arrowheads shown in Fig. 2. take situation B4for example, in this situation, it can be seen in Table 1 that "Opponent is in the eye sight, but out of the dogfight missile's attack range" and "Radar acquisition, and opponent in medium missile's attack range". Using arrowheads in Fig. 2, we can see if "Remained number of medium missiles/dogfight missiles are 0/n (no dogfight missile remained, M = 3, see Table 3)", tactical maneuver T3 can be executed; If "Remained number of medium missiles/dogfight missiles are n/x (M = 1)", tactical maneuver T4 can be executed. So one offensive tactical maneuver can be matched in every I and M.

Besides offensive tactical maneuvers, four defended tactical maneuvers were designed according to parameter D for target aircraft as follow:

T6: breaking away from the medium missile's attack range of opponent, executed when D = 2
T7: breaking away from the dogfight missile's attack range of opponent, executed when D = 3
T8: evading the medium missile's attack, executed when D = 4
T9: evading the dogfight missile's attack, executed when D = 5

When parameter M = 4, namely "Remained number of medium missiles/dogfight missiles are 0/0 (no missile remained)" in Table 3, the target aircraft cannot attack opponent any more, then a tactical maneuver should be obtained as:

T10: return back and exit combat, when M = 4, D = 1

These ten tactical maneuvers obtain elements of information, weapon use and maneuver flight in any air situation and can satisfy decision needs in auto air combat simulation. □

2.3   Reasoning and Development of Air Combat Tactical Decision

According to the logic relation of tactical maneuver T and the "integrated situations of air combat" I, The threat degree D and the remained missile M, an expert system using forward inference rules, namely "matching conditions -> conclusions (IF-THEN)" pattern [1]. Here matching conditions contains the input of reasoning machine of I, M, D, and conclusions are tactical maneuvers (T). The reasoning machine catches current I, D and M in air combat simulation, then touches off the matching rules in these conditions and searches corresponding "conclusions" T.

A rule in the rule library can be described by character as follow:

If [Opponent is out of the radar detect range, opponent is out of the eye sight, the aircraft is in A1–A3, B1–B3 of opponent aircraft, and Remained number of medium missiles/dogfight missiles are not zero]

Then [search and find tactical maneuver would be executed]

This rule can be described using parameter method in this paper as:

$$IF(I = A1 \& D = 1 \& (M = 1||2||3)) \rightarrow THEN(T = T1).$$

3   Development of Target Aircraft Tactical Maneuvers

3.1   Design of Tactical Maneuvers

Due to tactical maneuvers obtain elements of information, weapon use and maneuver flight, they can be executed based on flight maneuvers, situation judgment and weapon control. In order to execute tactical maneuvers, many models should be established and taken into the model library for use.

Take the search and find tactical maneuver T1 as example:

Maneuver conditions: Opponent is out of the radar detect range; opponent is out of the eye sight; Target aircraft is out of opponent's medium missile's attack range; Opponent's airborne air-to-air missile has not ejected; Remained number of medium missiles/ dogfight missiles are not 0/0.

Maneuver executed: first, the level straight flight maneuver of target aircraft is executed; the airborne radar and the eyesight search model are run at the same time; if the opponent aircraft is nod find for several minutes, take the level turn maneuver model of target aircraft and go on searching.

It is obvious that search and find tactical maneuver can be combined from level straight flight and level turn maneuvers, which integrated with airborne radar and eye search models.

3.2   Development of Tactical Maneuvers

In order to develop the tactical maneuvers in simulation system, the fundamental maneuver flight model [4] should be established first. The diagram of air-combat target aircraft's fundamental maneuver flight model is as follow (Fig. 3):

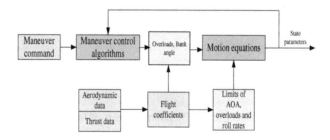

Fig. 3.   Diagram of target aircraft's maneuver flight model

According to the maneuver needed to be simulated, the model implements relevant control algorithm to get commanded over-loads and bank angle, then puts them into flight dynamic equations [5] to calculate state parameters of target aircraft.

The flight motion equations module includes several modules to calculate state parameters, such as data processing module (to get current aerodynamic coefficients), force calculation module (to get aircraft lift, drag and thrust), and module to enumerate dynamics and kinematics equations (to get state parameters).

14 control algorithms are designed for needs of target aircraft's maneuvering movement, including level flight, climb maneuver, dive maneuver, S-turn maneuver, Immelman turn maneuver, flip maneuver, etc. Each control algorithm is calculated in term of entry phase, implement phase and quit phase of each maneuver according to control rules of pilot.

The tactical maneuvers can be executed using maneuver-chain based on these flight maneuvers, the maneuver chain can be described by finite state machine [6], the finite state machine also called Maneuver Sequence Automation(MSA) [7], which can be described as:

$$MSA = \Phi\left(\sum, \varepsilon, Mini, \Sigma_f\right)$$

Here Σ and ε rely on air conditions and target aircraft flight dynamic characteristics; Mini can be understand as current flight maneuver; Σf can be understand as all flight maneuvers that may be taken. The MSA can be expressed using finite state machine as Fig. 4.

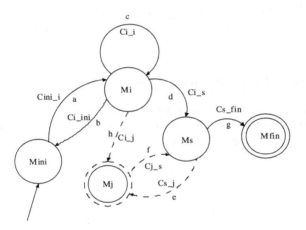

Fig. 4. Description of maneuver sequence automation

In Fig. 4, every node means the base flight maneuver of target aircraft, every arrowhead means connection to next flight maneuver, these arrowheads link relative flight manures and form chains. The initial flight maneuver is expressed as Mini; the last flight maneuver is expressed as Mfin. Take the flight maneuver Mi in Fig. 5 as example, when Mi is executed, all possible maneuvers linked with Mi are ready to touch off, when Ci_j is satisfied with executed condition, current flight maneuver become to Mj. By this way, the tactical maneuvers are successfully developed.

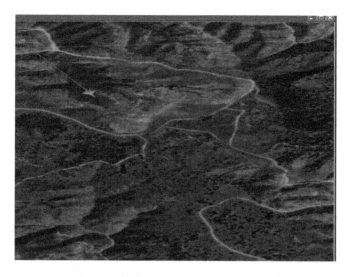

Fig. 5. Air combat simulation scene (Color figure online)

4 Simulation and Results

A simulation system was established by using Visual C++ with a scene system was also developed based on Open Scene Graph (OSG). In simulation conditions, red side is a simulator manipulated by pilot; blue side is a target aircraft using tactical decision expert system expressed in this paper. The simulation system can run in any air conditions.

Supposing the largest detection range of both sides are 100 km, the aircraft of red side loads 2 medium range interception missiles and 2 dogfight missiles; the target aircraft (blue side) loads no missile. The initial distance of each aircraft is 80 km; two aircrafts are head-on to each other. The countermeasure simulation process is shown in Fig. 5.

It can be seen in Fig. 5 that blue side (target aircraft) executed the "turn back and exit combat" (T10) tactical maneuver. Despite the opponent aircraft (red side) entered the detect range of its airborne radar, it does not execute other offensive tactical maneuvers such as BVR head-on and encounter (T2). This tactical maneuver decision is up to the actual behavior of pilot. It also can be seen that the "turn back and exit combat" (T10) tactical maneuver is executed by MSA to form maneuver chain "level straight flight – level turn – level straight flight" for target aircraft, and then run maneuver control algorithms and flight motion equations of target aircraft to implement air combat simulation.

5 Conclusion

Aiming at the need of reality target aircraft in air-combat simulation training, refer to tactics that pilot use in actual air-combat, integrated air-combat knowledge and rules from BVR(Beyond-Visual-Range) to WVR(Within-Visual-Range) were established in this paper. The simulation results show that the target aircraft air-combat tactics decision and maneuvers are in reason, This study can provide a high fidelity virtual opponent for simulation combat training, early-warning and detection, target recognition, information fusion etc.

References

1. Zhou, S.-y., Wu, W.-h., Zhang, N., Zhang, J.: Overview of autonomous air combat maneuver decision. Aeronautical Computing Tech. **42**(1), 27–31 (2012)
2. AO, Z.-g.: Artificial Intelligence and Expert System, p. 6. China Machine Press, Beijing (2007)
3. Gao, S.-y.: Multi-aircrafts air combat expert system and decision support system. Syst. Eng. Theory Pract. **8**, 76–80 (1999)
4. Yuan, K.-g., et al.: Development of air-combat target maneuver flight scene simulation system based on OSG. In: Second International Conference on Electronics, Communications, and Control, Zhoushan, China, pp. 1346–1349 (2012)
5. Gao, H., Zhu, P.-s., Gao, Z.-h.: Advanced Flight Dynamics, p. 6. National Defence Industry Publishing House, Beijing (2007)
6. Sun, P., Tan, Y.-x., Tang, L.: Visual modeling of combat entities behavior model rules based on finite state machine. Command Control Simul. **37**(2), 27–30 (2015)
7. Wan, L.-j., Yao, P.-y., Sun, P., Zhang, Y.-q.: Real-time evaluation method for flight manipulation in air countering. Fire Control Command Control **37**(7), 32–35 (2012)

Matching Suitability of Geomagnetic Aided Navigation Based on Spectral Moment Characteristics

Ting Li[✉], Jinsheng Zhang, Shicheng Wang, and Zhifeng Lv

High-Tech Institute of Xi'an, Xi'an, China
648033500@qq.com

Abstract. A novel matching-area suitability assessment method for geomagnetic matching aided navigation is proposed, which is based on spectral moment characteristics. With the analysis of profile spectral moment and the surface spectral moment, parameters of both homogeneity and isotropy are employed to analyze the effect of direction on geomagnetic three-dimension surface topography. Finally, simulations are made with the computing result of spectral moment parameters. Compared the matching effect of the Inertial Navigation System (INS) indicated path and the real path in the geomagnetic field contour map in different directions, a conclusion is reached that there is a good agreement between flight path and directions. Simulation results prove the proposed assessment method is effective.

Keywords: Matching suitability · Geomagnetic aided navigation · Spectral moment characteristics

1 Introduction

Geomagnetic navigation has become a popular aided navigation method in recent years, which uses the inherent properties of the geomagnetic field [1]. It is a supplementary navigation positioning by comparing the magnetic field data measured by geomagnetic sensor in real time and the reference map stored in computer. The geomagnetic navigation has desirable features of passive, non-radiation, all-time, all-weather, all terrain and low energy consumption, and it performs a good navigation capability while the vehicle is flying over the ocean, desert and plain, where there are little terrain features. Study found that matching precision is not only related to the matching algorithm, but also closely linked to the adaptation of selected matching area of a geomagnetic map [2].

Suitability of geomagnetic map is one of key technologies of geomagnetic aided navigation system. Selecting an area with significantly performance, good adaptability and high matching probability contributes a lot to real-time and location precision.

Methods on geomagnetic suitability are usually taken example by researches of scene suitability and terrain suitability. There are amounts of research papers about scene suitability abroad, but little about geomagnetic suitability. In China, in view of the problem of one-sided appraisal when using single character parameter to evaluate

© Springer Science+Business Media Singapore 2016
L. Zhang et al. (Eds.): AsiaSim 2016/SCS AutumnSim 2016, Part II, CCIS 644, pp. 297–305, 2016.
DOI: 10.1007/978-981-10-2666-9_29

geomagnetic map suitability, Wang et al. [3] applied the analytic hierarchy process to overall evaluation of geomagnetic suitability. Wang et al. [4] applied a multi-attribute decision making method based on maximum deviation and maximum entropy to the overall evaluation of suitability. Zhu et al. [5] proposed a comprehensive evaluation method based on multi-index fusion. Liu et al. [6] proposed a multi-characteristic parameter fusion selection method combining information entropy with project pursuit theory, which is presented in view of the disadvantage of one-sided appraisal for the selection method based on single geomagnetic characteristic parameter. Chen et al. [7] presented an improved algorithm for matching of multiple characteristic parameters. Kang et al. [8] proposed a selection based on geomagnetic entropy and magnetic variance entropy. Reference [9] presented a selection method of the geomagnetic adaptable matching area based on the geomagnetic co-occurrence matrix. Through the analysis of the profile spectral moment and the surface spectral moment, Li et al. [10] proposed a quantitative evaluation method, which is based on the application of fractal geometry theory. The second order spectral moment is employed to the research on the direction effect of three-dimension surface roughness grain this paper. A matching suitability method based on spectral moment characteristics is proposed, which has been proved effectively by simulations.

2   Description of Geomagnetic Field

Geomagnetic field is a vector field, any point in space can be described with seven geomagnetic elements, shown as Fig. 1.

Take the observation point as the ordinate origin. X, Y, Z stand for geographic north, geographic east and vertical component respectively. Geomagnetic field vector B in rectangular coordinates is projected into north component, east component and vertical component. H is the horizontal component of B, which points to geomagnetic north. F is the amplitude of B and is regarded as measure component in this paper. D and I are the two angles of magnetic field.

The main relationships among these components are as follows:

$$F^2 = X^2 + Y^2 + Z^2, H^2 = X^2 + Y^2$$

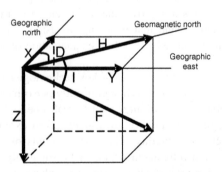

Fig. 1. Geomagnetic field characteristics

3   Three-Dimension Assessment Method Based on Spectral Moment Characteristics

Two-dimension stochastic process parameter and spectral analysis is widely used to demonstrate 2-D surface irregularities with the development of data processing technology. Power spectrum was employed to research since nineteen sixties and seventies [11, 12], which has been proven effective to present surface roughness.

3.1   Spectral Moment Characteristics of Geomagnetic Field

In rectangular coordinates, three-dimension surface is shown by two-dimension stochastic process function z(x, y). (x, y) represent the rectangular coordinates and z represents corresponding total intensity of geomagnetic field. The Fourier transform of z(x, y) can be written as:

$$F(f_x, f_y) = \int_{-\infty}^{\infty} \int_{-\infty}^{\infty} z(x, y) e^{-2\pi j(xf_x + yf_y)} d_x d_y \tag{1}$$

In Eq. (1), f_x, f_y represents spatial frequency in vertical directions. In reality, the length of area of geomagnetic contour map and sampling points are limited to a certain number. Assume that sampling points obtained at a certain interval Δx in X direction, and Δy in Y direction. Besides, the number of two directions is M and N respectively, so we can get the discrete spatial frequency:

$$f_u = u/(M\Delta x), \quad u = 0, 1, 2, \ldots, M-1 \tag{2}$$

$$f_v = v/(N\Delta x), \quad v = 0, 1, 2, \ldots, N-1 \tag{3}$$

two-dimension discrete Fourier transform:

$$F(f_u, f_v) = \frac{1}{NM} \sum_{k=0}^{N-1} \sum_{j=0}^{M-1} z(x_j, y_k) e^{-2\pi j(x_j f_u + y_k f_v)} \tag{4}$$

f_u, f_v represent spatial frequency in vertical directions.

Three-dimension surface can be composed of limited sampling points, and the corresponding discrete power spectrum density can be represented as:

$$G(u/(M\Delta x), v/(N\Delta y)) = \frac{|F(u/(M\Delta x), v/(N\Delta y))|^2}{MN\Delta x \Delta y} \tag{5}$$

In Eq. (5), $u = 0, 1, 2 \ldots\ldots M-1$, $v = 0, 1, 2 \ldots\ldots N-1$. For a discrete sampling surface, the zero and second order spectral moment of surface can be transformed as:

$$m_{pq} = \sum_{u=1}^{M/2} \sum_{v=1}^{N/2} (\frac{u}{M\Delta x})^p (\frac{v}{N\Delta y})^q G(\frac{u}{M\Delta x}, \frac{v}{N\Delta y}) \tag{6}$$

$$m_{00} = \sum_{u=1}^{M/2} \sum_{v=1}^{N/2} G(\frac{u}{M\Delta x}, \frac{v}{N\Delta y}) \tag{7}$$

$$m_{20} = \sum_{u=1}^{M/2} \sum_{v=1}^{N/2} (\frac{u}{M\Delta x})^2 G(\frac{u}{M\Delta x}, \frac{v}{N\Delta y}) \tag{8}$$

$$m_{02} = \sum_{u=1}^{M/2} \sum_{v=1}^{N/2} (\frac{v}{N\Delta y})^2 G(\frac{u}{M\Delta x}, \frac{v}{N\Delta y}) \tag{9}$$

$$m_{11} = \sum_{u=1}^{M/2} \sum_{v=1}^{N/2} (\frac{u}{M\Delta x})(\frac{v}{N\Delta y}) G(\frac{u}{M\Delta x}, \frac{v}{N\Delta y}) \tag{10}$$

Zero surface spectral moment m_{00} describes the height position displacement of points and can be regarded as height variance. The second order surface spectral moment m_{20}, m_{02} is the slope variance in the direction of coordinate axis X and Y. m_{11} represents covariance of both directions. When coordinate systems change, along with the change of surface spectral moment.

The second order surface spectral moment not only reflect amplitude distribution, but also reflect frequency characteristics, what's more, it is strongly dependent on grain direction of the measured surface. Consequently, the difference of directions of rough surface can be expressed by the second order surface spectral moment. Equations (8)–(10) are just several special cases, it is written as follows at any angle (assume it is α angle down from the positive X-axis):

$$m_2(\alpha) = m_{20} \cos^2 \alpha + 2m_{11} \cos \alpha \sin \alpha + m_{02} \sin^2 \alpha \tag{11}$$

3.2 Three-Dimension Evaluating Parameters

3.2.1 Homogeneity

Homogeneity of surface is defined as: distribution probability along the height, which is independent of measure position. It is considered poor homogeneous if some surface is uneven, for the opposite side, homogeneity is good if the surface is in at same height.

According to Longuet-Higgins's equation $m_n(\theta) = \sum_{q=0}^{n} m_{pq} \cdot C_n^q \cos^p \theta \cdot \sin^q \theta$, we can know that the zero order surface spectral moment is equal to profile spectral moment.

$$m_{00} = m_0(\alpha_i) \quad i = 1, 2, \ldots, n \tag{12}$$

Equation (12) demonstrates the homogeneity of surface clearly, that is to say, profile fluctuation variance is equal to height variance in all directions. Zero order surface spectral moment can reflect the height distribution variance of surface, and it is unequal to inhomogeneous surface. So we can evaluate the homogeneity of three-dimension surface in the following way.

$$H_{m0} = \frac{|\min\{m_{0i}\}|}{|\max\{m_{0i}\}|} \quad i = 1, 2, \ldots, n \tag{13}$$

H_{m0} is the homogeneity of the height distribution and m_{0i} stands for several translating profile spectral moments with zero order.

The second order surface spectral moment expresses slope distribution characteristics, and the homogeneity of three-dimension surface slope distribution can be defined as:

$$H_{m2} = \frac{|\min\{m_{2i}\}|}{|\max\{m_{2i}\}|} \quad i = 1, 2, \ldots, n \tag{14}$$

H_{m2} is the homogeneity of the slope distribution and m_{2i} stands for several translating the second order profile spectral moments.

3.2.2 Isotropy

Isotropy of random surface is the probability distribution of random surface's profiles remain unchanged in height direction when measuring coordinate-axis rotates. We get to know that isotropy of uneven surface can be expressed by the second order profile spectral moment. If the surface is isotropic, $m_2(\alpha)$ must have nothing to do with the angle α, that is

$$m_2(\alpha) = m_2 = \text{constant} \tag{15}$$

$\alpha = 0.5*\arctan(2m_{11}/m_{20} - m_{02})$ is the first derivative of the Eq. (15) versus α, besides, $m_{2\text{max}}$ and $m_{2\text{min}}$ can be obtained:

$$m_{2\text{max}} = \frac{1}{2}\left(M_2 + \sqrt{M_2^2 - 4\Delta_2}\right) \tag{16}$$

$$m_{2\text{min}} = \frac{1}{2}\left(M_2 - \sqrt{M_2^2 - 4\Delta_2}\right) \tag{17}$$

$M_2 = m_{20} + m_{02}$, $\Delta_2 = m_{20}m_{02} - m_{11}^2$, $M_2^2 = 4\Delta_2$ can be inferred by $m_{2\text{max}} = m_{2\text{min}}$. Above all, isotropy coefficient Λ is reached to describe the surface with anisotropy:

$$\Lambda = \frac{2\sqrt{\Delta_2}}{M_2} \qquad (18)$$

If $m_{11} = 0$, $m_{20} = m_{02}$, $\Lambda = 1$, the three-dimension surface is totally isotropic, on the contrary, $m_{11} = 0$, m_{20} or $m_{02} = 0$, $\Lambda = 0$ when the surface is not isotropic at all. So Λ ranges from 0 to 1, and the closer the value is to 1, the better the isotropy is. When we evaluate the anisotropy of three-dimension surface, for the same surface, not merely three profiles are measured, isotropic parameter can be get by the mean value of all:

$$\Lambda_{\text{average}} = \frac{1}{n}\sum_{i=1}^{n}\Lambda_i \qquad (19)$$

4   Simulation and Discussion

The geomagnetic reference map A is composed of high-density measurement data from the area of south sea in China. Taking total intensity F as matching characteristic and the data is stored as grid form. The 3-D and 2-D surface model is established in Fig. 2.

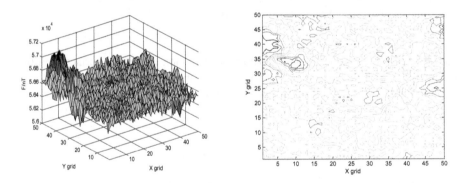

Fig. 2.   Three-dimension and contour map of Geomagnetic field

From part 3.1, the second order surface spectral moments of all directions can be plot in Fig. 3.

Figure 3 shows the strong difference of geomagnetic field surface, the maximal value can be got at the angle 87 and 267, and the minimum value can be get at 177 and 357. A random surface can be regarded as vast sine curves, which consist of various amplitude, different frequency and different phase. To a certain pure sine curve, height variance depends on the amplitude and slope variance equals to the product of amplitude and frequency. The second order spectral moments just represent the slope variance, furthermore, the second order surface spectral moment can reflect slope variance of surface, the second order profile spectral moment reflects slope variance of profile as well.

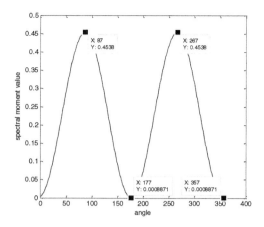

Fig. 3. The second order spectral moments

The calculations H_{m0}, $H_{m2} \rightarrow 0$ can be got from Eqs. (12)–(14), which indicate the poor homogeneity of reference map A. In addition, $m_2(\alpha)$ is not a constant but varies with the changing angle. Above all, A has anisotropy. Isotropy coefficient $\Lambda = 0.0871$ indicates the isotropy is poor as well. That is to say, navigation performance is closely related to directions. Directions would have great influence on matching effect. Simulation work would be done with ICCP (Iterated Closest Contour Point) method in the area A.

Parameter settings:
Vehicle's speed: 0.6 Mach;
Sampling frequency: 1 Hz;
Grid spacing: 200 m;
Magnetic measurement noise: white noise with mean value 0nT, $\sigma^2 = 20$ added to uniform noise range between −10nT and 10nT.
Matching sequence length: 10;
Maximal iteration number: 20.

When the angle between flight path and X-axis is 90, simulation result is shown in Figs. 4 and 5 show the result when the angle is zero.

Figure 4 shows a successful matching with error in one grid unit, while Fig. 5 shows that ICCP path fails to match the real path. It is proved again the direction has influence on matching effect. The second order spectral moment can provide reference for matching suitability analysis, with this method can improve path planning system preprocessing efficiency a lot.

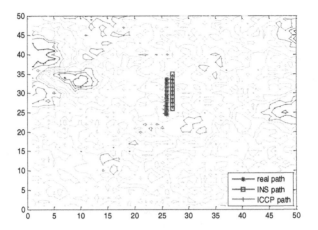

Fig. 4. Matching result when $\alpha = 90°$

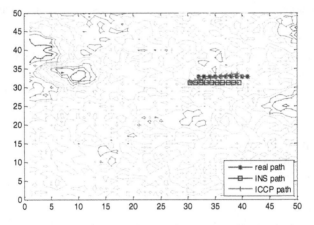

Fig. 5. Matching result when $\alpha = 0°$

5 Conclusions

An assessment method related to geomagnetic field suitability is proposed based on spectral moment characteristics by means of roughness assessment method of machining surface. Transformed the discrete data of geomagnetic field with Fourier method, then computed some parameters of 3-D magnetic field surface, such as power spectral density, the second order surface spectral moment and profile spectral moment. The isotropy has been proved poor by computing 3-D assessment parameters, and simulation results show that the area is sensitive to the direction, thus the proposed method is effective.

References

1. Guo, C.-F., Hu, Z.-D., Zhang, S.-F., Cai, H.: A survey of geomagnetic navigation. J. Astronaut. **30**(4), 1314–1319 (2009)
2. Ma, X.-J., Liu, H.-W., Xiao, D., Li, H.-K.: Key technologies of geomagnetic aided inertial navigation system. IEEE Intelligent Vehicles Symposium, New York, vols. 1, 2, pp. 464–469 (2009)
3. Wang, Z., Wang, S.C., Zhang, J.-S., Qiao, Y.-K., Chen, L.-H.: A matching suitability evaluation method based on analytic hierarchy process in geomagnetism matching guidance. J. Astronaut. **30**(5), 1871–1878 (2009)
4. Wang, P., Wu, M.-P., Ruan, Q., Yuan, H.-P.: Application of multi-attribute decision method in analysis of geomagnetic map suitability. Ordance Ind. Autom. **30**(8), 65–68 (2011)
5. Zhu, Z.-L., Yang, G.-L., Shan, Y.-D., Yang, S.-J., Wang, Y.-Y.: Comprehensive evaluation method of geomagnetic map suitability analysis. J. Chin. Inertial Technol. **21**(3), 375–380 (2013)
6. Liu, Y.-X., Zhou, J., Ge, Z.-L.: A projecting pursuit-based on selection method for matching region in geomagnetism navigation. J. Astronaut. **31**(12), 2677–2682 (2010)
7. Chen, L.-H., Wang, S.-C., Sun, Y., Zheng, Y.-H., Liu, Z.-G.: Matching of multi-dimensional feature elements in areas with smooth magnetic fields. J. Chin. Inertial Technol. **19**(6), 720–724 (2011)
8. Kang, C., Wang, M., Fan, L.-M., Zhang, X.-J.: Region selected of geomagnetic-matching navigation based on geomagnetic entropy and geomagnetic variance entropy. J. Basic Sci. Eng. **23**(6), 1156–1164 (2015)
9. Zhao, J.-H., Wang, S.-P., Wang, A.-X.: Study on the selection of the geomagnetic adaptable matching area based on the geomagnetic co-occurrence matrix. Geomatics Inf. Sci. Wuhan Univ. **36**(4), 446–449 (2011)
10. Li, C-G, Zhang, G-X, Yuan, C-L.: Evaluation of the isotropy of 3-D surface topograph. J. Mech. Eng. (1), 1–13 (1999)
11. Longuet-Higgins, M.S.: The statistical analysis of random moving surface. Philos. Trans. Roy. Soc. **249**, 321–384 (1957)
12. Nayak, P.R.: Random process model of Surface roughness measurement. Wear **26**, 165–174 (1973)
13. Li, C.-G., Shi, Z.-Y.: Spectrum moment characteristics of 3-D rough surface. J. Beijing Univ. Technol. **29**(4), 406–410 (2003)

Approach for Intelligent Rival-Air-Plane Threats Evading

Xiang Lei[(⊠)], AnXiang Huang, YuQiang Su, Chuan Ren,
HuiMin Cao, and XiaoWen Fen

Air Force Command College, Beijing, China
240669315@qq.com

Abstract. In the "man-aircraft" air combat simulation, the combat training of
the intelligent Rival-Air-Plane may advance the pilots' tactics. The intelligence
is represented in the two aspects: the intelligent attack and the intelligent evade
for the missile threats. This paper aims to use the shortest time when the
intelligent aircraft arrives the nearest boundary of the weapon attach zone as the
constraint condition, and further to plan out the optimal evasive route and
enhance the evasive intelligence. As well, a set of sample data validates the
simulation experiment, which is the scientific and feasible approach. Obviously,
it not only achieves requirements of the strong real-time combat simulation, but
also provides a reference of the actual combat missile to evade for the pilots.

Keywords: Weapon attach zone · Intelligent evasion · Real-time route
planning

1 Introduction

The air combat is fierce, agile and high-cost, it effectively uses the Air-Fight simulation
to improve the quality operations of the pilots. Whether the pilots in the Air-Fight
semi-simulation in the loop, or the fighters in embedded simulation, it is necessary to
assemble a certain intelligent virtual rival aircraft for the man-machine confrontation
training. That can increase the verisimilitude of the confrontation, as well as, improve
the operational capability of the pilots. The intelligence of the virtual aircrafts are
reflected in the intelligent attack and intelligent evade. I have preliminarily discussed
the trajectory planning when the intelligent aircrafts attack in the literature [1], the
detected probability as a weighting function is further used to plan out the optimal
attack trajectory, in a certain extent, the problems about how the virtual intelligent
opponents intelligently attack have been solved. While, this article is studying the
problems about how the virtual intelligent opponents intelligently evade. In recent
years, the relevant researches are mainly summarized as follows:

Literature [2] systematically expounds the defensive tactics maneuver strategies of
the multi-aircraft combat tactical expert system, which is based on the tactics theories
of the air combat summarized from the application of the basic theories and methods in
the expert system, and the actual experience of the air combat achieved by the experts.
Literature [3] proposes a solution of the closed loop that is based upon the multi-model
predictive control of the non-linear model, specifically, it adopts the maximum

© Springer Science+Business Media Singapore 2016
L. Zhang et al. (Eds.): AsiaSim 2016/SCS AutumnSim 2016, Part II, CCIS 644, pp. 306–314, 2016.
DOI: 10.1007/978-981-10-2666-9_30

likelihood approach to identify the guidance parameters and aerodynamic parameters of the attacking missiles, and deal with the problems of missile's unknown parameters, at the same time, the closed loop solution of control instructions enhances the robustness of control strategy. Literature [4] uses the maximum miss-distance as an index, adopts the direct multiple shooting method to solve the problems in the three-dimensional space. In Literature [5], Karelahti explains the optimization algorithm of the missile escape trajectory that is based on the optimization rolling time, and further adopts the approach of variable step length to extend the time window. At the same time, it also limits the growth of decision variables and processes the optimization calculation in the maximum miss-distance, intercept time, approximate speed, missile control energy, the off-axis Angle of missile seeker, Angle of sight rate etc.

From above, the literatures are generally based on the thoughts of the expert system and the trend prediction to determine the evasive strategies, but those do not effectively solve the problems of confrontational air combat. Additionally, the man-in-the-loop combat simulation training system is required a large amount of computation and strong real-time, so it is necessary to consider the project implementation of the algorithm and the time complexity of the algorithm when the algorithm is designed. This paper aims to use the shortest time when the intelligent aircraft arrives the nearest boundary of the weapon attach zone as the constraint conditions, then to adopt A star algorithm to identify the optimal position in the next simulation time, final to real-timely project the optimal route to evade, as a result, it will validate the effectiveness of the approach by simulation.

2 The Weapon Attach Zone Model

The objective of an air combat is to destroy the enemy air target. For that, it needs to ensure that there is an enemy target in the weapons attach zone [6], that is to say, there exists threats only when the target is in the weapons attach zone, and the optimal evasive route is away from the weapons attach zone as far as possible. The weapons attach zone of the missile refers to a space around the target area. In the weapons attach zone, the missile launched by the aerial carrier can meet the requirement of miss-distance, and destroy the target at a certain probability. There are many factors influence missile attach zone, including the missile maneuverability, the flight range of the missile, the guidance law of the missile, the target maneuverability, and the payload fighter's flight altitude and speed, etc. In practice, it generally adopts the polynomial fitting method for the calculation, which is introduced in literature [7]. When the target launches missile in the weapons attach zone, the missile will hit the target just as the target does not evasive maneuvers. While, if the target is evasively maneuvering, it is possible to escape from missile tracking.

The weapons attach zone is related to the target maneuver characteristics. It means that when the air-to-air missile launches, the weapons attach zone will change as with the changes of the target, and this zone is known as the dynamic attack zone of air-to-air missile. Specifically, the zone refers that the air-to-air missile is launching along the trajectory of the intercepting target for a period of time, and then hit the target of four-dimensional space zone with a certain probability, which is considering various constraints, such as the flight state of missile (fight's position vector and velocity vector, etc.), the working state of the engine, body mass, guidance navigation and control system, or other each subsystem [8]. Here are some changes of attach zone when a type of missile attacks in these two different ways [9] (Fig. 1).

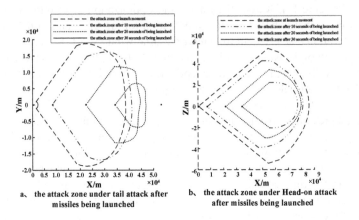

a、 the attack zone under tail attack after missiles being launched

b、 the attack zone under Head-on attack after missiles being launched

Fig. 1. The variable maps of the attach zone when the air-to-air missile launches

3 Approaches Description

In general, the area outsides the attach zone is non-threat. In the current situation, the virtual intelligent opponent aircraft escapes the attach zone of air-to-air missile as far as possible, and the optimal escape position is the boundary point of the maximum attach zone closed to the position of current aircraft. As shown in Fig. 2, it assumes that T is the time of air combat, O is the missile position, the elliptical area is the maximum attach zone of air-to-air missile, P is the target flight position, J is the closest point from P on the ellipse, the dotted line is the aircraft flight path from P to J. Obviously, at the time T, the virtual intelligent opponent plane needs to plan the optimal evade trajectory, and it needs to solve three major problems: first, how to quickly identify the boundary of attach zone at the time T? Second, how to determine the closest point from the boundary of attach zone? Third, on the basis of this point, how to project the optimal flight position in the next time?

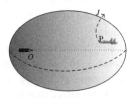

Fig. 2. The maximum attach zone to escape

There are three steps to solve these problems:

Step1: simplifying the model of the maximum attach zone.

In the air combat simulation system, if the information of any target can be obtained, and the maximum attach zone of missile in any time will be identified, this method is described by the literature [8]. While, due to the complexity of the calculation, the method can be reasonably facilitated for a quick solution in the simulation system. It assumes that at the time T, the maximum attach zone in actual is an irregular zone $G(x, y, z)$ in the three-dimensional space, and the irregular zone could be contained in a regular three-dimensional sphere, namely: $G(x, y, z) \in S(x, y, z)$, that is, if the virtual intelligent opponent aircraft escape successfully in $S(x, y, z)$,and it will success in $G(x, y, z)$.

In the actual combat, the maximum attach zone is real-time changing. The missile is an energy body when it launches, its energy is constantly reduced in the flight process, and the scope of the maximum attach zone is reduced as well. As a result, it only considers the major factors in the simplified model $S(x, y, z)$, such as the relative position and relative velocity between missile and aircraft at present, entry Angle and azimuth Angle, etc.

Step2: identifying the closest position to escape.

The shortest distance between one point and the curved surface: assuming that the current position of the virtual intelligent opponent aircraft is $P(x_i, y_i, z_i, h_i, p_i, r_i)$, the distance from P to the maximum attach zone is $D = P(x_i, y_i, z_i,) - S(x, y, z)$, so the corresponding coordinates of the shortest distance can be calculated:

$$\frac{\partial D}{\partial x} = P(x_i, y_i, z_i,) - S(x, y, z)|_x = 0$$
$$\frac{\partial D}{\partial y} = P(x_i, y_i, z_i,) - S(x, y, z)|_y = 0 \qquad (1)$$
$$\frac{\partial D}{\partial z} = P(x_i, y_i, z_i,) - S(x, y, z)|_z = 0$$

The three simultaneous equations will determine the closest coordinates (x_0, y_0, z_0) of the largest attach zone away from the current position.

Step3: identifying the optimal position in the next time.

For the intelligent opponent aircraft, the flight parameter in the next time is to evade missile tracking. Firstly, it is necessary to determine the alternative course angle and pitching angle, and they are related to the status and performance of the aircraft. The variation range of the aircraft's course angle is affected by the minimum turning radius of the aircraft, so the formula of the minimum turning radius is described in [10]:

$$R_{\min} = v_{\min}^2 \Big/ g\sqrt{n_{y_{\max}}^2 - 1} \qquad (2)$$

$$\theta_{head\ \max} = \arcsin(S_0 / 2R_{\min}) \qquad (3)$$

Formula (2): $v_{\min}$ is the minimum speed of the aircraft, $n_{y\ \max}$ is the maximum normal overload of the aircraft, according to the minimum turning radius and the step length of route planning, the maximum angle $\theta_{head\ max}$ will be calculated when the course changes.

Formula (3): S_0 is the step length of route planning.

In the range of course angle $[-\theta_{head\ max}, \theta_{head\ max}]$, $\Delta\theta_{head}$ is a unit, the current course angle is the initial value, and then A star algorithm is adopted to determine the closest position from the maximum attach zone, that is the optimal course.

The pitch angle's maximum range of variation depends on the climb rate of aircraft. During the application, the maximum average rate of climb can be used when the altitudes are different (Fig. 3).

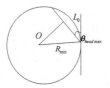

Fig. 3. Calculation of the maximum change angle of course

It is assumed that the plane's speed is constant, and the flight distance of the aircraft in a step is $v\Delta t$, so the next point coordinates are explained in the formula (4):

$$\begin{cases} x_{\Delta t} = x_{AO} + v\Delta t\ \cos(\theta_{pitch_i}) \times \cos(\theta_{head_i}) \\ y_{\Delta t} = y_{AO} + v\Delta t\ \cos(\theta_{pitch_i}) \times \sin(\theta_{head_i}) \\ z_{\Delta t} = z_{AO} + v\Delta t\ \sin(\theta_{pitch_i}) \end{cases} \tag{4}$$

Formula (5) shows the attitude parameters:

$$\begin{aligned} \theta_{head_{\Delta t}} &= \theta_{head_{AO}} + \theta_{head_i} \\ \theta_{pitch_{\Delta t}} &= \theta_{pitch_{AO}} + \theta_{pitch_i} \end{aligned} \tag{5}$$

The roll angle has little influence on the position, which can be neglected here. The flight parameters in the next time will be calculated as $P(x_{\Delta t}, y_{\Delta t}, z_{\Delta t}, \theta_{head\Delta t}, \theta_{pitch\Delta t})$. In the actual, the adjustment of exploration step will cycle in the next time.

4 Example Application

Air combat process is extremely complex, the simulation is not able to fully take all the factors into account. In a hardware man-in-the-loop simulation system is an effective way to improve the operational level. The man-in-the-loop combat simulation systems can validate this approach. Trainees launch missiles based on the position of intelligent opponent aircraft, the intelligent opponent adopts the proposed approach to plan its evasive route, and uses kill probability of missile as the evaluation function to review the effectiveness of evasive route.

The simulation condition is assumed as follows: "one-on-one" is used as the most basic air combat style, the missile uses the proportional guidance rate in the three-dimensional space to guide. Maximum acceleration of missile is 5 g, the initial speed is Vm = 300 m/s, the target travels at a constant speed Vt = 300 m/s; and then confrontation on the similar height ($H_{missile} - H_{target} < 500$ m) in an ideal external environment where regardless of the wind, temperature, electromagnetic interence etc.

For a certain type of missile, a regular ellipsoid is assumed to fit the maximum attach zone, the range of the dynamic attach zone after launching and its speed are positively proportional relationship, the equation $\frac{x^2}{a^2} + \frac{y^2}{b^2} + \frac{z^2}{c^2} = 1$ is using the ellipsoid for fitting, furthermore, a, b, c are related to the boundary of the maximum attach zone, so in order to facilitate the calculation, the relevant variables of the speed is represented in the simulation process.

The simulation process is described in Fig. 4, that is, when the system is ready, the first thing needs to judge if there is a missile in simulation environment. If no, keeping the current status of flight; if yes, judging further whether their distance is in the far field of the missile's maximum attach zone. When it is not in the maximum attach zone of missile, keeping the current status of flight; when it within, identifying the closest position of maximum attach zone. And then, the next position and posture will be calculated and adjusted on the basis of current position and posture. Therefore, conduct this calculation again and again until escape the maximum attach zone or is hit by a missile.

The deduction process of simulation in the air combat simulation is simulating, the simulation cycle is 40 ms. Through using The SAS's JMP software, the simulation data

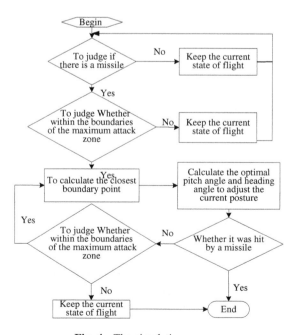

Fig. 4. The simulation process

fragments are recorded to draw the three-dimensional trajectory scatter diagram of the intelligent opponent aircraft and the missile, which can facilitate the analysis and visual display. Commonly, there are the evasive routes of intelligent opponent aircraft in the three attack ways.

In Fig. 5, when the intelligent opponent is lateral attacked, it will rise its altitude and turn flight, that aims to consistent with the direction of the missile.

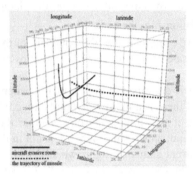

Fig. 5. The evasive route of lateral attack

In Fig. 6, the intelligent opponent will directly rise its altitude when it is tail attacked, that aims to consistent with the direction with the direction of the missile.

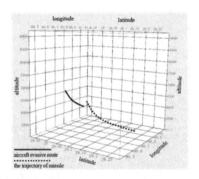

Fig. 6. The evasive route of tail attack

Figure 7 shows that when the intelligent opponent is head-on attacked, it will rise the altitude, and turn around to the opposite direction.

These simulation experiments explore that the two parameters $\Delta\theta_{head\ max}$ and $\Delta\theta_{pitch\ max}$ play a decisive role in the maneuverability of the aircraft, that is, the better maneuverability, the greater the two parameters. In a certain period of time, the large changes of aircraft position and attitude is conducive to evade the missile.

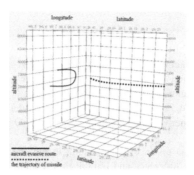

Fig. 7. The evasive route of Head-on attack

5 Conclusion

This paper aims to use the shortest time when the intelligent aircraft arrives the nearest boundary of missile's non-escape zone as the constraint condition, and to plan out the optimal route to evade. First of all, it studies the concept and the calculation method of the dynamic attach zone when air-to-air missile launches; second, it identifies the shortest distance of the aircraft away from the boundary based on the current situation; and then, it plans out the optimal azimuth angle and elevation angle in the next time, so as to determine the optimal position to avoid in the next time. In the simulation process, in order to reduce the overhead, the missile launch attach zone is simplified as a dynamic three-dimensional ellipsoid, at the same time, the program can be used to calculate the boundary points of the attach zone nearest aircraft, real-time deduction and simulation is carried out in air combat simulation system, it not only satisfies the requirements of the real-time air combat simulation system, but also effectively avoids the opponent missile, it embodies the intelligence of the opponent aircraft at a certain extent. Additionally, in the multi-machine war, the same way can be adopted as well to track the more missiles, identify the closed boundary points of their comprehensive attach zone to escape.

Improve the intelligence of the simulation target is of great significance to carry out an air combat training. When the missile launches, there is a large probability of being tracking if without any evasion, in another word, the evasion will reduce the probability of be tracking and to escape, therefore, so the reasonable evasion is necessary. While, how to evade is still a difficulty. In general, any model is designed by some rules and algorithms, but due to the process of air combat is extremely complex and strongly random, it is hard to establish an accurate model for simulation, which means, it is impossible to calculate with the consideration of all factors. So the approach proposed in this paper is largely simplified and assumed. For example, it usually decelerates and changes the sideslip angle to reduce the flight turning radius in actual flight, but the aircraft sideslip angle and the speed are not considered here. Likewise, the rage of attach zone is simplified. The application of this approach will be more effective if the maximum attach zone of the specific missile type can be accurately identified. But in actual combat, it is difficult to acquire the performance of enemy missiles, but the missile's velocity, direction and position.

References

1. Lei, X., Huang, A.-X., Feng, X.-W., Li, J.-S., Gao, Y.-P.: Approach for intelligent rival airplane real-time route planning. J. Syst. Simul. **25**(8), 1881–1885 (2014)
2. Gao, S.-Y.: Expert decision system for multiple-fighter air combat tactical maneuvering. Ph.D., The Air Force Command College of P.L.A., Beijing (1998)
3. Li, F., Yu, L., Zhou, Z., Fu, Z., Zhang, T.: The nonlinear model predictive control avoidance strategy of the fighter maneuver in endgame. J. Natl. Univ. Defense Technol. **36**(3), 83–90 (2014)
4. Raivio, T., Ranta, J.: Miss distance maximization in the end game. In: AIAA Guidance, Navigation, and Control Conference and Exhibit Proceedings, AIAA Paper: 2002-4947
5. Kamlaht, J., Virtanen, K., Raivio, T.: Near-optimal missile avoidance trajectories via receding horizon control. J. Guidance Control Dyn. **30**(5), 1297–1298 (2007)
6. James, S.M.: Real-Time Maneuvering Decisions for Autonomous Air Combat. Massachusetts Institute of Technology, Cambridge (2008)
7. Wu, W.-H., Zhou, S.-Y., Gao, L., Liu, J.-T.: Improvements of situation assessment for beyond-visual-range air combat based on missile launching envelope analysis. Syst. Eng. Electron. **33**(12), 2680–2685 (2011)
8. Wu, S.L., Nan, Y.: The calculation of dynamical attack zone of air-to-air missile after being launched. J. Projectiles, Rockets, Missiles Guidance **33**(5), 49–54 (2013)
9. Zhang, A.-K., Kong, F.-e.: Calculation and function of attack zone of air-to-air missile after launching. Electron. Opt. Control **23**(1), 74–79 (2016)
10. Zhu, B.-L.: Effectiveness Evaluation of Combat Aircraft. Aviation Industry Press, Beijing (1993)

Research on Construction and Evaluation Methods of the Operation Simulation Environment

Hui-min Cao, An-xiang Huang, Lei Xiang[✉], JinSong Li,
BaiGang Sun, and PeiHua Ye

Air Force Command College, Beijing, China
240669315@qq.com

Abstract. With the rapid development of computing science and the new military revolution, the concept of the battlefield environment has experienced a developing process from the "battlefield" to the "operation space" and to the "operation environment". Nowadays, the operation simulation environment is still mainly based on one or some certain aspect, and the construction haven't satisfied the need of operation training enough. This paper analyzed the process of operation simulation environment construction covering the aspects of geography, electromagnetic, information and meteorological, and further discussed the construction process of the operation environment in systematically. What's more, in view of the operation simulation environment elements, a comprehensive evaluation method was proposed to evaluate the operation simulation environment.

Keywords: An operation simulation environment · The construction · A comprehensive evaluation method

1 The Introduction

An operation environment refers to the land-based, the ocean, the sky, the space, and the contents of terrain, hydrology, weather and other natural conditions, as well as, the enemies' forces, facilities, weather, terrain, the electromagnetic spectrum and information environment. The research on an operation simulation environment is to provide the necessary data and models of battlefield environment for the operation simulation training, at same time, to improve the cognitive efficiency of the operational personnel, which final to provide a realistic possibility about the operational analysis, assessment and evaluation. In the United States, Europe and other countries, the battlefield environment simulation is considered as one significant content of the modeling and simulation in national defense and military domain. For instance, during the period of NATO strikes on Bosnia and Herzegovina, the U.S. Defense Department used the high resolution images taken by reconnaissance satellites and bureau of surveying and mapping provided the digital map of Bosnia and Herzegovina area, which are aim to simulate the environment of Bosnia and Herzegovina, and to apply the operation simulation for the flight training. These pilots who received the training have greatly improved their adaptability and operation success

© Springer Science+Business Media Singapore 2016
L. Zhang et al. (Eds.): AsiaSim 2016/SCS AutumnSim 2016, Part II, CCIS 644, pp. 315–324, 2016.
DOI: 10.1007/978-981-10-2666-9_31

rate. The United States MAK company developed operation simulation platform, including VR-Link, VR-Forces, Data-Logger and other major modules, which provide not only the battlefield environment but also the force generated environment. At present, most of the operation environment simulation remains one element or a few elements of the main building. MAK battlefield simulation platform is based on operation mission training simulation, it mainly describes the entity behavior in the battlefield environment of the specific simulation task, however, the description of some elements of the operation environment such as meteorological elements is not detailed enough, nor the construction of cultural environment involving politics, economy, and some other soft environment [4]. The Skyline Company in the United State developed a 3D battlefield environment that was mainly based on topography and surface construction. Using satellite images, digital elevation model (DEM) and the corresponding proportion of topographic map were to achieve the display of static battlefields natural environment, but it is lack of the complex dynamic environmental factors, such as meteorological environment and electromagnetic environment [5].

Based on the characteristics of modern warfare and the requirements of operation training, this paper sufficiently studied the factors, like the land, the sea, the air, the sky, the electricity and the network information, which are on all aspects of the overall comprehensive construction of operation simulation environment, and to improve the environment campaign simulation fidelity and applicability.

2   The Overall Design and Construction of the Battle Simulation Environment

2.1   The Natural Geographical Environment

The natural geographical environment contains a variety of natural elements in the actual, such as topography, hilly vegetation, and soil water. The natural environment model is a wide range and a complex structure, in other words, the natural environment on expression of the information relative to the purpose of simulation in terms of the degree of importance is different, likewise how much influence the amount of information on simulation credibility are not the same. Therefore, with the premise of maintaining a certain credibility, each part of fidelity of the natural environment models shall be reasonably determined, which as far as possible to reduce the burden of operation simulation environment. At the same time, we should pay more attention to avoid providing the operators with the important information that is more than a prototype system environment provided in modeling. From above, the correct evaluation of the natural geography environment simulation effect has become the most important issue in the demonstration and design. Meanwhile, the simulation model of the dynamic environment (such as topography, the destroyed object and rivers) is reality, real-time, and dynamic continuous change, which is integrated with the static visualization model, and to form a comprehensive and dynamic natural geographical environment finally.

2.2   The Electromagnetic Environment

The present warfare has become the joint operations of the "sea, land, air, sky, electromagnetic", and any military action must be in the electromagnetic environment. In the actual operation, the compound electromagnetic environment of battlefield is often formed by the interaction of several electromagnetic interference sources. Considering the various kinds of electromagnetic interference sources, they are divided into the natural and the man-made; the intentional and the unintentional; the radiation and the conduction. The battlefield electromagnetic environmental effects include electrostatic discharge, electromagnetic compatibility, electromagnetic sensitivity, hazards of electromagnetic radiation, lightning effect, electromagnetic countermeasure, interference and blocking, electromagnetic interference, electromagnetic vulnerability, electromagnetic pulse, radio frequency threats and so on [6]. Electromagnetic environment simulation mainly make use of computer to simulate the electromagnetic environment of arbitrary space-time in the realistic environment, it coordinates with geographical environment and weaponry of two confrontation sides, which ensures the troops to carry out vivid military exercises in complex electromagnetic environment. Due to the electromagnetic environment is changeable, it is very difficult to simulate by accurate mathematical model, but it can be described by establishing the statistical properties of mathematical model. Currently, the abroad have some mature software used to simulate electromagnetic environment, but it is still limited to a large amount of computations and storage requirements, as well as, the frequency range of the simulation is narrow, and electromagnetic distribution area is small.

2.3   The Meteorological Environment

The meteorological environment will directly affect the entire operational process, during which the use of tactics and selection of weapons and equipment are closely related to the meteorological conditions. For example, these photoelectric weapons, cruise missile, over the horizon radar and so on, are not only always influenced by conventional meteorological elements (like rain, cloud, snow) and macro weather environment, but also are sensitive to the influence of the atmospheric environmental factors (like cloud particle, aerosol, low-level wind shear, atmospheric electric field, atmospheric refraction, atmospheric turbulence and so on) and micro scale weather phenomenon [7]. The meteorological environment simulation is the comprehensive utilization of atmospheric environment model, weapon platform and weapon system simulation model and its environment model, it studies the impact of the atmospheric environment on the operational process and weapons, furthermore, the battlefield meteorological environment as the background analyzes the operation scenario and environmental impact, which is to realize the virtual reality expression of the battlefield meteorological environment, including graphical simulation data pretreatment, visualization of meteorological factors and weather system, battlefield situation analysis, image integration and interactive display.

2.4 The Frequency Domain Environment

The frequency domain environment covers all of the battle fields, like the sea, the land, the air, the sky, the cyber space. The frequency domain environment is a significant channel of battlefield information transmission, and it is also a material basis of the operational task executions (a battlefield command and communications, early warning and detection, weapon guidance, information investigation, force deployment, and maneuvering) and implementation prerequisite for action. The frequency domain environment simulation can be employed to train the troops whenever and wherever possible to use the crowded electromagnetic spectrum, even to seize or destroy the enemy electromagnetic spectrum. As well as, it is able to respond to the enemy's electromagnetic spectrum challenges, extend bandwidth, expand the available frequency band, contend electromagnetic spectrum rights, quickly adapt to the complex and volatile electromagnetic environment. The use of any electromagnetic wave need occupy a certain spectrum, the same frequency electromagnetic waves will interfere with each other, and that is to say, the power of electromagnetic waves will repress the smaller one. Electromagnetic in frequency domain is directly expressed as the electromagnetic spectrum map. It is to establish the mathematical model of frequency domain system simulation that has transient and steady-state characteristics to consistent with the simulation system. The corresponding differential equations and the larger step size, even and the reasonable accuracy of the simulation model are utilized for the modeling and simulation. Currently, the substitution method and matching method [8] are the common ways for the mathematical derivation, which take advantages of Matlab to convert the time domain signal into frequency domain, or use FEKO and HFSSD, the frequency domain electromagnetic simulation software, for the construction of the frequency domain electromagnetic model. In accordance with the requirements for battlefield environment simulation will finally provide a corresponding frequency domain environment.

2.5 The Electronic Information Environment

With the increasing upgrade of electronic warfare, the electronic warfare equipment and weapons for the confrontation between the two sides are becoming more and more. The distribution and status of the electronic warfare equipment and weapons of the categories of troops have their own characteristic. The arbitrary battlefield and spatio-temporal face with the signal density is from the tens of thousands per second to millions per second [8]. Each electronic warfare of the categories of troops has the different characteristics, the implementation of distribution covers all area of the land, the sea and the air. The simulation system of electronic warfare is achieved by the establishment of the simulation model library of electronic warfare equipment and weapon system, the aim is to simulate the basic working principle and working process of these equipment and weapons. Electronic warfare system simulation is currently using the functional simulation and signal simulation in these two ways.

2.6   The Infrared Environment

The infrared environment in the operation simulation environment contains the solar infrared radiation, the infrared radiation of the weapons and equipment, and some other background infrared radiation. In abroad, the research infrared simulation technology began in 1980s [9]. Using the computer to simulate the infrared environment, especially the infrared weapon system. So far, the common simulation platform has the joint modeling and simulation environment (JMASE), which can simulate the model of infrared radiation's mainly effect model based on the system requirements of the platform. The modeling method is also used to develop a model that is to calculate the infrared radiation effect of atmospheric transmission, or to model the infrared target, such as the target and the sensor. However, it is necessary to study the problems about how to link between these modules for the infrared environment modeling [10].

2.7   The Battlefield Threat Environment

The battlefield threat environment includes not only a variety of weapons platforms and the deployment of forces on the area of ground, air and sea, but also the internet connecting to the ground threats environment, the air threats environment, and the background interference environment. The battlefield threat simulation environment is operated by the computer that is generated by the manipulation forces and the computer intelligence forces. Actually, it is hard to encounter the tactical environment generated by the formation of operation maneuvers, what is more easily generated. The static elements in the threat environment can adopt the method of natural geographical environment for modeling and simulation. Generated force is able to adopt computer generated forces modeling based on the Agent. The method of modeling and simulation can generate a semi-autonomous force, intelligence forces and command forces. The first two models research has made some achievements, but for the generated model of command forces, it is complex and difficult to design and implement, which need further infiltration and development on it [11].

2.8   The Culture Environment

Modern warfare involves the military strength, the political, economic, diplomatic, cultural history and other aspects of the various countries. Particularly, the international community develops a war bill that is to prohibit attacks on the non-military targets or objects to operation. Therefore, during the establishment process of a operation simulation environment, it is required to accurately distinguish between the military targets and civil cultural facilities, especially for the churches, the schools, the hospitals, the charitable education institutions, DAMS, the embankments, and some other important civilian facilities. On the other hand, it must pay attention to the operational process to avoid the damage to the natural environment and social cultural environment [12]. The cultural environment mainly refers to the static objects with the single attribute that almost keep the unchanging position in operation. Hence, when processing the computer simulation, the targets' geometrical characteristics, attributes, and 3d rendering methods are setting out to build the digital model of the cultural environment, the complex geometric shape and surface texture [13] (Fig. 1).

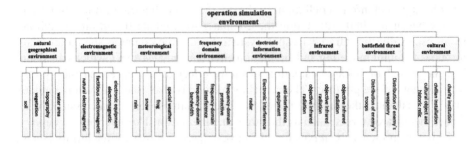

Fig. 1. The construction block diagram of operation simulation environment

3 Research on the Evaluation Method of Operation Simulation Environment

3.1 Analysis of the Characteristics of the Operation Simulation Environment

Currently, the existing evaluation methods generally include the AHP evaluation method, the subjective qualitative evaluation method and the feature analysis method [14]. The operation simulation environment relates to the computer simulation, the visual computing, the multimedia, the mathematical modeling, the graphics and the image processing technology, in view of the characteristics of the different environment, the different technologies are applied to build. When to evaluate the operation simulation environment, the utilization of quantitative methods for some environment module are carried out to accurately assess, and some other modules only depend on human's subjective feelings to evaluate, it cannot give a precise evaluation of the results. So the various methods should be adopted to evaluate it in accordance of the characteristics of the module. This paper puts forward a comprehensive evaluation method that is suitable for the simulation system based on the design and construction of operation simulation environment.

3.2 The Evaluation Method of the Operation Simulation Environment

As with the fidelity of simulation is required higher and higher, each element of the operation environment is considered more and more important. However, the simulation model of each element is complicated. A long time and the difficulties of the implementation of all elements will bring great burden for the entire simulation.

The various information of elements in the operation simulation environment has the different influence on the importance degree of the simulation purposes, like that the impact of the information quantity on the simulation credibility is not the same as well. Therefore, a very important issue in the operation environment simulation is to correctly evaluate the simulation effects of each element in the operation simulation environment, further to guide the whole simulation process.

3.2.1   The Quantitative Evaluation Method [1]

Assume that V is the operation simulation system that is composed of K elements, the system R is composed of l elements, there exists the similarities n between the system V and R, which constitute similar elements n, and then the value of each similar element is $q(u_i)$. Impact weight of each similar element on the system is β_i (β_i is normalization), as a result, the Quantitative fidelity of system V and R is $Q(V, R)$, it is defined as:

$$Q(V, R) = \frac{n}{k + l - n} \cdot \sum_{i=1}^{m} \beta_i \cdot q(u_i) \tag{2.1}$$

There are numerous technology and disciplines- involved in the operation simulation environment, the configuration of the simulation environment is different according to the different requirements of the operation training. While the operation simulation system is a very complex system composed of many elements, if using the formula (1.1) for each module in the simulation environment calculate the impact on the overall environment, the amount of calculation is quite large, the entire battlefield environment is divided into multiple levels and modules at once.

3.2.2   Hierarchical Division of the Operation Simulation Environment

The division of the elements of the operation simulation environment into modules is to reasonably evaluate the entire system. Specifically, the whole operation simulation environment will be divided into three layers [10].

1. The overall index layer
   According to the general requirements of the task, the operation simulation environment is designed.
2. The subsystem layer
   The constitution of the operation simulation environment is divided into the physical module and the functional module, there are eight modules in total, including the natural environment, the electromagnetic environment, the meteorological environment, the acoustic phonetic environment, the electronic information environment, the infrared environment, the cultural environment and the threat environment.
3. The subsystem index layer
   Refining each module. For instance, the electromagnetic environment is divided into the natural electromagnetic environment, the man-made electromagnetic environment, as well as the electromagnetic radiation of a variety of electronic equipment.

3.2.3   Multi-layer Weighted Evaluation [1]

Follow the three layers analysis, the whole operation simulation environment is evaluated by the method of multi-layer weighted evaluation. It assumes that the fidelity of the operation simulation system is $F(S)$, and then to choose subsystem layer index to calculate the impact of each subsystem on $F(S)$. The set of subsystems is assumed as $\{B_1, B_2, \dots, B_m\}$, the weighted value of each subsystem is $\{\alpha_1, \alpha_2, \dots, \alpha_m\}$, so the fidelity $F(S)$ is

$$F(S) = \sum_{i=1}^{n} \alpha_i \cdot F(B_j) \tag{2.2}$$

For each subsystem, the impact of each performance index on the fidelity of each subsystem is also evaluated. The detailed index of each subsystem is assumed as $\{\beta_1, \beta_2, \dots, \beta_m\}$, so the fidelity $F(B_j)$ is:

$$F(B_j) = \sum_{k=1}^{l} \lambda_k \cdot F(\beta_k) \tag{2.3}$$

In formula (2.3), λ_k and $(k \in \{1, 2, \dots, l\})$ are the weighted value of each index of the subsystem, which use the experts scoring and fuzzy mathematics methods to calculate.

3.2.4 The Weighted Value of Each Index of the Subsystem Calculation

The weighted value of each subsystem is calculated by the expert scoring and fuzzy evaluation methods. Assumed to invite k experts to give the scores of each index of the subsystem, in accordance of {very important, important, more important, in general, not important} and fuzzy reviews, so the numerical fuzzy matrix is:

$$\vec{v} = \begin{bmatrix} v_{11} & v_{12} & \cdots & v_{1m} \\ v_{21} & v_{22} & \cdots & v_{2m} \\ \cdots & \cdots & \cdots & \cdots \\ v_{k1} & v_{k2} & \cdots & v_{km} \end{bmatrix} \tag{2.4}$$

The average value is taken from the opinions of several experts, which will acquire the weighted value of each index of the whole operation simulation environment.

$$v_j = \frac{1}{k} \cdot \sum_{h=1}^{k} v_{kh} \tag{2.5}$$

Next, calculating the realistic and similarity system of each index: with N experts to evaluate the MIG index, in accordance of {like, more like, in general, not much, unlike}, so the numerical fuzzy matrix of the comments is:

$$\vec{P} = \begin{bmatrix} p_{11} & p_{12} & \cdots & p_{1m} \\ p_{21} & p_{22} & \cdots & p_{2m} \\ \cdots & \cdots & \cdots & \cdots \\ p_{n1} & v_{n2} & \cdots & p_{nm} \end{bmatrix} \tag{2.6}$$

Combining matrix $\vec{P}$ with the weighted value is to calculate the comprehensive evaluation value of Q

$$Q = \frac{1}{m} \sum_{j=1}^{m} \left(v_j \cdot \frac{1}{n} \sum_{i=1}^{n} p_{ij} \right) = \frac{1}{m \cdot n} \sum_{j=1}^{m} \sum_{i=1}^{n} v_j \cdot p_{ij} \tag{2.7}$$

Each person's subjective feeling on the same thing is not the same, or even completely opposite, that is the reason to carefully select experts, as soon as possible to expand the scope of the investigation, which is to judge the conclusion as objective as possible.

4 Conclusion

Modern military training and exercises are more highly relied on the simulation, the fidelity of the simulation system is becoming more required, especially for the operation environment simulation, its elements are increasingly complicated, the simulation constructing is more difficult, and the methods are more diverse. In this case, the difficulties of the simulation environment evaluation have gradually improved. This paper puts forward a comprehensive method to evaluate the operation simulation environment in modeling, which provides a feasible method for the evaluation of the operation simulation environment, as well as improves the credibility of the simulation system to a certain extent.

References

1. Huang, A.: Air War Virtual Battlefield Design. National Defense Industry Press, Beijing (2007)
2. Zhang, H., Tang, G., Wen, Y., Zhang, H., Luo, Y., Zhu, Y., Shang, Y.: Battlefield Environment Introduction, vol. 2. Science Press, Beijing (2013)
3. Zhang, G., Wei, Z.: Battlefield environment simulation. High-technology and Military 9 (2004)
4. Xie, B., Li, X.: Design of battlefield environment simulation system based on HLA. Command Control Simul. 31(4) (2009)
5. Chang, D., Qin, F., Li, B.: The research of three-dimensional battlefield environment simulation on 基 Skyline. Military Surveying 2 期 (2009)
6. Cheng, X.: Spectrum sharing technology in cognitive radio. Inf. Technol. 12 (2009)
7. Du, J., Liang, Q., Yao, F.: Evaluation method of visualization fidelity in virtual battlefield environment. J. Syst. Simul. 8 (2013)
8. Li, S.: Control System Simulation Technology
9. Su, C., Xi, H., Wang, W., Mao, W.: Integrated battlefield environment simulation based on multi-agent and HLA. Ordnance Ind. Autom. 30(6), 6 (2011)
10. Liang, S., Guo, G., Li, G.: Research on EO/IR environment simulation in JMASE. Comput. Simul. 7, 49 (2006)

11. Huang, K., Liu, B., Huang, J., Cao, X., Yin, Q., Gang, G.: A survey of military simulation technologies. J. Syst. Simul. **16**(9), 7 (2004)
12. Du, H.: Combat outpost battlefield environment simulation and virtual reality technology. Military College Laboratory Research **7**(384)
13. Common operation simulation engine design on solid model. Comput. Knowl. Technol. **3** (2010)
14. Sun, G., Yang, M., Liu, F.: A method for evaluating synthetic natural environment. Comput. Simul. **2**, 16 (2006)

The Development of Complex and Large System Based on Simulation Prototype

Zhiming Song[(✉)] and Xin Zhao

Systems Engineering Research Institute, CSSC, Beijing 100036, China
szm72@163.com

Abstract. The characteristics of traditional methods for complex and large system development were analyzed, in view of the deficiencies, a kind of engineering development method based on simulation prototype was put forward, and the implementation content, steps and keys during the whole product development process were described. Some key techniques such as the construction of simulation framework, complex object modeling, virtual experiment and simulation evaluation were analyzed, and the solutions are put forward. Practice has proved that the method deepens and optimizes the design of product significantly, excavates potential demands effectively, reduces the development cycle and development cost.

Keywords: Simulation prototype · Complex system · Development

1 Introduction

With the rapid development of the world science and technology, the development of modern industry product are more and more complicated, such as new aircraft, large ship, etc. This kind of product is complex and large system, which is on large scale, involves many professionals, uses new technologies. The traditional system development technologies and methods have been more and more difficult to meet the demand of modern engineering. The current information and digital technologies are promoting the innovation and progress of the engineering methods, especially the modeling and simulation technology have been gradually extensively and deeply applied to the development of complex system, used to display the image of product, validate the engineering design, etc. [1–3]. In the mid of 1990s the United States Defense Department established the SBA (Simulation -based Acquisition) as main technical route in the field of equipment development [4, 5]. In recent decades, great progress has been made in the field of simulation technology research and application in china. But compared with the international advanced, the gap is still large. Based on the theory of system engineering, exploring and establishing advanced research mode and methods have become the focus of the development for the high technology enterprise [6]. In a domestic major project, we have successfully explored and practiced a kind of development method based on simulation prototype, not only efficiently and successfully completed the research tasks, but also systematically established a new set of system development methods.

L. Zhang et al. (Eds.): AsiaSim 2016/SCS AutumnSim 2016, Part II, CCIS 644, pp. 325–335, 2016.
DOI: 10.1007/978-981-10-2666-9_32

2   The Analysis of Traditional Development Method

Traditional industrial product development takes the waterfall approach, the process of which is shown in Fig. 1. The essential feature of this method is based on the tests of "physical prototype". The main process included system designing based on special tools or even just based on document, making real prototype according to the design, testing the real prototype and founding insufficient, and then modifying the design, so loop iteration until the prototype meets the customer's requirements. Obviously, there are many shortcomings in this method: (1) Due to the complexity of the product system, the developers and even the users can't completely, correctly and accurately put forward demand in the early development phase. During the whole development process, with the deepening of the project the requirements of product will be added and changed. Especially after the real prototype production coming out, through the real tests, a lot of design defects will be exposed, or earlier demand have to be significantly modified and supplied. This development mode cannot adapt to the product which requirements may frequently change. (2) Each subsystem of the product is designed using the specific tools, the work is relatively isolated, a large number of problems of integrated interaction between the subsystems cannot be revealed and solved in time; Some professional lacking of appropriate tools even can only be designed based on the "document", the design of the system is "figurative" after all, the design depth and quality depends on the designer's mental perception, couldn't be perfect. Only when the physical prototype has been produced, many design errors are exposed. So the development cycle is greatly extended and the cost is increased. (3) The development of complex system generally involves much coordinated work between different profession. The traditional method is difficult to achieve the optimal combination of multiple subsystems. Even the parallel development unit finally cannot be integrated. (4) The characteristic of the traditional development mode is carrying out real tests on the physical prototype. However, the tests of complex systems will generally be constraint by many factors such as geography, time, weather, economic and even political, and the development cycle, found and quality are seriously affected.

3   The Simulation Based Development Method

3.1   Summary of Method and the Development of System Engineering Principle

In the whole process of product development, along with the designs gradually refinement, the corresponding granularity simulation system of the product is established, namely the simulation prototype, and the external environment of the product are modeled and simulated too, and then through dynamic simulation experiments, the design of the product can be verified. At the end of engineering design, the above simulation prototypes are very similar to the final product, almost all the functions, and even some performance of the product have been reflected. Project management organization and the users can evaluate the simulation prototype to confirm that the design of the product is correct or meet the requirements, equivalent to "virtually

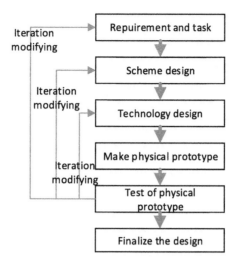

Fig. 1. The process of traditional method

delivery of products". Afterwards, the real physical prototype can be directly made according the final design, and real test still need to be carried out, in which some new defects may been found. But the product changes are certainly very little because that most design defects have been eliminated through a large number of simulation tests.

Hall model explained the principles of system engineering from three dimensions such as time, logic, knowledge [7], as shown in Fig. 2. The method of this paper emphasizes on developing corresponding simulation prototype and carrying out simulation test during different development phrase. It means that in the phase of planning, protocoling and development at the time dimension of the Hall model, simulation based design, development, test and verification are carried out after the traditional steps at the logical dimension. So three small "V" processes are amplified in time-logical dimensions plane, as shown in Fig. 2. Therefore, the method make a new development for the Hall model and the principle of system engineering by applying the simulation technology to system development.

3.2 Simulation in the Project Demonstration Phase

In simulation development mode, according to the preliminary argumentation and scenario of the future product, the simulation demo or deduction system are set up. Generally 3D modeling tools such as Creator are used to build high realistic entity shape model, high level real-time visual simulation platform such as VegaPrime are used to develop simulation demonstration system. The target image, working process and core characteristics of the future system are displayed in the form of 3D visual simulation. According to the complexity and fidelity of the simulation entities and scene, the computer can be single high-performance graphic workstation or distributed graphics workstations system, the display system can be one display screen or

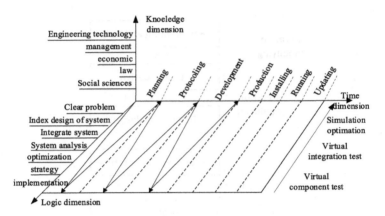

Fig. 2. Hall model

multi-channel projection. In the case of multi person interactive deduction, the simulation system need to be developed in the form of distributed interactive system, and each person in the simulation loop will operate a simulation node through the interaction equipment, meanwhile, the man-machine interface display and some visual 3D scenes are constructed for the persons. For the demonstration of the complex large scale system, the simulation record, playback, and evaluation nodes are needed to be constructed to record all the simulation process, playback conveniently and support the expert group assessment.

Through the auxiliary of the above simulation methods, the project demonstration report can be intuitively, conveniently and fastly deepen and improved. The user, project manager and developer can fully and deeply discuss, agree with each other based on the intuitive demonstration platform. The 3D entity models, behavior model and so on constructed in this stage can be used as the simulation resources for the subsequent stages.

3.3   Simulation in the Scheme Design Phase

After product demonstration the project enters into scheme design phase. In this phase the summary design of whole system is carried out, including the composition, main function, performance, working process and so on. In the early stage of this phase, the simulation prototype and the simulation running environment can begin to been built. Main work includes the following aspects: (1) Based on HLA distributed interactive simulation technology and standards, taking the preliminary reports and drawings of scheme design as input, the simulation system of prototype is directly developed in the HLA development environment according to the system composition, functions, working process and so on. The simulation system is named federation in HLA. The main work includes federal members modeling by using Simplicity tool [5], and integrating and operating in the RTI software environment. Each subsystem of the product can be simulated by independent federal members (named federate). The function, man-machine interface, interactive mode, work flow, etc. of each federate are as far as possible consistent with the real product. (2) By analyzing the working environment of the product, the federate which simulate the environment factors are constructed, such as synthetic natural environment (SNE), other entities interacting with the product system and so on. And then the simulation prototype can dynamic run by the support of these federates. (3) The simulation management node is built in the federation. It has two main functions. First it is used to initialize the simulation parameters, set up simulation conditions and model, etc., such as weather conditions, working conditions, the federal members joining or leaving federation, real-time or super real-time simulation, mode of people in the loop, etc. Second it is used to take controls in the process of the simulation, such as starting, pausing, recording, acceleration and so on. (4) The simulation recording and evaluation system is built in the federation, which is used to record the real time data of simulation process, playback the simulation process, show the simulation scene with arbitrary Angle of view through multi-channel projection system, and so on. All these effectively support expert group evaluation. Usually expert system and evaluation model are important parts of the simulation evaluation system. (5) For the products being operated based on visual, such as the air traffic control system, real-time visual simulation federate need to be constructed by using visual simulation technology. They receive simulation data from other federates and generate real-time working scene for the persons in the simulation loop to carry out the simulation test.

Above all, the simulation prototype of future product and the complete simulation test environment are available in the scheme design phase. People operate the simulation prototype just like operating the real product. So they can directly evaluate the merits and inadequate of system design, and find the potential demands. Then these comments and suggestion are submitted to the designer for optimization and modification. After the design improvements, the simulation federation can be conveniently and quickly modified because of the reusable and interoperable technical advantages of HLA. So the simulation federation always consistent with the design. Once again the simulation test is carried out to validate the new design. The above process is operated repeatedly and iteratively, as shown in Fig. 3, promotes the deepening and optimization of the design, until the result meets the desired level.

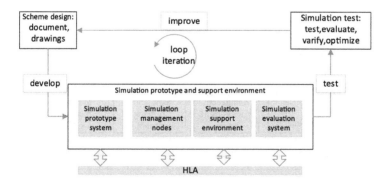

Fig. 3. The simulation method in the scheme design phase

3.4 Simulation in the Project Development Phase

The main work in the project development phase includes carrying out the detailed design of each subsystem, parts manufacture, component testing, system integration testing, and the real product testing and verification in real work environment. A natural way of thinking is that the simulation prototype of the scheme design phase will be constantly refined closely following the technical design, and the simulation test will be timely carried out to verify and optimize the design.

At this stage the subsystems of complex product generally need special tools to be designed, such as by using the EDSA tools to design power system, by using FLUENT tools to design fluid system, and so on. But the design results by these tools cannot be directly transplanted into federation based on HLA. This is also the main problems in multi-professional collaboration design and simulation. At present, Germany ITI company has developed the SimulationX simulation platform based on Modelica unified modeling and simulation standard, and it is compatible with the typical CAD, CAE tools such as CATIA, Pro/E, Adams and Simulink, etc. But it is only applicable to mechanical and electrical product development.

In view of this situation, the simulation prototype is refined by indirect mapping method. The design results by professional tools is extracted, and according the composition, function, operation process, etc., the simulation prototype of the scheme design phase is continued to deepen. For some common tools, data converter between the tools and federation can be developed to make professional design automatically convert to federate of the HLA side, as shown in Fig. 4. The simulation test is still carried out around the simulation prototype. When defects are found, the optimizing design is done in the tools environment, and the design results pass to the HLA system, and the simulation is run again, so loop iteration, until the result meets the final qualification. Finally, when the simulation prototype have reflects all the product features, the "virtually delivery" can be carried out. The project management group and the user evaluate the simulation prototype, finding insufficient and then the developers making batch correction, until the product pass the "acceptance". So the design state is cured down, and then enter manufacturing stage.

The manufacture and testing of product components, the system integration, and the product testing in real working environment can no longer rely closely on simulation prototype. Because most defects and hidden troubles have been eliminated and

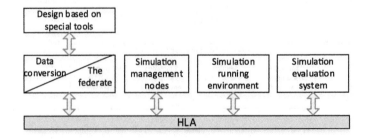

Fig. 4. The simulation in the project development phase

most implicit demand have been mined through large number of simulation experiments in the scheme and technical design phase, the improvement works for the product will be little at this stage. However, all changes must be recorded, and the simulation prototype will be adjusted accordingly.

For the testing of component, subsystem integration and real product, the simulation running environment can be used in whole or part as the supporting simulators. There are two key points in the implementation. First the real product will be joined the HLA federation to get support of running. Second the unified time system will be used in the whole system to ensure that each node is at the same time, and generally the timing equipment of real product is adopted. So the experiment in which virtual situation is combined with actual situation can be conveniently carried out and the real product integration tests are effectively aided.

3.5   The Simulation in the Maintenance Phase

The product maintenance stage begins after the product is delivered to the users. Because the simulation prototype is highly consistent with the real product, the developers can repeat the application problems of the product based on the simulation prototype system, and then research solutions to solve the problem quickly.

In general, the quantity of complex products are little but the operators are many. Almost all the operators need to be training because of the higher operating demands. The high-fidelity simulation training can be carried out by using the simulation federation. Not only the training time is significantly reduced compared with real training, but also the operator's operating skills and disposal ability for unexpected situations are be significantly improved, because the work conditions can be arbitrarily set up.

At the same time, the improvement requirements of product are deeply excavated through the large number of simulation running such as the simulation training, fault analysis and so on. They provide the important evidence for product improvement.

4   The Key Technology

4.1   The Overall Structure Design of Prototype Simulation System

The prototype simulation system of complex product is generally very large. Besides the prototype simulation of product, there are simulation support environment, simulation management nodes, evaluating nodes and so on in the federation. The Simulation prototype and support environment simulate different object, and the simulation nodes will deeply communicate and interact with each other during the simulation test. How to connect and integrate these nodes seamlessly is the basic problem of overall structure design. In addition, each node needs to be continuously refine and modify along with the deepening of the engineering design. And how to ensure that the simulation system and nodes are flexible and extensible is another important issue.

In view of these, the HLA distributed interactive simulation technology and standard are adopted to construct the overall system framework in the proposed method. The reasons are as follows. (1) At present, HLA is one of the best engineering standards to realize "reusable" and "interoperate" for the distributed interactive system. Complex systems are generally coordinately developed by different units, and there are large number of modification works during the development process. The multi people paralleling design and multi specialized subsystem integration are best supported by the HLA technology. So the simulation prototype can be constructed quickly, then through the simulation test and evaluation, the design is quickly improved. (2) Simulation prototype based on HLA only includes the main features of the real product, such as the functions, interfaces and so on. The details such as exception handling, handling of illegal input, the system stability index and so on are not considered. So the entanglements in unnecessary details are avoided in the early stage of design and the development cycle is greatly accelerated. (3) The development environment for HLA application is familiar to most developers, such as the Windows operation system, C++ language, large number of mature commercial tools and so on. Most importantly, because the communication is encapsulated, the large amount of underlying communication based on such as TCP/IP, CAN bus and so on are avoided, and the simulation prototype can be constructed quickly. (4) The particular business model can be programmed and tested in the simulation prototype, and the final results can be directly applied to the real products. When the simulation system and the product adopt the same language such as C, the model in simulation system can even be directly transplanted into the product.

In the method of this paper, pRTI1516 is adopted to build distributed simulation system. First the SOM table of each federate is established according to it's external data interface. Second the FOM table is set up by integrating all the SOM table. Third the framework of the overall federation and each federate are built by using Simplicity tool. During the simulation system design and development process, each node will strictly follow HLA standard, especially the simulation time strategy and data distribution rules.

In practice, some entities are too complex to be precisely model using digital method, or to be simulated in real time, in this case the physical effect devices are often adopted to simulate the entities. So the federal framework should be compatible with semi-physical simulation mode. In this method, the adapters connecting the HLA federation with physical effect device are developed. They communicate with physical devices based on the special mode such as CAN bus, etc., and communicate with the federation based on HLA rules. To solve the problem of time unity and synchronization, the time synchronization signal and time code of the timing equipment can be directly transported to every nodes in the form of a serial port, Ethernet, etc., and time is tested and synchronized in every simulation step.

4.2   Modeling of Complex Objects

In the development process of complex system based on simulation prototype, the difficulty includes two aspects: one is the simulation of the product itself. Due to multi professions and refinement, it is very difficult to establish a high precision model. The simulation prototype can be developed by using the mature, suitable auxiliary tools such as instrument tools, GIS tools, etc. The other is the simulation of external environment of the product. The running of product tightly couple with the external environment such as other related systems, synthetic natural environment and so on. The different conditions will lead to different work process and results. So, in order to achieve correct and effective test results, simulation credibility of the external environment need to be correspondingly guaranteed. In general, the external environment involves different professions, such as mechanical, electronic, electromagnetic, natural environment, etc. They should be modeled and simulated by professional developers [8], and the simulation granularity is depended on the requirements of the simulation prototype in different phase. Many factors have a huge impact on product operation, but it is difficult to be modeled, such as the sea state, air flow field behind the sailing ship, etc. They are quite changeable, and associated with each other, they have always been difficult problem in the field of modeling. For the synthetic natural environment, the model can be similarly built through extracting the change regulation of specific areas and time based on the statistical method. For the complex mathematical models such as radar model, the calculation are usually difficult in real time, and the physical equipment such as DSP can be adopted to simulate the complex object. For the large and sophisticated equipment such as aircraft, the whole simulation system can be developed by professional manufacturers and then integrated into the federation through the adapter. So the credibility of whole simulation system is guaranteed.

4.3 The Simulation Experiment Method of Virtual and Real Combination

On the traditional development mode, the test of complex system should generally follow the relevant test specification, and the test planning, test preparation, test implementation and solving the problems are carried out in turn.

When simulation experiment take place of the real experiment, the standards, methods and experience of real experiment should be thoroughly referenced. For the characteristics of "virtual", the key is to solve the following problems. (1) The simulation prototype and test environment need to be validated before the test to ensure that they meet the requirements of technical indicators and can reflect the working characteristic of real system. (2) It is necessary to demand professional person to operate the professional simulator to ensure the credibility of the virtual test. (3) The frequent iteration of "simulation running -modifying the product design and simulation system-simulation running again" is the main characteristic of simulation development, and the design, development and experiment need to be carefully coordinated and arranged. (4) The simulation test provides a convenient, intuitive and in-depth evaluation mean and it should be pay great attention to and fully used, so the optimization of product design can be deepened and speeded up.

4.4 The Evaluation Technique

There are two kinds of evaluation in the process of construction and application of the simulation system. One is the simulation credibility evaluation of the simulation system itself, another is the evaluation of product design through the simulation tests.

Simulation prototype and environment cannot be exactly the same as the real product and the environment. In the engineering practice, the model scope, granularity and credibility index of the simulation object need to be researched and determined. The models, simulation nodes and the whole simulation system should be Verify and validate by using VVA technology to ensure the validity of the simulation prototype and virtual experiment.

The virtual tests of simulation prototype include all aspects of the product design and application, such as equipment deployment, equipment function, interaction relations, the work flow, ability index, man-machine engineering and so on. It is necessary to establish special evaluation system to make quantitative analysis of the test results. The main work includes building evaluation model for relevant content and recording the appropriate data of test process.

For complex system, the evaluation model of comprehensive performance index should be established, and overall efficacy can be evaluated. Meanwhile, the experts in the evaluation system and the persons in simulation loop can also intuitively make subjective evaluations during the testing process. Especially when the users take part in the simulation tests, their opinions and suggestions are very important for the optimization of product design.

5   Conclusions and Future Work

The core characteristic of simulation prototype method is that the highly realistic "simulation prototype" is developed, and virtual tests are carried out, and then the product design is gradually and iteratively optimized according to the test results. So the modification work of physical prototype are reduced greatly. Meanwhile, just because the tests, evaluation, and modification are carried out based simulation prototype instead of the real physical prototype, the design ability and quality are also greatly improvement, and the development cycle, funds and risk are greatly reduced. This method of digital engineering development will surely replace traditional design method based on "physical prototype". The proposed method has been successfully applied to some domestic major project, the development cycle was significantly shortened, the cost was greatly reduced, and the product quality was effectively improved. Practice shows that this method is correct and feasible. Application level of foreign digital technology has reached the state of no drawings and full virtualization [3]. Based on the method in this paper, we will continue to increase application scope and depth of the digital simulation technology, and set up a set of rules and standards to unify the digital development program.

References

1. Sun, H.-J.: The modeling and simulation of digital technology application in the weapon equipment development abroad track. Digit. Mil. Ind. **2**, 47–51 (2011)
2. Xiong, G.-L., et al.: Collaborative Simulation and Virtual Prototyping, pp. 11–20. Tsinghua University Press, Beijing (2004)

3. Huang, N., et al.: The current situation and trend of development of military product virtual design technology. Digit. Mil. Ind. (1), 26–29 (2011)
4. Chen, X.-C., et al.: Equipment System Engineering, pp. 53–54. National Defence Industry Press, Beijing (2005)
5. Zhou, Y., et al.: HLA Simulation Program Design, pp. 30–35. Publishing House of Electronics Industry, Beijing (2002)
6. Xiao, S., Xudong, C., Li, Z.: Modeling framework for product lifecycle information. Simul. Model. Pract. Theory **18**(8), 1080–1091 (2010)
7. Li, H.-B., Zhang, C.-X.: Systems Engineering and Application. China Machine Press, Beijing (2013)
8. Li, B.-H., et al.: Some focusing points in development of modern modeling and simulation technology. J. Syst. Simul. **16**(9), 1871–1878 (2004)

Model Simulation of Melting Layer Based on Wind Profile Radar Data

Zhengyu Zhang[1,2(✉)], Zhengang Xue[2], Liren Xu[2],
and Taichang Gao[1]

[1] Institute of Meteorology, PLA University of Science and Technology,
Nanjing 211101, China
james9763@foxmail.com
[2] Beijing Institute of Applied Meteorology, Beijing 100029, China

Abstract. Based on the wind profile radar data during stratiform precipitation processes in Beijing, a model of melting layer which describes the spectral parameter features has been presented. This model is applied to the simulation of WPR FFT data using Gaussian distribution. The simulated WPR FFT data proved to be effective for presenting the echo signal of precipitation particles compared with real data. The application in WPR terminal software test indicates the practicability of this melting layer model in software improvement.

Keywords: Wind profile radar · Melting layer · Modeling · Simulation

1 Introduction

The melting process of ice particles in melting layer contributes to the sudden enhancement of radar reflectivity, which became known as the 'bright band'. Bright band is an important feature of stratiform precipitation, reflecting the evident ice-water transformation process in melting layer (Kain et al. 2000). In the past few decades, detections and studies of bright band have been gradually conducted using wind profile radar (WPR), which could provide full spectrum information of return signal (Ruan et al. 2002) and precise structure of melting layer (Shi et al. 2014) with higher resolution than Doppler weather radar. Acquiring accurate profiles of spectral parameter in melting layer and improving the capability to identify bright band could provide technical support for the study of eliminating the overestimation or underestimation of precipitation (Smith et al. 1986) and the recognition and forecast of stratiform precipitation (Kain et al. 2000), which has become one of the key concern in wind profile radar applications.

Through processing the power spectrum (FFT) data to calculate profiles of spectral parameters, various types of WPR terminal software are designed mainly for the purpose of acquiring physical quantities and real-time monitoring. Practices have proved that WPR terminal software can provide reliable and detailed wind field features. However, since the echo signal of precipitation particles is much greater than that of the turbulence (William et al. 2002), there still lacks effective testing measurements for the ability of software to effectively obtain realistic spectral parameter features in precipitation conditions.

L. Zhang et al. (Eds.): AsiaSim 2016/SCS AutumnSim 2016, Part II, CCIS 644, pp. 336–344, 2016.
DOI: 10.1007/978-981-10-2666-9_33

This paper proposes an improved model of spectral parameters in melting layer, the original version of which was introduced by author in previous paper (Zhang et al. 2016). More realistic WPR FFT simulation data is established by this improved model based on Gaussian distribution and then applied into a WPR terminal software test.

2 Spectral Parameter Features of Stratiform Precipitation

During July to October, 2014, the boundary layer WPR in Beijing has detected 32 obvious precipitation episodes. In order to establish the melting layer model based on features of spectral parameters, FFT data in eight typical stratiform precipitation episodes has been chosen to be pre-processed and analyzed. Figure 1 gives an example of stratiform precipitation episode in 12th Sept, 2014, which describes the average profiles of echo intensity, vertical velocity and spectral width during this stratiform precipitation. The profiles clearly reflect the phase transformation process of precipitation particle, thus the height space can be separated into solid area (I), upper melting area (II), lower melting area (III) and liquid area (IV), as Fig. 1 shows.

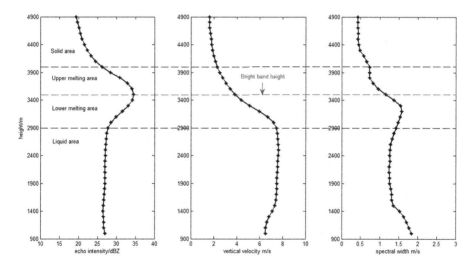

Fig. 1. Average WPR echo, vertical velocity, spectral width profiles during precipitation time in 12th Sept, 2014

Echo intensity has obvious variation in different phase region. In solid area, echo intensity increases slowly since ice particles have little change. In upper melting area, the melting of ice particle changes the permittivity, causing the increase of refractive index, which gives rise to echo intensity. In lower melting area, the collapse of ice structures contributes to the reduction of scattering cross-section. Additional, the acceleration of raindrops will form a divergence area of concentration, causing the decrease of the echo intensity. In liquid area, echo intensity changes little since the concentration remains stable when raindrops reach the terminal velocity.

For rain clouds body which has the presence of bright band, the height where maximum echo intensity value exists is usually defined as bright band height

(Huang et al. 2011). Generally, for stratiform precipitation, bright band height (H_{bright}) is located within the range of 2300 ~ 4400 m height, and both the top and the bottom height of melting layer (H_{top}, H_{bottom}) are no more than 600 m away from bright band height. The echo intensity at bright band height (Z_{bright}) is generally greater than 20 dBz, and that at the top of melting layer (Z_{top}) is usually 28 % less than Z_{bright}. Also, the echo intensity at the bottom of melting layer (Z_{bottom}) reduces usually 20 % less than Z_{bright}.

The falling velocity of precipitation particles changes insignificantly in solid area and liquid area, while increases sharply in melting area. The vertical velocity at bright band height (V_{bright}) is generally greater than 2 m/s, and that at the top of melting layer (V_{top}) is averagely 43.6 % less than V_{bright}. Also, the vertical velocity at the bottom of melting layer (V_{bottom}) increases averagely 80.1 % compared with V_{bright}.

Spectral width increases with the decline of height, reaching an maximum at the height of about 200 ~ 300 m above the bottom of melting area, then gradually decreases. Spectral width value at bright band height (W_{bright}) is usually around 1 ~ 1.5 m/s. and that at the top of melting layer (W_{top}) is averagely 30.9 % less than W_{bright}. Also, the vertical velocity at the bottom of melting layer (W_{bottom}) increases averagely 14.7 % compared with W_{bright}.

3   Simulation of WPR Data

3.1   Model of Spectral Parameters in Melting Layer

Based on the introduction of melting layer spectral parameter features in Chapter 2, a simulation program for model of spectral parameters in melting layer is established as following steps:

(1) The division of the height space
   The height space has been already separated into four particle phase areas in Chapter 2. According to the height resolution and the maximum detection height of the Boundary Layer WPR, the height space can be further divided into 59 range gates with a unit of 100 m.

(2) Assignment for spectral parameters
   In the original version of melting layer model which is proposed by author in the past, the spectral parameters were approximately viewed as linear variation with height in each area. In this improved model, the assigning method of spectral parameters has been modified: the spectral parameters in solid particle area (I) and liquid particle area (IV) can be viewed as linear variation with height, while those in the melting area (II, III) will be simulated by trigonometric functions for more realistic and accurate simulation output, as Fig. 2 shows.

Spectral parameters of every range gates can be assigned as following steps:

① Type initial values of melting layer spectral parameters: H_{bright}, H_{top}, H_{bottom}, Z_{bright}, V_{bright}, W_{bright}, the meaning of which has been mentioned in Chapter 2. Define $G(H(j)) = j$ as the range gate number at the height of $H(j)$, j = 1,2,3,...59.

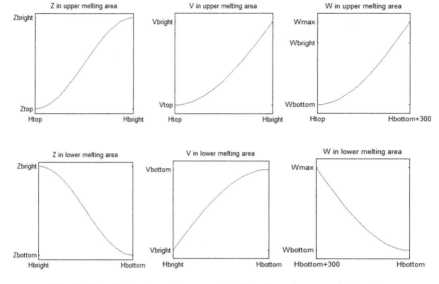

Fig. 2. Simulation in melting area (II, III) using trigonometric functions

② Calculate spectral parameters in melting area (II,III) using trigonometric functions,

$$Z(j) = \begin{cases} Z_{bright}[a_1 \cos b_1(j - G(H_{bright})) + c_1], & H_{bright} < h(j) \leq H_{top} \\ Z_{bright}[a_2 \cos b_2(j - G(H_{bright})) + c_2], & H_{bottom} \leq h(j) < H_{bright} \end{cases} \quad (1)$$

$$V(j) = \begin{cases} V_{bright}[a_3 \sin b_3(j - G(H_{bright})) + c_3], & H_{bright} < h(j) \leq H_{top} \\ V_{bright}[a_4 \sin b_4(j - G(H_{bright})) + c_4], & H_{bottom} \leq h(j) < H_{bright} \end{cases} \quad (2)$$

$$W(j) = \begin{cases} W_{bright}[a_5 \sin b_5(G(H_{bottom}) + 3 - j) + c_5], & H_{bottom} + 300 < h(j) \leq H_{top} \\ W_{bright}[a_6 \sin b_6(j - G(H_{bottom}) - 3) + c_6], & H_{bottom} \leq h(j) < H_{bottom} + 300 \end{cases}$$
$$\quad (3)$$

Where a, b, c are introduced in Table 1.

Table 1. Coefficient a, b, c of trigonometric functions (1) ~ (3)

No.	a	b	c
1	0.14	$\pi/(G(H_{top}) - G(H_{bright}))$	0.86
2	0.10	$\pi/(G(H_{bright}) - G(H_{bottom}))$	0.90
3	0.44	$\pi/[2(G(H_{top}) - G(H_{bright}))]$	1.00
4	0.81	$\pi/[2(G(H_{bright}) - G(H_{bottom}))]$	1.00
5	0.87	$\pi/[2(G(H_{top}) - G(H_{bottom}) - 3)]$	1.50
6	0.30	$\pi/6$	1.50

③ Calculate spectral parameters in solid phase area and liquid phase area (I, IV) using linear gradient K given in Table 2,

$$
Z(j) = \begin{cases} Z(G(H_{top})) - K_{Z_I}(h(j) - H_{top}), h(j) > H_{top} \\ Z(G(H_{bottom})) - K_{Z_{IV}}(h(j) - H_{bottom}), h(j) < H_{bottom} \end{cases} \tag{4}
$$

$$
V(j) = \begin{cases} V(G(H_{top})) - K_{V_I}(h(j) - H_{top}), (j) > H_{top} \\ V(G(H_{bottom})) - K_{V_{IV}}(h(j) - H_{bottom}), (j) < H_{bottom} \end{cases} \tag{5}
$$

$$
W(j) = \begin{cases} W(G(H_{top})) - K_{W_I}(h(j) - H_{top}), (j) > H_{top} \\ W(G(H_{bottom})) - K_{W_{IV}}(h(j) - H_{bottom}), (j) < H_{bottom} \end{cases} \tag{6}
$$

Table 2. Gradient K of spectral parameter in area (I) and (IV)

Area	K_Z ($dBz/100m$)	K_V (m · s^{-1}/100m)	K_W (m · s^{-1}/100m)
I	0.500	0.050	0.038
IV	−0.070	0.020	−0.001

For stratiform precipitation simulation of other season or even other region, statistics of local detecting data should be analyzed to reset the coefficients in Table 1 and Table 2 based on the variation of spectral parameters. The selection of initial values should be accordant with local practical situation as well.

3.2   Output of Simulated Power Spectrum Data (FFT)

Since vertical airstream in stratiform precipitation is weak and the echo signal of precipitation particles is much greater than that of turbulence, the power spectrum data can be approximately viewed as the echo signal of precipitation particles. According to previous studies (Wang et al. 2012 and He et al. 2014), the echo signals of precipitation particles can be fitted by Gaussian distribution. In order to simulate FFT data, the power spectrum distribution $S(v_i)$ can be expressed using Gaussian equation as,

$$
S(v_i) = a_i \exp\left[-\left(\frac{v_i - b_i}{c_i} \right)^2 \right], i = 1, 2, 3, \ldots, N \tag{7}
$$

where N is FFT points, a, b, c respectively represent peak height, peak position and half peak spectral width of power spectrum distribution $S(v_i)$, which can be obtained from the melting layer model.

For intuitive display and understanding, $S(v_i)$ could be further transformed into echo intensity spectral distribution,

$$Z_i(v) = CR^2 S_i(v), i = 1, 2, \ldots, N. \tag{8}$$

where R represents the distance from radar to scattering object,
$C = \dfrac{1024 \cdot \ln 2 \cdot \lambda^2 \cdot L}{\pi^3 \cdot P_t \cdot c \cdot \tau \cdot G^2 \cdot \theta \cdot \varphi \cdot \left| \dfrac{m^2 - 1}{m^2 + 2} \right|^2}$ is a radar constant determined by radar performance.

4   Case Analysis

(1)   Set performance parameter values of WPR as Table 3 gives.
(2)   Set 20 groups of initial values of melting layer parameter as Table 4 gives.

Table 3. Performance parameters of wind profile radar

Parameter	Value	Parameter	Value
Radar wavelength λ	231 mm	Pulse width τ	2.67 μs
Horizontal beam width θ	9°	FFT points N	128
Vertical beam width φ	10°	Coherent integration points J	120
Antenna gain G	24 dB	Pulse repetition frequency f	25000 Hz
Feeder loss L	26.5 dB	Peak power P_t	2 kW

Table 4. 20 groups of initial values of melting layer parameter

Group	H_{bright}	H_{top}	H_{bottom}	Z_{bright}	V_{bright}	W_{bright}
1	3600	4000	3200	28.72	3.2	1.0
2	3500	3800	3200	31.04	3.3	1.2
3	3500	3900	3100	33.32	3.6	1.4
4	3500	4000	3100	33.65	3.4	1.1
5	3600	4000	2400	33.16	3.1	1.8
6	3600	4000	3000	33.78	3.4	1.2
7	3500	4000	3000	34.92	3.6	1.2
8	3500	4100	2800	35.63	4.0	1.1
9	3500	4000	3100	36.08	4.2	1.5
10	3400	3900	2900	36.43	4.3	1.3
11	3400	3900	2900	36.74	4.4	1.3
12	3400	3900	2900	36.74	4.4	1.1
13	3400	3800	2900	36.02	4.3	1.2
14	3500	4000	3000	34.73	3.9	1.2
15	3500	3700	3000	33.55	3.6	1.1
16	3600	4000	3100	32.66	3.4	0.9
17	3600	3900	3100	31.48	3.2	1.0
18	3600	4000	3100	30.21	3.1	1.0
19	3600	3900	3200	28.98	3.0	1.2
20	3600	4000	3200	27.52	3.0	1.3

The values in Table 4 are acquired from real data in a stratiform precipitation in 1st Oct, 2014 using bright band identification algorithm designed by author in the past, making it possible to form contrast between simulated data and real data.

(3) Run the program. Figure 3 gives examples of group 1 and group 4, presenting the comparison between simulated data and the real data. Figure 3 shows that two groups of spectral parameter profile model are well related to real data. The simulated and the real-detected FFT data have similar features; both reveal the phase conversion process of precipitation particles in melting area

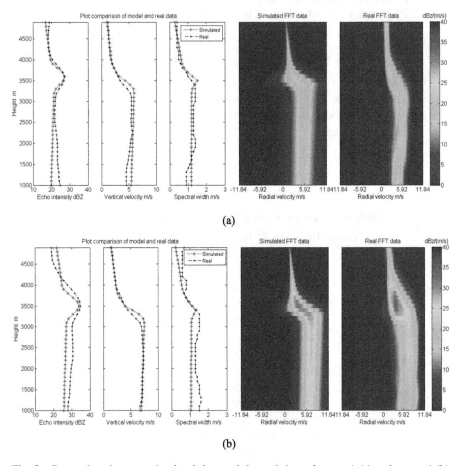

Fig. 3. Comparison between simulated data and the real data of group 1 (a) and group 4 (b)

The melting layer model has been proved to be of good effectiveness and reliability through the correlation test of 20 groups of simulated and real data as Fig. 4 shows. The average correlation coefficient of echo intensity, vertical velocity and spectral width in 20 groups of simulated and real data are respectively 0.8751, 0.9535 and 0.8443.

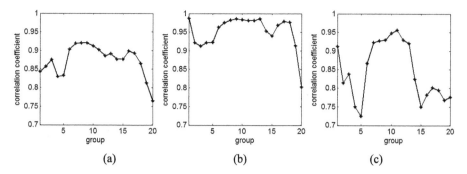

Fig. 4. Correlation coefficient of echo intensity (a), vertical velocity (b) and spectral width (c) in 20 groups of simulated and real data

5 Application in WPR Terminal Software Test

The simulated data is applied into a capability testament for data processing and bright band identification of a WPR terminal software (Aeolus V1.6, designed for LC-WPR). A sequence of continuous detecting data during stratiform precipitation has been fabricated using those 20 groups of simulated data in Chapter 4.

Import the simulated FFT data into the directory. Figure 5 shows the data processing results of the software.

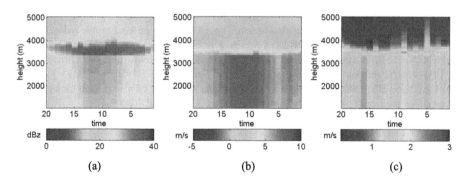

Fig. 5. Data processing results of echo intensity (a), vertical velocity (b) and spectral width (c) of simulated FFT data by WPR terminal software

Through processing the power spectrum (FFT) data to calculate profiles of spectral parameters, the WPR terminal software can effectively identified the bright band. However, the variation of spectral parameter values in several range gates under the melting layer is irregular to a certain extent. Besides, the values of vertical velocity and spectral width are slightly higher. These consequences might be related to the pre-processing algorithms for clutter suppression and signal scaling designed based on the standard of clear air turbulence echo, indicating the demand of further improvement for the adaptation of precipitation particle echo signal.

6   Conclusions

This paper develops a melting layer model based on WPR data of stratiform precipitation in Fangshan, Beijing, during July to October, 2014. Using Gaussian equation, 20 groups of simulated WPR FFT data were established as samples, each of which proved to be reliable compared with real WPR FFT data. The simulated FFT data could be effectively applied into the testament for bright band identification capacity of WPR terminal software, which indicates the practicability of this melting layer model in software improvement.

References

He, Y., He, P., Lin, X.M.: Raindrop size distribution retrieval from wind profile radar based on double-Gaussian fitting. J. Appl. Meteorol. Sci. **05**, 570–580 (2014)

Huang, Y., Ruan, Z., et al.: Study on bright band detection using wind profile radar. Plateau Meteorol. **05**, 1376–1383 (2011)

Kain, J.S., Goss, S.M., Baldwin, M.E., et al.: The melting effects as a factor in precipitation-type forecasting. Weather Forecasting. **15**, 700–714 (2000)

Ruan, Z., Ge, R.S., Wu, Z.G.: Method for detecting rain cloud structure with wind profiles. J. Appl. Meteorol. Sci. **03**, 330–338 (2002)

Shi, H.R., Li, F., et al.: Analysis on observations of precipitation phase changes using wind profile radar data. Meteorol. Mon. **10**, 1259–1265 (2014)

Smith, C.J.: The reduction of errors caused by bright bands in quantitative rainfall measurements made using radar. J. Atoms Ocean. Technol. **38**, 1214–1228 (1986)

Wang, S., Ruan, Z., Ge, R.S.: Simulation of return signal spectrum of wind profile radar. J. Appl. Meteorol. Sci. **23**(1), 20–29 (2012)

Williams, C.R.: Simultaneous ambient air motion and raindrop size distributions retrieved from UHF vertical incident profile observations. Radio Sci. **37**(2), 1024–1029 (2002)

Yu, L.J., Yao, Z.Y.: Studies on the microphysical characteristics of a stratiform cloud and its response to aircraft cloud seeding. Meteorol. Mon. **35**(10), 8–25 (2009)

Zhang, Z.Y., Xue, Z.G., et al.: Study of bright band model based on wind profile radar data. Chin. J. Stereol. Image Anal. **21**(2), 173–182 (2016)

Modeling of the Guidance and Control System for the Guided Ammunition

Peng Wang[1(✉)], Ge Li[1], Dongling Liu[2], Xibao Wang[1],
Xiaodong Zhu[1], and Kedi Huang[1]

[1] National University of Defense Technology, Changsha, Hunan, China
{wangpeng_nudt,geli}@nudt.edu.cn, xbwang1990@126.com
[2] Liaoning University, Shenyang, Liaoning, China

Abstract. The guided ammunition is a kind of ammunition that has the precise guidance system and high hitting probability. It has the advantages of low price and high precision. It is more and more widely applied in the combat. There are some differences of the working principle of the guidance and control system of the guided ammunition and the missile, so we need to model the guidance and control system of the guided ammunition individually. We built the guidance model and control model for the guided ammunition. Then we verified our model by running the digital simulation program. The simulation results prove the accuracy and effectiveness of our model. The model built in the paper can be used to model the guidance and control system for many other guided ammunitions. They can also be used in the computerized warfare simulation that the guided ammunition involved in.

Keywords: Guidance and control system · Guided ammunition · M&S · Digital simulation

1 Introduction

The ammunition is very important for the weapon system to destroy the targets. It has the advantages of low price, user convenience, violent firepower and so on [1]. However, the conventional ammunition has the limits of large dispersion area, poor precision and poor effectiveness [2]. The missile is a kind of precisely guided ammunition. It can make up for the limits of the conventional ammunition, but it also has the limit of high price [3]. If we replace the conventional ammunition with the missile, it would cause huge costs. Recently, the guided ammunition is more and more popular, and it can be used to fill the gap between traditional ammunitions and the missiles [4]. The guidance of the ammunition will be the main development tendency of the ammunition.

In this paper, we give the guidance and control model for a certain type of guided ammunition, and we use the digital simulation program to verify the accuracy of the model. The rest of the paper is organized as follows. In the next section, we give the dynamic model of the guided ammunition. We present the sight line axis system in Sect. 3.1. The computation of rotation rate of sight line and guidance command acceleration is given in Sect. 3.2. Section 3.3 details the computation of the control

© Springer Science+Business Media Singapore 2016
L. Zhang et al. (Eds.): AsiaSim 2016/SCS AutumnSim 2016, Part II, CCIS 644, pp. 345–353, 2016.
DOI: 10.1007/978-981-10-2666-9_34

signals for slipping turn. In Sect. 3.4, we describe the structure of the autopilot in details. Section 4 verifies the models by running the digital simulation program. Section 5 concludes our work.

2 Dynamic Model of the Guided Ammunition

As the guided ammunition doesn't have any engines, it uses the four actuators to control the all-moved control surfaces in the tail. The control forces and control moments are created by the rotation of the control surfaces [5, 6]. The mass center motion equation and the attitude motion equation in the emission axis system are as follows.

$$
\begin{bmatrix} \dot{x} \\ \dot{y} \\ \dot{z} \end{bmatrix} = \begin{bmatrix} v_x \\ v_y \\ v_z \end{bmatrix}
\tag{1}
$$

$$
\begin{bmatrix} \dot{v}_x \\ \dot{v}_y \\ \dot{v}_z \end{bmatrix} = \frac{1}{m} \begin{bmatrix} G_B \cdot (F_{xb} + F_{xc}) + F_{kx} + F_{ex} \\ G_B \cdot (F_{yb} + F_{yc}) + F_{ky} + F_{ey} \\ G_B \cdot (F_{zb} + F_{zc}) + F_{kz} + F_{ez} \end{bmatrix} + \begin{bmatrix} g_x \\ g_y \\ g_z \end{bmatrix}
\tag{2}
$$

$$
\begin{bmatrix} \dot{\omega}_{xt} \\ \dot{\omega}_{yt} \\ \dot{\omega}_{zt} \end{bmatrix} = I^{-1} \begin{bmatrix} M_{xb} + M_{xc} + M_{xd} + M_{xi} + M_{jx} \\ M_{yb} + M_{yc} + M_{yd} + M_{yi} + M_{jy} \\ M_{zb} + M_{zc} + M_{zd} + M_{zi} + M_{jz} \end{bmatrix}
\tag{3}
$$

$$
\begin{bmatrix} \dot{\phi} \\ \dot{\psi} \\ \dot{\gamma} \end{bmatrix} = I^{-1} \begin{bmatrix} \omega_y \frac{\sin \gamma}{\cos \psi} + \omega_z \frac{\cos \gamma}{\cos \psi} \\ \omega_y \cos \gamma - \omega_z \sin \gamma \\ \omega_x + \omega_y \sin \gamma tg\psi + \omega_z \cos \gamma tg\psi \end{bmatrix}
\tag{4}
$$

Here F_{xb}, F_{yb}, and F_{zb} are aerodynamic forces. F_{xc}, F_{yc}, and F_{zc} are control forces. F_{kx}, F_{ky} and F_{kz} are Coriolis inertia forces. F_{ex}, F_{ey} and F_{ez} are centrifugal inertia forces. G_B is the transition matrix from the missile body axis system to the emission axis system. g_x, g_y and g_z are the acceleration of gravity. M_{xb}, M_{yb} and M_{zb} are aerodynamical moments. M_{xc}, M_{yc} and M_{zc} are control moments. M_{xd}, M_{yd} and M_{zd} are damping moments. M_{xi}, M_{yi} and M_{zi} are inertia tensor torque. M_{jx}, M_{jy} and M_{jz} are hinge moments.

3 Guidance and Control Model of the Guided Ammunition

The guidance and control system of the guided ammunition is usually a multi-loop system, as well as a closed-loop control system. The larger closed loop at the outmost layer is the guidance loop including observation tracking device, instructions forming device, execution device and the projectile body. The attitude stability loop is the closed loop including the instructions forming device, execution device and the projectile body [7]. We usually name the devices in attitude stability loop except the projectile body as an autopilot [4].

The guided ammunition that we are studying uses the proportional navigation guidance method as its guidance law. The schematic diagram of the guidance signals is as shown in Fig. 1. Because the guided ammunition doesn't have any seeker, the rotation rate of sight line can't be obtained directly. But the guided ammunition is usually equipped with a navigation system, so we can get its position and velocity. With these values, we can obtain the equivalent rotation rate of sight line by using the mathematical methods. Now we will give the detailed description of the computation of the rotation rate of sight line and the guidance signals.

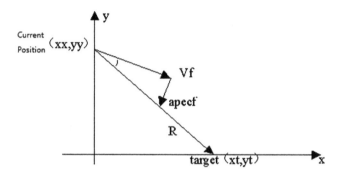

Fig. 1. The schematic diagram of guidance law in the pitch profile

3.1 Sight Line Axis System

By using the sight line axis system, we can expediently describe and compute the command acceleration. As it is shown in Fig. 2, the sight line axis system can be obtained by rotating the emission axis system. Here λ_p is the azimuth angle, and λ_t is the elevation angle. The axis transformation matrix S_g is given by Eq. 5.

$$S_g(\lambda_t, \lambda_p) = \begin{bmatrix} \cos(\lambda_t)\cos(\lambda_p) & \sin(\lambda_t) & -\cos(\lambda_t)\sin(\lambda_p) \\ -\sin(\lambda_t)\cos(\lambda_p) & \cos(\lambda_t) & \sin(\lambda_t)\sin(\lambda_p) \\ \sin(\lambda_p) & 0 & \cos(\lambda_p) \end{bmatrix} \qquad (5)$$

From Eq. 5, we can see that the azimuth angle and the elevation angle should be computed at the first step. We define the sight line vector $\vec{R}_s$ as the vector begins at the current position of the guided ammunition and ends at the position of the target.

$$\vec{R}_s = \begin{bmatrix} R_x \\ R_y \\ R_z \end{bmatrix} = \begin{bmatrix} xt - xx \\ yt - yy \\ zt - zz \end{bmatrix} \qquad (6)$$

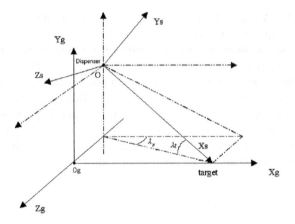

Fig. 2. The schematic diagram of sight line axis system

We can compute the azimuth angle with $\lambda_p = -tg^{-1}\left(\frac{R_z}{R_x}\right)$, and the elevation angle with $\lambda_t = tg^{-1}\left(\frac{R_y}{\sqrt{R_x^2 + R_z^2}}\right)$.

3.2   Rotation Rate of Sight Line and Command Acceleration

We decompose the guided ammunition's velocity vector into components V_1, V_2 and V_3 respectively along the X_s, Y_s and Z_s axis in the sight line axis system. The guided ammunition's velocity at arbitrary point in the sight line axis system is as shown as Fig. 3.

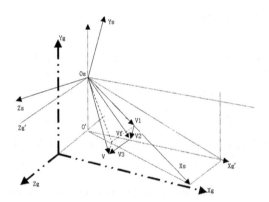

Fig. 3. The decomposition of guided ammunition's velocity

From Fig. 3, we can get the Eq. 7.

$$\begin{bmatrix} V_1 \\ V_2 \\ V_3 \end{bmatrix} = S_g\left(\lambda_t, \lambda_p\right) * \begin{bmatrix} V_x \\ V_y \\ V_z \end{bmatrix} \tag{7}$$

Here V_x, V_y and V_z are the three components of guided ammunition's velocity in the emission axis system. Now we can decompose the motion into the pitch plane and the yaw plane. Here the pitch plane is the plane denoted by $O' - O_s - X_s$, and the yaw plane is the plane denoted by $X_g - O_s - X'_g$. We calculate the corresponding command acceleration based on the proportional navigation guidance law on these planes.

The rotation rate of sight line in the pitch plane is $\dot{q}_f = -\frac{V_2}{|R_s|}$. By using the proportional navigation guidance law, the rotation rate of the velocity vector in the pitch plane is $\dot{\theta}_f = K_f * \dot{q}_f$, here K_f is the navigation ratio; $\dot{\theta}_f$ is the Z component of the angular rate vector of the velocity direction in the sight line axis system.

From the dynamic law $a = V \cdot \dot{\theta}$, we can get the expected command acceleration (control force) in the pitch plane as it is shown in Eq. 8.

$$a_{pecf} = |V_1| \cdot \dot{\theta}_f = K_f \cdot |V_1| \cdot \dot{q}_f = a_{ys} = -K_f \cdot |V_1| \cdot V_2/|R_s| \tag{8}$$

Similarly, we can get the rotation rate of sight line in the law plane as $\dot{q}_p = \frac{V_3}{|R_s|}$. The expected command acceleration (control force) in the yaw plane is shown in Eq. 9.

$$a_{pecp} = a_{zs} = -K_p \cdot |V_1| \cdot V_3/|R_s| \tag{9}$$

Now we have got two components of the command acceleration in the sight line axis system. In order to control the guided ammunition, we need to transform these signals in the sight line axis system into the signals in the body axis system. So we have Eq. 10.

$$\begin{bmatrix} x_b \\ y_b \\ z_b \end{bmatrix} = B_S \cdot \begin{bmatrix} x_s \\ y_s \\ z_s \end{bmatrix} \tag{10}$$

Here B_S is the transition matrix from the sight line axis system to the body axis system.

We can get the acceleration of the sight line by Eq. 11. Here B_N is transition matrix from the geocentric axis system to the body axis system.

$$\begin{bmatrix} a_{xb} \\ a_{yb} \\ a_{zb} \end{bmatrix} = B_S \cdot \begin{bmatrix} a_{xs} \\ a_{ys} \\ a_{zs} \end{bmatrix} - B_N \begin{bmatrix} 0 \\ -g \\ 0 \end{bmatrix} \tag{11}$$

3.3   Control Signals for Slipping Turn

In the Eq. 11, a_{ys} and a_{zs} are the known guidance signals. There is no clear requirements of a_{xs}, and it can be determined based on some specific needs. The apparent acceleration a_{xb} can't be controlled, but it can be measured. For the control of slipping turn, we make $\gamma_p = 0$, a_{yb} and a_{zb} are the control signals.

In order to get the control signals, we need to make a_{ys}, a_{zs}, λ_p, λ_t, a_{xb}, φ_p and ψ_p as known quantities obtained by computation or measurement. We should calculate a_{ys} and a_{zb} under the condition of $\gamma_p = 0$. Here a_{xs} can be got as an intermediate variable. From the first component equation of Eq. 11, we can get the Eq. 12.

$$a_{xb} = \begin{bmatrix} 1 & 0 & 0 \end{bmatrix} \cdot B_S \cdot \begin{bmatrix} a_{xs} \\ a_{ys} \\ a_{zs} \end{bmatrix} \tag{12}$$

Here we denote $B_{N1}^T = \begin{bmatrix} 1 & 0 & 0 \end{bmatrix} \cdot B_N = \begin{bmatrix} \cos \phi_p \cos \psi_p & \sin \phi_p & -\cos \phi_p \sin \psi_p \end{bmatrix}$. We also denote the following variables as it is shown in Eq. 13.

$$K_{xs} = B_{N1}^T \cdot N_g \cdot \begin{bmatrix} \cos \lambda_t \cos \lambda_p \\ \sin \lambda_t \\ -\cos \lambda_t \sin \lambda_p \end{bmatrix}, \quad K_{ys} = B_{N1}^T \cdot N_g \cdot \begin{bmatrix} -\sin \lambda_t \cos \lambda_p \\ \cos \lambda_t \\ \sin \lambda_t \sin \lambda_p \end{bmatrix},$$

$$K_{zs} = B_{N1}^T \cdot N_g \cdot \begin{bmatrix} \sin \lambda_p \\ 0 \\ \cos \lambda_p \end{bmatrix} \tag{13}$$

We can calculate a_{xs} by Eq. 14.

$$a_{xs} = \frac{a_{xb} + g_{xb} - K_{ys} \cdot a_{ys} - K_{zs} \cdot a_{zs}}{K_{xs}} \tag{14}$$

Here $g_{xb} = -\sin \phi_p \cdot g$. ψ_p, ϕ_p, γ_p are the 2-3-1 ordered eulerian conversion angles from the body axis system to the geographic axis system.

We denote $B_{s1} = S_g\left(\phi_p, \psi_p\right) \cdot N_g \cdot S_g'\left(-\lambda_t, -\lambda_p\right)$, and $B_{N1} = S_g\left(\varphi_p, \psi_p\right)$. So we can get Eq. 15.

$$\begin{bmatrix} a_{x1} \\ a_{y1} \\ a_{z1} \end{bmatrix} = B_{S1} \begin{bmatrix} a_{xs} \\ a_{ys} \\ a_{zs} \end{bmatrix} + B_{N1} \begin{bmatrix} 0 \\ g \\ 0 \end{bmatrix} \tag{15}$$

Based on $\gamma_p = 0$ and the second component and the third component of Eq. 11, we can get $a_{yb} = a_{y1}$ and $a_{zb} = a_{z1}$.

3.4   Structure of the Autopilot

The autopilot consists of three parts, namely the inertial device, the control circuit and the actuator system. The design of the autopilot is mainly based on the control theory. The structure of the autopilot is shown in Fig. 4. The autopilot has two important functions, one is executing the guidance orders sent by the guidance system, and the other one is keeping stability of the projectile body while flying.

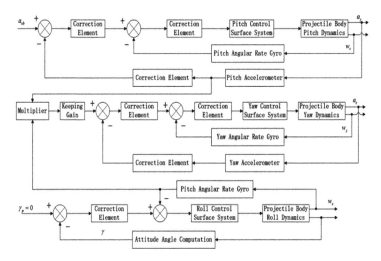

Fig. 4. The structure diagram of the autopilot

Usually the control signals of the three-channel rudder need to be transited into the control signals of the four-channel rudder. The transition method is shown by the Eq. 16.

$$\begin{cases} \delta_1 = (\delta_x - \delta_y + \delta_z)/4 \\ \delta_2 = (\delta_x + \delta_y + \delta_z)/4 \\ \delta_3 = (\delta_x + \delta_y - \delta_z)/4 \\ \delta_4 = (\delta_x - \delta_y - \delta_z)/4 \end{cases} \tag{16}$$

Here δ_x, δ_y, and δ_z are the output control signals of the three-channel rudders. δ_1, δ_2, δ_3 and δ_4 are the output control signals of the four-channel rudders.

4   Digital Simulation

We use the digital simulation program to simulate the guidance and control system of the guided ammunition, including the control model, guidance model and actuator model. We simulate the control model and the guidance model taking the time delay into consideration. The program also contains the model of the projectile body. The simulation cycle is 2 ms. The control cycle is 10 ms. The guidance cycle is 20 ms. The time delay of the control and guidance system is 20 ms.

The initial position of the guided ammunition is (0, 0, 10000), and the initial height is 10000 m. The initial velocity is 250 m/s. The position of the target is (50000, 0, 0). The simulation results of the guided ammunition are as follows (Figs. 5, 6, 7 and 8).

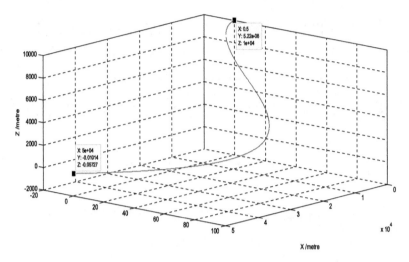

Fig. 5. The simulation result of the three-dimensional flight path

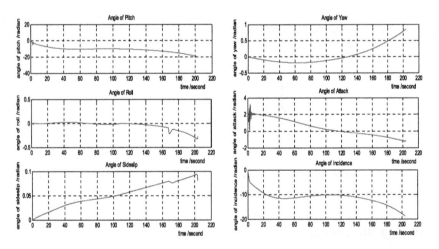

Fig. 6. The simulation results of the angles

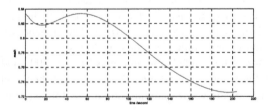

Fig. 7. The simulation result of the mach

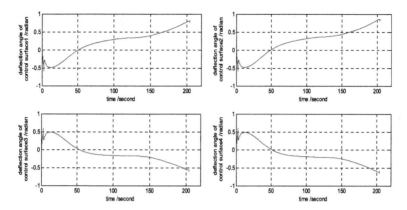

Fig. 8. The simulation result of the control signals

5 Conclusions and Future Work

In this paper, we create the model of the guidance and control system for a certain kind of guided ammunition. And we verify our model by running the digital simulation program. The simulation results prove the validity of the models. This model can be used in the digital simulation of other guided ammunitions such as airborne dispensers. At the current stage, the running of the model mainly depends on the digital simulation programs. In order to combining the model and the practical use of the weapons, we should put the model in the computerized warfare simulation, and test the operational effectiveness of the guided ammunitions in the combat system.

Acknowledgements. This work was supported by Grant 61374185 from National Natural Science Foundation of China. The authors thank the reviewers for their comment.

References

1. Deyong, K.O.N.G., Yongqi, G.A.O.: Vertification and validation of controlled trajectory for guided air ammunition. J. Proj. Rocket. Missiles Guid. **26**(6), 169–172 (2009)
2. Shousong, H.: Automatic Control Theory. National Defence Industry Press, Beijing (1999)
3. Zhiping, L., Fengqi, Z., Jun, Z.: Comment on design methods for modern missile autopilots. Aerosp. Control **24**(5), 91–96 (2006)
4. Cheng, Y.: Designment of the Autopilot of the Air-Defense Missile. Space Navigation Press, Beijing (1993)
5. Ma, J.: Principle of Missile Control System. Aviation Industry Press, Beijing (1996)
6. Wang, J., Lv, S., Zhang, M., Guo, R.: The design and simulation of the control system for a guided rocket. J. Proj. Rocket. Missiles Guid. **32**(1), 57–59 (2012)
7. Jia, P.: Ballistic of the Long-Range Rocket. National Defense University Press, Changsha (1993)

Research on the Maximum Allowable Advancing Step of a Distributed Flight Control Simulation

Yuhong Li, Chan Guo, Xiao Song, Ni Li, Guanghong Gong[✉], and Yaofei Ma

School of Automation Science, Beihang University (BUAA), Beijing 100191, China
ggh@buaa.edu.cn

Abstract. To finally guarantee the stability and real-time data transmission of network-induced distributed systems, the study of the maximum allowable advancing step of a constructive flight simulation is carried out. Firstly, time performance indicators of the flight dynamics model and the closed control system model are obtained by analyzing their dynamic characteristics in time domain, respectively. Then, the advancing step is calculated based on theory analysis. Finally, several groups of comparative experiments on standalone and distributed systems are conducted to demonstrate the control effects under different advancing steps. To apply the conclusions of this paper to distributed simulation systems can help to solve the unstable problem of distributed models and enhance the distributed simulation performance.

Keywords: Flight simulator · Distributed simulation · Maximum advancing step · Dynamic characteristics

1 Introduction

A distributed simulation system (DSS) is a computer network-based system. It connects computers and other simulation devices distributed in various locations through networking technologies to constitute an integrated whole, which is consistent in time and space [1].

As a typical DSS, a flight simulator enables to provide real-time flight simulation training with high fidelity, such as flight operations test flight, and risk monitoring and detection, etc. A simulator system includes many different high performance processing sub-systems that need communicating in real time [2], which has a rigorous requirement of the communication delay between these sub-systems. However, as a distributed system becomes more time-critical, the implementation spending is also higher. Simulator systems are getting larger and increasingly distributed in modern days to meet some demands, e.g., extensive application in large-scale [3]. As the result, the performance and the solution issues influenced by network latency have been increasingly prominent.

The problem of network communication time delay brings great limits for designs and applications of these distributed software systems, in which, the delay between nodes equals to the advancing step. When the step is not properly configured, a distributed system with independent simulation models running on each distributed node may

© Springer Science+Business Media Singapore 2016
L. Zhang et al. (Eds.): AsiaSim 2016/SCS AutumnSim 2016, Part II, CCIS 644, pp. 354–362, 2016.
DOI: 10.1007/978-981-10-2666-9_35

show the inconsistency of time and space [2]. This may lead to causal order violation, understanding ambiguity [4], unstable numerical algorithms [5] and fluctuant solutions.

For distributed simulator systems, existing literatures have mostly focused on their extensive application [6] and delay compensation [7]. However, little work has been documented in detail on the effect of the advancing step on system performance and how to determine the maximum step. The paper aims to explore a method for roughly determining the maximum advancing step of a flight simulator to guarantee the system stability based on analyzing dynamic characteristics of the system model.

The paper is organized as follows. Section 2 describes the considered flight simulation problem. Dynamic characteristics of the flight model and its closed-loop system on the longitudinal and on the lateral are analyzed in Sect. 3 from time domain, separately. On this basis, the maximum time performance indicators of the system are achieved. Section 4 presents theory analysis of the advancing step value. Then several groups of simulation comparison between the standalone and the distributed systems are conducted under different time steps. Section 5 concludes the paper with future prospect.

2 Problem Definition

The problem we discuss is derived from a flight simulator system shown in Fig. 1. The simulator runs a high-fidelity nonlinear model of the F-16 fighter aircraft. Its motion can be observed on a graphics terminal and pilot-in-the-loop simulations are supported. The simulation management platform, the visual system, the instrumentation system, and the consolidated natural environment module, as shown in the dashed sections, only send or receive data, and there is no two-way data interaction. The solid portion represents the flight dynamics and aircraft avionics system, completing the simulations of aircraft entity, navigation, guidance and control functions.

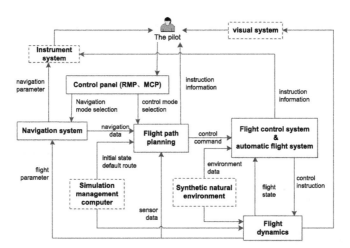

Fig. 1. Sub-models of flight simulator

Data transmits between the sub-models with solid lines, which form a closed loop in the overall structure in accordance with the feedback principle of the control system. In order to improve the overall efficiency of its distributed system, it's better to balance the load on computers as far as possible. The flight dynamics and the aircraft avionics systems in two separate computers share the demanding computational load in a synchronized manner.

Simulation results show that the distributed simulation results are worse than those of the standalone simulation with the same numerical algorithm. Similar problems also appear in other distributed systems, whose common feature is that each part of the simulation model is connected to form a closed loop via network. In order to solve the numerical algorithms divergence problem in distributed systems, we will take the above flight simulator system as an example to analyze essential reasons of the problem. And we will try to seek a general approach for the maximum advancing step of a distributed simulation system.

Factors that affect the performance of a DSS vary, we must first figure out the uncertainties of its performance deterioration caused by an intervention of network. It is summarized as network delay, packet loss and multi-packet transmission, etc. And network delay is one of the major problems as it determines the stability of a distribution system to a certain extent.

Network delay acting on DSSs with the result of divergent solution is in essence reflected by the stability of systems' delay differential equations. A generalized delay differential equation is

$$\begin{cases} \dot{y} = f(t, y(t), y(t - \tau_1), y(t - \tau_2), \ldots, u(t)) & t \geq t_0 \\ \qquad\qquad y(t_0) = y_0 \end{cases} \tag{1}$$

The data in the distributed flight simulation interacts by means of the UDP broadcast. Once the simulation management node sends and receives data, other computers push forward their models by an advancing step respectively. Therefore, the data delay time of each model from its preceding connected node is one advancing step. The impact of step on the simulator can be represented by

$$\tilde{X}(t) = AX(t) + BU(t - \tau) \tag{2}$$

Where τ represents the delay time, and the system performance gets worse as τ becomes lager [8]. If we do not properly configure the advancing step, the performance of the distributed system will be sharply declined, and even falls into instability [9]. The faster the system state $X(t)$ and the control input $U(t)$, the greater the influence of the step. Therefore, the dynamic performance time indicator of the system is an important parameter of delay differential equations.

3   Dynamic Analysis

Dynamic characteristics of the flight dynamic model and the closed control system model from time domain are analyzed, respectively. Time performance indicator which mostly reflects the effect of the advancing step between two connected simulation nodes in the distributed flight simulator is concentrated upon.

3.1 Dynamic Analysis of the Flight Dynamic Model

For the nonlinear aircraft model, the aerodynamic parameters change with altitude and Mach number, which bring much inconvenience to our analysis. An effective and widely used linearization partitioning approach is employed in analyzing the flight simulator model [10].

(1) Determination of the flight envelope and the operating points

Building a model of the 6-DOF nonlinear aircraft in MATLAB™ [11], the flight envelope through flight simulation tests is achieved. Through a series of horizontal straight flight tests, we record the minimum and the maximum level flight speeds in different heights. The determination of the ceiling and the maximum Mach number should consider some integrated factors such as structural strength and safety, so we select 18,000 m and 2 M as the maximum limits according to relevant technical documentations [12]. And operating points are uniformly selected throughout the flight envelope.

Taking the operating point (5000 m, 0.4 M) as an example, we will try to obtain the time performance indicators of the model in the following.

(2) Time domain analysis in the longitudinal mode

The small perturbation linearized model in the longitudinal direction is [13]:

$$
\begin{bmatrix} \Delta \dot{u} \\ \dot{w} \\ \dot{q} \\ \Delta \dot{\theta} \end{bmatrix} = \begin{bmatrix} \dfrac{X_u}{m} & \dfrac{X_w}{m} & \dfrac{X_q}{m} & -g\cos\theta_0 \\ \dfrac{Z_u}{m} & \dfrac{Z_w}{m} & \dfrac{Z_q}{m} & -g\sin\theta_0 \\ \dfrac{M_u}{I_y} & \dfrac{M_w}{I_y} & \dfrac{M_q}{I_y} & 0 \\ 0 & 0 & 1 & 0 \end{bmatrix} \begin{bmatrix} \Delta u \\ w \\ q \\ \Delta\theta \end{bmatrix} + \begin{bmatrix} \dfrac{X_{\Delta\delta_T}}{m} & \dfrac{X_{\Delta\delta_e}}{m} \\ \dfrac{Z_{\Delta\delta_T}}{m} & \dfrac{Z_{\Delta\delta_e}}{m} \\ \dfrac{M_{\Delta\delta_T}}{I_y} & \dfrac{M_{\Delta\delta_e}}{I_y} \\ 0 & 0 \end{bmatrix} \begin{bmatrix} \Delta\delta_T \\ \Delta\delta_e \end{bmatrix} \tag{3}
$$

There are two inputs in the vertical, elevator and throttle, and four state variables, airspeed, angle of attack, pitch rate and pitch angle. Although the time-domain analysis needs not linearization on the operating point, trimming at the reference state is necessary.

It has been known that the trim values at operating point (5000 m, 0.4 M) are $-4.781°$ of elevator, $9.039°$ of attack angle, and 0.819 of throttle.

Select the peak time t_p of vertical step responses as the time indicator, and eliminate the start time 10 s on the basis of the values in timeline. Time indicators in time domain are shown in the left column of Table 1.

(3) Time domain analysis in the lateral mode

The small perturbation linearized model in the lateral direction is [13]:

$$
\begin{bmatrix} \Delta \dot{u} \\ \dot{w} \\ \dot{q} \\ \Delta \dot{\theta} \end{bmatrix} = \begin{bmatrix} \dfrac{X_u}{m} & \dfrac{X_w}{m} & \dfrac{X_q}{m} & -g\cos\theta_0 \\ \dfrac{Z_u}{m} & \dfrac{Z_w}{m} & \dfrac{Z_q}{m} & -g\sin\theta_0 \\ \dfrac{M_u}{I_y} & \dfrac{M_w}{I_y} & \dfrac{M_q}{I_y} & 0 \\ 0 & 0 & 1 & 0 \end{bmatrix} \begin{bmatrix} \Delta u \\ w \\ q \\ \Delta\theta \end{bmatrix} + \begin{bmatrix} \dfrac{X_{\Delta\delta_T}}{m} & \dfrac{X_{\Delta\delta_e}}{m} \\ \dfrac{Z_{\Delta\delta_T}}{m} & \dfrac{Z_{\Delta\delta_e}}{m} \\ \dfrac{M_{\Delta\delta_T}}{I_y} & \dfrac{M_{\Delta\delta_e}}{I_y} \\ 0 & 0 \end{bmatrix} \begin{bmatrix} \Delta\delta_T \\ \Delta\delta_e \end{bmatrix} \qquad (4)
$$

There are two inputs in the lateral, aileron and rudder, and four state variables, side-slip angle, roll rate, yaw rate and roll angle. Through Lateral responses in time domain, time domain indicators are shown in the right column of Table 1.

Table 1. Dynamic time performance indicators of the aircraft model in time domain (tp/s)

In the longitudinal			In the lateral		
State variable	δ_e input	δ_T input	State variable	δ_a input	δ_r input
V	33.545	14.060	β	0.225	0.39
α	0.635	13.880	p	0.690	0.445
q	0.195	15.320	r	6.085	0.175
θ	15.760	32.285	ϕ	-	38.400

where, δ_e is elevator angle, δ_T is throttle deflection, δ_a is aileron angle, δ_r is rudder angel, V is airspeed, α is angle of attack, q is pitch rate, θ is pitch angle, β is sideslip angle, p is roll rate, r is yaw rate, ϕ is roll angle.

Since the roll angle cannot reach a steady state when ailerons deflect continuously, the roll angle response has no peak time. But it is clear that direct consequence of the roll torque acting on the flight is the roll rate, to which the roll angle is subject. Therefore, the dynamic characteristics are related, and the time indicator of the roll angle is larger.

3.2 Dynamic Analysis of the Closed-Loop Flight Control System

Dynamic analysis method of the closed-loop flight control system is the same with that of its open-loop system in Sect. 3.1. There are 6 control modes including pitch angle (θ) control, height (H) control, lifting speed ($\dot{H}$) control, airspeed (V) control, roll angle control (ϕ) and yaw angle (ψ) control.

From step curves under each control mode, the corresponding time performance indicators which have excluded the balancing effect are shown in Table 2. In order to fully understand the time indicator of the flight system, we should also study the dynamic characteristics of control surfaces and the throttle lever, which are the interface data of the control law and flight dynamics. The corresponding time indicators are shown in Table 2 in the last row.

In the closed-loop system, the controlled variables of the height control and the yaw angle control share a lower fast indicator while those of the roll angle control and pitch angle control are higher. The time indicator of roll angle control is the same with that of the yaw angle control in control variables, while the yaw angle control requires a longer time to come to the control effect.

Table 2. Dynamic time indicators of the closed-loop flight system in time-domain (ts/s)

Control mode	θ control	H control	$\dot{H}$ control	V control	ϕ control	ψ control
Controlled variables	2.42	16.45	4.71	1.80	1.27	26.09
Control variables	1.33	2.98	0.83	0.33	0.065	0.065

The above two tables present the time performance of the flight dynamics model and its closed-loop simulation model. In the control effect, the time indicator of the pitch angle control, the lifting speed control, the airspeed control in the longitudinal and the roll angle control in the lateral are faster. Control surfaces responds are more quickly in the lifting speed control, the airspeed control, the roll angle control and the yaw angle control. The fast performance of controlled variables and that of control variables are inconsistent, but the control variables are where the network delay takes effects directly.

4   Simulation Study

The flight simulator system includes continuous signal components (such as devices the pilot directly manipulates and the actuators), while the input and output signals of digital computers are in a digital format, so sampling is required before processing. The Shannon sampling theorem [14] points out that if the sampling frequency satisfies the condition

$$\omega_s \geq 2\omega_{max} \tag{5}$$

Then the sampled signal sequence can be restored to the original continuous signal without distortion.

Considering the stability of a practical closed-loop system and other design factors, the required sampling frequency should be higher than the theoretical minimum value. The rules of selecting a sampling frequency in engineering applications are as follows [15, 16].

If the controlled process contains a pure lag time τ, the sampling period T usually satisfies

$$T < (\frac{1}{4} \sim \frac{1}{10})\tau \tag{6}$$

If the closed-loop system has a homeostatic regulation time t_s, or a closed-loop natural frequency ω_n, it usually require

$$T < \frac{1}{10}t_s, \tag{7}$$
$$\omega_s > 10\omega_n$$

Based on the obtained dynamic characteristic data in Table 2, the sampling period of the flight simulation system in the case of zero delay time is

$$T < \frac{1}{10}t_s = \frac{1}{10} * 0.065\,s = 6.5\,ms \tag{8}$$

When using a fixed-step solver, to ensure that the numerical algorithm can give a numerical solution on each sampling time, the sampling time must be an integer multiple of the fixed step size, so the advancing step time satisfies

$$h = \frac{T}{n} \leq T < 6.5\,ms \tag{9}$$

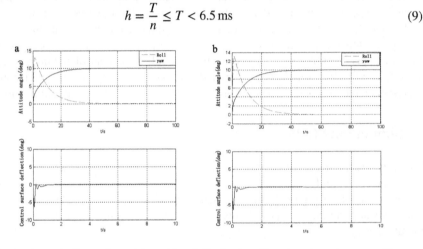

Fig. 2. Control effects of standalone (a) and distribution (b) under advancing step of 1 ms

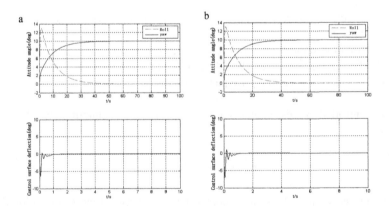

Fig. 3. Control effects of standalone (a) and distribution (b) under advancing step of 5 ms

According to the above theoretical results, four groups of comparative simulation experiments between standalone and distribution are carried out under the roll angle control mode, which is the fastest in system control variables. The simulation results of altitude angle (roll and yaw) and control surface deflection under the four advancing steps of 1 ms, 5 ms, 10 ms and 15 ms are shown in Figs. 2, 3, 4 and 5, respectively.

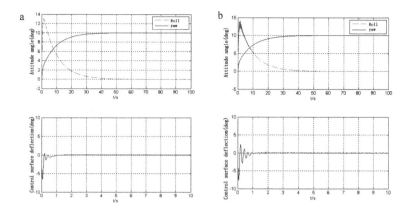

Fig. 4. Control effects of standalone (a) and distribution (b) under advancing step of 10 ms

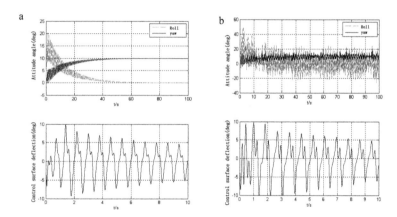

Fig. 5. Control effects of centralization (a) and distribution (b) under advancing step of 15 ms

It can be observed that the maximum step size of the standalone simulation is 10 ms. While in the distributed simulation with the same step, the control variable shows a strong fluctuation at beginning and still keeps fluctuating at its steady state, resulting in a high-frequency oscillatory in the aircraft's roll angle. When the step size increases to 5 ms, the distributed response is stable, but the control variable has a tendency to oscillatory. These simulation results show that the empirical formula (7) contains a certain amount of threshold. Moreover, the distributed simulation' threshold step is concluded to be a little smaller than half of the critical step in the standalone one.

5   Conclusion and Future Work

Based on dynamic characteristics analysis of the flight simulator model, several comparative simulation experiments are conducted by different advancing step. Results show
that the critical step in the distributed simulation is a little smaller than half of that in
the standalone condition. More work is expected to do as follows:

(1) The critical step could be worked out in the form of a theoretical formula although
     it is very difficult;
(2) Other ways to achieve the threshold time step such as applying a system partitioning
     approach could be tried.

References

1. Gong, Y.: The research of distributed virtual environment temporal consistency model and
    simulation technology. Master thesis, National University of Defense Technology (2005)
2. Zheng, S.P., He, J.F., Jin, J., Han, J.W.: DDS based high fidelity flight simulator. In: WASE
    International Conference on Information Engineering, vol. 1, pp. 548–551. IEEE Computer
    Society (2009)
3. Zhong, H.: Space-time consistency of large-scale distributed simulation system. Ph.D. thesis,
    National University of Defense Technology (2005)
4. Zhang, J.: Real perceive-based technology of time and space consistency in distributed virtual
    environment. J. Beijing Univ. Aeronaut. Astronaut. **36**(8), 969–978 (2010)
5. Hong, S.P., Yong, H.K., Kim, D.S., Kwon, W.H.: A scheduling method for network-based
    control systems. IEEE Trans. Control Syst. Technol. **2**(3), 318–330 (2002)
6. Rodrigues, C., Silva, D.C., Rossetti, R.J.F., Oliveira, E.: Distributed flight simulation
    environment using flight simulator X. In: Information Systems and Technologies. IEEE
    (2015)
7. Jiang, N., Huang, A.X., Li, J.S., Li, H.T.: Research on network time delay of collaborative
    fighting distributed simulation system based on HLA. J. Syst. Simul. **19**(14), 3234–3236
    (2007)
8. Li, B., Zhou, S.H.: Analysis of stability in distributed detection system with network delay.
    In: Second International Workshop on Education Technology and Computer Science (ETCS),
    vol. 1, pp. 317–320. IEEE (2010)
9. Xie, L.B.: Research on several issues of networked control systems. Ph.D. thesis, Huazhong
    University of Science and Technology (2004)
10. Etkin, B.: Dynamics of Atmospheric Flight. Dover Publications, New York (2005)
11. Garza, F.R.: A collection of nonlinear aircraft simulations in MATLAB, vol. 2, pp. 34, 36,
    39. Nasa Langley Research Center (2003)
12. Sonneveldt, L.: Nonlinear F-16 model description. Control and Simulation Division, Faculty
    of Aerospace Engineering. Delft University of Technology, Netherlands (2006)
13. Zhang, M.L.: Flight Control System. Beijing University of Aeronautics and Astronautics
    Press, Beijing (1994)
14. Cheng, P.: Automatic Control Theory. High Education Press, Beijing (2003)
15. Gao, J.Y., Xia, J.: Computer Control System. Tsinghua University Press, Beijing (2007)
16. Ma, Y.F., Song, X., Wang, J.Y., Xiao, Z.: A practical infrastructure for real-time simulation
    across timing domains. Math. Probl. Eng. **2015**, 1–12 (2015)

A Two-Stage Decision Model Based on Rough Set and Fuzzy Reasoning with Application to Missile Selection for Aerial Targets

Shanliang Yang[1]([✉]), Chuncai Wang[2], Mei Yang[1], Ge Li[1], and Kedi Huang[1]

[1] College of Information System and Management,
National University of Defense Technology, Changsha 410073, Hunan, China
yangshanliang@nudt.edu.cn
[2] Naval Academy Armament, Shanghai 200436, China

Abstract. Appropriate missile selection for hostile aerial targets is conceived as an important issue in military operations research. However, both roughness and fuzziness may exist in military data simultaneously due to the complexity of situation and subjectivity of human knowledge. Therefore, this paper presents a two-stage decision model based on rough set theory (RST) and fuzzy inference system (FIS) for missile selection. The LEM2 algorithm in RST is applied to derive decision rules. Next, a Mamdani fuzzy inference system is formed to identify the proper missile type depending on the Gaussian membership functions. Some experiments with respect to some practical parameters are performed to validate the proposed model. The computational results indicate that the proposed model is capable of producing high-quality solutions and is convenient to be incorporated in a military decision support software.

Keywords: Missile selection · Rough set theory (RST) · LEM2 algorithm · Mamdani fuzzy inference system · Gaussian membership function

1 Introduction

A proper missile selection for aerial targets is a very important issue in military operations research because improper missile selection would negatively affect the overall performance of the defense system [1]. Since the decisions on missile system are regarded as crucial to the outcome of battles, the selection process of missile system is a critical choice for military decision makers. With the rapid development of military technologies, it makes missile selection problem even more sophisticated and complex [2]. Selecting the appropriate missile system is a difficult and time-consuming process, requiring deep experience and advanced knowledge.

In previous researches, most scholars modeled the missile selection process as a multiple criteria decision-making (MCDM) problem because the performance evaluation of missile systems has multi-level and multi-factor features. For example, Metin et al. [3] developed an evaluation model based on the analytic hierarchy process (AHP) and the technique for order performance by similarity to

© Springer Science+Business Media Singapore 2016
L. Zhang et al. (Eds.): AsiaSim 2016/SCS AutumnSim 2016, Part II, CCIS 644, pp. 363–373, 2016.
DOI: 10.1007/978-981-10-2666-9_36

ideal solution (TOPSIS), to help the military commanders for the selection of the optimal missile system among a set of available alternatives. Wang [4] proposed a novel mathematical model based on the response surface method (RSM) and the grey relational analysis (GRA) to address the missile selection problem.

However, these publications have been concentrating on the features and performance ratings of missile systems, and ignoring all the associated information about the aerial targets. The selection methods for missile evaluation should pay more attention to the features of aerial targets. It is worth noting that both roughness and fuzziness may exist in military data simultaneously due to the complexity of situation and subjectivity of human knowledge. Therefore, this paper proposes a two-stage decision model based on rough set theory and fuzzy reasoning for missile selection. The LEM2 algorithm is applied to generate decision rules, and a Mamdani fuzzy inference system is formed to identify the appropriate missile type depending on the Gaussian membership functions. A case study is given to demonstrate the effectiveness and feasibility of the proposed model.

2   The Framework of Proposed Two-Stage Decision Model

In this section, we will present a two-stage decision model for tackling missile selection problem against aerial targets. The framework of proposed decision model consists of two phases: (1) Rules extraction based on rough set theory. (2) Missile evaluation based on fuzzy reasoning. The flow diagram of the proposed model is illustrated in Fig. 1. First, the training data are imported into the rough set model in order to obtain the necessary decision rules. In this process, various algorithms in database could be employed to execute rule learning [5]. Next, the missile data could be identified by using a Mamdani fuzzy inference system (FIS). Detailed information of the model framework is given hereunder.

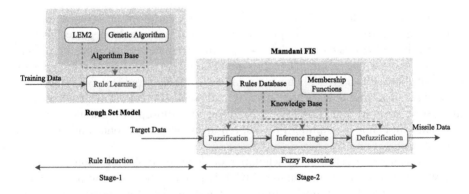

Fig. 1. Flow diagram of the proposed two-stage decision model.

The knowledge for missile selection include the basic properties of targets and missile systems. At the beginning of the proposed model, the original training data should be acquired from military experts. Although we may obtain massive amount of information about the application of missile systems, however, little valuable knowledge can be extracted from these rough data. Therefore, it is necessary to adopt rough set theory for achieving concise decision rules. The concise decision rules for missile selection are inducted by using LEM2 algorithm from military experts' original decision data. Finally, the extracted rules should be checked for compatibility and completeness.

After we getting the decision rules for missile selection, the next step is to identify the appropriate missile type for given target information. Generally speaking, there are countless aerial targets while organizing a large-scale battle. Hence, it is difficult to assign proper missiles for interception by using utilization of manpower. Accordingly, an evaluation methodology based on fuzzy reasoning is introduced in this procedure.

3 Rough Set Based Rule Induction for Missile Selection

The rough set theory (RST), which is introduced by Pawlak [6], is a powerful mathematical tool that can be utilized to help extract logical patterns and knowledge hidden in massive data. Rough set theory is very valuable in decision support systems for dealing with uncertain and vague information in classification problems, and has been widely applied in many fields, such as image analysis, supply chain management, fault diagnosis, network security, and financing risk credit evaluation [7]. In the context of the military domain, the primary advantages of RST are that it (1) identifies relationships that could not be discovered by using statistical approaches; (2) generates sets of decision rules from original data. Next, we will introduce the concept of decision rules defined in RST.

Definition 1 *(Decision Rules). Decision rules are induced so as to cover objects from probabilistic lower approximations of sets being classes or unions of decision classes. In general, a decision rule is a combination of the values of some attributes such that the set of all objects matching it is contained in the set of objects labeled with the same class [8]. Below, we define the syntax of a decision rule for the non-ordinal classification problem:*

$$R_k : (x_1 = M_{1,k}) \wedge (x_2 = M_{2,k}) \vee \cdots \wedge (x_n = M_{n,k}) \rightarrow (y = C_k) \qquad (1)$$

in which $M_{1,k}, M_{2,k}, M_{n,k}$ and C_k are the value contents of the attributes; the set $\{\vee, \wedge, \rightarrow\}$ of connectives represent disjunction, conjunction and implication, respectively.

In order to obtain the decision rules for missile selection, some rule induction algorithms have to be applied in RST. Decision rules are always induced from a given decision table that is subsequently transformed into a minimal set of rules [9]. Rough set rule extraction algorithms were implemented for the first time in a LERS (Learning from Examples based on Rough Set) system. In this study, the rough set LEM2 (Learning from Examples Module, version 2) is employed to generate decision rules for missile evaluation problem.

4   Missile Evaluation Based on Fuzzy Reasoning

Fuzzy reasoning finds applications in various areas, because it is much reliable and stronger than most of the classification methods. The idea of fuzzy reasoning is to map the input space to output space with the aid of set of "If-Then" statements called rules.

4.1   Selection of Input-Output Parameters

Missile evaluation procedure involves lots of parameters at a time. However, the most significant variables which affect the process are the features of aerial targets: Radar Cross-Section (RCS), horizontal velocity (V_H), vertical velocity (V_v), flying height (H), and accelerated speed (A_s). Therefore, we select these five parameters as the input variables of our two-stage decision model. Meanwhile, the purpose of this model is to determine the appropriate missile type in order to intercept with the hostile aerial targets successfully. So, we choose the missile type as our output variable.

4.2   Mamdani FIS Model

Two main types of fuzzy modeling schemes are Mamdani and Takagi-Sugeno-Kang (TSK) models. The primary difference between them is the form of consequent part [10]. In this paper, the Mamdani FIS model is employed to select correct missile to fire against aerial targets. The framework of Mamdani-type fuzzy inference system used in this study is depicted in Fig. 2. The Mamdani fuzzy inference system includes three components: a rule database, which contains a set of fuzzy rules; a database of membership functions used in the fuzzy rules; and a reasoning mechanism, which performs the inference process [11].

Fuzzification. The procedure of determining proper membership functions for fuzzy variables is called as fuzzification. A membership function (MF) is a curve that plots each point in the input space to a membership value between 0 and 1. Various types of curves are available for MF such as trapezoidal, generalized-bell, triangular, Gaussian, sigmoidal etc. [12]. In the fuzzification step, the Gaussian function was exploited to define the fuzzy sets. The Gaussian membership function could be expressed as

$$\mu_A(x) = exp\left(-\frac{(x-c)^2}{2\sigma^2}\right) \qquad (2)$$

where σ and c are adjustable parameters, denoting the width and centrality of the membership curve. In the fuzzy sets, linguistic variables of the uncertainties such as "Very High (VH)", "High (H)", "Medium (M)", "Low (L)" and "Very Low (VL)" are represented mathematically with the aid of MFs.

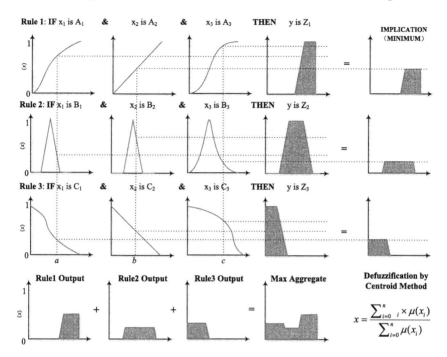

Fig. 2. The typical Mamdani-type fuzzy inference system used for missile selection.

Inference of Fuzzy Rules. If-Then type fuzzy rules convert the fuzzy input to the fuzzy output which in the defuzzification step are transformed into crisp data. In order to perform the fuzzy reasoning in the Mamdani FIS model, the logical "AND" and "OR" operators were handled as the "min" and "max" operations on the corresponding membership functions respectively [13]. Then, the aggregation of the rules was implemented by using the "max" operation on the consequent of the corresponding rules. These two operations could be defined as

$$\mu_{\tilde{A}\cap\tilde{B}}(x) = min\big(\mu_{\tilde{A}}(x), \mu_{\tilde{B}}(x)\big) \tag{3}$$

$$\mu_{\tilde{A}\cup\tilde{B}}(x) = max\big(\mu_{\tilde{A}}(x), \mu_{\tilde{B}}(x)\big) \tag{4}$$

Defuzzification and Thresholding. The final step of Mamdani FIS model is defuzzification in which the fuzzy output of inference engine is converted to crisp value using membership functions [14]. There exists many techniques to execute the defuzzification operation. Center of Area (COA) is the most common defuzzification technique among these approaches. In this study, COA method is exploited to make the crisp value for the output variable. In the COA method, the crisp value is obtained as follows:

$$x_{COA} = \frac{\int_x x\mu_A(x)dx}{\int_x \mu_A(x)dx} \tag{5}$$

where x_{COA} denotes the crisp value of output, and $\mu_A(x)$ represents the aggregated output membership function. The output of the model represents the appropriate missile type among various missile systems. The crisp output value itself however does not determine the missile type. Therefore, a thresholding module is developed to determine the proper missile type:

$$\text{MissileType} = \begin{cases} M_1 \text{ if output} \geqslant \text{threshold} \\ M_2 \text{ otherwise} \end{cases} \qquad (6)$$

5   Application Case Study

The validation of proposed two-stage decision model is initiated by taking the practical data from military experts. The Rough Set Exploration System (RSES) software toolset is introduced so that it is convenient to analyze the tabular datasets utilizing LEM2 algorithm. Meanwhile, the Fuzzy Toolbox of Matlab is indulged to execute fuzzy reasoning in the simulation of the proposed framework.

Table 1. Training data for missile selection versus aerial targets [15]

No.	Target	RCS (m^2)	V_H (m/s)	V_V (m/s)	H (m)	A_s (m/s^2)	Missile
1	TBM	1.5	2180	370	28500	40	M_1
2	AGM	1.7	1650	250	5000	22	M_2
3	CM	1.4	370	22	500	2	M_3
4	SA	0.8	1400	17	12000	2.5	M_4
5	SA	1	1650	19	20000	2.2	M_4
6	SA	0.3	800	18	7500	1.7	M_4
7	SA	0.4	1000	16	24000	3	M_4
8	SA	1.6	560	12	300	1.8	M_4
9	SA	0.75	600	30	16000	2.1	M_4
10	TBM	0.87	1650	450	28500	40	M_1
11	AGM	0.22	1700	500	650	25	M_2
12	AGM	1.64	1400	50	5000	19	M_2
13	AGM	0.8	1550	200	12400	22	M_2
14	CM	0.11	450	27	570	2.1	M_3
15	CM	0.33	150	18	700	5	M_3
16	CM	1.45	280	27	4800	4	M_3
17	SA	1.11	1900	30	9000	1	M_4
18	SA	0.76	1350	25	5000	1	M_4
19	SA	0.5	750	20	28900	1.5	M_4
20	SA	0.25	320	19	18000	2.2	M_4

5.1 Background and Problem Description

Selecting the optimal missile system among a set of alternatives is an unstructured, complicated problem with lots of factors that need to be considered. For a proper and effective evaluation of missile system, the military commanders may need a large amount of information to be analyzed and many elements to be taken into account. The training data in this paper is adapted from Lei's research [15], and the original tabular data is presented in Table 1.

As we can observe, the hostile aerial targets could be categorized into four classes: Tactical Ballistic Missile (TBM), Air-to-Ground Missile (AGM), Cruise Missile (CM), and Stealth Aircraft (SA). Each type of aerial target owes its unique features and needs different types of missile system to intercept, which are denoted by M_1, M_2, M_3 and M_4. The purpose of this study is to determine the appropriate missile type based on the detected information about the aerial targets.

5.2 Computational Results

The experimental studies have been carried out on a personal computer, and the computational results are discussed in the following sections.

Data Preprocessing. The proposed framework concerns with a selected group of military data from field experiments. Before handling the original data it is necessary to execute a series of preprocessing techniques to eliminate noise, and

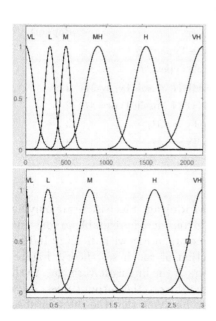
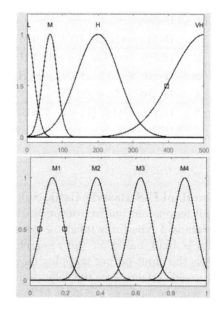

Fig. 3. Membership functions associated with the input and output parameters.

highlight information of interest. For the continuous data in this study, it is considerable to perform discretization operation on the raw data.

The input variable RCS could be divided into three regions based on its value (m^2): L([0,1]), M([1,2]), and H([2,3]). In the same manner, the input parameter V_H can be categorized into six regions (m/s): VL([0,200]), L([200,400]), M([400,600]), MH([600,1200]), H([1200,1800]), and VH([1800,2200]). With respect to the output variable, the missile type could be identified by using four intervals: M_1([0,0.25]), M_2([0.25,0.5]), M_3([0.5,0.75]), and M_4([0.75,1]). In this paper, the input and output variables are expressed with linguistic values. Meanwhile, simple Gaussian membership functions are employed for estimating the fuzzy membership degrees for the input and output parameters (see Fig. 3).

Rule Learning Using the RS LEM2 Algorithm. In general, it is rational to perform the attribute reduction operation before extracting decision rules from the data table. However, considering that there exists few data lists in our training data source, we will extract decision rules directly for missile selection from the original data table. The RS LEM2 algorithm is commonly included in the family of induction methods because it determines a minimal discriminant description. Therefore, the LEM2 algorithm is exploited in this paper to construct the decision rules set according to the discretized dataset. The partial decision rules for missile evaluation induced by LEM2 method are presented in Table 2.

Table 2. The partial rules extracted by LEM2 algorithm for missile selection

No.	Decision rule	Support
1	**IF** (V_V=VH) & (H=VH) **THEN** MissileType=M_1	2
2	**IF** (RCS=M) & (V_H=H) **THEN** MissileType=M_2	2
3	**IF** (RCS=L) & (V_V=L) & (H=VL) **THEN** MissileType=M_3	2
4	**IF** (RCS=L) & (H=VL) & (A_S=L) **THEN** MissileType=M_3	2
5	**IF** (V_H=H) & (V_V=L) **THEN** MissileType=M_4	3
6	**IF** (V_H=H) & (A_S=L) **THEN** MissileType=M_4	3

Mamdani FIS-Based Missile Selection Modeling. Since there are only five input parameters and one output variable, it is considered preferable to construct a Mamdani type fuzzy inference system. Therefore, a FIS with 37 fuzzy If-Then rules is built based on the research production of rough set theory. Figure 4 shows the input-output mapping for some pairs of the linguistic variables. In the discussed surface views the colours change according to the output values. As we can see, the surfaces are more or less smooth, implying that the rules database we built is reasonable.

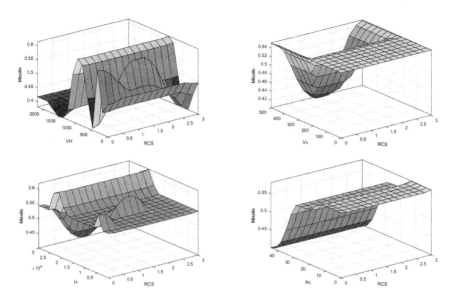

Fig. 4. Input-output mapping surface views for missile selection.

Table 3. Testing data for missile selection against aerial targets

No.	RCS (m^2)	V_H (m/s)	V_V (m/s)	H (m)	A_S (m/s^2)	Target	Missile
1	1.25	2000	480	27500	35	TBM	M_1
2	0.39	500	16	14000	5	SA	M_4
3	0.65	340	14	300	3.6	CM	M_3
4	0.72	1800	390	9000	24	AGM	M_2
5	0.51	300	15	11000	3	SA	M_4

The implication operation between two fuzzy sets is performed by taking the minimum value of the two membership functions. The Max aggregation operator is utilized to combine the fuzzy decision rules, while the COA method is used to estimate the crisp output value. Then the output values are mapped to generate the assigned missile type. The testing data is presented in Table 3 and the reasoning results are accordance with actual circumstances.

Take the first target for example, the input parameter vector could be identified as $I_1 = [RCS, V_H, V_V, H, A_S] = [1.25, 2000, 480, 27500, 35]$. We handled this vector as the input of Mamdani fuzzy inference engine, and the crisp output value equalled 0.248 (see Fig. 5). Based on the predefined threshold values, the target could be determined as a TBM and M_1 type missile will be launched to intercept with this target.

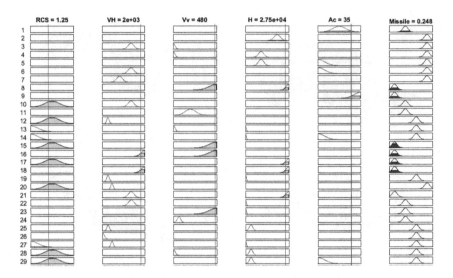

Fig. 5. The fuzzy inference result for TBM-type aerial target.

6   Conclusions and Future Work

This paper deals with the missile selection problem versus hostile aerial targets. In this study, we have presented an effective two-stage decision model for missile evaluation. In Stage 1, the training data are imported into the rough set model in order to obtain the necessary decision rules. In this procedure, LEM2 algorithm is exploited to carry out rule learning operation. In Stage 2, a typical Mamdani fuzzy inference system is constructed to execute fuzzy reasoning in order to determine the appropriate missile type for special aerial target.

In a word, the two-stage decision model consists of rule generation process by using rough set, and classification process through fuzzy inference. However, only Gaussian membership functions are utilized for the inference engine in this paper and other membership functions may also perform equally well. The future work may be concentrated on improving the developed model by making it into a versatile system that adapts itself to any kind of military data.

Acknowledgments. This work was supported by National Natural Science Foundation of China under Grant No. 61074108 & 61374185. The authors thank Zhonghua Yang and Rusheng Ju for their insightful comments which led to significant improvement of the manuscript.

References

1. Lee, J., Kang, S.-H., Rosenberger, J., Kim, S.B.: A hybrid approach of goal programming for weapon systems selection. Comput. Ind. Eng. **58**, 521–527 (2010)
2. Zhang, X., Jiang, J., Zhou, Y.: A hybrid approach of TOPSIS for weapon systems selection. Adv. Mater. Res. **850**, 432–436 (2014)

3. Dağdeviren, M., Yavuz, S., Kılınç, N.: Weapon selection using the AHP and TOP-SIS methods under fuzzy environment. Expert Syst. Appl. **36**, 8143–8151 (2009)
4. Wang, P., Meng, P., Song, B.: Response surface method using grey relational analysis for decision making in weapon system selection. J. Syst. Eng. Electron. **25**(2), 265–272 (2014)
5. Yang, S., Zhang, C., Wang, P., Xue, G.: Integrated decision making framework for weapon application under uncertain environment. In: International Information Technology and Artificial Intelligence Conference, pp. 468–472 (2015)
6. Pawlak, Z.: Rough sets. Inf. J. Comput. Inf. Sci. **11**, 341–356 (1982)
7. Tseng, T.-L., Huang, C.-C., Fraser, K., Ting, H.-W.: Rough set based rule induction in decision making using credible classification and preference from medical application perspective. Comput. Methods Progr. Biomed. **127**, 273–289 (2016)
8. Huang, C.-C., Tseng, T.-L., Fan, Y.-N., Hsu, C.-H.: Alternative rule induction methods based on incremental object using rough set theory. Appl. Soft Comput. **13**, 372–389 (2013)
9. Chen, Y.-S., Cheng, C.-H.: Hybrid models based on rough set classifiers for setting credit rating decision rules in the global banking industry. Knowl.-Based Syst. **39**, 224–239 (2013)
10. Ghanei, S., Faez, K.: Localizing scene texts by fuzzy inference systems and low rank matrix recovery model. Comput. Vis. Image Underst. **142**, 94–110 (2016)
11. Kwolek, B., Kepski, M.: Fuzzy inference-based fall detection using kinect and body-worn accelerometer. Appl. Soft Comput. **40**, 305–318 (2016)
12. Shams, S., Monjezi, M., Majd, V.J., Armaghani, D.J.: Application of fuzzy inference system for prediction of rock fragmentation induced by blasting. Arab. J. Geosci. **8**, 10819–10832 (2015)
13. Dey, S., Jana, D.K.: Application of fuzzy inference system to polypropylene business policy in a petrochemical plant in India. J. Clean. Prod. **112**, 2953–2968 (2016)
14. Camara, C., Warwick, K., Bruña, R., Aziz, T.: A fuzzy inference system for closed-loop deep brain stimulation in Parkinson's disease. J. Med. Syst. **39**, 155–165 (2015)
15. Yang, L., Yingjie, L., Jixue, H., Weiwei, K., Ru, C.: Techniques for target recognition based on adaptive intuitionistic fuzzy inference. Syst. Eng. Electron. **32**(7), 1471–1475 (2010)

Algorithm Research for Function Damage Assessment of Airport Runway

Guangping Zhang[1(✉)], Zhiwen Jiang[1], Yiping Yao[1], Bin Gan[2],
Wenjie Tang[1(✉)], and Cifeng Wang[3]

[1] College of Information System and Management,
National University of Defense Technology, Changsha, China
guangpinghust@163.com, tangwenjie@nudt.edu.cn
[2] Science and Technology on Complex
Land Systems Simulation Laboratory, Beijing, China
[3] National Space Science Center, Chinese Academy of Sciences, Beijing, China

Abstract. For airport runway, the specific battlefield target, the damage model is established. Based on damage data, this paper also proposes a method for airport runway damage assessment based on grid network scanning. It includes looking for the smallest aircraft landing window in the runway area, making up for the issue of identifying oblique landing window of the traditional algorithms, deciding the damage level of the airport runway, and assessing the function damage of airport runway. By computer simulation, the block situation of the airport caused by two different types of ammunition is analyzed. The paper makes airport runway damage assessment using different minimum landing window searching algorithm, and studies the significance of the oblique landing window on the assessment.

Keywords: Airport runway · Damage assessment · Minimum landing window · Grid network · Minimum ammunition consuming

1 Introduction

In modern warfare, "control of the air" is the key factor to achieve victory. The foreign armies usually see the airport as the focused target of the strategic air raid during the beginning of the war. Attack the airport runway, the main is to destroy the plane, destroy the runway, effective suppression of enemy air force to win the "control of the air" [1]. Because of the large area and the exposure, the airport runway is always the first and the most likely to get attacked.

At present, algorithms for searching the minimum landing window of the airport runway are studied both in the country and abroad. There are window scanning algorithm, two-point-comparison algorithm, grid matrix algorithm and regional searching algorithm [2–4]. These algorithms for choosing the minimum landing window of the airport runway are mostly focused on the cases that windows are paralleled to the runways. Very few of them considered the oblique landing window. Even if taking the oblique situation into consideration, they failed to give the detailed algorithm

© Springer Science+Business Media Singapore 2016
L. Zhang et al. (Eds.): AsiaSim 2016/SCS AutumnSim 2016, Part II, CCIS 644, pp. 374–384, 2016.
DOI: 10.1007/978-981-10-2666-9_37

because of the complexity of the oblique landing window. Therefore, it is urgent that related algorithms are to be studied.

In this paper, the damage model of airport runway is established, and a grid network scanning algorithm searching for minimum landing windows on the runway is proposed, making up to the oblique landing window identifying issues of the traditional algorithms, which is useful to the exploration of the function damage assessment method of the airport runway as a target.

2   Airport Runway Damage Model

Fixed-wing aircraft generally glides a certain distance on the runway before its landing or launching. The minimum landing window MLW) is the minimum area required for the landing or launching of the aircraft [5]. With the development of economy and construction industry, the area of the airport has been growing. Also, with the development of the space (military) technology, the performance of the aircraft has been improving, and the landing window is becoming smaller and smaller, which increases the difficulty of damaging the airports.

Aircraft generally land and launch along the longitudinal direction of the runway. The width direction of the runway is not suitable due to the limited width. Therefore, once the airport is attacked, there are two patterns of landing and launching [6]. One is along the runway direction, shown in Fig. 1(a), and the other is in a certain angle, shown in Fig. 1(b).

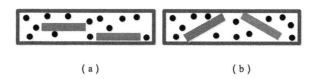

(a)   (b)

Fig. 1. Landing mode

Blocking the airport runway does not mean complete damage on every spot of the runway, but no intact area satisfied to the landing and launching requirements of the aircraft after the attack to the runway, which is seen as the success of blocking. On the contrary, the blocking is failed, and further attack is needed [7]. This model is mainly used to calculate the firepower distribution of the integral ammunition and cluster warhead attacking the runway. The compute process of the model is shown in Fig. 2.

2.1   Determine the Direction of Attack (Distance/Direction Partition Number)

(1) When the projection of the airport runway rectangle on the direction of the attachment wire between the fire unit and the geometric center of the runway

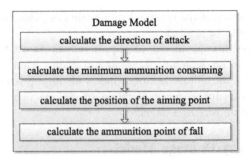

Fig. 2. Damage model compute process

(known as the ARTILLERY TARGET CONNECTION THREAD, ATCT) is larger than its projection on the direction that is vertical to the ATCT, the hit is called forward attack, and the parameters for the firepower distribution can be calculated as follows:

$$t = round(l/l_{min}); n = round(w/w_{min}); h = l/(t+1); I = w/(n+1) \quad (1)$$

(2) When the projection of the runway rectangle on the ATCT direction is less than the vertical direction, the hit is called lateral attack. The parameters can be calculated as follows:

$$t = round(w/w_{min}); n = round(l/l_{min}); h = w/(t+1); I = l/(n+1) \quad (2)$$

where t is the partition number of distance, n is the partition number of direction, l is the length of the airport runway, l_{min} is the length of minimum landing window, w is the width of the airport runway, w_{min} is the width of the minimum landing window, h is the distance-difference, I is the direction-difference, and *round* means rounding up to the nearest integer.

2.2 Calculate the Minimum Ammunition Consuming

The minimum amount of ammunition needed to attack the runway and successfully block the airport, making it unable to land or launch aircrafts is called Minimum Ammunition Consuming. In order to block the airport, all runways that are wider than w_{min} need to be destroyed. When the equation $N_{cw} = round[(w - w_{min})/(2r)]$ is satisfied, the airport is successfully blocked on the width-direction.

(1) Calculate the hitting probability of the integral ammunition
   (i) Guided integral ammunition. Calculate the hitting probability of single rounds of ammunition.

$$p_1 = 1 - 2^{-(0.5w/CEP)^2} \tag{3}$$

(ii) Unguided integral ammunition. Calculate the hitting probability of single rounds of ammunition.

$$p_1 = \hat{\Phi}\left(\frac{0.5l}{D\sqrt{E_d^2 + B_d^2}}\right) * \hat{\Phi}\left(\frac{0.5w}{D\sqrt{E_f^2 + B_f^2}}\right) \tag{4}$$

Where r is damage radius of the integral ammunition (cluster warhead), CEP is the guidance circular error probable of the integral ammunition (cluster warhead), E_d is the distance firing data error of the weapon, E_f is the direction firing data error of the weapon, B_d is the intensity for the ground distance of the integral ammunition (cluster warhead), B_f is the intensity for the ground direction of the integral ammunition (cluster warhead), D is shooting distance.

In the equation, the simplified Laplacian function is:

$$\hat{\Phi}(x) = 1 - \left(1 + \sum_{i=1}^{6} a_i (0.476936x)^i\right)^{-16} \quad (x \geq 0) \tag{5}$$

Where $a_1 = 0.0705$, $a_2 = 0.0423$, $a_3 = 0.0093$, $a_4 = 0.0002$, $a_5 = 0.0003$, $a_6 = 0.00004$.

(2) Calculate the hitting probability of the cluster warhead
  (i) Guided parent warhead. Calculate firing data error and ground density:

$$E_d = 0, E_f = 0, B_d = B_f = CEP/1.75 \tag{6}$$

(ii) Unguided parent warhead. Correct firing data error and ground density:

$$E_d' = E_d * D, E_f' = E_f * D, B_d' = B_d * D, B_f' = B_f * D \tag{7}$$

The hitting probability of single rounds of the cluster warhead:

$$p_1 = 1 - \exp\left(\frac{-\rho^2 R^2}{E_{dd}^2 + B_{dd}^2 + E_{ff}^2 + B_{ff}^2 + l_d l_f / \pi}\right) \tag{8}$$

In the equation,

$$E_{dd} = \sqrt{E_d'^2 + \frac{1}{P\eta} B_d'^2}, E_{ff} = \sqrt{E_f'^2 + \frac{1}{P\eta} B_f'^2} \tag{9}$$

$$B_{dd} = \sqrt{(1 - \frac{1}{P\eta})B_d'^2 + 0.152 \cdot \frac{\pi R^2}{4}}, \; B_{ff} = \sqrt{(1 - \frac{1}{P\eta})B_f'^2 + 0.152 \cdot \frac{\pi R^2}{4}} \qquad (10)$$

Where P is the number of launcher that involved in the shooting, η is the channel number of each launcher, and R is the scatter radius of the child warhead, $\rho = 0.4769$.

To sum up, to calculate the minimum ammunition consuming for blocking the runway is as follows:

$$N_{\min} = round(N_{cw} * K/p_1), \quad K = \begin{cases} t, & forward\,attack \\ n, & lateral\,attack \end{cases} \qquad (11)$$

2.3   Calculate the Position of the Aiming Point

Assuming the airport runway as an even rectangular target, a Cartesian coordinate system can be established with the two adjacent sides of the rectangle being the X axis (length) and the Y axis(width). When an ammunition satisfies the blocking condition on the width-direction, i.e. $N_{cw} = 1$, the forward blockade aiming point is centrosymmetrical to (x, y), the central of the runway and evenly distributed on the length-direction at equal intervals. Then coordinates of the aiming point is:

$$\begin{cases} x_i = x + dx * (i - (K+1)/2) \\ y_i = y \end{cases}, \quad i = 1, 2, \ldots, K$$

When an ammunition cannot block the runway on the width-direction, i.e. $N_{cw} > 1$, the lateral blockade aiming point is symmetric to the forward blockade aiming point (x_i, y_i) and evenly distributed on the width-direction at equal intervals. The coordinates of the aiming point is:

$$\begin{cases} x_{cw_j} = x_i + dz * (j - (N_{cw}+1)/2) \\ y_{cw_j} = y_i \end{cases}, \quad j = 1, 2, \ldots, N_{cw} \qquad (13)$$

Where $K = \begin{cases} t, & forward\,attack \\ n, & lateral\,attack \end{cases}$, $dx = \begin{cases} h, & forward\,attack \\ I, & lateral\,attack \end{cases}$, $dz = \begin{cases} I, & forward\,attack \\ h, & lateral\,attack \end{cases}$.

2.4   Calculate the Ammunition Point of Fall

(1) Calculate the point of fall of the unguided integral ammunition (parent warhead)

Convert firing/aiming error, ground density (scatter error), and other intermediate error into mean square error, according to the following equation:

$$\sigma = 1.5 * E * D \qquad (14)$$

we can calculate $\sigma_{Ef}, \sigma_{Bf}, \sigma_{Ed}, \sigma_{Bd}$.

Where σ is mean square error; E is intermediate error, Respectively corresponding to E_f, E_d, B_f, B_d.

When the number of firing ammunition for once shooting is n, firing/aiming mean square error σ_{Ed}, σ_{Ef} is sampled one time according to normal distribution, and scatter mean square error σ_{Bd}, σ_{Bf} is sampled n times according to normal distribution. The landing error of the n_{th} ammunition is: $\left(\sigma_f^{(n)}, \sigma_d^{(n)}\right)$.

$$\sigma_f^{(n)} = \sqrt{\sigma_{Ef}^2 + \sigma_{Bf}^{(n)^2}}, \sigma_d^{(n)} = \sqrt{\sigma_{Ed}^2 + \sigma_{Bd}^{(n)^2}} \tag{15}$$

Project $\left(\sigma_f^{(n)}, \sigma_d^{(n)}\right)$ onto the X axes and Y axes from the distance-direction and the vertical-direction, so that we get $\left(\sigma_x^{(n)}, \sigma_y^{(n)}\right)$. (The distance-direction is the direction of the attachment wire between the fire unit and the target, and the vertical-direction is the one that is perpendicular to it.)

(2) Calculate the point of fall of the guided integral ammunition (parent warhead)

Convert the circular error probable (CEP) into mean square error, then,

$$\sigma_x = \sigma_y = 0.9CEP \tag{16}$$

When the number of firing ammunition for once shooting is n, scatter mean square error σ_x, σ_y is sampled n times according to normal distribution. The landing error of the n_{th} ammunition is: $\left(\sigma_x^{(n)}, \sigma_y^{(n)}\right)$.

To sum up, the coordinates of the n_{th} ammunition is:

$$\left(x_n = x_0 + \sigma_x^{(n)}, y_n = y_0 + \sigma_y^{(n)}\right) \tag{17}$$

Where (x_0, y_0) is the aiming point.

(3) Calculate the point of fall of the child warhead
If the type of ammunition is cluster warhead, then the point of fall of the child warhead can be calculated according to the point of fall of each parent warhead.
   (i) Calculate the point of fall of the guided child warhead.
       The point of fall of child warhead is distributed straightly along the direction of ATCT with a scatter interval of $2r_{zdsb}$, which is the scatter diameter of child warhead. The starting point is the point of fall of parent warhead.
   (ii) Calculate the point of fall of the unguided child warhead.
       The child warhead evenly distributed in a square with an edge of $\sqrt{\pi}r_{zdsb}$, which takes the point of fall of parent warhead as a center.

3 The Algorithm for Assessing the Functional Damage Impact of the Airport Runway

3.1 Basic Idea

Assuming the airport runway as a uniform rectangle, the Cartesian coordinate system can be established with two adjacent sides of the rectangle as the X and Y axes. We can build a grid network that can cover the runway. When the four vertices of the grid window which makes up the grid network are all inside the runway, go through all the point of fall of the ammunition. If there are no points of fall of ammunition in one grid window, then it is an effective landing window. Find the effective landing windows. If there is none, the runway is blocked. Otherwise, the blockade has failed, and the number of effective landing windows should be recorded. Assessment process is shown in Fig. 3.

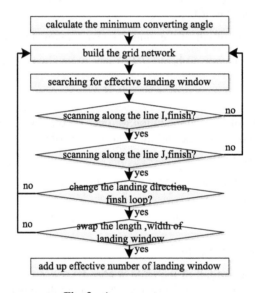

Fig. 3. Assessment process

3.2 Assessment Process

(1) Determine the minimum converting angle Δ_θ of the landing direction

Set the length of airport runway L, and the width of it W. Also, set the minimum length of landing window ξ, and the minimum width of it ω. The damage radius of ammunition is r. The length and width of the grid window are: $GridLong = \xi + 2 * r$, $GridWide = \omega + 2 * r$. Set the cycling flag $v = 1$ (v is a positive integer), the initial number of the runway windows $n_{ck} = 0$. Build the Cartesian coordinate system with two adjacent rectangular side as the X and Y axes, then the vertex coordinates in the clockwise direction of the airport runway is $(0,0)$, $(0,W)$, (L,W) and $(L,0)$.

According to the point of fall of every ammunition, the coordinate of the points of fall in the runway can be determined as $(x_1, y_1), \ldots, (x_n, y_n)$. Calculate the slope between any two points: $k_{ij} = \frac{y_i - y_j}{x_i - x_j}, i, j \in \{1, \ldots, n\}$.

The accordingly inclination angle is $\theta_{ij} = \arctan(k_{ij})$, then $\theta_{ij} \in (-\frac{\pi}{2}, \frac{\pi}{2}]$. Sort the angles in a descending order: $\theta_{(1)}, \ldots, \theta_{(m)}, \{m = \frac{n*(n-1)}{2}\}$. Calculate the difference of the two adjacent inclination angles after sorted, and denote the minimum difference as $\Delta_\theta > 0$.

(2) Build the grid network

Consider the two perpendicularly intersecting lines of the grid network. Denote the angle between the X-axis positive direction and one set of the lines (denoted as line J) as θ_{Jv}, and also denote the angle between the other set of the lines (denoted as line I) and the X-axis positive direction as $\theta_{Iv} = \frac{\pi}{2} + \theta_{Jv}$. According to the minimum difference Δ_θ, we can determine the inclination angle of the line J as $\theta_{Jv} = \frac{\pi}{2} - v * \Delta_\theta$.

Line J takes θ_{Jv} as the inclination angle to build the first grid line, with the point $(0, W)$ being the reference point, and builds the second grid line shifting to the right bottom with *GridWide* as an interval and so on. When the lines cover the airport runway area completely, the J lines are successfully built. The line I takes θ_{Iv} as an inclination angle, point $(0,0)$ as reference point, and *GridLong* as an interval to build grid network lines. It works like how we build line J. The grid network is shown in Fig. 4.

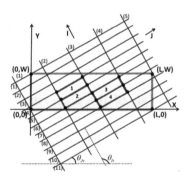

Fig. 4. Grid network

(3) Searching for effective landing window

Go through all the grid windows, When all of the four vertices of the window rectangle are in the airport area, see whether there are points of fall of ammunition in the window. If there is none, plus one to n_{ck}, and continue searching.

(4) Scanning along the line I

Move line J with an offset of r in the opposite direction of line I. Plus one to the offset number $J\_Advance$. When $J\_Advance > \omega/r + 1$, skip this step. Otherwise, rebuild the grid network and go to step (3).

(5) Scanning along the line J

Move line I with an offset of r in the direction of line J. Plus one to the offset number $I\_Advance$. If $I\_Advance > \xi/r + 1$, skip this step. Otherwise, make $J\_Advance = 0$, rebuild the grid network and go to step (3).

(6) Change the landing direction

Make $v + 1$. If $v > \frac{\pi}{2\Delta_\theta}$, skip this step. Otherwise, go to step (2).

(7) Swap the length and width of landing window

Swap the minimum length ξ and the minimum width ω of the runway landing window. Repeat the process above and sum the amount of landing windows of the two calculations, so that the damage situation of the runway can be determined and leveled. The level of damage is shown in Table 1.

Table 1. The level of damage

Amount of landing windows	Damage situation	Level of damage
0	Complete damage	4
1–4	Severe damage	3
5–10	Moderate damage	2
11–15	Minor damage	1
>15	No damage	0

4 The Results and Analysis of the Experiment

4.1 The Result of Simulation with Monte Carlo

Suppose that the airport runway is single-runway, with a length of $L = 3000$ m, and width of $W = 50$ m. The length of the minimum landing window is $\xi = 400$ m, and the width of it is $\omega = 25$ m. The distance between the firepower units and the airport runway is $D = 4800$ m.

Option one: Block the runway with guided cluster warhead. The *CEP* of the parent warhead is $CEP = 50$ m. The number of child warhead is 30. The damage radius of child warhead is $r' = 2$ m. The scatter radius of the child warhead is $r_{zdsb} = 40$ m.

Option two: Block the runway with guided integral ammunition. The *CEP* of the integral ammunition is $CEP = 50$ m, and the damage radius is $r = 40$ m.

Use different options to conduct the simulation experiment for 1000 times. Use traditional minimum landing and launching searching algorithms (considering only the paralleled landing windows) and the grid network algorithm to assess the damage situation of the airport runway. The results are shown in Tables 2 and 3.

Table 2. The grid network algorithm

Times		Level of damage					Blocking probability
		4	3	2	1	0	
Attack option	One	926	30	39	2	3	92.6 %
	Two	7	7	18	25	943	0.7 %

Table 3. Traditional searching algorithm

Times		Level of damage					Blocking probability
		4	3	2	1	0	
Attack option	One	988	7	3	1	1	98.8 %
	Two	72	93	98	119	618	7.2 %

4.2 Analysis

When using different options to block the airport runway, we can find out that for the ammunition that owns almost same capability of damage, the blocked effect is better when using the cluster warhead than the integral ammunition. Blocking the airport runway by cluster warhead is more efficient, while the consuming of the ammunition is lower. So it reduces the economic cost and can avoid duplication of hitting.

Using the traditional landing and launching searching algorithm to assess the airport runway may cause excessively high level of damage assessment due to large amount of oblique effective landing windows are not successfully identified. So the probability of the blockade is raised and the fidelity of the simulation is lowered. By the grid network scanning method, the oblique landing windows are quite identified, making up for deficiencies of the traditional window scanning algorithms not being able to recognize the oblique landing window. The grid network scanning algorithm is more strict in theory with higher precision, easier usage. And the fidelity of the simulation is improved.

5 Conclusion

According to the damage principle of the airport runway, this paper built a damage model of airport runway, and proposed a damage mechanism when attacking the airport runway. Focused on the issues that the traditional algorithms cannot quite identify the oblique landing windows, this paper proposed a minimum landing window searching algorithm based on grid network scanning. Through a series of experiments, we can see that this algorithm can precisely identify the oblique landing windows, and improve the fidelity of the simulation. Conducting experimental simulations by Monte Carlo method, this paper also analyzed damage situation about the airport runway destroyed by different types of ammunitions with the same damage ability. The results of the study provide as reference for the war.

References

1. Li, C.-G., et al.: Research on the series of existing window numbers of airport runway. Command Control Simul. **33**(6), 36–39 (2011)
2. Zhang, L.-Y., Wang, H., Han, Y.-J.: Study of damage simulation of penetration cluster warhead in blocking runway of airdrome. Tactical Missile Technol. **4**, 82–86 (2007)
3. Huang, H.-Y., Wang, Z.-M.: Calculation and analysis of the time of airstrips blockaded by cluster munitions. ACTA ARMAMENTARII **30**(3), 295–300 (2009)
4. Huang, H.-Y., et al.: Model for computing destruction probability of runway and calculating precision analyzing. J. Syst. Simul. **19**(12), 2661–2664 (2007)
5. Li, Z.-H., Ma, Y.-L.: Algorithms of blocking airdrome with cluster warhead. J. Syst. Simul. **18**(2), 862–864 (2006)
6. Yuan, Y.-J.: Research on destroy effectiveness of cluster warhead attacking the runway. Tactical Missile Technol. **1**, 34–37 (2000)
7. Su, G.-F., Wang, B.-S., Miao, Q.-G.: A study of the runway battle damage assessment. Fire Control Command Control **33**(11), 46–47 (2008)

A New Learning Method Study
of Military Simulation Data

Liang Tian[(⊠)], Shaojie Mao, and Shiqing Sun

Science and Technology on Information Systems Engineering Laboratory,
Nanjing, China
timoq2013@126.com

Abstract. In the paper, a new learning method is presented based on rough set (RS) and extreme learning machine (ELM) for military simulation system application. ELM is a recently proposed algorithm, which can random choose the parameters of hidden neurons and analytically determines the output weights of single-hidden layer feedforward neural networks (SLFNs). Multivariate discretization method is implemented to convert continuous military simulation data into discrete data firstly. RS is then employed to generate simple rules and to remove irrelevant attributes. Finally, ELM is used to evaluate the performance of the reduced data set. The experimental results demonstrate that with the help of RS strategy, our method can produce good enough generalization performance.

Keywords: Military simulation · Extreme learning machine · Rough set · Discretization

1 Introduction

In the future information based war, it is known that in the systems of all the services and arms an enormous potential of extractable information can exist. Information superiority and knowledge dominance are key points to win the future war. There has been a substantial growth in the amount of stored information in military systems, mainly due to the rapid development of military information construction. However, the large amount of stored data becomes impracticable for specialists to analyze through conventional methods.

We start this paper with a brief review of literatures related to research military data in Sect. 2. A description of the integrated methods is given in Sect. 3. Military simulation data preprocessing method is discussed in Sect. 4. Section 5 presents the experimental setup and details the results arrived at. Finally, Sect. 6 gives the conclusion.

2 Literature Review

Military data research has gained great importance and interest in recent years, especially in operations areas. To provide decision supports for commander, it is worth studying on how to effective learn massive data emerging in the operations. The data used in the equipment war gaming system are classified on the basis of introducing the

© Springer Science+Business Media Singapore 2016
L. Zhang et al. (Eds.): AsiaSim 2016/SCS AutumnSim 2016, Part II, CCIS 644, pp. 385–392, 2016.
DOI: 10.1007/978-981-10-2666-9_38

terms about Verification, Validation, Certification (VV&C), sort criterion of Authoritative Data Sources (ADS) is also put forward, as described by Wang et al. [1]. Li et al. [2] analyzed the characteristics of military data, according to the difference in data characteristics and functions for combat simulation, the methods to classify data based on their characteristics and functions were put forward, and the data sources for combat simulation were also discussed. Gao et al. [3] introduces a military simulation data aggregation framework of the extraction, transformation, transportation and loading (ETTL) based on MOM. As in [4], preliminary study on simulation data mining by rough set (RS) theory was done. RS enables finding the dependencies and the reduction of the number of attributes contained in military simulation data. Valuable results can be obtained by mining the battle simulation data, and the attributes which make a strong impact on performance of datasets learning can be found. However, given newly generated battle data, one cannot predict the classification results according to the method of [4].

Primary research of military simulation data has been done in the above literatures, and this paper will present deep research of military simulation data by integrated machine learning method: Extreme learning machine (ELM) and RS.

3 Integrated Methods

ELM [5–7] is a recently proposed machine learning algorithm to train neural network (NN) with only one hidden layer and the input weights and biases of the threshold networks in theory can be assigned randomly with continuous distribution probabilities. ELM algorithm can obtain good performance with high learning speed in many applications. In this work, RS theory is adopted to reduce the redundant attributes of military simulation dataset, and then ELM algorithm is employed to train this new dataset with optimal attributes subset.

3.1 ELM Review

For N arbitrary distinct samples $\{\mathbf{x}_i, t_i\}_{i=1}^{N}$, where $\mathbf{x}_i = [x_{i1}, x_{i2}, \ldots, x_{id}] \in \mathbb{R}^d$ and $t_i = [t_{i1}, t_{i2}, \ldots, t_{im}]^T \in \mathbb{R}^m$, a standard SLFNs with $\tilde{N}$ hidden nodes and activation function $g(x)$ are mathematically modeled as:

$$\sum_{i=1}^{\tilde{N}} \boldsymbol{\beta}_i g_i(\mathbf{x}_j) = \sum_{i=1}^{\tilde{N}} \boldsymbol{\beta}_i g_i(\mathbf{w}_i \cdot \mathbf{x}_j + b_i) = \mathbf{o}_j, \ j = 1, \ldots, N \tag{1}$$

Where $\mathbf{w}_i = [\mathbf{w}_{i1}, \mathbf{w}_{i2}, \ldots, \mathbf{w}_{id}]^T$ is the weight vector connecting the ith hidden node and the input nodes, $\boldsymbol{\beta}_i = [\beta_{i1}, \beta_{i2}, \ldots, \beta_{id}]^T$ is the weight vector connecting the ith hidden node and the output nodes, and b_i is the ith threshold of the hidden neuron, The standard SLFNs with $\tilde{N}$ hidden nodes and activation function $g(x)$ can approximate these N samples with zero error means that $\sum_{j=1}^{\tilde{N}} \|\mathbf{o}_j - \mathbf{t}_j\| = 0$. In this way there exists the parameter vector $\boldsymbol{\beta}_i$ such that:

$$\sum_{i=1}^{\tilde{N}} \beta_i g_i(\mathbf{w}_i \cdot \mathbf{x}_j + b_i) = \mathbf{t}_j, \quad j = 1, \ldots, N \tag{2}$$

and all N equations can then be written as the following matrix form:

$$\mathbf{H}\boldsymbol{\beta} = \mathbf{T} \tag{3}$$

where

$$
\begin{aligned}
&H(\mathbf{w}_1, \ldots, \mathbf{w}_{\tilde{N}}, b_1, \ldots, b_{\tilde{N}}, \mathbf{x}_1, \ldots, \mathbf{x}_{\tilde{N}}) \\
&= \begin{bmatrix} g(\mathbf{w}_1 \cdot \mathbf{x}_1 + b_1) & \cdots & g(\mathbf{w}_{\tilde{N}} \cdot \mathbf{x}_1 + b_{\tilde{N}}) \\ \vdots & \cdots & \vdots \\ g(\mathbf{w}_1 \cdot \mathbf{x}_N + b_1) & \cdots & g(\mathbf{w}_{\tilde{N}} \cdot \mathbf{x}_N + b_{\tilde{N}}) \end{bmatrix}_{N \times \tilde{N}}
\end{aligned} \tag{4}
$$

$$\boldsymbol{\beta} = [\boldsymbol{\beta}_1, \ldots, \boldsymbol{\beta}_{\tilde{N}}]^T \in \mathbb{R}^{\tilde{N} \times m}, \quad \mathbf{T} = [t_1, \ldots, t_{\tilde{N}}]^T \in \mathbb{R}^N \tag{5}$$

For given parameters $(\mathbf{w}_i, b_i)$, to train the SLFN is simply equivalent to find a least squares solution $\hat{\beta}$ of the linear system $\mathbf{H}\boldsymbol{\beta} = \mathbf{T}$ such that $\|\mathbf{H}\hat{\boldsymbol{\beta}} - \mathbf{T}\| = \min\|\mathbf{H}\boldsymbol{\beta} - \mathbf{T}\|$. The smallest norm least squares solution of the above linear system is:

$$\hat{\beta} = \mathbf{H}^{\dagger}\mathbf{T} \tag{6}$$

Where $\mathbf{H}^{\dagger}$ is the Moore-Penrose generalized inverse [8].

Thus a new learning method ELM can be summarized as follows:

Algorithm ELM

Input:

Given a training set $Z = \{(\mathbf{x}_i, t_i) \mid \mathbf{x}_i \in \Box^d, i = 1, \ldots, N\}$, activation function $g(x)$, and hidden node number $\tilde{N}$.

Training phase:

Step1: Randomly assign the weights $\mathbf{w}_i$ of input layer and the biases of output layer b_i, $i = 1, \ldots, N$.

Step2: calculate the hidden layer output matrix $\mathbf{H}$.

Setp3: Calculate the output weight $\boldsymbol{\beta}$ by $\boldsymbol{\beta} = \mathbf{H}^{\dagger}\mathbf{T}$, where $\mathbf{T} = [t_1, \ldots, t_N]^T$.

3.2 Rough Set

The notion of rough set (RS) theory was first introduced by Pawlak [9], which has become a popular pattern recognition tool for generating logical rules for prediction. It is widely recognized that rough set application have a great importance in various fields over the past decades, such as data mining and approximate reasoning, especially in the case of uncertain and incomplete data. Attribute reduction is one of the core contents in RS theory which means to find out the most informative attributes, remove the irrelevant or unimportant attributes with minimal information loss.

RS is the approximation of an uncertain set by a pair of precise concepts called lower and upper approximations. The lower approximation comprises of elements belonging to it, whereas the upper approximation of the set includes elements which are possible members of the set.

4 Data Preprocessing

The performance of the integrated method was evaluated on countermeasure simulation data of tank formation [4], which is exercised on medium undulating ground, hills, and Taiwan highland for digital armored battalion simulation system. The specification of the dataset is presented in Table 1.

Table 1. Parameters of simulation data

	W1	T1	S	V	W2	T2	F	P	R
1	Fine	Flat	Fast	More	Small	Short	Pool	Normal	High
2	Fog	Flat	Slow	Less	Small	Long	Better	Normal	High
3	Fine	Undulating	Slow	Less	Big	Long	Better	Normal	High
4	Fine	Flat	Slow	More	Small	Short	Better	Nervous	High
5	Fine	Undulating	Fast	Less	Big	Short	Better	Nervous	High
6	Fine	Flat	Fast	Less	Small	Short	Better	Normal	High
7	Fine	Undulating	Slow	More	Small	Short	Pool	Normal	Low
8	Fog	Flat	Fast	Less	Big	Long	Better	Nervous	Low
9	Fine	Undulating	Fast	Less	Big	Short	Pool	Nervous	Low
10	Fog	Flat	Slow	More	Small	Short	Pool	Nervous	Low
11	Fog	Undulating	Fast	Less	Small	Long	Better	Normal	Low
12	Fog	Flat	Fast	More	Big	Short	Pool	Normal	Low

From the Table 1, items 'W1', 'T1', …, 'Rc' represent 'Weather', 'Terrain', 'Speed', 'Vegetation', 'Wind', 'Time', 'Formation', 'psychology' respectively. ELM algorithm can be applied only to data sets composed of categorical attributes but attributes in Table 1 are continuous variables. Discretization process is important for char variables because it is less prone to variance in estimation from small fragmented data and it provides better performance for rule extraction. The main discretization process methods are: supervised [10], Hierarchical [11], Top-down [12] and multivariate [13]. The last one is employed in our work.

Multivariate discretization quantifies simultaneously multiple features. In the pre-processing phase, attribute 'Weather' is converted into two new attribute 'fine' and 'fog', which is shown in Table 2.

Table 2. Converted attribute of 'Weather'

Attribute	Fine	Fog
Weather = fine	1	0
Weather = fog	0	1

Based on examples shown in Table 2, other attributes are converted in Table 3.

Table 3. Discretization data set

W1		T1		S		V		W2		T2		F		P		R
1	0	1	0	1	0	1	0	1	0	0	1	0	1	1	0	1
0	1	1	0	0	1	0	1	1	0	1	0	1	0	1	0	1
1	0	0	1	0	1	0	1	0	1	1	0	1	0	1	0	1
1	0	1	0	0	1	1	0	1	0	0	1	1	0	0	1	1
1	0	0	1	1	0	0	1	0	1	0	1	1	0	0	1	1
1	0	1	0	1	0	0	1	1	0	0	1	1	0	1	0	1
1	0	0	1	0	1	1	0	1	0	0	1	0	1	1	0	0
0	1	1	0	1	0	0	1	0	1	1	0	1	0	0	1	0
1	0	0	1	1	0	0	1	0	1	0	1	0	1	0	1	0
0	1	1	0	0	1	1	0	1	0	0	1	0	1	0	1	0
0	1	0	1	1	0	0	1	1	0	1	0	1	0	1	0	0
0	1	1	0	1	0	1	0	0	1	0	1	0	1	1	0	0

5 Performance Evaluation

In our simulation study, sigmoid function is chosen for ELM algorithm with 6 hidden neurons. All the simulations are running in the MATLAB 6.5 (Windows version) environments with Intel 3.0 GHZ and 2G RAM. 20 repeated trials have been conducted for ELM on both original military simulation data set and reduced data set using RS strategy. The training data and testing data are randomly generated at each trial. For this problem, 50 % and 50 % samples are randomly chosen for training and testing at each trial, respectively. Correct classification rate (Testing accuracy) is used to evaluate the performance of all simulations.

5.1 Original Data Set Simulation

In this section, we first evaluate the performance of ELM classifiers on original military simulation data set, which is shown in Table 1. The simulation results are presented in Fig. 1.

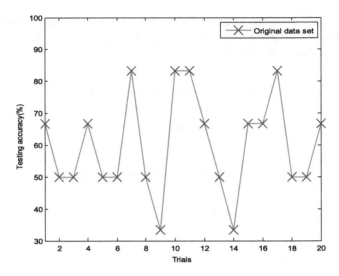

Fig. 1. Simulation results on original data set

From Fig. 1, in original data set simulations ELM can reach the testing accuracy no less than 50 % at 18 trials, and nearly half trials achieve 50 % testing accuracy. Generally speaking, the generalization performance of ELM on original data set is not so good.

5.2   Reduced Data Set Simulation

According to the RS strategy in [4], the number of attributes is reduced from 16 to 8 on military simulation data set, which is shown in Table 4. The simulation results are shown in Fig. 2.

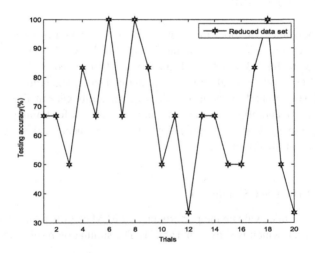

Fig. 2. Simulation results on reduced data set

Table 4. Reduced military simulation data set

W1		T1		S		F		R
1	0	1	0	1	0	0	1	1
0	1	1	0	0	1	1	0	1
1	0	0	1	0	1	1	0	1
1	0	1	0	0	1	1	0	1
1	0	0	1	1	0	1	0	1
1	0	1	0	1	0	1	0	1
1	0	0	1	0	1	0	1	0
0	1	1	0	1	0	1	0	0
1	0	0	1	1	0	0	1	0
0	1	1	0	0	1	0	1	0
0	1	0	1	1	0	1	0	0
0	1	1	0	1	0	0	1	0

From the Fig. 2, in the reduced data set simulations ELM can reach the testing accuracy no less than 83.33 % at 6 trials, which is better than 4 times obtained on original data set. The average testing accuracy over 20 trials is 66.667 %, while ELM classifier only achieves the average testing rate 60 % on original data set. This demonstrate that RS theory can significant improve the generalization performance of ELM algorithm.

6   Conclusions

This article has introduced an integrated learning method of RS and ELM for military simulation data set. ELM randomly chooses the input weights and analytically determines the output weights of SLFNs. Different from other learning algorithms, parameters in ELM classifier need not be tuned. The learning phase of ELM can be finished in less than seconds, and it can be used efficiently in real-time application. Significantly better results for the reduced data set are obtained by employing ELM classifier over crisp discretization. This method has the potential for further military application because it can provide real-time decision supports for commander in the battle.

References

1. Wang, L., Xue, Q., Meng, X.: The research of the data VV&C for the equipment war gaming based on the HLA. Comput. Eng. Appl. **21**, 200–202 (2006)
2. Li, M., Zhang, J., Che, W.: Research on data for combat simulation. Command Control Simul. **32**(4), 71–74 (2010)
3. Gao, H., Zhang, H., Chen, G., et al.: Research and implementation of military simulation. Fire Control Command Control **34**(2), 150–153 (2009)

4. Zhang, W.-m., Xue, Q.: Application of rough set in date mining of warfare simulation. J. Syst. Simul. **18**(2), 179–181 (2006)
5. Huang, G.-B., Siew, C.-K.: Extreme learning machine: RBF network case. In: Proceedings of International Conference on Control Automation, Robotics and Vision, pp. 1651–1663, December 2004
6. Huang, G.-B., Zhu, Q.-Y., Siew, C.-K.: Extreme learning machine: theory and applications. Neurocomputing **70**, 489–501 (2006)
7. Huang, G.-B., Chen, L., Siew, C.-K.: Universal approximation using incremental constructive feedforward networks with random hidden nodes. IEEE Trans. Neural Netw. **17**(4), 879–892 (2006)
8. Serre, D.: Matrices: Theory and Applications. Springer, New York (2002)
9. Pawlak, Z., Jerzy, G.B., Ziarkow, S.R.: Rough sets. Commun. ACM **38**(11), 89–95 (1995)
10. Dougherty, J., Kohavi, R., Sahami, M.: Supervised and unsupervised discretization of continuous features. In: Proceedings of the 12th International Conference on Machine Learning, pp. 194–202 (1995)
11. Kerber, R.: Discretization of numeric attributes. In: Proceedings of the Tenth National Conference on Artificial Intelligence, pp. 123–128. MIT Press, Cambridge (1992)
12. Hussain, F., Liu, H., Tan, C.L., Dash, M.: Discretization: an enabling technique. Technical report, School of Computing, Singapore, June 1999
13. Bay, S.: Multivariate discretization of continuous variables for set mining. In: Proceedings of the 6th ACM SIGKDD International Conference on Knowledge Discovery and Data Mining, pp. 315–319 (2000)

An OODA Loop-Based Function Network Modeling and Simulation Evaluation Method for Combat System-of-Systems

Zhe Shu[1(✉)], Quan Jia[2], Xiaobo Li[1], and Weiping Wang[1]

[1] College of Information Systems and Management,
National University of Defense Technology, Changsha, China
shuzhe7324175@gmail.com
[2] Nanjing Artillery Academy, The Chinese People's Liberation Army, Nanjing, China
jiaquan@nudt.edu.cn

Abstract. In this paper, we present a function network modeling technique and two capability evaluation indicators for combat system-of-systems (CSoS) based on OODA loop. The function network mainly describes the weapon entities and the function interaction between them, such as can-be-observed, can-orient, can-be-decided and can-act. After discussing the CSoS function network model and its generation algorithm, two indicators are proposed to evaluate CSoS capability. A case study on air strike CSoS modeling and simulation analysis is presented to validate proposed method and the indicators. Results show that the number of OODA loops is positively relevant to the CSoS capability, and entropy *TE* reflects the distribution of OODA loops covering enemy targets.

Keywords: OODA loop · Combat system-of-systems · Function network · Simulation · Evaluation indicator

1 Introduction

Under the condition of informationization, lots of information has penetrated to military actions so that different services, different combat units and different platforms on both sides of the campaign will be effective through information and become an effective, optimized integration. Neither will the Combat be a confrontation between a single branch of the military, nor between one combat unit or element any more. The future combat has almost all the characteristics of system-of-systems.

To understand the essence of the war, Boyd [1] defines a conceptual model as an "OODA" loop, which is short for observe, orient, decide and act. The OODA loop is deemed as a basic model to reveal the mechanism of combat system-of-systems (CSoS), and used widely in all levels and aspects of the war. Besides the OODA loop can not only describe and analyze the internal operational combat units' behavior, but also can be used to describe the interaction relationship between combat units. While OODA processes are neither described in detail nor formalized in any of Boyd's writings, and there is no precise introduction how to evaluate OODA loop.

© Springer Science+Business Media Singapore 2016
L. Zhang et al. (Eds.): AsiaSim 2016/SCS AutumnSim 2016, Part II, CCIS 644, pp. 393–402, 2016.
DOI: 10.1007/978-981-10-2666-9_39

The function network mainly describes the weapon entities and the function inter-action between them, such as can-be-observed, can-orient, can-be-decided and can-act. Combined with OODA loop, the function network can formalize CSoS to serve the system-of-system configuration design, evaluation, optimization, and other similar issues.

In this paper, a function network model is proposed based on OODA loop. According to the OODA loop concepts, there are presenting precise definition of CSoS function network model and three evaluating indicators to appraising the CSoS capability. A case on air strike is demonstrated to validate the application efficiency of the evaluating indi-cators in supporting the appraisals of CSoS capability.

2   Related Works

The OODA Loop was first proposed by U.S. Air Force Colonel John Boyd in the mid-1950s. Boyd took from his study the lesson that faster detection of the enemy's actions, assessment of their implications, and decision on how to respond could convey a significant combat advantage. This idea resonated with military thinkers around the world and there go a lot of follow-on models to modify OODA loop. This section reviews most modified OODA models and divided them into two categories, cognitive OODA model and combat OODA model.

2.1   Cognitive OODA Modeling

The cognitive OODA models pay more attention to decision making and C2 progress, with particular emphasis on extending the OODA model, including:

Keus [2] extends OODA to cooperative team working by embedding team func-tioning processes such as information distribution, task allocation, task balancing, authorization (of actions), and team assessment.

Bryant [3] considers OODA outdated as a model of human cognition. Based on advances in the cognitive sciences, such as goal-directed cognition, constructivist theo-ries of understanding, mental models, and critical thinking, Bryant proposes the Critique-Explore-Compare-Adapt (CECA) as a better descriptive model.

Rousseau and Breton [4] modify the OODA based on three principles: modularity, explicit feedback loops, and provision for team decision-making. Each module is a task-goal directed activity formed of Process, State and Control components.

Breton and Rousseau [5] expands each of the four processes in the M-OODA model to increase the level of cognitive granularity. Expansion incorporates theories and models from SA and RPDM, resulting in a Cognitive OODA (C-OODA) model of indi-vidual decision-makers.

Brehmer [6] proposes an amalgamation of Boyd's OODA model and the cybernetic approach, called Dynamic OODA (D-OODA). Brehmer notes that discussion of speed in the context of OODA focuses on one aspect: fast decision-making5. By contrast, cybernetic models include a representation of the environment that is affected by the decision-maker's actions. D-OODA preserves the prescriptive richness of the cybernetic approach in that it represents all the sources of delay in the C2 process. Moreover, D-OODA adds planning and sense-making to the original four OODA processes.

2.2 Combat OODA Modeling

The combat OODA models care more about the behavior of the whole, with particular emphasis on extending the OODA model, are including:

Jeffrey [7, 8] presented an information age combat model, which classified the forces in the battlefield into sensors, decision organs, influence organs and targets. And then he established a network model describing the relationships between these four parts in terms of information flow. Finally it made matrix analysis and operational evaluation of its system structures and their dynamics. Among them, the existed loops in the network in divided into four types.

Dr. Santiago [9] in Georgia Institute of Technology proposed a Digraph Modeling for Architectures on the basis of Cares' model. The model was established on the following two assumptions: the spectrum signature of system function diagram is relevant to the capacity of accomplishing a specific task; the centrality of the entity in function charts is relevant to the importance of modeling. The importance here refers to the contribution that the entity made on the overall structure. The impact of the changes in such entity behaviors on the architecture capacity is huge.

Michael points out that one of the difficulties in establishing the measurement of NCW [10–12] is the fact that NCW is a multifaceted issue involving technology, organizational structure, allegations and human factors (such as cognition and decision-making). A useful and comprehensive NCW measurement should not only be able to capture the degree distribution of the network, network topology and communication mode, but also includes situation communion levels and the quality of decisions which depend on the information provided by the network.

2.3 Summary

The modeling methods described in this section are pioneer and model of quantitative analysis in OODA modeling and evaluating. Based on the comparison of OODA with other process models and other authors' extensions of OODA, we could conclude that these models portray OODA loops from various dimensions, while they also have some limitations like that modeling methods can only model CSoS, but rarely analyze CSoS based on models.

3 Function Network Model and Evaluating Indicators

3.1 Function Network Modeling Based on OODA Loop

The modern combat loop theory deems that combat operation is an OODA loop involving observation, orientation, decision and action. Each combat side has a number of combat entities, such as sensor entity, control entity and engagement entity in Fig. 1.

- Sensor Entity: Weapons and equipments that carry out reconnaissance, monitoring and early warning missions, such as reconnaissance satellites, radar and etc.
- Control Entity: Weapons and equipments that carry out control and command missions, such as C4ISR, control vehicles and control centers etc.
- Engagement Entity: Weapons and equipment that carry out fire attack and electromagnetic interference missions, such as fighters, frigates, missiles and tanks etc.

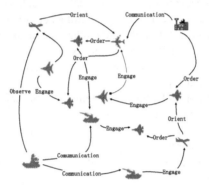

Fig. 1. A schematic diagram of CSoS

Then we can define four functions referring "can be observed", "can orient", "can be decided" and "can act" within these entities.

- Can Be Observed: Function that one side entities can be observed or detected by the other side sensor entities.
- Can Orient: Function that the same side sensor entities gather information to control entities or the communication between control entities.
- Can Be Decided: Function that the same side engagement entities can be ordered by control entities.
- Can Act: Function that one side engagement entities can attack the other side entities.

So we can abstract CSoS into a function network, which is delivered as $G = (N, E)$, where N is the set of nodes, and E is the set of functions between nodes. Furthermore, we can divide the N set into sensor nodes set, control nodes set and engagement nodes set, such as:

$$N = \{n_{s_1}^b, n_{s_2}^b, \ldots, n_{s_k}^b, n_{s_1}^r, n_{s_2}^r, \ldots, n_{s_i}^r, n_{c_1}^b, n_{c_2}^b, \ldots, n_{c_l}^b, n_{c_1}^r, n_{c_2}^r, \ldots, n_{c_j}^r, n_{e_1}^b, n_{e_2}^b, \ldots, n_{e_h}^b, n_{e_1}^r, n_{e_2}^r, \ldots, n_{e_g}^r\} \qquad (1)$$

where r is short for red side, b is short for blue side. Then s, c, e represent sensor, control and engagement nodes. While $i, j, k, l, h, g \in Q$ mean the numbers of nodes. The E set is a directed function set which exhibits the function relationship between different function nodes.

In the real world, a CSoS consists of thousands of entities and the interaction between entities is complicated and various. In order to study the law and rules hided in the CSoS, we make an algorithm of generating a CSoS function network as Fig. 2 showed. Since the OODA loop is studying the problem of CSoS against combat, the CSoS function network model should combine both side of red and blue in order to researching the against process.

Algorithm 1 Generation Algorithm for CSOS Function Network

Initialize

M_{num}: The number of the layer of control entities;
S: The set of all sensor entities;
S_{num}: The number of the sensor entity;
C: The set of all control entities;
C_0: The initial number of control entity;
C_{num}: The number of the control entity;
E: The set of all engagement entities;
E_{num}: The number of the engagement entity;
$P_{observed}$: The set of the probability of all the other side entities being observed by sensor entities;
P_{orient}: The set of the probability of sensor entities orienting all the same side control entities;
$P_{decided}$: The set of the probability of engagement entities being ordered by the same side control entities;
P_{act}: The set of the probability of engagement entities attacking all the other side entities
p_{o1}: The postulate standard probability of observation;
p_{o2}: The postulate standard probability of communication;
p_d: The postulate standard probability of decision making;
p_a: The postulate standard probability of attacking;
l: The layer label of each control entity;
$l \in M_{num}$;
Set $l = 1$;
Create C_0 control entities;
Add new created C_{num} entities into C;
Create S_{num} sensor entities;
Add new created S_{num} entities into S;
Create E_{num} engagement entities;
Add new created E_{num} entities into E;
While $l < M$ **do**
  For each control entity in the C_l set **do**
    Create new control entities;
    Add new created control entities into C_{l+1} set;
    Update C set;
  End Loop
  For each control entities in C set **do**
    If $p_{o2} < P_{C_{num}} \in P_{orient}$ **do**
      Add directed edges between control entities;
    Else
  End Loop
  For each sensor entities in S set **do**
    If $p_{o1} < P_{S_{num}} \in P_{observed}$ **do**
      Add directed edges from the observed entities to sensor entities;
    Else
  End Loop
  For each control entities in C set **do**
    If $p_d < P_{C_{num}} \in P_{decided}$ **do**
      Add directed edges from control entities to the same side engagement entities;
    Else
  End Loop
  For each engagement entities in E set **do**
    If $p_a < P_{E_{num}} \in P_{act}$ **do**
      Add directed edges between control entities;
    Else
  End Loop
  Update CSOSFN

Fig. 2. A generation algorithm for CSoSFN

3.2 Number Measurement of OODA Loop

Doctor Santiago [13] has mentioned in his dissertation that the spectrum signature of system function diagram is relevant to the capacity of accomplishing a specific task, proved the capability of eliminating the enemy unit can be estimated by measuring how many activity loops there are for the blues versus the reds through calculating the largest eigenvalue of its adjacency matrix, and demonstrated through the use of an agent-based simulation developed in NetLogo. Whereas, when applying this method to computing the capability of an architecture is to avoid overestimating the significance of the non-contributing loops, he pointed out that the contributing loops are determined by calculating the net λ_1, $\lambda_{1,net}$, as described in Eq. 2, where $\lambda_{1,inert}$ is the contribution to the λ_1 from the joint communication and order networks, since by themselves loops of these functions can exist, but produce no capability.

$$\lambda_{1,net} = \lambda_1 - \lambda_{1,inert} \tag{2}$$

After testing this method in Matlab, the conclusion is that there is just a positive correlation between λ_1 and loops, no linear correlation. The method of linear subtraction is not suitable for calculating the loops. Furthermore, the spectrum analysis of the adjacency matrix is just on a single time section, but the CSoS, which is evolving itself during the interaction, will have different adjacency matrix.

Therefore, based on the CSoS function network an algorithm is proposed to counting out the loops of both reds and blues, filtering the contributing loops and distinguishing the side with the simulation time step, as Fig. 3 showed.

```
Algorithm 2 Measurement Algorithm for OODA loop
1.  Initialization:
    Initialize CSOSFN of red and blue side;
    Mark both side nodes as S_red, C_red, E_red, S_blue, C_blue and E_blue;
2.  Loop Counting
    Set N as the number of all nodes;
    Set M as the number of counting loops;
    Set i as The starting point for the calculation of the number of loops;
   function circle_num = find_circle( M,u0,u,visit,circle_num,n )
      for i=1:N
         if M(u,i)==1
            if visit(i)==0;
               visit(i)=1;
               circle_num=find_circle(M,u0,i,visit,circle_num,n);
            end
            if visit(i)==1;
               if i==u0
                     circle_num=circle_num+1;
                     continue;
               else
                     continue;
               end
            end
         end
      end
      visit(u)=0;
      return M;
      end
3.  Loop Filtering
    Set N_j as the nodes collection of loop j, j ∈ M;
    Set M̃ as the number of filtering loops;
    for j=1:M
       if N_circle_num ∈ the same side;
          delete j;
       else
          continue;
       end
    end
    return M̃;
    end
4.  Loop Distinguishing
    Set R_k as the number of red nodes in loop k;
    Set B_k as the number of blue nodes in loop k;
     k ∈ M̃;
     Set M̃_red as the number of red loops;
     Set M̃_blue as the number of blue loops;
     for k=1:M̃
        if R_k > B_k;
           set M̃_red ← M̃_red +1;
        else
           set M̃_blue ← M̃_blue +1;
        end
        return M̃_red and M̃_blue;
        end
```

Fig. 3. A measurement algorithm for OODA loops

3.3 Load Balanced Analysis of OODA Loop

Measuring loops can get the situation that the red side weapons systems fall into the blue side OODA loops, while the number of some loops may be more and others are little, which led to redundancy or inadequate of the loops. Therefore it's need to make load balanced analysis to determine whether the number of loops is distributed evenly. In this study the distribution of entropy is proposed to measure the distribution of OODA loops.

Give the blue side loop length of up to L, set I as the number of the red side weapon systems, set n_i^L as the number of the blue side OODA loops which the red side weapon system i falls into, set p_i as described in Eq. 3.

$$p_i = n_i^L \bigg/ \sum_i^I n_i^L \tag{3}$$

Therefore the distribution of entropy is calculated in Eq. 4.

$$TE = -\sum_{i=1}^{I} p_i \ln p_i \tag{4}$$

where the more entropy TE goes, the better OODA loops' load is evenly distributed.

4   Case Study on Air Strike

The validity of two evaluation index as a measure of the ability of architectures to achieve a capability was studied by comparing the networks' index to an agent-based simulation created in MASS, which is short for multi-agent simulation system. MASS is driven by the time step and random multi-task oriented layer model for the evaluation of the use of C4ISR. And then, each agent runs commands in parallel threads of execution and follows the encoded cognitive code to control its behavior.

Based on MASS, an operation simulation scenario is proposed as an air strike happening in Iraq 2003 [14]. As shown in Fig. 4, the blue side is consisted of US - led multinational coalition, and the red is Iraqi air defenses. There is the force attachment for both in Fig. 5.

Fig. 4. A map of combat scenario situation. (Color figure online)

Due to the probabilistic nature of the modeling methodology, its ability to capture indicators cannot be studied by analyzing the CSoS function network, but a large number of function networks must be generated and analyzed to obtain statistical significance on the number of OODA loops. This means that the number of OODA loops for a given force structure are not a single value, but a distribution and therefore, when comparing

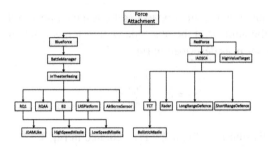

Fig. 5. A map of force attachment

the capability of a series of competing forces, it is not a trivial comparison between a handful of values. Meanwhile, for each function network, the entropy *TE* is unique.

In this case, recording the simulation process data and results, we can analyze the data to make some meaningful and interesting results. As shown in Fig. 6, comparing the number of OODA loops for the red and blue, the blue loops get earlier to the top than the red, and the number of blue loops is much higher than the red. In the end, the result shows that the red goes none and the blue survives, which is validated by the simulation result.

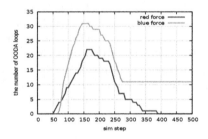

Fig. 6. A comparison of OODA loop of two side. (Color figure online)

An additional observation worth mentioning is shown in Fig. 7. We compare the results of different function networks, which have different target distribution for OODA loops, and the number of OODA loops. There are little singular points, which have OODA loops less than 10 in the picture, meaning that the less entropy *TE* comes into the decrease of the number of OODA loops.

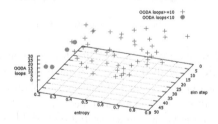

Fig. 7. A distribution of entropy *TE*

5   Conclusions and Future Work

In this paper, we propose the function network model for CSoS based on OODA loop. The function network is modeled within the Boyd's OODA conception in order to benefit from the capacity of representation of complex and dynamic situations and to keep explicit the notion of control inherent to the OODA loop model.

Meanwhile, a methodology to efficiently estimate the capability of CSoS has been described and demonstrated using a military proof-of-concept. The methodology incorporates OODA products and requires minimum effort to implement and execute the models, making it ideal to precisely evaluate a CSoS. The validity of using the number of OODA loops as a measure of CSoS's ability to achieve a capability has been demonstrated through the use of an agent-based simulation developed in MASS. Also, we have found some meaningful conclusion with the entropy *TE*.

As a final note, there may exist a calculating problem when the node of CSoS makes exponential explosion. Research efforts indicate that more information about the figures are contained about the relationship between indicators. This provides a large set of possible future avenues of research. Future work will focus in mining the relationships on the simulation process data.

References

1. Boyd, J.: A discourse on winning and losing. Maxwell Air Force Base, Air University Library Document, No. M-U, 43947, AL (1987)
2. Keus, H.E.: A Framework for Analysis of Decision Processes in Teams. TNO Physics and Electronics lab Hague (Netherlands) (2002)
3. Bryant, D.J.: Critique, Explore, Compare, and Adapt (CECA): A New Model For Command Decision Making. Defence Research Development, Toronto (2003)
4. Rousseau, R., Breton, R.: The M-OODA: a model incorporating control functions and teamwork in the OODA loop. In: Proceedings of the 2004 Command and Control Research Technology Symposium (2004)
5. Breton, R., Rousseau, R.: The C-OODA: a cognitive version of the OODA loop to represent C2 activities. In: Proceedings of the 10th International Command and Control Research Technology Symposium (2005)
6. Brehmer, B.: The dynamic OODA loop: amalgamating Boyd's OODA loop and the cybernetic approach to command and control. In: Proceedings of the 10th International Command and Control Research Technology Symposium, pp. 365–368 (2005)
7. Cares, J.R.: An Information Age Combat Model. Produced for the United States Office of the Secretary of Defense, USA (2004)
8. Cares, J.R.: The use of agent-based models in military concept development. In: WSC 2002. IEEE (2002)
9. Robinson, S.B., Li, Y., Nixon, J.N., et al.: Model Development of Large-Scale DoD System-of-Systems (2008)
10. Kilicay-Ergin, N., Dagli, C.: Executable modeling for system of systems architecting: an artificial life framework. In: 2008 IEEE 2nd Annual Systems Conference, pp. 1–5. IEEE (2008)
11. Kleijnen, J.P.C., Sargent, R.G.: A methodology for fitting and validating metamodels in simulation. Eur. J. Oper. Res. **120**(1), 14–29 (2000)

12. Starbird, S.A.: A metamodel specification for a tomato processing plant. J. Oper. Res. Soc. **41**, 229–240 (1990)
13. Balestrini, R.S.: A modeling process to understand complex system architectures (2009)
14. Biltgen, P.T.: A methodology for capability-based technology evaluation for systems-of-systems. Georgia Institute of Technology (2007)

Ontology Based Semantic Interoperation in Warfare Simulation

Chunguang Peng[⊠], Jianhui Deng, and Bo Zhang

Navy Arming Academe Postdoctoral Workstation, Beijing, China
ml5201116679@163.com

Abstract. Interoperation in warfare simulation actually represents that between the military field and the simulation field. The key problem in warfare simulation is that how military users can interact with simulation systems "naturally", namely how to realize the semantic interoperation. An ontology is a formal, explicit specification of a shared conceptualization, which can be used to resolve heterogeneous problems in information systems. First, three ontology-based interoperation approaches was evaluated and compared. Then, a new approach-Ontology based Online Semantic Interoperation was proposed. At last, an example was given to illustrate the approach.

Keywords: Interoperation · Warfare simulation · Ontology · Semantic

1 Introduction

As an important part of interoperation in warfare simulation, information interactions between the military field and the simulation field bridge military users and simulation systems. Currently, information interactions haven't employ natural languages completely, but adopt a type of middle language in terms of the real needs, such as HLA-SOM/FOM, ENA-LROM and so on. Semantic processing is taking a more and more important role, while syntactic processing is dominant currently. Ontology plays an important role in the process and provides a common and middle language for various interactions (human-system interactions or system-system interactions) [1, 2]. According to same ontology models, experts in different fields can come to an agreement on domain concepts and understand each other more easily, which provides the necessary condition for the cooperation of human and systems.

Interoperation in warfare simulation actually represents that between the military field and the simulation field. On this base, we brought an ontology based semantic method for warfare simulation interoperation. Section 2 describes the concepts of ontology. Section 3 describes three different ontology interoperation approaches. Section 4 presents two semantic interoperation methods based on ontology mappings. Section 5 gives an example to illustrate the method in Sect. 4. Finally, Sect. 6 concludes and presents the future research.

L. Zhang et al. (Eds.): AsiaSim 2016/SCS AutumnSim 2016, Part II, CCIS 644, pp. 403–412, 2016.
DOI: 10.1007/978-981-10-2666-9_40

2   Ontology Based Semantic Interoperation Approach

The popular definition of "ontology" is described by Studer in [3]: An ontology is a formal, explicit specification of a shared conceptualization. In nearly all ontology–based information systems, ontologies are used for the explicit description of the information semantics. But the way, how the ontologies are employed, can be different. In general, three different directions can be identified: Single Ontology Approaches, Multiple Ontology Approaches and Hybrid Ontology Approaches [4]. Therefore, there are also three different ontology-based interoperation modes in simulation systems, which can be used to solve problems of different levels.

2.1   Single Ontology Approaches

Single Ontology Approaches use one global ontology providing a shared vocabulary for the specification of the semantics (Fig. 1a). All information sources are related to one global ontology, which provides a uniform domain view for users.

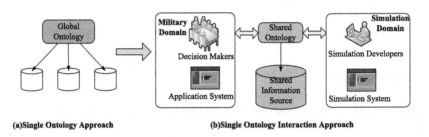

Fig. 1. Single ontology approaches

The global ontology based on shared domain information sources provides a global vocabulary and semantic specification for users in both military and M&S(Modeling and Simulation) domains. Users interact with system in the "same languages" (Fig. 1b). The construction of Single Ontology Approaches is simple but not adaptive dynamically. For example, if each domain view is different from each other, it's too complex to construct a common and minimal ontology commitment.

2.2   Multiple Ontology Approaches

In Multiple Ontology Approaches, each information source is described by its own ontology (Fig. 2a). Each local ontology interacts with each other through ontology mappings.

The advantage of Multiple Ontology Approaches is that no common and minimal ontology commitment about one global ontology is needed. Each source ontology can be developed without respect to other sources or their ontologies. This ontology architecture can simplify the integration task and supports the change, i.e. the adding and

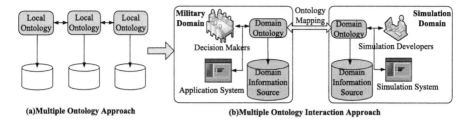

(a)Multiple Ontology Approach   **(b)Multiple Ontology Interaction Approach**

Fig. 2. Multiple ontology approaches

removing, of sources. For example, we can use CPR(Core Plan Representation) [5] and DeMO (Discrete Event Modeling Ontology) [6] to describe concepts in military and M&S domains, which will reduce the development and management work of ontology (Fig. 2b). The key of Multiple Ontology Approaches is to define the inter-ontology mapping. The inter-ontology mapping identifies semantically corresponding terms of different source ontologies. In practice the inter-ontology mapping is very difficult to define. It often depends on the quality of each domain ontology and mapping methods.

2.3   Hybrid Ontology Approaches

To overcome the drawbacks of the Single or Multiple Ontology Approaches, Hybrid Ontology Approaches were developed (Fig. 3a).

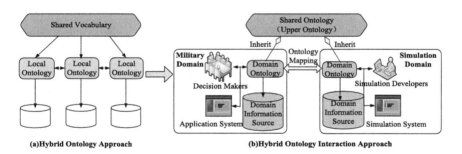

(a)Hybrid Ontology Approach   **(b)Hybrid Ontology Interaction Approach**

Fig. 3. Hybrid ontology approaches

Similar to Multiple Ontology Approaches the semantics of each source is described by its own ontology. But in order to make the local ontologies comparable to each other they are built from a global shared vocabulary. The shared vocabulary contains basic terms (the primitives) of a domain which are combined in the local ontologies in order to describe more complex semantics. Sometimes the shared vocabulary is also an ontology. There are ontologies in military and M&S domains respectively, but these ontologies are based on the global vocabularies including shared and essential concepts, which can simplify inter-ontology mappings (Fig. 3 b).

Recently, various ontologies have been developed in different fields. However, none of these fields has been able, on its own, to construct a standard, upper-level ontology. SUMO [7] (Suggested Upper Merged Ontology) is sponsored by IEEE SUO Working Group. The SUMO provides a foundation for middle-level and domain ontologies, and its purpose is to promote data interoperability, information retrieval, automated inference, and natural language processing. The SUMO consists of approximately 4,000 assertions (including over 800 rules) and 1,000 concepts.

There are some distinct advantages of the SUMO. First, developers need not start building specific ontologies from scratch, but they based on common and standard ontologies-SUMO. Second, they can build ontology mapping easily. SUMO may facilitate the matching level of models, and eliminate the heterogeneity of ontologies.

In general, Single Ontology Approaches need application fields associate with each other closely, which are not flexible and can't adapt to large and open environment. Once new sources are added, the global ontology should be changed. Nevertheless, the knowledge in application fields is not so restricted in Multiple Ontology Approaches and Hybrid Ontology Approaches. The approaches need effective ontology mappings. In addition, if ontologies are built based on common ontologies (SUMO), ontology mappings can be simplified.

3   Ontology Mapping Based Semantic Interaction Approach

This section introduces two types of semantic interoperation based on ontology mappings: Ontology Driven Simulation (ODS) and Ontology based Semantic Interoperation Online (OSIO).

3.1   Ontology Driven Simulation

ODS suggests a technique that establishes relationships between domain ontologies and a modeling ontology and then uses the relationships to instantiate a simulation model as ontology instances [8]. Techniques for translating these instances into XML based markup languages and then into executable models for various software packages are also presented.

ODS can be considered as an offline process of semantic interoperation. By using ODS, modelers can build simulation models effectively. The whole process can be divided into three phrases, as depicted in Fig. 4.

1. Mapping Phrase
   In this phrase, developers can create mappings between domain ontologies and modeling ontologies (e.g. DeMO). While these mappings are, on a technical level, similar to the mappings that often occur between domain ontologies, their purpose is different. The mappings that occur between domain ontologies are typically used to establish relationships (such as equivalence and subsumption) between two or more concepts. The concepts being mapped in ODS do not necessarily have obvious relatedness. In this case, relatedness will often not produce equivalences or subsumptions but rather connects concepts as analogs. These mappings are not

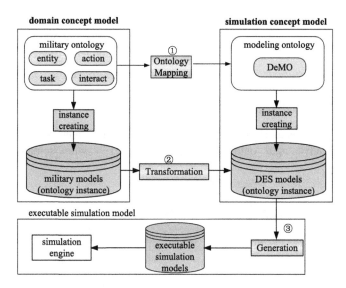

Fig. 4. Process of ODS

typically created during model composition but are created as a collaborative effort between domain experts and simulation experts prior to the development of models. While the primary purpose of these mappings is to facilitate ODS, they also have the side benefit of providing formalized documentation of the model development process.

2. Transformation Phases

   In this phrase, instances from domain ontologies are translated into instances that are used to represent a simulation model. Take an example for DeMO, instances from domain ontologies should be translated to DeMO instances based on different simulation strategies (e.g. Petri or Markov models).

3. Generation Phases

   After the transformation is complete, these instances generated can be used generate an executable simulation model, which is related with special simulation engines.

   The benefits of ODS are concluded as below:

1. Model developers and users have an agreed upon set of terms and concepts available throughout the development and use of a simulation model. This facilitates good communication between all of the entities involved in a simulation study and reduces the incidence of ambiguities.

4. DES(Discrete Event Simulation) models targeted for various simulation software packages or developed using various simulation world views can be represented in a common language.

5. Since models can be represented in a Semantic Web enabled language, the possibility exists for Web based DES model repositories.

6. Since much of the knowledge needed to develop a simulation model exists in the domain and the modeling ontologies, ODS is able to speed up model development by allowing the developer to assemble ontology components to create a model.

3.2   Ontology Based Semantic Interoperation Online

ODS can be considered as an offline process of semantic interoperation. Similarly, based on their advantages, ontologies can also be used in online semantic interoperation (Fig. 5).

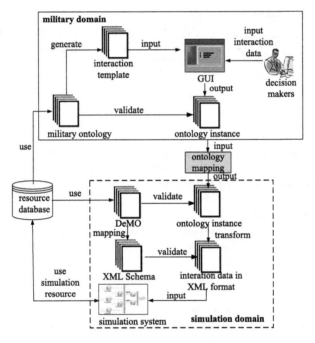

Fig. 5. Process of OSIO

OSIO works in both military and M&S fields. First, in the military field, some interaction templates are generated in terms of military ontologies. Decision-makers should fill in templates within the interface to generate ontology instances which can be validated according to their ontologies. Second, similar to ODS, military ontology instances are transformed to modeling ontology instances by ontology mappings. At last, in M&S field, modeling ontology instances should also be validated according to their ontologies. It is optional that ontology instances can be transformed to XML data with Ontology-Schema algorithms. Then XML Schema can be used to validate XML data. After that, the correct interaction data can be input to the system.

In OSIO, domain experts in both fields can use their own terms and concepts, which may reduce different meanings of the same thing and facilitate the reuse of domain models. Within the ontology reasoning, interaction data can be validated automatically, which is more efficient than checking manually.

It is noticed that modeling ontology instances can be transformed to XML data. The reason is that an ontology is different from a database schema. The differences are:

2. A language for defining ontologies is syntactically and semantically richer than common approaches for databases.
7. The information that is described by an ontology consists of semi-structured natural language texts and not tabular information.
8. An ontology must be a shared and consensual terminology because it is used for information sharing and exchange.
9. An ontology provides a domain theory but not the structure of a data container.

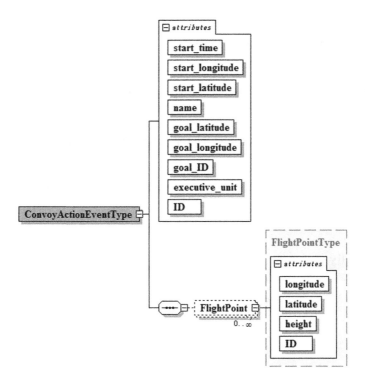

Fig. 6. Definition of ConvoyActionEventType in XML schema

4   Example

As an example, a model named Convoy Action is provided to illustrate OSIO. Decision-makers input an order (Convoy) to some unit in the simulation system. The Convoy Action class consists of a series of data properties, such as ID, name, start_longitude, goal_latitude, goal_ID, executive_unit and so on. There is also an object property-"has path". The domain of the property is Action, and the range is another class-FlightPoint. Properties of FlightPoint include properties as below: ID, longitude, latitude and height.

Decision-makers set values of these properties to generate the ontology instance. Since tasks in military domains can be considered simulation events, the ConvoyAction ontology is mapped to ConvoyActionEvent class (a subclass of Event in DeMO). We suppose that ConvoyActionEvent has same properties with ConvoyAction ontology, which will not affect the result. The ConvoyAction instance is described in A Appendix.

Figure 6 describes the XML Schema of ConvoyActionEvent generated by its ontology model. The Schema can remain the whole concept construction. Then the ontology instance is transformed into XML data (A Appendix).

It is obvious that the interaction data in XML format eliminate redundant terms in ontology languages, which is more concise, human-readable, and efficient to transfer.

5   Conclusions and Future Work

This paper represents the semantic interoperation in warfare simulation. By analyzing three different Ontology-based interaction approaches: Single Ontology Approaches, Multiple Ontology Approaches and Hybrid Ontology Approaches, we present the semantic interoperation method based on ontology mappings: Ontology Driven Simulation and Ontology based Semantic Interoperation Online. In the end, an example is discussed to describe OSIO method.

Future work includes the research on the ontology reasoning. The problem is how to use the ontology reasoning to validate the concepts and relations in domain ontologies.

A Appendix

The ConvoyAction instance is described as below:

```
<ConvoyAction rdf:ID="Action0201">
  <ID xml:lang="en">0201</ID>
  <start_longitude
rdf:datatype="http://www.w3.org/2001/XMLSchema#float">110.49</start_longitude
>
  <goal_latitude
rdf:datatype="http://www.w3.org/2001/XMLSchema#float">22.43</goal_latitude>
  <name
rdf:datatype="http://www.w3.org/2001/XMLSchema#string">Convoy</name>
  <goal_ID
rdf:datatype="http://www.w3.org/2001/XMLSchema#string">Airspace6</goal_ID>
  <start_latitude
rdf:datatype="http://www.w3.org/2001/XMLSchema#float">22.06</start_latitude>
  <start_time rdf:datatype="http://www.w3.org/2001/XMLSchema#datetime">2016-
02-24T15:14:11</start_time>
  <goal_longitude
rdf:datatype="http://www.w3.org/2001/XMLSchema#float">110.38</goal_longitude
>
  <executive_unit
rdf:datatype="http://www.w3.org/2001/XMLSchema#string">001</executive_unit>
  <has_path>
    <FlightPoint rdf:ID="FlightPoint_01">
      <latitude
    rdf:datatype="http://www.w3.org/2001/XMLSchema#float">22.25</latitude>
      <longitude
    rdf:datatype="http://www.w3.org/2001/XMLSchema#float">110.16</longitude
    >
      <height
    rdf:datatype="http://www.w3.org/2001/XMLSchema#float">8000</height>
      <ID xml:lang="en">01</ID>
    </FlightPoint>
  </has_path>
  <has_path>
    <FlightPoint rdf:ID="FlightPoint_02">
      <latitude
    rdf:datatype="http://www.w3.org/2001/XMLSchema#float">22.09</latitude>
      <longitude
    rdf:datatype="http://www.w3.org/2001/XMLSchema#float">110.05</longitude
    >
      <height
    rdf:datatype="http://www.w3.org/2001/XMLSchema#float">8000</height>
      <ID xml:lang="en">03</ID>
    </FlightPoint>
  </has_path>
  <has_path>
    <FlightPoint rdf:ID="FlightPoint_03">
      <latitude
    rdf:datatype="http://www.w3.org/2001/XMLSchema#float">22.45</latitude>
      <longitude
    rdf:datatype="http://www.w3.org/2001/XMLSchema#float">110.58</longitude
    >
      <height
    rdf:datatype="http://www.w3.org/2001/XMLSchema#float">8000</height>
      <ID xml:lang="en">03</ID>
    </FlightPoint>
  </has_path>
</ConvoyAction>
```

The ConvoyActionEvent in XML is described as below:

```
<ConvoyActionEvent          executive_unit="001"          goal_longitude="110.38"
start_latitude="22.06"      ID="0201"      goal_ID="Airspace6"      name="Convoy"
goal_latitude="22.43"  start_time="2016-02-24T15:14:11"  start_longitude="110.49"
xsi:noNamespaceSchemaLocation="Convoy.xsd"
xmlns:xsi="http://www.w3.org/2001/XMLSchema-instance">
    <FlightPoint ID="01" longitude="110.16" latitude="22.25" height="8000"/>
    <FlightPoint ID="02" longitude="110.05" latitude="22.09" height="8000"/>
    <FlightPoint ID="03" longitude="110.58" latitude="22.45" height="8000"/>
</ConvoyActionEvent>
```

References

1. Ma, W.-B., Wang, W.-G., Zhu, Y.: Development method of command and control domain modular ontology. Fire Control Command Control **12**(39), 50–53 (2014)
2. Peng, C.: Research on semantic interaction and dynamic reconfiguration based wargaming system concept framework and its key technologies. Ph.D. thesis, National University of Defense Technology, pp. 49–50 (2010)
3. Studer, R., Benjamins, V.R., Fensel, D.: Knowledge engineering: principles and methods. Data Knowl. Eng. **25**(122), 161–197 (1998)
4. Wache, H., Vogele, T., Visser, U., et al.: Ontology-based integration of information - a survey of existing approaches. In: Proceedings of IJCAI 2001 Workshop on Ontologies and Information Sharing, Seattle, WA, pp. 108–117 (2001)
5. Pease, A.C.: The JTF ATD core plan representation: request for comment. Armstrong Lab: AL/HR-TP-96-9631, Wright-Patterson AFB, OH, pp. 95–99 (1996)
6. Miller, J.A., Baramidze, G.: Simulation and the semantic web. In: Proceedings of the 2005 Winter Simulation Conference, SWC, USA, pp. 2371–2377 (2005)
7. Niles, I., Pease, A.: Toward a standard upper ontology. In: Proceeding of the Second International Conference on Formal Ontology in Information System, Ogunquit, Maine, USA, pp. 2–9 (2001)
8. Silver, G.A., Hassan, O.A.-H., Miller, J.A.: From domain ontologies to modeling ontologies to executable simulation models. In: Proceedings of the 2007 Winter Simulation Conference, WSC, USA, pp. 1108–1117 (2007)

An Efficiency Evaluation Model of Combat SoS Counterworks Based on Directed and Weighted Network

Tian Zhang[(✉)], Zhiyong Huang, Handong Wen, and Zhenfeng Bao

Air Force Command College, Beijing, China
27013061@qq.com

Abstract. To meet the military requirement of reconfiguration for optimization of combat SoS, the main purpose of this research is to propose an efficiency evaluation model of combat SoS counterwork based on the directed and weighted network. Firstly, combat SoS is proceed by a network description, according to the nature, state and interaction mechanism of the combat units, to judge whether it can form a link between two nodes, and ascertain the link weight. Secondly, set up the network evaluation index of combat SoS, and establish an efficiency evaluation model of combat SoS counterwork. Lastly, design an experiment for the test of model. The results show that the model could efficiently discriminate and estimate the change of effectiveness in Combat SoS counterworks which caused by the microscopic state change of combat units.

Keywords: Combat SoS counterworks · Directed and weighted network · Efficiency evaluation

1 Introduction

Informationized warfare is counterworks between combat SoS. The capability of combat SoS has become the basic form of informationized warfare; the efficiency of combat SoS counterworks directly determines the result of the war. Therefore, study on the inherent mechanism of combat SoS counterworks, which has important theoretical and practical significance.

Informationized combat SoS counterworks has many of the important problems, such as comparing the importance of different combat units in combat SoS, and reconfiguration for optimization of combat SoS, etc., which all need to use the efficiency of combat SoS as the basis and judgment standard. To this end, this paper proposes an efficiency evaluation model of combat SoS counterwork based on the directed and weighted network. The basic idea is described as: first of all, combat SoS is proceed by a network description. We regarded two confrontation sides in combat SoS as an integrated whole, and judge whether it can form a link between two nodes, and ascertain the link weight, which according to the nature, state and interaction mechanism of the combat unite; secondly, on the basis of the network description model of combat SoS, the network evaluation index of combat SoS is to be set up,

L. Zhang et al. (Eds.): AsiaSim 2016/SCS AutumnSim 2016, Part II, CCIS 644, pp. 413–423, 2016.
DOI: 10.1007/978-981-10-2666-9_41

those are different from the general network performance metrics; finally, the utilization of network evaluation indexes of the combat SoS is to establish an efficiency evaluation model of combat SoS counterwork, and designs an experiment for the test of model. The results of experiment explain that due to the change of macro countermeasure effectiveness caused by the microscopic state change of the combat unit, so the model will realize the efficient distinction and evaluation, which has good application prospects.

2   Related Works

In recent years, fruitful results about the study of combat SoS and the combat SoS effectiveness have been achieved by the application of complex networks, there are some representations: in June 2012, Liu Gang proposed a process and an algorithm for evaluating the complexity of architecture information flow. In May 2013, Qi Yanbo explained the network performance indicators of a new quantitative combat SoS, which are taking the quantitates of nodes and links to participate in the combat rings as indicators [10]. Additionally, Li RenJian designed a prototype tool framework that is based on the effectiveness and visualization analysis of system with weapon equipment system simulation test bed [3], and so on.

Based on the above research, many researchers have noted that the 'combat loop' is a basic unit of the efficiency of combat SoS, and its quantity has an important influence on the efficiency of the combat SoS counterworks; combat units of SoS cannot be abstracted into undifferentiated nodes which need to be appropriate to distinguish; as well as, it needs considered the operational time of combat represented by the combat loop. However, there are several issues mostly ignored in the previous researches: firstly, the efficiency of the SoS counterworks should be studied as a whole, whether the link is established between the combat unit and the target that depends on the two items; Secondly, the efficiency of the SoS counterworks should not only consider the quantity of combat loop, but the efficiency and distribution of the combat loop are also considered. Even if the combat SoS is equal to the number of combat loop, one party with the high efficiency will quickly achieved victory when it relies on the initial rapid attack; the combat SoS with the distribution of the combat loop that is more concentrated in the key objectives, its efficiency will be higher in the confrontation; Thirdly, the importance of nodes in combat SoS depends on many factors, so it cannot directly give weight for the modeling, etc. From the above, this paper indicates an efficiency evaluation model of the combat SoS based on directed and weighted complex network.

3   The Efficiency Evaluation Model

3.1   The Relevant Definitions of the Network Model

In order to facilitate the following discussion, the two sides of combat SoS counterworks is known as the Red and the Blue. Their combat SoS are known as the Red combat SoS and the Blue combat SoS, the perspective of modeling is based on the Red combat SoS.

Definition 1. Define $G(N,L,f,w,\eta)$ as the network model of combat SoS, and:

1. Define N as a set of network model nodes, $N = [v_1, v_2, \ldots, v_n]$;
2. Define L as a set of network model edges, $L = [e_1, e_2, \ldots, e_m]$;
3. Define f as a mapping function that the edge is mapped to nodes in network model, it determines the structure of the network, $f : L \to N \times N$; Define $f(v_1 \to v_2)$ as a directed edge from node v_1 to node v_2, v_1 is called the tail node, v_2 is called the head node.
4. Define w as a mapping function that the weight is mapped to the edge in network model, $w(v_1 \to v_2)$ represents the weight of the directed edge from the node v_1 to the node v_2;
5. Define η as overall correction parameter.

Definition 2. Define $T(v_1 \to v_2)$ as the time required for combat operations that is represented by the edge from the node v_1 to the node v_2.

Definition 3. Define $F_{Node} = \Gamma(Node_{label}, Node_{attribute}, Node\_status)$ as the describing function of node, then:

1. $Node\_label = \{ID, Class\_type\}$ is defined as the tag set of nodes, and:
   (1) ID is defined as identification badge of nodes, $ID = \{1, 2, 3\ldots n\}$, n represents the total numbers of combat units;
   (2) $Class\_type$ is defined as a type tag set of nodes, and:

$$Class\_type = \{S_{red}, D_{red}, A_{red}, S_{blue}, D_{blue}, A_{blue}\}$$

   Then $S_{red}, D_{red}, A_{red}$ refer to information acquisition node, command and control node, and attack node of the Red; and $S_{blue}, D_{blue}, A_{blue}$ refer to the nodes of the Blue, and the number of all kinds of nodes $S_{red}, D_{red}, A_{red}, S_{blue}, D_{blue}, A_{blue}$ are s, d, a, s', d', a'.

2. Define $Node_{attribute}$ is an attribute set of nodes, due to the attribute parameters of different types of combat units are not the same, so the elements of the collection $Node_{attribute}$ are relevant to $Class\_type$ of the collection $Node\_label$, the specific rules are as follows:
   (1) while $Class_{type} = \{S_{red}, S_{blue}\}$,
       then : $Node\_attribute = \{Range, Tranceform, L_{Capability}\ldots\}$
       (1) Define **Range** as the detection range of information acquisition nodes;
       (2) Define **Tranceform** as the time when Information acquisition node will obtain the information processing and return to the command and control nodes; $Tranceform_{S_{red}}$ is the capability of specified node S_{red}.
       (3) Define $L_{Capability}$ as ability matrix of information acquisition nodes, $L_{Capability\_S_{red}}$ refers to the ability of information acquisition that the information acquisition nodes for the Red (S_{red}) acquire the target $O_{red} = \{S_{blue}, D_{blue}, A_{blue}\}$. According to the number of various types of nodes, it knows that $L_{Capability\_S_{red}}$ is a matrix with the ranks number $s \times b$, s_{ij} is the element of a matrix, therefore, if the element i in the set of information acquisition nodes of the Red has not detection ability to the

element j in the target set O_{red}, so $s_{ij} = 0$. Otherwise, if the element i in the set of information acquisition nodes of the Red spend some time t to discover and locate the element j in the target set O_{red}, and $s_{ij} = t$. In a similar way, ability matrix of information acquisition nodes for the Blue can be defined as $L_{Capability\_S_{blue}}$.

(2) while Class_type = $\{D_{red}, D_{blue}\}$,
    then : Node_attribute = $\{MaxNumbe_A, T_{decision}, Range, \ldots\}$
  (1) Define **MaxNumbe$_A$** as the nodes that can command and control the maximum value of the attack node simultaneously;
  (2) Define $T_{decision}$ as the time spent by the command and control nodes starts from receiving information to make decisions;
  (3) Define **Range** as the range of charges for the command and control nodes in movement class;

(3) while Class_type = $\{A_{red}, A_{blue}\}$,
    then : Node_attribute = $\{Range, L_{Capability} \ldots\}$
  (1) Define **Range** as combat range of nodes in attack class;
  (2) Define $L_{Capability}$ as the ability matrix of combat unit in attack class, $L_{Capability\_A_{red}}$ refers to the attack ability about the set of attack notes A_{red} to the targets set $O_{red} = \{S_{blue}, D_{blue}, A_{blue}\}$, according to the number of various types of nodes, it knows that $L_{Capability\_A_{red}}$ is a matrix with the ranks number $a \times b$, a_{ij} is the element of a matrix, therefore, if the element i in the set of attack nodes for the Red has not attack ability to the element j in the target set O_{red}, so $a_{ij} = 0$. Otherwise, it is $a_{ij} = 1$. In a similar way, the ability matrix of attack nodes for the Blue can be defined as $L_{Capability\_A_{red}}$.

3. Define **Node_status** as the state set of nodes, the state of nodes mainly include the position, the speed, the subordinate command relations and so on, so:

$$Node\_status = \{Location, Velocity, Relationship\ldots\}$$

(1) Define **Location** as physical location of nodes, so:

$$Location(x, y, z) = g(t)$$

And x, y, z in the formula are the physical coordinates of the nodes in three-dimensional space.
(2) Define **Velocity** as the speed of nodes,
(3) Define **Relationship** as command relationship of combat SoS.

3.2   The Construction of Model

The key to construct the network model is to determine the edge mapping function f and the weight mapping function w, and these two functions is related to the node description function F_{Node}, they are described as:

$$\begin{cases} f(v_1 \rightarrow v_2) = f\{F_{Node}(v_1), F_{Node}(v_2)\} \\ w(v_1 \rightarrow v_2) = w\{f(v_1 \rightarrow v_2), F_{Node}(v_1), F_{Node}(v_2)\} \end{cases}$$

The edge mapping function f and the weight mapping function w are modeling in the following. Since the two functions are the judgment rule in the essential, the model is adopted by pseudo code description.

3.3 The Description and Determination Methods of the Edge

Arbitrary two combat units of the Red and the Blue combat SoS are recorded as the node v_1 and the node $v_2(v_1 \neq v_2)$, when $f(v_1 \rightarrow v_2)$ is the value of 0,it means there is no link from the node v_1 to the node v_2, or when $f(v_1 \rightarrow v_2)$ is the value of 1, it means that there are links between these two nodes. The edge mapping function f of the node v_1 to the node v_2 can be determined in accordance with the following methods:

Step 1. The classification parameters $Class\_type(v_1)$ and $Class\_type(v_2)$ are extracted separately from the node v_1 to the node v_2.

Rule 1 *while* $Class\_type(v_1) = S_{red}$, *then*

$\quad$ *if* $Class_{type(v_2)} = S_{red}$ *or* A_{red} *or* D_{blue} *or* A_{blue}, *then*

$\quad\quad Edge(v_1 \rightarrow v_2) = 0$

$\quad$ *else if* $Class_{type(v_2)} = D_{red}$, *and turn to step2.*

Step 2. The state parameter $Relationship(v_1)$ is extracted for the node v_1, and to determine $f(v_1 \rightarrow v_2) = 1$ or $f(v_1 \rightarrow v_2) = 0$;

else if $Class_{type(v_2)} = S_{blue}$, *and turn to step 3.*

Step 3. The state parameter $Location(v_1)$ is extracted for the node v_1, and the attribute parameter $Range(v_2)$ and $L_{Capability}(v_2)$, and The state parameter $Location(v_2)$ are extracted for the node v_2, so:

Rule 2 *while* $L_{Capability}(v_1 \rightarrow v_2) = 1$, *then*

$\quad$ *if* $Location(v_1) \subset \{Range(v_2), \ Location(v_2)\}$, *then*

$\quad\quad f(v_1 \rightarrow v_2) = 1$

$\quad$ *else if* $Location(v_1) \notin \{Range(v_2), \ Location(v_2)\}$, *then*

$\quad\quad f(v_1 \rightarrow v_2) = 0$

$\quad$ *else if* $L_{Capability}(v_1 \rightarrow v_2) = 0$, *then*

$\quad\quad f(v_1 \rightarrow v_2) = 0$

Rule 3 *while* $Class\_type(v_1) = D_{red}$, *then*

$\quad$ *if* $Class_{type(v_2)} = S_{red}$ *or* D_{blue} *or* A_{blue}, *then*

$\quad\quad f(v_1 \rightarrow v_2) = 0$

$\quad$ *else if* $Class\_type(v_2) = D_{red}$ *or* A_{red}, *then* turn to step 4.

Step 4. The state parameter $Relationship(v_1)$ is extracted for the node v_1, and to determine $f(v_1 \rightarrow v_2) = 1$ or $f(v_1 \rightarrow v_2) = 0$; *else if* $Class\_type(v_2) = S_{blue}$, then Repeat Step 3;

> **Rule 4** *while* $Class\_type(v_1) = A_{red}$, then
> > *if* $Class\_type(v_2) = S_{red}$ *or* D_{red} *or* A_{red}, *then*
> > $$f(v_1 \rightarrow v_2) = 0$$
> > *else if* $Class\_type(v_2) = D_{blue}$ *or* A_{blue},*then*turn to step 5.

Step 5. The attribute parameter $Range(v_1)$, $L_{Capability}(v_1)$ and the state parameter $Location(v_1)$ are extracted for the node v_1, as well as, the state parameter $Location(v_2)$ is extracted for the node v_2, so:

> **Rule 5** *while* $L_{Capability}(v_1 \rightarrow v_2) = 1$, *then*
> > *if* $Location(v_2) \subset \{Range(v_1), Location(v_1)\}$, *then*
> > $$f(v_1 \rightarrow v_2) = 1$$
> > *else if* $Location(v_2) \notin \{Range(v_1), Location(v_1)\}$, *then*
> > $$f(v_1 \rightarrow v_2) = 0$$
> > *else if* $L_{Capability}(v_1 \rightarrow v_2) = 0$,*then*
> > $$f(v_1 \rightarrow v_2) = 0$$
> > *else if* $Class\_type(v_2) = S_{blue}$, *then* *turn to step 6.*

Step 6. The link of $A_{red} \rightarrow S_{blue}$ (the similar situation for $A_{blue} \rightarrow S_{red}$) can represents a reconnaissance from the Reconnaissance node S_{blue} to the Attack node A_{red}, and also can represents an attack from the Attack node A_{red} of the Red to the Reconnaissance node S_{blue}, so it needs to discuss by two cases:

> **Rule 6 1)** *while* $A_{red} \rightarrow S_{blue}$ means S_{blue}'s investigation of A_{red}, then
> > Repeat Step3;
> **2)** *while* $A_{red} \rightarrow S_{blue}$ means A_{red} attack S_{blue}, then
> > Repeat Step5.

3.4   The Weight Determination Method of the Edge

Arbitrary two combat units of the Red combat SoS and the Blue combat SoS are recorded as the node v_1 and the node $v_2(v_1 \neq v_2)$, the weighting function $w(v_1 \rightarrow v_2)$ is the weight of the edges from the node v_1 to the node v_2, in accordance with the following methods, it is to determine the weight mapping function w of two node edge:

the classification parameter $Class\_type(v_1)$ and $Class\_type(v_2)$ are respectively extracted from the node v_1 and the node v_2, take the Red as example, from the above, the set of $f(v_1 \rightarrow v_2)$ value could be 1 as follow:

$$\{S_{red} \rightarrow D_{red}, S_{red} \rightarrow S_{blue}, D_{red} \rightarrow A_{red}, D_{red} \rightarrow D_{red}, D_{red} \rightarrow S_{blue},$$

$$A_{red} \rightarrow S_{blue}, A_{red} \rightarrow D_{blue}, A_{red} \rightarrow A_{blue}\}$$

The following rules are determined by the 8 kinds of link weight from the above.

Rule 1: $T(S_{red} \rightarrow D_{red}) = Tranceforms_{S_{red}}$
Rule 2: $T(S_{red} \rightarrow S_{blue}) = s_{ij}, s_{ij} \in L_{Capability\_S_{blue}}$
Rule 3: $T(D_{red} \rightarrow A_{red}) = T_{decision}$
Rule 4: $T(D_{red}(v_1) \rightarrow D_{red}(v_2)) = T_{decision}(D_{red}(v_2))$
Rule 5: $T(D_{red} \rightarrow S_{blue}) = s_{ij}, \quad s_{ij} \in L_{Capability\_S_{blue}}$
Rule 6:

(1) while $A_{red} \rightarrow S_{blue}$ expresses that A_{red} attack S_{blue}, then

$$T(S_{red} \rightarrow D_{red}) = \frac{Location(t_0)_{A_{red}} - Location(t_0)_{S_{blue}}}{v\{Velocity(t)_{A_{red}}, Velocity(t)_{S_{blue}}\}}$$

In a similar way, the weight of link between $A_{red} \rightarrow D_{blue}$ and $A_{red} \rightarrow A_{blue}$ will be acquired.

(2) while $A_{red} \rightarrow S_{blue}$ means that S_{blue} reconnoiters A_{red}, then $T(A_{red} \rightarrow S_{blue}) = s_{ij}, s_{ij} \in L_{Capability\_S_{blue}}$

Take the Red as an example, it studies the methods of determining the link weights in the above analysis. As their statuses of the Red and the Blue are equal in information warfare system countermeasure, the above rules are also established when the Red and the Blue exchange their logo.

To sum up, quintet $G(N, L, f, w, \eta)$ is a network model of combat SoS, in detail, The attribute of the element of the node set N is represented by the node description function F_{Node}, then:

$$\left\{ \begin{array}{c} F_{Node} = \Gamma(Node\_label, Node\_attribute, Node\_status) \\ Node\_label = \{ID, Class\_type\} \\ Node\_attribute = \{Range, L_{Capability}, MaxNumbe_A, T_{decision}, \ldots\} \\ Node\_status = \{Location, Velocity, Relationship \ldots\} \end{array} \right.$$

3.5   Networking Evaluation Index of Combat SoS

Base on the network model of combat SoS above, we put forward networking evaluation index of combat SoS as follow:

1. The number of network closed loop: The path starts and ends in the same node, which is known as the loop in the network, and the paper is defined as the closed loop in the directed network, the number of the closed loop in network refers to a sum number of all closed loop network.

2. The loop degree of node: The loop degree of a node is the number of closed loop which is composed of nodes. In the combat SoS, the node loop is one of the important indicators to measure the node's function.

3. The loop degree distribution of node: Define the loop degree distribution of node $P(k)$ as a number of nodes formed with combat loop k participating in the network.

4. The weight of the closed loop in the network: A sum of the weight of all links formed in a closed loop in the network.

5. The weight distribution of the closed loop in the network: The weight distribution of the closed loop in the network refers to the distribution of the weights of all the closed loop in the network, define $Q(k)$ as a number of the weight of closed loop k in the whole network.

3.6   An Efficiency Evaluation Model of Combat SoS Counterwork

From the above, the key indicators of an efficiency of information combat SoS counterwork, take the Red as an example, are sign convention:

1. N_{red}: The number of combat loop in the Red combat SoS;
2. N_{blue}: The number of combat loop in the Blue combat SoS;
3. $P_{red}(i)$: The efficiency distribution of combat loop in the Red combat SoS, $P_{red}(i)$ refers to the total number of efficiency of combat loop when the efficiency is i;
4. $P_{blue}(i)$: The efficiency distribution of combat loop in the Blue combat SoS, $P_{blue}(i)$ refers to the total number of efficiency of combat loop when the efficiency is i;
5. T_{blue_j}: The target's total number of efficiency of combat loop when an important degree is j in the Blue combat SoS;
6. T_{red_j}: The target's total number of efficiency of combat loop when an important degree is j in the Blue combat SoS;
7. E_{red}: The efficiency of the Red combat SoS;

An efficiency model in this formula:

$$E_{red} = \left(\frac{N_{red}}{N_{blue}}\right) \cdot \sum_{i=1}^{n} \left(i \cdot \frac{P_{red}(i)}{P_{blue}(i)}\right) \cdot \sum_{j=1}^{m} \left(j \cdot \frac{T_{blue}(j)}{T_{red}(j)}\right) \tag{1}$$

and: $\sum_{i=1}^{n} P_{red}(i) = N_{red}$; $\sum_{j=1}^{m} T_{blue_j} = N_{red}$

It can be known from the above formula, under the circumstance of the two sides have the equal strength, $E_{red} = 1$, which can use 1 as a reference:

When $E_{red} > 1$, the Red side has good post in the system confrontation;

When $E_{red} < 1$, the Red side has bad post in the system confrontation;

4 Design an Experiment

4.1 Ideas of the Experiments

Considering network model has the characteristics that the actual situation is highly abstract, and an amount of information is limited, the credibility will reduce when it tries to use the network model to simulate the complete process of combat. Therefore, this paper is based on a "combat scenario" in effectiveness evaluation of both Red and Blue combat SoS (Fig. 1 shows the network graph of both Red and Blue combat SoS in different operational stage), and to use the results of assessment as a benchmark. Then, when other factors remain unchanged, observe and compare their influence on the effectiveness of combat SoS by adjusting the values to variables. The principle of this method is described as: based on the construction of combat SoS network model, the different scenario variables is corresponding to the different input parameters of the model, which will change the structure of the network and the weights of corresponding link, and thus have an impact on the efficiency of combat SoS counterworks. This method will achieve more reliable results when the problems are large-scale and complex, furthermore, the experiments can be designed flexibly according to the various characteristics of other problems.

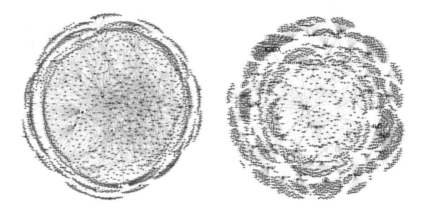

Fig. 1. The Network graph of both Red and Blue combat SoS (Color figure online)

4.2 The Background of Experiment

For A and B air combat platforms of the Red combat SoS, under the assumption that there are differences in capability of the mobility, situational awareness, command and control, it is to respectively use the number, different capabilities, deployment scheme of combat as the scenario variables, and study the effects of A and B combat platforms in different conditions on the efficiency of combat SoS counterworks.

1. Comparing the impact of combat units with different numbers. The confrontation state between the Red and the Blue are imaginary in a "scenario", when the number of combat units A and B are on the increase respectively, and the variations of combat efficiency will be observed in the Red combat SoS. Figure 2 (1) shows the results:

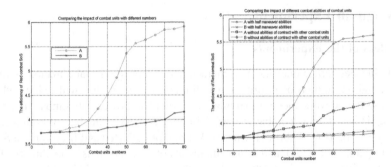

Fig. 2. (1) Comparing the impact of combat units with different numbers, (2) Comparing the impact of different combat abilities of combat units (Color figure online)

2. Comparing the impact of different combat abilities of combat units. The efficiency of the combat SoS are further analyzed on the combat platform A and B, under the circumstance where other conditions are unchanged, it is to assume that the maneuver abilities of combat unit A and B are respectively one half of the normal state, and also assumes the situations of whether they can interact information with other combat units, the results are shown in Fig. 2(2).

3. Comparing the impact of different deployment scheme of combat units. In order to investigate the effects of different deployment scheme of combat units, we compared the efficiency of the combat SoS in the three deployment scheme of combat unit A and B, this is in the circumstance where other conditions are unchanged. Figure 3(1) describes the deployment scheme. Figure 3(2) shows the results.

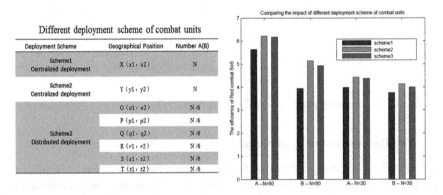

Fig. 3. (1) Different deployment scheme of combat units, (2) Comparing the impact of different deployment scheme of combat units

5 Conclusions

The results of experiments indicate that the different combat units have various effects on the efficiency of combat SoS counterworks in the case of the same increase in the number. This is related to the combat abilities of the combat unit, and the ability to communicate with other combat units is more important than the maneuverability. Moreover, the different combat units have various effects on the efficiency of combat SoS counterwork with the different deployment schemes.

As a result, an efficiency evaluation model of combat SoS counterwork built in this paper is able to distinguish the changes of microcosmic state of combat units, which realize the requirements of complex network modeling with macro properties through by the micro rules. In addition, this model has good scalability and extensive application, that is, on the basis of the different problems, it is to select the different sets of variables, and to evaluate an efficiency of combat SoS counterwork in the different situations.

References

1. Cares, J.R.: An Information Age Combat Mode. Office of the Secretary of Defense Publications, Pentagon City (2002)
2. Wang, X.: Complex networks: topology, dynamics and synchronization. Int. J. Bifurc. Chaos Appl. Sci. Eng. **12**(5), 885–916 (2002)
3. Li, R.-J., Si, G.: Visualizing analysis for effectiveness of system of systems based on network of networks. J. Syst. Simul. **6**(9), 1944–1955 (2014)
4. Ghoshal, G., Barabasi, A.-L.: Ranking stability and super stable nodes in complex networks. Nature **433**(7028), 895–900 (2011)
5. Opsanl, T., Riccaboni, M., Schiavo, S.: Structure and evolution of weighted networks. New J. Phys. **12**, 023003 (2010)
6. Deller, S.: Applying the information age combat model: quantitative analysis of network centric operations. Int. J. C2 **3**, 1–25 (2009)
7. Wang, Z., Ma, Y.C.: Research on network modeling of battle system of systems based on complex networks. Fire Control Command Control **08**, 40–47 (2011)
8. Hu, X.: On War System Engineering: Methodology Towards Information Age's War, 04 (2012)
9. Zhu, J., Liu, D.: Hyper-network model of combat system and use case. Command Control Simul. **04**, 13–16 (2013)
10. Qi, Y., Liu, Z.: Combat system of systems network modeling and networked effects analysis. Fire Control Command Control **05**, 66–69 (2013)

Modeling of Underwater Terrain Aided Navigation and Terrain Matching Algorithm Simulation

Shen Jian[1(✉)], Shi Jing[1], and Xiong Lu[2]

[1] Naval Academy of Armament, Beijing, China
sterrain@126.com
[2] Wuhan Ordnance N.C.O Academy, Wuhan, China

Abstract. In order to make an improved algorithm of good environmental adaptability and practicability, the simulation of three terrain matching algorithms were done on the condition of typical underwater navigation. Firstly, the differences of terrain aided navigation between on land and underwater were researched. Secondly, the underwater terrain aided navigation models were established as well as the underwater terrain aided navigation simulation of TERCOM, SITAN and ICCP. Finally, the influence of INS errors, measurement accuracy, and digital map resolution to algorithms performance were studied.

Keywords: Terrain aided navigation · Matching algorithm · TERCOM · SITAN · ICCP

1 Introduction

Underwater terrain aided navigation has the advantages of concealment, autonomy and weather resistance. It can provide the AUV with accurate position information without floating to surface which avoids voyage waste and location exposure. It is one of the popular underwater autonomous navigation technologies for civilian and military applications. At present, the research in developed countries, such as the United States, Britain, Sweden, Norway [1–4] has entered the experiment phase.

TERCOM, SITAN, ICCP are three kinds of typical terrain matching algorithm, of which the first two algorithms has been successfully applied in aircrafts [5–7]. Because of the marine environment is more complex than on land conditions, as compared with on land aircraft, the speed, measurement accuracy, data update rate and varying degrees of AUV is low. These negative factors restrict the underwater application of terrain matching algorithms. Therefore, Xin Tinghui, Zhang Li, Wang Dong, use different kinds of combination methods to enhance the applicability of the matching algorithms [8–10]. These combinations improve the performance of the algorithm, but the impact of underwater applications conditions are not considered which makes improve algorithm unstable. In order to make the improved algorithm has better environmental adaptability and practicability, the simulation of three terrain matching algorithms were done on the condition of typical underwater navigation.

© Springer Science+Business Media Singapore 2016
L. Zhang et al. (Eds.): AsiaSim 2016/SCS AutumnSim 2016, Part II, CCIS 644, pp. 424–432, 2016.
DOI: 10.1007/978-981-10-2666-9_42

2 Comparative Analysis of on Land and Underwater Terrain Aided Navigation

2.1 Movement Characteristics Analysis

Typically AUV navigation velocity is less than 10 kn, which means that the aircraft can get far more effective terrain profile data than AUV during the same period of time. Thus, a higher matching frequency on land conduces matching result convergence in a short time. In addition, the INS position error over time grow into a third power, since the vehicle speed is faster, the INS drift error can be assumed unchanged in each matching process. For AUV, due to the slow velocity, the INS drift error changes obviously in the initial matching process, which increases the complexity of the research problem to some extent.

2.2 Measuring Equipment Analysis

Aircrafts typically use radar or laser altimeter to get the terrain data with high accuracy and timeliness, while AUV use sonar to get the underwater topography. The speed of sound is low than electromagnetic waves and the sound beam is affect by water temperature, salinity, etc. which will reduce the real-time and accuracy of measurement. So the underwater terrain matching algorithm should have greater robustness and adaptability compared to the algorithm on land.

2.3 Digital Map Analysis

Due to influence of tides, sea conditions, ambient noise, sound velocity and silt deposition, underwater topographic survey is difficult, and the accuracy of the map is also lower than that on land. Generally digit map resolution measured by satellite and aerial plane is from 1 m to10 m, while the underwater digit map resolution measured by sonar is from 10 m to 500 m. Digit map accuracy of shallow areas or the coast is about 30 m, while the map accuracy of ocean areas is even up to 500 m or more.

3 Underwater Terrain Aided Navigation Model

Simulation model of underwater terrain aided navigation usually contain SINS model, measurement error model and underwater terrain DEM. In order to get an intuitive simulation results, models of underwater terrain aided navigation will be supplicated under the premise of validity.

3.1 SINS Simplified Model

SINS is the mainly navigation equipment of AUV, and during the terrain matching process, the depth and velocity are fixed. Since SINS can be regarded as an accurate dead reckoning system, the navigation system model can be simplified into a two-dimensional plane dead reckoning model [10] when studying the performance of terrain matching algorithm. The model is represents below:

$$
\begin{cases}
x'_n = x_0 + \sum_{i=0}^{n-1} \Delta x'_i = x_0 + \sum_{i=0}^{n-1} v'_i \bullet \Delta T \bullet \cos\left(\theta_0 + \sum_{i=0}^{n-i} \omega'_i \bullet \Delta T\right) \\
y'_n = y_0 + \sum_{i=0}^{n-1} \Delta y'_i = y_0 + \sum_{i=0}^{n-1} v'_i \bullet \Delta T \bullet \sin\left(\theta_0 + \sum_{i=0}^{n-i} \omega'_i \bullet \Delta T\right) \\
v'_i = v_i + u_{vi} \\
\omega'_i = \omega_i + u_{\omega i}
\end{cases}
\tag{1}
$$

Where (x_0, y_0) and (x_n, y_n) represent the position of AUV at t_0 (Initial matching time) and $t_n (n \geq 1)$, $\Delta x'_i$ and $\Delta y'_i$ are the displacement of AUV in the direction of X and Y. v'_i and ω'_i represent the velocity and angular rate provided by SINS at t_i. u_{vi} and $u_{\omega i}$ are the navigation deviation. v_i and ω_i are the actual speed and angular rate of AUV. θ_0 is initial heading angle of AUV. Since TERCOM algorithm requires stable course during matching process, in order to facilitate comparative analysis of the three algorithms, we set $\omega'_i = 0$. Equation (1) can be simplified as fellow:

$$
\begin{cases}
x'_n = x_0 + \sum_{i=0}^{n-1} \Delta x'_i = x_0 + \sum_{i=0}^{n-1} v'_i \bullet \Delta T \bullet \cos(\theta_0) \\
y'_n = y_0 + \sum_{i=0}^{n-1} \Delta y'_i = y_0 + \sum_{i=0}^{n-1} v'_i \bullet \Delta T \bullet \sin(\theta_0) \\
v'_i = v_i + u_{vi}
\end{cases}
\tag{2}
$$

The simplified SINS model above is the basis of matching calculation which provides velocity and location information of AUV when giving the initial position and course.

3.2 Simplified Measurement Error Model

The error of measurement system were caused by bathymetric sonar and pressure sensors on AUV [11].

$$
h' = h_r + h_l + \mu_r + \mu_l
\tag{3}
$$

Where h' is the terrain elevation of AUV position, h_r and h_l are the distances from AUV's position to surface and bottom respectively. μ_r and μ_l are the measurement errors of the pressure sensor and bathymetric sonar. μ_l is caused by sound beam bending, beam angle and relative motion which is the major error. μ_r is mainly caused by the tidal and surge. In this article, we assume that $\mu_h = \mu_r + \mu_l$ approximates normal distribution, the formula (3) can be expressed as:

$$h' = h_r + h_l + \mu_h = h + \mu_h \qquad \mu_h \sim N(0, \sigma_h^2) \tag{4}$$

3.3   Underwater Topography DEM

This article use real underwater depth data to establish the digital map which will be used for the follow-up matching simulation. Since the underwater terrain data is not based on the grid sampling, we will use interpolation method to product standard DEM model. The equation is expressed as follow:

$$\hat{h}(x, y) = \sum_{j=1}^{n} \lambda_j h_j^M \left[x_j^M, y_j^M \right] \tag{5}$$

Where $\hat{h}(x, y)$ is the depth of interpolation points, $h^M \left[x^M, y^M \right]$ is the depth set corresponding to the DEM grid which are surrounding the interpolation points. λ is the interpolation weights. Nearest neighbor interpolation, bilinear interpolation and bicubic interpolation are used generally. As a reference of [12], we use bilinear interpolation to establish the underwater DEM in order to avoid topographical variation overestimate.

4   Underwater Terrain Matching Algorithm Simulation

The Algorithm model of TERCOM, ICCP and SITAN can be found in references[4–9] which will be not described here. In the simulation, the matching sequence of TER-COM and ICCP is calculated with mean square difference (MSD):

$$\mathrm{MSD}(\tau_x, \tau_y) = \frac{1}{L} \int_{-\frac{L}{2}}^{\frac{L}{2}} [T_R(x, y) - T_M(x + \tau_x, y + \tau_y)]^2 dx \tag{6}$$

The ICCP iterative objective function is the minimum Euclidean distance between the depth date sequence and the nearest depth equal contour. Each measurement point in SITAN algorithm will be performed a matching operation, and 9 point neighboring measurement points is used to linearize the terrain. Underwater bathymetric maps and underwater terrain on simulation route is shown in Fig. 1:

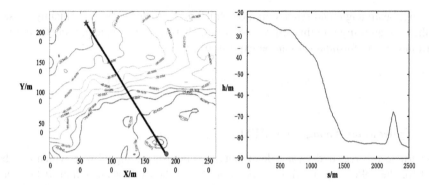

Fig. 1. Underwater bathymetric maps and underwater terrain on simulation route

As can be seen from the figure that the upper half region is shallower and the terrain is diversification significantly while the lower region is deep and flat.

The simulation parameters are shown as Table 1:

Table 1. Simulation parameters setting

Auv velocity	2 m/s	Initial position variance	(50 m, 50 m)
Initial velocity error	0.2 m/s	Measurement variance	0.01 m^2
Initial heading error	0.2°	Measurement interval	5 s
SINS variance (east, north)	(0.02 m/s, 0.02 m/s)^2 (0.1 m/s, 0.1 m/s)^2	Initial position variance	$\begin{bmatrix} (80\text{m})^2 & 0 \\ 0 & (80\text{m})^2 \end{bmatrix}$

4.1 The Influence of Navigation Error

The simulation parameters are shown in Table 1 and the resolution of underwater digital map is 6 m. 100 times of Monte Carlo simulation was done and the average error was calculated. The simulation results are shown in Fig. 2.

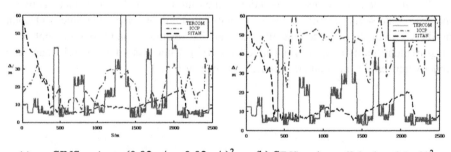

(a)   SINS variance (0.02m/s，0.02m/s)^2 (b) SINS variance (0.1m/s，0.1m/s)^2

Fig. 2. The matching error of the three methods in different navigation deviation

As can be seen from the Fig. 2, the SINS error affects the matching results of three algorithms to a different degree. For TERCOM and ICCP algorithm, the error accumulation exists in the depth data cache periods. Since each match process is in batch mode, the impact of SINS error is throughout the whole course. For SITAN algorithm, the matching method is based on recursive filtering, error cumulative can be inhibited effectively. The influence appears in the initial convergence stage. When it converged, SINS error deviation (within the afford scope of the EKF) had little effect on the matching result.

The figure also shows that TECOM performance is better than ICCP when SINS deviation increasing. This is mainly because the rigid transformation (rotation and translation) of ICCP algorithm cannot change the track shape. The difference between indicate track and real track is due to SINS deviation which affects the Iteration effect. In contrast, TERCOM's matching sequences are continuous map grid units. If the error is small compared to the grid resolution, TERCOM can still provide with better matching result.

As it can be seen from the curve trend, when the AUV enter into the flat area, matching errors of three algorithms is increasing of different degrees; TERCOM's matching error grows fast while SITAN is slower. The reason is that TERCOM only use measured depth sequence to estimate the position information while SITAN use both priori information and actual measurement for estimation.

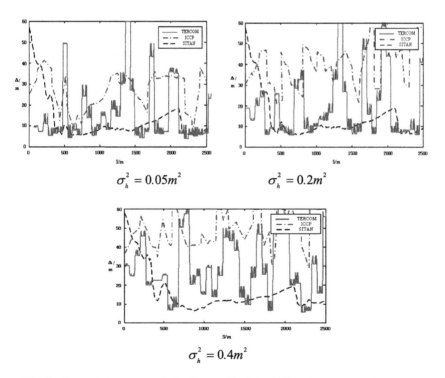

Fig. 3. The matching error of the three methods in different measurement accuracy

4.2   The Influence of Measurement Accuracy

The AUV navigation deviations of east and north are both $(0.02 \text{ m/s})^2$. measurement variance are 0.05 m^2, 0.2 m^2, 0.4 m^2. The remaining parameters are shown in Table 1. The simulation results are shown in Fig. 3.

As can be seen from the Fig. 3, ICCP matching error is increasing faster than the others. This reason is that the nearest equal depth sequences of ICCP are determined by indicate track depth sequences, if each measurement is not accurate, the nearest equal depth contours are also inaccurate. It will affect the rigid transformation process of indicate track and lead to an increasing matching error.

TERCOM is different from ICCP. Although TERCOM algorithm uses measurement sequences as the matching objects, the correlation operation of measurement sequence and terrain profile within the search area are calculated one by one. The batch processing calculated is an error average procession actually, which suppresses the influence of data error to some extent. Compared to TERCOM and ICCP algorithm, the influence to SITAN algorithm is minimal, but the convergence speed of matching result is slow and the error curve fluctuation significantly. This is mainly because EKF uses the posterior state to correct the priori estimate, in the early match, each state variables and their corresponding variance is large. The measurements with large observational error will impact the EKF convergence effect to a certain extent.

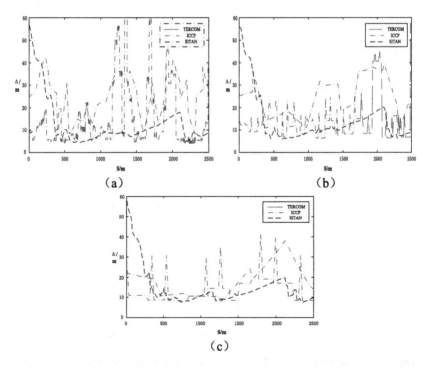

Fig. 4. The matching error of the three methods in different map resolutions. (a) The map resolution is 3 m, (b) The map resolution is 12 m, (c) The map resolution is 24 m

4.3   The Influence of Map Resolution

The digital map resolutions are 3 m, 12 m, 24 m. The measurement of TERCOM and ICCP were taken at intervals of 3 s, 10 s, and 18 s while the interval of SITAN is 5 s. The east and north navigation error of AUV is (0.02 m/s) 2 both. The measurement variance is 0.05 m^2. The other parameters are in Table 1. The simulation results shown in Fig. 4.

The matching result of TERCOM and ICCP become better when using the digit map of low resolution. The reason is that large distance of each measurement positions can reflect a better characteristic of topographic profile which reduces the influence of similar terrain in matching area. Thus, TERCOM and ICCP algorithm is suitable for a wide range 'rough search', while SITAN algorithm is more suitable for small-scale 'fine match'.

5   Conclusions and Future Work

SITAN has higher accuracy, less susceptible to bias and navigation Gaussian measurement noise. ICCP is influenced by navigation and measurement obviously, the match result is depends on the depth difference of measurement sequence and contour distribution to a great extent. The research above can provide us a comprehensive understanding the performance of typical terrain matching algorithms and improvement method.

References

1. Meduna, D., Rock, S., Mcewen, R.: Low-cost terrain relative navigation for long-range AUVs. In: MTS/IEEE, Quebec (2008)
2. Nygren, I.: Terrain navigation for underwater vehicles using the correlator method. IEEE J. Ocean. Eng. 29(3), 906–915 (2004)
3. Mcphail, S.: Autosub6000: a deep diving long range AUV. J. Bionic Eng. 6, 55–62 (2009)
4. Anonsen, K.B., Hagen, O.K.: An analysis of real-time terrain aided navigation results from a HUGIN AUV, Seattle (2010)
5. Tian, F.: Research on underwater terrain navigation model solving and navigation cell. Harbin Engineering University, Harbin (2009)
6. Liu, Y.: Technology study on seabed terrain matching navigation. Harbin Engineering University, Harbin (2009)
7. Yang, H.: Research on terrain matching algorithm based on ICCP for underwater vehicles. Harbin Engineering University, Harbin (2009)
8. Xin, T.: The research of terrain-aided underwater navigation. Northwest Polytechnical University, Xi'an (2004)
9. Zhang, L., Yang, H.: Research on assembled underwater terrain matching algorithm based on ICCP and TERCOM. J. Proj. Rockets Missiles Guid. 28(3), 230–232 (2008)
10. Wang, K., Yang, Y.: Method and equipment of terrain aided navigation, China (2008). CN 101339036A

11. Meduna, D.K.: Terrain relative navigation for sensor-limited systems with application to underwater vehicles. Stanford University, America Stanford (2011)
12. Rees, W.G.: The accuracy of digital elevation models interpolated to higher resolutions. Int. J. Remote Sens. 21(1), 7–20 (2000)

An Integrated Simulation System for Air-to-Ground Guided Munitions

Xiaodong Zhu[✉], Ge Li, Peng Wang, and Xibao Wang

School of Information System and Management,
National University of Defense Technology, Changsha, China
{zhuxiaodong,geli,wangpeng_nudt}@nudt.edu.cn, xbwang1990@126.com

Abstract. This paper proposes an integrated simulation system for air-to-ground guided munitions. Functionality and operating modes of the system are discussed. The structure design along with detailed analysis is given to illustrate its support for the whole process of simulation experiments. The simulation system comprised five subsystems, including experiment management system, data management system, mathematical simulation system, visual generating system and hardware-in-the-loop system. We propose a case study to illustrate the system's feasibility and advantages in terms of full flow of operating process simulation in real battlefield environment.

Keywords: Integrated simulation system · Air-to-ground guided munitions · Hardware-in-the-loop · Mathematical simulation · Visual generating

1 Introduction

The military mainly use air-to-ground guided munitions to accomplish air-to-ground precision strike missions. The hitting accuracy and damage effect of air-to-ground guided munitions, which is influenced by numerous factors, can affect air sorties directly and eventually cause impact on overall effectiveness of combat systems [1].

Battlefield environment have an influence on the performance of air-to-ground guided munitions. For instance, it reduces the accuracy of air-to-ground munitions when the military conduct shooting tests on the sea than on the land due to more complex conditions. In real battlefield environment, which is even more complex, the hitting accuracy will go further down. Besides, although most current air-to-ground guided munitions are human-in-the-loop missiles, the pilots who control those weapons are still lacking of effective training especially in battlefield environment. Limited live-fire experiments make it hard to get hold of the real performance of the munitions in complex battlefield environment.

Xiaodong Zhu—This work is supported by the National Nature Science Foundation of China (Grant No. 61374185).

© Springer Science+Business Media Singapore 2016
L. Zhang et al. (Eds.): AsiaSim 2016/SCS AutumnSim 2016, Part II, CCIS 644, pp. 433–440, 2016.
DOI: 10.1007/978-981-10-2666-9_43

So we present an integrated simulation system for air-to-ground guided munitions. There have been many related researches on air-to-ground simulation systems, but most of them focus on specific details, such as the architecture of certain mathematical models, the FOM/SOM design of HLA based simulation systems and so on. Besides, air-to-ground munitions simulation system is highly related to the certain type of the munitions. There is a lack of related works on the whole architecture of integrated simulation system for a certain type of air-to-ground munitions.

The system we proposed joints mathematical simulation system, hardware-in-the-loop simulation system, visual generating system, and management systems together through networks. It can be used during the development stage and after. When the munitions are in the development stage, the simulation system can use engineering-level simulation models and other critical components to conduct full flow simulation of the operational process in real combat environment to identify the disadvantage of the technical solution and critical components. When the munitions are handed over, the simulation system can conduct plenty of experiments to test the performance of the munitions. With enough experimental data, we can arrange live-fire experiments more effectively which will save much time and funds. In addition, in order to provide pilots an effective training environment, the system can simulate typical targets and situations on the battlefield such as terrain environment, marine environment, false targets, and electro-magnetic interference, etc. In general, the simulation system is designed for the military to get hold of the operational performance of the air-to-ground guided munitions precisely and to accelerate the fighting capability formation of new equipment.

This paper is structured as follows. In Sect. 2, we discuss the structure of the simulation system. Section 3 describes system operating modes. Section 4 presents detailed design of the system. Section 5 uses a case study to test the performance. Finally, we draw conclusion.

2   System Structure

The system should be capable of running trajectory simulation, controlling simulation, environmental simulation and damage simulation of air-to-ground television guided munitions to evaluate performance and effectiveness of the munitions in battlefield environment [1, 2]. To satisfy those needs, we design the structure of the system as shown in Fig. 1. The system comprises five subsystems including experiment management system, data management system, mathematical simulation system, visual generating system and hardware-in-the-loop system.

- The experiment management system is used to make the simulation mission plan, monitor the simulation running and provide post-mortem analysis of the experimental data.
- The data management system builds simulation experimental database which stores the process data and results data of simulation experiments.
- The mathematical simulation system builds mathematical models of variety of air-to-ground guided munitions, aircrafts, battlefield environment and typical targets.

It can run real-time and faster than real-time simulation to evaluate the effectiveness of the munitions.

- The visual generating system builds global terrain environment and interference environment. It builds detailed model of critical area near the target and along the air route by generating vivid 3D scenes.
- Hardware-in-the-loop simulation system builds real simulation environment of the critical components of the air-to-ground guided munitions and aircrafts such as seeker and missile attitude simulator.

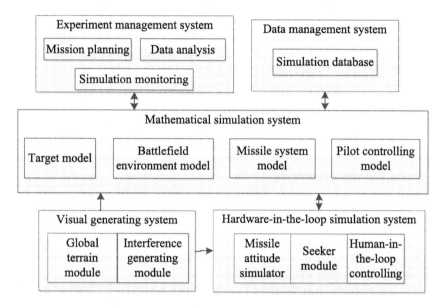

Fig. 1. Structure of integrated simulation system

Those five subsystems are connected to each other over a double-net structure, reflective memory network and infiniband network, so that the system can satisfy the need of low latency and high bandwidth.

3   System Operating Modes

In order to conduct diversified experiments, we design four kinds of operating modes for the simulation system. They are hardware-in-the-loop simulation for single weapon system, full digital simulation for single weapon system, Monte Carlo simulation for single weapon system, and joint simulation for multiple weapon systems.

- Hardware-in-the-loop simulation. Human controller and the critical components of the missile are linked into the system. With the help of mathematical models of the aircraft and environment, we build a real-time simulation system in this mode.
- Full digital simulation. This simulation is based on hardware-in-the-loop simulation. We use the physical units of missiles to adjust mathematical simulation models in

proper accuracy range. After adjustment and appropriate simplification, we can run real-time resolution of all mathematical simulation models of the missile on single computer.

- Monte Carlo simulation. After we have enough experimental data from human-in-the-loop simulation, we can turn human controlling activities into proper mathematical models in order to build full mathematical model for all operating process of the air-to-ground guided munitions. We can then conduct Monte Carlo simulation with full digital model which means we can complete large scale simulation calculation in a short time to improve the confidence of the simulation results.

- Joint simulation. The three kinds of simulation mentioned above can all be used in the simulation experiment of multiple weapon systems firing multiple targets. All the models of aircrafts and missiles share the same simulation time and space, and all simulation nodes are under unified management from the main control computer.

4   Detailed Design of the Simulation System

The simulation system comprises five subsystems. Due to limited space, we describe three of them including mathematical simulation system, hardware-in-the-loop simulation system, and visual generating system.

4.1   Mathematical Simulation System

The mathematical simulation system is the core of the whole simulation system. It provides the operating framework, takes control of the whole simulation process, and manages data exchanging among subsystems.

We design mathematical simulation system in two ways [3, 4]. On the one hand, it can run real-time resolutions of the missile system model and calculations of signal transmission which is related to the environment such as image transmission and satellite positioning. Besides, it simulates the prelaunch management action and controlling missile flight in human-in-the-loop way. On the other hand, the mathematical simulation system makes simulation plans, controls simulation process, and manages signal synchronizing and data exchanging among subsystems. In addition, it collects and stores simulation experiment data and is certainly capable of data analysis.

Based on the analysis above, we design the mathematical simulation system as shown in Fig. 2. The main control computer makes simulation plans, controls simulation process, and manages signal synchronizing and data exchanging. The mathematical simulation computer runs aircraft-missile weapon system model and environment model. Each mathematical simulation computer simulates one single weapon system and deals with environment signal transmission. We use reflective memory network to transfer the state data and target image of different simulation nodes while infiniband network is used to transfer monitoring command and data copies.

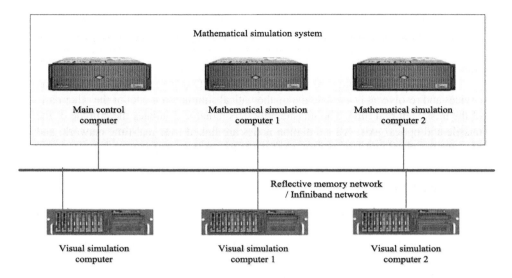

Fig. 2. Mathematical simulation system structure

4.2 Hardware-in-the-Loop Simulation System

The hardware-in-the-loop simulation system mainly focuses on identifying the mathematical simulation model of the given physical units, or adjusting the existing mathematical model with the help of physical units. It attaches missile units to the integrated simulation system to simulate the real working state of the missile. Besides, it can simulate the human interface and controlling process of the aircraft flight and weapon system to accomplish human-in-the-loop simulation.

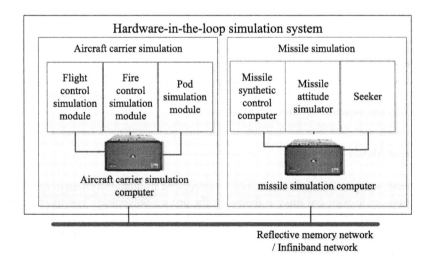

Fig. 3. Hardware-in-the-loop simulation system

The hardware-in-the-loop simulation system consists of real-time simulation computer, missile attitude simulator, weapon controlling device and other parts [5, 6]. All parts are connected over reflective memory network and infiniband network as shown in Fig. 3.

The simulation computers take participant in the I/O management of all simulation devices and resolve and calculate the mathematical simulation model of the other parts of the missile in real time. The missile attitude simulator simulates the attitude of the missile and optical axis. All simulation nodes are linked over real-time network, and time synchronized under management of the main control computer.

4.3 Visual Generating Simulation System

The visual generating simulation system can build a 3D global scene with global terrain database which can truly reproduce natural environment like ocean, land, weather, etc. Besides, it can also truly reproduce the battlefield environment. For instance, the system shows how sunlight and atmosphere affect the seeker of the missile and provides visual scene of the interference factors like smoke, dust, flame, etc. In addition, the system provides a 3D image of the movement of the aircraft carrier, missile and target. The structure of the system is as shown in Fig. 4.

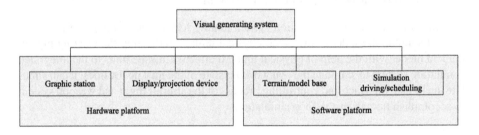

Fig. 4. Visual generating system

The system comprises two parts, one is hardware platform, and the other is software platform. The system uses high-performance graphic station to generate smooth 3D views and display/projection device to show them. Besides, it uses terrain/model base to provide visual support and simulation driving/scheduling to create real-time interactive virtual environment rapidly.

5 Case Study

In this case, we tested the performance of the integrated simulation system in full digital simulation mode with the missile flying by the pre-set waypoints. The main control computer initialized all simulation subsystems and controlled all systems during the process of simulation. The missile attacked a stationary target and we showed information on the moving trail and attitude angle of the missile.

5.1 Scenario Description

A fighter plane flew along the preset course carrying a certain type of the air-to-ground guided missile. When it reached the waypoint (−76000, 4000, 0), it fired the missile to attack the stationary target at the coordinate (0, 8, 0) on the ground. The missile used TV guidance during the flight with its seeker processing all the video images continuously and outputting control information after target recognizing.

5.2 Simulation Results

Here below are the coordinates of the waypoints, {(−76000, 4000, 0), (−45000, 2500, 0), (−40000, 2500, −1000), (−35000, 1000, −100), (−20000, 1000, 0), (−8000, 2000, 0), (0, 8, 0)}. The simulation results are shown in Figs. 6 and 7.

Figure 5 shows the moving trail of the missile. From the figure, we can see that this missile moved by all preset waypoints smoothly and hit the target eventually. Figure 6 shows information on the space attitude of the missile including the pitch angle, rolling angle, pitching trajectory and horizontal trajectory.

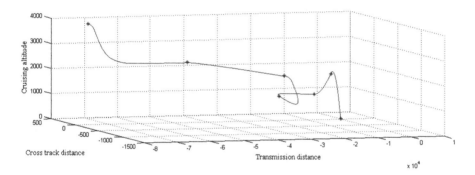

Fig. 5. The moving trail of the air-to-ground guided missile

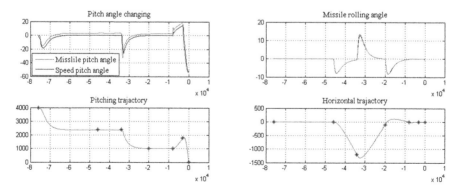

Fig. 6. The space attitude of the missile

From the two figures, we can see that this certain missile possessed a qualitative aerodynamic performance. In addition, we have proved the validity of the mathematical simulation model of the missile. The integrated simulation system can conduct all those kinds of simulation experiments by providing mathematical modeling, visual generating. However, it is still a primitive version and there is too much work left like promoting the visual effect, testing hardware-in-the-loop simulation, and so on.

6 Conclusion

In this paper, we proposed an integrated simulation system for the air-to-ground guided munitions. How to build the system is one of our main concerns. We designed the structure of the system consisting of five subsystems and presented details in three of them, mathematical simulation system, hardware-in-the-loop simulation system, and visual generating simulation system. We conducted a simple simulation experiment to test the performance of a certain missile and the results proved a primitive success in building the whole system.

However, in order to provide a reliable method to test the performance of the air-to-ground guided munitions in real battlefield environment, we still need to go further. In future work, we need to improve the quality of the visual generating system to make it seem more real. Besides, we need to test the hardware-in-the-loop simulation system and run more experiments on the whole system to perfect our design.

References

1. Mao, Z., Sun, L.G., et al.: Design and realization of air-to-ground TV-guided weapon simulation system. Syst. Simul. Technol. **6**(2), 140–146 (2010)
2. Zhang, Q.Z., Liu, J.Y.: Study of weapon system simulation on TV telecontrol missiles. Opt. Tech. **33**, 92–94 (2007)
3. Zhang, W.P., Wang, C.P., et al.: Analysis on simulated and tested system of countermeasure against laser guided weapon. Infrared Laser Eng. **35**, 353–357 (2006)
4. Li, P.B., Zhang, X.P., et al.: Using flight test data to validate the digital simulation model of homing guidance missile. J. Syst. Simul. **11**(3), 205–209 (1999)
5. Fan, S.P., Lin, D.F., et al.: Design and achievement of hardware-in-the-loop simulation system for guided shell based on laser semi-active seeker. Infrared Laser Eng. **2**, 394–397 (2014)
6. Yang, Y.L., Wu, X.Y., et al.: Design of hardware-in-the-loop simulation of flight control system for guided rocket. Fire Control Command Control **12**, 167–170 (2013)

Modeling and Simulation of Missile-Satellite Co-location System

Jia-zhen Duan$^{(\boxtimes)}$, Fei Cao, and Fu-zhong Bai

Rocket Force University of Engineering, Xi'an 710025, China
dbojue1989@163.com

Abstract. In order to improve the localization precision of airborne electronic reconnaissance equipment, Missile-satellite cooperative location method is proposed. First of all, the principle of this method is analyzed. Then the structure and process of location system is explained. At last, the feasibility of the system is proved and simulation is implemented in STK.

Keywords: Modeling and simulation · Cooperative location · STK · DOA

1 Introduction

With the development of electronic warfare (EW), it plays increasingly important role in modern warfare. Efficient attack of anti-radiation missile (ARM) depends on its precise position for enemy radiation source [1]. However, ARM is decoy easily when hit enemy radiation source. While building a anti-decoy system needs large cost and long time, electronic reconnaissance satellites can be used to help ARM get precise position of enemy because of their wide reconnaissance range and stability. Therefore, missile-satellite co-location technology is one of the effective way to improve the target position accuracy, it has a very important significance in actual combat [2].

2 Principle of Missile-Satellite Co-location

The DOA [3] method is used in missile-satellite co-location system. This method is finding direction of radiation source target on two or more platforms by direction-finding equipment which own high precision. Then establishing equation with known direction message of target and position message of platforms, solution of this equation is coordinates of radiation source target.

As shown in Fig. 1

$$\tan \theta_i = \frac{x - x_i}{y - y_i}, i = 1, 2 \tag{1}$$

According Eq. 1

© Springer Science+Business Media Singapore 2016
L. Zhang et al. (Eds.): AsiaSim 2016/SCS AutumnSim 2016, Part II, CCIS 644, pp. 441–449, 2016.
DOI: 10.1007/978-981-10-2666-9_44

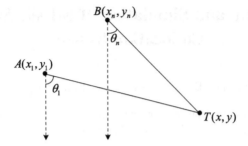

Fig. 1. Sketch map of direction finding cross localization

$$x_i - y_i \tan \theta_i = x - y \tan \theta_i \qquad (2)$$

In the case of n platforms, Eq. 2 can be simplified as Eq. 3

$$C = DX \qquad (3)$$

$$C = \begin{bmatrix} x_1 - y_1 \tan \theta_1 \\ x_2 - y_2 \tan \theta_2 \\ \vdots \\ x_n - y_n \tan \theta_n \end{bmatrix}, \quad D = \begin{bmatrix} 1, -\tan \theta_1 \\ 1, -\tan \theta_2 \\ \vdots \\ 1, -\tan \theta_n \end{bmatrix}, \quad X = \begin{bmatrix} x \\ y \end{bmatrix}, \quad \text{So the coordinates of}$$

radiation source is:

$$X = D^{-1}C \qquad (4)$$

3   Structure of Missile-Satellite Co-location System [4, 5]

As shown in Fig. 2, the positioning system consists of missile, satellite and enemy target. Supposed the missile can communicate with satellite as long as the satellite is in missile's vision field and communication process is not affected by other factors. Missile receive real-time messages of enemy radiation source from satellite during its flight process, these messages can help missile to track target more accurate and achieve precision hit. Specific processes are as follows (Fig. 3):

As the initiator, missile leads the whole process of co-location. The satellite has been running on its own track and keep continuous reconnaissance on the target area. The missile is launched at designated location at appointed time. The satellite sends real-time message of target within the time window given by missile. After that, the missile carries out the fusion of the target information provided by own seeker and satellite, then it calculates the target area, which provide favorable condition for the realization of precise strike (Fig. 4).

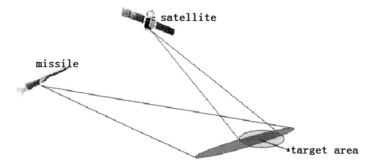

Fig. 2. Sketch map of missile-satellite co-location

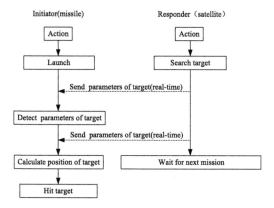

Fig. 3. Flow chart of missile-satellite co-location

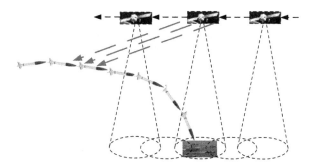

Fig. 4. Sketch map of missile-satellite co-location

4   Feasibility Analysis of Missile-Satellite Co-location

4.1   Communication Time Between Missile and Satellites Under Ideal Conditions [6]

4.1.1   Model of Satellite Motion

The position and velocity of the satellite are determined by six roots of satellite orbit (Fig. 5):

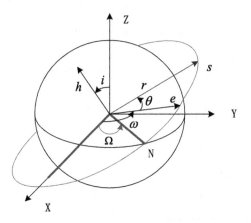

Fig. 5. Model of satellite motion

$$r = a(\cos \psi - e)e_0 + a\sqrt{1 - e^2} \sin \psi P_0 \tag{5}$$

$$v = -\frac{a^2 n}{r} \sin \psi e_0 + \frac{a^2 n}{r} \sqrt{1 - e^2} \cos \psi P_0 \tag{6}$$

$$e_o = \begin{bmatrix} \cos \Omega \cos \omega - \sin \Omega \sin \omega \cos i \\ \sin \Omega \cos \omega + \cos \Omega \sin \omega \cos i \\ \sin \omega \sin i \end{bmatrix} \begin{bmatrix} i \\ j \\ k \end{bmatrix} \tag{7}$$

$$P_0 = \begin{bmatrix} -\cos \Omega \sin \omega - \sin \Omega \cos \omega \cos i \\ -\sin \Omega \sin \omega + \cos \Omega \cos \omega \cos i \\ \cos \omega \sin i \end{bmatrix} \begin{bmatrix} i \\ j \\ k \end{bmatrix} \tag{8}$$

$$\psi - e \sin \psi = \sqrt{\frac{\mu}{a^3}} t_P = n t_P \tag{9}$$

4.1.2   Model of Missile Motion

Only consider the longitudinal motion of missile, the equations of motion can be written as:

$$\begin{cases} m\frac{dv}{dt} = P\cos\alpha - X - mg\sin\theta \\ mV\frac{d\theta}{dt} = P\sin\alpha + Y - mg\cos\theta \\ J_z\frac{d\omega_z}{dz} = M_z \\ \frac{d_x}{d_t} = V\cos\theta \\ \frac{dy}{dt} = V\sin\theta \\ \frac{d\vartheta}{dt} = \omega_z \\ \frac{dm}{dt} = -m_s \\ \alpha = \vartheta - \theta \\ \varepsilon_1 = 0 \\ \varepsilon_2 = 0 \end{cases} \qquad (10)$$

From above, there are 10 equations and 10 unknown parameters in this equation group, so it is consistent and can be handled independently.

4.1.3   Communication Condition Judgement Between Missile and Satellite [7, 8]

The initial judgement conditions are as follows (Fig. 6):

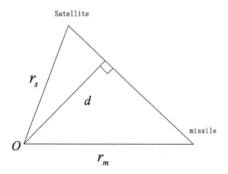

Fig. 6. Judgement condition1

The distance from earth's center to the straight line between missile and satellite is not less than the radius of earth R, $d \geq R$, but there is a special case (Fig. 7):

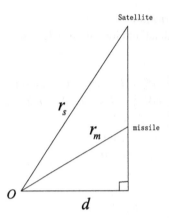

Fig. 7. Judgement condition2

Therefore, the judgement condition is modified as (Fig. 8):

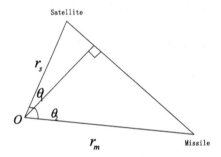

Fig. 8. Judgement condition3

$$
\begin{cases}
\theta_1 = \arccos(R/Rr_s) \\
\theta_2 = \arccos\left(\frac{R}{r_m}\right) \\
\theta_{\max} = \theta_1 + \theta_2 \\
\theta = \arccos\left(\frac{r_m \cdot r_s}{|r_m||r_s|}\right)
\end{cases}
\tag{11}
$$

As a result, the communication time period of the missile and satellite can be obtained.

5 Simulation in STK [9]

Parameter setting

Electronic reconnaissance satellites LD-1, LD-2, LD-3, LD-4, QS-1, QS-2, QS-3 are orbiting as designed. Missile launch site (108.985E, 19.176 N). Target ship (T) starting position (94.6031E, 51.74 N). Missile launching in Apr 5 2016 04:25:20 (Fig. 9).

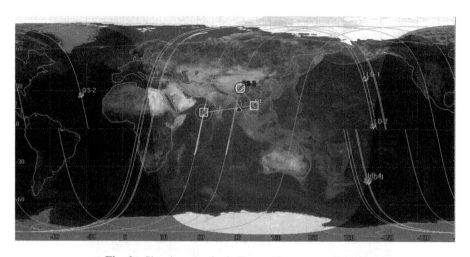

Fig. 9. Sketch map of missile-satellite communication

The simulation result shows that there are two satellites meet the communication requirements, and communication time is 673 s and 1037 s (Fig. 10).

```
DF-To-QS-1
----------
                    Access      Start Time (UTCG)           Stop Time (UTCG)          Duration (sec)
                    ------      -----------------------     -----------------------   --------------
                      1       5 Apr 2016 04:26:03.528     5 Apr 2016 04:37:16.972         673.444

Global Statistics
-----------------
Min Duration          1       5 Apr 2016 04:26:03.528     5 Apr 2016 04:37:16.972         673.444
Max Duration          1       5 Apr 2016 04:26:03.528     5 Apr 2016 04:37:16.972         673.444
Mean Duration                                                                             673.444
Total Duration                                                                            673.444
```

Fig. 10. Communication time of missile and QS-1

Under the condition of known satellite orbit, as long as the time is determined, the position of the satellite can be obtained, then the coverage of the satellite is known (Fig. 11).

```
DF-To-QS-3
----------
                    Access      Start Time (UTCG)           Stop Time (UTCG)          Duration (sec)
                    ------      -----------------------     -----------------------   --------------
                      1       5 Apr 2016 04:25:20.000     5 Apr 2016 04:42:37.048         1037.048

Global Statistics
-----------------
Min Duration          1       5 Apr 2016 04:25:20.000     5 Apr 2016 04:42:37.048         1037.048
Max Duration          1       5 Apr 2016 04:25:20.000     5 Apr 2016 04:42:37.048         1037.048
Mean Duration                                                                             1037.048
Total Duration                                                                            1037.048
```

Fig. 11. Communication time of missile and QS-3

The simulation result shows that only QS-3 can detect the target area, and the time period is overlapped with the missile's flight time, so only the QS-3 meets the conditions of missile-satellite co-location (Fig. 12).

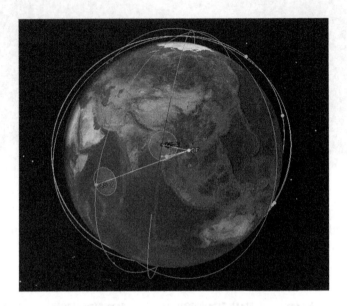

Fig. 12. Sketch map of satellite reconnaissance area

6 Conclusion

This article in view of insufficient localization accuracy of the anti-radiation missile. Principle, structure and process of missile-satellite co-location system under ideal communication condition is introduced, and proved the feasibility [10] of this method, the simulations is conducted in STK. However, actual battlefield is complex, achievement of missile-satellite co-location must depends on the rich resources of satellite and reasonable task scheduling. Believe that with the development of China's military modernization, large-scale, cross-platform joint operations can be implemented soon (Fig. 13).

```
Coverage for QS-3
-----------------

                    Access      Access Start (UTCG)        Access End (UTCG)          Duration (sec)   Asset Full Name
                    ------      -------------------        -----------------          --------------   ---------------
                       1        5 Apr 2016 04:25:36.877    5 Apr 2016 04:39:22.397          825.520     T
                       2        5 Apr 2016 06:07:33.536    5 Apr 2016 06:11:08.146          214.610     T

Global Statistics
-----------------
Min Duration           2        5 Apr 2016 06:07:33.536    5 Apr 2016 06:11:08.146          214.610     T
Max Duration           1        5 Apr 2016 04:25:36.877    5 Apr 2016 04:39:22.397          825.520     T
Mean Duration                                                                               520.065
Total Duration                                                                             1040.130
```

Fig. 13. Time of satellite reconnaissance target area

References

1. Haworth, D.P., Smith, N.G., Bardelli, R., et al.: Interference localization for EUTELSAT satellites - the first European transmitter location system. Int. J. Satell. Commun. **15**(4), 155–183 (1997)
2. Ho, K.C., Chan, Y.T.: Geolocation of a known altitude object from TDOA and FDOA measurements. IEEE Trans. AES **33**(3), 770–783 (1997)
3. Rieken, D.W., Fuhrmann, D.R.: Generalizing MUSIC and MVDR multiple noncoherent arrays. IEEE Trans. SP **9**(52), 2396–2406 (2004)
4. Zhou, Z.: The Modeling and Implementation of Electronic Reconnaissance Simulation System. Xidian University
5. Zhang, R.: Satellite Orbit Attitude Dynamics and Control. Beihang University Press, Beijing (2006)
6. Zhang, S.: Modeling and simulation of passive radar system. Master thesis, Xi'an Electronic and Science University, Xi'an (2011)
7. Xu, Z., Wang, G., Jiang, F., Zhang, R.: Application research of UML in electronic warfare simulation and modeling. Command Control Simul. **31**(5), 1 (2009)
8. Jingjuan, Z., Lifen, T., Juncheng, J.: New missile cooperative localization technology. J. Beihang Univ. **38**(9), 1149–1153 (2012)
9. Peng, R., Wang, G., Shi, J., Yuan, J.: Two bombs and collaborative localization feasibility study. J. Syst. Simul. **18**(5), 1118–1122 (2006)
10. Hu, L.: Passive Location, pp. 31–79. National Defense Industry Press, Beijing (2004)

Behavior Modeling of Air to Ship Fighter Based on Context-Based Reasoning

Ying-tong Lu[✉], Liang Han, Xiao Song, and Jiang-yun Wang

School of Automation Science and Electrical Engineering, Beihang University, Beijing, China
luciaxgd@163.com

Abstract. With the development of military intelligence training system, behavior modeling becomes the core technology in Computer Generated Forces (CGF). The Context-based Reasoning (CxBR) Framework facilitates building behavior model of Computer Generated Forces because of its visualization, maintainability and non-predetermination. However, it is limited in its ability to support models that include affective reasoning. In order to imitate human behavior more realistically, human affect comes to be considered. By adding two abstract classes to the original framework which are analogous to the Mission and Context classes, representing Mood and Emotion, improved CxBR framework can remedy this limitation and consider the affect. This paper validates the feasibility of the improved CxBR framework by building air to ship fighter system structure using conversion logic of production representation.

Keywords: Computer Generated Forces (CGF) · Behavior model · Context-based Reasoning (CxBR) · Air to ship fighter

1 Introduction

In the air-sea combat training system, the CGF (Computer Generated Force, CGF) is used mainly for pilots' tactical training. In order to improve pilots' strain capacity, the behavior model should be multivariate and uncertain. The introduction of artificial intelligence technology greatly improves the autonomy and authenticity of behavior. Main artificial intelligence technologies used in behavior modeling are Intelligent Agents, Soft Computing and Case Based Reasoning (CBR). Context-based Reasoning belongs to CBR. It is founded on the premise that humans make decisions based on a sub-set of their knowledge, which is referenced according to one's current environment or context. In other words, for any given situation, there are but a limited number of expected occurrences: therefore, one's actions and reactions are chosen from expected experiences based on past history [1]. Because of its visualization, maintainability, non-predetermination and high searching efficiency, CxBR is widely applied in behavior modeling.

In order to suit diverse engineering requirements, many kinds of modified frameworks have been put forward in recent years. Barrett described a Formation Class to allow modeling teamwork and collaborative behaviors in CxBR [2]. Stensrud and Barrett presented rigorous definitions of all terms and components applicable to CxBR

© Springer Science+Business Media Singapore 2016
L. Zhang et al. (Eds.): AsiaSim 2016/SCS AutumnSim 2016, Part II, CCIS 644, pp. 450–457, 2016.
DOI: 10.1007/978-981-10-2666-9_45

models along with a discussion on how and where these models store and execute tactical knowledge [3]. Liu and Huang integrated CxBR with professional system, fuzzy reasoning and database [4]. Stensrud et al. added emotional impact of context reasoning to improve the traditional CxBR framework [5]. In 2011, Chen applied the improved CxBR model to anti-submarine helicopters, and carried out the preliminary investigation on feasibility of the framework [6]. For a detailed explanation of CxBR please review [7]. For a detailed explanation of the CxBR framework prior to the improvement to facilitate affective modeling, please see [8].

This paper introduces an improved context-based reasoning framework which considered the affect, and applied it to air-ship fighter CGF. Using conversion logic of production representation, air-to-ship fighter CGF system structure is established. Finally, the feasibility of the theoretical framework gets a validation.

2   Traditional CxBR and Improved CxBR

This paper introduces traditional CxBR framework and improved CxBR framework with affect.

2.1   The Principle of Traditional CxBR

The basic idea of CxBR is that when an Agent tasks, it always experiences orderly through several different states. Agent requires a certain skill and action in each state. In general, the states change suddenly rather than gradually.

In CxBR, three levels of Context are defined: Mission Context, Main Context and Sub-Context, as shown in Fig. 1.

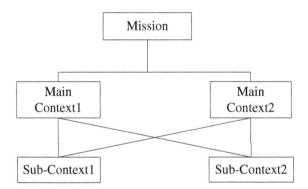

Fig. 1. Levels of context

Mission Context is the highest level and defines the tasks of Agent, including rang of mission, objects, plans and constraints (time, weather, rules of engagement) when performing specific tasks.

Main Context is the next lower level and is an essential element to control Agent, including functions, rules and a list of all Main Contexts that can be reached from the current Main Context. Main Contexts can transform between each other, for example, when plane detects the object, cruise state should be transformed to the state of tracking object.

Sub-Context is the lowest-level tactical process that usually occurs in a very short time, for example, in the state of attacking object, there are such actions as tension loading, climbing, missile release and glide. Sub-Contexts are mutually exclusive at the same time, but can be reused by different Main Contexts. Sub-Context is activated by rules defined in current Main Context and cancels its active state after completing the action.

Context can be seen as a representation of case knowledge, and it is the synthesis containing entity behavior, objects, characters, environments and knowledge of logic. Context can be abstracted to the implication body of relative information. Context has the following properties:

- Constraints: define all constraints restraining the Agent. Such as wind speed and atmosphere density of the battlefield environment, limitation of the force and the affect of the Agent.
- Mission: defines goals of the Agent. Such as Weapons such as warship launch hit probability reaches the specified array bit time.
- Mutual exclusion: defines exclusive events with the same level. Such as cruise and missile release. When the Agent is in the state of cruise, it is impossible to carry out actions of missile release.
- Transformation: defines exclusive events can transform with each other. Such as cruise and missile release. If the Agent detects the target and satisfies the condition of releasing missile in the state of cruise, the Agent can change the state to missile release.

In the Fig. 2, the traditional CxBR contains four abstract classes: AIP (Autonomous Intelligent Platform), Mission, Context and Inference Engine, which create an API (Application Program Interface) to facilitate modeling human behaviors. The AIP class provides an interface for modeling agents. The Mission and Context class provide the means for an agent to react and plan within a given scenario. The Inference Engine is used for simulate the process of matching facts.

Every agent is assigned a mission before simulation begins. The mission defines the high level goal the agent is expected to pursue for a given scenario, and specifies the contexts that will be applicable to the agent. Contexts provide the planning and reaction abilities of the agent and specify all the conditions to control the AIP's behavior in tactical simulation. Contexts also provide any other possible contexts which can be reached from the current active context. The current active Context searches for the next possible Context when the state changes. Once finds the next Context, the current Context will set it invalid and activate the new Context. AIP can be controlled intelligently by continuous conversions of Contexts. The relationship between contexts, missions and agents is shown in Fig. 3.

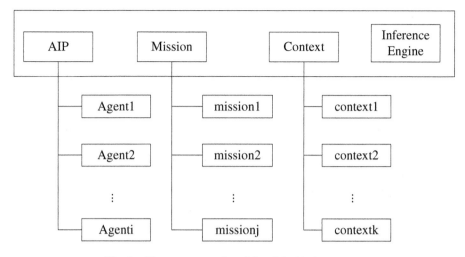

Fig. 2. Class structure of traditional CxBR framework

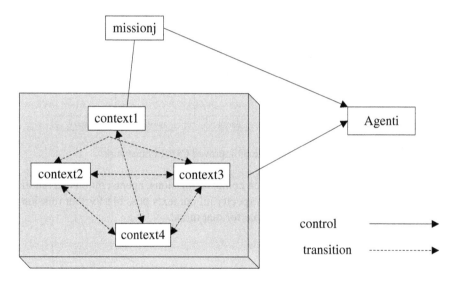

Fig. 3. Conversion diagram of traditional CxBR

CxBR packages process behavior and cognitive behavior in a particular state action, and reflects human skills and experience collection to control AIP.

2.2 The Principle of Improved CxBR

In a real human behavior, motivation and emotion have an important impact on cognitive behavior process. It will make CGF behavior modeling more realistic and increase the uncertainty of CGF behavior by considering affect impacts. This framework is suit to affective agents, such as pilots, drivers and athletes.

Most of the emotional upheaval human experience can be called affect. Two specific manifestations of affect are mood and emotion. Emotion can be induced by some certain reasons and its duration is short. For example, a pilot will have an emotion of happiness when he hits the target. However, if he cannot hit the next target, he will have an emotion of frustration. Six basic emotions include anger, fear, sadness, joy, nausea and surprises. Compared with emotion, mood cannot be induced by some certain reasons and its duration is longer. For example, a pilot maybe impatient in a rainy day, but we cannot find a certain reason case the mood. In majority, humans have two moods: positive and negative.

Improved CxBR framework is enhanced by adding the additional abstract classes to the traditional CxBR framework. The Improved CxBR framework includes Mood and Emotion. Relationship between mood and emotion is similar to that of the mission and context. In the same way, a mood specifies all possible emotions that an agent maybe experience. The class structure of improved CxBR Framework is shown as Fig. 4.

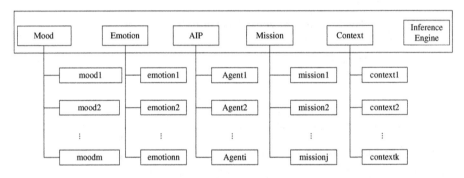

Fig. 4. Class structure of improved CxBR Framework

The conversion relationship between contexts, missions, agents, mood and emotion is shown in Fig. 5. As a mission must specify all contexts possible for that mission, a mood must specify all emotions possible for that mood.

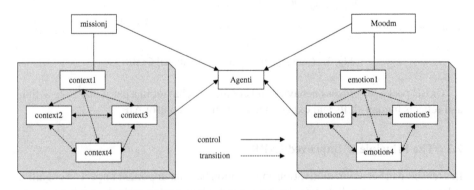

Fig. 5. Conversion diagram of improved CxBR

3   Air-Ship Fighter Behavior Model Based on Improved CxBR

3.1   Context Definition of Air-Ship's Fighter CGF

Air-ship fighter's behavior can be divided into five levels: the mission context, task context, subtask context, mood context and emotion context. Mission context is an overall goal in a tactical scenario, such as convoying, attacking ship with missiles, attacking ship with bombs and so on. Task context is a stage task taken to achieve the overall goal in a tactical scenario, such as cruise, tracking the target and missile release in the mission of attacking ship with missiles. Subtask context includes relatively independent and low-level tactical sub-actions, such as level flight, rising, missile, unloading, downthrust and rolling in the task context of missile release. Mood context is similar to mission context, and represent the mood state of the agent. Emotion context contains all emotions under the mood state. Mission context includes corresponding task context, and task context includes corresponding sub-task context. Similarly, mood context includes corresponding emotion context. Actions between these contexts are mutually independent.

3.2   Conversion Logic of Contexts

In the decision on attacking ship, current active context and sub-context control behavior of CGF. Context conversion is completed by the corresponding matching rules. When a context is activated, its corresponding rules are traversed all through in the simulation until a rule is matched then the conversion process is carried out, as a result, a new context is activated and its initialization function is called.

Rules' matching is used to realize relative recognition. This paper adopts production representation to achieve CxBR conversion logic.

The basic form of production representation is P-> Q or If P Then Q. Where P is the premise of production, and it is used to indicate whether the production is available; Q is a set of conclusions or operation, and it is used to indicate the deserved conclusion and operation when premise conditions P indicates are satisfied.

In the CxBR, P = {Context-Relative, Emotion} and Q = {Context-Action}.

For example, if the pilot find a destroyer in cruise with an emotion of fear, he might choose escape. On the contrary, if the pilot is in an emotion of confidence, he maybe chooses attack directly.

4   Architecture of Air-Ship Fighter CGF System

As shown in Fig. 6, architecture of Air-ship fighter CGF consists of two main parts: physical model and behavior model. Physical model and behavior model are realized with the development tool named Visual Studio 2010.

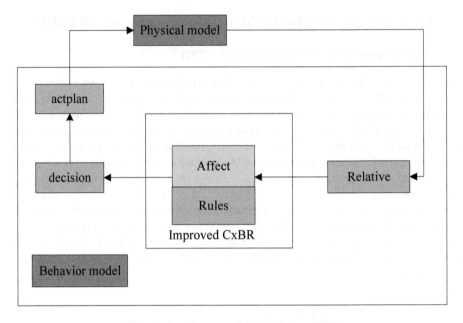

Fig. 6. Architecture of air-ship fighter CGF

4.1 Physical Model

Physical model reflects CGF's external capabilities, such as the performance of motor apparatus, fire system and detection equipment. Physical model consists of airplane model, weapon models and radar detection model. Among them, airplane model adopts limit parameter model which includes only six degrees of freedom kinematic equations. The advantage of using the limit parameter model is that dynamic model of the aircraft can be built without aerodynamic parameters. In another words, in order to describe movements and attitudes of aircrafts, building six degrees of freedom kinematics module is sufficient. There is no need to design the complex control law based on control surfaces, due to which, modeling complexity and workload can be greatly simplified.

4.2 Behavior Model

Behavior model reflects CGF entity's inherent "mental activity". In another words, behavior model describes the decision capability of the agent. Behavior model includes detection module, battlefield relative module, decision module based on improved CxBR and act planning module. According to the analysis of the battlefield relative, decision can be made based on improved CxBR which considers the influence of affect. Finally, action can be made according to the decision and physical model implements the action.

5 Conclusion

This paper introduced the traditional CxBR and adopted the improved CxBR adding affect module frame to build behavior model of air-ship fighter CGF, and applied production representation to achieve the context conversion logic, finally established the air-ship fighter CGF system structure to explore and verify preliminarily the feasibility of improved CxBR in air-ship fighter. This article battlefield environment in this paper is relatively simple, so the feasibility of the theory in a more complex environment has yet to be verified.

References

1. Guo, Q.-S., Yang, L.-G., Yang, R.-P.: Introduction of CGF. National Defense Industry Press, Beijing (2006)
2. Barrett, G.B., Gonzalez, A.: Modeling collaborative behaviors in context based reasoning. In: Working Report: Intelligent Systems Laboratory, University of Central Florida, Orlando (2002)
3. Stensrud, B.S., Barrett, G.C.: Context-based reasoning: a revised specification. In: Seventeenth International Florida Artificial Intelligence Research Society Conference (2004)
4. Liu, J., Huang, W.-B.: Research on decision modeling of antisubmarine warship based on CxBR. Comput. Simul. (2006)
5. Stensrud, B.S., Barrett, G.C., Lisetti, C.L., Gonzalez, A.: Modeling affect in context based reasoning. ResearchGate (2015)
6. Chen, T., Li, Z.-S.: Behavioral modeling of antisubmarine helicopter in the simulation of naval battle. Command Control Simul. (2011)
7. Gonzalez, A.: Context-based representation of intelligent behavior in training simulations. Trans. Soc. Comput. Simul. **15**(4), 153–166 (1998)
8. Norlander, L.: A framework for efficient implementation of context-based reasoning in intelligent simulation. Master's thesis, ECE Department, University of Central Florida, Orlando (1999)

Pilot Behavior Modeling Using LSTM Network: A Case Study

Yanan Zhou[1], Zihao Fu[2], and Guanghong Gong[1(✉)]

[1] School of Automation Science and Electrical Engineering, Beihang University
(BUAA), XueYuan Road No.37, HaiDian District, Beijing 100191, China
zyn_asee@126.com, ggh@buaa.edu.cn
[2] Alibaba Group, Beijing 100022, China
fllubo@qq.com

Abstract. Traditional behavior modeling methods rely on the knowledge representation derived from the induction and abstraction of subject matter experts, leading to the high barrier and long modeling period. To tackle this problem, we focus on a new behavior modeling approach, which extracts behavior knowledge from behavior data using recurrent neural network (RNN). A case study, take-off behavior modeling using long short-term memory (LSTM) network, was carried out in three phases: the data recording phase, the offline model training phase and the online model execution phase. A three-layer neural network was constructed to learn the pattern of take-off manipulations. The resulting take-off behavior model performed well to 'pilot' an airplane in the real-time test.

Keywords: Behavior modeling · Flight simulation · LSTM · RNN

1 Introduction

The importance of behavior model in the area of constructive simulation has been widely accepted [1], while it faces great challenges to build authentic behavior models. One of the major difficulties is the obstacle to access and represent the domain knowledge.

Deep understanding of the domain knowledge is pre-requisite for the modelers to utilize most of the present behavior modeling methods, including classical methods (e.g. rule-based method [2], finite state machine [3], etc.) and cognition-based methods (e.g. SOAR [4], ACT-R [5], etc.). As a consequence, the knowledge from subject matter experts (SMEs) is crucial to the quality of behavior model.

The present behavior modeling methods rely on the knowledge representation derived from SMEs' induction and abstraction. In this way, the threshold of behavior modeling becomes higher, and the modeling period becomes longer.

Besides, some kinds of behavior are difficult to model using traditional methods. For instance, the behavior knowledge of pilot behavior refers much to the pilot experience, which is beyond the representation ability of present modeling methods. To model pilot behavior, the SMEs have to firstly segment the behavior into several elementary stages, and describe the process and features of each stage; secondly, the

© Springer Science+Business Media Singapore 2016
L. Zhang et al. (Eds.): AsiaSim 2016/SCS AutumnSim 2016, Part II, CCIS 644, pp. 458–465, 2016.
DOI: 10.1007/978-981-10-2666-9_46

modelers would build the behavior model of each stage according to the knowledge described by the SMEs; at last, the modelers are able to join up the stages using modeling techniques such as flow diagram or finite state machine (FSM).

We focus on a new approach to model behavior, which extracts behavior knowledge from behavior data rather than relying on SMEs. Considering that pilot behaviors are mainly recorded in the form of sequence data, we adopt LSTM network, a kind of recurrent neural network, to learn the knowledge in the behavior data.

LSTM is able to process sequence data and handle the long term dependency in sequence data [6]. The state of art progresses of LSTM are mostly applied in the frontier domains of machine learning such as natural language processing (NLP) problems [7–9], speech recognition [10], handwriting recognition [10], polyphonic music modeling [10], text categorization [11], action recognition [12], automatic diagnose [13], etc. In this case study to model sequential behavior, we attempt to apply LSTM on pilot behavior modeling area.

This paper is organized as follows. Section 2 gives a brief review of RNN and LSTM, and introduces the method of modeling pilot behavior using LSTM. In Sect. 3, the detail of a case study to model take-off behavior using LSTM is demonstrated. Finally, a discussion is given in Sect. 4, and the future work is also introduced.

2 Method

2.1 Background: RNN and LSTM

RNN is a kind of neural network that process sequential data inputs. Different from ordinary forward Neural Network (NN), RNN can preserve part of the past information in the sequence, thereby discovering the long-term dependencies and sequence patterns [14].

Figure 1 is the structure of a typical RNN [14], and the equivalent structure which is unfolded in time. The RNN module's input comes from external input and the module state from the last time step. In this way, the output of RNN (o_t), depends on not only the input of present step (x_t), but also all the inputs of previous steps ($x_{t'}$, where $t' < t$).

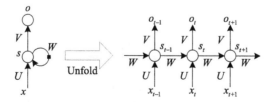

Fig. 1. The typical structure of RNN

Among all the variants of RNN, LSTM is one of the most widely-used one, which remedies the original RNN's defect of long-term memory by eliminating the gradient vanishing problem [6]. The unit module of LSTM is called the cell, illustrated in

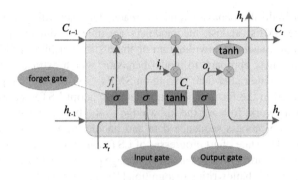

Fig. 2. The inside structure of a LSTM cell

Fig. 2 [15]. Each cell contains 3 filtering gates: the forget gate, the input gate and the output gate, corresponding to the three sigmoid layers in Fig. 2. The circles with '+' mark or '×' mark represent pointwise operations. The meanings of variables in Fig. 2 are as follows: x_t and h_t denote the input and output of the cell in time step t; C_t is the cell state; f_t, i_t and o_t are the outputs of forget gate, input gate and output gate respectively. Variables in Fig. 2 are updated according to the following formulas:

$$f_t = \sigma\left(W_f \cdot [h_{t-1}, x_t] + b_f\right)$$
$$i_t = \sigma(W_i \cdot [h_{t-1}, x_t] + b_i)$$
$$\tilde{C}_t = \tanh(W_C \cdot [h_{t-1}, x_t] + b_C)$$
$$C_t = f_t * C_{t-1} + i_t * \tilde{C}_t$$
$$o_t = \sigma(W_o \cdot [h_{t-1}, x_t] + b_o)$$
$$h_t = o_t * \tanh(C_t)$$

where σ denotes the sigmoid function, W_f, W_i, W_o and W_C are the weight matrices, and b_f, b_i, b_o and b_C are the bias vectors.

The state of art progresses of LSTM are mostly applied in the frontier domains of machine learning such as machine translation, speech recognition, etc. Gradient descent approach can be used to train the parameters of LSTM network, and RMSProp method is recommended in practice [16].

2.2   Pilot Behavior Modeling Using LSTM

Pilot behavior is the manipulations performed by airplane pilot in various flight situations, which is highly depended on the pilot's flying experience. For example, in the take-off stage (assuming that all the pre-take-off operations are finished), the pilot releases the parking brake at first, and pushes the throttle to increase thrust and begin the take-off run; when the running speed exceeds the rotation speed[1], the pilot gently

---

[1] Rotation speed is the speed at which the pilot begins to apply control inputs to cause the aircraft nose to pitch up, after which it will leave the ground [17].

pulls back the control wheel to raise the elevator which causes the airplane's nose to pitch upward slightly and the lift increases; as the airplane lifts clear of the runway, the pilot manipulates the control wheel to maintain the best rate-of-climb airspeed and the corresponding pitch angle; at last, as the desired altitude is reached, the airplane pitches downward to a level flight state. Analogously, the pilot behaviors in the course flight stage and landing stage are also series of sequential manipulations.

To model sequential behavior, traditional approaches normally use flow-based method or FSM, segmenting the behavior into several basic states and modeling the behavior state by state. However, profound understanding to the behavior is required.

In fact, pilot behavior can be modeled as a typical sequence to sequence learning model. Shown in Fig. 3, the LSTM module reads the flight state data as input at each time step, and outputs the corresponding manipulation data at the same time. As a consequence, the pilot behavior is represented as a mapping which maps the flight state sequence to the manipulation sequence. The output manipulation data depend on not only the present flight state, but also the history states, for the LSTM module is able to 'remember' the past flight states.

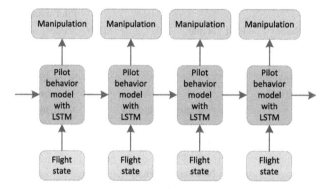

Fig. 3. Pilot behavior model with LSTM, which is a sequence to sequence learning model

3 Case Study: Aircraft Take-Off Behavior Modeling

To verify the pilot behavior modeling method, we conducted a case study that models take-off behavior using LSTM network. The configurations of the experiment are illustrated in Fig. 4. FlightGear, an open source flight simulator [18, 19], was adopted to provide authentic flight scenery and flexible control interfaces. The experiment was carried out in 3 phases: the data recording phase, the offline model training phase and the online model execution phase.

In the data recording phase, 10 sets of take-off flight data, which were produced by a pilot, were recorded from FlightGear at the frequency of 8 Hz. Listed in Table 1, the recorded data consists of flight state data and pilot manipulation data.

In the offline model training phase, a three-layer neural network was constructed. Shown in Fig. 5, the neural network contains two stacked LSTM layers and one dense layer (forward neural network layer with no recurrent connections). The 18-dimensional

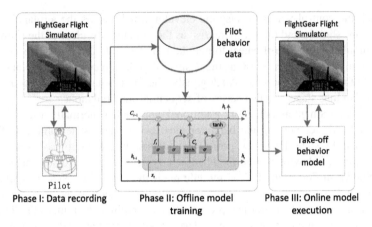

Fig. 4. The procedure of the experiment to model take-off behavior with LSTM

Table 1. Data recorded in the first phase: flight state data and pilot manipulation data

Flight state data						Pilot manipulation data	
Name	Unit	Name	Unit	Name	Unit	Name	Unit
Altitude	ft	Airspeed	kt	$\dot{v}$	ft/s^2	Normalized aileron control	–
Roll angle	deg	Vertical speed	ft/s	$\dot{w}$	ft/s^2	Normalized elevator control	–
Pitch angle	deg	u	ft/s	Normalized elevator position	–	Normalized rudder control	–
Heading angle	deg	v	ft/s	Normalized flap position	–		
Sideslip angle	deg	w	ft/s	Normalized aileron position	–		
Attack angle	deg	$\dot{u}$	ft/s^2	Normalized rudder position	–		

flight state variables are fed into the first LSTM layer, which has an 80-dimensional hidden layer; analogously, the second LSTM layer has a 30-dimensional hidden layer; the dense layer receives the output of the second LSTM layer, and maps it to a 3-dimensional output, which represents the pilot manipulation data.

It should be noted that the number of layers and the sizes of the hidden layers are determined empirically as a compromise. On the one hand, the more complexity the problem has, the more layers and larger hidden layer sizes will be preferred. On the other hand, large layer number and hidden layer sizes lead to slow convergence and more demand for training data. In general, the network structure is the result of several trial and error tests.

Using the flight state data as feature samples and flight manipulation data as target samples, the above network can be trained in the manner of supervised machine

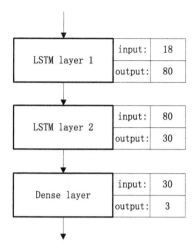

Fig. 5. Structure of the three-layer neural network

learning problem. We used mean squared error function as the objective function, and adopted the RMSProp method to optimize the parameters. After 100 episodes training with 10 sets of take-off flight data, as shown in Fig. 6, the elevator control output was able to fit the expected manipulation pattern. It should be noted that the aileron control output and the rudder control output were approximatively zeros all the time for the take-off scenario assumed no crosswind at the airport.

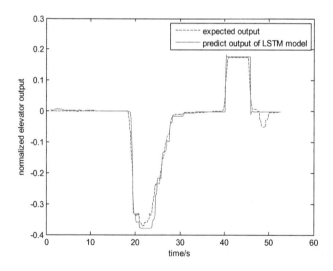

Fig. 6. The expected elevator control curve and the output curve after 100 episodes training with 10 sets of take-off flight data

After the offline training, the LSTM network can be used in the online model execution phase as the take-off behavior model to drive the flight model in FlightGear. The take-off behavior model was linked to FlightGear using generic I/O protocol of FlightGear via socket connection.

The profile of the online take-off flight is illustrated in Fig. 7. In order to evaluate the performance of the take-off behavior model quantitatively, 5 index parameters of the 10 sample flights and the online model execution flight are listed in Table 2. The index parameters are: the rotation speed (V_r), the maximum climb angle (θ_m), the average climb angle (θ_a), the level-off altitude (h_l) and the climb duration (t_c). As shown in Table 2, the index parameters of the online model execution fall in a reasonable area which is correspond to the sample flights.

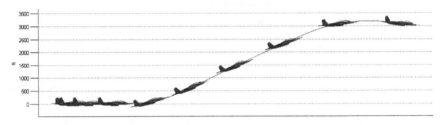

Fig. 7. The profile of the online take-off flight driven by the LSTM model

Table 2. The index parameters of the 10 sample flights and the online model execution flight

Groups		V_r/kt	θ_m/deg	θ_a/deg	h_l/ft	t_c/s
Sample flights	1	193.0	23.8	15.6	3078.7	26.5
	2	198.9	23.7	15.8	3215.5	31.1
	3	186.7	24.0	14.0	3047.5	30.2
	4	188.4	24.5	15.7	3098.0	27.7
	5	194.9	21.7	10.8	3056.7	37.4
	6	190.9	21.8	14.6	3077.0	27.9
	7	183.7	24.4	16.5	3195.0	26.7
	8	187.0	23.2	15.2	3101.9	26.3
	9	191.4	21.1	14.6	3063.9	27.0
	10	188.4	22.4	13.0	2946.3	31.0
	Average	190.3	23.1	14.6	3088.1	29.2
Online execution flight		192.6	22.5	14.9	3176.1	27.8

4 Discussion and Future Work

The resulting take-off behavior model performed well to 'pilot' an airplane in the real-time test. However, it is still far from a mature approach to model behaviors. Firstly, the design of neural network structure depends on the experience, which means amount of time-consuming attempts. Secondly, the recorded samples are extremely important for the quality of the resulting model. As a consequence, great effort should be made on the data recording phase. Last but not least, the computational efficiency of the neural network model should not be ignored to ensure the control without delay.

The future work aims to improve the pilot behavior model by collecting more behavior data samples in various flight environments and different types of airplane. Furthermore, more complex pilot behaviors, e.g. air combat maneuvers, will be modeled in the following research using the approach in this paper.

References

1. NATO Research and Technology Organisation: Human behavior representation in constructive simulation. Technical report RTO-TR-HFM-128 (2009)
2. Tian, S.C., Sun, F., Li, Z.Y., et al.: Research on CGF behavior modeling based on rule. Appl. Mech. Mater. **347**, 3056–3059 (2013)
3. Xiu-Luo, L., Huang, K., Xiao-Jun, Z.: The application of finite state machine in the CGF's behavior modeling. Acta Simulata Systematica Sinica **5**, 037 (2001)
4. Laird, J.E., Newell, A., Rosenbloom, P.S.: Soar: an architecture for general intelligence. Artif. Intell. **33**(1), 1–64 (1987)
5. Anderson, J.R., Matessa, M., Lebiere, C.: ACT-R: a theory of higher level cognition and its relation to visual attention. Hum.-Comput. Interact. **12**(4), 439–462 (1997)
6. Lipton, Z.C.: A critical review of recurrent neural networks for sequence learning. arXiv preprint arXiv:1506.00019 (2015)
7. Sutskever, I., Vinyals, O., Le, Q.V.: Sequence to sequence learning with neural networks. In: Advances in Neural Information Processing Systems, pp. 3104–3112 (2014)
8. Ghosh, S., Vinyals, O., Strope, B., et al.: Contextual LSTM (CLSTM) models for large scale NLP tasks. arXiv preprint arXiv:1602.06291 (2016)
9. Luan, Y., Ji, Y., Ostendorf, M.: LSTM based conversation models. arXiv preprint arXiv: 1603.09457 (2016)
10. Greff, K., Srivastava, R.K., Koutník, J., et al.: LSTM: a search space odyssey. arXiv preprint arXiv:1503.04069 (2015)
11. Johnson, R., Zhang, T.: Supervised and semi-supervised text categorization using one-hot LSTM for region embeddings. arXiv preprint arXiv:1602.02373 (2016)
12. Zhu, W., Lan, C., Xing, J., et al.: Co-occurrence feature learning for skeleton based action recognition using regularized deep LSTM networks. In: The 30th AAAI Conference on Artificial Intelligence (2015)
13. Lipton, Z.C., Kale, D.C., Elkan, C., et al.: Learning to diagnose with LSTM recurrent neural networks. arXiv preprint arXiv:1511.03677 (2015)
14. LeCun, Y., Bengio, Y., Hinton, G.: Deep learning. Nature **521**(7553), 436–444 (2015)
15. Christopher, O.: Understanding LSTM Networks (2015). http://colah.github.io/posts/2015-08-Understanding-LSTMs/
16. Keras development team. Keras documentation, usage of optimizer (2016). http://keras.io/optimizers/
17. Wikipedia. V speeds (2016). https://en.wikipedia.org/wiki/V_speeds/
18. Perry, A.R.: The flightgear flight simulator. In: Proceedings of the USENIX Annual Technical Conference (2004)
19. FlightGear development team. Introduction to FlightGear (2016). http://www.flightgear.org/about/

The Accuracy Enhancement of Angle Measurement for Compact RF/IR Compound Target Simulation System

Li Yanhong[1]([⊠]), Chen Dong[2], Tian Yi[1], Pang Xudong[1], and Zhang Li[1]

[1] Shanghai Electro-Mechanical Engineering Institute, Shanghai, China
lianhongg@126.com
[2] East China Normal University, Shanghai, China

Abstract. MMW/IR compound target simulation system can provide realistic millimeter and infrared signals in the occasion of performance verification for MMW/IR compound guidance missile. A reflector antenna arrangement with MMW/IR bispectral window is proposed for the MMW/IR compound target. Well, the edge diffraction of reflector which can cause angle measurement error seriously influences the uniformity of electric field. In order to enhance the accuracy, two reflector edge processing methods were given in this paper. Through the numerical calculation and comparison, the accuracy of angle measurement can be to 0.032° at 35 GHz. The edge processing can well oppress the edge diffraction and improve the uniformity of MMW field. And the edge processing can be used in the engineering of compound target simulation system design and development for HWIL simulation.

Keywords: Compact range system · Edge processing · Accuracy of angle measurement

1 Introduction

Compact range system is widely used in the measurement of antenna field and RCS for the advantage of short distance and high efficiency [1]. Here we design an MMW/IR compound target simulator based on the compact range system. That is to open a metal grid window in an offset parabolic antenna compact system for adding an infrared simulator. The window designed on the reflector can transmit IR radiation, and reflect MMW. Normally, compact range system including feed source, reflector and performance optimize. The main method for performance optimize is edge processing which can reduce the system edge diffraction. In engineering, serrated edge is normally used. The energy is reducing from root to tip gradually [2–4]. And curly edge is also another edge processing method. Here two edge processing method was given, and accuracy of angle measurement is compared, too.

© Springer Science+Business Media Singapore 2016
L. Zhang et al. (Eds.): AsiaSim 2016/SCS AutumnSim 2016, Part II, CCIS 644, pp. 466–472, 2016.
DOI: 10.1007/978-981-10-2666-9_47

2 MMW/IR Compound Target Simulator Based on Compact Range System

MMW/IR compound target simulator based on compact range system is seen in Fig. 1. An off-set reflector is intercepted by its parent reflector. The phase feed source is still on the point of parent reflector's focus. The max radiation direction is next to the center of off-set reflector, which can avoid blocking on the way of wave propagation for feed source and supports. In the center of reflector, there is a hole overlayed by metal grid which can transmit infrared radiation and reflect millimeter wave at the same time.

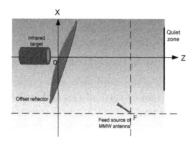

Fig. 1. The schematic diagram of a compact range system

In the rectangular Cartesian coordinates, the equation of the parent parabola is got by rotated of Z axis, that is

$$x^2 + y^2 = 4fz \tag{1}$$

Limited by five-axis table in the HWIL simulation system, the focal length is 400 mm. The aperture of parabola is a 500 mm side length of the square.

In order to measure the static electric field distribution in the quiet zone, we choose 950 mm from the center of reflective surface, 200 mm * 200 mm square observation of the electric field on the two axes to analyze amplitude and phase distribution. The horizontal axis and vertical axis are parallel to the X and Y axes, respectively. The geometric center of quiet zone is (0 mm, 0 mm, 950 mm).

In order to optimizing the performance of compact range system, reflective surface edge must be treated. The phase angle measurement is selected in order to calculate the angular accuracy in quiet zone closed 850 mm < z < 1050 mm by 5 mm as an interval. 5 mm is stepping to the quiet zone near field are applied to solve the electric field, thus 41 * 41 * 41 matrix will formed in the quiet zone for electric field analyze.

3 Electric Field Performance After Edge Processing

The infrared transmitting metal grid and ontology MMW reflective surface mix design was used in this paper. For the square reflector, curly edge and serrated edge processing structure designed as shown in Fig. 2.

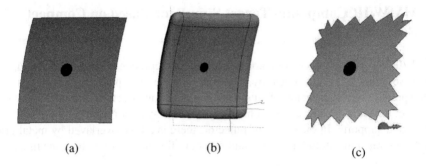

Fig. 2. Without edge processing reflective surface (a), the curly edge processing reflective surface (b) and serrated reflective surface (c)

The main polarization direction of feed source is y axis. The hierarchical fast multipole algorithm was used to calculate amplitude and phase of the electric field. The amplitude and phase on the two lines of vertical axis and the horizontal axis in the electric field is shown below (Figs. 3 and 4).

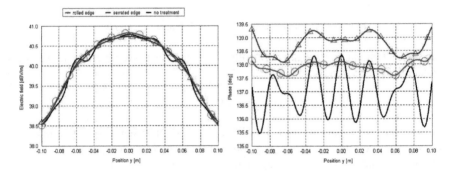

Fig. 3. Amplitude and phase on horizontal axis of quiet zone electric field

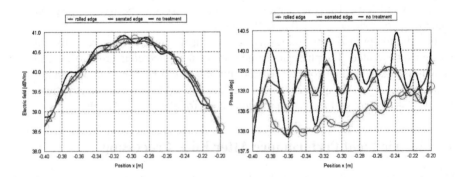

Fig. 4. Amplitude and phase on vertical axis of quiet zone electric field

Results show that the horizontal axis in the quiet zone, the phase peak-to-peak value of without edge processing reflector, curly edge processing reflector, and serrated processing reflector, is 2.91°, 0.77° and 1.29° respectively. The vertical axis in quiet zone, the phase peak-to-peak value of without the edge processing reflector, curly edge processing reflector, and serrated processing reflector, is 2.7°, 1.19° and 1.17° respectively. Results show that phase characteristic of edge treated reflector in quiet zone was optimized compared to reflector without edge processing apparently.

4   The Theory of Angle Measurement of Phase Comparison

4.1   Angle Measurement of Phase Comparison

Ideal far-field electromagnetic waves for the plane wave (the phase variation in the mouth of the receiving antenna faces less than 22.5°, the same to amplitude). The principle of angle measurement by phase comparison is shown in Fig. 5. Q1 and Q2 are the center of the seeker antenna, which are symmetrical about O' point. O' for the receiving antenna axis, the distance between the two receiving antenna is 2L. θ is target deviation angle (deflection angle for seeker antenna). The Phase difference of antenna receiving point is calculated by angle. Two receiver phase difference is

$$\Delta' = \frac{360}{\lambda} 2L \sin \theta \tag{2}$$

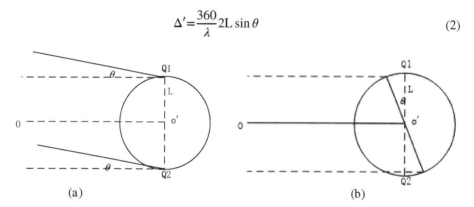

(a)   (b)

Fig. 5. Plane wave oblique incidence (a) equivalent of plane wave oblique incidence (b)

In the equations, Δ' is the output phase difference of seeker antenna, λ is the working wavelength.

According to the formula (2), the formula of calculating the accuracy of angle measuring by phase characteristic in quiet zone is

$$\theta = \arcsin(\frac{\Delta' \times \lambda}{360 \times 2L}) \tag{3}$$

4.2   Phase Estimation

For quiet zone sampling in the area of $\{(-100 < x < 100), (-100 < y < 100),$ $(850 < z < 1050)\}$, the $41 \times 41 \times 41$ matrix is got. A is 1×41. A is estimate sample as axial plane wave phase value. The value of A is from $-180°$ to $180°$, take modulus to $0°$ to $360°$.

For 35 GHz millimeter wave, the first axial plane wave front estimated P located in the axial direction 850 mm from reflector. Every 5 mm take a sampling point, there will be 41 axial sampling points, each axial plane wave front will vary as

$$\frac{5\,\text{mm}}{\lambda\,(\text{mm})} \times 360 = 210.14° \tag{4}$$

Among them, the speed of light is 299792458 m/s in the calculation. If relative dielectric constant of the air is changed, the small speed changes of light in the air will occur. B as axial wave front estimated vector = [P, P−210, ..., P−(n−1)210, ..., P−(41−1)210]. Again take modulus to B, make it into a range of $0°$ to $360°$.

To construct the objective function

$$\sum_{n\,=\,1:41} (A(n) - B(n))^2 \tag{5}$$

Taking the minimum, get the estimate Psudo at P.

5   Analyze of Angle Measurement After Edge Processing

The compound reflection model by serrated processing is established. According to the formula (4) get Psudo(1) = 12.77° at quiet zone z = 850 mm plane. According to Psudo(i)−Psudo (i + 1) = 210.14°, the phase estimate for each plane was known. The difference of 41 wave planes sampling average and estimated value as shown in Fig. 6. It's a linear decrease curve. The difference of first plane estimate and sampling average is 0.29°. The total 41 plane cumulative error is 0.58°. Average to each error between the two flat is 0.014°.

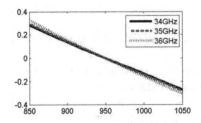

Fig. 6.   Difference of plane sampling average and estimated value

For error as shown in Fig. 6, it may be caused by calculation process and calculation parameter values. The wavelength of this calculation using the speed of light is

299792458 m/s as the international standard under vacuum. Well the calculation is in free space, if free space using air as the background medium, the speed will be slow. If the calculated using the speed of light is simplified the value of 300000000 m/s, the cumulative error of 41 plane is 5.2°. Average to each error between the two planes is 0.12°. So the impact of cumulative error caused by value factor would be greater.

For 41 planes, the difference between maximum sampling and estimated values in each plane as shown in Fig. 7(a), the maximum difference are within 1.83°. The difference between minimum sampling and estimated values in each plane as shown in Fig. 7(b), the maximum difference is within −1.93°. Sampling value of peak-to-peak each plane is less than 3.42°, the difference between the maximum sampling value and minimum sampling values in each plane as shown in Fig. 7(c). The standard deviation of sampling values is within 0.56° as shown in Fig. 7(d). The sampling values variance of each plane is squared by standard deviation, and the variance value is within 0.32.

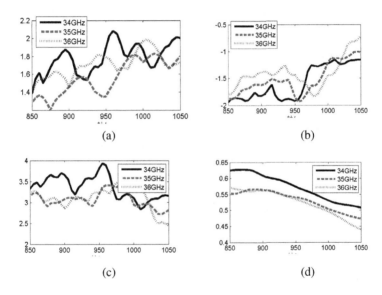

Fig. 7. Statistics of each plane

Known by the data above, from the analysis of phase, the millimeter wave in quiet zone has a certain error. But for the entire area it is a flat plane wave, and it can be used for phase sensitive unit test.

According to the sampling phase peak-to-peak values with the formula (3), the accuracy of angle measurement in each plane is shown in Fig. 8. The accuracy is within 0.032°.

The same method to get curly edge after processing of static field accuracy of angle measurement by phase is 0.025°.

The table below gives the accuracy of the results about the serrated edge and curly edge processing (Table 1).

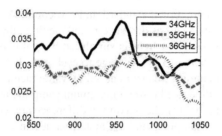

Fig. 8. Accuracy of angle measurement

Table 1. The accuracy of serrated edge and curly edge processing

Frequency	Accuracy of angle measurement/°	
	Serrated edge processing	Curly edge processing
34 GHz	0.038	0.027
35 GHz	0.032	0.025
36 GHz	0.032	0.028

6   Conclusions

MMW/IR compound target based on partial feedback structure is affected by environment, size of the structure greatly. So the edge treatment of the reflector improves the performance of quiet zone to a certain optimization. The accuracy of angle measurement is compared of electric field of two kinds of edge treatment. Through the calculation and analysis of angle measurement, the accuracy of angle measurement is within 0.032° at 35 GHz, which can achieve the purpose of engineering application. Follow-up it can guide dual-mode compound guidance hardware-in-the-loop simulation system to project implementation.

References

1. Jiong, Y.-Y.: Study of array antenna and millimeter wave CATR antenna. Xidian University dissertation, April 2011
2. Hui, Q.-S., Yu, H.-G., Bin, X.-H., et al.: High performance single reflector compact range. J. Beijing Univ. Aeronaut. Astronaut. **29**(9), 767–769 (2003)
3. Yaping, C., Houjun, S., Xin, L.: Optimization design method of electromagnetic characteristics for a novel infrared/millimeter wave co-aperture object simulator. J. Infrared Millimeter Waves **28**(5), 350–352, 366 (2009)
4. Bing, G.: Research on MMW/SMMW objects radiation characteristic and detection technology, Nanjing University of Science & Technology (2009)

Credibility Evaluation Index System Research of Optical Multi-mode Compound Guidance Simulation System

Qi Li[1(✉)], Tuo Ding[1], Ping Ma[2], Haisheng Zhao[1], Zhenhong Zuo[1], and Wei Li[2]

[1] Shanghai Institute of Mechanics and Electricity Engineering, Shanghai, China
irsl_sast@163.com
[2] Harbin Institute of Technology, Harbin, China

Abstract. Optical Multi-mode Compound Guidance Simulation System is developed for optical compound guidance system HWIL simulation application in lab environment. In order to appraise the HWIL simulation reliability, this paper analyses some influence factors of evaluation objects, and founds an index system of the Optical Multi-mode Compound Guidance Simulation System for credibility evaluation.

Keywords: HWIL simulation · Credibility evaluation · Index system · Optical Multi-mode Compound

1 Introduction

The Optical Multi-mode Compound Guidance Simulation System (OMCGSS) is a Hardware-In-the-Loop (HWIL) simulation system established for the demand of the development and test of optical compound guided missile. OMCGSS is used to simulate the whole target interception process of optical compound guided missile in a laboratory environment, to test the design validity and compatibility of the unit under test (UUT). As the credibility of HWIL simulation system direct decide the validity and authenticity of testing and simulation, so it should be properly analyzed for OMCGSS.

According to the requirement of the OMCGSS's credibility evaluation, and considering the composing and operational principle of OMCGSS, the credibility evaluation index system of the OMCGSS is founded, offered sustentation to evaluate the OMCGSS's credibility degree.

2 General Planning of Credibility Evaluation

OMCGSS consists of the real time simulation control system, the five-axis flight/target motion simulator (FMS), the target/decoy simulation subsystem, interface devices and the unit under test (UUT). Figure 1 is the composing and operational principles of OMCGSS.

© Springer Science+Business Media Singapore 2016
L. Zhang et al. (Eds.): AsiaSim 2016/SCS AutumnSim 2016, Part II, CCIS 644, pp. 473–482, 2016.
DOI: 10.1007/978-981-10-2666-9_48

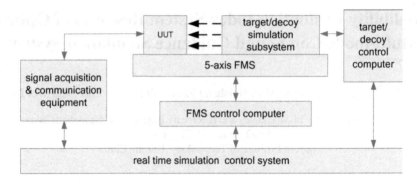

Fig. 1. OMCGSS's composing and operational principle

The OMCGSS's closed loop working principle is as follows: in the simulation frame time, firstly, the simulation computer acquires the helm-control order output from the guidance section, then substitutes the helm-control order into the missile body mathematical model to integrate, resolves the dynamic and kinematic model of the missile, and exports all kinds of parameters of the missile and the target, and then drives the optical compound target simulator to simulate the target's energy and release IR decoys, at the same time, drives the FMS to simulate projectile's attitude motion and LOS rate. The FMS follows the projectile's attitude motion order from the simulation computer, creates physical effect of movement for the gyro and the UUT, the UUT's tracing loop deals with the target radiation information it received, forms tracing order to control the UUT to track the target, the HWIL simulation is closed. Figure 2 is a general planning of the OMCGSS's credibility evaluation.

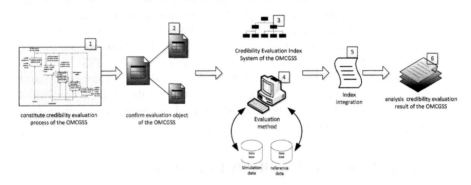

Fig. 2. OMCGSS's credibility evaluation general planning

Credibility evaluation of complex simulation system is noted for integrity, hierarchy, objective correlation and so on, for complete the credibility evaluation work better, an elaborate credibility evaluation process should be constituted, to definitize relative work in every phase of simulation system's credibility evaluation, to assure the credibility evaluation accomplished orderly and favorably. Figure 3 is the credibility evaluation process.

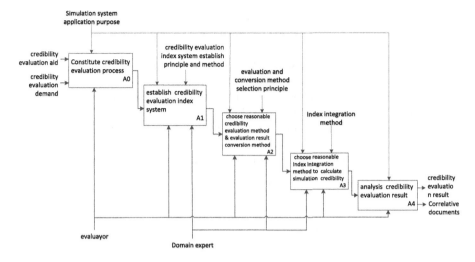

Fig. 3. Credibility evaluation process

3 Credibility Evaluation Index System

3.1 Evaluation Object

Evaluation object is the key of scope demarcation and range confirmation of credibility evaluation. To ascertain the evaluation object is the premise of analyzing credibility evaluation influencing factor of OMCGSS and establish credibility evaluation index

Table 1. Evaluation object decomposition of OMCGSS

Level 1 object	Level 2 object	Evaluation object
Target/decoy simulation subsystem	Target simulation system	Target radiation characteristic model
		Target simulator and controller
	Decoy simulation system	Decoy radiation characteristic model and motion model
		Decoy simulator and controller
Attitude simulation subsystem	5-axis FMS	Attitude simulation equipment (5-axis FMS)
		Host computer(FMS control computer)
Real time simulation control system	Simulation model	Missile body model
		Target motion model
		Missile target relative motion model
	Simulation computer	Digital simulator
Interface device and communication equipment	Signal acquisition card	UUT output signal→simulation computer
	HWIL facility drive	Simulation computer→simulation equipment
	Computer communication	Simulation computer→FMS host computer
		Simulation computer→target/decoy control computer

system. OMCGSS is a complex simulation system, it is difficult to carry through system-level evaluation directly for it. In order to make the evaluation maneuverable, system-level evaluation object should be decomposed.

According to composition and specific conditions, OMCGSS can be decomposed, and the evaluation object is determined. For whole OMCGSS, subsystem-level evaluation object contains target/decoy simulation subsystem, attitude simulation subsystem (5-axis FMS), real time simulation control system, body model, target motion model, missile target relative motion model, etc. Table 1 is the evaluation object decomposition of OMCGSS.

Aimed at the evaluation objects, their influence factor is presented in Table 2.

Table 2. Credibility influence factor of OMCGSS

Evaluation object	Credibility influence factor
Target radiation characteristic model	Relationship between missile target relative distance and target radiation energy
Target simulator and controller	Target point size and energy simulation
Decoy radiation characteristic model and motion model	Relationship between missile target relative distance and decoy separation angle or decoy radiation energy
Decoy simulator and controller	Decoy point size, position and energy simulation
5-axis FMS	3-axis tracing error, 2-axis tracing error, 5-axis error, response speed, load capacity
FMS control computer	Control signal precision, signal transmission speed, signal conversion precision
Missile body model	Displacement, speed in 3 directions of missile body, pitching angle, yaw angle, rolling angle, angle of attack, angle of side slip, etc.
Target motion model	Target position, speed, etc.
Missile target relative motion model	Angular altitude of LOS, azimuth angle of LOS, etc.
Digital simulator	Calculation speed, calculation precision, multi threading capability, interrupt handling capability, dada capacity, stable running time
Computer data transmission equipment	Transmission speed, transmission precision, reliable running time
UUT output signal→simulation computer	Acquisition speed, acquisition precision, conversion speed, conversion precision, transmission speed, transmission precision
Simulation computer→FMS host computer interface	Transmission speed, transmission precision
Simulation computer→target/decoy control computer interface	Transmission speed, transmission precision

3.2   Evaluation Index System

The most broadly used evaluation index system is the Two-Dimensional Index System (TDIS), which has two types of structures, multi-layer tree-structure and net-structure. Although establishing net-structure index structure is more complicated than the tree structure, its result on credibility is more convincing. Given the complexity of OMCGSS, the net index structure is more suitable in solving the credibility evaluation.

On the analysis basis of the OMCGSS credibility influencing factors, we use the Multiple Attribute Decision net to establish credibility evaluation index system. The definition of MAD net index system is as follows:

$$K = \{< N, V > ; < B, W > ; C; T\}$$ (1)

K is MAD net, N is node set, V is value set, B is the set of directed edge, W is weight set, C is condition set, M is threshold set. MAD net is shown in Fig. 4.

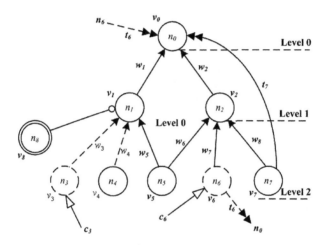

Fig. 4. MAD NET

The steps of establishing the index system of sub systems of OMCGSS are as follows:

- Target/Decoy simulation credibility evaluation index system

Target/Decoy Simulation System (TDSS) is used to simulate the compound optical feature of both targets and decoys. The credibility of TDSS can be obtained according to the consistency of simulation results and reference results. It is affected by target radiation model, decoy separation motion model, decoy radiation model and host computer missile/target relative motion model, etc. The evaluation index system is shown in Fig. 5.

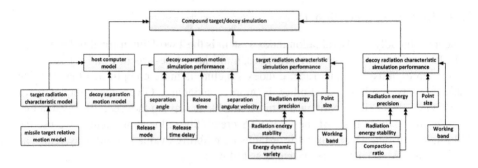

Fig. 5.   Compound target/decoy simulation

The target radiation characteristic model, decoy motion and radiation characteristic model can be verified by the UUT output data. The simulation performance target/decoy simulator and decoy separation motion can be evaluated using simulator test data and expert experience.

- 5-axis FMS credibility evaluation index system

5-axis FMS is used to simulate the attitude of missile (3 DoF) and target (2 DoF), which is one of the core sub-systems of OMCGSS. The credibility of FMS is influenced by host computer missile body model/target motion model/missile target relative motion model and FMS tracing precision/tracing speed/load capacity, etc. The evaluation index system is shown in Fig. 6.

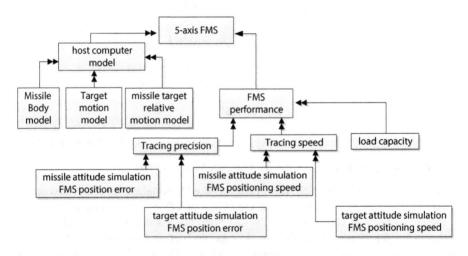

Fig. 6.   5-Axis FMS

Missile body model is used to drive the host computer digital simulation model, while target motion model is used to drive 2-axis FMS host computer digital simulation model. Missile/target relative motion model assists to drive 5-axis FMS host computer digital simulation model. The positioning error and speed of 3-axis FMS/2-axis target FMS and the load capacity can be calculated by using bool type.

• Real-time simulation control system credibility evaluation index system

Real-time simulation control system includes simulation computer and reflective memory network (RMN). OMCGSS linked all the HWIL facilities together though the VMIC RMN. Real-time simulation control system is used to deal with host computer model calculation, data recording, data conversation of OMCGSS. Figure 7 is the credibility evaluation index system of the Real-time simulation control system.

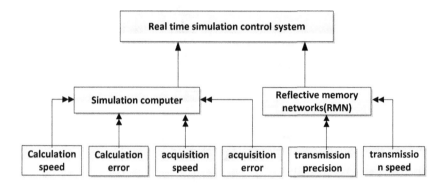

Fig. 7. Real time simulation control system

For the evaluation of simulation computer's calculation speed, calculation error, acquisition speed, acquisition error and RMN's transmission precision, transmission speed, we can give out evaluation result directly rely on whether or not the facilities' actual capability satisfy the simulation requirement.

• Missile body credibility evaluation index system

Through some analysis to the guidance system simulation process, we established the missile body credibility evaluation index system showed in Fig. 8.

The missile body model uses the general missile centroid/around centroid motion dynamic/kinematic model, put these twelve initial value into the dynamic/kinematic formula, includes X axis position, Y axis position, Z axis position, velocity, flight path angle, flight path azimuth angle, pitching angle, yaw angle, rolling angle, around X axis angular velocity, around Y axis angular velocity and around Y axis angular velocity, through numerical integration and simulation time advancement, these twelve variables' whole process simulation curve can be solved. Based on the missile body model calculation process, in credibility evaluation process, we usually do some consistency analysis of these twelve variables between the output curve and actual flight curve (or the specialist experienced curve), we can use the TIC method, grey correlation method, etc.

• Target motion model credibility evaluation index system

Through some analysis of the target motion model calculation process, we can establish the target motion model credibility evaluation index system showed in Fig. 9.

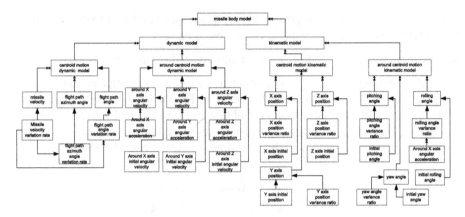

Fig. 8. Missile body model

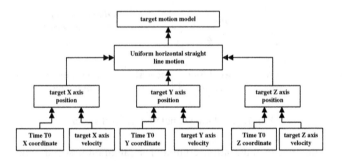

Fig. 9. Target motion model

Target motion model includes two sub-models, which are uniform horizontal movement and maneuver movement. Their weight is determined according to the ratio in simulation process. We use TIC method and grey correlation method to analyze the consistency of both simulation data and field measuring data on target motion speed and position in three directions. The consistency of target elevation angle ϑ_T, target azimuth angle ψ_T, flight path normal load ny, nZ, etc. can be analyzed by time-domain analysis. The coordination X, Y, Z during initialization should be consistent before simulation process.

- Missile/target relative motion model credibility evaluation index system

The missile/target relative motion model credibility evaluation index system, as shown in Fig. 10, is established by analyzing the calculation process of missile/target relative motion model.

Missile speed V, flight path angle θ, flight path azimuth angle ψ_v, missile flight path (x, y, z), etc. are already evaluated in missile body model, while target speed VT, target elevation angle ϑ_T, target azimuth angle ψ_T, target flight path (xT, yT, zT), etc. are evaluated in target motion model. The index of missile/target relative motion model includes LOS azimuth angle qH, LOS elevation angle qv, LOS angular velocity q, and can be evaluated by TIC method and grey correlation method.

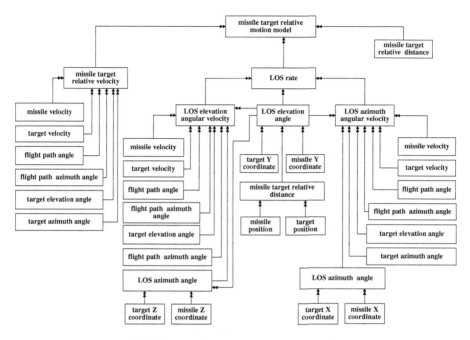

Fig. 10. Missile target relative motion model

- System credibility evaluation index system

According to the working mechanism of all sub-systems, we combine the evaluation index system of all sub-systems to establish OMCGSS credibility evaluation index system, as shown in Fig. 11.

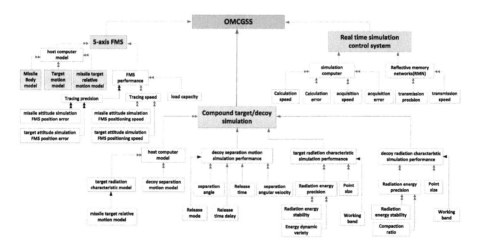

Fig. 11. Credibility evaluation index system of the OMCGSS

Based on MAD net, we analyze the influencing factors of OMCGSS credibility. According to the results, we established the credibility evaluation index system of missile body model, target motion model, 5-axis FMS and target/decoy simulation system, etc.

4 Summary

According of the characteristic of OMCGSS, the credibility evaluation index system is established, which provides an effective and feasible method for credibility evaluation of OMCGSS.

References

1. Wrobleski, J.J., Laack, D.R., Muessig, P.R.: An integrated approach to evaluating simulation credibility. In: ADA405051, August 2001
2. Lin, Q., Guo, Jing.: Accuracy analysis of distributed simulation systems. In: Proceedings of SPIE, vol. 7544 (2010)
3. Wei, L., Yang, M.: Research on simulation accuracy. Comput. Simul. 26(1) (2009)
4. Oberkampf, W.L., et al.: Estimation of Total Uncertainty in Modeling and Simulation, Sandia National Laboratories, Albuquerque, SAND2000-0824 (2000)
5. Nance, R.E., Sargent, R.G.: Perspectives on the evolution of simulation. Oper. Res. 50(1), 161–172 (2002)
6. Lou, S., Ren, J., Liu, L., Li, Z.: Research on the evaluation method for modelling and simulation of infrared imaging sensor. In: Proceedings of SPIE, vol. 9674 (2015)

Perceptual Modeling of Virtual Soldier in Military Game Based on Attention Theory

Jianjian Zhang$^{(\boxtimes)}$ and Long Qin

College of Information System and Management,
National University of Defense Technology, Changsha 410073, China
zjj9363@163.com

Abstract. An intelligent perceptual model is an essential component for a virtual soldier to simulate the attention mechanism in military games. Attention mechanism plays a critical role in the process of human evolution, enabling human beings to deal with information more efficiently by focusing on preferable objects and, at the same time, filtering the others. In this paper, we built a novel perceptual model for virtual soldiers based on attention theory. This model includes visual model and audial model. What's more, we designed the attention controller to decide virtual soldier's focus. The simulation tests show that by employing the proposed model, virtual soldiers gain more reasonable and efficient attention behaviour.

Keywords: Virtual soldier · Perceptual modeling · Attention · Military game

1 Introduction

In recent years, more and more military games appeared, which makes it very important that virtual soldier's perceptual model must be reasonable and believable. Virtual soldier's perception model directly affects the efficiency of simulation and the behavior of soldiers. In traditional military simulations, virtual soldier's perceptual models are relatively simple. Most of them use a whole perception of the environment, which does not meet the real battlefield situation. Under normal circumstances, more than 80 % of the human perceptions are acquired from the visual perception [1]. But on the real battlefield, other stimulates such as the gunfire et al. also has a great impact on soldier's attention. We proposed a suitable model for virtual soldier's perception in this paper, considering the special nature of military rule and battlefield environment requirements.

Much work about attention theory and virtual human perception model has been done. For example, Itti and Koch proposed computational model of visual attention [2–4]. This model calculates the saliency map, helping the attention theory get into the engineering filed for the first time. Tu in her research established a "focus attention" model for an artificial fish, enabling it to direct the senses and efficiently access to the most important information according to their action preferences and intentions [5]. However, the artificial fish model is too simple to simulate human attention mechanisms. Randall W. Hill has done a lot of work about attention theory [6–9]. He proposed a perceptual model combining bottom-up and top-down attention mechanisms, which

© Springer Science+Business Media Singapore 2016
L. Zhang et al. (Eds.): AsiaSim 2016/SCS AutumnSim 2016, Part II, CCIS 644, pp. 483–491, 2016.
DOI: 10.1007/978-981-10-2666-9_49

was used in the US military training system for a helicopter. This model is worthy for reference, although it's too simplex to only focus on tank and process information about tank. The models mentioned above cannot be directly used for virtual soldiers, so we built one in this paper.

In Sect. 2, we introduced attention theory and its development. In Sect. 3, we designed the attention model for virtual soldier. This is the main work done by us. Section 4 is the simulation part, we designed the experiment to improve our model's efficiency. In Sect. 5, we concluded our work.

2 Attention Theory

Visual attention mechanism is one of the most important feature in human visual system. In our daily life, the amount of information around us exceeds the maximum amount that our brains can handle. In order to handle the information efficiently, the human visual system evolved a mechanism, which was called visual attention mechanism, to filter and screen the information [10]. Attention mechanism can balance the perception and cognition, so it is an important result of human evolution. James studied the attention theory at the very beginning in the 1850s. At that time, this theory was regarded as one of the field in psychology. The study shows that, some stimulations can get our attention more easily, such as unfamiliar stimulation, strong stimulation and the expected stimulation [11]. The attention caused by scene is bottom-up attention, and caused by human's preference is top-down attention.

To explain the attention theory, psychologist proposed many attention models, like Broadbent's filter model [12], Deutsch's reacted selection model [13], Shiffrin's two-process theory [14], Treisman's spotlight theory [15], Treisman's feature integration theory (FIT) [16] and Wolfe's guidance search model [17]. The filter model and the reacted selection model have different view about the time when attention happens. The two-process theory describes the autonomous control of visual stimulus. Treisman's searchlight theory believes that the visual attention is based on space. However, another theory considers that the visual attention is based on object. Drawing on two-process model, Treisman's feature integration theory divides the data processing into two stages: pre-attention stage and attention stage.

Most of the previous modeling research has been focused on the bottom-up component of visual attention. While previous efforts are appreciated, the field of visual attention still lacks computational principles for task-driven attention [18]. In this paper, we did a research on virtual soldier's perceptual model on the battlefield. In this case, virtual soldier has his tactical purpose, so his attention is considered by top-down attention.

Top-down attention can be classified into at least three levels: spatial-level, feature-level, and object-level. People are more likely to notice the movement and close objects, which is the psychological foundation of spatial-level. Feature-level show that colorful and bright objects can attract attention easier. In the object-level, the objects being identified, human will focus on the things based on his acknowledge. Seif and Daliri [19] evaluated the potential signals of visual attention in feature-level. Shen et al. [20] did a research about visual working mechanism in object-level. In a virtual battlefield environment, the virtual soldiers should be able to recognize the objects, so we should use the object-level.

3 Virtual Soldier' Perceptual Model

In this section, we introduced the main frame of this model in first part. In part 2 and part 3, we built a visual model and an audial model for virtual soldier. In part 4, we designed the attention controller to decide virtual soldier's focus, which was our innovation.

3.1 Main Frame of the Perceptual Model for a Virtual Soldier

In the virtual battlefield, the virtual soldier can percept the environment and identify the objects from the database. The visual attention and audial attention are included in attention controller, which accepts the tasks and the identified objects. The memory model will accept the results provided by attention controller. After reasoning, a sequence will be produced to guide the action.

Figure 1 shows the procedure of a virtual soldier's perception: (1) Accept the mission, percept the virtual battlefield environment; (2) Attention controller process the mission and the identified objects; (3) The processed results guide the action after the reasoning model, and produce a feedback signal at the same time.

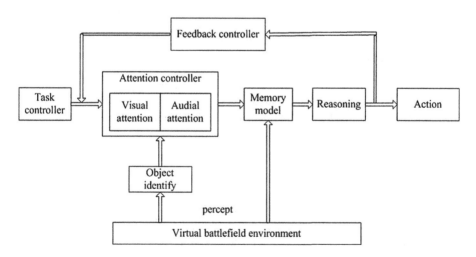

Fig. 1. Main frame of the perceptual model

3.2 Visual Model of the Virtual Soldier

Human's visual scope is limited because of the physiological characteristic. Generally speaking, our visual scope is an area of sector, whose angle in horizontal direction is about 60° and the same angle in vertical direction. In this paper, we simulated the visual limitation according to the visual model of geometry. The information of battlefield was obtained by inquiring the database. Figure 2 shows the human's visual model in geometry.

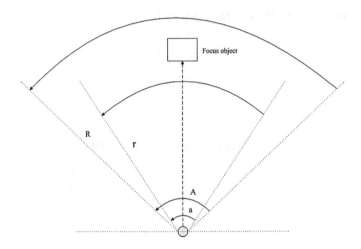

Fig. 2. The human's visual model in geometry

In Fig. 2, R is the effective radius of our visual scope and r is the best radius; A is the effective visual angle and a is the best visual angle. The objects in the visual field can be processed.

3.3 Audial Model of the Virtual Soldier

Under normal circumstances, our perceptual information is mainly from our vision, so most perceptual models ignore the audial perception. However, gunfire play a very important role in the battlefield. Different from vision, audition affected by the length and the intensity of sound. Hearing the sound, virtual soldier can identify the object's type and direction.

$$\text{Audial model}: V = k * v/d \tag{1}$$

V is the intensity of sound heard by virtual soldier, v is the real intensity of sound, d is the distance between virtual soldier and the place where sound come from, k is the factor of audition. In this paper, we set a threshold T. If V < T, virtual soldier will ignore this sound; if V >= T, virtual soldier will dispose it according to his mission. This audial model enable virtual soldier to be more intelligent.

3.4 Design the Attention Controller

Controlling the attention of virtual soldier, attention controller is an essential module in this perception model, because its decision is the foundation of virtual soldier's action.

In this paper, we set a value VAL to every object that can be detected by virtual soldier. Every objects' VAL is a dynamic value, which depend on the mission. The exact VALs are set according to the military rules and the experts' views in the military field.

Every time having accepted mission, virtual soldier will filtrate the objects that not in his visual field through spotlight-model. After that, the attention controller will inquire VAL of every object that in virtual soldier's perception according to the mission as Table 1 shows. Then, the attention controller will figure out virtual soldier's attention.

Table 1. Object in different missions has different VAL

	Mission 1	Mission 2	Mission 3	Mission 4
Object 1	VAL(1,1)	VAL(1,2)	VAL(1,3)	VAL(1,4)
Object 2	VAL(2,1)	VAL(2,2)	VAL(2,3)	VAL(2,4)
Object 3	VAL(3,1)	VAL(3,2)	VAL(3,3)	VAL(3,4)

However, if there are two same type objects in the vision, he will choose the one closer to him. After the mission is done, virtual soldier will wait for next mission.

Figure 3 shows the process flow of virtual soldier:

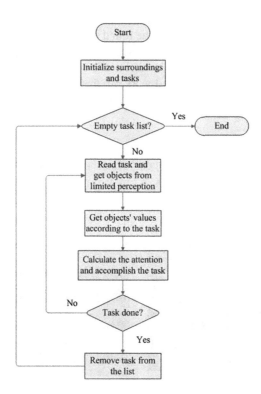

Fig. 3. The process flow of virtual soldier

4 Simulation

We simulated this model to test its feasibility and intelligence. With the help of Vega Prime, the simulation was showed as follows. Figure 4 shows the virtual battlefield, including hills, tanks, enemies, teammates, landmines and so on.

Fig. 4. The virtual battlefield

Mission 1: wipe out enemy. Because of the visual model, he only can see the objects in his view. Figure 5 shows that he found two tanks, an enemy (the green one), hills and many trees after the visual filter. What's more, he heard gunfire not far away. Table 2 shows the objects' VAL in this mission. Then, the attention controller calculate his focus according to his mission and work out that he should focus his attention on the enemy. After reasoning, he made his action to accomplish his mission. Figure 6 shows the enemy being killed.

Table 2. Different objects' values in Mission 1

Object	Enemy	Tanks	Trees	Hill	Gunfire
VAL	10	5	1	1	9

Fig. 5. Virtual soldier's vision (Color figure online)

Fig. 6. The enemy was killed

Mission 2: get into the trench. In the soldier's vision, there are a tank, six team-mates, a trench, a hill and many trees. Table 3 shows the objects' VAL in this mission. He worked out to choose the trench as his focus and get into it. Figure 7 shows virtual soldier's vision. Figure 8 shows he get into the trench at the bottom right.

Table 3. Different objects' values in Mission 2

Object	Tank	Teammates	Tree	Hill	Trench
VAL	2	2	3	5	10

Fig. 7. Virtual soldier's vision   **Fig. 8.** Virtual soldier in the trench

Mission 3: hide beside a tank. In the soldier's vision, there are two tanks, many trees, a hill and a house. Then, he inquire the objects' VAL according to this mission. The result was showed as Table 2. According to the rule, he chose a tank that closer to him as his focus. Figure 9 shows virtual soldier's vision, and Fig. 10 shows he hide beside a tank (Table 4).

The results show that this perceptual model enable the virtual soldier to be more intelligent.

Table 4. Different objects' values in Mission 3

Object	Tank 1	Tank 2	Trees	Hill	House
VAL	10	10	1	2	3

Fig. 9. Virtual soldier's vision   **Fig. 10.** Virtual soldier hide beside a tank

5 Conclusion

In this paper, considering the characteristic of the battlefield, we designed a perceptual model based on attention theory for virtual soldier. This model mainly consist of visual model and audial model. We put forward a method of attention control for virtual soldier that distribute different value for objects according to the mission. Finally, we simulated this model, and the virtual soldier showed more intelligent behavior.

There are two weaknesses in our model: 1: The VAL for each object is not so precise. 2: Memory model and feedback controller are simple in the simulation. Further aspects that are envisaged for future research concerns: 1: Do more investigation and give each object a more realistic VAL. 2: Optimize the memory model and feedback controller.

Acknowledgement. This work is sponsored by the National Natural Science Foundation of China under Grants No. 61473300 and No. 61573369.

References

1. Feng, H.: Research of Visual Attention Mechanism and Application. North China Electric Power University, Hebei (2011)
2. Itti, L., Koch, C.: Computational modeling of visual attention. Nat. Rev. Neurosci. **2**, 194–203 (2001)
3. Itti, L., Koch, C., Niebur, E.: A model of saliency-based visual attention for rapid scene analysis. In: IEEE Transactions on Pattern Analysis and Machine Intelligence, pp. 1254–1259 (1998)
4. Itti, L., Koch, C.: A saliency-based search mechanism for overt and covert shifts of visual attention. Vis. Res. **40**(10), 1489–1506 (2000)
5. Tu, X.: Artificial Fish – Artificial life method of Computer Animation. Tsinghua University Press, Beijing (2001)
6. Hill, Jr., R.: Modeling perceptual attention in virtual humans. In: Proceedings of the 8th Conference on Computer Generated Forces and Behavioral Representation, pp. 563–573. SISO, Orlando (1999)
7. Hill Jr., R.: Perceptual attention in virtual humans: towards realistic and believable gaze behaviors. In: Proceedings of the AAAI Fall Symposium on Simulation Human Agent, pp. 46–52. AAAI Press, Menlo Park (2000)
8. Hill Jr., R.W., Gratch, J., Marsella, S., Rickel, J., Swartout, W.R., Traum, D.R.: Virtual humans in the mission rehearsal exercise system. KI J. (2003). Special issue on Embodied Conversational Agents
9. Kim, Y., Hill Jr., R.W., Traum, D.R.: A computational model of dynamic perceptual attention for virtual humans. In: Proceedings of 14th Conference on Behavior Representation in Modeling and Simulation (BRIMS), Universal City, CA (2005)
10. Hu, R., Ding, J.: Processing mechanism of visual selective attention. Ergonomics **13**(1), 69–71 (2007)
11. Wu, X., Wang, Y.: Cognition and neurobiological model of visual attention. Trends Psychol. **3**(3), 16–22 (1995)
12. Broadbent, D.E.: Perception and Communication. Pergamon Press, London (1958)

13. Deutsch, J.A., Deutsch, D.: Attention: some theoretical considerations. Psychol. Rev. **70**(1), 80–90 (1963)

14. Schneider, W., Shiffrin, R.M.: Controlled and automatic human information processing: perceptual learning, automatic attending and a general theory. Psychol. Rev. **84**(2), 127–190 (1977)

15. Treisman, A., Schmidt, H.: Illusory conjunctions in the perception of objects. Cogn. Psychol. **14**(1), 107–141 (1982)

16. Treisman, A.M., Gelade, G.: A feature integration theory of attention. Cogn. Psychol. **V12** (1), 97–136 (1980)

17. Wolfe, J.: Guided search 2.0: a revised model of guided search. Psychon. Bull. Rev. **1**(2), 202–238 (1994)

18. Borji, A., Itti, L.: State-of-the-art in visual attention modeling. Patten Anal. Mach. Intell. **35** (1), 185–207 (2013)

19. Seif, Z., Daliri, M.R.: Evaluation of local field potential signals in decoding of visual attention. Cogn. Neurodyn. **9**(5), 1–14 (2015)

20. Shen, M., Huang, X., Gao, Z.: Object-based attention underlies the rehearsal of feature binding in visual working memory. J. Exp. Psychol. Hum. Percept. Perform. **41**(2), 479–493 (2015)

A Model on Airborne Radar in Look-Down Search Mode Based on Clutter Spectrum

Dazhi Qi[✉], Hucheng Pei, and Jinchang Tian

Beijing Electro-Mechanical Engineering Research Institute, Beijing 100074, China
Styx3b@163.com

Abstract. An effective model on airborne radar based on clutter spectrum is proposed in this paper. According to the simulation test, the calculating speed of the proposed model is close to that of the functional level radar model, and the simulation results of the proposed model are almost the same to that of the signal level radar model. The calculated quantity of the model proposed is much less than that of the signal level radar model. The model could be mainly used in simulation system with many airborne radars. In this paper, a simplified antenna model and a clutter spectrum model are proposed. The clutter spectrum is divided into four districts. The calculated quantity is further reduced since just one district's clutter energy will be computed. The effective model could be applied to some huge simulating systems, especially in multi-radar and multi-target scenarios where calculating speed is a significant factor.

Keywords: Clutter spectrum · Effective model · Airborne radar

1 Introduction

Clutter is a term used to define all unwanted radar returns. The nature of clutter necessarily varies with applications and radar parameters. Clutter in one scenario can be a desired target in another. The term "surface clutter" refers to surface echoes from a surface district illuminated by the radar. Airborne radars in look-down search mode is critical because the strong ground clutter echo, received both on antenna main beam and side lobes, usually increases the number of false alarms.

The process of calculating the surface clutter that returns to the airborne radar is complicated. Elaborated clutter models have been developed owe to the study of surface scattering and the characterization of clutter returns [1].

In the last few years, the availability of extremely fast workstations allowed computational models to be established on the foundation of enormous quantity of calculations performed in relatively short times. Consequently approximations and complex theory can now be displaced by mathematical model which are theoretically simple but computationally intensive.

In this paper we shall introduce such an airborne model which calculates faster with the simplified clutter spectrum. Its speed is close to that of the functional level airborne model and its detection result is nearly the same with that of the signal level airborne radar model. The model is applied to some huge simulation system with several airborne

© Springer Science+Business Media Singapore 2016
L. Zhang et al. (Eds.): AsiaSim 2016/SCS AutumnSim 2016, Part II, CCIS 644, pp. 492–499, 2016.
DOI: 10.1007/978-981-10-2666-9_50

radars and aircrafts. The simulation system needs models calculating in real-time and performing as the signal level airborne radar model.

2 Clutter Spectrum for Airborne Radar

In the design of the low altitude target detection, the clutter is the key factor of a simulation model. To detect a small target in the strong surface clutter, it is better to use the pulse Doppler radar. The pulse Doppler radar usually adopts frequency domain filter to suppress the clutter, because the frequency domain filter suppresses specific frequency signal. Mostly, the radar equation is commonly used in the functional level radar model. However, the functional level radar model reflects the Radar Cross-Section (RCS) and signal to noise ratio, without the clutter. Although the signal level radar model reflects the influence of the clutter, its speed of calculation is far away from the real time operation. So it is necessary to develop a simulation radar model which calculates fast enough with the influence of the clutter. It can be mainly used in the simulation system, which contains many airborne radars and a lot of targets, and runs in real-time.

Clutter spectrum is broadened due to the moving of the airplane and the fluctuation of terrain. The clutter spectrum is made up of three parts: the first part is the signal reflected from the surface where is irradiated by the antenna main beam, the second part is the signal reflected from the surface where is irradiated by the antenna side lobe, and the last part contains the signal reflected vertically from the surface and leaked from the emitter (Fig. 1).

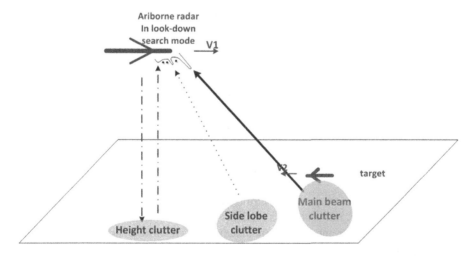

Fig. 1. Airborne radar in look-down search mode

The spectrum of the clutter generated by airborne radar is shown as blow. In the clutter spectrum, the power nearing f_0 frequency is much higher, because the power of the height clutter and the power leaked by the emitter make the signal power around the f_0 frequency reaches peak; due to the high gain of the radar antenna main beam, the energy of the main beam clutter is consequently much higher. Therefore, the power of target Doppler frequency in the main beam reaches another peak; the side lobe clutter is much lower because of the lower gain of the radar antenna side lobe, but, as the radar antenna side lobe covers a great width, the frequency range of the side lobe is consequently broadened (Fig. 2).

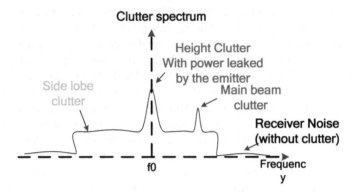

Fig. 2. The clutter spectrum

In order to simplify the character of the frequency domain of the clutter spectrum, the function f(x) can be used.

$$f(x) = \begin{cases} C_h, f_2 < x < f_3 \\ C_m, f_4 < x < f_5 \\ C_n, x < f_1 \text{ or } x > f_6 \\ C_s, x \in \text{others} \end{cases} \tag{1}$$

where x stands for frequency, domain $[-f_r/2, + f_r/2]$, and f_r means pulse repetition frequency, $f_1 < f_2 < f_3 < f_4 < f_5 < f_6$. C_h is the height clutter, C_m stands for main beam clutter, C_s as side lobe clutter and C_n the inside noisy power in the airborne radar. The airborne radar model is established on the function f(x).

3   A New Model Based on Clutter Spectrum

Taking advantage of the frequency spectrum characters of the clutter, and using the time and frequency domain information, a model is proposed to reflect the influence of the clutter on airborne radar, meanwhile run in real time. The flow diagram of the model is shown as below. First of all, the model calculates the distance and Doppler frequency inspected by airborne radar based on the location and speed of the airplane and target. Secondly, the model judges the specific clutter spectrum district where the target falls in according to the Doppler frequency shift. The model mainly processes the clutter energy in the specific field instead of time domain clutter energy of all the fields. Moreover, as the radar antenna model is simplified, and the calculation quantity of the clutter energy in the correlated clutter fields is low as known, the proposed model will be further speed up (Fig. 3).

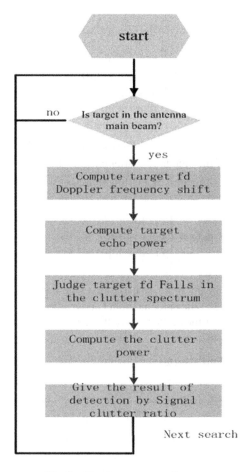

Fig. 3. The flow-process diagram

According to the flow diagram, the model has to collect the energy of the target signal and meanwhile judge the Doppler frequency of the target. The echo energy of the target can be calculated by using the following function.

$$S = \frac{P_t \lambda^2 G_1^2 \sigma_t}{(4\pi)^3 R^4} \qquad (2)$$

Where, P_t is the transmitted power, λ is the wavelength of the transmitted radiation, G_1 is the antenna gain in the main beam, σ_t represents the target RCS and R the distance between radar and target.

The following function can be used to calculate the Doppler frequency shift of the target.

$$f_d = \frac{2V_r}{\lambda} \tag{3}$$

Where V_r is the radial velocity, λ is the wavelength of the transmitted radiation.

According to the target Doppler frequency shift and the clutter spectrum, one can judge where the target echo falls in. The signal level radar antenna model usually established in the function sinc(). Here, a more simplified antenna model is proposed. The gain of the airborne radar is divided into three parts. The first one is G_1 the main beam gain corresponding to the main beam clutter; the second one is G_2 the first side lobe gain used for the calculation of the side lobe clutter energy; the third one is G_3 as other side lobe gain. The antenna is simulated by the function g(x) as below.

$$g(x) = \begin{cases} G_1, |\theta| < \alpha' \\ G_2, \alpha < |\theta| < \beta' \\ G_3, \beta < |\theta| < \gamma' \end{cases} \tag{4}$$

where α' stands for main beam angle, β' is the first side lobe angle, γ' represents other side lobe angle. According to the antenna model above, the clutter energy can be calculated based on the district of the clutter where the target Doppler frequency shift falls.

3.1 The District of Height Clutter

$$P_1 = \frac{P_t \lambda^2 G_3^2 \sigma_0}{(4\pi)^3 H^4} \tag{5}$$

Where P_1 stands for the height clutter power. σ_0 is the backscatter coefficient. The backscatter coefficient could be deducted by some backscatter model. The typical backscatter models, such as Ulaby model, GIT model and others, are not to be discussed in this paper.

Besides, part of the energy comes from the emitter; therefore, the clutter power can be calculated as blow:

$$C = P_1 + P_0 \tag{6}$$

Where P_0 represents the power from the radar emitter.

The Signal to Clutter Ratio (SCR) can be obtained. The detection result can be judged after comparing the SCR and SCR gate.

3.2 The District of Main Beam Clutter

According the radar equation, the clutter power per scatter cell can be calculated by

$$dP_2 = \frac{P_t\lambda^2 G_1^2 \sigma_0}{(4\pi)^3 R^4} \tag{7}$$

The shade of the airborne radar antenna main beam is ellipse. And the long axis of the ellipse is

$$a = \frac{R\beta}{\sin\alpha} \tag{8}$$

where β is the antenna man lobe width, α is the angle between the main beam and the surface.

The short axis is

$$b = R\beta \tag{9}$$

The district reflected on the surface is

$$S = \pi ab \tag{10}$$

Therefore, the main beam clutter energy is,

$$E = \iint S dP_2 \tag{11}$$

Since the clutter energy is obtained, the detection result can be judged after comparing the SCR and SCR gate.

3.3 The District of Side Lobe Clutter

According to the radar equation, the clutter power per scatter cell in the side lobe can be calculated by

$$dP_3 = \frac{P_t\lambda^2 G_2^2 \sigma_0}{(4\pi)^3 R^4} \tag{12}$$

According to the simplified antenna model, the side lobe shade is an ellipse ring. It is calculated by

$$S' = S_2 - S_1 \tag{13}$$

Where S_2 is the elliptical shade of the main beam and first side lobe, S_1 is the elliptical shade of the main beam. The reflected district of the side lobe is

$$E = \iint S' dP_3 \tag{14}$$

After the clutter energy calculated, the detection result can be judged after comparing the SCR and SCR gate.

3.4   The District Without Clutter

According to the simplified radar equation, the max range is calculated by

$$R' = R_{max} \cdot \sqrt[4]{\sigma} \tag{15}$$

The detection result can be judged after comparing the max detection range and the actual range.

4   Simulation Tests

A comparison test is done among the functional level model, the signal level radar model and the proposed model as mentioned above. The result of the test is shown as below (Table 1).

Table 1. A comparison test

	Functional level radar model	Signal level radar model	Model proposed in this paper
Radial velocity is close to Zero	Found	Lose	Lose
Radial velocity is low	Found	Lose	Lose
Radial velocity is close to the surface relative speed	Found	Lose	Lose
Radial velocity is high	Found	Found	Found

Setting consistent parameters in the three simulation model, a comparison test of calculating speed is done among the three kinds of model developed in Matlab. The result is shown in the following table (Table 2).

Table 2. The results of calculating speed

	Functional level radar model	Signal level radar model	Model proposed in this paper
Calculating speed	Run in real-time	Far away from calculating in real-time	Run in real-time

Even though using the C Program, the calculating speed of the signal level radar model is far away from the real time operation. The results above show that the performance of the model proposed in this paper is approximating the signal level radar model, and the speed of the model is close to that of the functional level simulation model.

It is appropriate for the large simulation systems, such as tactical simulation system with many airborne radars and targets.

5   Conclusion

An effective model on airborne radar based on clutter spectrum is proposed in this paper. Its calculating speed is close to that of the functional level radar model, and the simulation results are almost the same with the signal level radar model according to the simulation test. The calculation quantity of the model proposed is much less than that of the signal level radar model. The model could be generally used in simulation system with many airborne radars. In this paper, a simplified antenna model and clutter spectrum model are proposed. The clutter spectrum is divided into four districts. The quantity of calculation is further decreased since just one district's clutter energy is computed. But some value, such as signal to clutter ratio gate and clutter spectrum frequency gate, are not discussed in detail in this paper. The effective model could be applied in some huge simulating systems, especially in the multiple radars and targets scenarios where calculating speed is a significant factor.

References

1. Diani,M., Corsini, G., Berizzi, F., Calugi,D.: IEE Proc. Radar, Sonar and Navig. **143**(2), 113–120 (1996)
2. Goldstein, H.: Sea echo. In: Kerr, D.E., (eds.) Propagation of Short Radio Waves. MIT Radiation Lab. McGraw-Hill, New York (1951)
3. Trunk, G.V., George, S.F.: Detection of targets in non-Gaussian sea clutter. IEEE Trans. Aerosp. Electron. Syst. **6**, 620–628 (1970)
4. Fay, F.A., Clark, J., Peters, R.S.: Weibull distribution applied to sea clutter. In: Proceedings of the IEEE Conference Radar, London, vol. 155, pp. 101–104. IEEE Conference Publication (1977)
5. Goldstein, G.B.: False alarm regulation in log-normal and Weibull clutter. IEEE Trans. Aerosp. Electron Syst. **9**, 84–92 (1973)

Trajectory Modeling and Simulation of Anti-missile Interception of Warship Based Missile

Yunbo Gao[(⊠)], Liang Han, and Jiangyun Wang

School of Automation Science and Electrical Engineering,
Beihang University, Beijing, China
gaoyunbo923@buaa.edu.cn

Abstract. Air defense combat is one of the important parts in the research of surface ships. In the long-range missile intercepting maneuvering targets is a key link of warship air defense systems. Especially, in this paper, we mainly study for air defense intercept combat mission in CGF (Computer Generate Force) system, we study the designing and simulation of the ballistic of ship based-missiles adopt vertical launching mode. Aiming at the maneuver of the target, we do modeling and Simulation of interception trajectory model by using assumed target method. Finally, through the debugging operation with other CGF simulation against node, the feasibility of the model is verified.

Keywords: Vertical launch · Trajectory model · Interception strategy · Proportional guidance · Assumed target

1 Introduction

Surface ship formation air defense includes the systems of plan, organization and action in order to guarantee that warship formation intercept air target in full fire [1, 2]. With the emergence of high-tech weapons and equipment such as advanced mobile electronic warfare system and ship based unmanned aerial vehicle, constitute a new threat to the warship from the air. Especially, the development of stand-off launching and low altitude penetration concealment makes the depth of the ship to air detection and combat airspace compressed greatly. Therefore, the research on the key technology of warship air defense system to enhance the efficiency of air defense combat urgent needs.

References do corresponding research on some of the key issues of the problem. Some references aim on a part of air defense combat process. Such as early warning tasks in air defense operations discussed in paper [2], Duan considers on spatial grid as a unit of the corresponding effect of early warning and threat degree evaluation method; and then through the analysis of the actual demand, put forward to achieve alert succession mission patrol strategic planning model and, respectively, for the proposed multi master from the structure of a variety of group parallel genetic algorithm to solve the model. In paper [3], according to the fire strike rule, a multi-objective function model is set up by Wu, and a distributed genetic simulated annealing algorithm is

© Springer Science+Business Media Singapore 2016
L. Zhang et al. (Eds.): AsiaSim 2016/SCS AutumnSim 2016, Part II, CCIS 644, pp. 500–507, 2016.
DOI: 10.1007/978-981-10-2666-9_51

proposed to solve the model. The single target serial search method becomes a multi object distributed search method. In paper [4], according to the present situation of Integrated Support Engineering (ISL) of surface ship, Feng regards ship combat readiness as the research target, give out a cost effective rate of established fleet spare parts optimization model, and the fleet and spare parts cost constraints of operational requirements. These studies propose a large number of models and algorithms are all in strong pertinence. But what mostly they ignore macroscopically is the complete process of the combat operations. Although these references realize the model design of the whole process of warship formation air defense operation, they lack of quantitative analysis of the model.

Air defense combat system based on the task of intercepting new type of anti-ship weapons discussed above, has the characteristics of influencing factors, large amount of information, complex model and a wide variety of processes. The results of the trajectory planning of missile influence the interception capability. To propose a scheme for reference solving the phenomenon of "shipborne missile seasickness", we study on an interception strategy for vertical launching missile based on assumed target in this paper.

2 Vertical Launch Mathematical Model

The advantage of vertical transmission is that it can cover the whole range, get fast response and be simple to transmission. In this section, we give the ballistic model based on missile motion model.

2.1 Coordinate Systems Definition

There are two coordinate systems used in the whole process, geographic coordinate system and missile body-fixed coordinate system (Fig. 1).

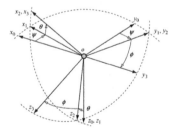

Fig. 1. Coordinate systems definition

- Ground coordinate system

The ground coordinate system S_g-$O_g X_g Y_g Z_g$ is fixed on the earth. O_g is randomly chosen on the ground, $O_g Z_g$ axis is downward along the direction of gravity direction; $O_g Y_d$ to south, and $O_g X_g$ to east;

- Missile coordinate system

Missile coordinate system S_b-$O_bX_bY_bZ_b$ is fixed on the body of the missile. O_b is at the missile centroid, O_bX_b is in the symmetrical plane of missile, pointing to warhead, O_bY_b is vertical to the symmetrical plane of missile, pointing to the right. O_bZ_b perpendicular to the plane of the OX_sZ_s.

- Coordinate system conversion

$$S_b = B_{3\times3}S_g$$

$$B = \begin{bmatrix} \cos\theta\cos\psi & \cos\theta\sin\psi & -\sin\theta \\ (\sin\phi\sin\theta\cos\psi - \cos\phi\sin\psi) & (\sin\phi\sin\theta\sin\psi + \cos\phi\cos\psi) & \sin\phi\cos\theta \\ (\cos\phi\sin\theta\cos\psi + \sin\phi\sin\psi) & (\cos\phi\sin\theta\sin\psi - \sin\phi\cos\psi) & \cos\phi\cos\theta \end{bmatrix} \quad (1)$$

θ, ψ, ϕ in the formula respectively indicate pitch, yaw and roll angle, which are the attitude angle of the missile.

2.2 Relative Motion Relationship

The target line of sight rotation speed in the ground coordinate is expressed by:

$$\omega_R = \frac{\vec{R} \times \vec{T}_{Vd}}{\left|\vec{R} \times \vec{R}\right|} \quad (2)$$

$\vec{R}, \vec{T}_{Vd}$ in the formula respectively indicate relative position and speed vector in the ground coordinate between missile and the target.

2.3 Interceptor Missile Theoretical Model

Although a total of six degree of freedom system describing the missile motion can be obtained with high accuracy, it requires a large amount of computation as well as stores a large number of aerodynamic parameters. System consists of mass trajectory of missile dynamics equations, around the centroid rotation dynamic equation group, missile motion of the center of mass of the kinematic equations, around the dynamical equations of motion of the center of mass, quality variation equation, geometrical equations and control equations, a total of 20 equations [6]. So it is not suitable for the general warship CGF system. In fact, the system uses a simplified five degree of freedom model. Five degree of freedom model of the simplified method is to ship blanks of flight trajectory procedure for ejection and guiding section, ignoring missile roll angle changes, considering only the yaw angle and pitching angle changes in the deregulated. Missile dynamics equations simplified using the limit parameter models are shown below.

$$\dot{V}_{xb} = \frac{F - mg \times sin\theta}{m} - \omega_y \times V_{zt} + \omega_z \times V_{yt}$$

$$\dot{V}_{yb} = \frac{Y + mg \times cos\theta \times cos\phi}{m} - \omega_z \times V_{xt} + \omega_x \times V_{zt} \qquad (3)$$

$$\dot{V}_{zb} = \frac{Z + mg \times cos\theta \times sin\phi}{m} - \omega_x \times V_{yt} + \omega_y \times V_{xt}$$

In this way interception missile in the process can be established as shown in Fig. 2.

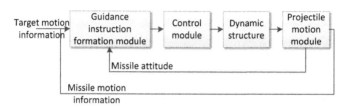

Fig. 2. Structure diagram of interception missile

Interceptor with vertical launching rose to a certain height, then keep flight in accordance with the established trajectory; while entry guidance stage, combined relative motion relationship, forms guidance law. The guidance law controls the missile to change the flight state, and to modify the trajectory according to the target's motion information until it meets the explosive conditions. In the guidance section, the attitude angle velocity is proportional to the rotation angle of the target in the flight process.

Meanwhile considering the different models of the missile, and the differences between different kinds of targets, each link of the ballistic model is set up.

2.4   Assumed Target Interception Strategy

The vertical transmission mode determines the operational mode of the missile to intercept the target after launch to a sufficient height. As for the super low altitude sea skimming flight target, due to the interference of the sea clutter and multipath effects, only can relatively accurate target location information be obtained. With the continuous improvement of the flight speed of the anti-ship missile, the time for the interceptor is getting shorter and shorter. Therefore, we study the method to improve the interception ability.

In this paper, we adopt the following strategies to solve the problem of the initial segment movement direction, so that the missile has been approaching to the target before entering the guidance stage. After the missile launches to the established altitude, an assumed target which is located on the line between the warship (detecting device on the warship) and the real target is introduced. The assumed target moves in the direction of the real target along the line of the detection line. The distance between the virtual target and the missile is kept in a small range. In this stage, the direction of missile's acceleration is pointed to the virtual target. In this way, missile can be pushed

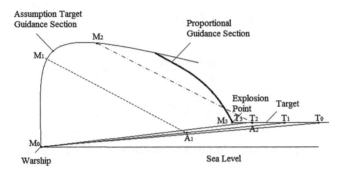

Fig. 3. Assumed target interception strategy sketch map in vertical plane

closer to the true target as the simulation advances without detecting detailed motion information of the target. As shown in Fig. 3.

$T_0 - T_3$ are points on target trajectory. Correspondingly, $M_0 - M_3$ are points on missile trajectory at the same time. A_1, A_2 are set to indicate the assumed target's position when target and missile are at the position of T_1, M_1 or T_2, M_2.

The location of an assumed target every moment can be calculated by formulas from the development of paper [7].

The distance between the assumed target and the missile is D. According to the relationship of mathematics, obtain X_{AI} on the detection axis along the line between the warship (detecting device on the warship) and the real target.

$$X_{AI} = X_{MI} + \sqrt{D^2 - Y_{MI}^2 - Z_{MI}^2} \tag{4}$$

The location of the assumed target in the ground coordinate can be calculated as shown below.

$$\begin{bmatrix} X_A \\ Y_A \\ Z_A \end{bmatrix} = \begin{bmatrix} cos\vartheta cos\mu & -sin\vartheta cos\mu & sin\mu \\ sin\vartheta & cos\vartheta & 0 \\ -cos\vartheta sin\mu & sin\theta sin\mu & cos\mu \end{bmatrix} \begin{bmatrix} X_{AI} \\ 0 \\ 0 \end{bmatrix} \tag{5}$$

ϑ, μ in the formulas indicate the altitude angle and the direction angle from the target to warship.

When target moves from point T_0 to point T_2, it keeps all the time that

$$|A_1 M_1| \approx |A_2 M_2| \tag{6}$$

When the assumed target moves along the line of motion, it is bound to rendezvous with the target. Meanwhile, the missile will detect and track with the target, and then the system transferred into proportional guidance section to intercept the target.

Guidance command in proportional guidance section satisfies

$$\omega_g = n\omega_R \tag{7}$$

Where $\vec{\omega}_g = (\vec{\omega}_{gx}, \vec{\omega}_{gy}, \vec{\omega}_{gz})$. Then let

$$\vec{\omega}_b = B\vec{\omega}_g = \left(\vec{\omega}_x, \vec{\omega}_y, \vec{\omega}_z\right) \tag{8}$$

Substitution (8) into (3), constitute guidance loop. The guidance system can guide the missile approaching to the target.

3   Simulation Results

- Simulation Approach

The ballistic model is embedded in the CGF system of surface ship while simulation processing. The workflow of the system is shown in the following figure.

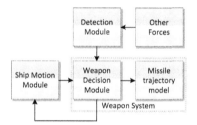

Fig. 4. Full set of simulation model

- Result Analysis

The interception process lasted 18 s. Miss distance takes less than 20 m.

Three dimensional trajectories, in horizontal plane and time variation curve of attitude angles are shown in Figs. 5 and 6.

In Fig. 7, as the pitching angle time curve shows, due to initial launching pitch angle cannot meet the needed overload of unloading phase. So the control system for the control of the missile quickly bows and keeps to the steady flight near the target. In Fig. 8 the yaw angle in the initial stage of rapid change, and then back again.

During the guidance process, the target is always in the range of the missile seeker. Seeker can intercept and track the target. Therefore, the missile has a large probability of intercepting target.

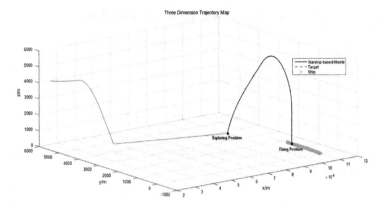

Fig. 5. Three dimensional trajectory

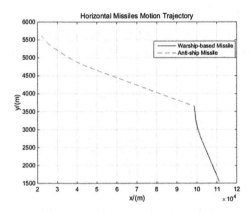

Fig. 6. Trajectories in horizontal plane

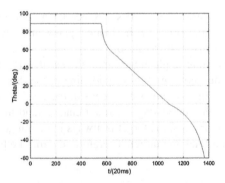

Fig. 7. Time variation curve of pitch angle

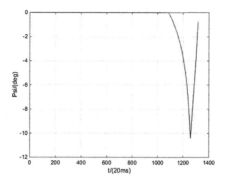

Fig. 8. Time variation curve of yaw angle

4 Conclusion

In this research, a mathematical trajectory model of warship-based missile adopting vertical launching is given. By the ballistic simulation, the long-range ballistic missile can be used in the terminal guidance to achieve the target of effective attack. Through the coupling simulation with other CGF nodes, verifies that the use of assumed target method in Interception stage can achieve the desired of anti-ship missile interception system. Although the anti-ship missile interception system designed in this way possibly has the disadvantages or shortcomings which we are not considered, this method values the prospect for deeply studied. This method plays a certain role in improving the accuracy of interception for vertical launching missile system [8].

References

1. Cheng, S.L., Wang, Y.A.: Research on the key technology of cooperative guidance air defense of warship formation. Ship Electron. Eng. (2016)
2. Cui, J.: Research on multi Agent based cooperative air defense intelligent planning. National Defense Science and Technology University (2013)
3. Duan, X.W., Gao, X.G., Li, B.: Research on the control strategy of air defense warning of the carrier based early warning aircraft in the comprehensive operational area. Syst. Eng. Electron. Technol. **1**, (2015)
4. Wu, K.H., Zhan, S.X.: Optimization of firefighting target assignment based on distributed genetic simulated annealing algorithm. Institute of Military Operation Analysis Research, The Academy of Military Science (2016)
5. Feng, S., Yang, Z.C.: Monte-Carlo simulating method for the spare parts allocation model centered availability of the single part system on naval ship. Ship Build. China (2005)
6. Wang, y., Liu, Y.L.: Evaluation method of path planning for six degree of freedom trajectory simulation. Trans. Beijing Inst. Technol. **4**, 2010
7. Zhou X F. Guidance strategy of air to air missile for carrier based anti-missile interception. Electron. Opt. Control **1** (2014)
8. Zhao, N., Si, X.C., Chen, T.: Research on the maneuvering target trajectory of long range missile attack in vertical launch. Appl. Sci. Technol. (2011)

An Air Combat Decision-Making Method Based on Knowledge and Grammar Evolution

Duan Yang[✉] and Yaofei Ma

School of Automation Science and Electrical Engineering,
Beihang University, Beijing, China
yangduan1991@126.com

Abstract. The problem of decision-making in autonomous air combat is widely studied in domains like military training, UAV operation, computer game intelligence, etc. In this paper, the Grammar Evolution (GE) approach is applied to derive proper tactics strategy in air combat. GE approach finds solutions in the form of structured programs based on evolution principles, and thus being possible to bridge domain knowledge with generic evolution process to form a general approach for decision-making problems. In our work, the basic GE approach is first tested with a problem-related BNF grammar, which regulates the mapping between the genotype and the programs (phenotype). We firstly test some simple situations to prove that GE can search for a right solution. Next, however, when combat with the enemy with the Min-Max strategy, we find it is inefficient to get robust strategy in the dynamic environment of air combat because the derived strategy often cover only a small portion of the whole decision space. To this problem, we propose some improvement measures in the next work.

Keywords: Air combat decision-making · Knowledge · Grammar Evolution · Combat simulation

1 Introduction

At present, the air combat has become a very important part of the modern warfare. With the transformation of modern air combat mode and the development of flight technology, the aircraft plays a more and more important role in the air combat. When both sides have equal equipment, the air combat decision will become the key factors for the combat outcome. And now, the aircraft and airborne weapons are increasingly advanced and the air combat space become more complex so that it's difficult for the pilot to make the optimize choice quickly. To reduce the load of pilot, improve the efficiency of the decision, to formulate a set of intelligent decision making plan is particularly important.

In many military simulations, the human-like decision making is critical to the credibility of the simulation results. The computer generated forces (CGF), which are usually used as alliance or opponent in simulated battlefield, are expected to behave like real human beings or be coincidence with military doctrines, to produce high confidence outcomes of the simulated scenario. Moreover, since the unmanned vehicles

© Springer Science+Business Media Singapore 2016
L. Zhang et al. (Eds.): AsiaSim 2016/SCS AutumnSim 2016, Part II, CCIS 644, pp. 508–518, 2016.
DOI: 10.1007/978-981-10-2666-9_52

are becoming important roles in the future battlefield, the human behavior modeling received more and more attentions and different modeling approaches are being explored aiming at high intelligent behavior that can handle complex missions autonomously.

The "traditional" approach to describe human behavior in military simulation is based on doctrines, or more generally, domain knowledge. The knowledge is integrated with different formulizations like production rules [1], finite state machine [2], and graph chart [3] etc. Some simulation platforms integrated comprehensive decision frameworks, for example the TacAir-Soar [4], BDI [5], Agent-fly [6],etc. These frameworks provide facilities to help the users to code, debug and compile the knowledge for available human behavior models. However, the lack of adaptability make these manually crafted models cannot adapt new knowledge automatically by self-learning. It has been proved that such models are difficult to be maintained when their sizes grow. Another consequence of non-adaptive is that the performance of behavior model is static and determined completely by the modeler. The continuous improvement based on historical data cannot be obtained in such case.

In order to overcome the disadvantages of the traditional approach based on domain knowledge, we will adopt an approach that is based on the domain knowledge, at the same time, combined with Grammar Evolution [7]. The Grammar Evolution, which is a branch of Genetic Algorithm, is based on Context-Free Grammar so that we can integrate the air combat decision-making knowledge into the Grammar Evolution. GE approach can generate air combat decision automatically and optimize it continually. GE can make connection between the Grammar, the domain knowledge, and the evolution progress so that with the evolution, new domain knowledge can be adapt automatically. And since the knowledge from GE is generated by computer, people don't need to design the strategy artificially. So the GE approach promises to be a general method.

2   Grammar Evolution

Grammar Evolution was originally put forward by O'Neil and Ryan [8]. It is a kind of Genetic Algorithm in essence. The core idea of GE approach is that user defines a context-free grammar (usually, the context-free grammar is based on Backus-Naur Form, BNF). The grammar can be used to establish the mapping relationship between genotype and phenotype. Here, the genotype usually consists of a series of digit while the phenotype, the decision knowledge, is usually a string. After the mapping process (i.e. the creation of the phenotype), the fitness score is calculated and assigned to each individual (phenotype) according to the given problem specification. These fitness scores are sent back to the evolutionary algorithm which uses them to evolve a new population of individuals.

One of the most unique feature of GE approach is that the GE is based on a context-free grammar, usually a BNF grammar, so that it provides convenience for us to combine the evolution with domain knowledge (the knowledge can be presented easily by context-free grammar).

2.1 The BNF

The Backus-Naur Form (BNF) is a set of symbols used to describe the rules [9]. A complete BNF should contain terminal nodes and non-terminal nodes. The non-terminal nodes will expand by the rules user defined until all the non-terminal nodes is expanded to terminal nodes. The non-terminal nodes are expressed by "<>". The string in quotes represent the string itself. And the string without any symbol represent the terminal nodes. Either item should be selected on both sides of the "|". ":=" equals "is defined as".

In air combat decision, the BNF we design should be able to expand into the form we need, just like mentioned above, that there are many "IF-ELSE" and they can nest with each other. The terminal nodes should contain the current situation and the action to perform. Besides, the BNF we designed should have good expandability so that the generated solution can cover more situation state. Now you can see a valid BNF as shown in Fig. 1.

<prog>::= <code>

<code> ::= <condition>

<condition>::="if("<expressions>") {"<line>"} else {" <line> "}"

<line> ::= <condition> | <op>

<expressions>::= expression1 | expression2 | expression3 | expression4

<op> ::= action1| action2 | action3 | action4 | action5

Fig. 1. Simple BNF to describe air combat decision

2.2 Grammar Evolution in Air Combat

Now we need to apply Grammar Evolution to the air combat. We design the program with the help of GEVA. GEVA is an open source implementation of Grammatical Evolution in Java developed at UCD' s Natural Computing Research & Applications group. GEVA can achieve the basic operation of Genetic Algorithm and the process genotype trans into phenotype. We design a BNF and use it to generate knowledge, the air combat strategy and then we perform a combat simulation experiment with the strategy to compute the fitness of this. This strategy is an individual in the evolution. In this way, we have lots of individual, in other word, we have one population here. So next, we do genetic operations to the population such as crossover, mutation, selection and so on, to search the optimal strategy. The flow of this method is shown in Fig. 2.

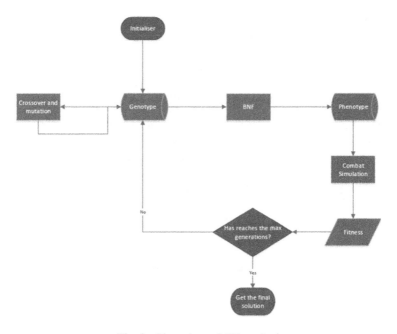

Fig. 2. Flow chart of GE method

3 Combat Simulation

3.1 Simulation Model

The air combat simulation in this article contains red fighters and blue. We are red and the enemy is blue. The aircraft three-dimensional motion equation is shown in the following:

$$\dot{x} = v \cdot cos\theta \cdot sin\psi \tag{4.1}$$

$$\dot{y} = v \cdot cos\theta \cdot cos\psi \tag{4.2}$$

$$\dot{h} = v \cdot sin\theta \tag{4.3}$$

$$\dot{\theta} = \frac{1}{mv}\{(L + \eta \cdot T_{max} \cdot sin\alpha) \cdot cos\phi - mg \cdot cos\theta\} \tag{4.4}$$

$$\dot{\psi} = \frac{1}{mv \cdot cos\theta}(L + \eta \cdot T_{max} \cdot sin\alpha) \cdot sin\phi \tag{4.5}$$

$$\dot{v} = \frac{1}{m}(\eta \cdot T_{max} \cdot cos\alpha - D) - g \cdot sin\theta \tag{4.6}$$

Where x, y and h is the fighter's space position. θ is the flight path angle, ψ is the yaw angle, and v is the velocity. L, D and T_{max} is the lift force, the drag force and the maximum thrust force respectively; η is the thrust control factor. α is the attack angle; ϕ is the bank angle. m and g is the mass and the gravity acceleration, which are assumed as const. The coordinate system is *East-North-Up*.

The aerodynamic force L and D is associated with multiple factors such as the aerodynamic coefficient, the attack angle, the air density, the equivalent cross-sectional area, etc. To simplify their computation, the follows are assumed:

- $L = mg \cdot f_n$, where f_n is the vertical overload of the fighter and is used as the control variable.
- $a = \frac{1}{m}(\eta \cdot T_{max} \cdot cos\alpha - D)$, where a is the axial acceleration and is used as the control variable.
- $\alpha \approx 0$, $\eta = 1$. Then we have the approximations of Eqs. (4.4)–(4.6):

$$\dot{\theta} \approx \frac{g}{v}(f_n \cdot cos\phi - cos\theta) \tag{4.7}$$

$$\dot{\psi} \approx \frac{g \cdot f_n}{mv \cdot cos\theta} \cdot sin\phi \tag{4.8}$$

$$\dot{v} \approx \frac{a}{m} - g \cdot sin\theta \tag{4.9}$$

The bank angle ϕ is controlled by the roll rate w, which takes either the maximum or the minim allowable value of w.

Both aircraft's goal is to occupy the advantageous position, to create conditions for shot down goals. The air state space is shown as the following type:

$$x = \{x_b, y_b, h_b, \phi_b, \psi_b, v_{zb}, x_r, y_r, h_r, \phi_r, \psi_r, v_{zr}\} \tag{4.10}$$

Here, the subscript r and b represent red and blue respectively, x is a state. The air state transition function is shown in the following:

$$s' = f(s, u_b, u_r) \tag{4.11}$$

This equation means that when state is s, the red and blue respectively perform the action u_r, u_b, then the state trans into s'. The actions are summarized for:

$$Action = \{turnleft_{up}, turnright\_up, turnleft\_down, turnright\_down, maitain\}, \tag{4.12}$$

The aimed state is the advantageous situation for us to shoot down the enemy. The aimed state should follow [10]:

$|AA| < \pi/3$, AA is the separating angle, it's the angle between the attachment of our plane and the enemy and the direction that the enemy moves towards. In this range, the kill probability our plane shoots from the tail is high.

$|ATA| < \pi/6$, ATA is the Radar Angle that is the angle between our plane's direction and the radar's direction. In this range, it's difficult to escape from our target for the enemy.

R is the distance between the enemy and us.

When one meet the above conditions, that's to say, it occupies the advantage situation. And if the time it occupies the advantage situation add up to a certain length, that means the combat end up with its victory.

3.2 BNF

Now we need to design the BNF grammar according to the give air combat model. First we need to determine the terminal nodes that contain the actions and the situation states. The BNF should contain five kinds of actions. They are {turn up and left, turn up and right, turn down and left, turn down and right, maintain}. And the situation state mainly involve these parameters, the separating angle AA, the radar angle ATA, the distance R, and the height difference H_d. At the same time we should consider the "IF-ELSE" form of the decision knowledge. So we can design the BNF just like Fig. 3:

```
<prog> ::= <code>

<code> ::= <condition>

<condition>::="if("<expressions>") {"<line>"} else {" <line> "}"

<line> ::= <condition> | <op>

<expressions>::="AA="<range1>" ATA="<range1>" R="<range2>"  Hd="<range3>

<range1>::=-180_-90|-90_0|0_90|90_180

<range2>::=0_1|1_2|2_3|3_5|5_10|10_

<range3>::=-1|1

<op> ::=  turnleft_up | turnleft_down | turnright_up | turnright_down |
maintain
```

Fig. 3. A valid BNF for air combat simulation

3.3 Fitness Function

GEVA adopt adjusted fitness function, that means, the fitness must be positive and the smaller value corresponds to the better individual. At the same time, the fitness should be able to reflect the result of the combat. So we can design the fitness function like this:

$$fitness = \begin{cases} \frac{1}{E} & (if\,win) \\ 1 + \frac{1}{\sum R_i} & (if\,not\,win) \end{cases} \tag{4.7}$$

Here, the fitness is a piecewise function that depends on whether it wins victory. E is the left energy when the combat ends. R_i is the reward value [10] of every state. We can get the result of the combat by judging whether the fitness is less than 1.

4 Experiment Result and Analysis

Here, we firstly performed experiments for some simple situations to test this method's viability. We choose two conditions (Fig. 4):

1   2

Fig. 4. Two simple initial conditions of air combat (Color figure online)

To simplify the progress, we make the blue fly along a straight line so that the time of simulation can be shortened and we can get the strategy quickly. What's more, by this way we can test whether the strategy we get is right more intuitively.

After the simulation, we get the strategies shown in Fig. 5:

```
1
if( AA= 90_180   ATA= 90_180   R= 3_5   Hd= -1 ) {
    turnleft_down
} else {
    maintain
}
```

```
2
if( AA= -180_-90   ATA= -180_-90   R= 1_2   Hd= -1 ) {
    if( AA= 0_90   ATA= 90_180   R= 10_   Hd= -1 ) {
        turnleft_up
    } else {
        turnright_up
    }
} else {
    if( AA= -90_0   ATA= -  90_0   R= 1_2   Hd= -1 ) {
        turnright_down
    } else {
        maintain
    }
}
```

Fig. 5. The strategies of the two simple conditions

And the track of the planes if shown in the Figs. 6 and 7.

As we can see from the above figures, obviously this method can get the right strategies for the simple conditions. Now we will test if it can get the strategy for the complex condition. We make the blue plane act with Min-Max method [10] to test if the strategy generated by GE approach can beat it. Here is the track of the combat. Here, we set three different types of initial situations (Figs. 8, 9 and 10):

In this experiment, considering that the velocity of both side is equivalent, to make it possible for that the red can beat the blue, we make the red a few superiority that the max of bank angle is larger than the blue's. As we can see from the above figures, when

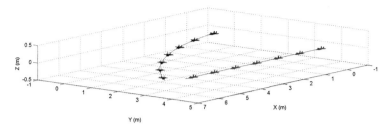

Fig. 6. The two dimension and three dimension track of the first conditions (Color figure online)

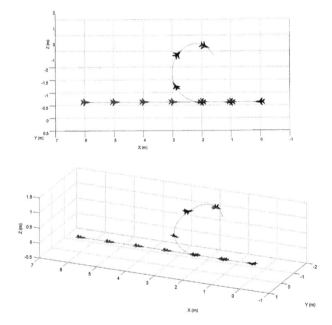

Fig. 7. The two dimension and three dimension track of the second conditions (Color figure online)

the blue acts following Min-Max method, the red, with the GE method, can beat the blue successfully. Because the red has some degree of advantages of property, the experiment can only prove that this method is valid. Whether the decision-making quality is stronger needs a further research. In fact, the strategy we've got so far is not so strong enough. Here are some possible reason. On one hand, the BNF grammar is too simple to describe the situation state accurately. To simplify the decision knowledge model and to shorten the simulation time we designed a simple BNF so that the strategy generated by it would not be powerful enough, or in other words, the knowledge base is perfect enough. On the other hand, in Grammar Evolution, the length of the genotype or the chromosome is limited so the length of the phenotype will be limited. This results in that the final strategy has difficulty in covering all the situations, so, it may not make the best choice in some specific situations.

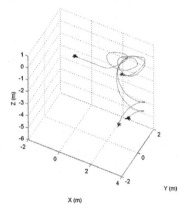

Fig. 8. The track of the combat of which the initial situation is the red occupying the advance. (Color figure online)

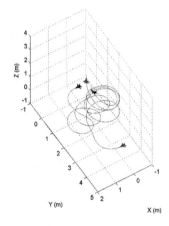

Fig. 9. The track of the combat of which the initial situation is balanced. (Color figure online)

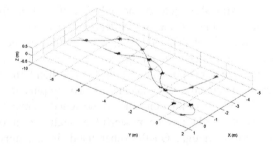

Fig. 10. The track of the combat of which the initial situation is the blue occupying the advance. (Color figure online)

To this problem, we have to improve our existing BNF grammar to make it be able to describe the combat state more accurately. For instance, the existing BNF grammar is only include the separating angle AA, the radar angle ATA, the distance R, and the height difference H_d. Next we can add the plane's attitude information. Also we should segment the states more accurately. At the same time, since the length of the genotype is limited, we must select the critical states artificially and evolve these states separately to make the final strategy cover the critical states as more as possible. So far we have proved that comparing with the traditional knowledge approach, GE has a certain degree of adaptability. But how to enhance the effect of decision should be further studied.

5 Conclusions and Future Work

In this paper, through the research we can find several advantages of GE approach. GE approach is a general method so that it can be combined with lots of problems in the field to search the optimal solution. In air combat problem, by designing different BNF grammar, the GE approach and combine with different aircraft model to make simulation of the air combat. Besides, through this way, the decision knowledge is generated by computer automatically so that it becomes more convenient for users because they don't need to design the knowledge by themselves. What's more, the knowledge generated by this way will be more complete and accurate. In addition, because of the universality of this method, when the type of plane or the parameters change, user only need to redesign the BNF and the related code rather than redesign the whole knowledge base. The GE approach will generate the new Knowledge according to the new BNF.

But we should find out that this method also has some disadvantages. If the aircraft model or the spatial becomes complex, in other words, more terminal nodes in BNF and related parameters is contained, the calculated quantity will be huge and the run time of the program will be very long accordingly. So how to promote the efficiency of the GE approach will be worth studying next.

References

1. Burgin, G.H., Sidor, L B.: Rule-based air combat simulation. No. TITAN-TLJ-H-1501. TITAN SYSTEMS INC LA JOLLA CA (1988)
2. Banks, S.B., Lizza, C.S.: Pilot's associate: a cooperative, knowledge-based system application. IEEE Expert **6**(3), 18–29 (1991)
3. Laird, J.E.: The Soar Cognitive Architecture. MIT Press, Cambridge (2012)
4. TacAir-Soar Goal/Operator Hierarchy. http://www.isi.edu/soar/ifor/agent/. Accessed 28 Dec 2015
5. Rick, E., John, T., Nitin, Y., et al.: A framework for modelling tactical decision-making in autonomous systems. J. Syst. Soft. **110**, 222–238 (2015)

6. Sislak, D., Volf, P., Kopriva, S., Pechoucek, M.: AgentFly: scalable, high-fidelity framework for simulation, planning and collision avoidance of multiple UAVs. In: Sense and Avoid in UAS: Research and Applications, pp. 235–264 (2012)
7. Nohejl, A: Grammar-based genetic programming. Department of Software and Computer Science Education (2011)
8. O'Neill, M., Hemberg, E., Gilligan, C., Bartley, E., McDermott, J., Brabazon, A: GEVA - Grammatical Evolution in Java (v2.0). Natural Computing Research & Applications Group University College, Dublin, Ireland, 13 June 2011
9. Harper, R.: Evolving robocode tanks for evo robocode. Genet. Program Evolvable Mach. **15**, 403–431 (2014)
10. Ma, X.: Research of many-to-many air combat intelligent decision. Beihang University Master Thesis (2014)
11. Ortega, A., de la Cruz, M., Alfonseca, M.: Christiansen grammar evolution: grammatical evolution with semantics. Trans. Evol. Comput. **11**(1) (2007)

Simulation Research on Missile Tracking Under the Guidance of Online Real Radar

Honglin Xu$^{(\boxtimes)}$, Weibo Chen, and Xiaolei Ning

Key Laboratory of Guided Weapons Test and Evaluation Simulation
Technology, China HuaYin Ordnance Test Center, Huayin, China
xhl-32jd@sina.com

Abstract. Aiming at the requirement of test and evaluation (T&E) on precision of missile target tacking under the guidance of radar, a virtual-real mixed simulation system is built up based on Xsim simulation platform. In the process, it involves some real equipment, such as radar and target. It solves some key technologies, including time-space consistency, data transmission and missile tracking trajectory modeling. In project, the test method of multiple virtual samples computing in a real time system running has been studied.

Keywords: Missile target tracking · Mixed virtual-real simulation · T&E

1 Introduction

During the flight initial and middle sections, the missile tracks a target using radar as guidance system. Once the missile closes to target, its optical-electronic seeker guides it to intercept the target more accurately. Therefore, research on missile flight under guidance of radar has great significance to weapon system analysis.

In the joint test of radar-reconnaissance and missile flight, it always brings the organizational complexity, huge cost and high safety risk. For example, it is impossible to conduct a missile attacking test with a manned aircraft target. Therefore, the missile flight simulation was applied in that test. Moreover, some difficulties exist in the process of modeling and simulation (M&S). For example, the error of radar-reconnaissance is especially uncertain. As shown in Fig. 1, the error curve of radar-reconnaissance is presented.

In a sense, it is difficult to describe the above error with traditional models. Therefore, it's insufficient to evaluate the influence of reconnaissance error in the flight process using digital simulation. In this paper, a virtual-real mixed simulation system is studied, based on Xsim simulation platform involving some real equipment, such as a radar and a helicopter (that is, a target). It breaks some technologies, such as time-space consistency, data transmission, the modeling of guiding flight trajectory. In practice, the performance of inconstant and the reliability of system both meet to the application requirement.

In the mixed simulation test, we applied a creative sampling method, that is, multiple samples of virtual missile flight were computed in a single running of real radar reconnaissance. Finally, the missile tracking precision was evaluated and some problems were discovered.

© Springer Science+Business Media Singapore 2016
L. Zhang et al. (Eds.): AsiaSim 2016/SCS AutumnSim 2016, Part II, CCIS 644, pp. 519–531, 2016.
DOI: 10.1007/978-981-10-2666-9_53

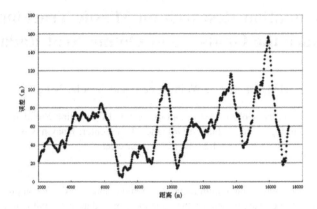

Fig. 1. The error variation curve under different distances

2 The Composition of Simulation System and its Running Link

Test system involves real equipment, virtual-real simulation resources, and some supplementary resources, and so on, as shown in Table 1.

Table 1. Equipment and resources of testing system

Index	Equipment and resource	Amount
1	Real radar	1
2	Real C2	1
3	Missile target tracking model	1
4	Target helicopter	1
5	Measuring system	2
6	Simulation platform	1
7	Testing network	1

There are two information links in the testing system, as shown in Fig. 2.

- In the first information link, radar firstly sends target information to the real intelligence network, then command and control (C2) system filters and analyzes the information. Subsequently, it will be injected into the missile control model through fiber high speed network. Of course, it is able guide the flight simulation under the XSim platform. In the process, the delay time of information link equals to real equipment network.
- In the second information link, the test data is gained from the GPS/infrared instrument. It records the target route, which is always viewed as the true value of target. Subsequently, these data will be injected into the evaluator.
- In our study, the main task of evaluating is to judge whether the target appears in the missile seeker field of view or not at the appropriate time. Considering the radar reconnaissance error, the missile is possibly committing to misdirection for the

duration of the flight. At the same time, it is impossible for the seeker to detect the target, as shown in Fig. 3.

3 Support Technology of Time-Space Consistency

3.1 Time Alignment

To ensure the credibility of the virtual-real testing system, it's necessary to keep the time-space consistency of real equipment, simulation system, testing system and their interfaces.

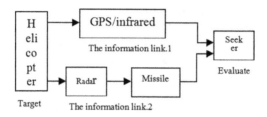

Fig. 2. The information link of system operation

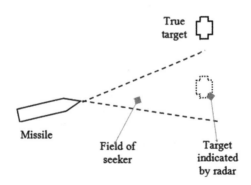

Fig. 3. Target outside the field of seeker view

4 Support Technology of Time-Space Consistency

4.1 Time Alignment

To ensure the credibility of the virtual-real testing system, it's necessary to keep the time-space consistency of real equipment, simulation system, testing system and their interfaces.

Generally, it's always not synchronize among the real equipment, system simulation and testing system, under the condition of combination operation. The phenomenon is caused by time base, which are always different among these systems. Therefore, it's necessary to keep the synchronization of data before starting an experiment. Generally, in virtual-real system, time alignment of physical data contains two parts: the alignment among different sensors, and the alignment among different systems. Meanwhile, the process of time alignment contains two steps.

Time alignment among different sensors in the same system.Each testing station uses IRIG-B receiver decoder to receive GPS signal, and trigger pulse of target helicopter will be sent to central station. Subsequently, it will be sent to sub-stations, which is viewed as the trigger signal to other equipment.

There are two main factors to affect the time alignment: one is the synchronization accuracy of IRIG-B decoder receiver, and the error is less than $5\,\mu s$ in a second sync pulse; the other one is sync accuracy of the trigger signal in testing station, because the delay time is always different among different testing stations. Generally, the error is always less than $10\,ms$, which can be revised by continual tests.

Time alignment among different systems

Usually, it's difficult to use a unified clock among different systems. Therefore, it's necessary to view a high-precision clock as the base time. Generally, the system mainly contains several sub-systems, such as real radar, real C2, simulation platform, and testing system. Especially, real radar, real C2 and center station are installed with GPS. Therefore, it only needs to install a GPS in the simulation platform, and the synchronization of the platform is achieved by the GPS signal of each sub-system.

There is a main factor to affect the time alignment. It is the transmission error of GPS among different systems, which is also less than $50\,\mu s$. Of course, it also meets to the alignment requirements of base time.

4.2   Space Alignment

The essence of space alignment is to choose a reference coordinate system, and it unifies the sensor data of different platforms to this coordinate system. As for the differences in the categories and locations of sensors and their coordinate systems, the observation values of the same object are also different. Therefore, it's necessary to unify the sensor data of different systems in space. Subsequently, all data will be unified to a same coordinate system, using the same measurement units.

In the process of space alignment, it contains several steps as follows:

- Firstly, a launching coordinate system is selected as the reference coordinate system in the process of space alignment;
- Secondly, the data format of the sub-systems is converted to the style of public reference coordinate system;
- Finally, experimental data are converted to the launching coordinates again.

5   Data Transmission

Generally, virtual-real experiment system mainly consists of real equipment, simulation model, and testing equipment. Meanwhile, the steps of data transmission include data capturing, filtering, analyzing and transmitting. For example, the experimental system is composed of real equipment, real target, real C2, simulation system and testing system, while the simulation system contains the models of launch vehicles and missiles. According to the experimental schema, target information will be sent to the intelligence network once the target is scouted by radar. Then real C2 will distribute task to the launch vehicles after ranking the danger of target information. Finally, launch vehicles gain the real-time coordinates from the intelligence network.

Therefore, in the process of transmitting target information from scout radar to simulation system, the first step is to intercept and capture data from intelligence network, the second step is to filter the target information of launch vehicle, the third step is to analyze encrypted information and convert it to usable information according to special rules, and finally launch vehicles receive the information which is able to support simulation. The process of data transmission and data transformation is shown in Fig. 4.

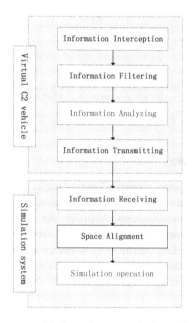

Fig. 4. The process of information transmission and transformation

5.1   Capturing Information

Capturing information is the process to gain messages which are sent to real C2 from radar. Under the premise of common communication, real C2 captures the target information by invoking capture function.

5.2   Information Filtering

Information filtering is the process to remove the useless information and save valuable information according to simulation requirements. In the interaction process, there are all kinds of messages, such as C2 information, data, orders, and target information.

According to the requirement of simulation system, most of information will be filtered. Finally, only target information is reserved such as time stamp, target velocity and target location, while other useless information is removed in the end. As shown in Fig. 5, it outlines some key codes of this algorithm.

```
void packet_handler(u_char *param, const struct pcap_pkthdr *header, const u_char *pkt_data).
{
    CNetDatasDlg *p=(CNetDatasDlg*)::AfxGetApp()->GetMainWnd();
    nDataSec=nDataSec+header->len;  //统计数据包的总大小
    ih = (ip_header *) (pkt_data+14);         //IP包
    unsigned char tmpbuf[1024]={0};
    int  tmplen = 0;
    switch(ih->proto)
    {
    case TCP_PROTO: //TCP包
        break;
    case UDP_PROTO: //UDP包
        uh=(udp_header*)((u_char*)ih+ip_len);
                for(int i=0 ;i<glcount;i++)
        {
        if (m_flag )    //找到匹配端口    p->g_jtsy 监听所有数据
        {
            datalength = ntohs(uh->len);  //长度大于8
if (datalength < 8)
                    return ;
    }
        if (finalSourceIp == m_tmpsourip) && ( m_tmpdesip==finalAimIp )
        {
            datalength = datalength - 8 ;
            m_data = ((byte*)ih+ip_len+8);
            if(p->g_zfsj)
            {
                p->TranlateProp(m_data,datalength,tmpbuf,&tmplen);
                p->SendToJTdata(tmpbuf,tmplen,1); //发送监听数据
```

Fig. 5. Key codes of information filtering

5.3 Information Analyzing

Generally, information is always encrypted in the real system. Therefore, it's necessary to analyze the target information based on special rules, and then the target information will be identified by simulation systems. Actually, the main task is to analyze the data which are sent to real C2 from radar. Usually, these data conforms to a certain protocol in binary format. Luckily, data transmitting software is able to analyze the message according to the protocol, and gain the desired target information. As shown in Fig. 6, it outlines some key codes of this algorithm.

5.4 Information Distribution

The main task of information distribution is to transmit the decrypted information to the simulation system through real-time network. Target information is distributed in the form of socket message, and the process conforms to a protocol. Additionally, key codes of this algorithm are shown in Fig. 7.

5.5 Information Receiving

The main task of information receiving is to receive real-time target information according to the network protocol, which is accepted by senders and receivers. Part of the program code is shown in Fig. 8.

```
typedef struct
{
    USHORT globno;    //目标编号
    USHORT globtype;  //目标类型
    UCHAR  ismove;    //目标可运动性
        time_t   time; //目标发送时间
    UINT    x;  //目标x值
    UINT    y;  //目标y值
    short   h;  //目标h值
}GLOBPROP;

void TranlateProp(unsigned char *rawdata,int rawlen,unsigned char *tdata,int *tlen)
{
    FetchFindTme(rawdata,&m_globdata);
    memcpy(tdata,(unsignedchar*)&m_globdata,sizeof(m_globdata));
    *tlen = sizeof(m_globdata);
}
BOOL FetchFindTme(unsigned char *msg,GLOBPROP *pNetMsg)
{
    char tmp[4]={0};
    if((char)(*(msg)>>3) == 1){
        //编号
        pNetMsg->globno = (unsigned char)*(msg) + (unsigned char)(*(msg+1) & 0x04);
        //发现时间
        pNetMsg->time = *(time_t *)msg;
            //运动性
        pNetMsg->ismove = ((unsigned char)((*(msg)>>3)));
        pNetMsg->speed = ((unsigned char)((*(msg)) >> 4)) ;
        //x坐标
        memset(tmp,0,4);
```

Fig. 6. Key codes of information analyzing

```
if(AfxSocketInit()==0)  //初始化socket
{
    MessageBox( _T("网络初始化失败") );
    return FALSE;
}
if( !m_LanSocket.Create( 0,SOCK_DGRAM,FD_WRITE,g_bdip ) )    //创建socket.
{
    MessageBox( _T("网络打开失败,网络断开或者端口冲突") );
    return FALSE;
}
m_LanSocket.SendTo(data,length,g_desport,g_desip);//发送接收 到的数据
```

Fig. 7. Key codes of information distribution

```
while( 1 )
{
    //接收消息,通过大小来判断是探测数据还是ask数据
    size_t length = mainThread->GetP()->ReceiveSock->receive_from(
        boost::asio::buffer(data, MAX_TRACK_DATA_LENGTH), sender_endpoint);
    if (length == TRACK_DATA_LENGTH)//接收探测数据
    {
        HRTrackDataInfo *dataInfo = GetTrackDataInfo(data, TRACK_DATA_LENGTH);
        if (!mainThread->CTrackBSE(*dataInfo, iterator))
        {
            delete dataInfo;
            continue;
        }
        delete dataInfo;
    }
    else if (length == SDisplayPDUSize)//接收ask数据
    {
        SDisplayPDU *displayData = GetEntityTruthDataInfo(data, length);
        if (!mainThread->CEntityTruthBSE(*displayData, iterator))
        {
            delete displayData;
            continue;
        }
        delete displayData;
    //发送导弹数据
        mainThread->MissilePosSend(iterator);
    }
}
```

Fig. 8. Key code of information receiving

5.6   Space Alignment

Space alignment is to verify the location parameters of target information. Finally, the location will be converted to the launching coordinate system. Part of the program code is shown in Fig. 9.

```
void HRHYModelUtil::ECEF2Shooting( TSVector3d ECEFPos, TSVector3d & ShootingPos )
{
    ECEFPos += DeltaECEF84;
    DOUBLE Lon, Lat, Alt;
    TSConversion::ECEFtoLLA(ECEFPos, Lat, Lon, Alt);
    DOUBLE XGaussProj, YGaussProj;
    DOUBLE LonDeg = RADTODEG(Lon);
    DOUBLE LatDeg = RADTODEG(Lat);
    TSConversion::GaussProjCal(LonDeg, LatDeg, YGaussProj, XGaussProj);
    DOUBLE TempX = XGaussProj - SHOOTINGGAUSSX + DeltaGaussX;
    DOUBLE TempY = YGaussProj - SHOOTINGGAUSSY + DeltaGaussY;
    DOUBLE XDirDeg = TSConversion::MilCoordToGeoCoord(Zero);
    DOUBLE XDir = DEGTORAD(XDirDeg);
    DOUBLE CosXDir = COS(XDir);
    DOUBLE SinXDir = SIN(XDir);
    ShootingPos.x = TempX * CosXDir + TempY * SinXDir;
    ShootingPos.y = Alt + 30;
    ShootingPos.z = TempY * CosXDir - TempX * SinXDir;
    ShootingPos += DeltaECEFtoShoot;
}
```

Fig. 9. Key codes of space alignment

5.7   Conclusion

Our experiment results show that the system response error in the time and space domain is less than 1 ms and 0.5 m respectively. The delay time of virtual-real system keeps consistent with the real system. Additionally, the reliability is also guaranteed by dozens of runs.

Finally, target information, verified by time-space alignment, will be used to guide the flight of missiles. Then target information, gained from the testing system, will be viewed as the real location of the target, which is also used to judge the success or failure of the missile tracking target.

6   Modeling on Flight Simulation

6.1   Modeling of the Tracking Flight

During the flight initial and middle sections, the missile flies to the target under the guidance of radar. The flight equations are follows:

$$\frac{dx}{dt} = V \cos \gamma \cos \psi$$

$$\frac{dy}{dt} = V \cos \gamma \sin \psi$$

$$\frac{dh}{dt} = V_m \sin \gamma$$

$$\frac{d\gamma}{dt} = (n_v - \cos \gamma)(g/V)$$

$$\frac{d\psi}{dt} = (n_h / \cos \gamma)(g/V)$$

Where,x, y, z are missile flight parameters. g is gravitational acceleration.n_v, n_h is calculated respectively by autopilot of missile, based on x_t and y_t,which are the target coordinates given by on-line radar and coordinates given by INS fixed to missile.

$$q_v = \sin^{-1} \frac{h_T - h_m}{\sqrt{(x_T - x_m)^2 + (y_T - y_m)^2 + (z_T - z_m)^2}}$$

$$q_h = \tan^{-1} \frac{y_T - y_m}{x_T - x_m}$$

$$n_h = \frac{K \dot{q}_h v}{g \cos \gamma}$$

Where, K is proportional coefficient. x_m, y_m, h_m are acquired from x, y, h by adding measuring error of INS. The optical-electronic seeker amounted the head of missile detects the target during flight period. If the target appears in the field of seeker view in appropriate distances, the missile tracking should be judged a success under the guidance of the radar.

6.2 Simulation on Multiple Sampling in a Single Test

With the Xsim simulation platform, the model of guided flight is built under the online guidance of radar, as shown in above equations. The missile will fly according to the three-dimensional equation of navigation. Combined with the information provided by sensors, such as the locations of target (by radar) and the positions of missile (by INS fixed to the missile), key parameters of flight can be calculated, such as nv and nh. It is able to calculate the Line-of-Sight angles of the missile relative to the target, and judge the precision of the missile tracking target under the guidance of radar.

Meanwhile, simulation tests also consider some important factors, such as the location of missile launch vehicle and the launching distance, INS error. The action of multiple affecting factors can be evaluated in a single virtual-real mixed simulation test.

- Distributed simulating multiple launch vehicles in different locations is used to evaluate for adverse effect of entry direction of the target.
- Sequential simulating launching missiles at uniform time interval for the duration of target moving are used to evaluate for the different effect of the launching distance.
- In a single Simulating launching, multiple trajectories of the missile flight are run based parallel computing in order to evaluate the missile tracking precision statistically. In the process, INS errors are input sampling based on amount of prior data.

By above strategies, it becomes a reality that we can obtain large sample data in a single virtual-real mixed test.

7 Case Study

7.1 Schema Description

In the schema, red force contains the radar and a C2 vehicle and 2 launch vehicles (each with some missiles). Blue force has a helicopter which always flies at a low altitude. In this experiment, reconnaissance radar, C2 vehicle and helicopter are real equipment, while launch vehicle and missiles are simulation models. As shown in Fig. 10, the battle begins from red battlefield. Subsequently, reconnaissance vehicle tries to search and identify the target, capture and rank the danger, and issue target information by intelligence network. The real C2 distributes the firepower according to the intelligence. Finally, launch vehicles open fire to the target according to the received order.

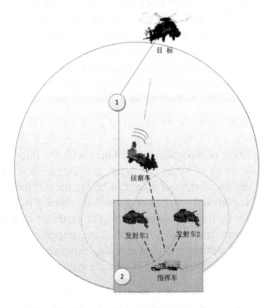

Fig. 10. The deployment diagram of scenario

7.2 Initialization

The initialization of simulation includes the parameters configuration of members and the layout of experiment schema.

The configuration of performance parameters is determined by the condition of experiments, such as ground temperature, humidity, wind, altitude and visibility. It needs to query the property database, gain the performance parameters under different condition, and initialize the simulation members. As for the real equipment, the parameters of models are gained from the testing values.

The editing work of experiment scenario is to initialize the categories and amount of weapon according to the experiment schema. The edit window is shown in Fig. 11, which allows users to add new members or modify existing information.

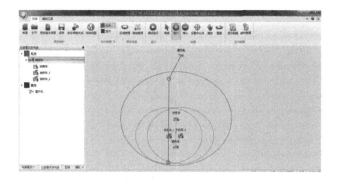

Fig. 11. Configuration and deployment of experimental scenario

7.3 Simulation Process

As shown in Fig. 12, a helicopter flies according to the scheduled flight route, and the radar keeps the real-time reconnaissance on the moving targets. Radar sends target information to the intelligence network once the target enters into the reconnaissance range. Then, these messages are filtered and analyzed by real C2, which will be injected into simulation models and guide the missile flight. Meanwhile, the moving route provided by GPS/infrared measuring system will be viewed as the real values, which is able to judge whether the simulation is successful or not. In our design, we assume that the target will be found by seeker once the guidance is successful.

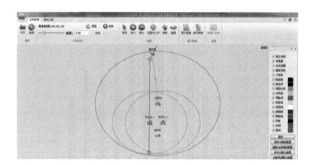

Fig. 12. Target entering into the reconnaissance range

As shown in Fig. 14, if a target enters into the effective range of missiles on the launch vehicle No.1, then it will launch missiles to attack. And the other is the same (Fig. 13).

In the simulation, two launchers are designed to launch multiple missiles. They aim at the same target, and the interval is 10 s. In this experiment, we will examine the tracking success rate under different launch either distances or directions.

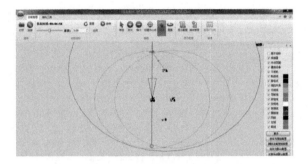

Fig. 13. A target enters into the effective range of missiles

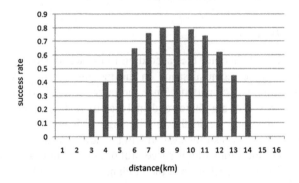

Fig. 14. The tracking success rate varied with launching distance, launch vehicle No.1

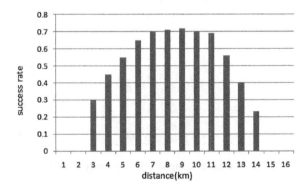

Fig. 15. The tracking success rate varied with launching distance, launch vehicle No.2

8 Conclusions

Based on the simulation outcomes, we obtained the tracking success rates to vary launching distance. It is presented in Figs. 14 and 15, corresponding to the launch vehicle No.1 and No.2, respectively.

To conclude, the tracking success rate keeps dropping as the launching distance either increasing or decreasing. Entry direction of the target has adverse effect on the tracking success rate.

References

1. Montgomery, D.C.: Design and Analysis of Experiments. Posts & Telecom Press, Beijing (2007)
2. Chen, B., Li, J., Shi, K.: Application of robust estimation in coordinates change between referenced-centric and GPS geocentric system. J. Kunming Univ. Sci. Technol. (2005). (SCI TECH Edn.)
3. Li, W., Shen, Y., Li, B.: Three-dimensional coordinate transformation with consideration of coordinate errors in two coordinate systems. J. Tongji Univ. (2011). (Natural science Edn.)

Study on Battlefield Situation Assessment Model of Simulation Entity Based on Stacked Auto-Encoder Network

Ou Wei[1,2(✉)], Guo Sheng-Ming[1], Liu Shao-Jun[1], and He Xiao-Yuan[1]

[1] Department of Information Operation and Command Training,
NDU, Beijing 100091, China
ouweiwlmq@163.com
[2] Urumqi Border Cadre Training Unit, Urumqi 830002, China

Abstract. Constructing the intelligent situation assessment model of entities based on deep neural network (DNN) according to simulations of human cognition and reasoning mode, is significant for improving the ability of quick response and scientific decision-making of entities in the virtual battlefield. Stacked auto-encoder (SAE) is a commonly used deep learning (DL) model, and its feature extraction process is similar to the way of commander when they assess the battlefield situation. Therefore, we construct the intelligent situation assessment model of the simulation entity based on SAE algorithm. Both the initial feature collection and coding method for the model input, and the knowledge encapsulation and pattern parse method for the model output are proposed to construct the datasets. Then, the proposed situation assessment model based on the SAE is trained by the training datasets. Comparing with the models based on multi-layer perceptron (MLP) and logistic regression classifier (LRC), the convergence and accuracy of the proposed SAE is much better than MLP and LRC, indicating that the battlefield simulation assessment model based on SAE is an effective intelligent model.

Keywords: Deep learning · Stacked auto-encoder · Simulation entity · Battlefield situation assessment · Feature representation

1 Introduction

Wargaming is known as "magic director of war" [1]. Since the 20th century, wargame system has developed from the traditional manual wargame into computer system with the development of information technology and military modeling and simulation technology [2]. Computer wargame system needs to construct lots of simulation entities with autonomous decision-making ability, to simulate human's perception, reasoning, decision-making behavior in battlefield and enhance the antagonism and immersed sense of wargaming. Therefore, it is significant for improving the quick-response and scientific decision-making ability for entities in the virtual battlefield by constructing the intelligent situation assessment model for entities based on deep neural network (DNN) [3].

© Springer Science+Business Media Singapore 2016
L. Zhang et al. (Eds.): AsiaSim 2016/SCS AutumnSim 2016, Part II, CCIS 644, pp. 532–543, 2016.
DOI: 10.1007/978-981-10-2666-9_54

At present, the commonly used situation assessment algorithms mainly include bayesian network, case based reasoning, fuzzy logic, genetic algorithm, D-S evidence theory, rough set theory, etc. Although these methods have achieved successes in some applications for battlefield situation assessment, there are still some limitations, such as the difficulty of knowledge acquisition, weak reasoning and self-learning abilities [4]. Artificial neural network(ANN) technology, with strong learning, association and distributed information processing functions, can effectively overcome the knowledge acquisition "bottleneck" of these above methods [5]. However, the traditional shallow layer ANN has the disadvantages of slow convergence rate, low calculation accuracy, high difficulty of feature extraction and network training. Deep learning (DL) network inherits traditional ANN but improves the feature learning ability of the model by building deep neural network (DNN) with multiple hidden layers, and reduces the difficulty of training the DNN by using layer wise pre-training method [6].

Stacked auto-encoder network (SAE) is a commonly used deep learning frame-work, and the auto encoder neural network (AENN) is the basic unit of SAE, which takes reconstruction error minimum as the optimization objective. Based on SAE algorithm, the intelligent assessment model of battlefield situation is constructed, the key information hidden in the input signal is extracted, and the redundant information of battlefield data is removed by layer-wised feature abstraction. The core idea of SAE is similar to the commanders' reasoning procedure when they assess the battlefield situation. Therefore, in order to improve the intelligent level of entities in virtual battlefield, we propose the basic framework of intelligent situation assessment model based on SAE. We further promote the method of initial feature collection and coding for input signals, and the mechanism of knowledge encapsulation and pattern parse for output signals, to construct the datasets. Finally, lots of contrast experiments are carried out to verify the proposed model's validity.

2 Problem Description

The interpretation of situation assessment (SA) is first appeared in the "art of war", and the meaning is to calculate and analyze the advantages and disadvantages of the enemy and us, so as to create a favorable military situation [7]. Situation assessment is the key chain of operational decision-making, and also the primary problem of constructing intelligent decision model of simulation entity. Situation assessment of simulation entity is to extract the key features automatically from the massive battlefield data by simulating the commander's thinking mode based on analysis, comparison and reasoning with real-time data in the virtual battlefield. The battlefield situation is usually highly uncertain and rapidly changed, entities need to draw conclusions with high dynamic, incomplete, even faked information by analyzing the type, status, behaviors of the entities in the local scope of time and space within a very limited time, to provide a reliable presupposition for planning its next operations and maneuvering direction [8, 9]. Therefore, the conceptual model of battlefield situation assessment can be described as formula (1).

$$BS = \{AD|T, S, At, St, Ac, Rl, En\} \tag{1}$$

In formula (1), *BS* is the current situation assessment results; *T* and *S* represent the time and space domain respectively; *St* is the attribute information of the entity, such as entity type, communication ability, killing ability, detection radius etc. *St* represents the state information of the entity, including the location, direction of movement, moving speed etc. *Ac* is the current behavior of entities, such as mobility, fire and defense; *Rl* is the relationship information between entities, including subordination relationship and the relationship between tasks, such as shield, support and cooperation; *En* represents the battlefield environment information, including topography, meteorology, hydrology, electromagnetic environment etc. *AD* represents the assessment conclusion based on the above information.

For a given entity, battlefield situation assessment requires a comprehensive consideration of the battlefield environment, entity's attribute, status and behaviors, as well as the relationship between entities in certain battlefield. These information are usually real-time, multi-dimensional and extremely complex. Therefore, the evolution law of battlefield situation is often seen as mysterious equations which can only be sensed but inexpressible, and it is difficult to be described, deduced or induced by quantitative methods with an explicit mathematical formula. This paper try to construct a standard formatted input signal to describe the entity's situation information, build a DNN model to simulate the thinking and reasoning mode of human, and then train the DNN to learn the commander's cognitive experience. Finally, the well-trained DNN is applied to assess the new battlefield situation and output the evaluation results for corresponding entities.

3 Basic Framework of Model

3.1 The Principles of Situation Assessment Model Based on SAE

A deep SAE network is formed by stacked AENN layers by feeding the latent representation found on the layer below as the input to the current layer, and lastly adding a logistic regression layer in the top layer [10].

The basic structure of SAE is as shown in Fig. 1. As shown in Fig. 1, each AENN unit includes an encoder and a decoder, and is pre-trained by minimizing the reconstruction errors of its input. Each layer of SAE is trained as an AENN independently by minimizing the reconstruction errors of its input (which is the output code of the previous layer). Once all layers are pre-trained, SAE is fining-tuned by minimizing prediction error on a supervised task, in which the logistic regression layer classifies the input signal according to labels. Then, the hidden relationship between the input signal and high-level abstraction features could be built.

Situation assessment is a reasoning process, in which the dross are discarded, and the essential are extracted, and the false are eliminated, and the truth is retained [11]. The feature extraction process of SAE is a procedure of feature extraction from the low level to high level and from the specific to the abstract, which is similar to commanders' reasoning mode when they assess battlefield situation. Therefore, in this paper,

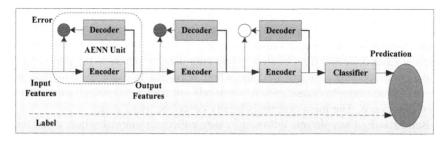

Fig. 1. The network structure of stacked auto-encoding

we construct the entity's situation assessment model based on the SAE algorithm, which combines unsupervised feature extraction and supervised network training method. The situation assessment model of entity can not only capture the deep characteristics of the evolution of battlefield situation, but also simulate the rule of the behavior and cognition of human in the war.

3.2   Technology Framework of Situation Assessment Model Based on SAE

The situation assessment model based on SAE is shown in Fig. 2, which mainly includes two tasks. One is to construct a deep SAE network, which consists of a lot of AENN units and is trained by sample dataset extracted from battlefield data. And the second is to integrate the trained situation assessment model into simulation entities' model to make entities in virtual battlefield imitate what human does in real battlefield. Then the entities would have the ability to assess the battlefield situation in local temporal domain by self-learning and self-adapting.

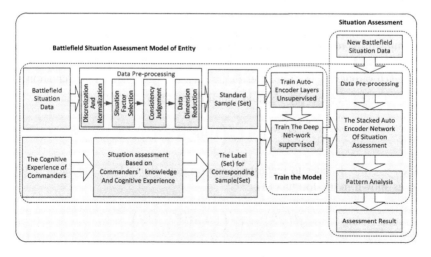

Fig. 2. The framework of situation assessment model based on SEA

As shown in Fig. 2, the situation assessment model based on SAE uses both unsupervised feature extraction and supervised knowledge learning methods. Firstly, we use layer-wise unsupervised method training SAE network with a lot of unlabeled sample dataset collected from battlefield situation data, to optimize the parameters of the network; Secondly, we fine-tune the whole networks by supervised method with parts of labeled sample dataset, where the labels are added according to human cognitive experience. The main process is briefly described as follows:

Build standard sample sets followed by data collection, normalization, consistency check and data dimension reduction in sequence with the historical battlefield situation data generated by the wargame system.

Select samples randomly from the standard sample sets, and add labels according to human cognitive experience, to build labeled sample datasets.

Optimize the parameters of SAE with unsupervised layer-wise training method through minimizing the reconstruction error using the unlabeled sample set.

Fine-tune the parameters of SAE with supervised training method by minimizing prediction error with labeled datasets.

The left part of Fig. 2 describes the battlefield situation assessment process of SAE model. The model includes several steps, collect and pre-process data from the virtual battlefield data sets, evaluate battlefield situation by training SAE, and then parse the pattern and output the assessment results. In the above framework, AENN model, data abstraction and encoding method, knowledge expression and pattern parse mechanisms are key technologies of this intelligent situation assessment model. In the next section, we will briefly introduce those technologies.

4   Design and Implementation of Key Technologies

4.1   Design of Auto-Encoder Neural Network [10, 12]

AENN is the core component of the SAE, and its function is to extract the main feature of the input signal by minimizing the reconstruction error. The core idea of training AENN is as follows: firstly, the input signal is encoded to get the output feature, which is the implicit expression of the main characteristics of original signal. Secondly, the output features are used to reconstruct the original signal.

For each sample $x^{(i)}$ in sample set $\{x^1, x^2, \ldots, x^{(m)}\}$, the latent representation $y^{(i)} = f(x^{(i)})$ is firstly calculated by sigmoid function, as shown in the formula (2):

$$f\left(x^{(i)}\right) = 1 \Big/ \left(1 + e^{-\left(Wx^{(i)} + b\right)}\right) \tag{2}$$

Then use the decoder to reconstruct the original signal from the latent representation, as shown in the formula (3).

$$f'\left(y^{(i)}\right) = 1 \Big/ \left(1 + e^{-\left(W'y^{(i)} + b'\right)}\right) \tag{3}$$

In the formula (3), W and W' respectively represent the weights matrix of input layer and hidden layer, which usually satisfy $W' = W^T$; b and b' denote the bias vector of the input layer and the hidden layer, respectively. W and W', b and b' is the main parameters of AENN, denoted as $\theta = \{W, W', b, b'\}$.

In this paper, we use the Log-Likelihood Negative (NLL) function to define the reconstruction error $e^{(i)} = L(x^{(i)}, z^{(i)}, \theta)$, as shown in the formula (4).

$$e^{(i)} = -\sum_{k=1}^{d} \left(x_k^{(i)} \log\left(z_k^{(i)}\right) + \left(1 - x_k^{(i)}\right) \log\left(1 - z_k^{(i)}\right) \right) \tag{4}$$

Here, d represents the sample dimension, and $e^{(i)}$ represents the reconstruction error of a single sample. Average error is used to measure the reconstruction cost of the sample set, as shown in the formula (5).

$$\bar{c} = \frac{1}{M} \sum_{i=1}^{M} \left(e^{(i)} \right) \tag{5}$$

M is the number of samples in a sample set.

5 Stochastic Gradient Descent Algorithm

Gradient Descent (GD) [13] algorithm is a simple, effective training algorithm of ANN and is widely used in machine learning and numerical optimization. GD algorithm measures the reconstruction cost by the average error of sample set, which is calculated as formula (6).

$$\nabla_\theta J(\theta) = \frac{1}{M} \sum_{i=1}^{M} \left(\nabla_\theta L\left(x^{(i)}, y^{(i)}, \theta\right) \right) \tag{6}$$

Since GD algorithm needs to calculate the gradient of each sample, the computational complexity is $O(M)$. Because the size of sample set of battlefield situation assessment is very large, calculating all samples' gradient will consume a lot of computing resources, resulting in low efficiency. Therefore, stochastic gradient descent (SGD) algorithm [12, 13] is introduced to overcome this issue. The core idea of SGD is to extract a small subset of samples from the whole sample set, calculate the average gradient (denoted as g) of this subset, and then use it to estimate the gradient of whole sample set, as shown in the formula (7).

$$g = \frac{1}{M_B} \sum_{i=1}^{M_B} \left(\nabla_\theta L\left(x^{(i)}, y^{(i)}, \theta\right) \right) \tag{7}$$

Here, M_B is the number of samples in subset, which is denoted as $B = \{x^{(1)}, x^{(2)}, \cdots, x^{(M_B)}\}$.

g will represent expectation gradient of the entire sample set commendably as long as the distribution characteristics is guaranteed because this subset is sampling from the entire sample set randomly. Usually, it satisfies $M_B < < M$, it will greatly reduce the computational complexity by using SGD algorithm.

5.1   Feature Representation and Sample Coding

In order to train the deep SAE model, we need to address two key issues: the first is feature representation, namely how to describe the state space of input signal. In other words, what information should be extracted from battlefield data, and how to encode samples to construct standard sample space; the second is knowledge expression and pattern parse, which are how to determine the SAE solution space, or the mean of classification pattern in battlefield situation assessment.

For feature representation, the more information extracted from the battlefield data, more comprehensive the description of the battlefield situation will be, and the higher the dimension of corresponding input signal will become. However, if the dimension of the input signal is too high, it will increase the difficulty of constructing the sample set and the difficulty of training the DNN, which will lead to more storage occupation and more time consuming. Therefore, we should take the storage space, processing time and other limits into account when constructing the sample set.

For these reasons, a situational data extraction and encoding method for simulation entity is presented in this paper. When extracting information from battlefield data, we mainly consider the battlefield environment, the attributes and real-time state of current entities, as well as a certain number of entities who are interacting or will interact with current entity (such as 10 friends and 10 enemies, the specific quantity needs to be determined according to the actual situation), then these information is encoded as a unified format, as shown in Fig. 3.

In Fig. 3, the encapsulated information for each entity primarily includes the entity's types (x_k), attributes (x_{at}), state (x_{st}), behavior (x_{ac}), and the distance (x_d) between the entity and its interacting ones. The dimensions of x_k, x_{st}, x_{ac} and x_d are all equal to 1, and the length of x_{at} is denoted as L_{at} ($L_{at} > 1$). In the virtual battlefield, a sample in samples set corresponds to a set of input signals of SAE, and represents situation information of an entity's. Therefore, the length of a sample is $L = L_B + (N_e + 1) * L_e$, where $L_e = 4 + L_{at}$, N_e is the number of correlative entities, and L_B is the length of code which describes the battlefield environment. In this paper, we take $L_B = 12$, $L_{at} = 5$, and $N_e = 16$, hence $L_e = 9$, and $L = 12 + (2 * 8 + 1) * 9 = 165$.

5.2   Knowledge Expression and Mode Parse Mechanisms

In this paper, we use the approach of layer-wise feature abstraction to simulate the feature extraction and reasoning process of human when they assess the battlefield situation. At the same time, in order to learn cognitive experience of human, we use the labeled samples to train the situation assessment model based on SAE by supervised method. Therefore,

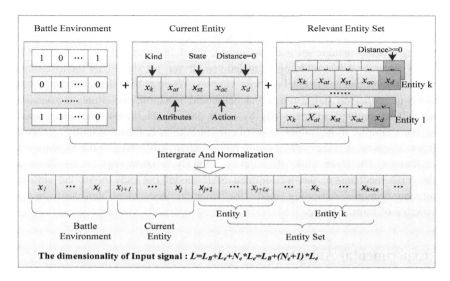

Fig. 3. The structure of input signal

how to represent the human cognitive pattern as the sample's label, and explain the classification mode represented by this labels in situation assessment, are the key issue of SAE when apply it to actual situation assessment.

When a commander assesses the situation, he usually extracts key features from battlefield data firstly, and then combines them with his cognitive experience, and finally draws the conclusion of the merits and demerits of the battlefield situation. And commander's cognitive experience mainly implies in the past evaluation results. Therefore, we need to convert these cognitive experiences into knowledge, and package them as sample's labels. Here, we divide the result of battlefield situation judgments into several levels and labeled from 0 to 7. The corresponding knowledge expression and mode parse mechanism is shown in Fig. 4.

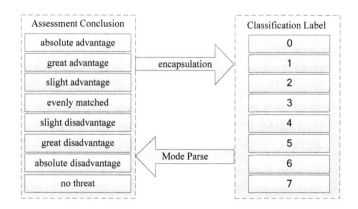

Fig. 4. Knowledge encapsulation and mode parse

As shown in Fig. 4, the situation judgment conclusion of entity is divided into eight levels, including absolute advantage, great advantage, slight advantage, evenly matched, slight disadvantage, great disadvantage, absolute disadvantage and no threat in the local area etc. When building a labeled sample set, we should set the assessments conclusion of human as the label of those samples. Whereas the intelligent model based on SAE is applied to judge the actual battlefield situation, the situation assessment result will be mapped automatically by mode parse mechanisms from the output of SAE. For example, if the output value of current SAE is 2, the corresponding result of situation assessment is the current entity holds a slight advantage in the local time and space domain. Therefore, under the support of the above knowledge encapsulation and mode parse mechanism, the well-trained SAE model not only holds the ability of simulating human's reasoning mode for situation assessment, but also own the knowledge of human being.

6   Experimental Analysis

6.1   Data Preparation and Parameter Settings

Battlefield situation samples are randomly generated by the wargame system, including 80000 training samples, 2000 validating samples and 2000 test samples, which are corresponding to the training datasets, validation datasets and test datasets. In addition, according to the experience of people's cognitive, we add labels (In order to avoid arbitrariness, we adhere to certain principles) for all validation and test samples, and parts of train samples (randomly selected 8000 in train set).

In order to verify the validity of the algorithm, three groups experiments were carried out. The first group is to use multi-layer perceptron (MLP) [12], logistic regression classifier (LRC) [13] and the SAE algorithm proposed in this paper to assess the intelligent situation respectively, and then compare and analyze the results. The second group is to try different parameters of hidden layers of SAE model to optimize the structure of the model. The third group is to test the above models with datasets from virtual battlefield. The parameters of these algorithms are shown in Table 1.

Table 1. Parameters Setting of SAE, MLP and LRC

Algorithm	Parameter settings
SAE	Pre-train epochs $ep_1 = 100$, pre-train learn rate $\zeta_2 = 0.02$, train epochs $ep_2 = 2000$, fine-tune learn rate $\zeta_1 = 0.02$, batch size $N_B = 200$, hidden layers number $HN = 1$, hidden layers sizes $HLZ = [512]$
MLP	Learn rate $\zeta_1 = 0.02$, train epochs $ep'_2 = 2000$, batch size $N'_B = 200$, hidden layers number $HN' = 1$, hidden layers sizes $HLZ' = [512]$
LRC	Learn rate $\zeta''_2 = 0.02$, train epochs $ep''_2 = 2000$, batch size $N''_B = 200$

6.2   Performance Comparison Between SAE and Other ANN

In order to facilitate comparison, MLP and SAE are only include one hidden layer, the number of neuron nodes are set to 512, a number of experiments are conducted respectively, the validation errors are counted when those ANNs are trained, the statistical results are shown in Fig. 5.

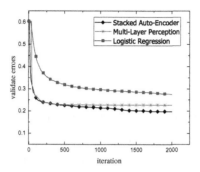

Fig. 5. Comparison of validation errors of different algorithms

As shown in Fig. 5, when training these ANNs, all these algorithms can quickly converge, where the decline rate of validation error of SAE is the fastest. From the overall performance, after 2000 times iteration, the validation errors of SAE, MLP and LRC algorithms are 19.6 %, 23.1 % and 27.8 %. Obviously, the performance of SAE is better than that of MLP and LRC, the proposed SAE holds a higher accuracy and a faster convergence rate than MLP and LRC.

6.3   The Influence of Different Network Depth on Performance

In order to analyze how the depth of network influences the performance, we set up different depth for the proposed SAE: (1) Single hidden layer with the number of hidden nodes 512; (2) 2 hidden layers with the number of hidden nodes [256, 256]; (3) 3 hidden layers with the number of hidden nodes [256,128,128]. All the sums of hidden nodes number are set to a constant value (512), and the other parameters keep in accordance with 5.1 section. The statistical results were shown in Fig. 6.

Seen from Fig. 6, the validation error of SAE network with two hidden layers is significantly decline faster than the SAE network with only one hidden layer. Identically, the validation error of the SAE network with three hidden layers is less than two hidden layer SAE network, while the rate of validation error decline faster. Therefore, it will effectively improve the convergence speed and computational accuracy by increasing the depth of SAE network appropriately while the number of hidden nodes keeps unchanged.

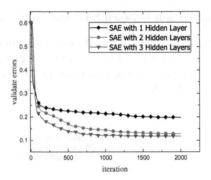

Fig. 6. The performance of SAE with different depth

6.4   Test Performance Comparison Between Different Algorithms

In order to verify the effectiveness of the proposed SAE, we construct the intelligent situation assessment model of simulation entity using the well-trained ANNs which mentioned above respectively, and then test the reliability of the corresponding algorithms. These experiments are based on the same sample set (which contains 2000 new samples) for testing, and the statistical results are shown in Fig. 7.

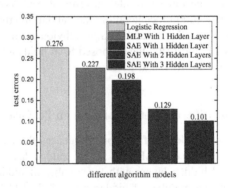

Fig. 7. Comparison between test errors of different models

Figure 7 shows the statistical errors between the assessment results by manual and ANNs mentioned above respectively. This figure shows that the test error of LRC, MLP and SAE are all less than 30 %. All of these algorithms manifest a good performance, but the performance of SAE is much better than that of MLP and LRC. In addition, the SAE model with 3 hidden layers holds the best performance, whose test error is about 10.1 %, showing a high accuracy and reliability in the application test.

7 Conclusion

Situation Assessment is a key step of autonomous decision-making, and it is also the basis for entities to plan the future actions. Therefore, it is significance for improving the quick response and scientific decision-making ability of entities in the virtual battlefield by constructing intelligent situation assessment model based on DNN to simulate human's cognitive experience and reasoning mode. SAE is a commonly used architecture of deep learning, and the feature extraction procedure of SAE is similar to the commander's reasoning process when they assess the battlefield situation. As illustrated above, an intelligent situation assessment model based on the SAE is constructed, and the effectiveness of this model is verified by lots of experiments. Our future work will continue to focus on how to improve the calculation accuracy of SAE and how to collect initial feature of battlefield situation.

Acknowledgment. This work is supported by the National Natural Science Foundation of China under Grant No. U1435218 & 61403401 & 61374179 & 61273189 & 61174156 & 61174035 and the Project supported by military graduate students under Grant No. 2015JY035.

References

1. Perla, P.P.: The Art of Wargaming, pp. 1–21. Naval Institute Press, Annapolis (1990)
2. Blank, D.: Military wargaming: a commercial battlefield. Jane's Def. Wkly. **2**, 5–9 (2004)
3. Perla, P.P., Mcgrady, E.D.: Why wargaming works. Naval War Coll. Rev. **64**(3), 111–133 (2011)
4. Zhuo, Y., He, M., Gong, Z.: A rough set analysis model of network situation assessment. Comput. Eng. Sci. **34**(3), 1–5 (2012)
5. Schmidhuber, J.: Deep learning in neural networks: an overview. Neural Netw. Off. J. Int. Neural Netw. Soc. **61**, 85–117 (2015)
6. Fukushima, K.: Training multi-layered neural network neocognitron. Neural Netw. **40**, 18–31 (2013)
7. Minford, J.: The art of war. New Engl. Rev. Middlebury Ser. **23**(3), 5–28 (2002)
8. Li, Y., Liu, G., Lao, S.Y.: A new interpretation of battle field situation and battle situation assessment. Fire Control Command Control **37**(9), 1–5 (2012)
9. Endsley, M.R., Garland, D.J.: Situation Awareness Analysis and Measurement, pp. 23–29. Lavorence Erlbaum Associates (2000)
10. Tse-Tung, M.: On practice. In: Selected Works of Mao Tse-Tung, vol. 1 (1951). **16**(1), 295–309
11. Vanhoucke, V.: Adaptive auto-encoders: US, US8484022[P] (2013)
12. Deep learning tutorial. http://www.cs.nyu.edu/~yann/talks/lecun-ranzato-icml2013.pdf
13. LeCun, Y., Ranzato, M.: Deep learning tutorial. In: Tutorials in International Conference on Machine Learning (ICML13). Citeseer (2013)

Methods of Analyzing Combat SoS Coordination Pattern Based on Temporal Motif

Wenfeng Wu$^{(\boxtimes)}$, Xiaofeng Hu, Shengming Guo, and Xiaoyuan He

Department of Information Operation and Command Training,
National Defense University, Beijing 100091, China
autumn_wwf@aliyun.com, xfhu@vip.sina.com,
30706732@qq.com, binglingl922@sina.com

Abstract. In this paper, a temporal network model of system of systems (SoS) coordination is constructed and an algorithm of detecting corresponding temporal motif is designed according to the dynamics and evolution of SoS coordination. By the use of war gaming data, four methods including contrary analysis of temporal motif density in the whole process, the evolution analysis of temporal motif's density, the analysis of correlation between motif density and operational task measure, generation analysis of SoS coordination pattern are used to analyze the characteristics of SoS coordination pattern, which will be a helpful reference for research in dynamics and evolutionary of SoS coordination.

Keywords: Temporal motif · SoS coordination · Coordination pattern

1 Introduction

Network sciences have been extensively studied with diverse empirical datasets ranging from manmade to natural systems since the discoveries of small-world [1] and scale-free networks in 1990s [2]. This has led to better understanding of interactive patterns and dynamics behind the great amount of behavior data. However, traditional researches mostly focused on the static network analysis with measures such as node degree, length of shortest path, efficiency [3], etc. while most empirical systems show dynamics and evolution in temporal dimension [4]. Some alternative methods to study dynamics and evolutionary of complex system recur to aggregated static network or multi time slice network, which reveal topologies' dynamics only. But recent researches have witnessed that many human activities have the feature of non-Poissonian temporal bursts [4], which shows that temporal transitivity and reachability among interactive activities have strong correlation to social contagion and immunization strategies. So a key issue to understand the dynamics and evolution is to research a system from both topological and temporal perception. We use temporal network approach [4–6] and measure of temporal motif to study the combat system of systems (SoS) coordination.

The whole confrontation between opposed combat SoS has become the main form of joint operation in information warfare, while SoS coordination is the source of

© Springer Science+Business Media Singapore 2016
L. Zhang et al. (Eds.): AsiaSim 2016/SCS AutumnSim 2016, Part II, CCIS 644, pp. 544–554, 2016.
DOI: 10.1007/978-981-10-2666-9_55

generating the whole capability and also the main form of SoS constitutes' networking interactivities [7]. We define SoS coordination as the coordinated actions of constitutes including diverse combat units, elements, and systems according to the purpose and goal of higher headquarters with shared battlefield situation information. Since SoS coordination has the property of whole emergency and dynamic evolution which are typical complex characteristics, its description should consider both temporal evolution and networking interactive relations.

A temporal network characterize both topological and temporal dynamics of a complex dynamic system by appending time label to edges, e.g., an edge $e_i = (n_{i,1}, n_{i,2}, t_i, \delta_i)$ means an coordination between node $n_{i,1}$ *and node* $n_{i,2}$ during the time interval from t_i to δ_i. Since the coordination activity is mutual and its value is derived from more than one operation activity, we suggest that the edge has no direction and one node can simultaneously participate in more than one event, and this article mainly focuses on undirected temporal network, which is not consist with the research in [5].

Temporal network has been widely used in Scientific Collaboration Network [8], biological network [9], email network [10], disease protein networks [11], etc., and has uncovered some networking interaction and dynamic evolution properties which cannot be described with static network only, and provide beneficial references for studying the evolution process of SoS coordination.

Different measurements of temporal network represent different aspects of network, and general measurements are extended from static network directly, e.g., degree, temporal path lengths, temporal connectivity, degree centrality, betweenness, efficiency, etc. this paper mainly analyze SoS coordination patterns based on temporal motifs. SoS coordination pattern is the feature of several coordination activities showed simultaneously in temporal and topological dimension, which can help to find the mechanism of SoS capability generation and provide criterial to predict activity of SoS constitutes.

2 Temporal Model of SoS Coordination

Since entities in SoS always have more than one attributes, the coordination among different entities have different forms in different combat domains, e.g., observation in information domain, orientation and decision in cognitive domain, action in physical domain, and cross-coordination across different domains. Since commander is dominating in the contrary of combat SoS, we regard that the coordination in information or physical domain is the reflection of decision coordination in cognitive domain, and action coordination in physical domain is the final effect of the other two domains. By analyzing the coordination in physical domain we can somewhat detect the dynamics and evolution of other two domains.

From the view of combat effect, relationships between two operational actions can be divided into temporal and spatial. A temporal relationship means sequence existed in time, while a spatial relationship means the position relationship between two actions. For the convenience of studying, we assume that if the time interval between two combat actions is not greater than ΔT and the distance of their targets is not greater than ΔD there is a coordination.

One operational action has 6 attributes, such as the operation unit name *Unit*, start time *Starttime*, end time *Endtime* (*Endtime* $\geq$ *Starttime*), and target name Target, target latitude *LAT*, target longitude *LON*, which can be expressed in a 6-tuple as following:

$$Action(Unit,\ Starttime,\ Endtime,\ Target,\ LAT,\ LON) \tag{1}$$

So, if $Action_1$ and $Action_2$ meeting the following requirements:

$$\begin{cases} \|Starttime_1 - Starttime_2\| \leq \Delta T \\ \|(LAT_1, LON_1) - (LAT_2, LON_2)\| \leq \Delta D \end{cases} \tag{2}$$

Then, we conclude that there is a coordination *Coordinate* between $Action_1$ and $Action_2$. A *Coordinate* has four parameters including two combat units $Unit_1$ and $Unit_2$, the start time of beginning the coordination $Starttime = min\ (Starttime_1, Starttime_2)$, and the end time of coordination $Endtime = max\ (Endtime_1, Endtime_2)$. So, *Coordinate* can be expressed with a 4-tuple as following:

$$Coordinate(\ Unit_1, Unit_2, Starttime, Endtime) \tag{3}$$

The construction of SoS coordination temporal network in physical domain of one side based on operational data is listed in Fig. 1.

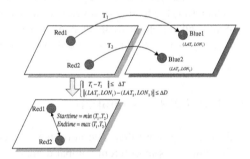

Fig. 1. The construction of SoS coordination temporal network in physical domain

By the criterion of Eq. (2), we can build a temporal network of coordination from magnanimous war gaming data. Unlike the edge in static network or real operational coordination order, the coordination is constructed from operational action data. The node in the coordination temporal network represents the combat unit in a coordination, the edge represents the relationship of coordination, and the time labels represent the start time and end time of the coordination.

3 Definition of Temporal Motifs

Motifs are defined as classes of isomorphic subgraphs in static network and have been used in protein networks [12], software networks [13] and brain network [14] to capture the relationship between mesoscopic structure and specific function. Connection is the basis of static motif, while its definition in temporal network is different and relevant to topology and temporal sequence both, so we should redefine related conceptions in temporal networks before defining temporal motifs.

- Temporal Adjacency
  We consider two coordinations temporal adjacent if they have at least one common operational unit and their happen time durations have intersection. This definition is not consist with [5] which require the time difference between the end time of the first edge and the start time of the second edge is no longer than Δt. The reason is that an operation action always take a long time, and temporal adjacency means the two coordinations are performing the same task, e.g. firing at the same target. Figure 2(a) is a temporal network with an event sequence $\{e0, e1, e2, e3, e4, e5\}$. Since $e0$ and $e1$ have a common node B, and the end time t_0^e of $e0$ is later than the start time t_1^s of $e1$, the two events are temporal adjacent. Similarly, $e0$ is temporal adjacent to $e1$, $e2$, $e3$. But $e0$ is not adjacent to $e5$, because the end time t_0^e of $e0$ is earlier than the start time t_5^s of $e5$. With regard to $e4$, though the end time t_0^e of $e0$ is later than the start time t_4^s of $e4$, $e0$ is not temporal adjacent to $e4$ for they have no common node.
- Temporal connected
  If there exists an event sequence between two coordinations, and every two neighbor events are temporal adjacent, we regard them temporal connected. In Fig. 2(a), $e3$ is temporal connected to $e5$ because $e3$ and $e4$, $e4$ and $e5$ are all temporal adjacent, and $e3$, $e4$, $e5$ are obey the time order.
- Temporal connected subgraph
  We call a temporal subgraph is connected when its two arbitrary events are temporal connected.
- Valid Temporal subgraph
  If there exists at least one temporal connected path between arbitrary two events in a temporal connected subgraph, the subgraph is a valid temporal subgraph. An additional requirement is that all the events relevant to the node within the time boundary of the path should be included[1]. Figure 2 shows the valid temporal subgraph example, (d), (e) and (f) are valid temporal subgraphs, while (b) and (c) are not. The reason to (b) is that the relevant event $e2$ to B is not included in the subgraph, and with regard to (c), though the events relevant to D are all included in the subgraph, $e2$ is not temporal connected to $e4$ or $e5$. We can get the number of various classes of subgraphs by counting isomorphic valid temporal subgraphs.
- Temporal Motif

---

[1] This is the same as the definition taken by Kovanen et al. [5]

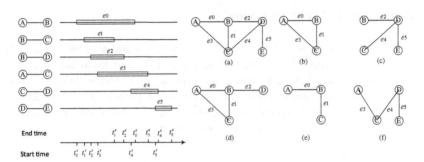

Fig. 2. The definition of valid temporal subgraphs

There are at least two different definitions of temporal motif [5, 15], this paper defines temporal motif as classes of isomorphic valid temporal subgraphs, and the isomorphism means the two networks have both similar topology and identical temporal order of edges, but name, type, direction and real time label of edges or nodes are neglected.

This paper concentrated on 3-event temporal motifs, which may have 2, 3 or 4 nodes in one motif. Taking no account of the node types and direction, there are 22 classes of motifs, and their structure and relevant ID are listed in Fig. 3.

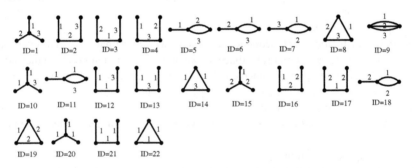

Fig. 3. The structure and relevant IDs of different temporal motifs

From the definition of temporal motif, it is easy to find that if two events share a common node, it is apparent that the two coordinations are attacking the same target. That is to say the time sequence label depict the transmission of coordinations, e.g. the labels of three edges in No.1 motif represent the time sequence, and four nodes means four different operational units. The topology of No.1 is a typical star structure, which means the transmission of coordination is sequential and shows a centrality. In No.12 motif, it is evident that earlier two coordinations happened at the same time, while the third coordination is the closest neighbor to the earlier two coordinations. We can conclude that earlier two coordinations induced and triggered the third coordination or coordination transmit from the earlier two to the third and three events construct a link structure.

4   Algorithm for Detecting Temporal Motifs

Obviously the first task of detecting temporal motif is to find valid temporal subgraphs according to the definition of temporal motif. Then we can calculate the quantity and density of different temporal motifs by mapping valid temporal subgraph to temporal motif. The full algorithm includes 3 parts, the first part is to identify the valid temporal subgraph, the second part is to find valid edges to a given edge, last part is to identify the isomorphism of a valid temporal motif and a temporal motif. 3 parts are accomplished by three algorithms shown below.

Algorithm 1: Find all the valid temporal subgraphs in temporal network G and use start time of the edge to mark all the edge. The parameter Edge_max denotes the number of edges that a subgraph should have, and Valid_subgraph_list is a list for storing all the detected valid temporal subgraphs.

```
Input: Edge_max, G
Output: Valid_subgraph_list
Function FindValidSubgraph(G, Edge_max)
  Valid_subgraph_list= Φ
  elist=G.edges()  //find all the edges in G
  graph_found= Φ
  ecount=0
  for one_edge in elist:
    if (graph_found! =Φ)&&(ecount< Edge_max):
      FindValidEdges(elist, graph_found)// modify graph_found
      ecount= ecount+1
    else if  ecount>= Edge_max:
      if  Valid_subgraph_list== Φ:
        Valid_subgraph_list.append(graph_found)
      else if  Valid_subgraph_list!= Φ:
        for one_graph_found in graph_found:
          is_in=False//bool variety initialization
          for one_graph_valid in Valid_subgraph_list:
            if one_graph_found == one_graph_valid:
              is_in=True
              break
          if is_in==False:
            Valid_subgraph_list+=one_graph_found
  return Valid_subgraph_list
```

Algorithm2: Find valid edges(earlier nearest, later nearest, and simultaneous) in the edge list elist of temporal network G to each edge in each subgraph of the detected subgraph list graphlist_found, and append the valid edge to each subgraph to construct a new subgraph with one more edges. Then substitute and renew the subgraph list graphlist_found. Iterate the process until the number of edges reach Edge_max in Algorithm1.

```
Input:   elist, graphlist_found
Output:  graphlist_found
Function  FindValidEdges(elist, graphlist_found)
   graphlist_temp=Φ
   for one_graph in graphlist_found:
      edge_list_temp=Φ
      for one_edge in one_gaph:
         find all the nearest edges to one_edge in elist and add
to edge_list_temp
      for one_edge_nearest in edge_list_temp:
         one_graph_temp=one_graph.add_edge(one_edge_nearest)//add
edge to graph
         graphlist_temp= graphlist_temp.append(one_graph_temp)
   graphlist_found = graphlist_temp//renew graphlist_found
   return graphlist_found
```

Algorithm 3: Classify valid temporal subgraphs by mapping them to all the temporal motifs. First we should convert the time label of each edge to temporal sequence for the same format as temporal motif. Then call graph isomorphism algorithm to determine which temporal motif is isomorphic to temporal subgraph and calculate quantity and density of the temporal motifs. The isomorphism algorithm we use is vf2 [16]. The parameter temporal_motif_dict is a dictionary with the keys of temporal motifs, and the values are the IDs.

```
Input: G, temporal_motif_dict
Output: temporal_motif_list
Function  Match_motif(G, temporal_motif_dict)
   temporal_motif_list=Φ
   G_sequential=Convert_sequence(G)
   for one_motif in temporal_motif_dict.keys():
      if one_motif is temporal isomorphic to G_sequential:
         temporal_motif_list.append(one_motif)
   return temporal_motif_list
```

5   Experiment on War Gaming Data

This article uses war gaming data as the basis to analyze SoS coordination patterns for the real operation data is always hard to get. War gaming data is the most similar as to real data, because it not only simulates all the dimensions and full time of a whole war, it also incorporates great amount of commanders' commanding and controlling data which reflect human actions and autonomy in real world. Based on the action data we can construct the SoS coordination temporal network.

The task in the scenario of certain example war gaming data is joint fire attacks with a combat time of 10 h. We mainly consider coordination of firing actions including artillery and missile.

5.1 Contrary Analysis of Temporal Motif Density in the Whole Process

Statistical data of temporal motif density of both red and blue sides are listed in Table 1. It is easy to find that the characteristic of red side is prominent for the top 5 classes occupies 71 % of all the temporal motifs, while the characteristic of blue side is not highlighted with the proportion of only 45 %. The top 5 temporal motifs of red side are {12, 16, 20, 1, 2}. From the view of motif structure, 12, 16 and 2 are all "Link" structure which occupies 48 % of all the motifs, while 20 and 1 are "Star". We classify these structure into two as the "group-influenced effect" (multi simultaneous coordinations induce a new coordination) and "trigger effect" (one coordination leads to more than one later) based on temporal sequence. The top 5 classes motifs {2, 1, 12, 8, 6} of blue side show different topologies (link, star, and triangle) which have similar density but sequential transmission pattern from the view of temporal sequence because these top 5 motifs are all temporal sequential, so we call this is "sequential transmission effect".

Table 1. Temoral motif density of both sides in the whole time(top = 10)

Order	Red Side		Blue Side	
	DENSITY	ID	DENSITY	ID
1	0.2318	12	0.1081	2
2	0.1596	16	0.0996	1
3	0.1201	20	0.0910	12
4	0.0952	1	0.0853	8
5	0.0945	2	0.0754	6
6	0.0810	15	0.0697	16
7	0.0449	21	0.0597	7
8	0.0446	10	0.0583	5
9	0.0381	14	0.0526	14
10	0.0239	3	0.0441	18

5.2 Evolution of Temporal Motif's Density

Table 1 provide a view of the whole process, but if the whole operational process is divided into several time slices, we can see the evolution of each temporal motif, shown in Fig. 4. The 12 and 16 motifs which are the top class in Table 1 are not always prominent, their proportions of density changes over time, shown in Fig. 4.

No.12 is the most popular between 4:30 and 5:30, No.1 is the most popular between 5:30 and 7:30, No.12 and No.16 are both the most popular between 7:30 and 9:30, No.1 reoccupies the top position after 10:00. If we regard the process to their structures, the prominent coordination pattern experiences a process from Link to Star and return to Link.

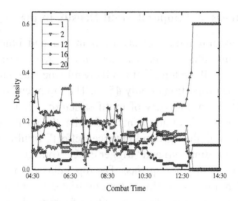

Fig. 4. The evolution of red side's temporal motifs. (Color figure online)

5.3   Analysis of Correlation Between Motif Density and Operational Task Measure

The purpose of analyzing temporal motif is to capture insight into the operational process, so we instinctively resort to task measure. The most general measure is combat success, which means the achievement of one side's operational action to the other, such as the declination of enemy's strength, or people and weapon loss. In this article we use the declination of blue strength for red side.

By calculating the correlation of the motif density and red combat success, we find the most matched two motif IDs are 12 and 1 with the correlation coefficients −0.779 and 0.654, shown in Fig. 5. We can conclude that these two motifs reveal the prominent coordination patterns, as they show best correlation to task measure.

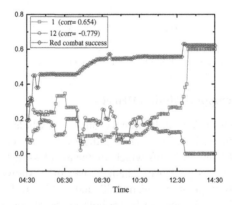

Fig. 5. Correlation of red side's temporal motifs and combat success. (Color figure online)

5.4   Generation Analysis of SoS Coordination Patterns

Complex system theory regards that the property in higher levels of a complex system are the emergency of behaviors in lower levels. So if we regard the motifs with less edges are lower levels and the motifs with more edges are higher levels, we conclude that motifs with less edges generalize the motifs with more edges. By analyzing the generation process, we will gain deeper insight into the rule of SoS coordination. Table 2 lists the top 4 classes of 4-edge temporal motifs and their possible generation relationship with 3-edge motifs (the classes are so many that the result is not full).

Table 2. Density of red side's temporal motifs and their generation (top = 4)

The motif densities listed in Table 2 are not high enough as to too many classes. But from the view of possible generations of 3-edge motifs, No.12, 16 and 20 are the dominant motifs, which are also dominant in 3-edge motifs.

6   Summary

SoS coordination is a kind of typical interaction, which is inherently dynamic and evolving with time. Temporal motif takes into account both the topology and temporal sequence and can depict SoS coordination more accurately and comprehensively and help people insight into the dynamical and evolutionary mechanism of SoS. In this paper, we propose a new approach for detecting recurrent patterns by temporal motifs, and give four different methods to analyze temporal motif based on war gaming data, which demonstrates the validity of the approach.

Four methods reflect different roles of temporal motifs respectively, and should be selected according to specific issues. The first method is mainly used to detect certain temporal motif closely associated to certain combat mission throughout the whole period, but it is likely to ignore the dynamics in time dimension. The second method is mainly used to find such temporal motifs which have high relations to certain actions in the whole process, and the disadvantage is that it will take a lot of time analyzing the relation between events data and motifs data. The third method is always used in mining the key coordination pattern, but the diversity of combat mission performance metrics will reduce the efficiency. The fourth method can be used to find the mechanism of certain behavior mode, but it will also neglect the dynamics just as the first.

References

1. Watts, D.J., Strogatz, S.H.: Collective dynamics of "small-world" networks. Nature **393**, 440–442 (1998)
2. Barabasi, A.L., Albert, R.: Emergence of scaling in random networks. Science **286**, 509–512 (1999)
3. Newman, M.E.J.: The structure and function of complex networks. SIAM Rev. **45**, 167–256 (2003)
4. Holme, P., Saramäki, J.: Temporal networks. Phys. Rep. **519**, 97–125 (2012)
5. Kovanen, L., Karsai, M., Kaski, K., Kertesz, J., Saramäki, J.: Temporal motifs in time-dependent networks. Stat. Mech. **11**, P11005 (2011)
6. Zhang, Y., Wang, L., Zhang, Y.Q.: X Li.: Towards a temporal network analysis of interactive WiFi users. Europhys. Lett. **98**, 68002 (2012)
7. Hu, X.F., Yang, J.Y., Si, G.Y., et al.: War Complex System Simulation Analysis & Experimentation. National Defense University Press, Beijing (2008)
8. Spiliopoulou, M.: Evolution in social networks: a survey. In: Aggarwal, C.C. (ed.) Social Network Data Analytics. Springer, US (2011)
9. Fraser, H.B.: Modularity and evolutionary constraint on proteins. Nat. Genet. **37**(4), 351–352 (2005)
10. Kim, H., Tang, J., Anderson, R., Mascolo, C.: Centrality prediction in dynamic human contact networks. Comput. Netw. **56**(3), 983–996 (2012)
11. Huang, H.Y., Lee, E., Liu, Y.T., Lee, D., Ideker, T.: Network-Based classification of breast cancer metastasis. Mol. Syst. Biol. **3**(140), 1–10 (2007)
12. Lee, W.P., Jeng, B.C., Pai, T.W., Tsai, C.P., et al.: Differential evolutionary conservation of motif modes in the yeast protein interaction network. BMC Genom. **7**, 89 (2006)
13. Zhang, L., Qian, G.Q., Zhang, L.: Network motif & triad significance profile analyses on software system. WSEAS Trans. Comput. **7**, 756–765 (2008)
14. Sporns, O., Kötter, R.: Motifs in brain networks. PLoS Biol. **2**(11), e369 (2004)
15. Lahiri M., Berger-Wolf, T.Y.: Structure prediction in temporal networks using frequent subgraphs. In: Proceedings of the 2007 IEEE Symposium, Computer Intelligent Data Mining (CIDM), Honolulu, HI, USA, pp. 35–42 (2007)
16. Cordella, L.P., Foggia, P., Sansone, C., Vento, M.: A (sub)graph isomorphism algorithm for matching large graphs. IEEE Trans. Pattern Anal. Mach. Intell. **26**(10), 1367–1372 (2004)

Test Data Fusion Based on Importance Sampling Mechanism

Xiaolei Ning[1(✉)], Yingxia Wu[1], Hailin Zhang[1], and Xin Zhao[1,2]

[1] Key Laboratory of Guided Weapons Test and Evaluation Simulation Technology, China, HuaYin Ordnance Test Center, Huayin, China
ningxiaolei21@163.com
[2] Shang Hai Jiao Tong University, Shanghai, China

Abstract. Flying test and simulation test are the main means in weapon test range to estimate the performance of equipment. Flying test has a high credibility while the sample size is too small, which is contrary to simulation test. It is an effective method to use the two data to estimate collectively. In this paper, we put forward a new test data fusion method based on importance sampling mechanism, which treats the flying test distribution as the true distribution, and the simulation test distribution as the proposal distribution. So we give a new frame and strategy on how to fuse the two different kinds of test data. Numerical computations show the feasibility of the improved method.

Keywords: Data fusion · Flying test · Simulation test · Bayesian estimation · Importance sampling mechanism

1 Introduction

Weapon test and evaluation aims at checking the qualification of equipment during its development time mainly by the means of equipment flying test traditionally. However, as the price of the single weapon becomes more expensive and the usage profile of the weapon system becomes more complex, the flying test reveals the following shortcomings. Firstly, big size flying test costs a lot; secondly, the limited flying test cannot cover all the usage profile of weapon system; thirdly, the test can't be accomplished under the boundary and extreme conditions. Besides the flying test, simulation technique is the only test method that can describes the closed-loop characteristics of missile weapon system, which has already been parallel to the flying test as its rapid development in ordnance test field. Comparing with the flying test, simulation test is of flexibility, economy, repeat ability and indestructibility. More importantly, the simulation test can get more test information than flying test and its operation is not restricted by the test environment, test time and test space which are the major factors that influences the flying test efficiency.

Considering the above advantage, the range test engineers show great interests in simulation test, because it can make up the deficiency of flying test. While on the way of the population and application of simulation test in checking the performance of weapon system, they find two main technical difficulties which are the evaluation of the credibility of the simulation test system and the fusion of the flying test data and the

© Springer Science+Business Media Singapore 2016
L. Zhang et al. (Eds.): AsiaSim 2016/SCS AutumnSim 2016, Part II, CCIS 644, pp. 555–565, 2016.
DOI: 10.1007/978-981-10-2666-9_56

flying test data. For the latter one, we put forward a test data fusion method based on importance sampling mechanism, which admits the flying test distribution as the true distribution, and the simulations one as the proposal distribution. So we give a new frame and strategy on how to fuse the two different kinds of test data.

2 Mathematical Description of Test Data Fusion

Let $x_{1:M}$ as the flying test data and $y_{1:N}$ as the simulation test data, where M, N are the sample size respectively. Normally, M is small while N is big.

What need to do is to find out a good method to get more accurate performance evaluation based on $x_{1:M}$ and $y_{1:N}$, that is how to estimate more precise numerical characteristic of the true distribution with $x_{1:M}$ and $y_{1:N}$. As is shown in Fig. 1.

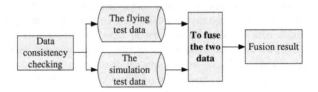

Fig. 1. The conduct procedure of test data fusion

3 Problem Analysis and Procedure Determination

Sample size over 30 is treated as large one. The procedure for fusing both flying and simulation test data interactively is the below, and shown in Fig. 2.

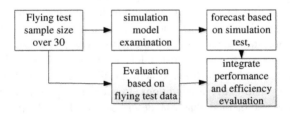

Fig. 2. The conduct procedure of big sample size flying test data and simulation test data fusion

Step1.   Use the flying test data to assess the index of reliability and hit probability
Step2.   Use the flying test data to examine the validity of simulation model
Step3.   Use simulation test to forecast the equipment performance

When the flying test data sample size is under 30, especially the minimum sample size, the statistics based on the limited samples will lead to the risk of inaccurate evaluation. Simulation test data then can be used for amendment to lessen the estimation error and raise the evaluation confidence. As is shown in Fig. 3.

4   Test Data Fusion Based on Importance Sampling Mechanism

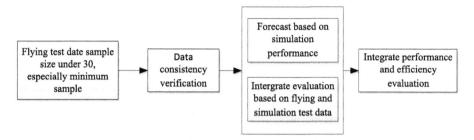

Fig. 3. The conduct procedure of small sample size flying test data and simulation test data fusion

4.1   Importance Sampling Mechanism

The most successful case of importance sampling is to solve the complicated integral problems. The integral problem is stated as

$$I = \int h(x)dx \tag{1}$$

Where $h(x)$ is a non-linear and transcendental function. To solve formula 1, we need to transform it into formula 2 according to importance sampling method.

$$I = \int \frac{h(x)}{g(x)} g(x)dx \tag{2}$$

It is easy to sample from $g(x)$ which is usually called importance distribution function or proposal distribution. Using Monte Carlo method, the computation of formula 2 can be indicated as

$$I = E\left(\frac{h(x)}{g(x)}\right) = \sum_{i=1}^{N} \frac{h(x_i)}{g(x_i)} x_i = \sum_{i=1}^{N} w_i(x_i)x_i \tag{3}$$

Where $w_i(x_i) = h(x_i)/g(x_i)$ is called importance coefficient.

Actually, the difficulty of importance sampling is how to find an accurate proposal distribution. If the distribution is not good, $w_i(x_i)$ will be zero. Then the samples will be useless and have no contributions to the estimated results.

4.2   Feasibility Analysis of Test Data Fusion Based on Importance Sampling Mechanism

Test data fusion problem is that we can obtain data from the flying test and simulation test on which we can estimate the true distribution of product performance that is unknown based. Where simulation test data sample size is big and we can get stable distribution. And also the simulation test system usually has certain credibility, so we can take the simulation distribution as proposal distribution in importance sampling mechanism and choose samples from simulation distribution to estimate the unknown product performance.

4.3   Test Date Fusion Mechanism Based on Importance Sampling

Let $\pi(x)$ be the true posterior distribution, $\pi_1(x)$ be flying test distribution and $\pi_2(x)$ be simulation test distribution. Based on the importance sampling, $\pi(x)$ can be treated as a series of weighted sampling $(w_i, x_i), i = 1, 2, \cdots$. Where x_i is the sample from the proposal distribution; $w_i = \pi(x)/\pi_2(x)$ is the importance coefficient. In this way, we avoid the key problem of importance sampling and choose the simulation distribution as the proposal test distribution. Whereas, the difficulties only lies in the computation of $w_i(x) = \pi(x)/\pi_2(x)$.

Here are some feasible solutions to calculate importance coefficient.

(a) Approximate computation using $\pi_1(x)$

$$w_i(x) = \frac{\pi_1(x)}{\pi_2(x)} \tag{4}$$

(b) Approximate computation using the weighted results of $\pi_1(x)$ and $\pi_2(x)$.

$$w_i(x) = \frac{rand \times \pi_1(x) + (1 - rand) \times \pi_2(x)}{\pi_2(x)} \tag{5}$$

The test data fusion of flying test and simulation test based on importance sampling mechanism is thus given by the following.

Step 1.   Inspect the consistency between the flying and simulation test samples.

(a) Method one: Check whether the flying test sample lands within the interval estimation of the simulation test.
(b) Method two: Check the consistency of the parameters between the flying test distribution and the simulation test distribution.
   a. Check the consistency of variance.
      Using F test method, the criterion for the consistency of variance is

$$F_{1-\frac{\alpha}{2}}(n_1 - 1, n_2 - 1) < F < F_{\frac{\alpha}{2}}(n_1 - 1, n_2 - 1) \tag{6}$$

Where $F = \left(S_1^*\right)^2 / \left(S_2^*\right)^2$.

It should be illustrated about variance. Since $P = \int_{-R}^{R} dy$ $\int_{-\sqrt{R^2-y^2}}^{\sqrt{R^2-y^2}} f(x,y)dx = 4 \int_0^R dy \int_0^{\sqrt{R^2-y^2}} f(x,y)dx$, the change of polar

coordinates $x = R \cos \alpha$ and $y = R \sin \alpha$,   and   then $P =$
$\frac{2K}{\pi} \int_0^{\pi/2} \frac{1}{\cos^2 \alpha + K \sin^2 \alpha} dy \left\{ 1 - \exp\left[-\frac{R^2}{2\sigma_x^2} \left(\cos^2 \alpha + K \sin^2 \alpha \right) \right] \right\} d\alpha$ where
$K = \sigma_x/\sigma_y$.
The final formula is

$$P = 1 - \exp\left(-\frac{K}{2\sigma_x^2} R^2 \right) = 1 - \exp\left(-\frac{R^2}{2\sigma_x \sigma_y} \right)$$

Use mean-value theorem and condition as $P(R \to \infty) = 1$.
The drop point of missile is decided only by the parameters σ_x, σ_y.
The smaller the parameters σ_x, σ_y are, the larger the possibility of the missile landing within the circle of radius R is. For the fixed σ_x, σ_y, $R = \sqrt{-2\sigma_x\sigma_y \ln(1 - P)}$ can be used to computer the maximum radius of missile drops. When $\sigma_x = \sigma_y = \sigma$, then $CEP = R_{\max} = \sqrt{2\ln\sigma} = 1.177\sigma$. CEP is the radius of half of samples dropping in the circle, which means the hit rate lower than 0.5. To raise the hit rate to more than 0.5, then $\sigma = CEP/1.177$.
For the given target, the size is 2.3 m × 2.3 m, and the hit probability is 90 %, then $\sigma = R_{\max}/[-2\ln(1 - P)]^{1/2} = 0.5359$.

b. Check the consistency of mean value.
Accepting mean value consistency, the difference between the two test data should be not more than

$$|\bar{x}_1 - \bar{x}_2| < t_{\frac{\alpha}{2}}(n_1 + n_2 - 2)\sqrt{\frac{1}{n_1} + \frac{1}{n_2}} s^* \tag{7}$$

Where $s^* = \sqrt{\frac{1}{n-1}\sum_{i=1}^{n}\left(x_i - \frac{1}{n}\sum_{i=1}^{n} x_i \right)}$.

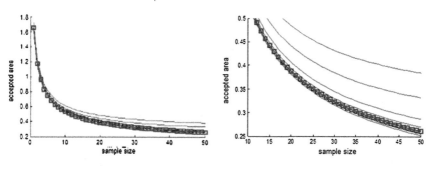

(a) full figure   (b) detailed drawing

Fig. 4. The impacts of sample size on acceptance region

Figure. 4 shows the flying test sample size and the simulation test sample influence the region of acceptance. X-axis shows the quantity of flying samples. The red variable curve shows quantity of simulation test samples which are large ones.

Step 2.   Use importance sampling strategy to approximate the posterior distribution.

Conclusion: Considering variance s^* and $t_{\frac{\alpha}{2}}(n_1 + n_2 - 2)\sqrt{\frac{1}{n_1} + \frac{1}{n_2}}$ together, if consistency check goes well, then the mean difference should be no more than 1, which is influenced by the flying test sample size most.

5   Numerical Calculation

5.1   Test Method

Take sample set x_i from the true distribution normrnd (ZM, ZF, N, 1). ZM is the mean; ZF is the variance; N is the sample size of flying test. Take sample set from proposal distribution normrnd (ZM + dZM,ZF + dZF, M, 1) which has certain errors, then simulate the simulation test distribution. dZM and dZF are the difference between simulation distribution parameter and real distribution parameter.

5.2   Comparative Method

Method 1:   point estimation
Method 2:   bootstrap method
Method 3:   randomly weighing bootstrap method
Method 4:   mean value
Method 5:   Bayes estimation
Method 6:   estimation based on importance sampling strategy

5.3   Criterion on Performance Estimation

Same sample data are tested in different methods for 100 times individually. Assess superiority of each method with estimation error

$$Error = \frac{1}{Monte}\left(\sqrt{\sum_{i=1}^{Monte}(\hat{z}_i - ZM)^2}\right) \tag{8}$$

Where *Monte* is test times and equals to 100. Obviously, the smaller the error is, the better the method. $\hat{z}_i$ is the estimate value of different method.

5.4   Test Procedure

Case one:
The true distribution is N (0.86, 1);
The flying test distribution: $X \sim N$ (0.85, 1), Sampling size is M (3–50);
The simulation test distribution: N (0.9, 0.9).

Table 1 shows the estimation of the true distribution using different methods. According to Table 1, it is obvious that the estimation accuracy of the proposed method is higher than Bayes method. Figure 5 plots estimation error changes of different methods as sampling size. The yellow line is the Cramér-Rao lower bounds.

Table 1. Estimation of the true distribution based on different methods

Algorithm	1	1'	2	3	4	5	6	7
M = 3	0.4975	0.0816	0.6519	0.5087	0.2482	0.3501	0.2544	0.0305
M = 5	0.3353	0.0900	0.4121	0.3386	0.1741	0.2686	0.1762	0.0221
M = 10	0.2596	0.0772	0.2978	0.2641	0.1295	0.2291	0.1260	0.0234
M = 20	0.1756	0.0821	0.1980	0.1792	0.1046	0.1661	0.1050	0.0244
M = 30	0.1615	0.0845	0.1815	0.1616	0.0924	0.1550	0.0907	0.0288
M = 50	0.1178	0.0893	0.1235	0.1180	0.0772	0.1152	0.0949	0.0245

notes 1' stands for the mean of simulation test data;7 is the limitation of 6.

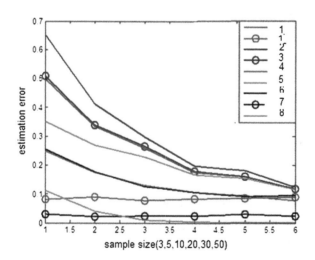

Fig. 5. Plot of evaluated error - sample size

Case two:
The true distribution: N (0.85, 0.6);
The flying test distribution: $X \sim N$ (0.85, 0.6), Sampling size is M;
The simulation test distribution: N (0.4, 0.75).

Table 2 shows the true distribution estimation based on 6 different methods. According to Table 2, it is obvious that the estimation accuracy of the proposed method is higher than Bayes method. Figure 6 plots estimation error changes of different methods as sampling size. The yellow line is the Cramér-Rao lower bounds.

Table 2. Estimation of the true distribution using different methods

Algorithm	1	1'	2	3	4	5	6	7
M = 3	0.2633	0.3414	0.3411	0.2601	0.1948	0.1956	0.2336	0.0634
M = 5	0.2145	0.3525	0.2623	0.2095	0.1906	0.1765	0.2289	0.0551
M = 10	0.1697	0.3562	0.2978	0.1916	0.1765	0.1479	0.2085	0.0617
M = 20	0.1020	0.3434	0.1096	0.1023	0.1638	0.0957	0.1984	0.0713
M = 30	0.0874	0.3482	0.0956	0.0874	0.1801	0.0847	0.1982	0.0606
M = 50	0.0597	0.3455	0.0638	0.0593	0.1740	0.0582	0.1914	0.0568

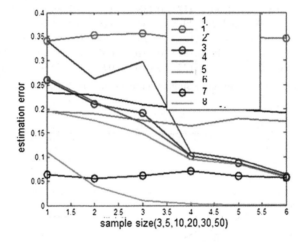

Fig. 6. Plot of evaluated error - sample size (Color figure online)

5.5 Results Analysis

From the above numerical computation, we can conclude

(a) For case 1, the estimation precision of simulation test is better than point estimation of the flying test data. And the new method gets better estimated accuracy than Bayes method;

(b) For case 2, the estimation precision of simulation test is bad. Under the condition of small sample, the new method gets better estimated accuracy than point estimation method, bootstrap method. But with the sample size gets larger; the accuracy of new methods is lower than other methods.

6 Further Improvement of the New Method

The reason why the estimation effect of new method goes bad as sample size raising in situation 2, is originally the absence of variation about sample size N in Gaussian sum distribution (the algorithm is rand, 1-rand) to simulate true posterior distribution. So putting the sample size into the fusion cage can improve the new method to approximate the posterior distribution. Besides, according to analysis, estimation error is also related to the credibility of the simulation models. The improvement strategy is

$$w_i(x) = (rand, \pi_1(x), \pi_2(x), N, C) \tag{9}$$

Where C is the credibility. When N gets larger, the weight of $\pi_1(x)$ gets bigger; C gets bigger, the weight of $\pi_2(x)$ gets larger. A feasible way is

$$zh1 = (1/Ds * Ds/NN)/(1/Ds * Ds/NN + 1/0.4/0.4);$$

$$zh2 = rand; \tag{10}$$

$$zh = zh1 * (1 - gama) + zh2 * C;$$

However, formula 10 is a simple procedure; better strategy would be the core of the improvement. We take two examples to exam the improvement.

For above case 1, set C = 0.9. The results are shown in Fig. 7. The estimation error curve waves for different sample size ranging 3 to 50 in different methods.

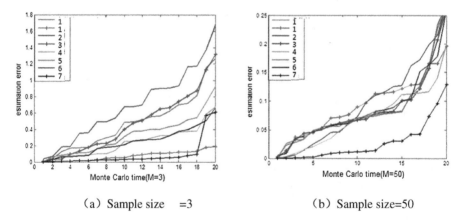

(a) Sample size =3   (b) Sample size=50

Fig. 7. Plot of sample size - estimation error

For above case 2, set C = 0.2. The results are shown in Fig. 8.

From above numerical computation, we can conclude:

(a) From Figure 9 and 10, the improved method overcomes the shortcoming of big estimation error that originated from the poor credibility to some extent.
(b) The improved method is the best estimation way to the small sample size test.

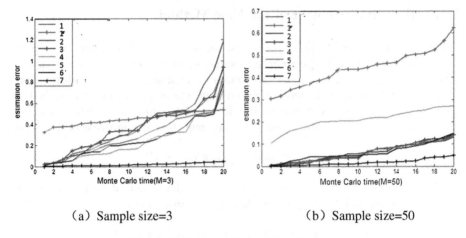

(a) Sample size=3   (b) Sample size=50

Fig. 8. Plot of sample size-estimation error

7 Conclusion

(a) The limited estimation error of the new method is nearest to the Cramér-Rao lower bound which is the minimum estimation error based on samples.

(b) The new method especially fit small sample estimation problems. It gets more accurate estimation results than point estimation, bootstrapping method, randomly weighing bootstrap method and Bayes Bootstrap.

(c) To increase the credibility of the simulation model can improve the estimation accuracy of Bayes method and importance estimation algorithm. For the two methods, importance estimation algorithm is more sensitive to the credibility. And to add the quantity of flying test samples can improve the estimation accuracy of all estimation algorithms. When the flying test samples size is over 30, all the estimation results are close to the numerical characteristics of the true distribution.

(d) Besides, it is a question worthy of deep thinking that if the credibility of the simulation test system is quite high, the result of simulation test is most accurate of all, so why we need the fusion method?Because any fusion method finally leads to a sub-optimal estimation result, according to the test data analysis.

At last, we emphasize that the difficulties are how to compute the samples weight so that it can approximate the true posterior distribution. The computing strategy is rather simple in this paper. If we can develop more subtle weighing methods, it is possible to be close to the Luo-cramer lower bound for estimation error. We expect senior experts proficient in Monte-Carlo sampling strategy carry out in-depth theoretical research and exploration, which are worthy of further follow-up studies.

References

1. Zhang, S.-F., Cai, H.: Fusion of information of multiple sources in Bayesian analysis. J. Syst. Simul. **12**(1), 54–57 (2000)
2. Xiaojun, D., Zhengming, W.: Evaluation and analysis of small-sample missile test based on characteristic variables. Acta Armamentarii **24**(3), 367–372 (2003)
3. Deng, H., Zha, Y.-B.: Research on applying simulation credibility into weapon system appraisal. Acta Simulata Systematica Sin. **17**(7), 1566–1568 (2005)

Inspiration for Battlefield Situation Cognition from AI Military Programs Launched by DARPA of USA and Development of AI Technology

Zhu Feng[1,2(✉)], Hu Xiaofeng[1], Wu Lin[1], He Xiaoyuan[1], and Guo Shengming[1]

[1] The Department of Information Operation and Command Training, National Defense University, Beijing 100091, China
zhufeng_83@126.com
[2] No. 93682 Unit of PLA, Beijing 101300, China

Abstract. Battlefield situation intelligent cognition is very important for the warfare, but this kind of technology is very hard for breakthrough. 'Deep Green' program which is launched by DARPA of USA to study military intelligent command and operation for modern warfare is unsuccessful. The key problem is that the technology of battlefield situation intelligent cognition is no breakthrough. Later on, USA pays more attention to the AI technology applied in the military filed, especially in the cognition intelligence aspect. The supported money from DARPA is increased apparently year by year. As some new technologies, such as Big Data and Bayesian Deduction, especially Deep Learning technology, are presented, and these new technologies are applied in the wider and wider range of domains, the development of the AI technology takes a big step forward. We also find some researches on the Deep Learning technology is applied in the situation cognition. Therefore, some significant inspirations for battlefield situation cognition in the military domain can be brought to us. In the paper, the main AI military programs launched by DARPA are combed and analyzed. Big Data, Bayesian Deduction and Deep Learning contained by the AI technology are introduced. Especially, the research status of Deep Learning and its applications in the situation cognition are generalized. On the basis of that, the researches on the military battlefield situation cognition based on the AI technology are prospected according to some relative knowledge.

Keywords: Battlefield situation cognition · DARPA · AI · Deep learning · Inspiration

1 Introduction

In 2007, 'Deep Green' program was launched by DARPA (Defense Advanced Research Projects Agency) of USA, in order to study military intelligent command and operation for modern warfare [1, 2]. However, this program is unsuccessful. The key problem is that the battlefield situation intelligent cognition is no breakthrough. As well

L. Zhang et al. (Eds.): AsiaSim 2016/SCS AutumnSim 2016, Part II, CCIS 644, pp. 566–577, 2016.
DOI: 10.1007/978-981-10-2666-9_57

known, the battlefield situation intelligent cognition is very important for modern warfare. In fact, the cognition contains several steps, such as awareness, comprehension, assessment, prediction and so on.

Later on, USA pays more attention to the AI (Artificial Intelligence) technology applied in the military filed, especially in cognition intelligent aspect. They consider the AI technology as the disruptive technological force in the future warfare and the one of the best weapons for keeping the advantage in the next turn of the military competition all over the world. The Defense Department of USA firstly proposed the 'Third Offset Strategy' for keeping their hegemony and chairman position [3–5]. In their declaration, they point out that the AI technology is the key drive of this strategy and it is also the 'High Tech Holy Grail' of the whole strategy. Hence, DARPA have be launching lots of the relative programs to explore the key technologies and the application prospects of the AI technology applied in the military domain, especially in intelligent cognition aspect. According to the reports, the supported finance and force are increased and enhanced apparently year by year. In recent years, the whole supported finance from DARPA is closed to the 10 billions, where the budget of the program about cognitive system is over 5 billions.

Nowadays, the battlefield has been in the Big Data age. The plenty of complex information can be contained in the battlefield. The non-linear, unsure and emergence characteristics are shown sufficiently. Hence, we must consider the battlefield situation as the complex system [6–8]. However, the traditional AI technology based on the simple or linear method is not suitable for researching the complex battlefield situation intelligent cognition. It will bring the quite difficulty for the technological breakthrough of battlefield situation intelligent cognition. It needs to explore and study to this technology as soon as possible.

As the development of the AI technology is greater and greater. Big Data [9], Bayesian Deduction [10–12], especially Deep Learning technology [13–15], are presented one by one. At the same time these new technologies are applied in the wider and wider range of domains. It can be seen that the development of the AI technology takes a big step forward. These technologies are not the traditional method, but can be suitable for those complex questions. At the same time, we also find some researches on the AI technology, especially the Deep Learning technology, is applied in the situation cognition. Hence, we can say that the progress of the AI technology can bring the valuable chance to research the complex military questions, especially for the battlefield situation intelligent cognition. However, it still needs a lot of efforts and a long time to gain the breakthrough.

Aimed at the analyzed above, in the paper, the main AI military programs launched by DARPA are combed and analyzed in Sect. 2. The Big Data, Bayesian Deduction and Deep Learning contained by the AI technology are introduced in Sect. 3. Especially, in this part, the research status of Deep Learning and its applications in the situation cognition are generalized. On the basis of that, the researches on the military battlefield situation cognition based on the AI technology are prospected according to some relative knowledge in Sect. 4. Last, some conclusions are given.

2 AI Military Programs Launched by DARPA

In 2007, 'Deep Green' program which is the one of the important AI research programs was launched by DARPA [1, 2]. The main idea of this program is that the autonomous assistant decision-making system is attempted to exploit. By using this system, the function of autonomous intelligent assessment and decision-making based on the data can be realized. However, battlefield situation cognition is the precondition on the assessment and decision-making. No battlefield situation effective cognition is impossible for the assessment and decision-making. In fact, 'Deep Green' program is not successful faced on the bottleneck problem about intelligent processing of Big Data, especially about battlefield situation intelligent cognition. The main unsuccessful reason of 'Deep Green' program is that the comprehension and processing capability of computer for the battlefield data is further poorer than the human's cognition level.

Aimed at this problem, several relative research programs about the AI technology applied in the military domain are launched by DARPA step by step. In order to support the application technology, some research programs in the basic field are launched firstly. These programs are stated generally as follows [5].

In 2008, 'Machine Reading' program was launched to address the prohibitive cost of handcrafting information by replacing the expert and associated knowledge engineer. And some systems are exploited to "read" natural text and insert it into the AI knowledge bases especially encoded to support subsequent machine reasoning. Later on, this program is improved, adjusted and renamed as 'Machine Reading and Reasoning Technology'. It is developing the enabling technologies to acquire, integrate, and use high performance reasoning strategies in knowledge-rich domains. In 2009, 'Deep Learning' research program was launched. The main purpose of this program is that more hidden and valid features are attempted to extract from lots of un-supervised sound, video, sensor and text datum obtained from the battlefield. At the same time, these extracted features will be utilized for the pattern recognition and feature classification to perform the abnormal surveillance, to describe the associated relationship especially the time relationship of the events. In 2010, 'Insight' program was launched to develop the new capabilities for automated exploitation and collection management. It will emphasize several areas, mainly including model-based correlation, adversary behavior modeling, threat network analysis tools to automatically combine data across sources and manage uncertainty, and tools to integrate human and machine processing, including visualization, hypothesis manipulation, and distributed social intelligence. In 2012, 'XDATA' program was launched to develop computational techniques and software tools for analyzing large volumes of data, both semi-structured and unstructured [16]. It also will develop open source software toolkits that enable flexible software development supporting and users processing large volumes of data in timelines commensurate with mission workflows of targeted defense applications. In the same year, 'DEFT (Deep Exploration and Filtering of Text)' program was launched to enable automated extraction, processing, and inference of information from text in operationally relevant application domains. A key DEFT emphasis is to determine the implied and hidden meaning in text through probabilistic inference, anomaly detection, and disfluency analysis. In 2013, 'Probabilistic Programming for Advancing Machine

Learning (PPAML)' program was launched to create an advanced computer programming capability that greatly facilitates the construction of new machine learning applications in a wide range of domains. The key enabling technology is a new programming paradigm called probabilistic programming that facilitates the management of uncertain information. The research results of these program above can be benefit for the research on the of the AI technology applied in the military domain, especially in the important aspect of the battlefield situation cognition.

Furthermore, some research programs about the AI technology applied in the military domain. The key questions occurred in these programs are all that the battlefield situation intelligent cognition and autonomies decision-making are expected to attempt to realize breakthrough by using the AI technology, the complex network and system-of-system analysis technology, and so on. The detailed demonstrations can be expressed generally as follows.

In 2013, 'Afanda' plan program was launched. The main purpose of this program is that some armies consisted of lots of the robots are established. These robots, as the human's simulation, can be controlled by human's brain like Afanda in the film. They can act instead of the officials and soldiers of human for emerging in the real battlefield, in order to realize zero-casualty indeed in the future warfare. In 2014, 'Distributed Battle Management (DBM)' program was launched to develop distributed mission-driven architectures, protocols, and algorithms for battle management (BM) in the contested environment. The architecture will enable rapid reaction to ephemeral engagement opportunities and maintain a reliable BM structure, despite limited communications and platform attrition in continuously evolving threat environments. This program also will incorporate highly automated decision-making capability while maintaining vital human-on-the-loop operator approval. In the same year, 'Plan X' program was also launched. This program will develop technologies to enable comprehensive awareness and understanding of the cyber battlespace as required for visualizing, planning, and executing military cyber warfare operations. It will extend operationally meaningful measures to project quantitatively the collateral damage of executed cyber warfare missions. In 2015, both the deputy secretary of Defense of USA Robert Work and the DARPA director Arati Prabhakar have ever announced that 'human-machine collaboration (also informally named as semi-Sagittarius)' program will be attracted and launched. This program will develop an organic symbiosis whole produced by the fusion of human and machine deeply. This organic symbiosis whole can have the advantage of the precision of machine and the sharp of human at the same time. By using this whole, the cognition speed and quality of human can be improved apparently to make decision and action rapidly and validly. It is valuable to noticed that this pattern of 'human-machine collaboration' is considered by Defense Department of USA as the 'High Tech Holy Grail' of the 'Third Offset Strategy' which is adverse for the development of China and Russian. Later on, Arati Prabhakar also has announced the other important 'Cognition Electronic Battle' plan. This plan attempts to identify, examine, classify and counter-check captured enemy radar signal autonomously by using the Deep learning technology.

Although so many supported finance and force are cost for researching the AI technology applied in the military domain, the advanced effects are not apparently due to these programs are difficult, especially the battlefield situation intelligent cognition and autonomous decision-making being very complex resulting in still no breakthrough.

3   Advanced Development of AI Technology

The AI technology is one branch of the subject of Computer Science. Its main purpose is that the intelligent behavior will be realized through exploiting and producing intelligent machine and system to analog and extend human's intelligence by using the artificial method and technology [17]. The AI subject mainly contains the Machine Learning, Data Mining, Knowledge expression, Autonomous Deduction, Brain-like Intelligence, Expert System, and so on. The further purpose of the AI technology is that the human's intelligence level will be reached by artificial method and technology. Hence, this technology will be faced on the large challenge.

Recently, the development of the AI technology is greater and greater, especially Big Data, Bayesian Deduction, Deep Learning technology and so on are proposed and applied in a wide range of domain. These technologies can bring the valuable chance to perform intelligent military researches; especially can bring the wishes for the breakthrough of the battlefield situation intelligent cognition.

3.1   Big Data Technology

Big Data is not only the data column is large, but has the more important value. Usually, Big Data has the '4 V' characteristics [18–20]. Firstly, it has the large volume. Its orders of magnitude can be reached to TB, PB even over EB. Secondly, it has the apparent variety, which contains the many kinds of information with different structures, and it can be existed with different information carriers. Thirdly, it has the high velocity data flow, resulting in the processing speed should be in the reasonable time. Fourthly, it has the high value or veracity. In fact, the noise is usually within Big Data. Hence, Big Data will be shown as high value and low density and the value contained by Big Data is real. In addition, the other definition of Big Data from processing method aspect is given by Wiki. That is Big Data is a kind of particular data. The cost time of capturing, managing and processing this kind of data by using the conventional methods and tools will be over the acceptable limit.

Big Data not only is shown as '4 V' characteristics, but also bring the novel research thought and approach to us. The revolutionary advances can be stated as follows. Firstly, the local data analysis is transformed to the global research. Secondly, the pure data analysis is transformed to the complex research due to Big Data is very complicated and has lots of unsure information. Thirdly, the causality analysis is transformed to the correlation research. Fourthly, the simple analysis is transformed to deep and indirect research. We can say that the most important contribution of Big Data is science research thought and approach for us.

Nowadays, Big Data is popularly attracted and applied in many fields, such as internet, news and image research and so on. Most of famous companies, such as Baidu and Alibaba, have built Big Data structure to supply services for users. In the military domain, Big Data have the other particular features, such as the strong confidentiality, confusion, and jamming and so on, besides '4 V' characteristics. Hence, several more strict requirements will be suggested for these Big Data in the military domain.

3.2 Bayesian Deduction Technology

Despite remarkable advances in machine learning, two aspects of human conceptual knowledge have eluded machine systems [10]. Firstly, for most interesting kinds of natural and manmade categories, people can learn a new concept from just one or a handful of examples, whereas standard algorithms in machine learning require tens or hundreds of examples to perform similarly. Secondly, people learn richer representations than machines do, even for simple concepts, using them for a wider range of functions, including creating new exemplars, parsing objects into parts and relations, and creating new abstract categories of objects based on existing categories [21].

It needs to use the Bayesian Program Learning (BPL) framework, capable of learning a large class of visual concepts from just a single example and generalizing in ways that are mostly indistinguishable from people. This framework brings together three key ideas, i.e., compositionality, causality, and learning to learning. As programs, rich concepts can be built "compositionally" from simpler primitives. Their probabilistic semantics handle noise and support creative generalizations in a procedural form that naturally captures the abstract "causal" structure of the real-world processes that produce examples of a category. Learning proceeds by constructing programs that best explain the observations under a Bayesian criterion, and the model "learns to learn" by developing hierarchical priors that allow previous experience with related concepts to ease learning of new concepts [22]. In short, BPL can construct new programs by reusing the pieces of existing ones, capturing the causal and compositional properties of the real-world generative processes operating on multiple scales.

The Bayesian Deduction technology can provide the new and valid thought and theory for the development of the AI technology.

3.3 Deep Learning Technology

A. General Introduction. In 2006, the new research field which is Deep Learning was proposed in the AI subject [13–15]. The origin of Deep Learning is a kind of the classical artificial NN (Nerve Network) technology. The deep network obtained by using Deep Learning has the same net structure feature as the artificial NN. Hence, we can call the deep network as DNN (Deep Nerve Network). Essentially, DNN has the multi-layer sensor structure, due to it simulates the process of analysis and study process of human's brain [23].

It is helpful for enhancing the precision of the data identification and classification by using the Deep Learning method to find the descriptions of the essential features of the data, through compressing layer by layer after multiple combining and mining for the data at the low layer. The main advantages of Deep Learning are stated as follows.

Firstly, it has the strong non-linear processing capability to solve those problems which are hardly to describe reasonably by the several simple linear method. Secondly, lots of hidden information behind the Big Data can be mined deeply by using the Deep Learning due to this technology has some characteristics of comprehension layer by layer and autonomous analysis or extraction. Thirdly, Deep Learning also has the well memory characteristic, which can offer potential support for those cognition problems needed prior knowledge.

Nowadays, Deep Learning has brought the disruptive revolution in the many fields, such as the image, sound, voice, vision processing and natural language comprehension and so on. At the same time, it has also brought some breakthroughs about the intelligent decision-making and society behavior analysis [24–26].

B. *Applied in the Situation Cognition.* Abroad, on the basis of the 49 kinds of Atari video games, especially Super Mario game, are concurred successfully by using the Deep Learning technology [27, 28], the program AlphaGo of DeepMind of Google company has beaten South Korean professional Lee Sedol, considered by many to be the world's strongest player [29–31]. That is to say the computer with the AI technology plays the Go equivalent of a world champion. The key technology of AlphaGo is Deep Learning. In this technology, the Go situation comprehension and awareness can be realized to complete every decision-making. In Araki Shoko's research, the real-world sound environments can be aware to comprehend its situation and to separate the useful sound and the noise effectively by using the Deep Learning model [32]. The robustness of the useful sound mixed with noise is analyzed by Yoshioka T. and Gales M.J.F. using the acoustics Deep Learning model [33]. There are also some relative researches such as taxi route prediction [34], autonomous drawing [35], and editing news draft [27] and so on.

Interiorly, the traffic situation based on the big traffic data is aware to research the traffic flow prediction problem by Yisheng Lv and his accompaniers [36]. The prediction method based on the Deep Learning technology which considers the spatial and temporal correlations inherently is proposed by them to achieve the superior performance. The unified speaker-dependent speech separation and enhancement system based on the Deep Learning method is researched by Gao Tian and his accompaniers [37]. The indoor scene recognition method for mobile robots combining global and saliency region features is researched to propose by NIU Jie and his accompaniers [38]. Aimed at the problem of network situation awareness with Big Data, the feature extraction algorithm based on the Deep Learning method for dimension curse to comprehend situation is proposed by CHEN Zhen and her accompanies [39]. In [40], some general conclusions about research on cyberspace situational awareness are shown.

These elucidations above are not only shown as the advanced development of the AI technology, but also the some valuable gifts for the researches on battlefield situation cognition with the AI technology.

4 Inspiration for Battlefield Situation Cognition with AI Technology

In the military domain, the battlefield situation can be defined as the statuses, changes and development trends of all kinds of elements of all sides in the war [41–43]. The battlefield situation cognition can be described as three steps. Firstly, a piece of visual graph is achieved which is consisted by combat action, event, time, position, force and so on, according to the battlefield situation at that moment. Secondly, the distribution of the combat forces, battlefield environment and combat intention and maneuverability of enemy which are obtained from the visual picture of battlefield are effectively combined together to analyze and deduce the reason of occurred event in the war. Thirdly, the force structure and employment character of enemy are evaluated, according to deduced results. Aimed at the battlefield situation cognition with the AI technology, some inspirations with are shown as follows.

4.1 Research Thought Based on Data Analysis

In the Big Data age, the conventional research approach with math model for battlefield situation considered as the complex system will be not competent, due to some especial characteristics of Big Data, such as non-linear, unsure and emergence characteristics and so on. Hence, the research approach will be transformed to data analysis. According to the different research thoughts and methods of the Big Data technology, some other important characteristics of battlefield situation data, such as the integration, correlation, complexity and deepness and so on, should be more regarded. At the same time, some conventional processing methods for battlefield situation data such as local, causality, purity and simplicity analysis and research and so on should be used as the assistants.

4.2 Tactical Level Cognition Based on Bayesian Deduction Technology

In the battlefield, the confrontation on the tactical level is a kind of combats with a narrow range and a low layer, such as whether the different capabilities of combat entity are valid, or how well are these capabilities, containing the capabilities of awareness, attack, supplement, jamming, early warning and spying and so on. It can be said that the confrontation on the tactical level usually is the comparatively explicit combat action, where those compositionalities, causalities and relative elements are generally sure. Therefore, the Bayesian Deduction technology can be considered as the effective tools to analyze battlefield situation on the tactical level to achieve cognition results. When the Bayesian Deduction technology is utilized, the statistic methods orienting Big Data should be applied to obtain the relative probabilities.

4.3   Campaign Level Cognition Based on Deep Learning Technology

The researches on the campaign level cognition can be carried out, on the basis of researches on the tactical level cognition. The campaign level battlefield contains so many kinds of different systems with the different combat missions, and the complicated interaction of these different systems will bring lots of unsure, complex and emerging features to the campaign level battlefield. Hence, the campaign level battlefield must be considered as the complex system to research. When the researches on the campaign level battlefield situation cognition are executed, the Deep Learning technology with some especial advantages can play the important role to mine and describe the hidden and emerging information and to complete the complex processing. The deep neural network constructed by using the Deep Learning technology is consisted of plenty of basic elements, i.e. neural units, and their connections, i.e. synapses. Those tactical level cognition results and their some interactions can be considered as the basic elements and their connections, respectively. Based on these conformations and a mass of trainings, the battlefield situation cognition on campaign level can be attempted to explore.

As stated above, the schematic sketch of the research inspiration of the battlefield situation cognition with the AI technology can be described in Fig. 1.

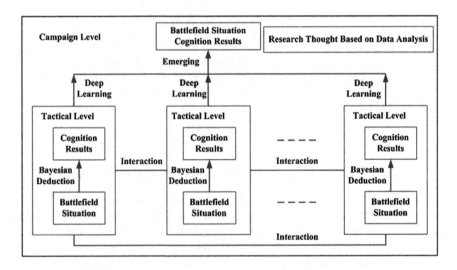

Fig. 1. Sketch of inspiration of battlefield situation cognition with AI technology

Last, we refer to the views of Professor HU who is the chief engineer of War Game system in China [30]. The rapid development of the AI technology has brought the wishes of the intelligent warfare to us. Although, there is the long distance between the intelligent warfare and us and there are lots of unknown or unimaginable things, we must get ready for orienting its coming. It is the inevitable formula of the development and revolution of the warfare.

5   Conclusions

In the paper, some key issues and helpful inspirations are embroidered on the important military problem about the battlefield situation cognition with the AI technology to discuss. The main contents can be stated as the following these aspects. Firstly, the main AI military programs launched by DARPA are combed and analyzed. From these we can find that the researches on the military problem with the AI technology have been high-regarded by USA, where the key problem of the battlefield situation intelligent cognition is still no breakthrough. Secondly, Big Data, Bayesian Deduction and Deep Learning contained by the AI technology are introduced. Especially, the research status of Deep Learning and its applications in the situation cognition are generalized. From these we can see that the advanced development of the AI technology can bring the important wishes for the researches on battlefield situation cognition with the AI technology. Thirdly, the researches on the military battlefield situation cognition based on the AI technology are prospected. The relative schematic sketch of the research inspiration is given. This paper can provide some lessons and thoughts for researches on the development of the AI technology applied in the military domain of USA, the advanced development of the AI technology and the problem of the battlefield situation intelligent cognition.

Acknowledgement. The authors would like to thank the associated editors and the anonymous reviewers for their helpful comments and suggestions. This work is supported by the National Natural Science Foundation of China (No. 61374179 and U1435218).

References

1. Zhou, Y., Huang, J., Huang, K.: A study on impact of 'deep green' on command and control. Fire Control Command Control **38**(6), 1–5 (2013)
2. Zhou, Y., Huang, J., Huang, K.: Review on Key Technology in Deep Green. J. Syst. Simul. **25**(7), 1633–1638 (2013)
3. http://mp.weixin.qq.com/s?
4. Volner, R.: Chasing autonomy: how much is enough and how much is too much. In: 19th ICCRTS
5. DARPA. Department of Defense Fiscal Year (FY) 2012–2016 President's Budget Submission (Unclassified). Defense Wide Justification Book
6. Hu, X., Zhang, Y., Li, R., Yang, J.: Capability evaluation problem of networking SoS. Syst. Eng. Theory Pract. **35**(5), 1313–1317 (2015)
7. Hu, X., He, X., Rao, D.: A methodology for investigating the capabilities of command and coordination for system of systems operation based on complex network theory. Complex Syst. Complex Sci. **12**(2), 9–17 (2015)
8. Jia, J., Wu, Y., He, X., Hu, X.: Operation cooperative relation modeling based on hypergraphs. J. Nat. Univ. Defense Technol. **37**(3), 185–190 (2015)
9. Hu, X., He, X., Xu, X.: Simulation in the big data era-review of new ideas and new theories in the 81st Academic Salon of China association for science and technology. Sci. China Inf. Sci. **44**(5), 676–692 (2014)

10. Lake, B.M., Salakhutdinov, R., Tenenbaum, J.B.: Human-level concept learning through probabilistic program induction. Science 350(6266), 1332–1339 (2015)
11. Zhao, X., Yao, P., Zhang, P.: Application of dynamic bayesian network in battlefield situation assessment. Electron. Opt. Control 17(1), 44–47 (2010)
12. Tong, S., Pang, S., Yang, J., Hua, H.: Status and prospect of applications of bayesian networks in warfare. Command Control Simul. 32(5), 1–4 (2010)
13. Hinton, G., Salakhutdinov, R.: Reducing the dimensionality of data with neural networks. Science 313(5786), 504–507 (2006)
14. Hinton, G.E., Deng, L., Yu, D., et al.: Deep neural networks for acoustic modeling in speech recognition. IEEE Signal Process Mag. 29(6), 82–97 (2012)
15. LeCun, Y., Bengio, Y., Hinton, G.: Deep learning. Nat. Rev. 521, 436–444 (2015)
16. Lang, Y., Kong, L.: The U.S. government released big data research and development initiative science research. Informationization Technol. Appl. 3(2), 89–92 (2012)
17. Shi, Z.: Artificial Intelligence. China Machine Press, Beijing (2016)
18. Li, G.J.: The scientific value of big data research. Commun. CCF 9, 8–12 (2012)
19. Big_data[EB/OL]. http://en.wikipedia.org/wiki/Big_data (2012)
20. Meng, X.F., Ci, X.: Big data management: concepts, techniques and challenges. J. Comput. Res. Dev. 50, 146–169 (2013)
21. Jern, A., Kemp, C.: Cognition Psychology 66, 85–125 (2013)
22. Braun, D.A., Mehring, C., Wolpert, D.M.: Structure learning in action. Behav. Brain Res. 206, 157–165 (2010)
23. Yin, B., Wang, W., Wang, L.: Review of deep learning. J. Beijing Univ. Technol. 41(1), 48–59 (2015)
24. Li, W:. The research and application of deep learning in image recognition. Dissertation of Degree of postgraduate of Wuhan University of Technology, Hubei, Wuhan, May, 2014
25. Lin, T.H., Wang, C.C.: Deep learning of spatio-temporal features with geometric-based moving point detection for motion segmentation. In: 2014 IEEE International Conference on Robotics & Automation (ICRA), Hong Kong, China, 31 May–7 June 2014, pp. 3058–3065 (2014)
26. Huang, Y., Wu, R., Sun, Y., Wang, W., Ding, X.: Vehicle logo recognition system based on convolutional neural networks with a pretraining strategy. IEEE Trans. Intell. Transp. Syst. 16(4), 1951–1960 (2015)
27. Mnih, V., Kavukcuoglu, K., Silver, D., et al.: Human-level control through deep reinforcement learning. Nature 518, 529–533 (2015)
28. https://mp.weixin.qq.com/s?__biz=MzI3MTA0MTk1MA==&mid=400876473&idx=2&sn=0f43a12d58bbfc07711954ffff163978&scene=1&srcid=1206Ri2LlY6BKM1LlThmPlYo&pass_ticket=ExFOJ3Ghj9aFYvJUmAH%2F6B7UgqKH25HY3J3%2FruMePi6zxmsbebjRoVHfAbdlvDdy#rd
29. Silver, D., Huang, A., Maddison, C.J., Guez, A., Sifre, L., van den Driessche, G., et al.: Mastering the game of go with deep neural networks and tree search. Nature 529, 484–489 (2016)
30. Hu, X.: Triumph of AlphaGo and Wishes of Future Warfare Evolution. Xinzhiyuan, 18th March 2016
31. Google masters Go. Nature 529, 445–446 (2016)
32. Shoko, A., Masakiyo, F., Takuya, Y., Marc, D., Miquel, E., Tomohiro, N.: Deep learning based distant-talking speech processing in real-world sound environments. NTT Tech. Rev. 13(11) (2015)
33. Yoshioka, T., Gales, M.J.F.: Environmentally robust ASR front-end for deep neural network acoustic models. Comput. Speech Lang. 31(1), 65–86 (2015)

34. de Brébisson, A., Simon, E., Auvolat, A., Vincent, P., Bengio, Y.: Artificial neural networks applied to taxi destination prediction, pp. 1–12. arXiv:1508.00021v2 [cs.LG], 21 September 2015
35. http://www.zhihu.com/question/32011032
36. Lv, Y., Duan, Y., Kang, W., Li, Z., Wang, F.-Y.: Traffic flow prediction with big data: a deep learning approach. IEEE Trans. Intell. Transp. Syst. **16**(2), 865–873 (2015)
37. Tian, G., Jun, D., Li, X., Cong, L., Li-Rong, D., Chin-Hui, L.: A unified speaker-dependent speech separation and enhancement system based on deep neural networks. In: 2015 IEEE China Summit and International Conference on Signal and Information Processing, SIP, China, pp. 687–691, 12–15 July 2015
38. Niu, J., Bu, X., Qian, K., Li, Z.: An indoor scene recognition method combining global and saliency region features. Robot **37**(1), 122–128 (2015)
39. Chen, Z., Xia, J., Bai, J., Xu, M.: Feature extraction algorithm based on evolutionary deep learning. Comput. Sci. **42**(11), 288–292 (2015)
40. Gong, Z.H., Zhuo, Y.: Research on cyberspace situational awareness. J. Soft. **21**(7), 1605–1619 (2010)
41. Sun, R.: Research and Implement of Technologies for Situation Assessment. Dissertation of Degree of Postgraduate of Xidian University, Shaanxi, Xi'an, January 2009
42. Lei, Y.: Research on Situation and Threat Assessment Based on Intuitionistic Fuzzy Reasoning. Dissertation of Degree of Doctor of Xidian University, Shaanxi, Xi'an, October, 2005
43. Wang, Y.: Situaiton Assessment Using Probabilistic Graphical Model. Dissertation of Degree of Postgraduate of Beijing Institute of Technolog, Beijing, December 2011

Intelligent Behavior Modeling on Information Delivery of Time-Sensitive Targets

Chi-Jung Jung and Il-Chul Moon[✉]

Department of Industrial and Systems Engineering,
KAIST, Daejeon 305701, South Korea
{wjdclwjd,icmoon}@kaist.ac.kr

Abstract. This thesis introduces a case study of utilizing the decentralized partially observableMarkov decision process (DEC-POMDP) in modeling information delivery behavior under the network centric warfare settings. The deployed troops are modeled as bounded rational agents, and they have different communication success possibilities in the long range and the short range. Our DEC-POMDP model indicates how to deliver time-sensitive target information from the monitoring agent to the headquarter through multiple bridging agents. The bridging agents should intelligently decide which information to transmit through the long range or delegate the transfer to other agents via short range communications. Our models shed light on the improved information delivery behavior that are inferred from the DEC-POMDP model with simulation based experiments. We expect that this research would play a role in improving Tactics, Techniques, and Procedures (TTP) in the field operation.

1 Introduction

Deep infilteration scout units conducting enemy area survelliance should maintain the minimum communication as well as ensure the information delivery to a distant headquarter. This information is considered high reliability and plays an important role in influencing the quality of determined strategy. On the battle field, there are many factors to lower the success rate of the communication equipment, and terrain factors make up a large proportion of the diruption factors. For instance, there is a place that reduces the success probability of the communication; and an opposite situation also exists. Traditional approach is always trying to use the long-range radio communication for the information delivery to the headquarter, and the team which is situated in such challenging position would not be able to deliver the information on time.

This paper suggests an alternative approach compared to the traditional one by adopting an emerging network structure with a short-range communication radio. In particular, while an AM radio set for long-range communication is influenced by external factors; a FM radio set for short-range has a short distance range but is robust to external disrupting factors, such as the terrain. This paper

© Springer Science+Business Media Singapore 2016
L. Zhang et al. (Eds.): AsiaSim 2016/SCS AutumnSim 2016, Part II, CCIS 644, pp. 578–587, 2016.
DOI: 10.1007/978-981-10-2666-9_58

proposes a communication model where a unit with an adverse AM communication condition delivers a information via the adjacent unit with good reception for AM communication using FM communication. The proposed model can help increase the amount of gathered information in order to ensure a quick tempo of the surveillance operation.

The purpose of this study is to derive an optimal policy through the proposed communication model and analyze whether it is actually effective. We model (1) the scout units as agents and (2) the success probability of the communication as environments. These agents operate in the bounded situational awareness phase, and the agents are decentralized and independent.

To reflect the process where agents obtain partial observations from the environment to improve the level of situation awareness and select the optimal action using observations, the partially observable Markov decision process (POMDP) is used. [1,2] However, the sole application of POMDP does not model the separated agents' context. Therefore, decentralized agents act with the other operational agents in mind wihtout their actual context. This leads us to adopt the decentralized partially observable Markov decision process (DEC-POMDP). The agents behave by following DEC-POMDP models, and the team performance of the agents were measured in the agent-based simulation environment [3].

2   Previous Research

Markov decision processes (MDPs) provide a foundation for much of the work on stochastic planning. [4] Researchers in this area have studied the extensions of the basic model that are suitable for multi-agent systems. In multi-agent systems, agents have their own policies, and there are two perspectives of multi-agent policies: centralized ones and decentralized ones. While the centralized policies specify the decision of the agents according to the global system state, the decentralized policies, which correspond to the decisions of situated agents, must assume only a partial knowledge of the system in each agent and must deal with the communication explicitly. [5] Fig. 1 shows the key difference between a centralized policy and a decentralized policy. A centralized policy assumes the global state as the starting point, but in a decentralized policy, the global state is not automatically observed by the agents. [6]

Our simulation scenario requires that agents are placed in a decentralized situation and are generally autonomous. Bernstein [8] extends the POMDP model to allow multiple distributed agents to each receive local observations and base their decisions on these observations. Becker [9] studied one way to avoid this complexity obstacle, which is to exploit the structure of the domain offered by some special classes of DEC-MDPs. In that model, two agents operate independently but are tied together through a reward structure that depends on both of their execution histories. Goldman [10] proposed DEC-POMDP with communication (DEC-POMDP-COM). In that study, he presents an analytical model to evaluate the tradeoff between the cost of communication and the value of the information received. Becker [11,12] also studied a class of DEC-MDPs that

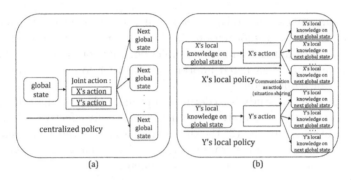

Fig. 1. Figure (a) shows the way to solve the problem under such a policy in a two-agent system with agent X and Y. The expected utility of the next state in Figure (a) can be calculated using a standard policy evaluation algorithm for Markov decision processes. It can be handled as a big state simply composed of each agent's states. [7] However, Figure (b) shows the process of problem solving under a decentralized environment. At any time step, each agent decides what local action to take and gains some observations from it (if any). Using those observations, local knowledge is updated and the agent enters the next state with it.

restrict the interactions between the agents to a structured, event-driven dependency. He focused on the property that the number of dependencies is much smaller than the number of states for many problems.

3   Methodology

This section describes how to implement the two models that move under the various input variables from the combat environment. Specifically, we describe the planning process, which can offer a policy to each agent using DEC-POMDP with prior settings from the information of the combat environment. Figure 2 shows the concept map of this research.

3.1   Rational Behavior Model

DEC-POMDP is a formalism when a rational agent with bounded situation awareness behaves in a decentralized situation [13]. Here, we formalize the ten-agent control problem as a cooperative and decentralized decision problem.

Tuples of Model. The inference on our DEC-POMDP model on communication provides an action policy on how to create such an emergent communication network. Our DEC-POMDP model is defined by a tuple $< S, A, \Omega, P, O, R >$, where $S = s_1 \times s_2 \times ... s_N$ is a finite set of world states. $A = a_1 \times a_2 \times ... \times a_N$ is a finite set of actions that consist of the AM communication attempt and request to another agent using FM. Ω is the set of all observations for each of the agents, P is a transition function, O is the observation function, and R is a reward function.

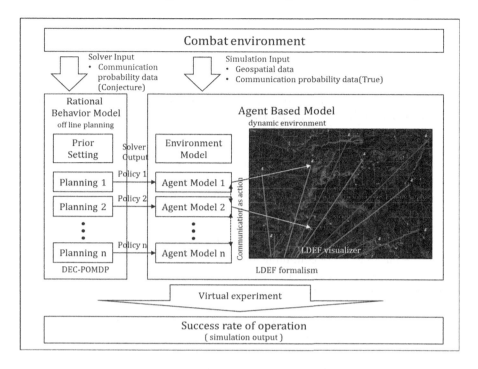

Fig. 2. Concept map of this research

State. In order to consider information of another agent's state, we define s_i as $s_i = < E_i, C^{AM,i}, C_i^{FM,j}, C^{AM,j}, Ready^j, Wait^j >$ where s_i is the state of $agent_i$, $E_i \in \{DecisionMaking, Operating, Success, Failure\}$ is the mission state of s_i, $C_i^{FM,j}$ is the success probability of communication between $agent_i$ and $agent_j$. So $C_i^{FM,j}$ is influenced by terrain properties. $Ready^j$ is the readiness condition of $agent_j$ to relay $agent_i$'s request. So $Ready^j$ is the binary value and $Ready^j = 1$ when $agent_j$'s mission is accomplished. And $Wait^j$ is the information whether $agent_j$ is already relaying another agent's requests. The agent has exact knowledge on t_i and E_i, but a probabilistic belief on $C^{i,j}$, $Ready^j$, and $Wait^j$. Therefore, we use belief states with partial observation about $C^{AM,i}, C_i^{FM,j}, C^{AM,j}, Ready^j$, and $Wait^j$ after actions.

$s_i = < E_i, C^{AM,i}, C_i^{FM,j}, C^{AM,j}, Ready^j, Wait^j >$, $i \neq j, j \in N = \{index\ of\ agents\}$

$E_i \in \{DecisionMaking, Operating, Success, Failure\} = \{E^d, E^o, E^s, E^f\}$

$C^{AM,i} = $ AM communication probability of $agent_i$

$C_i^{FM,j} = $ FM communication probability between $agent_i$ and $agent_j$

$C^{AM,j} = $ AM communication probability of $agent_j$

$Ready^j$ = binary value whether $agent_j$ already accomplished the mission($i \neq j$)

$Wait^j$ = binary value whether $agent_j$'s AM equipment is already used by someone.

E, which is the initial letter of engagement, means the state of operation that the agent currently behaves in. So the agent has one of 4 state of E, including *decision making, operating success, and failure* state. *Decision making* means a moment where the agent makes a decision to choose one action among various options. *Operating means* that after *decision making*, the agent takes some action and waits for observation. So the agent stays in this *Operating state* until observation is obtained. *Success* is a state where the agent obtains a observation where the AM communication is successful and report is delivered to HQ. And if the agent cannot obtain successful observation until the time is over, the agent's E makes a transition to *failure* regardless of any other condition.

C is the initial letter of communication probability. Its subscript is the sender of the action, which is placed on the first superscript. The second superscript means the receiver of the action. So $C_i^{FM,j}$ means the short range radio communication between $agent_i$ and $agent_j$ using FM radio equipment. This value of C is important because it is used in the process of state transition and determines the expectation value on next reachable state.

Because every agent basically provides priority to its own mission, the agent that has already succeeded can handle another agent's request. *Ready* is the probability of whether the agent of the superscript is ready to relay for another agent's request. $Ready^j$ has a binary value, which is 1 or 0 so if $agent_j$ succeeded at once, and $Ready^j$ is updated as 1 and never changes because the agent's success state never changes.

$Wait$ means the probability that the waitline of the agent, which can handle another agent's request has no user and is thus available. $Agent_i$ recognizes that $agent_j$'s waitline is empty and $agent_j$ can help $agent_i$ at once, and so the value of $Wait_i^j$ is updated as 1 and never changes. The reason that value is never changed is different from the value of $Ready$, because the agent that firstly recognizes that $Wait_i^j$ is 1 has priority to use $agent_j$.

An agent has exact knowledge on E, but a probabilistic belief on C, $Ready$, and $Wait$. Therefore, the agent should update its belief on C, $Ready$, and $Wait$ until E is updated to E^s or E^f to make a rational decision at the most. So we need the belief state $b_i = < E_i, \hat{C}^{AM,i}, \hat{C}_i^{FM,j}, \hat{C}^{AM,j}, \hat{Ready}^j, \hat{Wait}^j >$ as belief on state s_i. In this tuple, $\hat{Ready}_i^j$ does not mean the binary value but the probability that $agent_i$ already accomplished the mission. This is also true with $\hat{Wait}_i^j$. It means that $agent_i$'s equipment is already used by someone. In this context, there might be some gap between the real value and the conjecture. And the agent's conjecture can be changed according to the observation of the next state after taking action because the agent uses $\hat{C}_i, \hat{Ready}^j$, and $\hat{Wait}^j$ as a transition probability instead of $C_i, Ready^j$, and $Wait^j$; the accuracy of them is important to make a right decision.

Belief State Update. Because C is not deterministic and the information about C is partially observable, we require belief states on its estimation. Belief states about the success probability of a communication equipment are continuous, and we can present it as a distribution form. Among these tuples, the update of the conjecture C is a very important part. So $\hat{C}_i$ can be defined as the conjecture of success probability of the related equipment. $\hat{C}_i$ can be presented as the distribution form of belief on the success probabilities of communication, which has the value of 0 to 1. Hence, C can be expressed as probability density function (PDF) form on continuous probabilities. From the property that the vector of belief state has the value from 0 to 1, the PDF of the Beta distribution is suitable because the Beta distribution has an x axis, which has a value of 0 to 1, and the total area under the density curve equals a probability of one. Then the belief state update is as follows:

$$b(C) \sim beta(\alpha, \beta)$$

$$b^{ao}(C') = \frac{P(o|C', a)}{P(o|b, a)} \int_0^1 (P(C'|C, a)b(C)) \, \mathrm{d}C$$

$$P(o|b, a) = \int_0^1 (P(o|C', a))(\int_0^1 (P(C'|C, a)b(C)) \, \mathrm{d}C) \, \mathrm{d}C'$$

And to calculate the state transition probability, the values of the vector should be converged to one value. That expectation value can be obtained as follows:

$$\hat{C}' = \int_0^1 (b^{ao}(C') \times C') \, \mathrm{d}C'$$

After the update is done, the agent can use C value as the transition probability in the transition function. Initial vector values of belief state are defined from a distribution that has a communication success probability of the equipment as the mean value and value of 0.005 as the variance value.

4   Results

Figure 3 shows some of the experimental cases from a visualized tool during a specific period of simulation. Agents' behavior can be explained well by Fig. 3. After beginning operation, all agents try to communicate with AM. After 10 min, every agents gets messages of success (agents 5, 6, 7, 9 : mission accomplished), but the rest have failed. First, because the AM trial has failed, agents 1, 2, 3, 4, 8, and 10 should act to maximize their probability of success. At the same time, agents 1, 3 and 4 take action with AM as soon as they receive negative messages, but agents 2, 8, and 10 try to connect to adjacent agents, which may be succeed. After three minutes, agent 2's FM attempt is successful but agent 1 is not ready to relay. Agent 8's FM try is successful and agent 7's mission is already done. However, agent 10's FM try has failed. Thus, agent 2 who thinks agent 1 cannot help agent 2 to try to communicate by itself. So agent 8 asks agent 7 to relays information so that agent 7 relay it. Agent 10 tries to

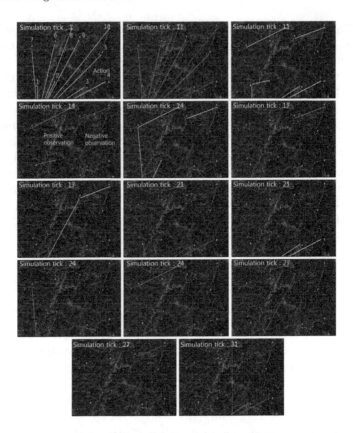

Fig. 3. The screenshots of the virtual experiment in arbitrary area of Gangwon-do. Red spot represent agent, and HQ is represented as one point of outer area of the map. Yellow line is attempt at AM communication, FM and Relay. Red line is negative observation from trying (yellow line). On the contrary, green line is the positive observation from trying (yellow line). Thus, after the related time of trying is passed, the red or green line is followed after the yellow line. One simulation tick correspond with one minute. (Color figure online)

engage in FM communication again. Then, agent 10 gains a positive observation from it after three minutes and asks agent 9 to relay. After three minutes, the agents who try to do AM communication 10 min before gets the observation that agent 1 has succeeded (agent 1 : mission accomplished) but agents 3 and 4 have failed again. Thus, agents 3 and 4 try AM one more time. Three minutes later, agent 2 and agent 7 obtain a negative and positive observation in the AM trial respectively (agent 2 : mission failed, agent 7 : mission accomplished). Agent 7 shares these contents with agent 8, which is waiting to use FM (agent 8 : mission accomplished). At 27 min, agent 9 has a negative observation about the AM trial at 14 min and share this with agent 10 (agent 10 : mission failed). At 31 min, agent 3 is finally succeeded (agent 3 : mission accomplished), but agent 4 is not (agent 4 : mission failed). In this one experimental case, agents 1, 3, 5, 6, 7, 8 and 9 are accomplished; their missions finally succeed, but those of agents 2 and 4 have failed. Agent 8 has succeeded using relaying, but agent 10 has failed in spite of using relaying.

Table 1. Standardized coefficient for the regression analysis by the success rate of operation after simulation against experiment variable factors. ($\dagger\dagger$: $p < 0.01$, $\dagger$: $p < 0.05$)

Experiment variable name		Standardized coefficient
Regression on success rate of operation	AM success probability of agent with good reception	0.102
	AM success probability of agent with bad reception	0.644
	Ratio of teams located at good reception in a group	0.699
	Degree of over-estimation	−0.585
Adjusted R Square		0.714

Regression analysis in metamodeling is used to analyze which factors contribute to the performance measure. Table 1 shows the meta-model from the results of simulation. The table entries indicate standardized coefficient values by the number of successful operations against experiment variable factors. This meta-model shows that all of four variables, i.e., AM success probability of agent with good reception, AM success probability of agent with bad reception, ratio of teams located at good reception in a group, and degree of over-estimation, are independent variable. No relay method in relay decisio-making is meaningless to investigate the effect of the degree of over-estimation; for the fourth independent variable, relay method with DEC-POMDP is used only. However, AM success probability of the agent with good reception has less of an influence on the result than the others do. According to this analysis, the ratio of teams located in good reception in a group and the AM success probability of an agent with bad reception are the most influential factors. It means that helping the agent who has no or short waitline is advantageous to agent which needs to help, and the AM success probability of one's own equipment is always important for robust and flexible correspondence. The sign of the fourth variable means that the smaller the overestimation is the better the operations.

5   Discussion

In this study, we made a solver named rational behavior model using DEC-POMDP formalism. In addition, when we follow the policy created in this solver, it was confirmed that this has better performance than current doctrine in various given environments. From this research, we hypothesize that this quantitative analysis and the action policy could be our improved Tactics, Techniques, and Procedures (TTP) in the field operation. Also, this method can be applied not only to an enemy area operations in depth but also the whole theater, which consists of an ad-hoc network. This proposed model in this paper has a number of limitations. Firstly, the improved method of applying a more complex system will be necessary. It will be possible using the features of the domain, as shown in this study, but it has the disadvantage that it can be applied only in special cases. A more general and improved approximation or heuristic algorithm is required. Secondly, as mentioned, the research on the agent's belief state update model requires more.

Acknowledgment. This research was supported by the Korean ICT R&D program of MSIP/IITP (R7117-16-0219, Development of Predictive Analysis Technology on Socio-Economics using Self-Evolving Agent-Based Simulation embedded with Incremental Machine Learning).

References

1. Sondik, E.J.: The optimal control of partially observable Markov processes. No. SU-SEL-71-017. Stanford Univ Calif Stanford Electronics Labs (1971)
2. Kaelbling, L.P., Littman, M.L., Cassandra, A.R.: Planning and acting in partially observable stochastic domains. Artif. Intell. **101**(1), 99–134 (1998)
3. Bae, J.W., Lee, G., Moon, I.-C.: Formal specification supporting incremental and flexible agent-based modeling. In: Proceedings of the 2012 Winter Simulation Conference (WSC). IEEE (2012)
4. Puterman, M.L.: Markov Decision Processes: Discrete Stochastic Dynamic Programming. Wiley, New York (2014)
5. Russell, S., Norvig, P.: Artificial Intelligence: A Modern Approach. Prentice Hall, Englewood Cliffs (1995)
6. Xuan, P., Lesser, V.: Multi-agent policies: from centralized ones to decentralized ones. In: Proceedings of the First International Joint Conference on Autonomous Agents and Multiagent Systems: part 3. ACM (2002)
7. Bellman, R.: A Markovian decision process. No. P-1066. RAND CORP SANTA MONICA CA (1957)
8. Bernstein, D.S.: The complexity of decentralized control of Markov decision processes. Math. Oper. Res. **27**(4), 819–840 (2002)
9. Becker, R., et al.: Transition-independent decentralized Markov decision processes. In: Proceedings of the Second International Joint Conference on Autonomous Agents and Multiagent Systems. ACM (2003)
10. Goldman, C.V., Zilberstein, S.: Optimizing information exchange in cooperative multi-agent systems. In: Proceedings of the Second International Joint Conference on Autonomous Agents and Multiagent Systems. ACM (2003)

11. Becker, R., Zilberstein, S., Lesser, V.: Decentralized Markov decision processes with event-driven interactions. In: Proceedings of the Third International Joint Conference on Autonomous Agents and Multiagent Systems, vol. 1. IEEE Computer Society (2004)
12. Becker, R.: Solving transition independent decentralized Markov decision processes. J. Artif. Intell. Res. **22**, 423–455 (2004)
13. Wiering, M., van Otterlo, M. (eds.): Reinforcement Learning: State-of-the-Art, vol. 12. Springer Science & Business Media, New York (2012)

Design and Application of Exterior Ballistics Simulation and Data Analysis Tool for EMRG

Dongxing Qi, Ping Ma[✉], and Xiaobing Shang

Control and Simulation Center, Harbin Institute of Technology,
Harbin, People's Republic of China
{Qidongxing01,shangxiaobing1}@163.com, pingma@hit.edu.cn

Abstract. The general structural design and operation process of the existing electromagnetic railgun (EMRG) simulation tools are defective. Aiming to solve the problems, including functional singleness, poor extensibility and inflexibility, the EMRG exterior ballistics simulation and data analysis tool is designed and developed in this paper. Firstly, in order to realize its functions, the requirement analysis of exterior ballistics simulation and data analysis is presented and the overall structural design and operation process of this tool are obtained. Secondly, this comprehensive tool is developed by Microsoft Visual Studio 2010, and based on the modularization theory, the tool realizes exterior ballistics simulation according to the six-DOF model, applications in various data analysis methods and report generation, etc. Finally, the application case shows that the tool can meet the requirement of the simulation and data analysis of the EMRG exterior ballistics and it is easy to operate. Therefore, the tool has significance to the study of the EMRG exterior ballistics.

Keywords: Electromagnetic railgun · Exterior ballistics simulation · Data analysis · Sensitivity analysis

1 Introduction

Electromagnetic railgun (EMRG) is a typical representative of the electromagnetic emission weapons. As a new concept of weapon-system, it has the advantage of faster response and higher damage [1] compared with conventional guns. The simulation of exterior ballistics and data analysis are the two important components in EMRG research. The former part, simulation of exterior ballistics, not only play a wide and important role in the design of EMRG, tabulation and compilation, but also in model validation, combat and equipment simulation [2]. And the other part, EMRG data analysis, it refers to process of depth analysis and conclusion of data produced from the simulation of EMRG system in advance with the appropriate method [3]. The data analysis methods, specially, include sensitivity analysis [4–7], linear regression analysis [8], variance analysis [9, 10], principal component analysis [11] and typical correlation analysis [12]. Therefore, EMRG exterior ballistics simulation and appropriate analysis method selection will be valuable for the whole system construction and evaluation.

© Springer Science+Business Media Singapore 2016
L. Zhang et al. (Eds.): AsiaSim 2016/SCS AutumnSim 2016, Part II, CCIS 644, pp. 588–596, 2016.
DOI: 10.1007/978-981-10-2666-9_59

Nevertheless, the problems at present mainly exist in two aspects. Firstly, researches in this field are still limited to the exterior ballistics simulation, experiment design and its data analysis. Furthermore, it's difficult to complete the integrated exterior ballistics simulation and data analysis research [13–15]. Secondly, the lack or the inappropriate design for overall design in the exterior ballistics simulation and data analysis tools, leads to awkward ability in extension and reoperation for the software. According to the two aspects, on one hand, for the improvement of efficiency of exterior ballistics simulation and data analysis, so as the management in distribution of simulation resource, it's a very must to design auxiliary tool. The tool should be designed from two aspects of functional structure and running process to support corresponding research. And on the other hand, with the deep research of the exterior ballistics simulation and data analysis, the tool's general and comprehensive requirements of the users are becoming more and more strictly. Thus, in order to simulate the exterior ballistics of the electromagnetic gun easily and efficiently, as well as analyze the simulation data accurately and effectively, it's very essential to develop a comprehensive tool.

This paper aims at the research status of EMRG system and the problems which exist in exterior ballistics simulation and data analysis tools. A comprehensive tool is drawn up and developed based on requirement analysis of exterior ballistics simulation and data as well as modularization theory, using Visual Studio 2010. This tool makes up of database management, exterior ballistics simulation, experimental design, data analysis and analysis report generation, and other functions. Finally, the application case results show the feasibility and effectiveness of the tool, and the tool can provide a foundation for EMRG weapon system research.

2   Requirement Analysis of Exterior Ballistic Simulation and Data Analysis Tool

As the first part of software development, requirement analysis aims to determine the specific tasks of software design and performance requirement based on the target of clients. According the problems existing in the field of exterior ballistics simulation and data analysis at present, the tool should include the functions as below.

- Exterior Ballistics Simulation
  Firstly, to deal with the enormous data produced from the simulation, it demands on unified database in EMRG ballistics simulation for effective utilization and storage, which stores the data from experiment for its query, addition, deletion, so as its writing and reading, display, etc.

  Secondly, Established on the basis of theory of probability and mathematical method of statistics, experiment design is supposed to be a kind of economic and scientific techniques. Due to both outside and inside inevitable effect, suitable plan for the experiment should be set in advance for researchers to achieve the best result.

  In the last, the model of EMRG exterior ballistics describes the process of projectile's movement after leaving the railgun with a high speed in the atmosphere. It is the foundation of exterior ballistics simulation and the characteristic analysis of ballistics. Researchers need to consider EMRG's shooting range, high altitude flight, the variation of the earth curvature and gravitational acceleration. Supported by the Six-DOF model of projectiles, the simulation of exterior ballistics is realized. According to the initial input, the simulation can get the accurate result of the output, so as to be convenient for the firing accuracy analysis of the exterior ballistics and the evaluation of the whole system.

- Data Analysis

    Due to enormous data produced by the simulation experiment with various parameters, researchers need to analyze the effect to results produced by the different factors, like effect on firing accuracy. And it demands on the tools of exterior ballistics simulation and data analysis for data's introduction, standardization, analysis method choose, process and analysis.

- Report Generation

    In the last step, after the exterior ballistics simulation and data analysis, all data from the simulation and data analysis need to be stored for query and filing, which demands the tool can support automotive report generation.

3 Design of Exterior Ballistics Simulation and Data Analysis Tool

Overall design is a very important step in the process of completing the development of software tools. After the requirement analysis of the exterior ballistics simulation and the data analysis tool of the EMRG, it is essential to design the tool from many aspects. So this section will describe the problem from two aspects which are the tool's design of the functional structure and the running process.

3.1 Design of the Function Structure

According to the demand of users, the exterior ballistics simulation and data analysis tools are mainly divided into exterior ballistics simulation module, data analysis module and report generation module. In the tool, each module is closely related to the database. Users can manage the database through the interactive interface of each module and transfer the corresponding data and parameters to each module, and then the simulation data analysis results are got. There are two aspects in exterior ballistics simulation module which are database connection and exterior ballistics simulation. Various functions have been well implemented in this module, such as database management, configuration of parameters, aerodynamic configuration, test design management and model calculation. Data analysis module is composed of three parts that are data statistical analysis, data preprocessing and sensitivity analysis. In this module, firstly, the function of data statistics analysis includes variance analysis and regression analysis. Lately, the function of data preprocessing consists of singular point elimination, normal test and correlation analysis. Furthermore, sensitivity analysis function includes sensitivity analysis method selection and sampling method selection. The function of the specific module is shown in Fig. 1.

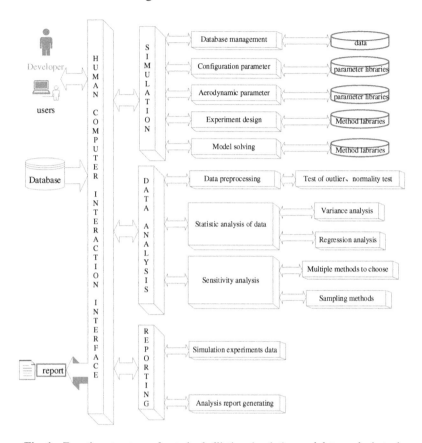

Fig. 1. Function structure of exterior ballistics simulation and data analysis tool

3.2 Design of the Running Process

Based on the function of each module in the tool, the corresponding running process is designed. Firstly, based on the requirement analysis, the content of the two aspects which are exterior ballistic simulation and data analysis is confirmed. Secondly, the database is established by using different EMRG simulation parameters in the parameter library and factor library. And then choose the reasonable and effective experimental design method to get the experimental design of the exterior ballistic simulation model solving. So we can get the simulation data for the data analysis through model solving. The data are preprocessed, and the singular value is removed. In the same time, the normality of the data is tested, and the correlation is analyzed. Based on the processed data, the analysis is carried out, such as investigating the effect of some input to output, and the credibility of the model dynamic output. Furthermore, choose the appropriate analysis method, which are statistics analysis or sensitivity analysis. Finally, the useful data generated in the analysis process is saved into the resource database and the data analysis report will be generated according to the requirement. The specific flow is shown in Fig. 2.

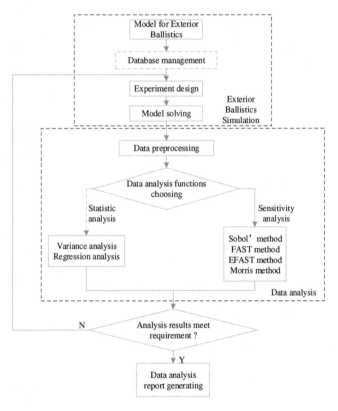

Fig. 2. The flow of exterior ballistics simulation and data analysis tool

4   Application of Exterior Ballistics Simulation and Data Analysis Tool

According to the requirement analysis and design scheme of the exterior ballistics simulation and data analysis tool, this section modularizes the comprehensive tool for exterior ballistics of EMRG by Visual Studio 2010 platform of the ribbon interactive interface in every stage. Then the tool is applied in the case of EMRG's firing accuracy analysis. In the case, with the purpose of researching the influence of model output according to the uncertain input factors of the model, firstly, six factors determinedly have an impact on ballistic range are extracted based on the prior knowledge. In the last, the influence of each input factor on the firing accuracy is obtained by the tool. The following are the analysis and instructions of exterior ballistics simulation, data analysis, Generation report management which are all key module functions respectively.

4.1 Exterior Ballistics Simulation

Two main functions of database connection and exterior ballistic model simulation are realized well in exterior ballistics simulation module. The database connection includes new database establish, existing databases connection and database login, in order to make it more convenient for data import, storage and output. Exterior ballistics model simulation includes configuration parameters, aerodynamic configuration, test of designing management and model calculation function, users can adjust the environment parameters, projectile parameters and aerodynamic parameters as desired. After setting the environment variables and other factors, the user can choose the reasonable design method and the solution in exterior ballistics simulation interface, and the corresponding output results can be obtained by solving the model.

The experiment design methods include Monte Carlo Sampling, Latin Hypercube Sampling and user-defined methods. And the simulation model is based on Six-DOF model of projectiles. Those motion equations are dynamic equations of projectile's centroid, dynamic equations around the centroid, kinematics equations of the centroid, kinematics equations around the centroid, etc. The relevant equations are shown in reference [16], and the interpretations are omitted here due to the limitation of paper's number. The database connection and management interface is shown in Fig. 3. And in Fig. 4, which is the exterior ballistics simulation interface, we choose the Monte Carlo experiment design method, set the sampling times are 100. Then model solving is completed and the scatter diagram in two directions is drawn.

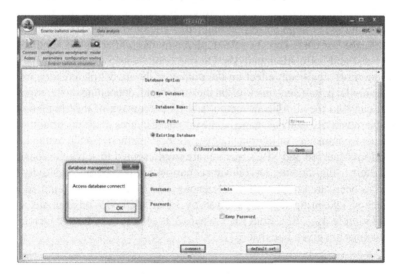

Fig. 3. Database connection and management interface

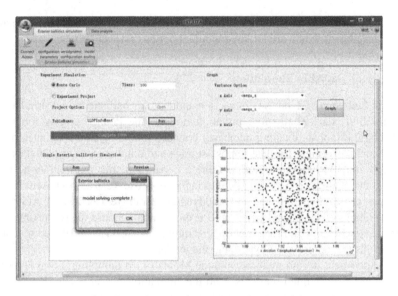

Fig. 4. Exterior ballistics simulation interface

4.2 Data Analysis

The key module for data analysis includes three functions, data statistics analysis, data preprocessing and sensitivity analysis. The data statistics analysis includes data information, analysis of variance and regression analysis and other functions. This module uses the traditional statistical methods to analyze the fluctuation of simulation data series which is defined the discreteness. Data preprocessing is a way for the user preprocess the simulation data through corresponding data validation method to ensure the simulation rationality of data. This module implements the outlier test of simulation data, normality test and correlation analysis. On one hand, sensitivity analysis method can find out the most significant effect on the output of the model parameters, in order to correct the model parameters quickly. On the other hand, depending on the experimental results, it can find the significant factors and its percentage of the simulation output through the sensitivity analysis, namely, the influence degree of the uncertainty of simulation system parameters on output indexes. Sobol' method, FAST method, EFAST method Morris method and SRCs method are implemented to solve the sensitivity of the parameters in this module. The relevant equations of the previous sensitivity analysis methods has been already showed in reference [16, 17], thus they are omitted here. As showed below, take firing accuracy analysis by Sobol' method as an example, assuming the gained sample $A_{N \times r}$, $B_{N \times r}$ from LHS, where N is sample size, k is the factor number, some equations are given like that

$$f_0 \approx \frac{1}{N} \sum_{j=1}^{N} f(A)_j \quad V + f_0^2 \approx \frac{1}{N} \sum_{j=1}^{N} f^2(A)_j \tag{1}$$

$$V_i + f_0^2 \approx \frac{1}{N} \sum_{j=1}^{N} f(A)_j f\left(B_A^{(i)}\right)_j \quad V_{-i} + f_0^2 \approx \frac{1}{N} \sum_{j=1}^{N} f(A)_j f\left(A_B^{(i)}\right)_j \tag{2}$$

where under the condition of A is unchangeable, change the i'th column of B into A to get $A_B^{(i)}$, and the same method to get $B_A^{(i)}$. Thus the first-order sensitivity S_i and total sensitivity S_{Ti} of the parameter i can be written as

$$S_i = V_i / V \quad S_{Ti} = 1 - V_{-i} / V \tag{3}$$

Firing accuracy analysis by Sobol' method interface is illustrated in Fig. 5. Set the sample size is 500, and factor size is 6, and then the simulation results can be obtained in the table. Analyze the sensitivity of longitudinal dispersion and lateral dispersion, respectively. The experimental results are viewed in the table and histograms.

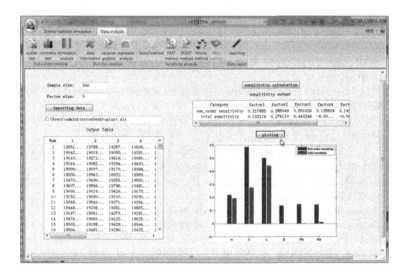

Fig. 5. Firing accuracy analysis by Sobol' method interface

4.3 Report Generation

According to the data obtained from the simulation, visual simulation results, assessment of the shooting and hit probability calculation results, the user, by calling Microsoft word for the report generation, can achieve corresponding report generation by user-defined or default method to make them convenient to check and record.

5 Conclusion and Future Work

This paper aiming at the problems, which include the single-functionality, as well as unreasonable structural design of existing exterior ballistics simulation and analysis tools, divides whole tool into a number of modules, reduce the coupling among each module, and guarantees the close of the internal relations in each module. This tool comprehensively considers each part from the whole process, including data management, exterior ballistics, experiment design, data analysis and report generation, etc. The application case indicates that the tool can fulfill the researches requirement of exterior ballistics simulation and data analysis of the EMRG system. Furthermore, its operation is convenient, and it plays a very important supporting role in the research of EMRG. Though the tool has realized the functions above, it is still defective in some fields. And in the future, it seems to be a promotion to make its expansion in data analysis, enhancement in auxiliary tools interface and visualization, etc.

References

1. Fan, C.-Z., Wang, W.-K.: The development of electromagnetic railgun. J. Yanshan Univ. **31**(5), 377–386 (2007)
2. Wang, H.-J., Cao, Y.-J., Wang, C.-X.: Review of the development of the electromagnetic railgun in the United States Navy. Ship Sci. Technol. **32**(2), 138–143 (2010)
3. Luan, W.-P., She, Y.-X., Wang, B.: AMI Data Analysis Method. J. Chin. Electr. Eng. **35**(1), 25–36 (2015)
4. Sobol, I.M.: Theorems and examples on high dimensional model representation. Reliab. Eng. Syst. Saf. **79**(2), 187–193 (2003)
5. Cukier, R.I., Fortuin, C.M., Shuler, K.E.: Study of the sensitivity of coupled reaction systems to uncertainties in rate coefficients. Chem. Phys. **59**, 3873–3878 (1973)
6. Saltelli, A., Tarantola, S., Chan, K.P.S.: A quantitative model independent met hold for global sensitivity analysis of model output. Technometrics **41**, 39–56 (1999)
7. Morris, M.D.: Factorial sampling plans for preliminary computational experiments. Technometrics **33**, 161–174 (1991)
8. Yi, F.: Linear return analyzed with MATLAB. Softw. Tech. **23**(1), 68–69 (2004)
9. Yang, X.-y.: Discussion of variance analysis: the single factor variance analysis. Exp. Sci. Technol. **11**(1), 41–43 (2013)
10. Lv, D.-l., Cao, Z.-y., Deng, B., Wang, Y.-f.: Application of variance analysis in model validation. Comput. Simul. **23**(8), 46–48 (2006)
11. Nie, H.-z., Nie, S., Qiao, Y., Lv, P.: Comprehensive decision-making of alternative transmission network planning based on principal component analysis. Power Syst. Technol. **34**(6), 134–138 (2010)
12. Sun, Y.: An empirical study on the influencing factors of customer life cycle based on canonical correlation analysis. J. Anhui Polytechnic Univ. **26**(3), 80–83 (2011)
13. Bologna, M., Marracci, M., Micheletti, R., et al.: Resonant shield concept as alternative solution inrailguns. In: 2014 17th International Symposium on Electromagnetic Launch Technology (EML), pp. 1–5. IEEE (2014)
14. McNab, I.R.: Minimization of the input power for a long railgun. IEEE Trans. Magn. **39**(1), 498–500 (2003)
15. McNab, I.R., Crawford, M.T., Satapathy, S.S., et al.: IAT armature development. IEEE Trans. Plasma Sci. **39**(1), 442–451 (2011)
16. Xiao-bing, S.: Research on firing accuracy analysis and evaluation techniques of electromagnetic railgun exterior ballistic, pp. 7–29. Harbin Institute of Technology (2015)
17. Ling-yun, L.: Research on sensitivity analysis methods and tool based on simulation experiments, pp. 7–16. Harbin Institute of Technology (2013)

Inverse Modeling of Combat Behavior with Virtual-Constructive Simulation Training

Doyun Kim, Do-Hyeong Kim, and Il-Chul Moon[✉]

Department of Industrial and Systems Engineering,
KAIST, Daejeon 305701, South Korea
{maybedy,dhkim.aai,icmoon}@kaist.ac.kr

Abstract. Modeling combat behavior is an important, yet complicated task because the combat behavior emerges from the rationality as well as the irrationality. For instance, when a soldier confronts a dilemma on accomplishing his mission and saving his life, it is difficult to model his ongoing thoughts with a simple model. This paper presents (1) how to reconstruct a realistic combat environment with a virtual-constructive simulation, and (2) how to model such combat behavior with the inverse reinforcement learning. The virtual-constructive simulation is a well-known simulation application for soldier training. Previous works on this virtual-constructive simulation focuses on a small number of entities and mission phases, so it was difficult to observe the frequent behavior dilemma in the field. This work presents a large scale and a complete brigade-level operation to provide such synthetic environment to human player. Then, our second work is observing the com-bat behavior through the virtual-constructive simulations, and modeling the behavior with the inverse reinforcement learning. Surely, we can observe the descriptive statistics of the observed behavior, but the inverse reinforcement learning provides calibrated weights on the valuation on hypothetical rewards from conflicting goals. Our study is the first attempt on merging the large-scale virtual constructive simulation and the inverse reinforcement learning on such massive scale.

1 Introduction

1.1 Introduction

Modeling behavior of combat entities is a challenging task because of their complex reasonings as well as instinctive reactions. Firstly, the reasonings and the reactions becomes the latent dynamics of behavior that is only to be observed as a resulted mixture of the two separate dynamics. Secondly, the drivers of the reasonings and the reactions are diverse, and the drivers consist of intrinsic information, such as the states of the combat entities, the task assignment, as well as external contexts, such as the formation of the friendlies and the detection of the opposition forces. These two challenging factors require the combat entity behavior models to incorporate both probabilistic aspect and guidance by human experts.

© Springer Science+Business Media Singapore 2016
L. Zhang et al. (Eds.): AsiaSim 2016/SCS AutumnSim 2016, Part II, CCIS 644, pp. 597–606, 2016.
DOI: 10.1007/978-981-10-2666-9_60

The most recent and popular approach on this problem is using the Markov decision process, or MDP, in the behavior modeling. MDP [1] provides a probabilistic framework on the behavior modeling, and a modeler can provide a guidance by modifying the rewards per the state and the action of the combat entities. The role of MDP is maximizing the reward by choosing an action to make a state transition toward a state providing further reward. To adopt this in the combat entity modeling, a modeler should enumerate (1) the possible state list, (2) the action list of the combat entity, (3) the probabilistic transition of the states through the actions, and (4) the reward for each state. While MDP provides the natural framework for the probabilistic behavior modeling, the hurdle is not removed, but transformed. The previous problem of moderating the intrinsic reaction, the rule-guided behavior, and the rational behavior is just becoming the reward design of the MDP formulaton. Therefore, using MDP does give a niche start on modeling the combat behavior, yet it does not provide a complete answer.

One way of modeling this complicated reward in MDP is learning from the observations on the subject-matter experts' behaviors. This approach is called as inverse reinforcement learning, or IRL. IRL maintains the utilization of MDP, but the reward structure is supervised by the human training examples [2,3]. The result of IRL, which is the estimated reward function of the experts, becomes a soft guidance to the autonomous agent in the simulation. The IRL approach is generally used in a simple context, such as a scroll action game, and this approach is not used in a complicated defense simulation as in this paper [4,5].

This paper applies the IRL based behavior modeling to the logs of virtual-constructive simulation, or VC simulation [6,7], that is a human-in-the-loop combat simulation. A tank in the VC simulation is operated by a human, who can be either subject-matter experts or non-experts, and we learn and contrast the reward functions from the two different groups of operators. This provides a deeper understanding in what would be the rational of individual combat entity behaviors, and this understanding will contribute the combat behavior modeling of autonomous agents with the MDP framework.

2   Problem Formulation

IRL is a technique to derive an estimated reward function from the observed entity behavior [3]. This paper formulate and apply to the modeling on a tank's combat behaviors through IRL. The below is the definition of MDP and IRL before we apply the framework to the combat domain.

2.1   Markov Decision Process and Reinforcement Learning

MDP is a probabilistic framework to model a sequence of behavior, or a *plan* [1]. This has become the fundamental building block of reinforcement learning and stochastic control theory [8]. MDP assumes that an agent makes a rational decision based upon the perceptions on environments and the available actions given the agent's state. MDP is defined with the below five tuples.

$$< S, A, T, R, \gamma >$$

Here, S is a set of states that an agent's full information is described at the temporal moment; A is a set of actions that are available to the agents; T is the state transition probability given the agent's current state and the executed action at the moment; R is the reward function per the visited state; and γ is the discount rate of the future reward. The transition probability and the reward function is formally defined as the below.

$$T(s, a, s') = Pr(S_{t+1} = s' | A_t = a, S_t = s)$$

$$R(s, a) = E[R_t | S_t = s, A_t = a]$$

Solving a MDP model is finding the most optimal policy, which is $\pi^*(s) = a$, that yields the highest cumulative reward over time. The optimal policy can be obtained through either value or policy iterations that are the approximation method for the optimization. During the MDP problem solving, the cumulative value on each state given the policy, $V^\pi(s)$, is useful information to derive.

$$V^\pi(s) = max_a[R(s, a) + \gamma \sum_{s' \in S} T(s, a, s')V^\pi(s')]$$

Now, reinforcement learning releases the assumption on the prior knowledge of the transition, T and the reward, R. Then, the reinforcement learning should estimate the transition and the reward, and the learning should optimize as the estimation becomes mature. Given that agents have bounded rationality on the situated world, the reinforcement learning becomes a closer depiction on the world. Basically, the estimation on the transition and the reward requires the exploration phase of the agents, and the agents start developing its policy as the perceived world becomes complete. We can apply the maximum likelihood estimation, or MLE, or the maximum a posteriori, or MAP, to estimate the distribution of the transition probability. The reward can be recorded per a state visit.

2.2   Inverse Reinforcement Learning

Inverse reinforcement learning, or IRL, is the opposite problem of the reinforcement learning. IRL estimates the reward function by observing the expert's behavior while reinforcement learning estimates the reward from the perception. This is called an inverse problem because reinforcement learning ultimately derives the behavior policy from the estimated reward, but the policy is assumed latently given in the IRL setting. In contrast to reinforcement learning, IRL derives the reward function from the behavior of experts who are considered to behave optimally.

In notations, one of IRL is solving a MDP\R model. MDP\R consists of the same tuples in MDP. However, compared to MDP, there are three different aspects that are (1) no information on T and R, (2) R as a linear sum of modeler defined feature functions, and (3) the available observation on (S_t, A_t) from experts.

$$R(s, a) = w\phi(s, a) = w_1\phi_1(s, a) + w_2\phi_2(s, a) + \cdots + w_d\phi_d(s, a)$$

The above formula indicates the structure of the reward function, R, and the feature functions, $\phi_i(s)$. The linear-sum weights of the feature functions, w_i, are the targets of learning in the IRL setting. The feature functions are the factors contributing to the determination of rewards, and the modelers supply such factors in conjunction with the action and the state in MDP\R.

The inference on w_i utilizes the linear programming for the optimization. The below formula is an objective function of the linear programming.

$$\underset{\hat{w}}{\text{maximize}} \sum_{\pi \in \Pi} p(V^{\pi_E}(s_0) - V^\pi(s_0))$$
$$\text{subject to } |\hat{w}_i| \leq 1 \qquad\qquad i = 1, 2, \cdots, d$$

The objective function maximizes the difference between the cumulative value function of $V^{\pi_E}(s_0)$ and $V^\pi(s_0)$ by indicating that $V^{\pi_E}(s_0)$ should be the most optimal in any given $\pi \in \Pi$ because π_E is given by the expert. Now, this becomes an iterated problem because the compared policy set in the linear programming has huge possible cases of policies. One approach is bootstrapping the possible policy by turning this into an iterative problem. We setup a simple policy at the start, and we infer the $\hat{w}$ from the linear programming. Then, by using the inferred reward function, we solve the MDP model to find an additional policy to maximize the reward. The additional policy and the previous policy becomes a combined set of policies for the next iteration. This approach is applicable when we only observe the expert's state-action pairs, a M sequences actions and each sequence with H state-action pairs, without knowing the expert's policy, π_E, because we only need V^{π_E} in the below.

$$V^{\pi_E}(s_0) = \frac{1}{M} \sum_{m=1}^{M} \sum_{t=0}^{H-1} \gamma^t R(s_t^m, a_t^m) = \frac{1}{M} \sum_{m=1}^{M} \sum_{t=0}^{H-1} \sum_{i=1}^{d} \gamma^t w_i \phi_i(s_t^m, a_t^m)$$

3   Virtual-Constructive Simulation and IRL Application

This section introduces the virtual-constructive simulation that produces the expert behavior sequences. Firstly, we provide an overview on the combat simulation interoperating virtual and constructive models. Secondly, we describe how to apply the inverse reinforcement learning to the simulation.

3.1   Virtual-Constructive Combat Simulation

The virtual-constructive simulation, or VC simulation, is an interoperating simulation with a constructive model and a virtual model. The constructive model

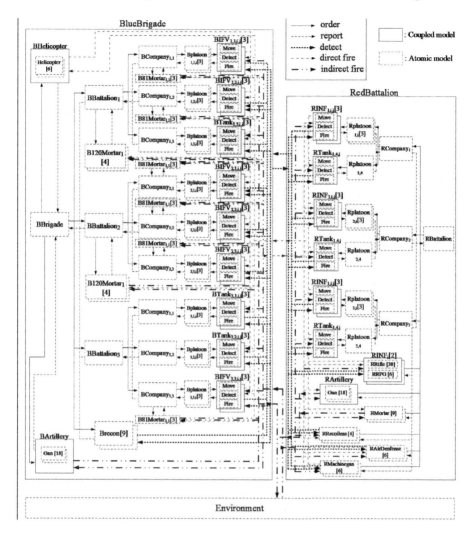

Fig. 1. DEVS hierarchy of constructive simulation

describes the behavior of various and diverse combat entities. The combat entities in the constructive model behaves autonomously in the decentralized fashion, so our constructive model follows the paradigm of agent-based modeling.
While there are multiple approaches in modeling agents, our simulation uses the
descriptive and rule-based approach. Particularly, we use the DEVS formalism to
explicitly formalize the behavior rules [9,10]. The DEVS formalism has two different types of models: coupled models and atomic models. The coupled models
collectively creates a hierarchy of simulation models by coupling the inputs and
the outputs of models. The atomic models become an individual state-transition
model that becomes the basic building blocks of the hierarchy. Figure 1 is the

Fig. 2. (Top-Left) Constructive simulation screen-capture, (Top-Right) Operation picture for command and control, (Bottom-Left) Virtual tank simulation, (Bottom-Right) Virtual helicopter simulation

DEVS model hierarchy of our constructive simulation. The hierarchy has three major components: the blue mechanized brigade, the red fortified battalion, and the combat environment. Each component except the environment has (1) command and control models, such as brigade, platoon, company models, etc. and (2) combat entity models, such as BIFV (blue infantry fighting vehicle), BTank, etc.

The virtual simulation is a detailed simulation of entities controlled by a human in a well-described virtual environment. For example, Fig. 2 shows the virtual simulation of a tank and a helicopter. As the figure shows, the tank and the helicopter are controlled by a human who can be subject-matter experts. This virtual simulation alone can be a good model for individual combat exercise or gaming. However, when the virtual simulation becomes a single simulation interoperating the constructive simulation, the virtual simulation becomes an interface of interacting with agents in the constructive model, and this is the critical aspect of the VC simulation.

3.2   Inverse Reinforcement Learning of Combat Behavior

Now, we model the IRL problem of the tank behavior learning in our VC simulation. The inputs are the observed multiple sequences of state-action pairs from the VC simulation operated by a human subject. Then, we need to define the MDP\R formulation. The most basic information to define is the state of the agent. The below is a state variable that represent the combination of various information in the simulation context.

$$S = (Dir_{Goal}, Dir_{Company}, Ind_{North}, Ind_{East},$$
$$Ind_{South}, Ind_{West}, Ind_{Fire}, Ind_{Hit}, Ind_{Damage})$$

Table 1. Reward feature function of IRL in our VC simulation

Binary feature function	Binary condition	Description
$\phi_{\{1,2,3,4\}}(s)$	$ind_{\{north,east,south,west\}} = ture$	Detection of an enemy entity in {north, east, south, west}
$\phi_{\{5,6,7,8\}}(s)$	$ind_{\{north,east,south,west\}} = ture$ $ind_{Fire} = true$	Detection of an enemy entity and a weapon fire in {north, east, south, west}
$\phi_{\{9,10,11,12\}}(s)$	$dir_{Goal} =$ $\{north, east, south, west\}$	The assult objective location is in {north, east, south, west}
$\phi_{\{13,14,15,16\}}(s)$	$dir_{Company} =$ $\{north, east, south, west\}$	The center of affiliated tank company is in {north, east, south, west}
$\phi_{\{17,18\}}(s)$	$ind_{Hit} = \{false, true\}$	Enemy hit by our weapon fire is {false,true}
$\phi_{\{19,20\}}(s)$	$ind_{Damage} = \{false, true\}$	My hit by an enemy's weapon fire is {false,true}

Dir_{Goal} indicates the relative $\{north, east, south, west\}$ of the final assault location by setting the heading of the controller tank as the exact North. We discretize the direction into four category to reduce the problem complexity. Similarly, $Dir_{Company}$ indicates the relative $\{north, east, south, west\}$ of the center of the affiliated tank company. $Ind_{\{north,east,south,west\}}$ indicates the detected enemy location. Ind_{Fire} is a boolean of the weapon fire. Ind_{Hit} is a boolean case of striking enemy with my fire. Finally, Ind_{Damage} is a boolean case of being hitted by enemy fires. This state definition is correlated to the reward features in Table 1. This is total $4 \times 4 \times 2 \times 2 \times 2 \times 2 \times 2 \times 2 = 2^{11} = 2048$ states.

Now, we define an action set with five actions: moving forward, turning right, turning left, moving backward, and weapon fire. After defining the action and the state, we can estimate the transition probability as the below. The transition probability is factorized into four different components to model the conditional independence. Each probability component is a simple maximum likelihood estimation on the observed sequence.

$$
\begin{aligned}
T(s, a, s') &= Pr(S_{(t+1)} = s' | A_t = a, S_t = s) \\
&= Pr(dir'_{Goal}, dir'_{Company} | a, dir_{Goal}, dir_{Company}) \\
&\quad \times Pr(ind'_{North}, ind'_{East}, ind'_{South}, ind'_{West} \\
&\quad\quad | a, ind_{North}, ind_{East}, ind_{South}, ind_{West}) \\
&\quad \times Pr(ind'_{Fire} | a) \times Pr(ind'_{Exact} | a) \\
&\quad \times Pr(ind'_{damage} | a, ind_{North}, ind_{East}, ind_{South}, ind_{West})
\end{aligned}
$$

Finally, we have to define the reward function for the learning. We modeled the reward function as a linear combination of feature functions in Table 1. The below formula is the articulation of the linear combination. What we expect

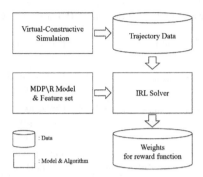

Fig. 3. Analysis process of using Virtual-Constructive simulation and Inverse Reinforcement Learning

from the mixing IRL and VC simulation is the key reward feature of the subject-matter experts' planning. Figure 3 illustrates this analysis process of IRL and the VC simulation.

$$R(s) = w \cdot \phi(s) = \sum_{k=1}^{20} (w_k \phi_k(s))$$

4   Experiment Design and Result

We experimented the behavior of combat entities with two categories of human operators: military experts and civilian. The number of subjects are three for each side, totaling six subjects. For the meaningful simulation operation, we provided a significant monetary reward for the subjects per each replication. The subject takes one tank of the blue side and assigned to complete the object assigned to the battalion that the tank is assigned. The objective is the battalion-level, so the single tank cannot achieve the goal, which means that the subject should work with the autonomous simulation combat entities. We changed the assigned battalion for three times. Each subject ran the simulation for 24 times.

Figure 4 shows the difference between the reward feature function weights in four different aspects. The displayed feature functions were selected based upon the largest difference between the civilian and the military. This could be considered as the reward difference coming from regarding the VC simulation as either a game or a training simulator. The military personnel chose to stay away from the engagement when the civilians are indifferent because the feature function on the enemy detection in the north and the weapon fire is much lower in the military compared to the civilian. However, this does not mean that the military personnel are not located at the spearhead of their company because the military prefer to put the center of the company behind of his tank, see Table 2.

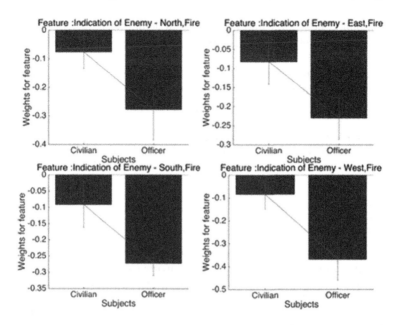

Fig. 4. Weights on the feature function on the engagement at north, east, south, and west. (Top-left, Top-right, Bottom-left, Bottom-right). The engagement is defined as detecting an enemy and firing a weapon.

Table 2. Five reward feature functions with the top five difference between the civilian and the military

Feature	Feature label	Weight difference	Civilian average	Military average
1	Indication of Enemy - North	1.944	-0.063 ± 0.927	-2.007 ± 1.526
15	Direction of Company - South	1.369	0.093 ± 0.948	1.462 ± 1.909
16	Direction of Company - West	1.271	-0.099 ± 0.838	-1.370 ± 0.915
12	Direction of Goal - West	1.259	-0.392 ± 0.428	-1.651 ± 0.618
2	Indication of Enemy - East	1.148	-0.279 ± 0.521	-1.427 ± 1.273

5   Conclusion

To our knowledge, this study is the first study of explaining a subject-matter expert behavior with a large-scale VC simulation and IRL. Previously, IRL is used in a simple setting, for instance an arcade game, a simplified highway driving, etc. Or, IRL has been used to teach a limited number of instructions, such as flipping a helicopter and hovering. Participating in a battle field with a military training is different from gaming or following a simple set of instructions. There is a rational part as well as an instinctive part, and sometimes a mandatory part, in the combat behavior. This research tells how to unfold such mixture of behavior by learning the subject-matter experts behavior in a virtual environment.

Acknowledgment. This research was supported by the Korean ICT R&D program of MSIP/IITP (R7117-16-0219, Development of Predictive Analysis Technology on Socio-Economics using Self-Evolving Agent-Based Simulation embedded with Incremental Machine Learning).

References

1. Bellman, R.: A Markovian decision process, pp. 679–684 (1957)
2. Russell, S.: Learning agents for uncertain environments (extended abstract). In: Proceedings of the 11th Annual Conference on Computational Learning Theory (COLT), pp. 101–103 (1998)
3. Ng, A., Russell, S.: Algorithms for inverse reinforcement learning. In: Proceedings of the Seventeenth International Conference on Machine Learning, pp. 663–670 (2000)
4. Ziebart, B., Maas, A., Bagnell, J., Dey, A.: Maximum entropy inverse reinforcement learning. In: AAAI, pp. 1433–1438 (2008)
5. Abbeel, P., Ng, A.Y.: Apprenticeship learning via inverse reinforcement learning, In: Proceedings of the 21st International Conference on Machine Learning (ICML), pp. 1–8 (2004)
6. Wood, C., López, P.J., Garcia, H.R., van Geest, J.: Developing a federation to demonstrate the NATO live, virtual and constructive concept. In: Proceedings of the 2008 Summer Computer Simulation Conference, p. 25. Society for Modeling and Simulation International (2008)
7. Tolk, A., Boulet, J.: Lessons learned on NATO experiments on C2/M&S interoperability. In: IEEE Spring Simulation Interoperability Workshop. Citeseer (2007)
8. Sutton, R.S., Barto, A.G.: Reinforcement Learning: An Introduction. The MIT Press, Cambridge (1998)
9. Zeigler, B.P., Praehofer, H., Kim, T.G.: Theory of Modeling and Simulation, p. 510 (2000)
10. Bae, J.W., Moon, I.-C.: LDEF formalism for agent-based model development. IEEE Trans. Syst. Man Cybern. Syst. **PP**(99), 1 (2015)

Visualization and Virtual Reality

Human Action Recognition Based on Angle Descriptor

Ling Rui[1], Shiwei Ma[1(✉)], Lina Liu[1,2], Jiarui Wen[1],
and Bilal Ahmad[1]

[1] School of Mechatronic Engineering and Automation, Shanghai University,
NO.149, Yanchang Rd., 200072 Shanghai, China
{ruiling0812,linaliu-126,wenjiarui2010}@163.com,
{masw,abilali}@shu.edu.cn
[2] School of Electrical and Electronic Engineering,
Shandong University of Technology, Zibo, Shandong, China

Abstract. A simple and effective method for 3D skeleton based action recognition is proposed in this paper. Instead of taking the whole skeleton joints as the input, we select several active joints to represent the entire action which motion ranges are relatively large via evaluating their variance and give them different weights. Then by calculating the angles between these joints and the center joint in their three projections produces a feature set at each frame which is applied in a bag-of-words to form the 2D array. The final features are cascaded by these 2D arrays. During this process, the feature numbers can be reduced effectively. The random forest is utilized to classify different actions. Experiments on MSR-Action3D dataset demonstrate that our approach is able to achieve the state-of-the-art performance with high recognition rate and computational efficiency.

Keywords: Action recognition · 3D skeleton joints · Angle descriptor · Random forest

1 Introduction

Human action recognition has been a popular research filed of computer vision due to its wide applications in human-computer interaction (HCI), robot vision, game control, video surveillance, and so on [1]. Despite the significant research efforts over the past decades, it remains a challenging problem considering of intra-class variation, occlusion and some other factors.

At the beginning of the action recognition research area, traditional studies mainly focus on the recognition from video recorded by 2D cameras. Unfortunately, the 2D data is sensitive to illumination changes, occlusions and background clutter. Moreover, 2D cameras cannot fully catch the human motion in 3D space. Recently, depth sensor such as Kinect can provide us 3D depth data of the scene. Unlike the wearable devices, none of the landmarks are required to wear in order to capture the 3D locations. Besides, it is cost-effective and robust to illumination changes which can also offer reliable 3D joint coordinates using estimation algorithms. So there are more attentions

© Springer Science+Business Media Singapore 2016
L. Zhang et al. (Eds.): AsiaSim 2016/SCS AutumnSim 2016, Part II, CCIS 644, pp. 609–617, 2016.
DOI: 10.1007/978-981-10-2666-9_61

are paid to the skeleton based action recognition. Raviteja et al. [2] consider the human skeleton as a connected set of rigid segments and represent actions in the lie group by special Euclidean group. Similar idea is proposed in [3], which divide the K-best estimated joints into five body part for the spatial-temporal structures. Yong et al. [4] tanning the hierarchical recurrent neural network for each part of the body to obtain five subnets. The final representations of the skeleton data are fed into a single-layer perceptron to make the decision. In [5] histogram of oriented displacements (HOG) is computed in all frames of one action. Each displacement in the trajectory votes with its length in a histogram of the orientation angles. Human skeletons are represented in [6], covariance descriptors are addressed using the 3D joint locations and the joint trajectories are modeled using a temporal hierarchy. In [7], a histogram of 3D joints descriptor in a frame is computed, a dictionary is built and the temporal modeling is done by HMM.

In this paper, we exploit the skeleton joints 3D locations to develop an interpretable action recognition approach. Five key joins are estimated by evaluating the standard deviation of each joint of an action after normalization. In order to represent the actions, angle descriptor is used to calculate the angles between the key joints and the center joint in each frame in their three projections. The angle range is divided into 8 bins to account the number of the corresponding angles. The final action features are cascaded by these angles of five key joints and random forest is applied to classify the actions. We demonstrate the advantages of our method by our experiments. The results show that our proposed method outperforms various skeleton based human action recognition approaches.

2 Angle Descriptor

Our proposed method is based on the skeleton joints from MSR Action3D dataset containing 20 joints which is shown in Fig. 1. The data contain three streams which represent the 3D point(x, y, z) where X is the horizontal axis, Y is the vertical axis and Z it the distance between a joint and the sensor. The angle descriptor is proposed to

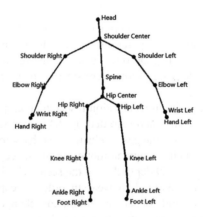

Fig. 1. 20 skeleton joint locations and names

represent human actions in this paper. The three dimension skeleton joints are projected on three orthogonal Cartesian planes (XY, YZ and ZX).

The angle between the vector of key joint to the center joint and X-axis on three projections is calculated. Figure 2(a) shows the angle θ of vector OJ and X-axis on XY plane, where J is one key joint of one frame and O is the center joint. Value θ ranges between 0 and 360 which is divided into 8 bins, and each bin cover 45 degree. The bag-of-words model is utilized to accumulate the number of angle in each bin to achieve the histogram. Every angle descriptor of one key joint contains three histograms of three projections, as shown in Fig. 2(b). The final angle descriptor is cascaded by all the histograms of the key joints.

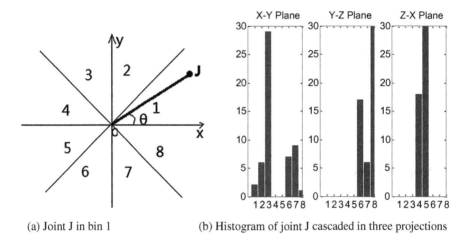

(a) Joint J in bin 1   (b) Histogram of joint J cascaded in three projections

Fig. 2. Angle descriptor of joint J

Among the 20 joints, the motion range of five vertex joints including head, right hand, left hand, right foot and left foot is relatively large. So they are chosen to be the key joints. As we can see in Fig. 3, the standard deviation of the right hand and right elbow is much larger than others which indicate that the movement of these two joints is larger. Since these two joints are very close to each other, choosing one of them is enough for us to describe the motion change.

For different actions, the motion range of these key joints is different from another one. So we give the angle descriptor F different weight.

The final feature is defined as followed,

$$F = \{\alpha_1 f_1, \ \alpha_2 f_2, \ \alpha_3 f_3, \ \alpha_4 f_4, \alpha_5 f_5\}. \tag{1}$$

Here, f_1 to f_5 refer to the key joints: right hand, left hand, head, right foot and left foot respectively, and α is the corresponding weight. As shown in Fig. 3, the standard deviations of right wrist and right hand are relatively higher than those of other joints. So we set α_1 1 and other weights 0.

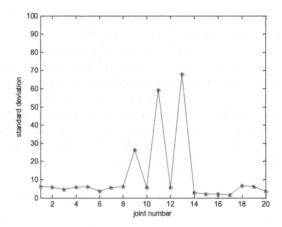

Fig. 3. Standard deviation of 20 joints in high wave action

The angle descriptor obtains the spatial changed of the key joints which has a clear physical meaning. It shows how much angle the key joint moves from one frame to another.

3   Proposed Method

A new skeleton feature angle descriptor is proposed in this paper. Figure 4 shows the overview of our action recognition system. Before feature extraction, normalization of the row data is used to make the 3D joint locations invariant to the camera parameters. We subtract the hip center joint J_h from the other joints by the following equtations,

$$J_o = [J_1 - J_h, \ldots, J_N - J_h] \tag{2}$$

$$J_i = (J_x, J_y, J_z). \tag{3}$$

Where $i \in \{1, \ldots, N\}$, and N is the total number of skeleton joints.

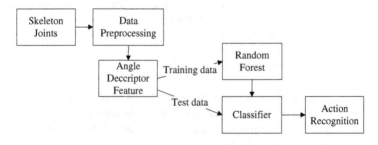

Fig. 4. Overview of the proposed method

3.1   Feature Extraction

After data preprocessing step, angle descriptor for each action is calculated and fed to the bag-of-word model.

The bag-of-word model is employed to account the number of angles in each bin. Since the lengths of actions are different from the others, the following weight factors are used as below:

$$tf_{w,d} = \frac{n_w}{\sum_j n_j} \tag{4}$$

$$idf_{w,d} = \log \frac{|(D)|}{|\{d : w \in d\}|} \tag{5}$$

where $f_{w,d}$ refers to term frequency, n_w is the frequency of words in the action sequence, $\sum_j n_j$ is the number of whole words in the document, and $idf_{w,d}$ refers to inverse document frequency, $|D|$ is the number of all documents, $|\{d : w \in d\}|$ is the number of documents containing word w. $f_{w,d}$ can eliminate the different length of actions. $idf_{w,d}$ can re-determine the weight of different words according to their importance. The importance for a word in an article is proportion to the frequency in this article and in inverse proportion of the frequency in all articles.

In order to capture the temporal evolution, a temporal pyramid is applied. In the first level, the entire sequence is used to construct a part of the feature. In the second level, the entire sequence is divided equally into three parts and each of them is used to obtain the second three parts of the angle descriptor. The final feature is the concatenation of the four parts as shown in Fig. 5.

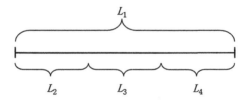

Fig. 5.   2-level temporal pyramid of the feature

3.2   Action Classification

Random forest has excellent performance in classification tasks, especially in multi-classification. In a random forest, each node is split using the best among a subset of predictors randomly chosen at that node. This counterintuitive strategy turns out to perform very well compared with many other classifiers, including discriminate analysis, support vector machines and neural networks. It shows strong robustness with respect to large feature sets and has good predictive performance even when most predictive variables are noise. Since our feature is linearly independent in this paper, the randomly choosing subsets can train the forest well. Besides, it is very user-friendly in the sense that it has only two parameters needs to train: the number of variables in the random subset at each node and the number of trees in the forest, and is not very sensitive to their values. In this paper, random forest is applied for classifying the proposed angle feature and the experiment results show the efficiency of this classifier.

4   Experiments

We first evaluate the performance of the proposed approach on the public MSR-Action3D dataset and compare our results to some exist methods to demonstrate the advantages of the proposed approach.

4.1   MSR-Action3D Dataset

MSR-Action3D dataset [8] is used in this paper which includes 20 actions by 10 subjects and each subject performs one action 2 or 3 times. We use the 20 joints positions shown in Fig. 1 which are available in [9]. The actions are divided into 3 action sets as shown in Table 1. Each set has 8 actions with some overlap between action sets. Figure 6 shows some key frames of three actions including high arm wave, hand clap and side kick in the MSR-Action3D dataset.

Table 1.   Classification accuracy on MSR-Action3D using 3-fold method

Set	Accuracy(%)
AS1	92.6
AS2	95.4
AS3	96.2
Mean	94.7

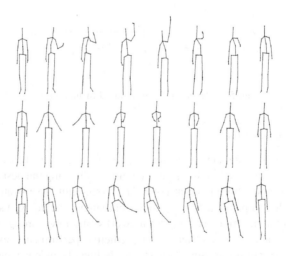

Fig. 6.   Some key frames of three actions in MSR-Action3D dataset which are high arm wave, hand clap and side kick

4.2 Results and Discussion

In order to compare the effect of different characteristics of the algorithm, Leave-One-Out method (LOO) is used to evaluate the experiment result. The experiments are conducted for 10 times, excluding one subject in each run. Using this method allows us utilize as much data as possible for training. At the same time, it can help us find problematic subjects and analyze the reason of the classification errors.

Table 2 shows the recognition rate on MSR-Action3D dataset for the three subsets AS1, AS2 and AS3. We can see clearly that the accuracy of three subsets is relatively high and the average accuracy is up to 94.7 %. Subset AS1 is a little lower may because of the similarity of the right hand action. Better performance on subset AS3 indicates that the proposed representation is better in modeling complex actions.

The confusion matrix of the 20 actions is shown in Table 3. The misclassifications mainly occur among several very similar actions. For example, the action "hammer" is misclassified to the action "forward punch". Some of the "forward punch" actions are not horizontal but slant which may cause the angle descriptor of these two actions some resemblance. The action "draw tick" and "draw" have some overlap parts of some frames. Despite all this, there are 14 actions completely classified. Among the 20 actions, we can see that the more complex actions which involve more motion changes in different body part have higher accuracy rate is due to the weight of factor α. The weight factor gives the active joint heavier weight which enhances the angle descriptor to represent the actions better. At the same time, it can eliminate some of the noise of the data.

Table 2. Confusion matrices of the proposed approach on MSR-Action3D dataset (%)

	High arm wave	horizontal arm wave	hammer	hand catch	forward punch	high throw	draw x	draw tick	draw circle	hand clap	two hand wave	side-boxing	bend	forward kick	side kick	jogging	tennis swing	tennis serve	golf swing	pickup & throw
high arm wave	100																			
horizontal arm wave		100																		
hammer			70.4	22.2	7.4															
hand catch	11.1		85.2			3.7														
forward punch			18.5		74.1	7.4														
high throw			3.7		7.4	88.9														
draw x	3.7		7.4				77.8	11.1												
draw tick								100												
draw circle									100											
hand clap										100										
two hand wave											100									
side-boxing												100								
bend													100							
forward kick														100						
side kick															100					
jogging																100				
tennis swing																3.7	96.3			
tennis serve																		100		
golf swing																			100	
pickup & throw																				100

Table 3 summarizes the state-of-art perfomance on the MSR-Action3D dataset. We achieved 94.7 % accuracy and outperform the [5] over 2 %. The results calidate the applicability of the angle decriptor of the actions on this dataset. It contains more information of the action sequence and recovers the key joints both temporally and spatially. With the random forest, it can trainning and testing in a very short time. Therefore, the effictiveness of our approach is forested by its simplicity compared to the other method, which shows its practical advantage. For the weakness of the arm-hand action part, more information should be used to classify.

Table 3. Classification accuracy comparison for MSR-Action3D dataset

Method	Accuracy(%)
Hidden Markov Model [10]	63
Eigen Joints [11]	81.4
Action Ensemble [12]	88.2
HOD Descriptor [5]	91.26
HOJ3D Feature [7]	90.9
Proposed Method	94.7

5 Conclusion

In this paper, the angle descriptor framework for action recognition based on 3D skeleton joint is presented. Cascade of the angle descriptor in three projections can effectively reduce the dimension of the 3D row data. Moreover, the use of temporal pyramid can capture the temporal evolution. The combination of the whole feature contains both spatial and temporal information which can represent the action well. The normalization of the data before feature extraction ensures the scale-invariant. Recognition accuracy employing the proposed feature with random forest outperforms some published method on the public MSR-Action3D dataset. Experimental results have clearly shown the promising performance of the proposed method and also the advantages of using 3D skeleton joints which is physical interpretable, compact and computationally efficient.

Rotation invariance is very important in action recognition. The proposed approach is view dependent. However, with the help of 3D skeleton locations, new reference coordinate can be redefined, for example, choosing the line of left and right shoulder in X axis as the new X axis to correspondingly transform the coordinates of skeleton joints.

References

1. Koutník, J., Schmidhuber, J., Gomez, F.: Evolving deep unsupervised convolutional networks for vision-based reinforcement learning. In: Conference on Genetic and Evolutionary Computation (ACM), pp. 541–548 (2014)

2. Vemulapalli, R., Arrate, F., Chellappa, R.: Human action recognition by representing 3D skeletons as points in a lie group. In: IEEE Conference on Computer Vision and Pattern Recognition, pp. 588–595. IEEE (2014)
3. Wang, C., Wang, Y., Yuille, A.: An approach to pose-based action recognition. In: IEEE Conference on Computer Vision and Pattern Recognition, pp. 915–922. IEEE (2013)
4. Dum, Y., Wang, W., Wang, L.: Hierarchical recurrent neural network for skeleton based action recognition. In: IEEE Conference on Computer Vision and Pattern Recognition, pp. 1110–1118. IEEE (2015)
5. Gowayyed, M.A., Torki, M., Hussein, M.E.: Histogram of oriented displacements (HOD): describing trajectories of human joints for action recognition. In: International Joint Conference on Artificial Intelligence(IJCAI), pp. 1351–1357 (2013)
6. Hussein, M.E., Torki, M., Gowayyed, M.A.: Human action recognition using a temporal hierarchy of covariance descriptors on 3D joint locations. In: International Joint Conference on Artificial Intelligence(IJCAI), pp. 2466–2472 (2013)
7. Xia, L., Chen, C.C., Aggarwal, J.K.: View invariant human action recognition using histograms of 3D joints. In: IEEE Computer Society Conference on Computer Vision and Pattern Recognition Workshops (CVPRW), pp. 20–27. IEEE (2012)
8. Li, W., Zhang, Z., Liu, Z.: Action recognition based on a bag of 3D points. In: IEEE Computer Society Conference on Computer Vision and Pattern Recognition Workshops (CVPRW), pp. 9–14. IEEE (2010)
9. http://research.microsoft.com/en-us/um/people/zliu/ActionRecoRsrc/default.htm
10. Lv, F., Nevatia, R.: Recognition and segmentation of 3-D human action using HMM and multi-class AdaBoost. In: Leonardis, A., Bischof, H., Pinz, A. (eds.) ECCV 2006. LNCS, vol. 3954, pp. 359–372. Springer, Heidelberg (2006)
11. Yang, X., Tian, Y.L.: Eigen joints-based action recognition using naive-bayes-nearest-neighbor. In IEEE Computer Society Conference on Computer vision and pattern recognition workshops (CVPRW), pp. 14–19. IEEE (2012)
12. Wang, J., Liu, Z., Wu, Y., Yuan, J.: Mining actionlet ensemble for action recognition with depth cameras. In: IEEE Conference on Computer Vision and Pattern Recognition (CVPR), pp. 1290–1297. IEEE (2012)

Research on Satellite Simulation for Mobile Terminals

Qi Su[⊠], Xin Lin, and Qipeng Hu

School of Automation Science and Electrical Engineering, Beihang University, Beijing, China
{suqi2014,lx}@buaa.edu.cn, w18679104034@126.com

Abstract. With the development of Internet+, developing an application of satellite simulation which executes on mobile terminals has an important significance for engineers to get visual knowledge of spaceflight. The application design and implementation method of satellite simulation software are discussed. A framework of satellite simulation system is presented, the modules and workflow of the satellite simulation system are described. Approaches to create the starry background of the satellite operation, environment lighting of the earth and the orbits of satellites in the software are presented in detail. The software uses Unity3D platform to create 3D simulation environment, uses SGP4/SDP4 orbit prediction models to calculate orbits of satellites, and uses databases to store TLE data.

Keywords: Mobile terminals · Satellite simulation · Unity3D

1 Introduction

The research of simulation is one of the effective ways to reduce the risk and cost of production. Since the beginning of the aerospace industry in 1950s, simulation technology has been widely used in aerospace engineering. Up to nowadays, the development of spaceflight simulation has experienced the following stages: physical simulation, analog machine simulation, digital machine simulation, multimedia simulation and visual interactive simulation, etc. In recent years, with the deepening of the scientific research and the breakthrough of the technology of computer hardware and software, the development and application of the simulation technology has been promoted to a new stage, and plays an important role for the development of space industry.

Nowadays, concept of "Internet+" affects deeply on technology research. Traditional industries are undergoing significant changes when fusing with the Internet technology. As intelligent mobile terminals has got a very big development on data storage, computing capability and the image processing ability, some spaceflight simulation and scenario demonstration executed on computers originally can be realized on mobile terminals. The research working on applying spaceflight simulation on mobile terminals has an important significance for aerospace engineering.

This paper researches application design and implementation method of the satellite simulation software. A framework of satellite simulation system is presented, modules and workflow of the satellite simulation system are described. Approaches to create the

L. Zhang et al. (Eds.): AsiaSim 2016/SCS AutumnSim 2016, Part II, CCIS 644, pp. 618–624, 2016.
DOI: 10.1007/978-981-10-2666-9_62

starry background of the satellite operation, environment lighting of the earth and the orbits of satellites in the software are presented in detail.

2   Application Design

The satellite simulation application system for mobile terminals uses Unity3D platform as the foundation of the development and implementation and is intend to be applied to Android platform. The Unity3D platform has cross-platform features. Applications developed on the Unity3D platform can be planted to multiple platforms, such as Android, iOS, Windows and so on [1]. Therefore, different from the general development of the Android applications, the design and implementation of the satellite simulation application system for mobile terminals are carried out according to the Unity3D platform [2, 3].

2.1   Framework Design

With consideration of maintainability, reusability and extensibility of the system, the satellite simulation application system for mobile terminals uses a four-layer framework which introduces a service layer into the classical three layers framework: presentation layer, business logic layer and data access layer (Fig. 1).

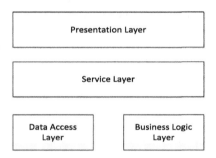

Fig. 1.   The software framework

The functions of the four layers in the software framework include,

Presentation Layer: Gets input information and operations of user, and returns the specific business data to user. The purpose of the presentation layer is to accomplish interaction between the system and user.

Service Layer: Provides business logic entry to presentation layer, defines interface service forms and completes services by calling the interfaces. It also needs to manage interactive behaviors of all business logic objects.

Business Logic Layer: Accepts data transfer object (DTO) transferred through the service layer, processes the incoming DTO according to the business rules, returns the processed data to the service layer and provides business logic behaviors for business logic objects.

Data Access Layer: Provides access interfaces to local data and remote data.

The relationships among four layers are listed as below.

The presentation layer collects input information of user and transfers the information to service layer by calling the interfaces. The service layer analyzes the information to get required services of user. For services that service layer can react directly, such as the rotation and scaling of the scene, service layer provides them to presentation layer and responds to the user's operations. For services that business logic layer and data access layer need to participate in, the service layer gets relevant data from data access layer, or feeds back some related data to presentation layer directly, or transfers data to the business logic layer by DTOs to perform relevant business rules. The business logic layer processes DTOs according to the corresponding business rules and sends the processed information back to the service layer. The service layer processes the feedback data and updates data in the presentation layer, and then responds to user's operations.

2.2   Modules Design

The satellite simulation application system for mobile terminals is composed of three main modules, the satellite simulation environment module, the satellite orbit prediction module and the satellite simulation database module. The modules of the software are shown as Fig. 2.

(1) Satellite Simulation Environment Module

Satellite simulation 3D environment is the window that shows to user and matters a lot to user's experiences. To some extent, it is the most important part of the satellite simulation application system. The module is designed based on Unity3D platform [4]. It is composed of several modules: UI module, to get user's input data and show corresponding data of satellites to user; skybox module, to create starry background of 3D environment; lighting module, to create lighting effect of 3D environment; dynamic model load module, to load 3D models of satellites according to user's input; satellite orbit draw module, to show satellite orbit in the 3D environment; scene control module, to control the scene demonstration reacting to user's operation.

(2) Satellite Orbit Prediction Module

Satellite orbit prediction is the core function of the satellite simulation application. The calculation accuracy and speed of the orbit prediction algorithm have a direct impact on the accuracy of orbit simulation and experiences of the user. Because calculation accuracy is inversely proportional to calculation speed, the orbit prediction algorithm should take balance between these two indicators. The module is designed to adopt NORAD two-line element(TLE) data as the data input of orbit prediction, and SGP4/SDP4 orbit model, which can produce very accurate results when used with current NORAD TLE data, as the core algorithm solution to calculate satellite position and velocity in earth inertial coordinate system [5].

(3) Satellite Simulation Database Module

The satellite simulation databases are an important part of satellite simulation application system for mobile terminals. The databases store satellite orbit data, two-line element(TLE) data, and provide data support for satellite orbit prediction.

The module is designed to develop three databases: SQLite database, LAN database, and Cloud database. The SQLite database is designed to install on the mobile terminals. When using SQLite database, users can accomplish satellite simulation within mobile terminals independently, and there is no need to connect internet. The LAN database is designed to be laid in the LAN. When using LAN database, users need to connect to the database through WLAN to get orbit data and accomplish satellite simulation. The Cloud database is designed to be laid in the Cloud. When using Cloud database, users need to connect to the database through Internet and accomplish the satellite simulation dependent on the orbit data stored in the LeanCloud database.

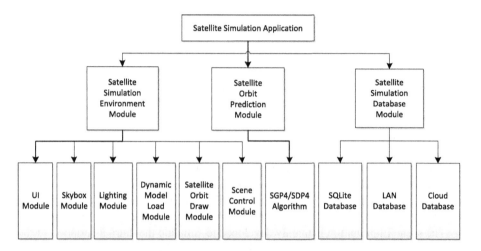

Fig. 2. The software modules

All above three modules are dependent on each other and work together closely to make sure that satellite simulation application system for mobile terminals executes correctly.

3   Application Implementation

The satellite simulation application system for mobile terminals is developed on Unity3D platform. Unity3D is developed by Unity Technologies and allows the user to easily create 3D visual simulation, architecture visualization, real-time 3D animation and other types of interactive content. It is a multi-platform integrated virtual reality development tools and a fully integrated virtual reality engine. The visual editor features of Unity3D are what you see is what you get. The developer can create the relevant scenes according to the real needs [6].

3.1 Starry Background

The starry background is developed on the basis of a component called *Skyboxes*. The thought of the skyboxes is putting the whole scene in a large cube and every plane of the cube is a square with the texture mapping. When the scene camera is put into the large cube, the scope of the field looks like in the real scene environment.

Methods as shown below are adopted to create the starry background,

(1) Get the coordinates of celestial body at a given moment through the ephemeris and map the coordinate data in the universe to the surface of a celestial sphere;
(2) Set a viewpoint at the center of the celestial sphere and divide what is seen at the viewpoint into six same-size seamless images;
(3) Import the prepared starry background images into Unity3D platform as assets which are used to construct starry background and change the images' properties to meet the needs of starry background to be constructed.
(4) Create a *material* in the Unity3D platform and set the material created in the *skybox* mode. Add reference assets to the skybox cube material at the right position and render the starry background environment in 3D scene.

3.2 Scene Illumination

Lighting is an important part of a scene and determines the color and atmosphere of 3D environment. There are four standard types of light source: directional light, point light, spot light and area light. Each light source has its unique properties, and developers can adjust position and direction of the light to construct an actual scene illumination.

The scene illumination is mainly developed to simulate the diurnal variation of the lighting on the Earth's surface. When satellites operate in the 3D environment, use scene lighting to reflect the satellites are operating in the sunlit side or the sunless side of the Earth. Generally the light from sun to earth is treated as parallel light. Considering that the directional light is close to parallel light, use the directional light to simulate the sun light and set the origin position of the light to infinity and the direction of the light orientation to the Earth in the scene. Add the sun lens to the light to simulate the sun and use the technology of dynamic shadows in the scene to realize the sunlit side and the sunless side on the Earth's surface (Fig. 3).

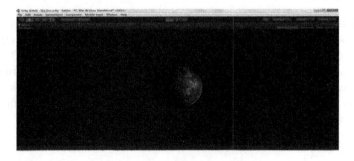

Fig. 3. The simulation environment

3.3   Scene Control

The application development based on Unity3D platform is using object-oriented method and modular modeling method. Every *GameObject* created in Unity3D platform has at least one *Transform* module. Through the *Transform* module, position and posture of the entity model in 3D environment can be obtained, changed and updated. If *Rigidbody* or *Collider* module was added to a gameobject, the gameobject could support rigid body features or collision detection.

Entity model features in 3D environment are organized by modules. Through modules, develop the scene control effect in 3D scene. Create an EmptyObject at the original point of the scene and drag the scene mainCamera object onto it in the Hierarchy View to create a Parent-Child relationship between the two objects. On the basis of the Parent-Child relationship, update the posture of the EmptyObject to realize the scene rotation control. Based on the field of view of the cameras, develop the scene scaling control. The field of view for the cameras represent the scope that the cameras can see. The larger the field of view, the larger the area of the scene the observer can see. At the same time, the smaller the object is in the scene. When *Transform* module added to the Camera gameobject, we realize the rotation and scaling of the scene, changing viewpoints and fields scopes. When *Transform* module added to satellite gameobjects, we realize the simulation of satellite operation in 3D scene.

3.4   Model Loading

For the 3D models created out of Unity3D platform, when they are imported into Unity3D platform, the engine will automatically create Prefabs for them. The prefabs, similar to the public class in object-oriented languages, can be loaded directly into different scenarios in the project. Using the prefab in project development can improve the efficiency of scene management and production.

Make 3D satellite models outside Unity3D platform and transform them to the format that Unity3D supports. Import satellite models into Unity3D and organize them in the form of prefab. If need to load a satellite model into the 3D scene, Unity3D engine would create an instance of the prefab assets. Most of work that we should do is writing scripts to control the process of instantiation.

3.5   Orbit Drawing

We choose SGP4/SDP4 orbital model as the core algorithm solution to calculates satellite location and velocity in the earth orbit [7]. In accordance with the SGP4/SDP4 model published by NORAD, program and realize it in the project in C/C++ programming language. To use it in the mobile terminals, compile the model as. so shared library and use the orbit model to produce the latitude, longitude and altitude of the satellites in the ECI coordinate system and transform the LLA data to the coordinate data of the scene coordinate system. Use a structure array to store the solution result and transmit the structure array to a third-party plug-in which is compatible for Unity3D platform to draw the orbit of the satellite operating in the scene (Fig. 4).

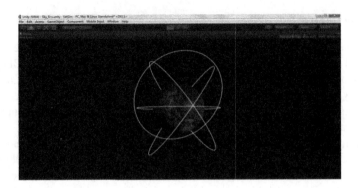

Fig. 4. Satellite simulation scene

4   Conclusions and Future Work

We study the framework and the modules of the satellite simulation application system for mobile terminals and elaborate the implementation method of some key modules. This paper is an explore for the spaceflight simulation carried out based on mobile terminals and make sure that it is possible for more complex spaceflight simulation task to be developed for mobile terminals. There are a lot of work to do in the future.

References

1. Zhu, H.-J.: Virtual roaming system based on Unity3D. Comput. Syst. Appl. **21**(10), 36–39 (2012)
2. Kim, S.L.: Research on the 3D game scene optimization of mobile phone based on the unity 3D engine. In: 2011 International Conference on Computational and Information Sciences (ICCIS), pp. 875–877. IEEE (2011)
3. Stamford, J.: Design and implementation of virtual interactive scene based on unity 3D. Adv. Mater. Res. **317**, 2162–2167 (2011)
4. Jin, L.: Research on visual simulation system of guided bomb. North University of China, May 2015
5. Liu, Y.-F.: Research on low earth orbit spacecraft orbit prediction strategy based on SGP 4 model. Harbin Institute of Technology, June 2009
6. Blackman, S.: Beginning 3D Game Development with Unity: All-in-One. Multi-Platform Game Development. Tsinghua Publishing, China (2015)
7. Diao, N.-H., Liu, J.-Q., Sun, C.-R., Meng, P.: Satellite orbit calculation based on SGP4 model. Remote Sens. Inf. **27**(4), 64–70 (2012)

Viewpoint Scoring Approach and Its Application to Locating Canonical Viewpoint for 3D Visualization

Li Che[1,2(✉)] and Fengju Kang[1,2]

[1] School of Marine Science and Technology,
Northwestern Polytechnical University, Xi'an, China
cheli@mail.nwpu.edu.cn
[2] National Key Laboratory of Underwater Information Process and Control,
Xi'an, China

Abstract. In this paper, a novel viewpoint scoring method based on multi-attribute fusion is proposed. The perceptual model of viewpoint preference is explored from geometry and visual perception aspects. Modified mesh saliency entropy is presented as the crucial intrinsic geometric attribute. Several digital image factors which have influence on human visual perception form the viewpoint perception attributes. Evolution algorithm is utilized to select the canonical viewpoint automatically and intelligently. Experimental results demonstrate that the canonical viewpoint obtained by the proposed method contains more visible salient features and better conforms to human visual perception characteristic. Moreover, the method has high efficiency and requires no user interaction.

Keywords: 3D visualization · Canonical viewpoint · Viewpoint attribute · Visual perception · Particle swarm optimization

1 Introduction

The criteria for viewpoint quality estimation in existing literature can be classified into two categories: geometric information based criteria and visual information based criteria. Geometric information based viewpoint quality estimation criteria use geometric information, such as project area of surface [1], geometric area [2], distance-histogram entropy [3]. etc. to measure the goodness of the viewpoint. These algorithms are simple and have high efficiency. The main drawback is that the best viewpoint depends on the polygonal discretization. The attention of the measure will be heavily attracted by a high discretized region. Visual information based optimal viewpoint selection algorithm emerged in recent years. Evaluation factors mainly used in the current literature are curvature [4], mesh saliency [5], shape/detail view descriptor [6], relief saliency [7] and Skeleton-Based [8]. These evaluation factors can extract visual features of the objects in the scene and better conform to human visual habit. The disadvantage is that ignoring geometric information and the calculation is more complicated. During the last few years, researchers explored artificial intelligent (AI) techniques in visualization to accelerate the computing efficiency. Particle Swarm

© Springer Science+Business Media Singapore 2016
L. Zhang et al. (Eds.): AsiaSim 2016/SCS AutumnSim 2016, Part II, CCIS 644, pp. 625–633, 2016.
DOI: 10.1007/978-981-10-2666-9_63

Optimizer (PSO) [9] was used to select the optimal viewpoint intelligently. The modified PSO algorithm GA-PSO [10] was used to select the optimal combination of resolution levels of objects for 3D scene. Other algorithms such as shuffled frog leaping [11] and ant colony [12] were integrated into the process of best viewpoint selection.

In this paper, we explore the viewpoint attribute from not only geometry information perspective, but also visual perception perspective. The combination of the viewpoint attributes form a novel viewpoint scoring approach named viewpoint pertinence with the aim of finding the canonical viewpoint. Such a combination inherits the strengths of each attribute while compensating for their individual disadvantages. We place the viewpoints on the viewpoint sphere, the problem between the size of viewpoints set and the efficiency of algorithm is balance by utilizing evolution algorithm in the process of viewpoint optimization. By graphics processing unit (GPU) acceleration, algorithm efficiency is greatly improved.

The rest of the paper is structured as follows: Viewpoint attribute and mathematical models are given in Sect. 2. The novel viewpoint scoring method is given in detail in Sect. 3. In Sect. 4, intelligent viewpoint selection framework is presented. Experimental results and comparison studies to verify the capability of the proposed method are shown in Sect. 5. Conclusion and future work are given in Sect. 6.

2   Viewpoint Attribute

In this section we describe a set of viewpoint attributes from visual perception and computer graphics perspective, and we combine these attributes to form a more effective and accurate viewpoint quality evaluation metric than any one or a few measures taken alone. In Table 1, we enumerate the viewpoint attribute, each attribute is selected from the previous literature which is generally recognized by most scholars or inspired by former presented one.

Table 1. Viewpoint attribute

A_1	**Surface curvature attribute**	*Mesh saliency entropy*
A_2	**surface area attribute**	*Viewpoint entropy*
A_3	**Visual perception attribute**	*Luminance*
A_4		*Chrominance*
A_5		*Texture Details*
A_6		*Spatial Location*
A_7	**Scene information attribute**	*Image information entropy*
A_8	**Object weight attribute**	*Object Visible Priority*

2.1   Surface Curvature Attribute

A1: *Mesh saliency entropy.* Local structural features information of 3D model depends on the mean curvature, because the mean curvature tensor field can express the visual characteristic of 3D model. We combine the information entropy theory and face curvature to build a novel viewpoint quality metric named mesh saliency entropy.

We use the Gaussian-weighted mean curvature of vertices proposed by Lee [13] to calculate mean curvature.

Face curvature of 3D object is determined by the average curvature of its corresponding vertices. Assuming that the Gaussian-weighted mean curvature of vertices v is $\zeta(v)$, we define the saliency of the triangle T_i as follows:

$$\zeta(T_i) = \frac{1}{3}\sum_{v \in T_i} \zeta(v) \tag{1}$$

To reflect the change in projected area of the triangle due to perspective projection, we use the angle between surface normal vector and the line of sight as adjustable parameters, the modified saliency is defined as follows:

$$\zeta'(T_i) = \zeta(T_i) \cdot P_f \tag{2}$$

Where $P_f = abs(V_d \cdot N_f)$, it represents the projection weight of triangle face f in the visual plane. V_d is the view vector and N_f is the normal vector of triangle face f.

The saliency entropy for a given viewpoint is defined as follows:

$$S(T,p) = -\sum_{i=1}^{N_T} \frac{\zeta'(T_i)}{\sum_{T \in s}\zeta'(T_i)} \log \frac{\zeta'(T_i)}{\sum_{T \in s}\zeta'(T_i)} \tag{3}$$

2.2 Surface Area Attribute

A2: *Viewpoint entropy*. Introduced by Vazquez [1], this attribute combines probability distribution of projected areas of mesh faces and Shannon entropy to qualify the information of a viewpoint. Among the metrics that have been introduced for measuring the object visibility in the 3D scene from a camera position, the viewpoint entropy is the most valid metric up to now.

2.3 Visual Perception Attribute

A3 ~ A6: From the perspective of visual psychology, the vision is a kind of positive feelings behavior, not only relates with the physiological factors, but also depends on psychological factors. The research on human visual system shows that several digital image factors (luminance, chrominance texture details, spatial location factor, etc.) have strong influence on human visual characteristic. So we use these four visual perception factors as the viewpoint attributes and mathematic model of attributes A3 to A6 refer to literature [9].

2.4 Scene Information Attribute

A7: *Image information entropy*. Image information entropy is a statistical form of character, which reflects the average amount of information in the image. Color histogram of image is seen as the probability density function. In [14], image information entropy was used to evaluate viewpoint quality. We use image information to measure the information richness of the corresponding viewpoint.

2.5 Object Weight Attribute

A8: *Object Visible Priority*. This attribute gives the visible priority to each individual model in the 3D scene. In conformity to the weight of objects, the viewpoint position is controllable. Thus attribute A8 is useful to express the detailed part or recognition of a certain object. A8 expresses the importance for each object in the scene, the value is determinate either by user or LOD level of the object in the scene.

3 Viewpoint Scoring Method

In this section, a novel criterion for viewpoint goodness measurement named Viewpoint Pertinence is proposed. The definition of the novel metric contains not only geometric criterion, such as visible projected area, surface curvature, but also non-geometric criteria such as, visual perception, scene information are taken into account. In our precious work, a novel viewpoint quality evaluation metric named Region Weighted Information Entropy (RWIE) [9] was proposed. The novel criterion combines visual perception and information entropy theory which make viewpoint quality evaluation result more conform to human visual habits. So, we use RWIE to represent viewpoint attribute A3 to A7.

We use the attributes enumerated in Table 1 to formalize the Viewpoint Pertinence as expression (4), thus the viewpoint quality can be quantified. An adequate combination of these attributes could give a good measure of viewpoint quality.

$$Vp(S,p) = w_1 \sum_{i=1}^{N} S_i(T,p) + w_2 \sum_{i=1}^{N} V_i(S,p) + w_3 \sum_{i=1}^{N} p_i + w_4 \sum_{j=1}^{M} W_j \times E(R_j) \quad (4)$$

Where w_i is the weight of each attribute of Viewpoint Pertinence which is determined by Analytic Hierarchy Process (AHP) algorithm. N presents the number of models

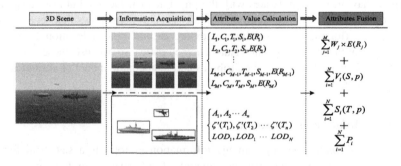

Fig. 1. Implementation process of Viewpoint Pertinence

contain in a scene, M presents the number of equal sized regions that the viewpoint image is divided. Figure 1 presents the implementation process of Viewpoint Pertinence.

According to Fig. 1, the overall computational process of Viewpoint Pertinence Vp for the given viewpoint Vp_i is showed by Algorithm 1.

Algorithm 1: Computing the Viewpoint Pertinence Vp for the given viewpoint (S,p)

M:The number of image segmentation regions with equal size

N:The number of object in scene

$\quad\quad W_j \leftarrow 0, \ E(R_j) \leftarrow 0, \ V_i(S,p) \leftarrow 0, \ S_i(T,p) \leftarrow 0, \ P_i \leftarrow 0$

$[\,w_1, w_2, w_3, w_4\,]$←Attribute weight determination using AHP

For $(i=0; i<N; i++)$

$\quad$ Compute mesh saliency entropy $S(T, p)$, viewpoint entropy $V(S, p)$, Visible Priority P;

End for

For $(j=0; j<M; j++)$

$\quad$ Compute the perception factors (L, C, T, S) and image information entropy $E(R)$;

$\quad$ Compute the weight W_j for each region after normalization;

End for

$Vp(S, p)$ ←Attributes value accumulate;

---

4   Viewpoint Selection Using PSO Algorithm

In order to eliminate the number of viewpoint quality evaluations, thus improve the efficiency of the optimal viewpoint searching process, we adopt we adopt the random weight PSO to select the canonical viewpoint intelligently and automatically. In the previous literature, viewpoints are located on the viewpoint sphere [9], which have a fixed distance from the center of the sphere. Differ from previous method, we define the view distance R as a variable within a certain range. The viewpoint set contains different view direction and distance, these viewpoints can be represented by multi-resolution hierarchy.

The standard PSO algorithm can easily drop into local optimum and has the low convergence speed, we use random weight PSO to overcome these shortcomings. In modified PSO, velocity and position of each particle is updated by Eqs. (5) and (6).

$$v_{im}^{k+1} = w \times v_{im}^k + c_1 \times Rand() \times (p_{im}^k - x_{im}^k) + c_2 \times Rand() \times (p_{gm}^k - x_{im}^k) \quad (5)$$

$$x_{im}^{k+1} = x_{im}^k + v_{im}^k \quad (6)$$

Where c_1 and c_2 are the learning factor. w is weight coefficient. The random weight w is defined as:

$$\begin{cases} w = \mu + \sigma \times N(0,1) \\ \mu = \mu_{\min} + (\mu_{\max} - \mu_{\min}) \times rand(0,1) \end{cases} \tag{7}$$

Where $N(0,1)$ represents a random number of standard normal distribution. μ_{max} is the maximum value of the mean value of the random weight, μ_{min} is the minimum value. σ is the variance of the mean value of the random weight.

The basic process of the algorithm is as follows:

Step1.   Enter the initial viewpoints candidate set, random weight PSO parameters and the viewpoint sphere parameters, then encoding viewpoints into particles in PSO;

Step2.   Update particle velocity and position by random weight PSO algorithm to achieve particle evolution;

Step3.   Decoding particles to obtain the corresponding viewpoint coordinate, render the scene for each alternative viewpoint respectively;

Step4.   Evaluating the viewpoint image quality by using Algorithm 1 to calculate the fitness value of each particle, then update the *pBest* and *gBest*;

Step5.   If the iteration termination condition is reached, then output canonical viewpoint, otherwise return to step 2), update the particles, into a new round of iterations

Iteration termination condition is stable residuals or the maximum number of iterations.

5   Experimental Results and Analysis

We use three models (aircraft, ship and sea) to form the test scene. Through the AHP analysis, the weight of four attributes is $w = \{0.2053\ 0.2594\ 0.1137\ 0.4216\}$. Viewpoint distance R has 4 resolution levels, angle θ has 30 resolution levels, δ has 10 resolution levels. So the number of the candidate viewpoints is 4*10*30. The viewpoint image is 800*600, and divided into 48 blocks with equal size of 100*100 pixels. The initial viewpoint location covers the top, front, back, left and right direction of the viewpoint sphere, but the viewpoint distance is randomly selected. Table 2 shows the corresponding parameters setting of adaptive weight PSO in the process of viewpoint selection.

Table 2. Parameters setting of random weight PSO

Population size	Dimension	Maximum iterations number	μ_{max}	μ_{min}	σ	C_1, C_2
6	3	50	0.8	0.5	0.2	2, 2

Fig. 2 a shows the change of fitness value of six particles in the iterative process. The average fitness and optimal fitness curve of the six particles is showed in Fig. 2 b. From Fig. 2, we can see each particle gradually close to the optimal solution in the evolutionary process, the entire process is toward the better solution program, and the viewpoint quality is getting better and better. The canonical viewpoint is obtained by the fourth particle in the 22nd generation. The rendered image of obtained canonical viewpoint is showed in Fig. 3 b.

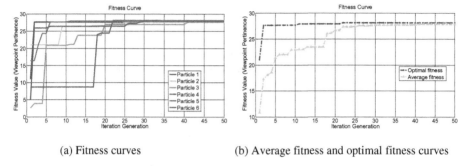

(a) Fitness curves   (b) Average fitness and optimal fitness curves

Fig. 2. The fitness curves of six particles

In the same experimental environment condition, we compare the canonical the viewpoint selected by the proposed algorithm with the algorithm in [14]. Fig. 3 a is the optimal viewpoint selected by method in [14] and Fig. 3 b is by our algorithm.

(a)   (b)

Fig. 3. Optimal viewpoint selection by algorithm in [14] and proposed algorithm

Image information entropy is used in graphics area to represent the information richness of an image. We can see although viewpoint image contains more information of the scene but it does not conform to human observation habits. The selected viewpoint distance is too far to see the objects of the scene clearly and the small object (aircraft) is submerged in scene background. So the canonical viewpoint obtained by image information entropy can easily affected by scene background.

The proposed algorithm considered not only geometric information, human visual perception characteristics are taken into account. From Fig. 3 b, we can have a more comprehensive understanding of the scene than Fig. 3 a. The canonical viewpoint selected by our algorithm contains enough geometric information to understand what are the objects and the shape. Meanwhile, the definition of Viewpoint Pertinence contains chrominance and luminance information, so we can see the bright part of the aircraft and the left ship. From geometry and visual perception aspects, the canonical viewpoint selected by our algorithm is superior to algorithm in [14].

6   Conclusions and Future Work

In this paper, we present a novel viewpoint scoring method based on multi-attribute fusion. The perceptual model of viewpoint pertinence is formalized as a combination of viewpoint attributes which are believed to be significance for viewpoint selection. Random weight PSO is introduced to eliminate the reluctant viewpoint evaluations, and by GPU acceleration the efficiency and speed of algorithm is improved. The canonical viewpoint obtained by the proposed method contains more visible salient features and better conforms to human visual perception.

There are many potential attributes of viewpoint preference described in the literature, we will explore and enrich the classes of viewpoint attributes. Moreover, we will use this method in a number of applications, such as trackball controls and extensions and camera orbits optimization.

References

1. Vázquez, P.P., Feixas, M., Sbert, M.: Viewpoint selection using viewpoint entropy. In: Proceedings of the Vision Modeling and Visualization Conference, pp. 273–280 (2001)
2. Feixas, M., Sbert, M., Gonz, F.: A unified information-theoretic framework for viewpoint selection and mesh saliency. ACM Trans. Appl. Percept. 6(1), 1–25 (2009)
3. Weiguo, C., Ping, H., Hua, L.: Canonical viewpoint selection based on distance-histogram. J. Comput. Aided Des. Comput. Graph. 22(9), 1515–1521 (2010)
4. Honnglei, H., Jing, L., Guangzheng, F.: A hybrid measure of viewpoint scoring using visual perception and information entropy. J. Comput. Aided Des. Comput. Graph. 23(5), 732–740 (2014)
5. Yubo, T., Hai, L., Hujun, B., Feng, D., Gordon, C.: Structure-aware viewpoint selection for volume visualization. In: IEEE Pacific Visualization Symposium, PacificVis, pp. 193–200 (2009)
6. Bin, P., Shuai, W., Wei, C.: Perceptual-based automatic viewpoint selection. J. Comput. Aided Des. Comput. Graph. 23(5), 732–740 (2011)
7. Yongwei, M., Hongjun, W., Huahao, S.: Best viewpoint selection driven by relief saliency entropy. J. Comput. Aided Des. Comput. Graph. 23(12), 2033–2039 (2011)
8. Shi, Z., Yu, L., Ahmed, A.: A kinematics significance based skeleton map for rapid viewpoint selection. Res. J. Appl. Sci. Eng. Technol. 4(17), 2887–2892 (2012)
9. Che, L., Kang, F.: Visual perception based regional weighted information entropy to intelligent viewpoint selection for 3D visualization. J. Comput. Inf. Syst. 11(23), 8699–8709 (2015)
10. Che, L., Kang, F.: Intelligent combination of discrete LoD model for 3D visualization based on visual perception and information entropy fusion. J. Syst. Simul. 27(8), 1815–1823 (2015)

11. Yousai, Z., Bin, W.: Optimal viewpoint selection for volume rendering based on shuffled frog leaping algorithm. In: IEEE International Conference on Progress in Informatics and Computing, pp. 706–709 (2010)
12. Yousai, Z., Li, X.: Viewpoint optimization based on ant colony algorithm for volume rendering. J. Jiangsu Univ. Sci. Technol. **27**(3), 270–274 (2013)
13. Lee, C.H., Varshney, A., Jacobs, D.W.: Mesh saliency. ACM Trans. Graph. **24**(3), 659–666 (2005)
14. Wu, Z., Zeng, Y., Liu, Z., et al.: Viewpoint optimization method for 3D visualization based on particle swarm optimization. Comput. Eng. Appl. **51**(17), 168–172 (2015)

Self-collision Detection Optimization Method in the Arm Clothes Simulation

He Bing, Lv Yue[✉], and Jing Mi

School of Computer Science and Engineering, Beihang University, Beijing, China
lvyue2014@buaa.edu.cn

Abstract. This paper implements the self-collision detection optimization during the clothes simulation, including the high-level and low-level tailoring optimization. During the high-level tailoring stage, this paper firstly implements the basic high-level tailoring in combination with the hierarchical bounding box algorithm and continuous normal vector cone information. On this basis, this paper implements the high-level tailoring optimization based on the radiation angle. Finally, this paper implements the high-level tailoring optimization based on the isolated set. During the low-level tailoring stage, this paper firstly implements the low-level tailoring optimization based on the characteristic distribution. In addition, this paper also implements the low-level tailoring optimization based on the non-coplanar filter. Experiment result shows that the two level tailoring optimization method in this paper can effectively cut off the redundant and non-collision primitive pair and further improve the efficiency of self-collision detection.

Keywords: Cloth simulation · Low-level tailoring · Self-collision detection · High-level tailoring · Algorithm optimization

1 Introduction

Collision detection is the most time consuming part in the dynamic simulation of clothes. In order to implement optimization of self-collision detection, the researchers propose a series of optimization methods, including the high-level tailoring optimization and low-level tailoring optimization methods.

High-level tailoring is made on the triangle plane to obtain all candidate triangle pairs (PCTPs) possibly occurring collision through cutting off the area and triangle pairs which will not occur collision, and the most common method is the hierarchical bounding box algorithm. As for self-collision tailoring, Barbic and James [1] proposed a subspace culling method for reduced deformation and Zheng and James [2] use energy-based certificates for arbitrary deformation. Volino [3] judged the self-collision state of meshes through the profile test. Provot [4] proposed the normal vector cone method to effectively cut off the non-collision area, and this method is only applicable to the discrete collision detection. Tang [5] expanded the normal vector cone method to the continuous collision detection to calculate the continuous normal vector cone information in the whole time step. Low-level tailoring is made on the primitive pair plane to

© Springer Science+Business Media Singapore 2016
L. Zhang et al. (Eds.): AsiaSim 2016/SCS AutumnSim 2016, Part II, CCIS 644, pp. 634–641, 2016.
DOI: 10.1007/978-981-10-2666-9_64

cut off the redundant and non-collision primitive pairs and obtain all candidate primitive pairs possibly occurring collision. Many techniques have been proposed to reduce the number of elementary tests between the triangle primitives [6]. Hutter and Fuhrmann [7] proposed the primitive bounding box method to effectively cut off the non-collision primitive pairs. Curtis [8] proposed the representative triangle to eliminate the redundant primitive pairs through uniquely distributing each primitive feature to a triangle containing it. Tang et al. [9], proposed the filter method to filter out the non-coplanar primitive pairs.

2   High-Level Tailoring Optimization

This paper firstly implements the basic high-level tailoring in combination with the hierarchical bounding box algorithm and continuous normal vector cone information On this basis, this paper implements the high-level tailoring optimization based on the radiation angle and cuts off the non-collision triangle pairs in cluster through the radiation angle test. Finally, this paper implements the high-level tailoring optimization based on the isolated set and cuts off the adjoining triangle pairs in the candidate triangle pairs through establishment of isolated sets, so as to further improve the efficiency of self-collision detection.

2.1   Basic High-Level Tailoring

During the self-collision detection, this paper implements the basic high-level tailoring by combining the hierarchical bounding box algorithm with the continuous normal vector cone information. During the traverse process of hierarchical bounding box, this paper firstly uses the continuous normal vector cone information to cut off the non-collision areas, implements the intersection test of bounding box in remaining area and cuts off the disjoint area and triangle pairs in bounding box, so as to obtain all candidate triangle pairs possibly occurring collision. In order to use the continuous normal vector cone information in the hierarchical traverse process, each node in the hierarchical bounding box contains two additional attributes: semi-cone angle and cone axis vector axis.

2.2   High-Level Tailoring Optimization Based on the Radiation Angle

The tailoring idea based on the radiation angle is: if there is an observation point in the given closed manifold mesh and all triangles in this mesh is completely visible to this point (namely, the connection line from the observation point to each triangle will not intersect with other triangles), then this mesh will not occur collision.

This paper improves the skeleton-driven radiation angle tailoring method proposed by Wong [10], and implements the high-level tailoring optimization based on radiation angle in combination with the hierarchical bounding box algorithm and continuous normal vector cone information.

This paper arranges two observation points at the center of upper arm and lower arm in accordance with the structural features of the arm clothes meshes, and the initial location of observation points shall be determined in accordance with the boundary points on the upper and lower end faces of the arm mesh. The mesh is divided into two clusters in accordance with the relative location of the center point on the connection line between the triangle and two observation points, and each cluster corresponds to an observation point. This paper defines two cross sections at the initial location of observation point to cut out loops in the arm meshes and obtain two section loops. In each time step, the location and speed information of observation point can be obtained by a group of vertex interpolation of the corresponding section loop.

During the pre-processing stage, we determine the observation points, implement clustering of meshes and construct the hierarchical bounding box for each cluster of mesh.

During the collision detection stage, we firstly update the hierarchical bounding box of each cluster, update the location and speed information of the observation points and make classifications of observation points for the triangles in each cluster of mesh. Then, implement the detection in and among clusters to obtain all triangle pairs possibly occurring collision. Detection in cluster is to detect the self-collision state in cluster by performing radiation angle test on each cluster of mesh. If all triangles in the cluster are the positively directed triangles, this cluster will not occur collision and shall be cut off. If there is negatively directed triangles or non-directional triangles, detect the collision status of triangle to obtain all triangle pairs possibly occurring collision in the cluster. Detection among clusters is to use the algorithm based on the hierarchical bounding box to obtain all triangle pairs possibly occurring collision among clusters through the intersection test of hierarchical bounding box.

2.3   High-Level Tailoring Optimization Based on the Isolated Set

As the bounding boxes of adjoining triangle pairs always intersect with each other, the efficiency of high-level tailoring is low. During the final step of high-level tailoring, this paper implements the tailoring optimization based on the isolated set [5] and cuts off the adjoining triangle pairs in the candidate triangle pairs.

Establish the isolated set during the preprocessing stage. Only the upper and lower end face of the arm clothes mesh are not closed, boundary element is a few and the quantity of primitives in the isolated set is also a few. During the collision detection stage, cut off all adjoining triangle pairs during the high-level tailoring process to obtain all non-adjoining triangle pairs with intersecting bounding boxes, so as to form the candidate triangle pairs. If the bounding boxes of two leaf nodes intersect with each other during the intersection testing of hierarchical bounding box, judge whether two triangles are adjoined (namely whether they contain the common vertex). If only two triangles are not adjoined, one candidate triangle pair can be formed; otherwise, cut off this triangle pair.

After the high-level tailoring optimization on the basis of the isolated set, the candidate triangle does not contain adjoined triangle pairs. The primitive pair distributed by the candidate triangle pair and the primitive pair in the isolated set for the candidate primitive pair together and can be used for the subsequent basic intersection test.

3   Low-Level Tailoring Optimization

During the low-level tailoring stage, this paper firstly implements the low-level tailoring optimization on the basis of characteristic distribution. Cut off the redundant primitive pairs through the characteristic distribution, implement the intersection test of primitive bounding box when distributing primitive pairs to the candidate triangle and cut off the non-intersecting primitive pairs of the bounding box. In addition, this paper implements the low-level tailoring optimization based on the non-coplanar filter, filter out the non-coplanar primitive pairs in the time step through the non-coplanar test, further reduce the quantity of candidate primitive pairs and improve the efficiency of self-collision detection.

3.1   Low-Level Tailoring Optimization Based on the Characteristic Distribution

As the vertex/edge of mesh is shared by several triangles, the primitive pairs have redundancy. In order to eliminate the redundant primitive pairs, Curtis [8] proposed the idea of representative triangle and uniquely distributed each vertex/edge of mesh to one triangle containing it.

The primitive hierarchical bounding box method proposed by Hutter and Fuhrmann [7] can effectively cut off the primitive pairs not intersecting with the primitive bounding box. The tailoring efficiency is high, but the requirement of maintenance of several primitive hierarchical bounding boxes affects the simulation efficiency. In order to make use of the advantage of high tailoring efficiency of the primitive hierarchical bounding box method, this paper implements the low-level tailoring optimization based on characteristic distribution in combination with the representative triangle mechanism and primitive bounding box during the low-level tailoring stage. This paper firstly implements the characteristic distribution and use the representative triangle mechanism to cut off the redundant primitive pairs. When distributing the primitive pairs to the candidate triangle pairs containing the compatible characteristic pairs, calculate the bounding box of primitives, implement the intersection test of primitive bounding box and cut of the non-intersecting primitive pairs of the primitive bounding boxes.

The low-level tailoring optimization method in this paper implements the intersection test of primitive bounding box during the distribution of primitive pairs and cuts off the non-intersecting primitive pairs of the primitive bounding box, which further improves the efficiency of low-level tailoring. Comparing with the primitive hierarchical bounding box method, the low-level tailoring optimization method in this paper does not need to maintain several primitive hierarchical bounding boxes and has high simulation efficiency. The low-level tailoring optimization method in this paper is implemented as follows:

Pre-processing stage:

Add two attributes in the data structure of each triangle to respectively record the quantity of characteristic vertexes and characteristic sides distributed to this triangle. Implement the characteristic distribution of mesh by using the greedy algorithm and traverse each triangle in order. If there is undistributed primitive (vertex and side) in this triangle, it shall be distributed to this triangle. During the characteristic distribution process, the vertex list and side list of each triangle shall be re-arranged so as to make the distributed characteristic primitive in the front part of the vertex/edge list.

Collision detection stage:

In each time step, distribute the candidate primitive pair which will implement the subsequent basic intersection test to the candidate triangle pairs obtained through high-level tailoring. The distribution process is as follows:

Step 1: firstly judge whether the candidate triangle pair contains compatible characteristic pairs. If at least one triangle is distributed to one or several vertexes or two triangles are distributed to one side or several sides, then this triangle contains the compatible characteristic pairs and continues the step 2. If these two triangles don't contain compatible characteristics pairs, skip these triangle pairs.

Step 2: implement the intersection test of primitive bounding box when distributing the primitive pairs.

(1) Each vertex represented by the triangle A implements the VF primitive bounding box intersection test with the triangle B. If the primitive bounding boxes intersect with each other, it will form a VF candidate primitive pair;

(2) Each vertex represented by the triangle B implements the VF primitive bounding box intersection test with the triangle A. If the primitive bounding boxes intersect with each other, it will form a VF candidate primitive pair;

(3) Each characteristic side represented by the triangle A implements the EE primitive bounding box intersection test with each characteristic side represented by the triangle B. If the primitive bounding boxes intersect with each, it will form an EE candidate primitive pair.

3.2 Low-Level Tailoring Optimization Based on the Non-coplanar Filter

Continuous self-collision detection. Basic intersection test consisting of 6 VF primitive pairs and 9 EE primitive pairs shall be implemented for each candidate triangle, and each basic intersection test shall be divided into 2 steps: coplanar test and internal test. The coplanar test shall involve 4 vertexes no matter for the VF primitive pair or EE primitive pair, and the primitive pairs will possibly have collision only when 4 vertexes are coplanar. Provot [4] proposed that univariate cubic equation shall be solved for the coplanar test of 4 vertexes. If it can be judged in advance that the 4 vertexes will not be coplanar within the time step, the primitive pair will certainly not have collision and can be cut off, so it is unnecessary to solve the univariate cubic equation to implement the coplanar test.

If the vertex is always at the same side of the triangle during the whole time step for the VF primitive pair, this VF primitive will not have collision. This is because the vertex and triangle during the whole time step will not be coplanar and will not have intersection. Thus, if the two sides have not intersection during the whole time step for the EE primitive pair, this EE primitive pair will not be coplanar. Tang [9] proposed the non-penetrating filter method which is to implement the non-coplanar test of primitive through calculating the projection distance and filter out the non-coplanar primitive pairs within the time step.

At the final step of low-level tailoring, this paper implements the low-level tailoring optimization based on the non-coplanar filter and cut off the non-coplanar primitive pairs within the whole time step through the non-coplanar test, so as to further reduce the quantity of candidate primitive pairs and improve the collision detection efficiency. During the collision detection stage, implement the non-coplanar test of the VF primitive and EE primitive within each time step through calculating the projection distance of primitive pairs.

4 Experiment Result

In our experiments, we use a PC with a Intel Xeon CPU and 4G of memory. There are 693 vertexes and 1,345 triangular facets used for arm clothes mesh here. Taking one gesture for example, the quantity and simulation frame rate of the candidate triangular pairs (PCTPs) see below.

4.1 Experiment 1: High-Level Tailoring Optimization

In the high-level tailoring stage, we firstly implement the basic high-level tailoring in combination with the hierarchical bounding box algorithm and continuous normal vector cone information. In order to improve the tailoring efficiency, we implement the high-level tailoring optimization based on the radiation angle to obtain all candidate triangle pairs possibly having collision. Final step: implement the tailoring optimization of the isolated set to cut off all adjoining triangle pairs in the candidate triangle pairs through establishment of the isolated set, so as to further improve the self-collision detection efficiency.

The basic high-level tailoring experiment result is shown in the Fig. 1(a), and the high-level tailoring optimization experiment result is shown in the Fig. 1(b). The high-level tailoring optimization experiment result based on the isolated set is shown in the Fig. 1(c). Red triangles are used for marking the triangle in the detected candidate triangle pairs. We can see that comparing with basic bounding box method, the quantity of candidate triangular pairs tested by our high-level tailoring optimization method is much smaller. The simulation frame rate is improved by 14 times in fact. We improved the skeleton-driven radiation angle method of Wong and cut off adjoining triangle pairs. The simulation efficiency by our method is 6 times higher than that of Wong and moreover, the candidate triangular pairs are much less. Comparing the tailoring method of Tang which only employs orphan set, since we processed self-collision tailoring to each cluster through radiation angle test, the candidate triangular pairs tested by our method is only a half of that tested by Tang's method, with simulation frame rate similar to that of Tang's.

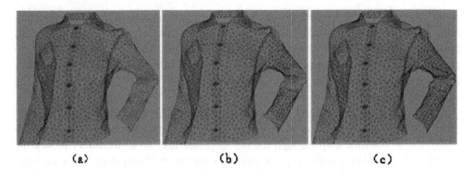

(a)   (b)   (c)

Fig. 1. Experiment result of high-level tailoring optimization method in this paper (Color figure online)

4.2 Experiment 2: Low-Level Tailoring Optimization

During the low-level tailoring stage, this paper firstly implements the low-level tailoring optimization based on the characteristic distribution. On this basis, this paper implements the low-level tailoring optimization based on the non-coplanar filter and respectively analyzes the experiment results.

Table 1 shows the comparison of quantity of primitive pairs and simulated frame rate. We can see that, comparing with basic low-level tailoring method, the quantity of candidate primitive pairs tested by our method decreased sharply and simulation frame rate has been improved by 3 times. Comparing with the tailoring method based on representative triangular mechanism of Curtis, since our method has filtered out non-coplanar primitive pairs and tested even fewer candidate primitive pairs, with high-level culling efficiency. Our low-level tailoring optimization method is lower than Tang's in terms of simulation frame efficiency. But since our method has cut off redundant primitive pairs that do not intersect with primitive bounding box, fewer candidate primitive pairs have been tested. Thus, it is better than Tang's method in terms of culling efficiency.

Table 1. Comparison of different low-level tailoring optimization methods

	Quantity of VF	Quantity of EE	Frame rate
Basic low-level tailoring	1122	2056	12.70
2008 Curtis	74	45	32
2011 Tang	44	338	37.54
Method in this paper	31	137	34.22

5   Conclusion

During the high-level tailoring stage, this paper firstly implements the basic high-level tailoring in combination with the hierarchical bounding box algorithm and continuous normal vector cone information. On this basis, this paper implements the high-level tailoring optimization based on the radiation angle. Finally, this paper implements the high-level tailoring optimization based on the isolated set. The high-level tailoring optimization method of this paper can greatly improve the self-collision detection efficiency. During the low-level tailoring stage, this paper firstly implements the low-level tailoring optimization based on the characteristic distribution. In addition, this paper also implements the tailoring optimization based on the non-coplanar filter. The low-level tailoring optimization method in this paper can further improve the self-collision detection efficiency.

Acknowledgement. This work is supported and funded by the National Natural Science Foundation of China (61272346).

References

1. Barbič, J., James, D.L.: Subspace self-collision culling. ACM Trans. Graph. (TOG) **29**(4), 81 (2010). ACM
2. Zheng, C., James, D.L.: Energy-based self-collision culling for arbitrary mesh deformations. ACM Trans. Graph. **31**(4), 13–15 (2012)
3. Volino, P.: Collision and self-collision detection: efficient and robust solutions for highly deformable surface. In: Computer Graphics, SIGGRAPH 1995. Proceeding, pp. 137–144 (1995)
4. Provot, X.: Collision and self-collision handling in cloth model dedicated to design garment. Graph. Interface, 177–189 (1997)
5. Tang, M., Curtis, S., Yoon, S., et al.: ICCD: interactive continuous collision detection between deformable models using connectivity-based culling. IEEE Trans. Vis. Comput. Graph. **15**(4), 544–557 (2009)
6. Govindaraju, N.K., Knott, D., Jain, N., Manocha, D., et al.: Interactive collision detection between deformable models using chromatic decomposition (SIGGRAPH, 2005). ACM Trans. Graph. **24**(3), 991–999 (2005)
7. Hutter, M., Fuhrmann, A.: Optimized continuous collision detection for deformable triangle meshes. In: Proceedings of WSCG07, pp. 25–32 (2007)
8. Curis, S., Tamstorf, R., Manocha, D.: Fast collision detection for deformable models using representative triangles. In: Proceedings of the 2008 Symposium on Interactive 3D Graphics and Games, pp. 61–69. ACM (2008)
9. Tang, M., Manocha, D., Tong, R.: Fast continuous collision detection using deforming non-penetration filters. In: Interactive 3D Graphics and Games, pp. 7–13. ACM (2010)
10. Wong, S.K., Lin, W.C., Hung, C.H., et al.: Radial view based culling for continuous self-collision detection of skeletal models. ACM Trans. Graph. **32**(4), 96 (2013)

3D Finite Element Modeling and Simulation of Nonlinear Ultrasonic Evaluation for Steel Damage

Yanyan Liu, Linwen Zhang, Haojie Yuan, and Shiwei Ma[✉]

Shanghai Key Laboratory of Power Station Automation Technology,
School of Mechatronics Engineering and Automation, Shanghai University,
Shanghai 200072, China
{yyliu2014,masw}@shu.edu.cn, 274517590@qq.com,
yhjdapple@163.com

Abstract. This research develops a theoretical method to evaluate the creep damage in a 91 steel with ultrasonic nonlinear technique. A three-dimensional finite element model is built to simulate the creep damage of steel P91 and the ultrasonic wave propagation through the degraded material. The nonlinear parameter is calculated from the amplitude of the second harmonic component of ultrasonic waves which is caused by the micro-structural changes of the material. Both the experimental and theoretical results show that the nonlinear parameter increases with the increase of temperature. The results show the feasibility of the model to evaluate the early stage of the degradation of materials by using ultrasonic nonlinearity.

Keywords: Nonlinear ultrasound · Finite element model · Creep damage · Steel P91

1 Introduction

Recent studies are demonstrating the potential of nonlinear ultrasound to quantitatively detect and characterize the micro-structural changes in metals, such as incensement of crystal size, slip and dislocation of the intercrystalline. In this technique, high amplitude ultrasonic wave of a particular frequency is excited to propagate through the material. The harmonics which are due to the interaction of ultrasonic waves with the micro-structures are used as the indication of the degradation of materials. The nonlinear parameter is calculated by the ratio of the second harmonic amplitude to that of the square of the fundamental amplitude [1–5].

To date, many researchers have applied nonlinear ultrasonic technique to detect and characterize the creep damage in metals under laboratory conditions [6–15]. Hurley experimentally found that nonlinear ultrasonic parameter increases and ultrasonic longitudinal phase velocity remains the same, with the increase of carbon content for a series of quenched martensitic steels. These results show that the observed increase in nonlinear parameter can be attributed to dislocation-related effects in the material. Deng analyzed the nonlinear effect of primary Lamb wave propagation for assessing accumulated fatigue damage in aluminum sheets and experimentally found that the effect of second harmonic generation by Lamb wave propagation is very sensitive to the

L. Zhang et al. (Eds.): AsiaSim 2016/SCS AutumnSim 2016, Part II, CCIS 644, pp. 642–650, 2016.
DOI: 10.1007/978-981-10-2666-9_65

accumulation of fatigue damage of solid plates. Ehrlich experimentally characterized the creep damage in a welded steel pipe section using a nonlinear ultrasonic technique. Matlack used the nonlinear ultrasound to measure microstructural changes due to the radiation damage in steel. Studying the above listed researches, it is found that most of them measure the damage in metal by using nonlinear ultrasonic techniques experimentally. There has been no systematic work reported on the theoretical model of using ultrasonic nonlinearity to examine the microstructural creep damage and the stage of creep for steel P91.

This research proposes a three-dimensional finite element model to simulate the ultrasonic wave propagation through the creep damaged P91 steel. The nonlinearity parameter is used as an indicator of the thermal damage of the material, which is calculated from the amplitudes of the fundamental and second harmonic wave.

2   Experiment and Analysis Method

2.1   Experiment Setup

The experiment is conducted by the nonlinear ultrasonic measurement system (RITEC RAM-5000 SNAP) with longitudinal wave probes of 5 and 10 MHz. The diameter of the probe is 1.27 cm. The schematic of the system is shown as Fig. 1, which consists of an amplifier, attenuator, filters, transducers, and a dual channel digital oscilloscope (Tektronix DP04032). One of the transducer acts as a transmitter, and the other acts as a receiver. The transmitter (T) is a narrowband p-wave Lithium Niobate transducer with a center frequency of 5 MHz, and the receiver (R) is a broadband p-wave Lithium Niobate transducer with a center frequency of 10 MHz. ULTRAGEL II was used as the couplant. In the experiment, the transmitting and receiving transducers are always on the same axis to avoid the energy loss. A 5 MHz single-frequency sinusoidal pulse with cycles of 5 and width of 1 μs is used as excitation, as the pulse width of the excitation signal should be less than the travel time of the ultrasound through the sample in order to reduce the disturbance from equipment and random noise. The sample is made of steel 91 (9CrMoVNb), which has a size of 4 cm × 4 cm × 2 cm.

2.2   Nonlinear Ultrasonic Theory

It is well known that ultrasonic wave interacts with the micro-structural changes and micro-cracking, and as a result of this interaction, part of the wave is converted into harmonics. As damage increases, larger amplitudes of harmonics are generated.

Assume that the nonlinear constitutive relationship of the material is described by Eq. (1):

$$\sigma = E\varepsilon(1 + \beta\varepsilon + \cdots) \tag{1}$$

where E is Young's modulus and β is the higher order nonlinear elastic coefficient. For small strain deformation, the equation of motion can be written as

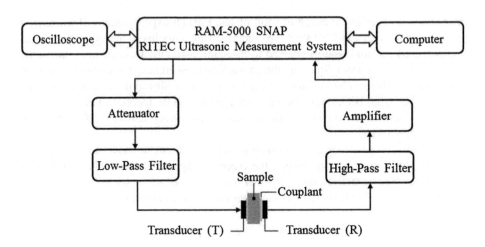

Fig. 1. Schematic of ultrasonic measurement system

$$\rho\frac{\partial^2 u}{\partial t^2} = \frac{\partial \sigma}{\partial x} \tag{2}$$

where ρ is the density of material in the unperturbed state, x is the propagation distance of sound wave, u is the displacement. For the small strain deformation considered here, the normal strain in the x-direction is $\varepsilon(x, t) = \partial u(x, t)/\partial t$, Eq. (1) can be written as

$$\rho\frac{\partial^2 u}{\partial t^2} = E\frac{\partial^2 u}{\partial x^2} + 2E\beta\frac{\partial u}{\partial x}\frac{\partial^2 u}{\partial x^2} + \cdots \tag{3}$$

To solve the above equation, the displacement u is assumed to contain two parts: the initial wave and the first-order perturbation solution, as follows:

$$u = u_0 + u' \tag{4}$$

Assuming u_0 is a single frequency sinusoidal wave,

$$u_0 = A_1 \cos(kx - \omega t) \tag{5}$$

where k is the wave number, ω is angular frequency, and A_1 is the amplitude of wave.
The perturbation solution up to the second-order is

$$u = u_0 + u' = A_1 \cos(kx - \omega t) - A_2 \sin 2(kx - \omega t) \tag{6}$$

Where $A_2 = \frac{\beta}{8}A_1^2 k^2 x$.

The second term in the above equation represents the second harmonic frequency component. It is seen that the magnitude of the second-order component A_2 depends on β, which represents the nonlinear characteristics of degraded material. For constant k and x, β can be normalized as

$$\beta' = \frac{\beta k^2 x}{8} = \frac{A_2}{A_1^2} \tag{7}$$

In this study, β' is defined as the nonlinear parameter.

2.3 3D Finite Element Model

Based on the above theory, a 3-dimensional finite element model is developed by COMSOL Multiphysics. The simulation is conducted in two steps: (1) the creep evolution of a material by using the transient analysis of Nonlinear Structural Materials Module, which is based on the Norton Law; (2) the ultrasonic wave propagation through the creep-damaged material by using the transient analysis of Acoustic Module, where the displacement of material calculated from step (1) is used as initial conditions.

Figure 2 shows the mesh of the system in 3-D. It's know that the finer the mesh size, the more accurate the simulation results. Because of the limitation of our computer's addressable memory for calculation, the maximum mesh size is around 15 % of the wavelength. The larger rectangular block represents the steel sample with a size of 4 cm × 4 cm × 2 cm, while the small cylinders at two sides represent the transmitted and received transducers with a diameter of 0.9 cm and thickness of 0.1 cm, respectively.

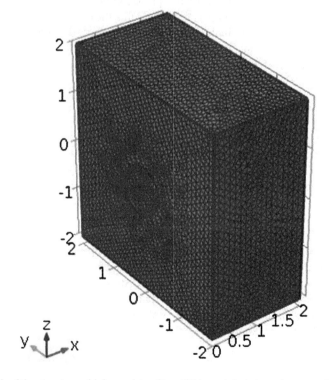

Fig. 2. Mesh of the structure which consists of two lithium niobate transducers and a rectangular block sample of P91 steel.

In this study the simulation is focused on the sound wave propagation through the damaged material, which is computed by the Acoustic Module (the second step). For a time-harmonic wave, for which the pressure varies with time as

$$p(x, t) = p(x)e^{i\omega t} \tag{8}$$

The 2nd-order Westervelt equation is used as the nonlinear wave equation to solve the wave propagating in the steel sample as follows:

$$\frac{1}{\rho c^2} \frac{\partial^2 p}{\partial t^2} - d_a \frac{\partial p}{\partial t} + \nabla \cdot \left(-\frac{1}{\rho}(\nabla p) \right) = \frac{\beta}{\rho^2 c^4} \frac{\partial^2 p^2}{\partial t^2} \tag{9}$$

where p is the ultrasonic pressure, c is the speed of sound, d_a is the damping term due to the wave attenuation, β is the nonlinear parameter.

The boundary conditions of the 3D model are: the interface between the transducer and steel sample is pressure boundary, and the rest of the sound field boundaries are plane wave radiation boundaries. The excitation conditions for the transducer are: a 5-cycle sine pulse with the frequency f of 5 MHz and the amplitude of $A_0 = 10^5$ Pa. And the density of and sound speed in steel P91 are 7780 kg/m^3 and 6087 m/s. The displacement of material calculated from the Nonlinear Structural Materials Module is used as the initial conditions for the nonlinear wave propagation equation in Acoustic Module. Because when ultrasonic wave propagates in the solid, the propagation velocity not only depends on the sound velocity in the material, but also depends on the displacement of material and its nonlinear characteristics.

3   Results and Discussion

The sample P91 exhibits the creep behavior under a thermal treatment of one hour at 970 °C. The distribution of the ultrasonic wave propagation in the steel sample at time of $4.4e^{-6}$s after the thermal treatment is analyzed. Figures 3 and 4 shows the distribution of acoustic pressure field inside the sample and at the central cross-sectional surface, respectively. It is seen that the ultrasonic waves decay very fast during the propagation in the steel sample because of high attenuation. The frequency spectrum of the received ultrasonic wave at transducer R is analyzed, as shown in Fig. 5. It is seen that a second-order harmonic component is generated at the frequency of 10 MHz, where the fundamental wave with a frequency of 5 MHz. The harmonic component indicates the material's nonlinearity after the thermal treatment. This is because the micro-structural changes in the damaged material cause the distortion in the ultrasonic wave, and this material's nonlinearity leads to the generation of the second- harmonic wave component.

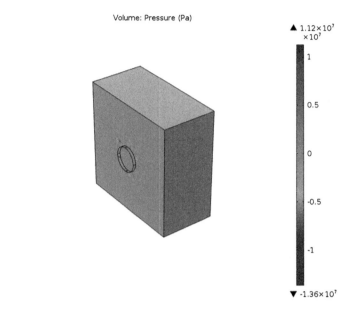

Fig. 3. Distribution of acoustic pressure field in the sample.

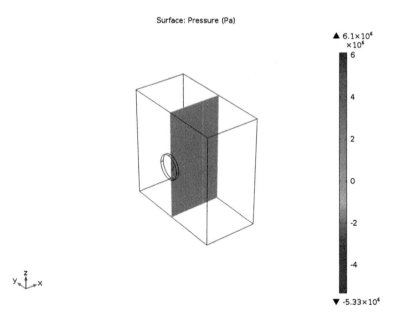

Fig. 4. Distribution of acoustic pressure field at the central cross-section of the sample.

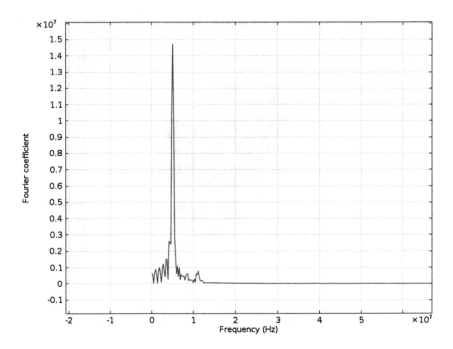

Fig. 5. Frequency spectrum of received ultrasonic wave.

The experimental and theoretical relationships between the normalized nonlinear parameter and temperature for steel P91 is presented in Fig. 6. The measurement was conducted on five different samples under one hour thermal treatment at five different

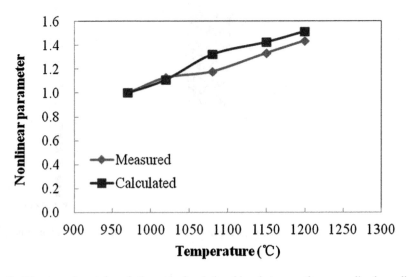

Fig. 6. The experimental and theoretical relationships between the normalized nonlinear parameter and temperature.

temperatures of 970 °C, 1020 °C, 1080 °C, 1150 °C and 1200 °C, respectively. 16 measurements on the nonlinear parameter of each sample were averaged to improve the signal-to-noise ratio. The theoretical calculation is based on the same conditions. It is observed that the nonlinear ultrasonic parameter increases with the increase of temperature for both the simulated and measured results. This is because when temperature increases, the speed of the movement of dislocation and sliding of grain boundary increases, and the diffusion coefficients increase as well, all of these microstructural changes attribute to the nonlinearity of the creep-damaged material. Therefore, it can be expected that the degree of material degradation can be evaluated by using the nonlinearity of the ultrasonic wave.

4   Conclusions

In summary, a method to theoretically determine the creep damage of steel P91 by nonlinear ultrasonic technique is proposed. A three-dimensional finite element model is built to simulate the creep evolution and ultrasonic wave propagation through the degraded material. The propagation of ultrasound through the creep-damaged sample causes the generation of the second-harmonic component of wave. The nonlinear parameter is calculated from the amplitude of the second-harmonic wave. Both the experimental and theoretical results show that the nonlinear parameter increases with the increase of temperature. As the damage increases, the magnitude of the nonlinear interaction also increases. Thus the nonlinear ultrasonic parameter can be used to express the relative change of the material's nonlinearity in order to evaluate the early stage of the degradation of mechanical properties and micro-damage of the materials. Although more experimental and theoretical work are needed to develop a general method for the evaluation of the early stage degradation, the feasibility of using this finite element model by nonlinear ultrasound for such purpose is clearly demonstrated in this study.

Acknowledgement. This work is funded by National Natural Science Foundation of China (61171145) and Shanghai Young Eastern Scholar (QD2015030).

References

1. Shui, G., Wang, Y.: Ultrasonic evaluation of early damage of a coating by using second-harmonic generation technique. J. Appl. Phys. **111**(12), 124902 (2012)
2. Bermes, C., Jocobs, L.L., Kim, J.Y., et al.: Cumulative second harmonic generation in lamb waves for the detection of material nonlinearities. AIP Conf. Proc. **894**, 177–184 (2007)
3. Ma, S., Yuan, K.: Ultrasonic nondestructive evaluation to the thermal fatigue damage of SUS306 stainless steel. Tech. Acoust. **27**(2), 206–209 (2008)
4. Jhang, K.-Y.: Nonlinear ultrasonic techniques for non-destructive assessment of micro damage in material: a review. Int. J. Precis. Eng. Manufact. **10**(1), 123–135 (2009)
5. Shui, G., Jacobs, L.J., Qu, J., et al.: A Rayleigh wave technique to measure the acoustic nonlinearity parameter of material. AIP Conf. Proc. **975**, 1267–1274 (2008)
6. Hurley, D.C., Balzar, D., Purtscher, P.T., et al.: Nonlinear ultrasonic parameter in quenched martensitic steels. J. Appl. Phys. **83**(9), 4584–4588 (1998)

7. Jeong, H., Nahm, S.-H., Jhang, K.-Y., et al.: A nondestructive method for estimation of fracture toughness of CrMoV rotor steels based on ultrasonic nonlinearity. Ultrasonics **41**(7), 543–549 (2003)

8. Deng, M., Pei, J.: Assessment of accumulated fatigue damage in solid plates using nonlinear Lamb wave approach. Appl. Phys. Lett. **90**(12), 121902 (2007)

9. Ehrlich, C., Kim, J.-Y., Jacobs, L.J., et al.: Experimental characterization of creep damage in a welded steel pipe section using a nonlinear ultrasonic technique. AIP Conf. Proc. **1430**, 292–298 (2012)

10. Matlack, K.H., Kim, J.-Y., Wall, J., et al.: Using nonlinear ultrasound to measure microstructural changes due to radiation damage in steel. Proc. Meet. Acoust. **19**(1), 045023 (2013)

11. Barnard, D.J., Dace, G.E., Buck, O.: Acoustic harmonic generation due to thermal embrittlement of Inconel 718. J. Nondestr. Eval. **16**(2), 67–75 (1997)

12. Nagy, P.B.: Fatigue damage assessment by nonlinear ultrasonic material characterization. Ultrasonics **36**(1–5), 375–381 (1998)

13. Hurley, D.C., Balzar, D., Purtscher, P.T.: Ultrasonic nonlinearity parameter in precipitate-hardened steels. AIP Conf. Proc. **497**, 413–418 (1999)

14. Nazarov, V.E., Kolpakov, A.B.: Experimental investigations of nonlinear acoustic phenomena in polycrystalline zinc. J. Acoust. Soc. Am. **107**(4), 1915–1921 (2000)

15. Jaya Rao, V.V.S., Kannan, E., Prakash, R.V., et al.: Fatigue damage characterization using surface acoustic wave nonlinearity in aluminum alloy AA7175-T7351. J. Appl. Phys. **104**(12), 123508 (2008)

Research on Simulation Scenario Entity Transform Based on Visually Mapping

Xin Wang[✉] and LaiBin Yan[✉]

College of Information System and Management,
National University of Defense Technology, Changsha, Hunan, China
wangxin201604@126.com, Lbyan2000@163.com

Abstract. Simulation scenario is the data base of simulation system. The current simulation scenario can often be applied to single simulation system. There are problems like the low reusability of old simulation scenario, long time when the large number of entities are created and so on. This paper studies the mapping relationship of simulation objects between different specifications, visually saving this mapping relationship to the data dictionary, and through the simulation object instantiation and data query to transform old entities to new entities that simulation system is able to identify. In MAXSIM Simulation System Development, this way greatly reduce the simulation scenario development time and ensures the accuracy of the data.

Keywords: Simulation scenario · Visually mapping · Entity transform

1 Introduction

Simulation scenario is the digital base of simulation system which makes system run smoothly. It's also the key part of the simulation system. The present simulation scenario is firstly set by the military technical personnel after they make a good military scenario, and then technology personnel according to certain standards, cost a lot of time to convert it into data simulation scenario data. However, due to the various groups of the simulation scenario description, development methodologies and final data format is not exactly the same understanding, making big difference between simulation scenarios.

To achieve the simulation system you want to reuse the given data and avoid developing simulation scenario authoring software when simulation rules transform, we need to do the research on the simulation scenario conversion technology and by this simulation scenarios of different standardized descriptions can be quickly transformed. Simulation entity as the key part of simulation scenario is the core of this paper. This paper will focus on different simulation scenario type set of entities, attributes, and the same simulation entity mapping relation dictionary under different description specifications, and then by querying the mapping dictionary, the old simulation entities will be converted as new simulation entities that can be identified by simulation system.

The rest of this paper is organized as follows. Section 2 describes the related work. Section 3 introduces how to get the correspondence between the entity classes and their

© Springer Science+Business Media Singapore 2016

L. Zhang et al. (Eds.): AsiaSim 2016/SCS AutumnSim 2016, Part II, CCIS 644, pp. 651–659, 2016.

DOI: 10.1007/978-981-10-2666-9_66

attributes and save as dictionary. Section 4 uses the mapping dictionary to quickly generating simulation entities. Section 5 concludes the whole work of this paper.

2   Related Work

Recently, there is a lot of research on the simulation scenario conversion. Chao-yang Liu et al. come up with the conversion technology based on MDA. This technology can well realize the transformation of independent model in different scenarios, but for the "heterogeneous" problem with different description specification (Due to the description of the simulation scenario, development methods and the understanding of the final data format are from different groups, it makes database are different from each simulation member's database and storage modes) it is not a very good solution. The transformation of heterogeneous object classes is unrealizable. Meiyan Zheng etc. want to set the data conversion interface based on HLA, it implements from military scenario to simulation scenario, together with the method of mapping, convert military conceptual entity to simulation data entity. It has a good reference for how to transfer different simulation entities under different description specification. Wenzhen Li etc. present an air force scenario description based on the Agent, used to generate scenario quickly. But this scenario generation was more by simulation personnel through contrast military scenario in manual configuration software, cannot realize quickly generate of scenario entity.

The present scenario transformation research mainly exist the following problems:

(a) Can't solve the "heterogeneous" problem due to different description specification and different entities in different simulation scenario.
(b) In the process of simulation scenario transformation, object instantiation can only be made by time-consuming manual configuration.

This paper takes MAXSIM simulation system as the background, study on the simulation object visualization mapping technology under different description specification, form a mapping dictionary which can store the same simulation object under different specification mapping relation. By querying the mapping dictionary, converts the old simulation scenario entity to new simulation entities that system can identify, to realize the transformation of the simulation scenario entity.

3   The Simulation Object Visually Mapping

"The simulation object visually mapping" is to achieve visually configuration simulation object classes and their attributes and to form the corresponding "dictionary". To provide a data basis for simulation scenario conversion, this chapter will introduce simulation object visually mapping technology from three aspects:the implementation principle, implementation method and software implementation. Its work mode is shown in Fig. 1.

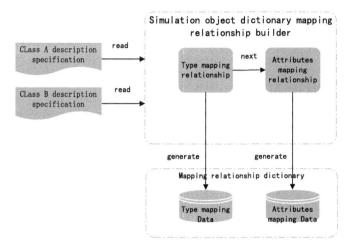

Fig. 1. The simulation object visually mapping

3.1 The Principle of Implementation

Under the description of the different specification, the same simulation objects such as aircraft may have different names, like "aircraft", "plane", "airplane" etc. The structure may be different as shown in Fig. 2. Two different scenario describe plane using XML data format specification.

```
<PlatformList>
 <Platform TKBID="01" TypeName=" aircraft-1 ">
  <SensorList>
   <Sensor Num="1",  TKBID="0102",Name="SPS-10" />
   <Sensor Num="2",  TKBID="0112",Name="SIR" />
  </SensorList>
 </Platform>
</PlatformList>
```

```
<PlatformList>
 <Platform SID="71"  Name=" plane-1 ">
  <equipList>
   <SenseList>
    <Sense Num="1",  SID="012",Name="SPS-10" />
    <Sense Num="2",  SID="112",Name="SIR" />
   </SensorList>
  </equipList>
 </Platform>
</PlatformList>
```

Fig. 2. The same plane at different specifications

You can see that all are an instance of the plane but their names are different and attributes of organizational relationships are also different. The left side call it "aircraft", and the right side is "plane". The sensor suite of left side is directly mount on Sensor List, the right side is mounting on Sense List in equip List. This different specification makes left side of the aircraft cannot be used directly by the right side of the simulation scenario. But we can see that they have the same physical meaning— "airplane",mounting on the same sensor—SPS-10 SIR and if they have other properties, they are also the same.

What we need to do is to save the "same physical meaning" and form a data document. When the computer reads the document, it will know "aircraft = plane". When the computer reads Sensor List, knows is "my sense list".

3.2 Implementation Method

Figure 2 as an example, realize visualization of simulation object mapping must solve the following problems:

(a) How to make the computer know the aircraft and the plane are equivalent.
Technicians know both are the same when they see name, but the computer doesn't know, so you need to "tell" computer "aircraft = plane". Because of storage and query difficulty, name as the matching characters is not available. We can see, no matter use which description, if you want the simulation scenario data can be read by the simulation system, each kind of simulation object has a unique identification code, so what we have to do is to get the identification code as a symbol of the query matches.

(b) How to make the computer know corresponding relations between properties of aircraft and plane.
Such as "speed" in aircraft may be defined as "cruising speed" in plane, we need to do is to find the corresponding relations. Due to the different description in the specification, the attributes of simulation object maybe is different under the XML data structure. Some may be as a class of child nodes, others may be the properties of the nodes. In order to improve the speed of the query, we read its name as a match. Although there will be repeated in the data ("Speed", "weight" and other general properties), but querying speed will get a lot of ascension.

(c) How to save this mapping relationship, to form a data document that can be identified by the computer.
Use tree data structure to store the mapping relationship. The mapping relationship of object classes as the parent node, the corresponding relation of attributes as child node. When the simulation entity generator query "dictionary", by iterating through the parent node to find the simulation object, and instantiation, find the corresponding relation of attributes from child nodes quickly.

The specific work process is shown in Fig. 3:

3.3 The Simulation Object Mapping Dictionary Builder

According to the above design, this paper designs generator software of simulation object mapping dictionary. It contains the following functions:

- Read two kinds of description specification: class A and class B. And displayed in the form of tree.
- Can easily match the simulation object types, properties under two description specifications, and generate the corresponding matching data.

It's working interface as shown in Fig. 4.

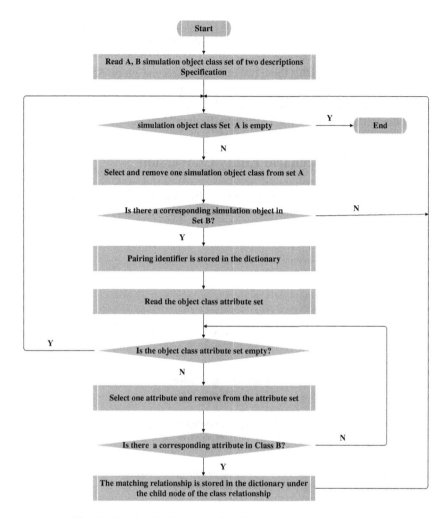

Fig. 3. Simulation object visually mapping technology processes

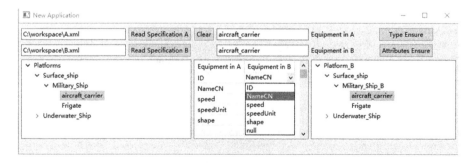

Fig. 4. Simulation object class mapping dictionary builder interface

Firstly, it will read the two specifications A and B. In the right and left sides, entity classes are displayed as tree structure. Secondly, double-click the entity class on the left side and then double-click the corresponding entity class on the right. Click the "Type Endure" button. It indicates that these two classes is the same entity. After that, attributes of these two entity classes will be shown in the middle. And then, select the corresponding properties in the drop-down menu B. If the attribute you do not need, you can select "null". In the end, click the "Attributes Endure" button.

4   The Simulation Scenario Entity Conversion

The simulation scenario entity conversion is by querying the mapping dictionary, instance initialization, achieving quickly convert the old simulation entities to new simulation entities.

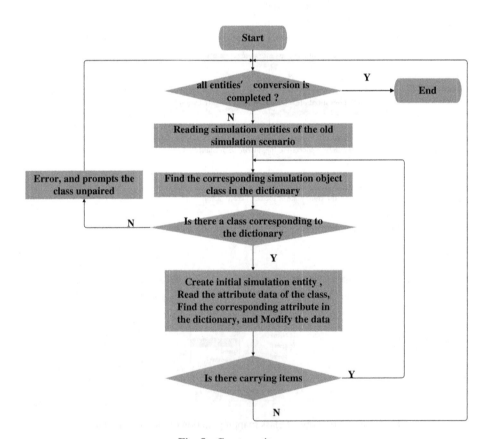

Fig. 5.   Create entity process

4.1 Implementation Method

Entities in the simulation scenario mainly consist by types, properties, carrying relationship, etc. To transform all entities in the simulation scenario, we need to do the following works:

- All entities can find the corresponding simulation object instantiation.
- All entities after conversion are not lack of attributes. (Can run in a new simulation system).

Format stored "simulation object mapping dictionary" can satisfy the demand for the first item, when you read the class A primitive entities in the simulation scenario data types, querying the dictionary to find the corresponding class B simulation objects and then instantiate it.

Because of the different description specification, there may be some properties exist in new scenario but not in the old scenario, so meaningful initial values are needed to meet the needs of the new scenario. When the first creation is instantiation, by coping built initial instance, then read the corresponding attributes to modify it.

Its working process is shown in Fig. 5.

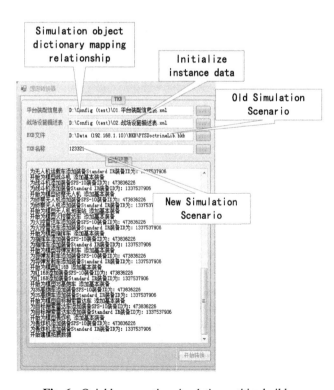

Fig. 6. Quickly generating simulation entities builder

4.2   Software Implementation

According to the above design, this paper designed simulation scenario entity conversion based on different description. Figure 6 shows the scenario entity conversion interface.

By reading the simulation object mapping dictionary, initialize the instance data of new simulation object, the old data simulation scenario, etc. Enter new name of the entity, click start conversion.

4.3   Validation

The process of making scenario data in MAXSIM simulation system, 17 kinds of 367 entities, costs 22 min to finish transformation. Visually mapping relationship of entity and attributes costs about 16 min. Generating entities only cost 3 min, and other 3 min are for operating software, inputting names of files and other things. The proportion of each part is shown in Fig. 7.

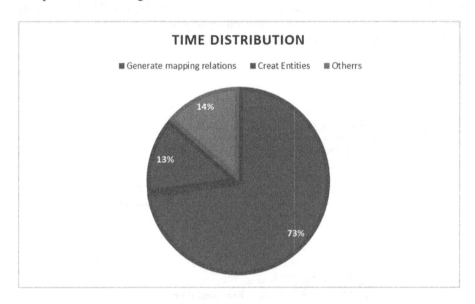

Fig. 7.   Time distribution

5   Conclusion

Through the research of simulation scenarios conversion technology based on different description specification, we can make the original scenario entity quickly generated under new description specification and ensure the correctness of the data, enables the simulation technology personnel to focus on the development of simulation system, regardless of the specific military technologies.

This technology has been practiced in MAXSIM simulation system. In making a new simulation scenario, fully use the existing simulation scenarios, save much time of making scenario, improving the progress of research and development.

Acknowledgment. We appreciate the support from State Key Laboratory of High Performance Computing, National University of Defense Technology (No. 201303-05) and Research Found for the Doctoral Program of Higher Education of China (No. 20124307110017).

References

1. Liu, C.-y., Chen, W.-t., C., Zhang, W.: Research on simulation scenario transform based on model driven archite. Control Autom. **27**(4) (2011)
2. Liu, Z.-w.: Research on standard description method of simulation scenario. Inf. Technol. (7) (2012)
3. Mei, Y.-z., Yao, Y.-p., Yang, J.-y., Peng, Y.-w.: Research on HLA-based scenario data interface. J. Syst. Simul. (2006)
4. Li, W.-z., Wan, X.-d., Li, Y.-l., Zhang, D.-h., Xue, Y.-y.: Research and implementation of operation simulation scenario based on XM. Comput. Technol. Devel. (2013)

A Motion Segmentation Based Algorithm
of Human Motion Alignment

Meng Zha[1], Zhigeng Pan[1(✉)], and Mingmin Zhang[2]

[1] Digital Media and Human Computer Interaction Research Center,
Hangzhou Normal University, Hangzhou, China
floristt@l26.com, zgpan@cad.zju.edu.cn
[2] School of Computer Science and Technology,
Zhejiang University, Hangzhou, China
zmm@cad.zju.edu.cn

Abstract. As a classic method of human motion alignment, original Dynamic Time Warping algorithm may cause poor effects while applied in the field of human motion blending, such as motion pause and motion distortion. To address this problem, we propose a motion segmentation based method of human motion alignment. We first make use of Isomap which is a classic algorithm in manifold learning to reduce dimensionality of all the motion frames in the original motion samples. Then we can obtain the segment of different motion samples by making use of the extreme point of all the corresponding low-dimensional coordinates of motion frames. Finally we apply Dynamic Time Warping method in the corresponding segments of different motion samples respectively to achieve refined alignment results. We conduct contrast experiment between our algorithm and traditional method, the result shows that our method can eliminate motion pause and motion distortion phenomenon caused by traditional method and make significant improvement in the application of human motion blending. The generated motion samples have a high degree of both fidelity and fluency.

Keywords: Motion alignment · Motion blending · Dynamic time warping · Isomap · Motion segment

1 Introduction

The control and synthesis of 3D human motion have been one of the hot spots in the research field of computer graphics all along. And with motion capture technology being widely used in the field of digital entertainment and system simulation, data driven human motion technology has increasingly become an important research topic in the field of computer animation. Benefiting from many large-scale 3D human motion database been established, the importance of mining the value of existing motion capture data and make good use of them is becoming increasingly prominent.

Motion data pre-processing has always been the previous step of reuse of motion data. Motion data pre-processing also includes a variety of forms, such as: motion denoising, motion space warping, motion alignment, etc. The major purpose of motion denoising is

L. Zhang et al. (Eds.): AsiaSim 2016/SCS AutumnSim 2016, Part II, CCIS 644, pp. 660–670, 2016.
DOI: 10.1007/978-981-10-2666-9_67

to eliminate the generated noise data which are caused by the defects of motion capture equipment, the commonly used methods include linear time invariant filter [1, 2], the Kalman filter [3–5] and some data driven filter [6, 7]. Motion space warping is mainly in order to adjust the spatial coordinates of the moving segment or the whole direction, so that the data can be processed in a unified coordinate space [8].

Motion alignment aims to find the temporal correspondence between different motion clips. After that, different motion clips can have a high degree of similarity in logic, and it has been the crucial step of much follow-up work, such as motion blending [9], motion synthesis [10] etc. Dynamic time warping [11, 12] is the most common algorithm used in motion alignment, and there are also some variants of this algorithm, such as iterative DTW [13] and incremental DTW [14] etc. All these DTW based motion alignment methods that mentioned above have a common characteristic, they all aim to seek overall corresponding relations between different motion clips. And furthermore, they calculate the matching path with minimum weight value to achieve the correspondence relation between two motion samples. But all these above methods also have a common drawback. Most of the time the original motion samples contain multiple motion segments, it means that the original motion samples may contain multiple cycles or a periodic motion inside can continue to be subdivided into different phases of movement. In these cases traditional motion alignment methods may not get good performance. While applied in motion blending, traditional DTW based alignment algorithms often result in apparent motion pause phenomenon and serious motion distortion due to the unsatisfactory motion alignment results. In [15] the original DTW algorithm is also adjusted and it achieves great improvement in the application of motion retrieval.

Due to the high dimensionality of 3D human motion data, it is difficult to deal with them directly. Dimensionality reduction technology is often used as a key step, and has been widely used in the field of human motion synthesis and human motion control. In [16], the application of different data dimensionality reduction techniques in the field of data driven human animation is reviewed. Generally speaking, dimension reduction techniques can be classified into two categories: linear dimensionality reduction and nonlinear dimensionality reduction. While linear dimension reduction technique mainly includes PCA [17] (Principal Component Analysis) and ICA [18] (Independent Component Analysis). [19] uses PCA to reduce the dimension of motion capture data, and interpolation operation is implemented in low dimensional space to control the movement of avatar. [20] proposed a method that could automatically calculate the weight of the principal components, thus it can effectively generate new human animation which does not exist in the original database. All these methods mentioned above are to reduce the dimensionality of original motion data through PCA, and then synthesize high dimensional target motion by optimizing the low dimensional parameters. The advantages of these methods are that the calculation is easy to implement, but due to the linear assumption, the effect is not good enough when they are applied to complex motion types. While the ICA method aim to find the demographic independent components, in order to achieve the purpose of reducing the dimension. The effectiveness of this method depends on the assumption that the low dimensional signals extracted are as independent as possible [21] uses ICA technology to decompose the motion, make it break down into the stylized component so that the user can choose the appropriate stylized component to realize the motion editing. In [22], motion data is decomposed into several sub spaces to express the movement style, in order to generate stylized motion. But due to the high spatial and temporal correlation within human motion data, the application of ICA method is often limited, and it is used commonly in the field of stylized motion synthesis.

Taking into account that the complexity of real human motion data are always very high, and often exhibiting a significant nonlinear characteristics, linear dimension reduction technology may not achieve good results. For this reason, the nonlinear dimensionality reduction technology represented by manifold learning has been introduced into the field of 3D human animation in recent years. Manifold learning is a typical nonlinear dimensionality reduction techniques, it is based on this hypothesis: high dimensional data are not distributed in flat Euclidean space, but are distributed in low dimensional manifold which embedded in high dimensional space. Manifold learning can reveal the essential characteristics of the original motion data, and it can be used to obtain a simple and intuitive expression of the original data. In [23], the SOM method is used to obtain the low dimensional representation of high dimensional motion data, and the inverse mapping is obtained by RBF function training, which can generate high dimensional motion data from the low dimensional samples. The disadvantage is that when the number of original samples is sparse, it may cause distortion in the reconstruction of high dimensional motion. In [10] Isomap [24] is implemented to reduce the dimension of the original high-dimensional motion data and to construct a low dimensional semantic motion parameter space. Then users can specify some sample points in the low dimensional space and weighted coefficient will be imposed on the original high dimensional samples so that new high dimensional human motion can be synthesized.

In this paper we combine with manifold learning algorithm and traditional motion alignment algorithm. Firstly, we use Isomap algorithm to map the original motion data with high dimensionality into a low dimensional space, and then we can achieve motion segmentation based on low dimensional distribution of mapped motion frames. Finally we conduct DTW algorithm between segmented corresponding motion clips to fulfill motion alignment. The motion alignment results are applied to motion blending and comparison experiment with traditional alignment method are conducted. Experimental results show that our algorithm can effectively eliminate the phenomenon of motion pause and motion distortion which are caused by traditional alignment method when applied in motion fusion. The final motion samples synthesized by our alignment method are of high degrees of both fidelity and fluency.

2   Isomap Based Motion Segmentation

2.1   Construction of Low Dimensional Embedded Manifold by Isomap

The motion capture data used in this paper is composed of a series of discrete and ordered sequence frames. Each single frame is composed of 31 nodes, including the root node, which form a skeleton model of human body. The root node has three translational motion components and rotational motion components which control position and orientation of the whole model. While the non-root nodes have at most three rotational degrees of freedom, which represent the rotation angle in the local coordinate system that is bound to its parent node. The formula is expressed as follows:

$$Motion = \{Frame_1, Frame_2, \ldots Frame_m\} \tag{1}$$

$$Frame(t) = \{Pos_{root}(t), Ori_{root}(t), R_1(t), R_2(t), \ldots R_n(t)\} \tag{2}$$

As indicated earlier, the dimension of each single frame of human motion pose sequences are very high, there are usually more than 60 dimensions. The high dimensionality of the original motion sample frames has brought great inconvenience to our analysis and process. And meanwhile it is not conducive for us to dig out the essential characteristics of motion sequences. But on the other hand, despite the high dimension of the original motion data, for many types of motion, we can always abstract simple semantics to describe and summarize the complex 3D human motion itself. Taking two walking samples with different stride-length for example, despite the complexity of these two motion sequences, we can extract the essential semantic features from them through observation, namely, the amplitude in which avatar swings arm and the stride-length with which avatar walks. Furthermore, taking into account that both of them have a high degree of consistency, we can even describe these motion samples by even one single dimensional semantics.

The existing manifold learning algorithm is designed to find the potential low dimensional manifold structure and related parameters. Isomap [24] is a typical non-linear manifold learning algorithm, which can find the potential low dimensional parameter space embeded in the high dimension space. The main idea is to calculate the geodesic distance of the sample points on the manifold to take the place of Euclidean distance, the purpose of which is to preserve the inherent manifold structure in the original data. And then MDS algorithm is utilized to solve the low dimensional coordinates. With respect to LLE [25] algorithm which aims at keeping the relationship between neighboring point, Isomap can keep the global characteristics of the sample points and its effectiveness has achieved validation in many fields such as face images, gestures distribution and 3D object detection. In this paper, we apply Isomap algorithm to map the the original motion frames to a low dimension parameter space, and the specific algorithm steps are as follows:

(1) Extraction and representation of motion data. Firstly, a corresponding motion clip with the same period is extracted from the two original motion samples respectively, which is used as the original data. The motion data is represented as mentioned before, each sample frame data contains root node's POS_{root} vector representing position and ORI_{root} vector representing direction, as well as R_i vector representing the rotational degrees of freedom of various non-root nodes.

(2) Constructing the original distance matrix of motion frame data M_{disc}. Calculate the distance between any two frames from the extracted motion data frame by frame:

$$Disc(frame_i, frame_j) = \sum_{k=1}^{n} \|R_{ik} - R_{jk}\| * Weight_k \tag{3}$$

Where n represents the number of non-root nodes, and considering that different bone nodes have different weight values for the whole movement, so we should also take the corresponding weight coefficient values into account while calculating the frame distances. The general rules are: the closer to the root node, the higher is the weight coefficient value, and vice versa. After we achieve the distances between frames, we will get the original distance matrix:

$$M_{disc}(i,j) = Disc(frame_i, frame_j) \tag{4}$$

(3) Construct geodesic distance matrix $M_{geodesic}$ based on the original distance matrix M_{disc}. Firstly we get the solution of corresponding weight matrix M_{weight} according to the original distance matrix M_{disc}:

$$M_{weight} = \begin{cases} M_{disc}(i,j), & if \quad frame_j \in N_{kth}(frame_i) \\ MaxDisc, & if \quad frame_j \notin N_{kth}(frame_i) \end{cases} \tag{5}$$

In this step, the minimum K_{th} nearest neighbor algorithm is used to get the local neighborhood of every single frame. Then Dijkstra algorithm is used to solve multiple sources shortest path between every sample frame, and the geodesic distance is simulated by the distance of path, finally the geodesic distance matrix $M_{geodesic}$ can be obtained, and the first half part of the Isomap algorithm is completed:

(4) MDS algorithm is then used to get the final low dimensional manifold coordinates of all the original motion frame data. Assuming that the n*n matrix D is obtained from the original high dimensional motion data, and this distance matrix is actually the matrix $M_{geodesic}$ which obtained in the 3rd step. We aim to achieve the solution of the n*q matrix X in the low dimensional parameter space after projection. Here we use a n*n matrix B as a intermediate, let matrix B = XX^T, and as a result:

$$b_{ij} = \sum_{k=1}^{n} X_{ik}X_{kj} \tag{6}$$

$$d_{ij}^2 = \|X_i - X_j\|^2 = X_i^2 + X_j^2 - 2 * X_i * X_j = b_{ii} + b_{jj} - 2 * b_{ij} \tag{7}$$

Furthermore:

$$\sum_{i=1}^{n} d_{ij}^2 = T + n * b_{jj} \tag{8}$$

$$\sum_{j=1}^{n} d_{ij}^2 = T + n * b_{ii} \tag{9}$$

$$\sum_{i=1}^{n} \sum_{j=1}^{n} d_{ij}^2 = 2n * T \tag{10}$$

(Among these T is the trace of medium matrix B, that is $T = \sum_{i=1}^{n} b_{ii}$, and we can constrain $\sum_{i=1}^{n} X_{ik} = 0$), From the above formulate, we can get result as follows:

$$\sum_{i=1}^{n} d_{ij}^2 / n = T/n + b_{jj} \tag{11}$$

$$\sum_{j=1}^{n} d_{ij}^2 / n = T/n + b_{ii} \tag{12}$$

$$\sum_{i=1}^{n} \sum_{j=1}^{n} d_{ij}^2 / n^2 = 2 * T/n \tag{13}$$

Also we can get this result from formula (7):

$$b_{ij} = -0.5^* \left[d_{ij}^2 - (b_{ii} + b_{jj}) \right] = -0.5^* \left[d_{ij}^2 - \sum_{i=1}^{n} d_{ij}^2/n - \sum_{j=1}^{n} d_{ij}^2/n + \sum_{i=1}^{n} \sum_{j=1}^{n} d_{ij}^2/n^2 \right] \tag{14}$$

Since d_{ij} is already known, then matrix B can be obtained. And because the matrix B is a real symmetric matrix, it is bound to be able to be orthogonal, assuming that $B = V*A*V^T$, then the $X = V * \sqrt{A}$ is just what we seek. In this paper, we let q be 2, that is, the low dimensional projection space is a plane.

2.2 Motion Segmentation

Motion sequences tend to show periodic variations, and they often have the same or similar high dimensional motion poses at the same stage of different periods. Besides, in a internal movement cycle, the poses sequences also presents the difference. After dimensionality reduction by Isomap algorithm we expected the distribution of low dimensional sample parameters should be consistent with the original motion segmentation in semantic level.

In this paper, we use the extreme points of low dimensional distribution curves to divide the motion. Table 1 shows the comparison result between artificial segmentation and automatic segmentation by our method. We can see that these two kinds of results are quite close, and therefore it confirms the validity of our method.

Table 1. Performance comparison of different motion segmentation methods

Motion semantics	Right foot step forward	Left foot step forward	Right foot keep-up
Automatic	0–52	53–104	105–150
Artificial	0–55	56–112	113–150
Motion semantics	Right foot step forward	Left foot step forward	Right foot keep-up
Automatic	151–231	232–313	314–350
Artificial	151–237	238–311	312–350

3 Motion Alignment

As mentioned before, motion alignment aims to find the temporal correspondence between different motion clips and then different motion clips can achieve a high degree of similarity in logic. DTW algorithm is one of the most common time sequence alignment algorithm, and it is designed to find an optimal path between different time series. It has already been widely applied in the field of speech recognition, computer vision, etc. Each point in the path represents the matching relationship between the sample sequence points. This matching relationship obtained by the path can ensure that the distance between those two sequences is minimum, in other words, any distance calculated by other corresponding relationship must be greater.

In this paper, we apply DTW algorithm to the corresponding motion clips which have already be segmented, aiming to seek the corresponding relationship between them, and the algorithm steps are as follows:

(1) Two motion clips are expressed as follows:
   $Motion_1 = \{Frame_{a1}, Frame_{a2}, ..., Frame_{an}\}$; $Motion_2 = \{Frame_{b1}, Frame_{b2}, ..., Frame_{bn}\}$ Firstly, we calculate the frame distance between the two sequences frame by frame. The process of calculation is similar as formulas (3) and (4), but the difference is that here two different motion data are never mixed together but separated. In other words, we calculate the distance between the frame from motion 1 and the frame from motion 2, and then M_{disc} is obtained.

(2) Then we obtain the solution of DTW weight matrix M_{dtw_disc} through the distance matrix M_{disc}, details are as follows:

$$M_{dtw\_disc}(i,j) = min \begin{cases} M_{dtw\_disc}(i-1,j) + M_{disc}(i,j) \\ M_{dtw\_disc}(i,j) = min \, M_{dtw\_disc}(i-1,j-1) + k^*M_{disc}(i,j) \\ M_{dtw\_disc}(i,j-1) + M_{disc}(i,j) \end{cases}$$

$$(15)$$

(3) Finally we solve the path matrix M_{path} to get the final matching relationship. In the last step, during the process of building the DTW weight matrix, we need to record all the selected path obtained from the formula (15). As a matter of fact, there are only three possibilities for the path between the elements in the matrix: (I–1, J) → (I, J); (I, J–1) → (I, J); (I–1, J–1) → (I, J). After we get the path of all the elements in the DTW weight matrix, it means we obtain the final path from the starting point (1, 1) to the ending point (m, n). Every single point in this path represents the corresponding matching relation between two motion frames.

The experimental results of motion alignment are shown as below, in which the length of 1st motion sample is 150, and the length of the 2nd motion sample is 200. Figure 1 shows the motion alignment result using original DTW algorithm while Fig. 2 shows the alignment result using our method, which combines DTW algorithm with motion segmentation. From the experimental results we can see that using DTW algorithm along can result in that many different frames mapped into the same frame of the other motion in the final alignment results, which will lead to motion pause and motion distortion phenomenon in the subsequent motion fusion. While by combining the DTW algorithm with motion segmentation the alignment result we get is much better. We can see from Fig. 2 that the situation of one frame corresponding to n frames has been improved a lot compared to Fig. 1. Although in the situation that two motion samples to be aligned having different lengths, the final alignment results will surely appear some n:1 cases, but as long as n is not that big, it will cause much smaller negative impact on the subsequent motion fusion.

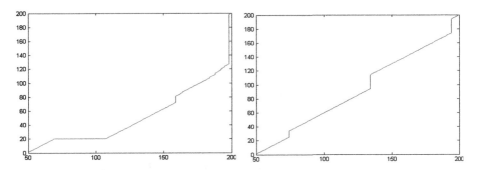

Fig. 1. Alignment result using original DTW   **Fig. 2.** Alignment result using our method

4   Experimental Results

Motion blending refers to that utilizing the existing motion capture data samples as input, weighting different original sample data with different values and then generating a new motion that owns a fusion of different styles inherited from different original samples, the specific formula is as follows:

$$\text{Motion}_{\text{new}} = f(\omega_i; m_i) = \sum_{i=1}^{n} \omega_i m_i \tag{16}$$

In order to verify the effectiveness of our method, we take the motion blending result as a evaluation rule of motion alignment algorithm. We conduct motion blending on two walking motion with different stride-length, and comparative experiments are also implemented between original DTW algorithm and our method. The original motion sample m1 is a series of walking motion sequences with normal stride, and the sequence length is 150 frames; the other original motion sample m2 is a walking motion sequences with exaggerated stride, its sequence length is 200 frames. Finally, in order to analyze experimental results more carefully, we conduct comparison experiments with different weighted fusion coefficients as follows: (1) $\omega 1 = 0.8$, $\omega 2 = 0.2$; (2) $\omega 1 = 0.5$, $\omega 2 = 0.5$; (3) $\omega 1 = 0.2$, $\omega 2 = 0.8$.

Table 2. Performance comparison of different motion alignment methods in motion blending

Weighted	Index	DTW	Our method
(0.8, 0.2)	Fidelity	Serious distortion during 56th–104th;127th–167th frames	Very high
	Fluency	Serious pause during 171st–221st frames	Slight pause during 25th–34th; 94th–113rd frames
(0.5, 0.5)	Fidelity	Serious distortion during 53th–127th; 134th–194th frames	Very high
	Fluency	High	Slight pause during 29th–33rd, 105th–116th; 193rd–200th frames
(0.2, 0.8)	Fidelity	High	Extremely high
	Fluency	Serious pause during 22nd–58th frames	No pause at all

Table 2 presents the motion blending comparison result between two algorithm with 3 groups of different weighted fusion coefficient. From the experimental results we can see that while applied in motion blending, original DTW alignment algorithm can cause serious motion distortion phenomenon, including:feet be off ground, slide, etc., besides the motion pause phenomenon is very serious. On the contrary, the visual effect of the motion samples generated by our method has greatly improved. The fidelity of motion is very high, and occasionally there is slight movement pause phenomenon yet.

5 Conclusions and Future Work

Original DTW motion alignment algorithm can result in motion pause and motion distortion when applied to human motion blending. To address this problem, this paper proposes a new motion alignment algorithm based on the segmentation of human motion. We first utilize Isomap algorithm to projected the original motion sample frames into a low dimensional parameter space; then with the help of the extreme points in the low dimensional space, we can obtain motion segmentation; finally we conduct DTW algorithm on the corresponding motion segment respectively to achieve the final alignment result. Experimental results show that our method can simply and effectively overcome the defects caused by traditional alignment method, and can achieve significant improvement in the visual effect of final generated motion samples.

Nevertheless, there is occasionally slight movement pause phenomenon yet while using our method, and we will step forward to improve our algorithm to seek a higher degree of fluency and fidelity in the final result.

Acknowledgement. This project is supported by Key Project of National Natural Science Foundation of China (Grant No. 61332017); Project of National Science and Technology Supporting Plan (Grant No. 2015BAK04B05).

References

1. Lee, J,H., Shin, S.,Y.: Motion fairing. In: Proceedings of the Computer Animation, pp. 136–143. IEEE Computer Society Press, Los Alamitos (1996)
2. Lee, J., Shin, S.Y.: A coordinate-invariant approach to multiresolution motion analysis. Graph. Models **63**(2), 87–105 (2001)
3. Shin, H.J., Lee, J., Shin, S.Y., et al.: Computer puppetry: an importance-based approach. ACM Trans. Graphics **20**(2), 67–94 (2001)
4. Tak, S., Ko, H.S.: A physically-based motion retargeting filter. ACM Trans. Graphics **24**(1), 98–117 (2005)
5. Lee, J.H., Shin, S.Y.: General construction of time-domain filters for orientation data. IEEE Trans. Vis. Comput. Graphics **8**(2), 119–128 (2002)
6. Wang, J., Drucker, S.M., Agrawala, M., et al.: The cartoon animation filter. ACM Trans. Graphics **25**(3), 1169–1173 (2006)
7. Yamane, K., Nakamura, Y.: Dynamics filter - concept and implementation of online motion generator for human figures. IEEE Trans. Robot. Autom. **19**(3), 421–432 (2003)
8. Kovar, L., Gleicher, M.: Flexible automatic motion blending with registration curves. In: Proceedings of the ACM SIGGRAPH/Eurographics Symposium on Computer Animation, pp. 214–224. Eurographics Association Press, Aire-la-Ville (2003)
9. Park, S.I., Shin, H.J., Kim, T., et al.: On-line motion blending for real-time locomotion generation. J. Vis. Comput. Anim. **15**(3–4), 125–138 (2004)

10. Wang, Y.J., Xiao, J., Wei, B.G.: 3D human motion synthesis based on nonlinear manifold learning. J. Image Graphics **15**(6), 936–943 (2010)
11. Kovar, L., Gleicher, M.: Flexible automatic motion blending with registration curves. In: Proceedings of the ACM SIGGRAPH/Eurographics Symposium on Computer Animation, pp. 214–224. Eurographics Association Press, Aire-la-Ville (2003)
12. Bruderlin, A., Williams, L.: Motion signal processing. In: Proceedings of the 22nd Annual ACM Conference on Computer Graphics and Interactive Techniques, pp. 97–104. ACM Press, New York (1995)
13. Hsu, E., Pulli, K., Popovic, J.: Style translation for human motion. ACM Trans. Graphics **24** (3), 1082–1089 (2005)
14. Park, S.I., Shin, H.J., Shin, S.Y.: On-line locomotion generation based on motion blending. In: Proceedings of ACM Siggraph Symposium on Computer Animation, pp. 105–111. IEEE Computer Society Press, Los Alamitos (2002)
15. Pan, Z.G., Lv, P., Xu, M.L., et al.: A survey on low-dimensional space expression for human motion data and character animation generation. J. Comput. Aided Des. Comput. Graphics **25**(12), 1775–1785 (2013)
16. Liu, X.M., Liu, D., Hao, A.M.: Human motion data retrieval based on dynamic time warping optimization algorithm. Pattern Recognit. Artif. Intell. **25**(2), 352–360 (2012)
17. Hotelling, H.: Analysis of a complex of statistical variables into principal components. J. Educ. Psychol. **24**(7), 498–520 (1933)
18. Oja, E., Hyvarinen, A., Karhunen, J.: Independent Component Analysis. Wiley, Hoboken (2001)
19. Glardon, P., Boulic, R., Thalmann, D.: PCA-based walking engine using motion capture data. In: Proceeding of Computer Graphics International, pp. 292–298. IEEE Computer Society Press, Los Alamitos (2004)
20. Urtasun, R., Glardon, P., Boulic, R., et al.: Style-based motion synthesis. Comput. Graphics Forum **23**(4), 799–812 (2004)
21. Shapiro, A., Cao, Y., Faloutsos, P.: Style components. In: Proceedings of Graphics Interface, pp. 33–39. Canadian Information Processing Society Press, Canada (2006)
22. Liu, G.D., Pan, Z.G., Lin, Z.Y.: Style subspaces for character animation. Comput. Anim. Virtual Worlds **19**(3–4), 199–209 (2008)
23. Lee, C.-S., Elgammal, A.: Human motion synthesis by motion manifold learning and motion primitive segmentation. In: Perales, F.J., Fisher, R.B. (eds.) AMDO 2006. LNCS, vol. 4069, pp. 464–473. Springer, Heidelberg (2006)
24. Tenenbaum, J.B., de Silva, V., Langford, J.C.: A global geometric framework for nonlinear dimensionality reduction. Science **290**(12), 2319–2323 (2000)
25. Roweis, S.T., Saul, L.K.: Nonlinear dimensionality analysis by locally linear embedding. Science **290**(12), 2323–2326 (2000)

Research on Virtual-actual Design Environment of Command Compartment

Shengxiao Zhang[✉], Wenyuan Xu, Hao Li, Li Guo, and Dongmei Zhao

China Shipbuilding Industry Systems Engineering Research Institute, Beijing, China
asheng2003@qq.com

Abstract. The design environment of command compartment is developed based on the physical compartment and virtual scenes, and can be used for design and simulation training for command and control systems. The characteristics of the traditional virtual cabin are analyzed. A cost-effective hardware architecture is designed according to the construction target of the semi physical command cabin. A design method of the design environment of command compartment based on virtual reality is presented. And the key technologies of multi-channel virtual scene generation are analyzed and studied.

Keywords: Virtual-actual · Command compartment · Multi-channel · Virtual scene

1 Introduction

Ship is moving offshore structures. Due to the requirements of the sea voyage and task, taking into account the special requirements of various dynamical systems, command and control system, weapon system, platform system, many compartments are designed inside the ship and the structure is quite complex. With the continuous development of large ships, its internal complexity is also increasing, and the importance of design of cabin environment and related system is gradually highlighted. Especially for the command cabin, the deployment of equipment and the interaction with the external operating entities are the key issues to be considered in the process of system design. By traditional design method based on text and pictures, the comprehensive design view can't be provided, so there are difficulties in the demand communication. The virtual-actual technology can be used to build an effective platform for the design visualization of the command cabin, and it is of great significance for the design, test, training and assessment of the ship command and control system [1, 2].

The virtual reality combination of the command compartment design is to build an environment of the command ship's operation, with high sense of immersion and inter-action, based on the relevant physical and computer. Digital design and simulation training of the conductor can be carried out in the realistic environment of approximate actual combat and the design level of the cabin command system can be enhanced. It is also great helpful for the improvement of the training command personnel in the complex operation situation of the disposal and decision-making ability.

© Springer Science+Business Media Singapore 2016
L. Zhang et al. (Eds.): AsiaSim 2016/SCS AutumnSim 2016, Part II, CCIS 644, pp. 671–679, 2016.
DOI: 10.1007/978-981-10-2666-9_68

2   Related Research and Analysis

On the research of virtual design environment, MTI Lincoln Laboratory in the United States as early as 1960s has begun the application of virtual reality technology research and developed the HMD system. The US Defense Advanced Research Projects Agency has been working on a virtual battlefield environment known as SIMNET since the 1980's. The "virtual naval warfare command center" developed by the US Navy can realistically simulate the environment which is almost completely similar to the real ship combat command center and trainees can be immersed in the "real" battlefield. The British navy has begun to use the virtual ship for technical demonstration, design improvement and interface verification since 2000. In China, the application of virtual reality has become more and more extensive. For example, the virtual display and simulation of the cabin can be completed in the "ship cabin environment simulation lab" of Harbin Engineering University, using the virtual 3D simulation technology.

But there are some problems that can't be ignored in the existing system. On the one hand the real world is isolated by the virtual reality, and is conflict with the way humans perceive the outside world. On the other hand, the existing systems are generally implemented using high-end graphics workstations for graphics rendering, and a high resolution multi professional projector fusion for three-dimensional scene display, so the Implementation and maintenance costs are high. In order to overcome the above problems, the virtual reality technology is used to superimpose the virtual object or non-geometric information about the real object generated by computer onto real-world scenarios, enhancing the real world. Because the link between the real world and the real world is not cut off, the interaction is more natural. At the same time, the use of commercial personal computer and large screen display to achieve the generation and display of the three-dimensional scene, the cost of the system can be greatly reduced. The design and implementation of the semi physical command compartment based on the technology is introduced in this paper.

3   Application Scenario Analysis

Compared to a fully digital virtual cabin, designers do not need to wear glasses and other external devices in the semi physical command compartment based on the virtual-actual technology. So the interaction is more natural, causing no dizziness and discomfort, and is able to meet the needs of a long time interactive design, supporting multi station design and evaluation of personnel and training. In addition, the use of commercial personal computers and monitors instead of high-end graphics workstations and projection display devices, greatly reducing the cost of the realization of the virtual design environment. A variety of application purposes can be achieved based on the combination of the actual situation and the semi physical command cabin.

Generally, there are three main aspects.

- The design and evaluate environment of command and control system
  According to the ship cabin structure design and command console layout, the design evaluation environment of command and control system is built. In the process of system design based on the environment the designers and users can design together, provided a visual communication platform. Designers can quickly build command and control prototype system in the environment, so that users can evaluate the function and application process of the system in a virtual environment which is consistent with the application scenario. The demand can be cured in the early stage of system design, which avoids the progress lag and cost waste caused by the change of system realization.
- Construction of command and control simulation training system
  Command and control system operator plays a very important role in the process of the system. The semi physical command cabin can be used in the construction of command and control simulation training system. Through computer realistic reproduction of the environment, users are immersed in the digital environment. The scene in the real cabin environment that is not easy to meet and the executive control command can be simulated so that the special emergency disposal ability can be trained.
- Construction of a test environment for command and control prototype system
  The ship command and control system needs to be carried out on the land before the delivery of the real ship. In this stage, the semi physical command cabin combined with the actual situation can provide a virtual scene for the system, similar to the field test environment. According to the external interface of the command and control system, the operation of the related entities is simulated. A visual test method for the assessment test is provided, especially is of great significance for the test evaluation of relative position of real space.

4   Architecture Design

A perfect cabin design environment should be composed of the hardware and the software with a high degree of simulation as a supporting architecture, and should be extended. The hardware equipment is composed of semi physical compartments, image rendering equipment, display equipment and network equipment. The software system is composed of three dimension scene system, scenario database, command system prototype, communication middleware and so on. The multi-channel visual system with large field of view is developed, which is used to run on the multi graphics computer, being able to provide the command personnel with a sense of immersive cabin scene. So the operation process and the spatial position information of the relevant entities can be obtained. In this paper, a ship borne aircraft cabin tower is an example and the structure of the system is as shown in Fig. 1.

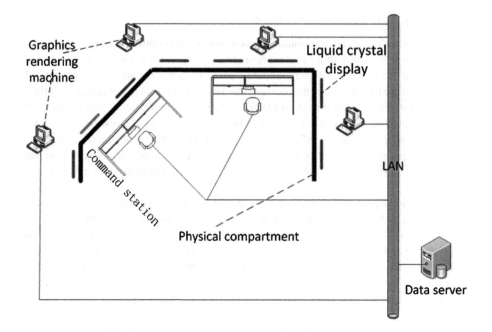

Fig. 1. General structure of semi physical cabin

The shipboard aircraft cabin tower design environment is based on the steel physical cabin structure. The liquid crystal display is hung on the window of the cabin, and is used as a display terminal of the virtual scene. Three dimensional scene is synchronous rendered by the four computer distributed in the compartment. Each computer is connected to two LCD monitors, and each channel is responsible for the rendering of the virtual scene of the two windows. Command station and data server is communicated through the LAN network, and the simulation program running on the data server based on command and scenario is to generate entity state information. The information is send to the graphics computer through the network, driving the movement of the entities of the virtual scene. Its system operation flow is as shown in Fig. 2.

In the process of system design, multi-channel visual rendering is achieved by dividing a large angle of view scene into a plurality of continuous parts of each other and each section is rendered, then a complete picture is formed. The design of display parameters of multi - channel scenes is the key to the realization of this system.

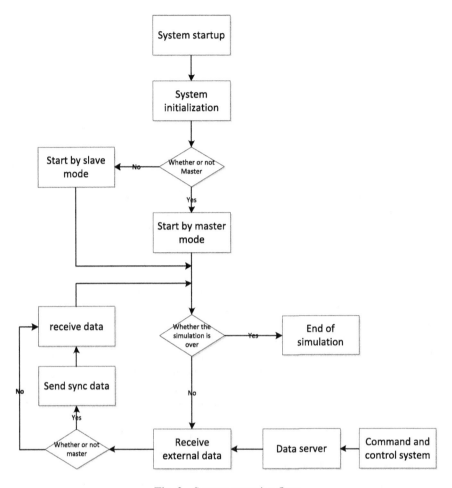

Fig. 2. System operation flow

5   Mosaic and Display of Multi-channel Three-Dimensional Scene

5.1   Setting for Line of Sight in Single Channel

According to the projection screen types, the display types of the multi-channel large FOV are divided into three categories, such as a flat screen, a curtain, a column, or a ball [4]. It is as shown in Fig. 3.

In addition to the middle channel, it is necessary to go through the shear transformation in the generation of visual images by imaging computer in other channels, when using plane screen in the multi-channel visual system. Then the image is correct when projected onto the plane screen. The imaging computer of the multi-channel system and the multi-channel system of the curtain is used to generate the visual scene in the same way. All objects need to be projected onto a plane that is perpendicular to the line of sight. Therefore, when the image is displayed on the screen, the geometric correction of

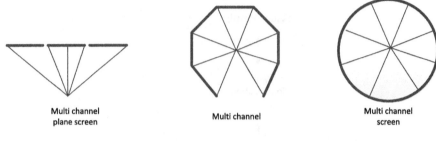

Fig. 3. Projection type

the image is needed to ensure that the image is not deformed. In this paper, the display hardware in the semi physical command cabin is a combination of plane and fold, no curtain. So the planar liquid crystal display with the function of non-geometric correction can meet the requirement of system design. But it is needed to calculate the line of sight direction of each channel according to the cabin structure diagram to ensure the matching of the image of each channel.

Perspective projection is usually used to observe the scene in the visual simulation system. In perspective projection, the view frustum is truncate table vertex in the center of the projection of the pyramid that is a parallel to the bottom surface of the plane cut off at the top of the pyramid. In perspective projection, the line of sight direction should be the line between the point of view and the intersection point of the straight line across the bottom rectangle. The vertex position of the visual body is consistent with the view point, and the view point of each channel of the multi-channel visual system is exactly the same. Therefore, the best viewing position of the observer in the multi-channel visual system development must be first determined. In the design of the ship borne aircraft cabin tower, according to the cabin structure layout and use of demand, the intersection (x, y) of the L1 edge and the L2 edge is selected as the initial viewpoint position of the multi-channel scene, as shown below.

The length of L1, L2, L3 and L4 is known, and the length of the window is a, the window spacing is d, the edge distance is d1 and the two angles are α, β. So $x = L2/2$, $y = L1/2$.

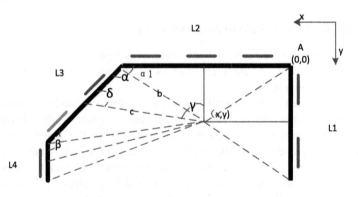

Fig. 4. Definition of coordinate of field of view

Set the direction of the line of sight forward L1 side is 0°, the counter clockwise is positive, then L2, L3, L4's direction of the line of sight respectively is:

The direction of the L2 side line of sight is 90°;

The direction of the L3 side line of sight is 90 + γ degrees, which can be solved by the following formula to obtain the γ angle value.

$$\gamma = 270 - \alpha - \delta;$$
$$b/\sin\gamma = c/\sin(\alpha - \alpha 1);$$
$$b2 = (L2/2)2 + y2;$$
$$c2 = b2 + (L3/2)2 - b*L3*\cos(\alpha - \alpha 1);$$
$$\sin\alpha 1 = y/b;$$

The direction of the L4 side line of sight can be obtained by solving the equations using the classical formula of plane geometry in the same way, and it is not repeated.

5.2 Calculation of Field View Angle Parameters of Single Channel

In OpenGL, there are two ways to set up the single channel field of view, which are symmetric field of view and asymmetric field of view, as shown in Fig. 5. For multi-channel visual system, due to the limitation of the cabin structure, viewpoint can only be located in a small number of symmetric line of sight. Therefore, the unified field of view angle parameters of each single channel is set up by using the non-symmetrical field of view, including four parameters such as, left field angle, right field angle, top field angle and bottom field angle. Based on the coordinate definition in Fig. 4 and the known length and angle, the value of top, right, bottom and left can be obtained by using the knowledge of triangle geometry. The setting of single channel field of view can be completed by the function glFrustum(left, right, bottom, top, 1, 35000). In this example, the VegaPrime software is used as the generation engine of

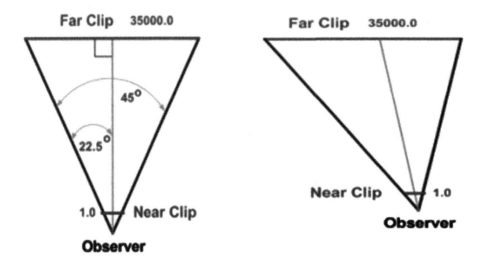

Fig. 5. Definition of symmetric and asymmetric field of view

3D scene, its line of sight direction and field of view angle parameter value can be directly set in FOV Angle and offsets in Lynx Prime.

5.3 Display of Multi-channel Three-Dimensional Scene

For the multi-channel visual system composed of a plurality of computers, each computer is rendered as a part of the scene. It is relatively independent, so it is needed to set up the mechanism to coordinate the scene drawing of each computer. Most existing visual drivers uses the server - client mode to solve the problem, setting a microcomputer as the control center of the visual display client. Shipboard aircraft cabin tower design environment is taken as an example. The four computer number is set to 1 to 4, No1 is set as the central control server, used to connect the data server, receiving the control command, related job entity trajectory and state data. The microcomputer 1 simultaneously will need to synchronize the entity information and the scene command to send to other visual clients through the radio, and control the synchronous update display after receiving the feedback information.

In actual engineering practice, due to the unavoidable factors such as the mechanical machining error, the calculated field angle parameters according to the theory will exist certain deviation, such as inter channel coherence of scene geometry line. It is needed to be further fine-tuned. For ship cabin design environment, the pitch angle and the upper and lower field angle can be adjusted by the sea level line to ensure the continuity of the actual 3D scene.

6 Conclusion

The common PC cluster and the liquid crystal display as the generation and display of the virtual scene is used in the design method of the semi physical command cabin. With the 1:1 physical structure of the actual command compartment, a multi-channel visual simulation system with high immersion and high cost is set up, and a new method is provided for the engineering realization of the virtual design environment. The overall structure of the design environment is designed in this paper and the basic concepts and key technologies of multi-channel scenario generation are analyzed. It is of guiding significance to the realization of the digital design environment of the ship command and control system.

In view of the movement situation in the next, the relative position of the observer in the cabin can be obtained by using the position locating device. And a dynamic computing library for single channel field of view is developed in order to make the best view position of the multi-channel scene consistent with the observer position.

References

1. Song, Z.-M.: Application of VR technology in development of shipborne C2 system. J. Syst. Simul. **23**(08), 1729–1733 (2011)
2. Qiao, C.-L.: Study of synchronization technique for multi-tiled display system. J. Syst. Simul. **19**(15), 3437–3439 (2007)
3. Gong, L.: Virtual warship compartment environment design. Comput. Digit. Eng. **42**(4), 725–727 (2014)
4. Zhang, W.-M.: Research on division of three-dimensional scene in multi-channel visual simulation system. J. Inf. Eng. Univ. **09**(02), 153–155 (2008)
5. Yin, Y.: Research on simulation system based on virtual reality technology for handling underwater vehicle in deep sea. J. Harbin Eng. Univ. **26**(04), 435–439 (2005)

Analysis on the Deviation of the Position and Color Based on Kinect Scanning Modeling

Shan Liu, Shiying Cui, Zhengliang Zhu$^{(\boxtimes)}$, and Guanghong Gong

School of Automation Science and Electrical Engineering,
Beihang University, Beijing, China
965807575@qq.com, 835100937@qq.com,
{zhuzhengliang, ggh}@buaa.edu.cn

Abstract. Kinect is an instrument that can interpret specific pictures with relatively high precision. In this paper, we utilize proper mathematical methods based on the point cloud data from Kinect 2.0 we tested before to analyze the deviation of Kinect scanning. By using Pearson Correlation Coefficient, regression model and Fuzzy Comprehensive Evaluation Method, we manage to analyze the deviation from both the position deviation and color deviation. Our work suggests the important parameters of Kinect—Elevation and Vertical Dimension. When searching for ways to reduce deviation of the color of the measured object, we should not only be concentrated on the optimized combination of the two parameters but also take the relation between vertical dimension and position accuracy into consideration.

Keywords: Kinect · Vertical dimension · Elevation angle · RGB · Chromatic aberrance

1 Introduction

Kinect is an instrument that can interpret specific pictures with relatively high precision. The deviation of the point cloud mainly comes from two aspects: the position information and the color information. In this paper, we utilize proper mathematical methods based on the point cloud data from Kinect2.0 we tested before.

First we use plane fitting to analyze the position deviation. By measuring the standard deviation of axis y toward different vertical dimension, we get the quadratic relation between vertical dimension and plane coordinate.

Then we consider the deviation of Kinect from color information perspective.

In the first step, we use Pearson Correlation Coefficient to reach the correlations among the value of R, G and B. The value of R, G, and B have strong correlations separately between each other.

As it cannot fit to the randomized procedure, we build a regression model and set elevation as argument and the value of R, G, B separately as dependent variable. From the regression equation sets, we can safely draw the conclusion that elevation has strong influence on RGB.

Furthermore, by using Fuzzy Comprehensive Evaluation Method, we consider the RGB value from both elevation and vertical dimension. We work out that the important

© Springer Science+Business Media Singapore 2016
L. Zhang et al. (Eds.): AsiaSim 2016/SCS AutumnSim 2016, Part II, CCIS 644, pp. 680–690, 2016.
DOI: 10.1007/978-981-10-2666-9_69

color of the measured object and the miscellaneous color have the same affected extent. Thus, higher accuracy of the object's own color surely means the higher deviation of miscellaneous color.

Therefore, our work suggests the important parameters of KINECT—Elevation and Vertical Dimension. When searching for way to reduce deviation of the color of the measured object, we should not only be concentrated on the optimized combination of the two parameters but also take the relation between vertical dimension and position accuracy into consideration.

2 Model Building

2.1 Model Preparation

1. When studying the measurement error of Kinect, our modeling is based on preceding tests. Using Kinect, we manage to measure the RGB values and position information of three different papers, which are red, blue and green respectively, all of them with peak brightness (255) in ideal condition. In the measure of each paper, three data sets are collected featured with different vertical dimensions.
2. Due to the large quantity of the collected point cloud data, Lewitt Criteria is adopted in preprocessing the point cloud data. In a specific data set, for example, the R value data set, when the difference between some value and the arithmetic mean value of its data set is three times larger than the data set's standard error, it becomes doubtful and should be rejected.

Standard deviation σ is calculated by the formula as.

$$\sigma = \sqrt{\frac{\sum_{i=1}^{N}(x_i - \mu)^2}{N}} \tag{1}$$

Where μ is the mean value of the value x_1 to x_N, and N is the number of samples.

After the preprocessing of the data sets and filtration of irrelevant ambient point cloud information, the number of valid data in each data set is controlled from 30000 to 40000 (Fig. 1).

The Coordinate System of the Kinect. The internal coordinate system is shown in Fig. 2. X, Y, Z are the three coordinates the Cartesian coordinate system.

2.2 Model I: Analysis of Vertical Dimension and RGB Deviation

The Relation Between the Precision of Point Cloud and Horizontal Scanning Distance. In our experiment, we find that, from 0.8 meters to 4 meters, with the increase of the horizontal scanning distance, the precision of the scanning imaging

Fig. 1. Rebuilding object surface in meshlab

correspondingly declines, other things being equal. In order to quantify the relation between the object's positioning information and the linear distance from the object to Kinect, the object surface with a fixed vertical distance to the Kinect is measured repetitively, and that distance is altered many times to avoid accidental error. Then, standard deviation σ is introduced, whose specific relation with the horizontal distance is calculated. For data processing, calculation and analysis, we employ Kinect for Windows SDK 2.0 as the driver, utilizing Meshlab to acquire image and transform it to point cloud data. Then, the data sets are dealt with plane fitting by Matlab. Finally, the relation is figured out with statistical methods in modeling.

The objects of the experiment are papers with great surface smoothness. We measure with Kinect every 0.1 meters in the range from 0.8 meters to 4 meters. Thus, we come up with the variation relation of the standard deviation to the distance. The plane fitting is performed using least square method on Matlab, coming up with a certain functional relation. In addition, to avoid disturbances arising from ambient light and the surface's color itself, we conduct the experiment in darkness and three different-colored papers are measured.

The relation between the standard deviation and the horizontal distance of the coordinate Z is shown in Figs. 2, 3 and 4 below.

$$f(x) = p1 * x^\wedge 2 + p2 * x + p3 \tag{2}$$

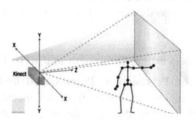

Fig. 2. The coordinate system of Kinect

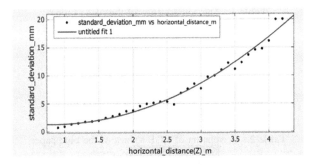

Fig. 3. The relation between the standard deviation and horizontal distance Z (Red) (Color figure online)

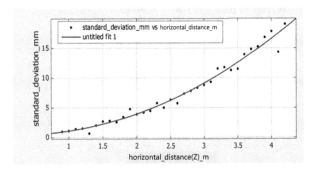

Fig. 4. The relation between the standard deviation and horizontal distance Z (Green) (Color figure online)

RMSE is Root Mean Square Error. Analyzing the relation between the horizontal distance and the standard deviation of the plane axis, we can get the strong quadratic relation between vertical dimension and plane coordinate (Fig. 5 and Tables 1, 2, 3 and 4).

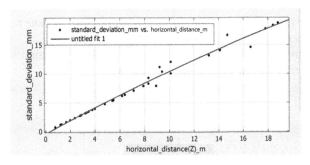

Fig. 5. The relation between the standard deviation and horizontal distance Z (Blue) The consequence of the plane fitting is as follows. (Color figure online)

Table 1. The consequence of the plane fitting

Coefficients	Red	Green	Blue
p1	1.525	1.148	−0.008438
p2	−2.457	−0.5772	1.166
p3	2.318	0.5148	−0.3888
RMSE	0.7309	0.8499	0.7298

Table 2. Correlation of RGB values of the blue paper

	B1	B2	B3
R&G correlation	0.9243	0.9809	0.9196
G&B correlation	0.7727699	0.81285166	0.64181676
R&B correlation	0.52	0.72889	0.375672
Number of data	32576	39765	37282

Table 3. Correlation of RGB values of the green paper

	G1	G2	G3
R&G correlation	0.740908	0.3757	0.595429
G&B correlation	0.942179	0.846523	0.8515
R&B correlation	0.866846	0.701404	0.866777
Number of data	34814	38672	36884

Table 4. Correlation of RGB values of the red paper

	R1	R2	R3
R&G correlation	0.380184	0.414257	0.22789
G&B correlation	0.955662	0.935964537	0.916591
R&B correlation	0.417651	0.454978	0.228453
Number of data	33068	38075	36032

2.3 Model II: Correlation Study of RGB Values Based on Pearson Correlation Coefficient

We incorporate *Pearson Correlation Coefficient* by SPSS to calculate the correlation of different RGB values. The consequence is as follow:

For the sample $x_i(i = 1, 2, \cdots, N)$, N is the number of samples. The Pearson Correlation Coefficient can be calculated as follow.

$$\gamma(x, y) = \frac{\sum_{i=1}^{n}(x_i - \bar{x}) \times (y_i - \bar{y})}{\sqrt{\sum_{i=1}^{n}(x_i - \bar{x})^2}\sqrt{\sum_{i=1}^{n}(y_i - \bar{y})^2}} \tag{3}$$

Where, $\bar{x}$ and $\bar{y}$ is the mean value of the samples.

Conclusions can be drawn:

1. When color A is predominant in a paper, color B and color C appear to be strongly correlated. For example, if the R value is the highest when measuring a paper, the G value and the B value are likely to be strongly correlated
2. The correlation between the value of G and B is strong in all the experiments. Referring to paper concerning color production of KINECT, we know that it will compare the real color to its own pattern by choosing the nearest value of the gray grade. The gray grade of green and blue are nearer than that of red and each of them. Thus the much strong correlation between green and blue should better be neglected if we have other alternatives when making statistical analysis. Basically, there is no correlation between the number of collected data and the RGB values, which means their correlation is random.

It is shown above that the correlation between every two of the three RGB values cannot be neglected. Therefore, the three RGB values cannot be studied separately. Since our research focus on Kinect is the chromatic aberration when scanning plane figure, we do not take depth measurement into consideration.

Error Analysis of Elevation Angel and RGB Values. We study the correlation between elevation angle and the horizontal distance Z between Kinect and the measured point in this part.

We use SPSS on preprocessed data to calculate the elevation angle and the Distance between Kinect and Collected Point.

The elevation angle θ and the standard deviation σ are as follows.

$$\theta = arctan(\frac{z}{\sqrt{x^2 + y^2}}) \tag{4}$$

$$\sigma = \sqrt{\frac{\sum_{i=1}^{N}(x_i - \mu)^2}{N}} \tag{5}$$

Where x, y, z are the coordinates.

It is demonstrated from the data analysis that the y value remains basically the same with very small oscillation, and now y can be preliminarily determined as vertical distance.

Using SPSS, we calculate the Pearson Correlation Coefficient and the analysis is shown in the following Table 5:

Table 5. The pearson correlation coefficients

B1	B2	B3
0.954922	0.875502	0.940529
G1	G2	G3
0.938499	0.880586	0.943017
R1	R2	R3
0.942679	0.892383	0.943964

It can be seen from the table that the distance and elevation angle is strongly correlated. Therefore, we deem that they bear identical statistical characteristics, so we can choose only one independent variable – elevation angle.

Regression Analysis of Elevation Angle and RGB Deviation by SPSS. Because of the strong relevance between each two of the RGB values, RGB value cannot be an independent variable separately in multiple regression, or it will lead to poor fitting effect.

We take elevation angle as the independent variable to solve the regression equation of the three RGB values respectively.

For blue paper, its RGB value is (0, 0, 255) in ideal condition, and the result displayed is (37.5877, 68.1969299, 180). Due to the deviation brought by display cards and other factors, we cannot acquire relatively accurate RGB value of a paper. Assuming the standard value is (a, b, c) and the real value is (A, B, C), their deviation is the absolute value of simple subtraction. Attributing to the translation invariance of linear regression, we can conduct the regression using the real value (A, B, C) directly.

If the original data is not processed, the F test value F will be found to be 0, which means they have no obvious characteristics. After browsing all data, we found the deviation among every hundreds of data to be very small with upper or lower disturbances. To deal with that, every 1000 data is combined in a data group, and the mean value of each group represents the whole group. Then, we conduct F test and T test on new data groups, and the results from SPSS are eligible, so we can build linear regression function for simulation (Table 6).

Table 6. Results of regression analysis by SPSS

Linear regression equations		
Blue paper	Red paper	Green paper
y = 0.14x + 0.027	y = 0.35x + 0.009	y = 0.29x + 0.031
y = 0.23x + 0.015	y = 0.28x + 0.014	y = 0.34x + 0.022
y = 0.18x + 0.019	y = 0.44x + 0.001	y = 0.38x + 0.041

The regression equations above show that the elevation angle is strongly positively correlated with RGB values regardless of the color of the paper.

The Distribution Feature of the Deviation of RGB Values and Elevation Angle. In order to analyze the distribution feature of the deviation of RGB values, we use function H to quantify the deviation of RGB values. The function H is defined as.

$$H = (R - \bar{R})^2 + (G - \bar{G})^2 + (B - \bar{B})^2$$

Where, R, G, B and R̄, Ḡ, B̄ represents the value and the mean value of R, G, B, respectively.

Similar to what we have done in the **Error Analysis of Elevation Angel and RGB Values**, every 1000 data is combined in a data group, and the mean value of each group represents the whole group.

Then, we use Matlab to plot the relation between the deviation of RGB values H and the elevation angle of different groups of the collected data and use curve fitting to figure out the distribution pattern. We choose two groups of the distribution figure to display as follows (Figs. 6 and 7).

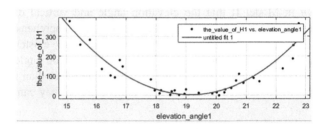

Fig. 6. The distribution of the value of H (Group 1)

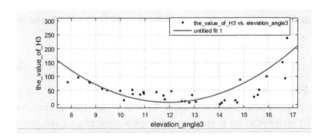

Fig. 7. The distribution of the value of H (Group 2)

The distribution of deviation well follows the quadratic distribution. The consequence of the plane fitting is as follows (Table 7).

$$f(x) = p1 * x^2 + p2 * x + p3 \tag{6}$$

RMSE is Root Mean Square Error. As we can see, the deviation of RGB values reaches its minimum in a certain degree range. Although the certain degree range varies in different groups of data, the distribution feature, which is, quadratic distribution, remains the same. We can use this feature to diminish the chromatic aberrance of Kinect in our future study.

Table 7. The consequence of the curve fitting

Coefficients	Group 1	Group 2
p1	21.23	7.346
p2	−812.6	−175.5
p3	7781	1056
RMSE	37.18	49.86

2.4 Model III Analysis of Kinect's Distance and Elevation Angle Based on Fuzzy Comprehensive Evaluation

We have known in Model II that the elevation angle and vertical dimension have certain influence on the error of the RGB values, so Fuzzy Comprehensive Evaluation can be adopted for analysis. Take the blue paper for example, the existence of negative correlation between vertical dimension and the range of elevation angle is significant. However, we analyze the certain degree of elevation angle rather than the range of it, which does affect or be affected by the vertical dimension, so they can be considered respectively.

Alternative Object Set. Paper of different color has different alternative object set. For the blue paper, since we have concluded in Model I that the value of R and the value of G are strongly correlated, we can approximately determine that the deviation of color is only influenced by the value of B and the value of R. The value of G is not considered because of the strong correlation between the value of B and the value of G, which will definitely effect experiment result.

Thus, the alternative object set $X = \{X_1, X_2\} = \{$The Value of B, The Value of R$\}$.

Determine the Factor Set. The set of various decision factors affecting the alternative objects is called the Factor Set, denoted by U. After the preliminary analysis in Model II, the distance between Kinect and the measured object and the elevation angle are chosen as the major influencing factors to assess its operation stability, constituting the factor set $U = \{U1, U2\}$, where U1 and U2 represents the vertical dimension and elevation angle respectively.

Determine the Weight Vector. The weight set demonstrates to which extent different factors influence the accuracy of the coloring of Kinect. The weight vector is featured by polarity and nonnegative:

$$a_{ij} \geq 0, \ \sum Q_{ij} = 1, \ j = 1, 2 \ldots \ldots n$$

Obviously, from the correlation analysis in Model II, the elevation angle is significantly more influential than the vertical dimension to the deviation of RGB values. Therefore, the corresponding weight set is $A = \{0.7, 0.3\}$.

Determine the Evaluation Set. The assessment of stability is classified into two types: high (H) and low (L). That is V = {V1, V2} = {H, L};

We firstly study the value of B:
A fuzzy mapping is drawn from the above (Table 8):

Table 8. Membership degree of each index

Index	B	X1	R	X2
Membership	H	L	H	L
U1	0.65	0.35	0.8	0.2
U2	0.7	0.3	0.7	0.3

$$U1 \rightarrow \delta(VX1) = (0.65, 0.35) \tag{7}$$

$$U2 \rightarrow \delta(VX1) = (0.7, 0.3) \tag{8}$$

Then, the evaluation matrix is drawn:

$$R = \begin{pmatrix} 0.65 & 0.35 \\ 0.7 & 0.3 \end{pmatrix} \tag{9}$$

Using the M ($\wedge$, $\vee$) model, we calculate B:

$$B = AoR = (0.65, 0.35), \tag{10}$$

There is no need of normalization processing here.
The evaluation set V is quantified in 1-score-sysytem and C = (0.9, 0.1).
Then, the comprehensive evaluation value Y is calculated in the formula:

$$Y = B \cdot C_T = 0.62 \tag{11}$$

For the value of R, it can be calculated in the similar procedure:

$$Y = (0.7, 0.3) * C_T = 0.66$$

Result of Model III. From the period of building and testing the Fuzzy Comprehensive Evaluation Model, we can safely draw the conclusion that when combining the influence of elevation angle and vertical dimension, the comprehensive evaluation value of the important color (Blue) and the miscellaneous color is the same. Thus, it means that the smaller deviation of important color will lead to the bigger deviation of miscellaneous color.

3   Conclusion

From the mathematical methods based on real result to KINECT experiments, we can draw two basic conclusions as follows:

- The regression equations in Model II can vividly show the strong positive quadratic correlation between the elevation angle and the value of RGB, named the deviation of RGB. The parameters of the quadratic function varies with the change of the horizontal distance Z.
- The random deviation of the surface position will get larger along with the longer vertical dimension, and the deviation is proportional to the square of vertical distance. The optimal vertical dimension that can reach a respectively accuracy varies from 0.8 meters to 2.3 meters, under which the standard deviation of the surface smoothness is constricted under 1 cm.

References

1. Him, Y.M., Theobalt, C., Diebel, J., et al.: Multiview image and TOF sensor fusion for dense 3D reconstruction. In: IEEE International Conference on Computer Vision Workshops: ICCV Workshops, kyoto, Sept. 27–Oct. 4, 2009. IEEE (2009)
2. Meglar, E.R.: Arduino and Kinect Projectsts, pp. 23–34. Apress, New York City (2012)
3. Giles, J.: Inside the race to hack the Kinect. New Sci. **208**(2789), 22–23 (2010)
4. Chang, Y.J., Chen, S.F., Huang, J.D.: A Kinect-based system for physical rehabilitation: A pilot study for young adults with motor disabilities. Res. Dev. Disabil. **32**(6), 2566–2570 (2011)
5. Jose-Juan Hernandez-Lopez, et al.: Detecting objects using color and depth segmentation with Kinect sensor. Procedia Technology 196–204 (2012)

The Framework of Inspection Layers of CT and MRI Human Brain Datasets by Bimanual Gesture Interaction

Yiyi Deng, Zeqing Fu, Xin Jia, Bin Gao, and Yanlin Luo[✉]

College of Information Science and Technology, Beijing Normal University, Beijing, China
luoyl@bun.edu.cn

Abstract. We proposed methods for 3D visualization and inspection of different layers corresponding to different tissues. First, we give pipeline of extraction the MRI human brain datasets. Then we present the design of trapezoid opacity transfer function and present the framework of visualization for the CT and segmented MRI datasets, based on CUDA-based real-time volume ray-casting. Furthermore, we inspect its inner layers via virtual lenses by intuitive bimanual gesture interaction, achieving the focus+context visualization. Finally, the performance of our framework verified effective by our experiments.

Keywords: CT (Computed Tomography) · MRI (Magnetic resonance imaging) · Volume visualization · CUDA- based volume ray-casting · Bimanual gesture interaction

1 Introduction

MRI and CT are two powerful techniques for assessing the brain. MRI can provide cross-sectional and longitudinal high-resolution images of soft tissue in brain with obvious contrast, while CT can display the cross sections which are perpendicular to the body long axis and present bone and muscle better. What's more, MRI is more time-consuming and costly than CT. Therefore, they differ in functions for medical study, and their datasets are always processed in different methods.

3D visualization and inspection of the human brain volume dataset is the further critical step, which is also essential to the modern medicine and its application. It helps users efficiently understand both the shape characteristic and the internal geometry structure of the volumetric datasets [1]. Currently, most studies for volume visualization focus on real-time rendering algorithm, which achieved particularly rapid development as the GPU innovation [2].

In volume rendering it's difficult to simultaneously visualize interior and exterior structures, and it's necessary to design layer inspection to show each organization individually. Rezk-Salama et al. put forward an opacity peel rendering algorithm basing on depth peeling [3]. This algorithm solved the problem of occlusion in volume data. Basing on this algorithm, Liang Ronghua et al. put forward a delamination volume rendering algorithm. Liang's algorithm improved the accuracy of stratification and got great draw peeling effects [4, 5].

© Springer Science+Business Media Singapore 2016
L. Zhang et al. (Eds.): AsiaSim 2016/SCS AutumnSim 2016, Part II, CCIS 644, pp. 691–699, 2016.
DOI: 10.1007/978-981-10-2666-9_70

In the meanwhile, rendering performance alone is not sufficient to ensure that users understand volume visualizations intuitively [6]. Actually providing effective interaction techniques to ensure that users understand volume visualizations intuitively has become a hot research topic [7]. There are two basic fashions for volume interaction. One employs a 2D or 3D controller device, the other is touchless fashion which allows the user to manipulate on the display with their bare hands. Touchless interface is a primary paradigm of natural user interface and quantities of application need it to support the specified scenario, by which users apperceive and interact with volume data in a more natural and intuitive way.

In this paper, we mainly make four contributions. First, we present method of the extraction of human brain MRI dataset. Second, we design the framework of visualization of MRI and CT respectively. Then, we propose layer inspection of the MRI and CT datasets by intuitive bimanual gesture interaction via virtual lenses. Finally, some experiments are conducted to analyze the differences of visualization and inspection results between MRI and CT. The paper is structured as follows. Section 2 describes our method. Section 3 shows our experiment result. Section 4 gives some conclusions and ideas of future work.

2   Methods

There are several differences of visualization and interaction methods between MRI and CT. The first one is that CT datasets don't need to be processed from NIFTI dataset into RAW dataset. According to their differences we propose the following methods to achieve our framework for two kinds of datasets.

2.1   The Extraction of MRI Human Brain Datasets

We apply the FSL (FMRIB Software Library v5.0) to automatically extract the brain tissues and divide the brain image. The extraction method consists of following four steps.

Step 1. Extract the brain from the whole dataset

We used automated brain extraction method for human brain MRI data by BET method (Brain Extraction Tool)in FSL, which deletes non-brain tissue from an image of the head after inputting T2 images.

Step 2. Segment the brain into different tissues

The extracted brain images are spatially normalized using FAST method (FMRIB's Automated Segmentation Tool), which segments the 3D image into different tissue types, whilst also correcting for spatial intensity variations. Thus the human brain was segmented into some tissues such as grey matter, white matter and CSF (cerebrospinal fluid). The density threshold of these brain tissues are overlapped in some intervals.

Step 3. Take linear transformation

By statistics of the three tissues, we get the density of cerebrospinal fluid ranging from 1 to 1892, the grey matter ranging from 16 to 1129 and the white matter ranging from 286 to 1361. Hence we took linear transform for the density values of three tissues with non-overlapping region. The density values of CSF remain in [1,1892], the grey matter mapped from [16,1129] to [1900,3013] and the white matter mapped from [286,1361] to [3020,4095].

Step 4. Merge

After the linear transformation, we merge the data of three tissues into a result of the brain and finally input the data into MIPAV by which converting the MRI volume NIFTI dataset to MRI volume RAW dataset.

2.2 Transfer Functions Designed for the CT and Segmented MRI Volume Datasets

In direct volume rendering, it's essential to show different part of volume dataset, by build a mapping relationship from voxel to the corresponding optical characteristics.

This critical step is implemented by transfer function, which might be simple slope, piecewise continuous function, or in any other forms. The transfer function affects the final quality of output image directly. Meanwhile, intuitive transfer function improves the efficiency of adjusting parameters.

In the early transfer functions, scalar threshold was used as the basis for dividing the materials, mapping to different color and opacity value. This early method is simple and particle, but doesn't perform well in boundary, because the scalar threshold of some different materials too close to be categorized. To make up for this imperfection of one-dimensional tracker function, some researchers proposed multi-dimensional transfer function, which is based on scalar value, gradient value, curvature, and spatial association information. However, as the dimension increasing, it can cause high complexity and heavy computation. So we propose an improved one-dimensional transfer function, a trapezoid-shaped function which has a better performance for layer control.

Transfer Function Designed for CT Datasets. In CT scalar datasets, materials can't be divided precisely only based on single scalar threshold, and there must be the scalar threshold coincidence of several data. As for the trapezoid transfer function, the trapezoidal waist corresponds to the overlapping threshold interval of multiple materials. To study the different expression in linear form in accordance with the actual distribution of material in the region is the key to solve the problem.

We described the transfer function as multiple trapezoid, and each one represents one classification such as boon, skin, and muscle. Assume that the number of categories is K, and the trapezoid is expressed as $B_j = [b_{j,0}, b_{j,1}, b_{j,2}, b_{j,3}]$ with color value C_j and maximum opacity A_j. In fact, there's an overlapping area between two neighboring materials, as we illustrated in Fig. 1.

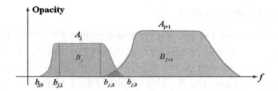

Fig. 1. Illustration of overlapping area

Take a ray V starting from viewpoint as an example, let f_i be the scalar value correspond to sampling point p_i on V, $fi \in Bm(m = 1, 2, \dots, K - 1)$, the weight w_i is defined by the following equation

$$
w_i = \begin{cases}
g\left(\dfrac{f_i - b_{m,0}}{b_{m,1} - b_{m,0}}\right), & f_i \in [b_{m,0}, b_{m,1}] \\
1, & f_i \in [b_{m,1}, b_{m,2}] \\
1 - g\left(\dfrac{f_i - b_{m,2}}{b_{m,3} - b_{m,2}}\right), & f_i \in [b_{m,2}, b_{m,3}]
\end{cases}
\tag{1}
$$

where g(t) is the cubic function of the value in [0,1], $g(t) = t^2(3 - 3t)$.

According to Eq. (1), we can get the opacity value α_i of p_i

$$
\alpha_i = \begin{cases}
g\left(\dfrac{f_i - b_{m,0}}{b_{m,1} - b_{m,0}}\right)A_m, & f_i \in [b_{m,0}, b_{m,1}] \\
A_m, & f_i \in [b_{m,1}, b_{m,2}] \\
\dfrac{\left[1 - g\left(\dfrac{f_i - b_{m,2}}{b_{m,3} - b_{m,2}}\right)\right]A_m + g\left(\dfrac{f_i - b_{m+1,0}}{b_{m+1,1} - b_{m+1,0}}\right)A_{m+1}}{A_m + A_{m+1}}, & f_i \in [b_{m,2}, b_{m,3}]
\end{cases}
\tag{2}
$$

where the last part is the opacity value of the overlapping $[b_{j,1}, b_{j,2}]$.

As supposed the color c_i of p_i can be got from the color of B_m, $c_i = \alpha_i T_m$, so we can get accumulated value of its opacity and color according to conventional ray-casting algorithm by the following equation

$$
\begin{cases}
c_i^* = c_{i-1}^* + (1 - \alpha_{i-1}^*)\alpha_i c_i \\
\alpha_i^* = \alpha_{i-1}^* + (1 - \alpha_{i-1}^*)\alpha_i
\end{cases}
\tag{3}
$$

where α_i^*, c_i^* are the accumulated opacity and color corresponding to one viewing ray through the pixels into the field volume implemented by one thread in CUDA.

Transfer Function Designed for the Segmented MRI Volume Datasets. For MRI datasets, we illustrated it in Fig. 2 in which one trapezoid expresses one band or layer for the segmented human brain MRI data. Each band has no overlapping region. There are three bands corresponding to CSF, the white matter and the grey matter.

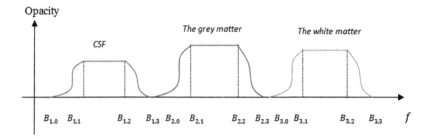

Fig. 2. Illustration of three bands

B_j is defined as above. Because different bands are corresponding to different separated tissues, so B_j and B_{j+1} ($j = 1, 2, \ldots, K - 1$) has no overlapping region. The opacity α_i of p_i is defined by the following equation

$$
\alpha_i =
\begin{cases}
g\left(\dfrac{f_i - b_{m,0}}{b_{m,1} - b_{m,0}}\right) A_m, & f_i \in [b_{m,0}, b_{m,1}] \\
A_m, & f_i \in [b_{m,1}, b_{m,2}] \\
[1 - g\left(\dfrac{f_i - b_{m,2}}{b_{m,3} - b_{m,2}}\right)] A_m & f_i \in [b_{m,2}, b_{m,3}]
\end{cases}
\tag{4}
$$

We can get the accumulated opacity and color α_i^*, c_i^* according to conventional raycasting algorithm by the Eq. (3).

We use the above transfer function in which more details are shown to get better effects of volume rendering and effective layer control when performing volume exploration using the layer filter interaction tool.

2.3 The Framework for Visualization of CT and MRI Human Brain Datasets

The framework for visualization is described in Fig. 3. As for the MRI datasets, we process it as Sect. 2.1 and then input the volume datasets into data cache. As for the CT data, we can input the dataset into the data cache directly.

The framework for visualization is similar to our previous work depending on different transfer function design [8], and here we integrate the CT and segmented MRI datasets. It exploits the CUDA framework and the hierarchical structures such as octree for both compression of volume data and speed optimization of ray casting process. In the beginning of raycaster, we need to determine the thread index in CUDA, and then resample in the volume if it intersects with the viewing ray. Data mapping means from data properties to optical properties specifying the RGBA. We adjusted the opacity and color according the tools specification if it is inside the ROI, else take data mapping from our transfer function defined in Sect. 2.2. Phong illumination model is used for shading before accumulating the color. Because all threads run at the same time and process the data, the performance is greatly increased and real time.

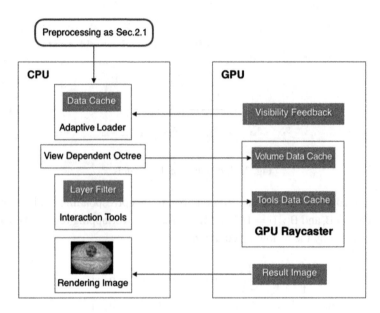

Fig. 3. The framework of visualization

2.4   Inspection by Bimanual Gesture Interaction via Virtual Lenses

In order to achieve better inspection of human brain structure by our visualization framework mentioned above, we design bimanual gesture to manipulate the volume model with layer filter tool.

Layer Filter Tool. For facilitating inspection of interior and exterior tissues, we define the virtual lenses as layer filter for 2D inspection. According to above simplified model, the volume dataset is divided into two parts including 3D ROI described as shaded parts in Fig. 4 which is the intersection of a cone with the window of virtual lenses as base and the viewpoint, and the whole volume datasets. In ROI, we modify the opacity α_i of p_i in (0, 1] for selected band and 0 for others bands before compositing as Eq. (3). Outside ROI and inside the view frustum the conventional CUDA-based volume rendering is used.

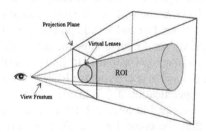

Fig. 4. Diagram of virtual lenses

Bimanual Gesture Design. In order to simultaneously visualize interior and exterior structures and get the region of interest, the layer filter and intuitive hand gestures are need to manipulate the human brain volume datasets directly. We develop natural and intuitive exploring fashion. The concept of natural means various, intuitive, memorable and practical, which is argued through mimicking aspects of the real world or drawing on our existing tendencies in the areas of communicative, gesticulate, deictic, and manipulative behaviors and actions [9].

We propose the bimanual gesture for operating human brain volume model and the interactive tool simultaneously. Using an open hand pose as shown in Fig. 5(a). The user can rotate and move the left hand as the non-dominant hand with natural hand pose to achieve a 6DOF motion of the human brain volume model. The right hand is regarded as the dominant hand to control an interactive tool as shown in Fig. 5(b), and can change the visible layer by moving in a circular motion. When interacting with both hands, the working space is limited, so finger movements are considered as much as possible to achieve the manipulation of the volume datasets.

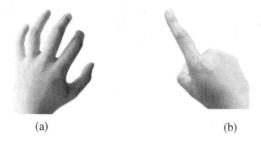

(a)   (b)

Fig. 5. Bimanual gesture interaction for both volume model and layer filter. (a) Natural open bending pose for 6DOF manipulating the volume model. (b) Point pose to control the layer filter

3   Experiment Result

We get the human brain CT and MRI T1 imaging using a Siemens Trio Tim scanner at Beijing MRI Center for Brain Research. It is a $168 \times 206 \times 128$ with 16 bit volumetric dataset. We have implemented our algorithm on an Intel Core 2 Quad CPU Q9400 @ 2.66 GHz equipped with 4 GB of RAM on Windows 7 using OpenGL and CUDA 3.0. The graphics card is a NVIDIA GeForce GTX 760 with 1 GB of RAM memory. We use a Leap Motion sensor to track hand motion data and provide 3D object coordinates with millimeter accuracy at 120 Hz.The system is written in C++ using SDK V2.3.1 for Windows provided by Leap Corporation and uses CUDA parallel architecture to accelerate calculation for real-time rendering of the volume dataset.We can maintain an interactive frame rate with an average of 100 fps.

Figure 6 are the results of using virtual lenses for inspection of different layers of CT datasets in (a) bones, (b) muscle, (c) skin of the brain structure (d) in ROI. Figure 7 are results of using virtual lenses for inspection of different layers of MRI human brain in (a) CSF, (b) the grey matter, (c) the white matter and (d) the image of brain with three tissues.

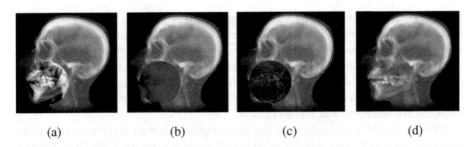

(a)   (b)   (c)   (d)

Fig. 6. Virtual Lenses for inspection of different layers of CT dataset

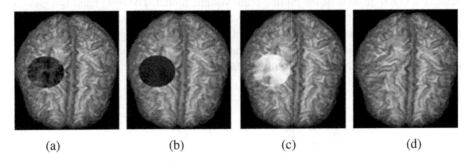

(a)   (b)   (c)   (d)

Fig. 7. Virtual Lenses for inspection of different layers of MRI dataset

We use our designed bimanual gestures as shown in Fig. 5 to operate the volume model and the interactive tool simultaneously by Leap Motion sensor, with two different cameras for touch-free motion sensing. The Leap Motion system detects and tracks hands and fingers. The device operates in an intimate proximity with high precision and tracking frame rate. But it cannot identify a specific static gesture directly. As shown in Fig. 8, we used a spot as a metaphor of layer filter in order to explore different structures of volume dataset. A point pose (see Fig. 5(b)), with index finger pointing to the screen, provides a convenience greatly to using the tool. The user can change the position and the size of this

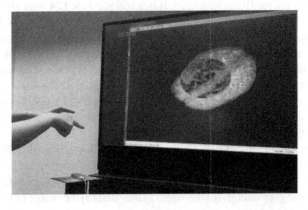

Fig. 8. Bimanual gesture interaction with the MRI human brain volume model

region by moving index finger in the physical space. In addition, our system can achieve different layer exploration as shown in Figs. 6 and 7(a)–(c) by moving index finger in a circular motion, based on our transfer function design described in Sect. 2.2.

4 Conclusions and Future Work

We combine the human MRI brain extraction and the trapezoid functions with non-overlapping region to display its different layers. The segmented MRI dataset and non-segmented CT can be efficiently and easily adapted to CUDA-based volume ray-casting in our framework. The results strongly depend on our trapezoid opacity transfer function design, in which the different trapezoid functions are designed. By intuitive bimanual gesture interaction via virtual lenses, the inner layers are inspected in focus region with semi-transparent out parts by focus+context visualization.

Although the original data we used are not from the same person, our methods and framework can be applied to CT and MRI datasets from the same person. One of our goals in future is to extend to our methods to other MRI and CT volume dataset with more bands. Also we hope to expand to projection based virtual environments toward a more natural interface for cooperative inspection supporting multi-modal interaction and multi-user.

Acknowledgements. This work is supported in part by a grant from the National Natural Science Foundation of China (No. 61472042), the Beijing Natural Science Foundation (4152028) and the Fundamental Research Funds for the Central Universities (No. 2013YB70).

References

1. Gallo, L.: A study on the degrees of freedom in touchless interaction. In: ACM SIGGRAPH Asia Technical Briefs, pp. 1–4 (2013)
2. Gobbetti, E., Marton, F., Iglesias-Guitián, J.A.: A single-pass GPU ray casting framework for interactive out-of-core rendering of massive volumetric datasets. Vis. Comput. **24**(7–9), 797–806 (2008)
3. Rezk-Salama, C., Kolb, A.: Opacity peeling for direct volume rendering. Comput. Graph. Forum **25**(3), 597–606 (2006)
4. Liang, R.H., Li, C., Wu, F.L., et al.: Layered peeling algorithm of direct volume rendering for medical dataset. J. Compu.-Aided Des. Comput. Graph. **21**(10), 1381–1386 (2009). (in Chinese)
5. Wu, F.L., Huang, X.P., Liang, R.H., et al.: Opacity peeling for medical data based on volume membership. J. Comput.-Aided Des. Comput. Graph. **22**(10), 1810–1816 (2010). (in Chinese)
6. Laha, B., Sensharma, K., Schiffbauer, J.D., Bowman, D.A.: Effects of immersion on visual analysis of volume data. IEEE Trans. Vis. Comput. Graph. **18**(4), 597–606 (2012)
7. Hanqi, G., Ningyu, M., Xiaoru, Y.: WYSIWYG (What You See is What You Get) volume visualization. IEEE Trans. Vis. Comput. Graph. **17**(12), 2106–2114 (2011)
8. Luo, Y.L.: Distance-based focus+context models for exploring large volumetric medical datasets. IEEE Comput. Sci. Eng. **14**(5), 63–71 (2012)
9. Wigdor, D., Wixon, D.: Brave NUI World: Designing Natural User Interfaces for Touch and Gesture, pp. 65–72. Elsevier, Amsterdam (2011)

Author Index